The Complete Guide to
Linux System
Administration

Nicholas Wells

THOMSON

COURSE TECHNOLOGY

Australia • Canada • Mexico • Singapore • Spain • United Kingdom • United States

The Complete Guide to Linux System Administration

is published by Course Technology.

Managing Editor
William Pitkin III

Product Manager
Amy M. Lyon

Developmental Editor
Deb Kaufmann

Production Editor
Brooke Booth

Senior Manufacturing Coordinator
Trevor Kallop

Senior Marketing Manager
Karen Seitz

Technical Editor
Serge Palladino

Quality Assurance Management
John Freitas

Associate Product Manager
Sarah Santoro

Editorial Assistant
Jennifer Smith

Cover Design
Abigail Scholz

Text Design
GEX Publishing Services

Compositor
GEX Publishing Services

Disclaimer:
Course Technology reserves the right to revise this publication and make changes from time to time in its content without notice.

The Web addresses in this book are subject to change from time to time as necessary without notice.

Linux is a registered trademark of Linus Torvalds. Linux+ is a trademark of CompTIA.

ISBN- 13: 978-0-619-21616-0
ISBN- 10: 0-619-21616-6

BRIEF Contents

TABLE OF
Contents

Introduction

Linux is now the fastest growing server operating system in the world, according to analysts such as IDG and Gartner Group, with a market share that has outpaced Macintosh. Millions of Internet sites and internal servers are run on Linux, and billions of dollars are generated in Linux-related revenue for companies like IBM, Hewlett-Packard, Dell, Red Hat Software, and others. Linux also continues to expand its technical prowess by adding high-end features and spreading globally into new market niches. Many world governments now mandate that Linux and other open source software be considered before money is spent on commercial alternatives. Because most networks include multiple operating systems, any system administrator planning for a long term career is well-advised to include Linux as a core competency to offer to potential employers, many of whom have already installed Linux and are looking for staff to maintain it.

This book guides you through the basics of Linux technology and trains you as a system administrator to maintain a Linux server that other users rely on for e-mail, Web, database, networking, or other system services. The book begins by introducing basic Linux concepts that may be unfamiliar to you, and then explains the installation and use of a Linux-based computer from the viewpoint of a system administrator.

This book cannot cover everything there is to know about Linux. Instead, it presents the basics of many areas, with enough theory and practice that, after reading it and completing the exercises and review questions included in each chapter, you should feel comfortable working on a Linux system and be able to locate additional utilities, and additional documentation about utilities, to enable you to progress in your knowledge of Linux (and in your career) with a solid foundation. Although this book was designed with a classroom setting in mind, nothing in it requires that setting, and many Linux users (the author included) were self-trained, without the guidance that a good instructor can provide. This book is based on a two-volume set: *Guide to Linux Installation and Administration, Second Edition* and *Guide to Linux Networking and Security*. It replaces the first volume and includes most of the core concepts and utilities of the second volume (it's also larger than either one alone); if you need more detailed information about networking and security, you should consult the second volume or another specialized text. This volume assumes you have never seen a Linux system, but that you are familiar with basic computer operation, such as entering commands, using a mouse to selecting graphical items on screen, and working with removable discs and CD-ROMs.

One aim of the material presented here is to prepare you to pass a Linux certification exam, which will demonstrate to potential employers that you have mastered important theoretical and practical knowledge about Linux-based computers. Several certification programs for Linux are currently available. The material in this book maps to three of the most popular Linux certification programs: Red Hat Certified Technician (RHCT), Linux Professional Institute (LPI) Level I, and Linux+ from CompTIA. It also maps to the first two (of four) exams of the SAIR/GNU Linux Certified Administrator Level 1 certification. The objectives for each certification program, Web site references where you can obtain official information, and cross-references to relevant chapters and sections in this book, are provided in the appendices to this book. These certification exams are generally multiple choice tests that you can take at a testing facility near your home or school after paying a fee. More advanced certification programs are available from Red Hat Software, LPI, and SAIR/GNU, but having any one of these certifications makes a very strong statement to potential employers about your knowledge of Linux.

The Red Hat certifications, which are generally considered the most challenging, are also more expensive and less widely available—they require that you perform hands-on system administration tasks in a lab setting. Because of this, and the market-leading position of Red Hat Software, the focus in this book has been on Red Hat's products, specifically the Fedora version of Linux. Users will find that nearly all of the knowledge obtained in this book is easily transferred (usually with no modification) to other versions of Linux. The exceptions are Red Hat specific graphical utilities, which the reader may encounter in any event in a future job setting.

The inclusion of Fedora Linux in this book is a compromise of sorts. A more realistic training environment would suggest using Red Hat Enterprise Linux, which is the basis for the Red Hat Software certification exams and which is widely used in large organizations. Though the cost of Red Hat Enterprise Linux doesn't permit its inclusion here, Fedora is the technology core from which Red Hat Enterprise Linux is taken. Fedora is a completely free operating system that can be downloaded from the Internet (see *fedora.redhat.com*). Except for technical support options and a few high-end management features (and the color of the installation screens), Fedora is similar enough to Red Hat Enterprise Linux to be considered a clone for training purposes.

This book uses an "onion skin" or layered approach to learning about Linux. Instead of beginning with a subject, such as user accounts, and disgorging all there is to know about them, leaving the reader with no context of when that information is useful (and perhaps little memory of it), this layered approach introduces a number of concepts on a superficial level, so that they fit together in a useful fashion. Other concepts are added, and the text then returns with more depth to explore important concepts that were introduced initially. Thus, for example, user accounts are mentioned in Chapter 1, explored more fully in Chapter 4, and are the subject of a "full" discussion in Chapter 11, once the context for the utilities and policies have been fully set out.

The Intended Audience

This book is intended for students and professionals who need to install Linux and understand basic system administration, networking, and security-oriented tasks on UNIX or Linux-based servers. Though it begins with the conceptual foundations of operating systems and some historical notes on Linux, the focus is on practical, hands-on descriptions of system administration tasks and the utilities—both command-line and graphical when available—that an administrator would use to complete daily work managing a Linux-based server. This book is ideal as the text for introductory courses on operating systems and system administration; it assumes the reader has no experience with Linux and only minimal experience with Windows-based computers. The text and pedagogical features are designed to provide an interactive learning experience, so that further self-study of Linux documentation, Internet documents, and computer industry resources will prepare readers for more advanced education or work assignments in system and network administration. Each chapter includes Hands-On Projects that lead readers through various tasks in a step-by-step fashion. Each chapter also contains Case Projects that place readers in the role of problem solver, requiring them to apply concepts presented in the chapter in a situation that might occur in a real-life work environment.

The chapter on installing Linux has been moved from a more "traditional" location at the beginning of the book to a place in the middle of the text. This is intended to allow students to become familiar with the command line and graphical environments before tackling the more advanced tasks of installing the operating system. Most computers today come with an operating system installed (Linux can also be purchased this way), and most beginning system administrators will not be called upon immediately to install a new system. Readers working on their own should feel free to jump immediately to Chapter 8 to install their new Linux systems, referring back to earlier chapters if questions arise. On most newer computers, installing Linux can be done in about 15 minutes by pressing the Enter key repeatedly (though Chapter 8 isn't written for the 15-minute version).

In a classroom or lab setting, the ideal situation would be for students to begin working with the installation done by a previous class until they reach Chapter 8. At that point, having a certain comfort with the operating system, they would re-install their systems and continue working through the more advanced chapters of the book. The next class to use the computers could then continue to use those systems, as installed, until they read Chapter 8. If the lab network makes it convenient, it is of course handy to re-install Linux on each computer at the beginning of each semester to avoid students having problems because of changes made by overambitious students the previous semester. Fedora supports the Kickstart and network-based installation techniques that should make repeated installation on multiple systems fairly painless.

Chapter Descriptions

The chapters in this book discuss the following topics:

Chapter 1, "Introducing Linux" introduces the free software model and provides a basic history of UNIX and Linux, with some comparisons to other operating systems and descriptions of the features of Linux. It then guides you through logging in and starting to use the Linux command-line and graphical desktop environments.

Chapter 2, "Exploring the Desktop" describes how to use the GNOME and KDE desktop interfaces to interact with Linux files and utilities. It illustrates basic desktop configuration and introduces commonly used graphical utilities, such as the file manager, text editor, and popular productivity applications.

Chapter 3, "Using the Shell" focuses on the command-line environment, showing usage tips and introducing the bash shell, including variables, data redirection operators, and the vi text editor.

Chapter 4, "Understanding Users and File Systems" introduces these two key areas of system administration work. User accounts are discussed as they relate to file systems, inodes, links, and file permissions. File system management is also introduced, including partitions, mounting file systems, and archive management.

Chapter 5, "Understanding Text Processing" explains how to use a collection of command-line utilities to manipulate text files in simple and complex ways. Regular expressions are taught, as are the *sed* and *awk* text processing programs. This information is then used as the basis for more advanced training in the vi editor at the end of the chapter.

Chapter 6, "Managing Processes" defines a Linux process at the kernel and shell levels and describes how to use command-line and graphical utilities to view and control those processes. Process scheduling is also discussed using *cron* and *at*.

Chapter 7, "Using Network Clients" discusses how to use a number of different networking tools to work remotely with a Linux system. Tools include *ssh*, r-utilities, and *telnet*. Data services such as rsync and FTP are introduced, and basic network diagnostic tools are discussed in the context of these network client operations.

Chapter 8, "Installing Linux" begins by reviewing Linux hardware requirements and how to configure hard disk space for a Linux operating system. The text then describes the installation process step-by-step, including how to select among the options presented, and how to start up and use the system after the installation is completed.

Chapter 9, "Understanding System Initialization" explains how standard PC computers start up and how the Linux kernel begins to operate at boot time. The boot loader that launches the kernel is discussed, along with the *init* program and the important service control scripts that are part of the initialization process for all Linux systems.

Chapter 10, "Managing Software Packages and File Systems" describes how to install and manage utilities and applications using the RPM or Debian package format. Both graphical and command-line utilities are discussed. Advanced file system management is then introduced, including using multiple file system types, checking the integrity of existing file systems, and creating file systems on newly installed hardware.

Chapter 11, "Managing Users" discusses daily management tasks related to user and group accounts, such as creating, disabling, and modifying accounts, as well as issues related to resource consumption and user security.

Chapter 12, "Configuring Networks" describes how to configure networking on a Linux system using command-line or graphical utilities. Basic routing and name resolution issues are introduced, along with more topics such as DHCP, IP aliases, and a lengthy section on networked printing in Linux.

Chapter 13, "System and Kernel Management" covers a number of system administration tasks such as maintaining backups, using RAID and volume management, monitoring system logs, and maintaining an updated kernel. Kernel modules are introduced, as is the basic process for recompiling the kernel.

Chapter 14, "Writing Shell Scripts" teaches how to create scripts using the bash shell, including using positional variables, conditional statements, and various types of loops. Shell script examples from an installed system are mentioned, and basic debugging techniques are introduced. Tools used in other types of programming, such as Perl and C++, are touched upon.

Chapter 15, "Advanced Topics and Troubleshooting" discusses a number of topics that readers will want to learn more about as they continue their study of Linux: advanced graphical configuration, including remote graphical access; the basics of system security; simple configurations to use popular network services; and troubleshooting hints and techniques.

Appendix A, "Red Hat Certified Technician Objectives" lists all certification objectives for the Red Hat Certified Technician (RHCT) program from Red Hat Software, with each objective mapped to a chapter and heading in this book.

Appendix B, "Linux Professional Institute LPI Certification–Level 1 Objectives" lists all certification objectives for the Linux Professional Institute (LPI) Level I certification program, with each objective mapped to a chapter and heading in this book.

Appendix C, "SAIR/GNU Linux Certified Administrator (LCA) Level 1 Objectives" lists all certification objectives for the SAIR/GNU LCA Level 1 certification program. The objectives for all four exams are provided, with each objective in the first two exams mapped to a chapter and heading in this book.

Appendix D, "Linux+ Certification Objectives" lists all certification objectives for the CompTIA Linux+ certification, with each objective mapped to a chapter and heading in this book.

Features

To aid you in fully understanding networking concepts, this book includes many features designed to enhance your learning experience.

- **Chapter Objectives.** Each chapter begins with a detailed list of the concepts to be mastered within that chapter. This list provides you with both a quick reference to the chapter's contents and a useful study aid.

- **Illustrations and Tables.** Numerous illustrations of Linux utilities as well as conceptual diagrams help you to visualize and better understand Linux tools and technical concepts. In addition, the many tables included provide concise references on essential topics such as command options and online information resources.

- **Chapter Summaries.** Each chapter's text is followed by a summary of the concepts introduced in that chapter. These summaries provide a helpful way to recap and revisit the ideas covered in each chapter.

- **Command Summaries.** Each of the Linux utilities introduced or discussed in the chapter is shown in italic boldface as it is introduced. Those utilities are summarized in table form at the end of the chapter, with a brief description of the utility and a sample command.

- **Key Terms.** All of the conceptual terms within the chapter that were introduced with boldfaced text are gathered together in the Key Terms list at the end of the chapter. This provides you with a method of checking your understanding of all the terms introduced.

- **Review Questions.** A list of review questions is included to reinforce the ideas introduced in each chapter. Answering these questions will ensure that you have mastered the important concepts.

- **Hands-On Projects.** Although it is important to understand the theory behind the Linux operating system, nothing can improve upon real-world experience. To this end, along with thorough explanations, each chapter provides numerous Hands-On Projects aimed at providing you with practical implementation experience and real-world solutions.

- **Case Projects.** Located at the end of each chapter are several case projects. To complete these exercises, you must draw on real-world common sense as well as your knowledge of the technical topics covered to that point in the book. Your goal for each project is to come up with answers to problems similar to those you will face as a working system or network administrator.

Text and Graphic Conventions

Wherever appropriate, additional information and exercises have been added to this book to help you better understand the topic at hand. Icons throughout the text alert you to additional materials. The icons used in this textbook are described below.

The Note icon draws your attention to additional helpful material related to the subject being described.

Each hands-on activity in this book is preceded by the Hands-On icon and a description of the exercise that follows.

Tips based on the author's experience provide extra information about how to attack a problem or what to do in real-world situations.

The Caution icon warns you about potential mistakes or problems and explains how to avoid them.

The Case Projects icon marks case projects, which are more involved, scenario-based assignments. In these case examples, you are asked to implement independently what you have learned.

Instructor's Resources

The following supplemental materials are available when this book is used in a classroom setting. All of the supplements available with this book are provided to the instructor on a single CD-ROM.

Electronic Instructor's Manual. The Instructor's Manual that accompanies this textbook includes additional instructional material to assist in class preparation, including suggestions for classroom activities, discussion topics, and additional projects.

Solutions. Contains solutions to all end-of-chapter material, including the Review Questions, and where applicable, Hands-On Projects.

ExamView®. This textbook is accompanied by ExamView, a powerful testing software package that allows instructors to create and administer printed, computer (LAN-based), and Internet exams. ExamView includes hundreds of questions that correspond to the topics covered in this text, enabling students to generate detailed study guides that include page references for further review. The computer-based and Internet testing components allow students to take exams at their computers, and also save the instructor time by grading each exam automatically.

PowerPoint Presentations. This book comes with Microsoft PowerPoint slides for each chapter. These are included as a teaching aid for classroom presentation, to make available to students on the network for chapter review, or to be printed for classroom distribution. Instructors, please feel at liberty to add your own slides for additional topics you introduce to the class.

Figure Files. All of the figures in the book are reproduced on the Instructor's Resources CD in bit-mapped format. Similar to the PowerPoint presentations, these are included as a teaching aid for classroom presentation, to make available to students for review, or to be printed for classroom distribution.

SOFTWARE CD-ROMs

The Complete Guide to Linux System Administration comes with the Fedora Core 2 version of the Linux operating system software. This software, which is a free software project sponsored by Red Hat Software, Inc., is also available as a free download. You can use the included CDs in accordance with the license agreement. The Fedora version of Linux is substantially equivalent to Red Hat Enterprise Linux, except for the technical support options (Fedora provides none) and a few advanced management utilities. For more information about the Fedora Project, visit *http://fedora.redhat.com*. For more information about Red Hat Software, Inc., and their Linux operating system products and training and certification programs, visit *www.redhat.com*.

Lab Requirements

The Hands-On Projects in this book help you to apply what you have learned about Linux. The following section lists the minimum hardware requirements that allow you to complete all the Hands-On Projects in this book. In addition to those requirements, students must have administrator (root) privileges on their workstations in order to complete many of the projects.

Although this book includes a copy of the Fedora Core 2 version of Linux, the Linux certification programs that the book tracks to are not focused on Fedora per se. The information in the book applies, in most cases, to all current versions of Linux, such as SUSE/Novell, Xandros, Debian, TurboLinux, Mandrake, and many others. The exceptions occur in some of the utilities used as examples and in the location of certain files in the directory structure. Those users preparing for the Red Hat Certified Technician examination are advised to research features specific to Red Hat Enterprise Linux on the Red Hat Software web site (*www.redhat.com*). Those preparing for other certification programs should be well-served by the information in this book, because those other programs are oriented to a more "generic" understanding of Linux, not tied to a specific vendor's version. In any case, the Hands-On Projects will work for the most part as written on other versions of Linux.

Minimum Lab Requirements

Hardware

- Each student workstation and each server computer requires at least 64 MB of RAM, an Intel Pentium or compatible processor running at 200 MHz or higher, and a minimum of 2.4 GB of free space on the hard disk. More memory and hard disk space is useful, but these figures will allow Linux to be installed as directed in the chapter text and run smoothly. If you have less space available than this, you can make alterations to the recommended packages to be installed as listed in Chapter 8, and alter some of the projects as needed to bypass software that is not installed on your system. (For example, recompiling the kernel requires that a number of large packages be installed.) In labs with very limited equipment, a text-only workstation can be created that will still permit learning about many features of Linux without exploring the graphical utilities or desktop interfaces.

- It may be useful to have workstations in a lab networked together, though detailed instructions and troubleshooting on network configuration are not provided in this book. No particular cabling system or speed requirements apply. Internet access or the ability to communicate with another workstation is assumed for several of the book's Hands-On Projects (this is noted in the introduction to any such project). If Linux is installed in a lab with newer computers and networking hardware installed, networking is generally very easy to set up using the basic descriptions in Chapters 7 and 8.

- Care should be taken that security is not compromised in allowing workstations to access the Internet through a larger organizational LAN. Linux includes many utilities that, if used carelessly, are likely to make administrators on the LAN quite unhappy. (None of these utilities are the focus on this book, but they are available on the default system nevertheless.)

Software

- Fedora Core 2 version of Linux

ACKNOWLEDGMENTS

The idea for this book started with Course Technology's Managing Editor, Will Pitkin, who thought we could take the best from my two previous Linux books, revise them with the latest material, and map it to all of the popular Linux certifications. The Linux world never sits still for long, but all things considered, the book came together quite smoothly, thanks to the patience and hard work of a lot of very skilled people. As the philosopher Spinoza said, "All things excellent are as difficult as they are rare," and so, having vouched for the difficult part, I hope you will conclude that we have achieved the rare part as well.

This is the fourth book I have worked on with my good friends, Product Manager Amy Lyon and Development Editor Deb Kaufmann. Both are always a pleasure to work with and excel at handling all the details so that I can concentrate on the content of the book without worrying about the myriad other steps that go into making the finished product come together so well. Amy has cheerfully juggled my changing academic and travel schedule in addition to managing all the reviewers and editorial steps during a very hectic year (for both of us) when I seemed to provide a new reason for delays in every e-mail. Deb has presented me with a conundrum of sorts. On the one hand, I watch my writing craft improve, even as I focus on new technologies and utilities, because of her careful editing, constructive comments, and extra-mile fixes of my often harried prose. On the other hand, I might easily conclude, working with such assistance, that I don't really need any skill—anyone could create a decent book with Deb backing them up. My tremendous thanks to them both.

I had less direct contact with other members of the team—I simply saw their reports and incorporated all their suggestions. Having now written about 15 books, I know of no publisher that shows such attention to detail as the professionals at Course Technology. It is obvious they take pride in their work and are concerned that the end-product be the most accurate, useful, and attractive that it can be. Production Editor Brooke Booth and copyeditor Mark Goodin adeptly maneuvered through my schedule and my prose, keeping both flowing smoothly. MQA (quality assurance/testing) team lead John Freitas headed a group that included Marianne Snow, Danielle Shaw, Chris Scriver, and technical editor Serge Palladino. Their efforts often went beyond what I considered their "job" as they worked to save me time and improve the book you're reading.

Amy also recruited several instructors to review the initial Table of Contents and each chapter as writing progressed. I considered their input invaluable in tailoring the material presented here to the needs of students, based on their many years of experience in the classroom. My thanks to each of them:

Tim Chappell	Dona Ana Branch Community College
Nick LaManna	New England Technical Institute of Technology
Chris Spreitler	Vatterott College
Dave Venable	Boise State University

As I recall, while writing this book, I completed law school, started a new job, took the bar examination, sold my own home, and moved my family across the country. I can therefore hardly mention the patience of my editors without mentioning the patience of my dear wife, Anne—encouraging, supportive, hard-working, interested in the project... but glad it is finished.

Nick Wells

1

INTRODUCING LINUX

After reading this chapter and completing the exercises, you will be able to:

♦ Describe how Linux was created and how it compares to other operating systems

♦ List versions of Linux currently available

♦ Outline the skills required and challenges facing a system administrator

♦ Log in and begin using a Linux system

♦ Explore a Linux file system from the command line

♦ Locate additional information about commands you want to use or learn about

In this chapter you learn how Linux was first created and how it differs from other popular operating systems. That background provides a foundation for learning about the ways that Linux is currently sold and its place in the larger information technology market. You also learn about Linux certification programs such as the Red Hat Certified Technician program.

You then learn about working as a system administrator: what a system administrator does each day, what skills a good system administrator possesses, and what challenges (both technical and nontechnical) each day brings.

In the last three sections of this chapter, you begin working with Linux, logging in and using the command line and graphical tools to explore the file system. You also find out how to locate help on the commands that you learn about.

A Brief History

If you are like most users, your experience with computers is limited to working on one of the popular graphical computers such as an Apple Macintosh or a computer running Microsoft Windows (NT, XP, ME, 2000, and so on). Linux was developed as an alternative for people whose computing needs require something other than the platforms with which most people are familiar.

To appreciate the features and benefits that Linux offers, you need to understand what an operating system is, and how an operating system interacts with the applications that you run on your computer (such as your word processor or Web browser).

Understanding Operating Systems

Early computers were **hard wired**, meaning that instructions telling the computer what to do were arranged in the wires and other components that made up the computer. Because of this, a computer was able to complete only a single task—the one that it was hard wired to perform. For example, a computer might be designed to accept two numbers as inputs and add those numbers together. A computer that was hard wired for this task could not subtract one number from the other without being rebuilt by rearranging the wires in the computer. As more powerful computer hardware became available, computer scientists demanded more flexibility. Once computers included the capability both to store information and to alter it electronically, computer designers could create software. **Software** is a collection of instructions that control the tasks that a computer performs. Unlike a hard-wired system, software can be changed without disassembling the computer and applying a soldering iron to the wiring. Obviously, this was real progress compared to hard-wired systems.

Early software programs contained every instruction that a computer needed to complete a given task. Before long, however, programmers decided it would be more efficient to create reusable software that provided core functionality such as reading keystrokes from the keyboard or writing characters to a screen. Specialized programs could then be written more quickly by taking advantage of these core functions.

A set of core functionality that many programs can use to control a computer is called an operating system. Although operating systems have advanced a great deal in the last 50 years, the basic purpose remains the same: an **operating system** is software that helps other programs control the computer hardware and interact with users.

With an operating system to take care of common tasks, programmers can more easily write applications. An **application** is a software program that provides a service to the person using the computer, rather than simply controlling the computer's hardware. For example, word processors and accounting software are applications. So are Web browsers and e-mail readers. In the case of a Web browser, the operating system manages networking, the keyboard, the screen display, and dozens of other issues. The programmer who created the

Web browser is free to focus on problems specific to the browser, such as how to process Web pages or how to store Web page bookmarks.

The operating system controls applications running on the computer. An application cannot act without "permission" from the operating system. But as long as the applications avoid unreasonable requests (such as "delete everything in memory"), the operating system spends most of its time acting on requests of the applications. Figure 1-1 shows the relationship of the user, the application software, the operating system, and the computer hardware.

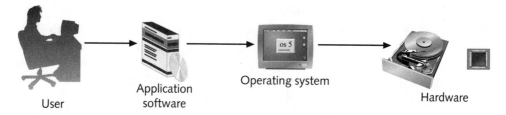

Figure 1-1   The relationship between the user, applications, operating system, and computer hardware

Operating System Functions

Although they vary in appearance and functionality, all operating systems have similarities. For instance, all operating systems are likely to include the following functions:

- Initialize (or prepare) the computer hardware so that the operating system and other programs can function correctly.

- Allocate system resources, such as memory and processing time, to the programs that are using the operating system.

- Keep track of multiple programs running at the same time.

- Provide an organized method for all programs to use system devices (such as the hard disk, printer, and keyboard).

An operating system consists of multiple parts or components. The most essential part is the kernel. Additional components assist the kernel in managing the computer's resources and in controlling application software. The following is a list of the major components of an operating system:

- **Kernel**: The core of the operating system, which allocates computer resources such as memory and CPU time between multiple applications

- **Device drivers**: Software that permits the kernel to access hardware devices such as a keyboard, mouse, hard disk, scanner, or network card

- **Shell**: Software that accepts input from a user via a command line and processes that input to manage system resources

- **Utility programs**: Software programs that manage the hardware and operating system features. A utility is similar to an application such as a Web browser, but the purpose of a utility is to manage the computer system rather than perform a task that is independently useful (such as display a Web page or calculate a mortgage payment).

- **Graphical user interface** (**GUI**; sometimes called a graphical interface or a **desktop interface**): Software that provides a mouse- or pointer-driven interface in which graphical applications can operate using menu bars, buttons, and over-lapping graphical windows.

The precise line between an operating system component and an application is vague. For example, many utility programs are included when you install an operating system, but they may also fulfill specific needs you have such as searching for a word or downloading e-mail. But this vagueness won't cause you any problems if you understand the purpose of an operating system and its components as outlined above.

The UNIX Operating System

UNIX is an operating system originally created at AT&T Bell Labs (now part of Lucent Technologies) in the early 1970s by Ken Thompson and Dennis Ritchie. It was designed to control networked computers that were shared by many users. UNIX development has continued since it was first introduced, and versions of UNIX are currently sold by dozens of large companies, such as IBM, Hewlett-Packard, and Sun Microsystems. The Internet was developed on UNIX and is still based around the UNIX operating system.

 One reason that many versions of UNIX exist is because of government restrictions on what AT&T—being a monopoly at the time—could do with technology that it developed. Today you will sometimes see reference to "*nix" or "unices," meaning all of the versions of UNIX collectively. If something is compatible with most unices (most versions of UNIX), it is also likely compatible with Linux, as described later in this section.

Ironically, the features and low cost of Linux (which is basically a version of UNIX, as explained shortly) are effectively driving UNIX out of the market. Computer hardware and software companies that formerly based much of their business on selling UNIX are now switching their support to Linux. Two examples are HP and IBM.

UNIX initially did not include a graphical interface. The operating systems provided only character-based screens, which required the user to type commands at the keyboard. Eventually, graphical interfaces were developed for each operating system. These graphical interfaces provided core graphical functionality that other programs could draw upon. The leading graphical interface for UNIX was called the **X Window System**. This system is still in use today and is also used for graphical displays on the Linux operating system.

The Free Software Foundation and the GNU Project

In 1983, during the heyday of UNIX popularity, **Richard Stallman** at the Massachusetts Institute of Technology founded an organization called the **Free Software Foundation (FSF)**. Stallman's motivating idea was that users should have complete freedom in how they use software—the people selling software shouldn't control what users could do with that software. He proposed that companies and individuals could make money by charging for services and customization, but that the software itself should not be restricted in its distribution by a standard commercial license agreement. To back up his opinions, Stallman and those working with the FSF created hundreds of utilities that ran on most versions of the UNIX operating system and distributed them freely around the world. This effort was called the **GNU Project**. (GNU is a recursive acronym that stands for GNU is Not Unix; it is pronounced with a hard g, guh-new.) With the GNU Project, Stallman intended to create a completely free version of UNIX, written from scratch.

NOTE One of the best known products of the GNU Project is the C language compiler called **gcc**. This is a software program for converting C language programming instructions into code that a computer can execute. The gcc compiler is the most widely used, highly regarded compiler in the world.

For more information about the philosophy of free software and the relationship between GNU and Linux, visit *www.fsf.org*.

Perhaps more far reaching than the free software produced by Stallman's efforts has been the software license that Richard Stallman designed for the GNU Project. A **software license** is a legal definition of who can use a piece of software and how it can be used. Stallman introduced the **GNU General Public License**. Often abbreviated as the **GPL**, this license is very different from a standard commercial software license:

- When the author of a piece of software decides to license it under the GPL, the author agrees to give away the source code to the software. The **source code** is the set of human-readable programming instructions used to create the program. For non-GPL commercial software, only the machine-readable **binary code** used to execute a program is distributed. By including the source code, the software author makes it possible for anyone to modify the original program.

- Anyone who obtains a copy of the software is licensed to redistribute it in any form they choose (on CD-ROM, via the Internet, in retail stores, and so forth). They can even charge money for it. But they must license everything they distribute under the GPL—they cannot impose restrictions on anyone who obtains the software from them.

- Any modifications to the source code (a derivative work of the original program) must be licensed under the GPL as well.

The last point here is sometimes referred to as the "viral" nature of the GPL—any changes to the code are also "infected" with the GPL. Once you start with software licensed under the GPL, you can't get away from it. On the other hand, some have mistakenly assumed that any program that is used with GPL software is also infected. That is not the case. For example, if you wrote a business software application for Linux and used a standard commercial license, running on Linux doesn't mean that your software is part of the same collection of source code as Linux itself.

NOTE   Software called "system libraries" may be shared by both free programs and commercial programs operating in memory at the same time. The use of these libraries is covered by a separate version of the GPL called the Library GPL (or the **LGPL**).

TIP   Software licensed using the GPL is sometimes called **copyleft**; it is copyrighted material, but using a license that is very different from standard licenses that restrict distribution.

Some software is placed in the public domain by its author. **Public domain** means that no one has the copyright to the software. Most things produced by the U.S. government are in the public domain because they were produced using tax dollars. If software is in the public domain, anyone can modify it, keep the modifications secret, and copyright the modifications under a standard commercial software license. But the GPL is a type of license, with copyright maintained by the software author. GPL is very different from software in the public domain, though some journalists have confused the two concepts.

The GPL was not the first license to allow free redistribution of software. Nor will it be the last. Other similar licenses are used for the Berkeley version of UNIX (called FreeBSD), the Apache Web server, the PERL programming language, the X Window System, and many other programs.

NOTE   The name **OpenSource** is often used to refer to software licensed under the GPL. The OpenSource initiative is a consortium of people who support free software principles, but they have approved many different licenses as being valid expressions of those principles. The Free Software Foundation, which maintains the GPL, makes a distinction between the GPL and the term OpenSource, though in practice they are used synonymously in the Linux industry. For more information, visit *www.opensource.org.*

Linux Arrives

While the GNU Project was creating utilities for UNIX, a college student in Helsinki, Finland, named **Linus Torvalds** wanted access to his own UNIX system (UNIX has always been popular on many college and university campuses). But like most students, he couldn't afford the huge computer and expensive software required to run UNIX. Torvalds decided to create a UNIX-like operating system kernel for his IBM-compatible PC as a school project. This in itself would not be different from the efforts of many other students working to create something useful and save a few dollars—it was also similar to Stallman's plan, though Torvald's started with the kernel instead of the utilities.

Instead of trying to complete this project on his own, Torvalds solicited help via the Internet. Soon hundreds of programmers around the world were working together to create a new UNIX-like operating system kernel. (For a photograph of Torvalds, see Figure 1-2.) Their work was dubbed Linux, in honor of Linus, the founder of this cooperative software development project. (Most people pronounce Linux with a short i sound, lin-nucks; some say lee-nucks; Linus' pronunciation matches neither of these exactly, being Finnish, but he has never seemed concerned with how it is pronounced.)

Figure 1-2   Linus Torvalds, originator of the Linux kernel

Stallman had started with the utilities; Torvalds with the kernel. Stallman had a complete philosophical agenda; Torvalds didn't want to pay for UNIX. Between them, they created the pieces necessary for rapid development of Linux.

Because of its community-oriented nature, Torvalds decided to released the Linux kernel under the GPL. The GPL allowed Linux to develop rapidly because everyone who worked on the project knew that they would benefit from everyone else's efforts: because they were all working on the same program, the GPL guaranteed that everyone's work would be shared. The result was rapid progress in a friendly, professional atmosphere.

TIP

Recently, legal challenges to Linux and the GPL have been mounted by a UNIX company named SCO. Though considered unlikely to succeed by most legal experts, these court battles are highlighting the benefits of Linux and also defining how Linux and other free software programs will be used in years to come. For more details on this subject, visit *www.groklaw.net*, *www.osdl.org*, or a Linux news site such as *www.linuxtoday.com* or *www.linuxworld.com*.

Linux kernel development follows a standard model used by hundreds of free software projects. To begin a project, a person identifies a need and begins writing a program, just as Torvalds did. At some point, the software developer announces the project on the Internet. Developers who share an interest in that project respond, and soon they begin to work together on different parts of the project. One programmer or team of programmers might develop the user interface, another the networking capabilities. Another group might work on documentation for the software. All of the individual developers and writers communicate through e-mail to share code, documentation, and their views on how the project should move forward.

After the software being developed reaches a certain level of stability, the person leading the project releases the software (including the source code) on the Internet. This part of the process has become both easier and more formalized in recent years. Most projects have their own Web site (many through the *sourceforge.net* site) and announce their progress on news sites affiliated with free software. Two of the most widely visited sites are *slashdot.org* and *freshmeat.net*.

Since the inception of Linux, the source code has been distributed via the Internet site *ftp://ftp.funet.fi*, based in Finland, and many other sites around the world.

NOTE

After a software project (or an update to it) has been announced, people download the source code and try out the program. Some of those people send back information about problems they have encountered (software bugs). The team of developers fixes the bugs, occasionally working with other developers who have submitted bug fixes or specific enhancements to the software. These fixes and enhancements are the basis for the next version of the software, which may be announced and released anywhere from a few days to many months later.

A security flaw was discovered in one open source program in late 2003. The flaw was identified at 2 a.m. By 6 a.m., several patches had been distributed around the world.

TIP

Although Linus Torvalds continues as the leader of Linux kernel development, the kernel is no longer dependent on him alone. He has several key associates charged with maintaining various parts of the kernel, and hundreds of others who regularly contribute programming code or suggestions.

Sometimes a participant in a free software project decides that he or she doesn't like the direction the project is going. If the larger project membership doesn't share his or her views, that person can start a new project based on the existing source code. This is sometimes called **forking** the source code. Forking is how many new projects begin. For example, suppose a group of developers is working on a driver for a network card. A new card from the same company is announced. One of the developers decides he would like to work on a driver for that project. He starts a new team, using the original team's source code as a beginning point. Because no one is being paid, everyone chooses to work on whatever is most interesting to them.

Motivating Free Software Developers

As Linux is discussed in business and computer publications, those unfamiliar with the software development model used by Linux and other free software ask a reasonable question: "Why would so many people devote so much effort to something without expecting any reward? It just doesn't make sense."

Of course, the business world that asks these questions is driven mainly by money, and when considering money alone, free software development does not make much sense. Linux developers, however, have other motivations:

- Creating a piece of software often fills a developer's specific technical need. Because they may have used the work of other free software developers at some point, releasing their own work as free software is a way to thank everyone who has made their life easier.

- Developers who create the highest quality, most useful programs are regarded very highly by their peers in the free software community. The respect of like-minded professionals whom you respect in turn is a powerful motivating factor.

- The Linux community and other similar online communities devoted to products such as the Apache Web server are very popular in the news. Participating in free software development gives a sense of contribution and community to developers. What begins as a small project to fulfill a developer's own technical requirements may be discussed in the *Wall Street Journal* a year later.

- As products such as Linux receive increased support from mainstream software vendors (such as IBM and Hewlett-Packard), experience with Linux is a valuable boost to any developer's resume. Having your name associated with the development of a widely known, free software project indicates both proven technical ability and strength at working in a team and organizing the work of others.

The Strengths of Linux

Although the ability to use Linux without paying for it is an incentive to many people, large businesses would not choose Linux for this reason. Indeed, businesses generally prefer to pay for software in exchange for having someone to turn to for technical support, upgrades, and other services. These organizational users select Linux over competing products because it is a high-quality operating system. Some of the features for which Linux is highly regarded include:

- *Stability*: Linux servers are known for being able to run for months or even years without needing to be restarted. (The site *www.netcraft.com* has impressive statistics regarding Linux as a Web server.)

- *Security*: Having source code available has meant that the occasional security flaw in open source software is located and repaired more quickly than is typical for commercial products.

- *Speed*: Linux makes very efficient use of hardware, from very small systems to very large. (An excellent resource to study speed comparisons between Linux and Windows systems is *www.kegel.com/nt-linux-benchmarks.html*.)

- *Cost*: Linux is free, but most users pay something for it, as discussed in the next part of this chapter. Still, the price paid is generally much lower than a competing solution based on commercial software. Many studies have been done on the **total cost of ownership (TCO)** for various products. The TCO includes the cost of the software plus the ongoing cost to maintain, support, and upgrade it. Red Hat Software has done many studies to show the favorable TCO for Linux-based business solutions.

- *Multiprocessing and other high-end features*: As the popularity of Linux grows, it continues to add features that were formerly found only in systems costing many thousands of dollars. These include the ability to run on computers with multiple microprocessors (**multiprocessing**), support for numerous new hardware devices, and other features you will read more about later in this book. (See, for example, the information at *www.redhat.com/software/rhel/features/*.)

- *Applications*: Linux now boasts a long list of general purpose and specialized applications, including office suites (similar to Microsoft Office), powerful database tools, and Internet applications. Many of the largest software vendors have created Linux versions of their products. You can also run many Windows programs directly on Linux using special utilities.

LINUX IN THE MARKET

In this section you learn about how Linux is packaged and sold, including the specific products offered by Red Hat Software, the current market leader. You also learn about Linux certification programs.

Linux Distributions

The Linux kernel alone doesn't provide the functionality of a full-blown operating system. To be really useful, a complete system ought to include:

- Hardware drivers to permit Linux to work with numerous peripheral devices such as printers, network cards, digital cameras and scanners, DVD drives, and so on

- Installation programs to make it easy for users to set up all the Linux files on a computer

- Networking and system administration utilities to monitor and configure how the operating system functions

- A graphical environment (a desktop interface), along with graphical tools to manage the operating system

- Personal productivity applications such as a word processor, calculator, calendar, CD player, and clock (perhaps even some games)

- Documentation describing how to perform system administration tasks, how to operate the graphical interface, and many other tasks

A "productized" version of Linux that includes the operating system kernel along with many or all of the above components is called a **Linux distribution**. A Linux distribution typically includes thousands of individual programs that run on Linux. Most are related to managing the Linux system—in other words, they are **system utilities**. Many of these system utilities are taken from the GNU Project. For this reason, some people refer to a Linux distribution as the GNU/Linux operating system. Using a packaged Linux distribution, nontechnical individuals can install and use Linux. Figure 1-3 shows how different components are collected into a Linux distribution.

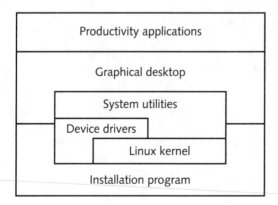

Figure 1-3   Many components together create a Linux distribution

Many companies have created Linux distributions. In accordance with the GPL, these companies include in their distributions the source code for the Linux kernel, as well as for most of the other utilities in the distribution. They can charge as much as they choose for their Linux distributions; because the software is freely available from other sources, one view of Linux companies is that they act essentially as packaging services that save users the trouble of downloading and configuring a large number of files.

The fact that the programs in a Linux distribution are free has, for the most part, kept prices for Linux quite low—generally between $2 and $100. Because the Linux kernel and utilities offered by the many Linux vendors are practically identical, vendors use commercial components (such as specialized utilities) or services (such as technical support) to make their products more attractive to consumers. Red Hat Enterprise Linux, described shortly, is one example of this. Table 1-1 lists several Linux distributions. You can find detailed information about the hundreds of Linux distributions available around the world by visiting *www.distrowatch.com*. A good source for inexpensive CDs of Linux distributions is *www. cheapbytes.com*.

Table 1-1 Popular Linux Distributions

Name	Comments	Web site
Red Hat Linux	The most widely used distribution, from Red Hat Software; currently sold as Red Hat Enterprise Linux, in several versions for different markets and hardware configurations	*www.redhat.com*
Fedora	A distribution based on Red Hat Linux, but entirely free (no commercial version exists)	*fedora.redhat.com*
SUSE Linux	Very popular in Europe; originally produced by SUSE, a German company, which was recently acquired by the networking software company, Novell	*www.suse.com*
Debian	A noncommercial Linux distribution targeted specifically to free software enthusiasts. Debian does not have a company behind it. It is created and maintained by developers of free software	*www.debian.org*
Xandros	Focused on providing a desktop operating system to replace Microsoft Windows	*www.xandros.com*
Linspire (formerly Lindows)	Focused on providing a desktop operating system to replace Microsoft Windows (also the target of a lengthy trademark lawsuit by Microsoft, in which Lindows/Linspire has so far prevailed)	*www.linspire.com*

Red Hat Software

Because one of the purposes of this book is to prepare you to take the Red Hat Certified Technician exam, you should know more specifics about the Linux products offered by Red Hat Software.

Until late 2003, Red Hat Software sold Red Hat Professional Linux, a fairly low-cost but highly regarded distribution that had advanced to version 9 by that time. Red Hat Software then changed its product line by creating the Fedora distribution as a free product and technology seedbed. By maintaining the Fedora distribution, Red Hat continues to provide financial support to many developers creating the Linux kernel and other free software. The commercial focus for Red Hat Software is now Red Hat Enterprise Linux, which is available in three different configurations:

- *WS (workstation):* A product designed for power users who want to use Linux at their Intel or compatible (x86) desktop. This version does not include most of the Internet server technology provided in other Linux distributions, such as a Web server and e-mail server. A separate version called Red Hat Professional Linux is a low-cost version of the Enterprise Linux WS product. It is sold through retail stores and corporate resellers, but you cannot purchase technical support beyond basic installation support.

- *ES (enterprise server):* A midrange server product for Intel x86 and compatible computers that includes Internet server software such as a DNS server and e-mail server

- *AS (application server):* A high-end server product similar to the ES product, but which is available for seven types of hardware, including IBM mainframes (model S/390)

TIP

For simplicity, the term Red Hat Linux is used throughout this book to refer to Linux products from Red Hat Software. Specific products or differences between products are noted when appropriate.

Red Hat Enterprise Linux is sold as a subscription service. Suppose you purchase a copy of Red Hat Enterprise Linux ES with a Basic service agreement via the Red Hat Web site at *www.redhat.com.* You can immediately download and install the operating system, or you can also order a media kit (for about $25) that includes CD-ROMs and basic documentation such as an installation guide. After you install the operating system, it maintains contact with Red Hat Software via the Internet. Any security fixes, package upgrades, or other information needed to keep your system running smoothly and securely are downloaded and configured through this **Red Hat Network (RHN)** service.

You should become familiar with the different Red Hat products by reviewing the detailed information available at *www.redhat.com/software.* Note that the software included with Red Hat Enterprise Linux is not very different from that included with any other Linux distribution. Red Hat has added several powerful utilities, but the key to their success has been the service and support they offer to large companies using Linux. For example, the Enterprise Linux AS product, which can cost from $2500 to $18,000 per copy, provides one-hour response time for critical problems, 24 hours per day, seven days per week. The Red Hat training and certification programs, discussed later in this section, are also an important factor for businesses that consider using Linux, because they ensure knowledge-able staff to maintain the organization's Linux systems.

Hardware Requirements

Linux systems can run on very minimal hardware. You can run a Linux system using a computer with a 133 MHz CPU, 16 MB of RAM, and 100 MB of hard disk space (or perhaps even less, depending on what you wanted to do with the Linux system). Major distributions such as those listed in Table 1-1, however, typically recommend that your computer have a minimum of about 1 GB of free disk space and 64 MB of RAM. This permits you to use the graphical system and install a large number of commonly used software packages.

Realistically, if you are purchasing a newer computer, you are likely to have 128 MB of RAM and 20–40 GB of hard disk space at a minimum. More hard disk space permits you to install more applications, so you can add functionality to a server, store more data files, or just experiment with fun programs on your desktop. More RAM typically makes your system run faster because the Linux kernel uses the extra memory to store information from the hard disk, improving performance.

Red Hat provides specific recommendations for Enterprise Linux installations. It recom-mends 256 MB of RAM (a maximum of 8 GB for Enterprise Linux ES and 64 GB for Enterprise Linux AS), a 300 MHz CPU, and 800 MB of free disk space (a maximum file system size of 1 TB). Visit *www.redhat.com/software/rhel/configuration/* for information about Enterprise Linux requirements and an interesting summary of the capabilities of Linux.

Version Numbering

The version numbers associated with Linux products can be confusing. Each release of the Linux kernel is assigned a version number. Each component of a Linux distribution is also assigned a version number by the team that develops that component. The Linux distribu-tions themselves also have version numbers, which are chosen for marketing reasons, based on how often the distribution is updated.

Most users select the latest available version of the distribution that they choose to use. For example, Red Hat Enterprise Linux 3 is the latest version of Red Hat Linux available as of this writing. But the version number of the Linux kernel is also important because it defines some of the key capabilities of the operating system, such as what hardware is supported and what security model is used. The kernel version includes three parts:

- A major version number, which changes very rarely. The major version of Linux has been 2 for the last six or seven six years.

- A minor version number, which changes infrequently, perhaps every 10–18 months. Even-numbered minor versions are stable operating systems that are used for creating commercial Linux distributions. Odd-numbered minor versions are development versions of Linux that should not be used except by experienced Linux users because they may crash at any time. Development versions of Linux are interim releases—they allow advanced users to experiment with new features before they are stable.

- A patch-level number, which changes very frequently for development versions of Linux, perhaps once per day or once per week. For stable versions of Linux, this number changes only a few times (usually six to 10 times in a year) as problems are located and fixed to make the stable Linux kernel even more solid.

A version number for the Linux kernel might look like this: 2.6.3. This is a stable release of the kernel (as indicated by the 6). It is also patch level 3, indicating that the 2.6 kernel has had several minor updates for stability or improvements in hardware support. Another Linux kernel version might look like this: 2.7.67. In this case the second number is odd, indicating that it is a development release of the kernel, which should not be used in a business environment. The 67 indicates that 67 versions of this release have occurred, each with fixes or enhancements added by the kernel developers. After a certain number of enhancements have been added and made stable, the kernel developers will decide to release a kernel version 2.8.0. The process then begins again as they work on adding new features with the 2.9 series of kernels.

 Don't run the development kernels on your servers unless you want to experiment with new features that might crash your system. Commercial Linux distributions always use stable Linux kernel releases.

CAUTION

Linux distributions created by groups like Debian, Red Hat Software, and SUSE are composed of thousands of programs. The version of the Linux kernel included with a product is important, but a separate version number for each component could also be mentioned, for example, the version number of the Apache Web server or the version of the gcc compiler. To avoid the need to specify which version of each component is included in a distribution, vendors of commercial Linux distributions assign a version number to the distribution as a whole. For example, the Fedora Core 2 distribution contains a 2.6.5 Linux kernel. The 2 designation was decided by the group that put together the distribution; it has no relation to the version of the kernel or any other package. It does provide a shorthand for users, however, as anyone who has Fedora Core 2 can easily determine which version of other programs they are using by consulting the Fedora Web site (*fedora.redhat.com*).

Don't worry about the version number of a distribution when comparing products. Instead, look at the versions for the individual components that matter most to you, including the Linux kernel, the graphical system, and specific services you need to use. You can get information about all these specific version numbers from the vendor's Web site.

Linux Certification

One of the best ways to show potential employers that you have Linux skills is to obtain a Linux certification. A certification provides a standard by which employers can judge how much you have learned. It also gives them some assurance that you have some hands-on experience and familiarity with a broad range of technical issues that present themselves to a typical system administrator.

Industry Certification Programs

As outlined in the Preface, several Linux certification programs are available, including the following:

- Red Hat Software offers the Red Hat Certified Technician program, plus a more advanced Red Hat Certified Engineer program. See *www.redhat.com/training*. Objectives for this program are listed in Appendix A of this book.

- The Linux Professional Institute (LPI), a consortium of software industry companies (the most prominent being IBM), offers an LPI certification program with three levels: LPIC1, LPIC2, and LPIC3, for junior, intermediate, and senior system administrators, respectively. See *www.lpi.org*. Objectives for this program are listed in Appendix B of this book.

- SAIR/GNU, originally developed by a professor at the University of Mississippi, offers a Linux Certified Administrator (LCA) certification. See *www. linuxcertification.org*. Objectives for this program are listed in Appendix C of this book.

- CompTIA offers a Linux+ certification program. See *www.comptia.com*. Objectives for this program are listed in Appendix D of this book.

- Novell offers a Novell Certified Linux Engineer program, which builds on the LPI certification (or equivalent experience). See *www.novell.com/training*.

Among these programs, Red Hat certification is focused on Red Hat Enterprise Linux products; Novell's program focuses on SUSE Linux (which Novell now owns) and its integration with Novell's other networking software products; all the other certifications are vendor neutral, meaning that they try to provide information that applies to any of the major distributions of Linux.

Many other companies, of course, offer Linux training. Most recognize the value of certification in the job market and tie their instruction to one of the programs just listed.

Red Hat's Certification Program

Red Hat's certification program is very highly regarded, in part because certification is quite difficult to obtain. The exam consists of both multiple choice questions and a hands-on exercise. Basically, you sit down at a system that has been "broken." You must diagnose and repair the problems. Red Hat appears to take a perverse pride in the average failure rate of about 40% among test takers, though most people do well on the multiple choice portion.

The result, however, is that anyone who has passed the Red Hat exams is assumed to have a very strong technical foundation in Linux.

The Red Hat training program consists of three courses (though they are reconfigured and bundled in various ways with differing course numbers):

- *Course 033 Operator:* A class for a person with no prior Linux or UNIX experience
- *Course 133 Technician:* A class for those with experience in Linux or UNIX to the level of a competent operator
- *Course 253 Engineer:* An advanced class for experienced Linux system administrators. Much of this class focuses on networking services and security.

Anyone can take either the Red Hat Certified Technician (RHCT) or Red Hat Certified Engineer (RHCE) exam as often as they wish simply by paying the fee. Red Hat recommends, however, that a student have the equivalent of Courses 033 and 133 before taking the RHCT exam, and the equivalent of all three courses before taking the RHCE exam. Because taking a Red Hat exam costs several hundred dollars, sufficient preparation is highly recommended. A useful list of questions and answers is available at *www.redhat.com/ training/rhce/rhce_faq.html.*

THE WORK OF A SYSTEM ADMINISTRATOR

Although most Linux distributions can be downloaded free of charge, Linux is increasingly part of the information technology infrastructure of large organizations. These organizations require employees with Linux expertise to manage, sell, and work on those systems. Knowledge of Linux can therefore set you on the path to a fulfilling and profitable career.

Careers in Linux

Examples of the work you can do with a strong understanding of Linux and its related technologies include: system administrator, network administrator, software engineer, trainer, technical writer, product marketing, and business consultant.

Even if you are not seeking a job in a field directly related to Linux, many companies now recognize Linux expertise as a sign of generally strong computer knowledge. Such companies list knowledge of Linux as a qualifying skill for many types of jobs, including training, marketing, sales, and technical management.

You can visit any of the following Web sites to research jobs related to Linux by entering the keyword "Linux":

- *www.dice.com*
- *www.careerjournal.com*

- *www.monster.com*
- *www.careerbuilder.com*

The Duties of a System Administrator

The role of a system administrator within any organization is simple: make technology work and continue to work for those who do the "real work" of the organization. The term "real work" isn't meant to downplay what the system administrator does—to the contrary, all the powerful technology that an organization invests in is useless without the knowledge that a system administrator brings. Your goal as system administrator is to enable others to use the benefits that technology can provide.

While others develop software programs or hardware devices with great potential, the system administrator ties hardware and software into complete, operational systems that can increase productivity, lower costs, or otherwise benefit those who use the technology.

The system administrator keeps these systems running efficiently as new pieces are added, changes occur, and reconfigurations and failures alter the face of the original systems. The job of the system administrator is primarily practical. It requires perseverance, patience, curiosity, creativity, problem-solving skills, and technical knowledge. To be truly successful as a system administrator, you must continue to increase both the breadth (number of subjects) and depth (expertise in a subject) of your technical knowledge. If you don't, new problems will come along that you won't know how to solve. At the same time, you will lack the ability to integrate new technologies into your systems or to determine how they apply to your environment.

A term you will often hear is **MIS**, meaning **management of information systems**, or **manager of information systems** if applied to an employee.

A system administrator generally works as part of the **Information Systems (IS)** or **Information Technology (IT)** department of an organization. In a large organization, this group reports to a **chief information officer (CIO)**. In smaller organizations, a group of system administrators might consult other company officers to make decisions about information technology. The IS or IT department is typically concerned with two areas:

- *Internal information systems*: The computers on each employee's desk, the software they have installed, the networks that connect them together, and the user accounts to which employees log in. Internal systems normally include telephones as well, which are often computer-based and integrated with other computer systems.

- *Organizational information viewed by the public over the Internet*: Web servers, FTP download servers, e-mail servers, and similar public services

In technology organizations (such as companies that develop software or sell computers or telecommunications equipment), the team that develops software and hardware for sale to others is not part of the IS or IT department. Figure 1-4 shows the position of a system administrator in a typical small or large company.

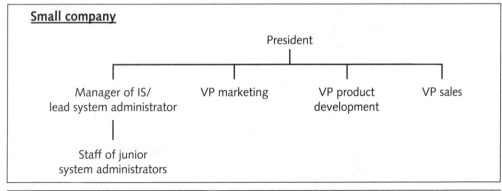

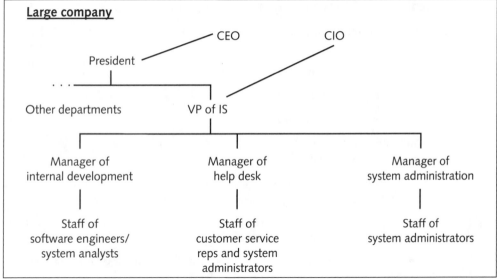

Figure 1-4   The position of a system administrator within large and small companies

System administrators typically have two- or four-year college degrees with a specialization in computer science, information technology, or a related field. A few junior system administrators are self-taught or have completed a short program of intense technical training. But most employers prefer the longer training that a two- or four-year degree provides, especially when hiring someone without previous work experience. Such a degree also improves your opportunity for promotion within an organization, either to more responsible system administrator positions or to related work such as programming, systems analysis, or management.

Most system administrators work with people as much as they work with technology. They may work primarily with a group of technical colleagues in the IT department, but they also are likely to interact with most of the organization as they answer questions, solve technical problems, train users, install software, and so forth. The employees of the organization are the clients or customers of the system administrator.

In larger organizations, the tasks of working with end users and maintaining the systems are divided into different areas. For example, an IS team may manage internal servers, while a Web team maintains Internet sites, and the **help desk** team directly solves problems for **end users** (those who use computer systems to accomplish their daily work). In such an environment, you, as a system administrator, can focus on the particular area that best suits your interests and skills, be it networking, server software, graphical productivity applications, or different types of computer hardware. Many of the same technical skills and problem-solving abilities are required for all of these areas.

Typical Tasks Performed by a System Administrator

As a system administrator, the tasks for which you are responsible can vary considerably based on factors such as:

- Your expertise and specific job position
- Your seniority in an organization
- The size of the organization

The following list shows some of the tasks that are part of a system administrator's job description in many organizations.

- Create new user accounts and make changes in existing user accounts, such as granting new access permissions as assignments change.
- Maintain system hardware, including installing new hardware to increase system capacity, replacing damaged systems, or upgrading obsolete components.
- Train end users to use new systems, software, or procedures effectively.
- Perform occasional or recurring tasks that keep the system running smoothly. Some of these are routine, such as backing up files; others require more creativity, such as determining why system response time has slowed, or tracking down an intruder from the Internet.
- Document the system so that other system administrators can understand how it is configured and how it operates. This might include informing others of how applications are configured, where backup files are stored, and which users have had specific problems with certain hardware or applications. This task is often related to the next one.

- Define procedures and policies related to how systems are administered at your site. Among other things, a system administrator might need to define backup procedures (see Chapter 13, "System and Kernel Management"), user guidelines (see Chapter 11, "Managing Users"), a disaster plan, or privacy and security policies (see the Course Technology companion volume to this book to be published in 2005.)

- Recover from emergencies. Get the system running again after a power outage, hardware failure, employee problem, or natural disaster.

- Plan systems. When working within small organizations or departments, or as you gain experience in a large organization, you may be asked to decide on new hardware purchases or plan for future system components or designs to meet anticipated needs.

Ethics, Privacy, and the Law

Working as a system administrator involves many ethical issues that may not be evident at first. As a system administrator you have control—full or partial—over an organization's computer systems. Implicit in this responsibility is a great deal of trust on the part of both the company (its officers, managers, and owners) and the individual employees who use the systems that you manage. The way you view this trust determines how effective you are as a system administrator. For example, if you cheat on school tests or certification exams, or pirate software (make unauthorized copies), you show your disregard for the legal and ethical norms that make employers comfortable trusting you. A professional reputation lost by such acts is very hard to regain.

Employers pay you to maintain their systems in a way that contributes to the success of their organization. Your role also has an important effect on individual users. Although you may be working behind the scenes most of the time (and probably should be if things are running smoothly), remember that your fellow employees count on your work in order to do theirs. A lack of preparation or accuracy on your part can lead to company-wide downtime, corrupted or lost files, malfunctioning printers, and so forth. As a result, other employees may not be able to be productive. Everyone in a modern office relies on the work of a good system administrator every workday.

With this influence over the work of others comes the potential for abuse. For example, as the system administrator with root privileges on the Linux server, you have the ability to:

- Play practical jokes that could cause trouble for users and make them mistrust the computer system.

- Read users' e-mail and the files in their home directories.

- Alter company or personal files.

- Send falsified messages as if they came from other users.

- Erase ("lose") files on the system.

- Delay fixing a system problem or helping an employee with a simple question.

- Neglect security measures that would protect sensitive data.

These actions are unethical because they invade others' privacy and impede the work of your employer. Most are also illegal and would make an unscrupulous system administrator subject to criminal prosecution. But as you might suspect, some unethical actions are likely to go undetected, especially if you are the sole person in a company with expertise in Linux.

 An excellent resource on legal issues related to technology is *www.gigalaw.com*.

TIP

To have a successful career as a system administrator, you should decide at the outset on a few guidelines for your relationships with employers and the fellow employees whose systems you manage. Your self-made guidelines might include statements such as these:

- I realize that I know more about the systems I manage than others, but I also realize that they know more about their job functions and what they need from their computer systems.

- I understand that other employees and managers trust me to handle their technology needs so they can be productive.

- I know I can never read files that do not belong to me personally unless I am required to do so as part of a legal proceeding or to comply with a publicly acknowledged company policy.

- I must treat other employees as my clients. My success as a system administrator depends on their satisfaction with my work, not on how much I know about technology.

Occasionally, a rogue system administrator decides to configure systems so that no one else can figure out how everything is put together. This is sometimes done in the name of job security: "They can't fire me," this kind of system administrator reasons, "or the entire company will have to shut down."

In fact, however, your best route to success as a system administrator (not to mention peace of mind) comes through making your employer successful. This allows you to grow professionally by accepting additional responsibility and embracing technical opportunities. If you train yourself well, you need never feel compelled to make implied threats of holding your employer "hostage" because you are the only person who can maintain the computer systems. Remember these two rules:

- Good jobs are always available for well-trained technical people; don't base ideas of job security on working at a single company. Instead, build a reputation as both a technical expert and a personable employee so that potential future employers will be eager to hire you and past employers will be sorry they lost you.

- If you haven't trained yourself well, you're not worth keeping as an employee. Your employer can then replace you with someone who is not being territorial under the guise of "job security." The true expert is always able to set up efficient, standardized, well-documented systems and have a solid career based on managing those systems.

To read more about working as a system administrator, visit the **System Administrators Guild (SAGE)** at *www.sage.org*. SAGE is part of the USENIX group, an organization for people who work with advanced computing systems (see *www.usenix.org*). USENIX and SAGE have tremendous resources for system administrators.

TIP

In relation to the topics in this section, consider reviewing the SAGE Code of Ethics at *http://sageweb.sage.org/resources/publications/code_of_ethics .html*.

Starting to Use Linux

In this section, you start using Linux. Ideally, you should have access to a computer with Linux installed as you read these sections.

NOTE

If you are not working in a classroom or lab, you may need to jump ahead to Chapter 8 ("Installing Linux") to install Linux yourself. Because installation is a fairly advanced topic, several chapters of foundational material are provided so you can better understand the installation process.

Logging In

Before you can do anything in Linux, you must **log in** to the system. When you log in, you identify yourself to the operating system so that it knows you are authorized to use the system, and which parts of the system to permit you to access. Unlike some older versions of Windows that you might have used, you cannot access any features of Linux without logging in.

Each person who uses a Linux system typically has his or her own user account. A **user account** is a set of permissions to use the system, with an associated user name and password. You must have a valid user name and password in order to log in. If you are working in a classroom or lab, your instructor should provide you with a user name and password. If you have installed your own Linux system, you should have created a user account (with a user name and password) when you installed Linux.

Linux operates in two modes: graphical and text. The text mode provides only a simple prompt at which you type your user name, press Enter, then type your password and press Enter. If you log in using a valid user name and password, you see a command-line prompt such as this:

```
[nwells@inverness nwells]$
```

At this prompt, you can enter commands to start programs or interact with the system. An explanation of each part of this prompt is provided later in this chapter. When you are working in this mode, you are using a **console**.

More commonly, you log in to Linux using a graphical login screen. This screen appears automatically after you turn on the Linux-based computer (after many lines of start-up information scroll by). When you enter your user name and password in the text boxes provided, you see a graphical desktop, similar to the one shown in Figure 1-5. This desktop interface is your main working environment.

Figure 1-5   The GNOME desktop interface

Graphical Environments

The desktop interface used by default on all major Linux distributions is very similar to the interface of any Microsoft Windows or Apple Macintosh computer. The Linux desktop interface can be reconfigured in many ways (as described in later chapters), but its basic operation is straightforward. Two different desktops are popular on Linux systems: the **KDE desktop** and the **GNOME desktop** (guh-NOME). Both of these desktops include the following basic features:

- A taskbar containing numerous icons across the bottom of the screen

- A main menu that you access by clicking on the icon in the lower-left corner of the screen (at the same location as the Start button in Microsoft Windows operating systems)

- Multiple levels of menus that group programs together by subject

- Desktop icons that you can double-click to access commonly used programs

- Multiple overlapping windows that you control using your mouse. Each window can be moved, resized, and so forth.

Opening a Terminal Window

From within the graphical desktop (the GUI, or the desktop), you can start a text-mode interface—a **terminal window**—that resembles a console. From this window you can enter commands from the keyboard.

TIP

A terminal window is also known by other names: a **command-line interface (CLI)** or an **xterm window**. Xterm (EX-term) is the name of one popular program that provides a terminal window in UNIX and Linux.

To start a terminal window in Red Hat Linux, click the main menu button in the lower-left corner of the desktop—it is the icon with a Red Hat on it. When the menu appears, click System Tools, and then click Terminal on the submenu that appears. A terminal window appears. You can also open a Terminal window by right-clicking the background of the desktop and selecting Open Terminal from the context menu that appears. You can open as many terminal windows as you want by repeating these steps. (See Figure 1-6.)

EXPLORING THE FILE SYSTEM

Manipulating files and directories is a large part of what you do on a computer, whether as a regular user or as a system administrator. For example, you search directories for a file, you open that file to review or change its contents, and you save an updated version of the file. This section describes some basic concepts and tools (both text-based and graphical) that enable you to access files on a Linux system.

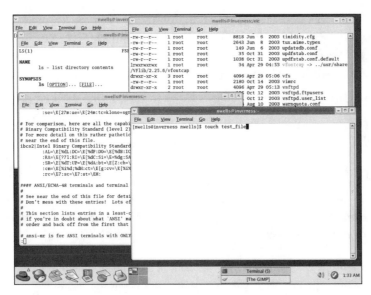

Figure 1-6 A graphical desktop with multiple open terminal windows

File System Concepts

Information stored on your computer is organized into files, each with a name and other attributes such as size and a creation date. To make it easier to keep track of thousands of files, they are organized into directories, which are similar to file folders that arrange files into groups. Each file has a name—a file name. Each directory also has a name. You should remember the following points about Linux file names and directory names:

- Names are case sensitive. If you name a file or directory using uppercase letters, you must use uppercase the next time you refer to that file or directory: The file names "test," "Test," and "TEST" can refer to three different files.

- Names can be long—up to 256 characters—and can contain multiple periods, numbers, spaces, and punctuation marks in addition to uppercase and lowercase letters. You cannot, however, use a forward or backward slash within a file name. For clarity, if a file name contains unusual characters, especially spaces, you generally enclose the file name in quotation marks. (Examples are shown later in this section.)

- Names can include file extensions, but these don't have the same importance as in Windows. For example, a Linux configuration file may not have an extension, or it may end with .conf, or some other file extension. (A **file extension** is the last part of the file name after a period.) The names of Linux program files don't include any file extensions (such as .exe or .com in Windows).

Multiple levels of directories are arranged in a branching treelike structure, in which one directory leads to other directories. Each directory can contain both files and other directories. When one directory contains another directory, that relationship is expressed by calling the first a **parent directory** and the second a **subdirectory**, or **child directory**. The subdirectory may also be the parent directory to another directory—a subdirectory—that it contains.

A list of directories is called a **path**. Each subdirectory in a path is separated by a forward slash.

> In Windows, a backward slash (\ ) is used to separate directories in a path. You must use a forward slash (/) in Linux.
>
> **CAUTION**

You can specify a path in two ways:

- *Use an* **absolute path**: Start the path with a forward slash and include every subdirectory starting from the root directory.
- *Use a* **relative path**: Do not start the path with a forward slash. The path is then assumed to be relative to the directory in which you are currently working.

An example can help illustrate absolute and relative paths. Suppose you are working in a directory called /home/nwells. You want to refer to the directory /home/nwells/documents. You could use the absolute path, /home/nwells/documents, or the relative path, documents. Suppose you were working in a directory called /usr/share/doc and wanted to refer to the /home/nwells/documents directory. You could use the absolute path, /home/nwells/documents, or the relative path, ../../home/nwells/documents. The relative path changes based on where you are working in the file system; the absolute path does not change. You decide which is more convenient as you work.

The double period (..) in the above example refers to the parent directory. So the path ../../home instructs the system to go to the parent directory of the one you're working in, then go to its parent directory, then look for a home directory at that point.

Every file, directory, and device in Linux is accessed as part of a single directory structure. Linux does not have separate drives such as A:, C:, and D:, as you find in Microsoft Windows systems. Instead, you access different hard disks or floppy disks by looking in different subdirectories. The parent directory for all of these is the root directory, which is represented by a single forward slash: (/). All Linux configuration files are located in subdirectories of the root directory. All devices are also associated with a file name located in a subdirectory of the root directory. As a system administrator, much of your work consists of managing the status, contents, and location of files and directories.

> The /root subdirectory is the home directory of the root user account. Don't confuse this with the root directory, /. For clarity, it's helpful to refer to the /root subdirectory as "slash-root," or "root's home directory."
>
> **TIP**

By default, Linux includes a standard set of subdirectories when first installed. Table 1-2 lists these subdirectories. Some versions of Linux may contain subdirectories of the root directory that are not listed here. For example, several versions of Linux use an /opt directory for storing optional applications.

On newly installed Linux systems, the directory that contains the greatest number of files and subdirectories is the /usr subdirectory. This subdirectory contains system utilities, the files for the graphical system, documentation files, and much more.

The names of standard Linux subdirectories are not intuitive, but each has a distinct purpose that has been refined through years of UNIX and Linux development. This well-known directory structure ensures that programs can interact with each other because they can locate files in customary locations on any Linux system. You will become familiar with the arrangement and purpose of standard Linux files and directories as you explore your system using the graphical and command-line tools described in the following sections.

Table 1-2   Standard Linux Subdirectories of the Root Directory

Directory	Contents
/bin	Executable programs, typically including system utilities
/boot	Files used to initialize Linux when the system is booted, such as the Linux kernel
/dev	File names that are linked to hardware resources (devices)
/etc	Configuration files, especially those used by system utilities and network services such as e-mail, Web, and FTP
/home	Home directories for all regular user accounts
/lib	System libraries (described later in this chapter) used by many Linux programs, especially system utilities and the Linux kernel
/root	Files used by the root user (the superuser account). This is the home directory of that user account. It is separate from the /home directory so that actions taken on /home (as described later) do not affect the root user's files.
/sbin	Executable programs used only by the root user
/tmp	Temporary files created by any user or program on the system
/usr	Files used by all regular users on the system, including data, programs, and documentation
/var	Variable (changing) information created by system utilities and network services; examples include system log files, e-mail messages, and files waiting to be sent to a printer

Managing Files with Graphical Utilities

Your Linux desktop includes a file manager that makes it easy to manage files and directories. The **file manager** on your GNOME desktop is a graphical program called **Nautilus**. This program displays the contents of a directory as a collection of icons or file names and lets you manage files and directories using menus, mouse clicks, and dialog boxes.

TIP

The descriptions here refer to the GNOME desktop interface, which is the default in Red Hat Linux. The KDE Desktop provides almost identical functionality in a program called Konqueror.

1

To open a Nautilus window, choose Browse Filesystem on the main menu.

File managers help you interact with many parts of Linux. They often resemble (and can act as) Web browsers as well. To view files and directories in the root directory using Nautilus, enter a forward slash (/) in the Location text box, then press Enter. The contents of the root directory are shown in the Nautilus window. You can change to a new directory or see the contents of many types of files by double-clicking any icon representing that directory or file. Some key operations you can perform within Nautilus are described in the next section.

In addition to entering a path in the Location text box, you can double-click a directory icon to view the contents of that directory. When you click the Up button in the toolbar of Nautilus, you see the contents of the parent directory (you move up the directory tree by one level).

Your personal working area in Linux is called your home directory. A **home directory** is the subdirectory where all of your personal files are stored, as well as configuration information and program settings specific to your user account. The Home button on the Nautilus toolbar takes you to your home directory, which is located by default in the /home directory, in a subdirectory with your user name. The home directories for all regular user accounts on a Linux system are stored in the subdirectory /home. For example, if your user name is abutler, your home directory would be /home/abutler.

You can view information in a directory either in the form of icons (the default—see Figure 1-7) or as a list of detailed information about each file and directory.

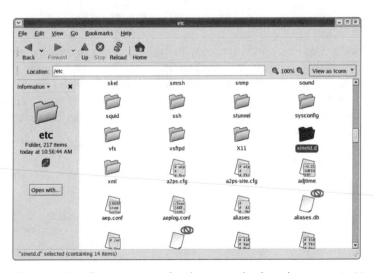

Figure 1-7   The contents of a directory displayed as icons in Nautilus

When you select to view icons or a detailed list, that setting only affects the directory you are viewing. To change the default so that all directories are shown using a list of details, choose Preferences on the Edit menu. On the Views tab, under Default View, change the View new folders using option to List View. (See Figure 1-8.)

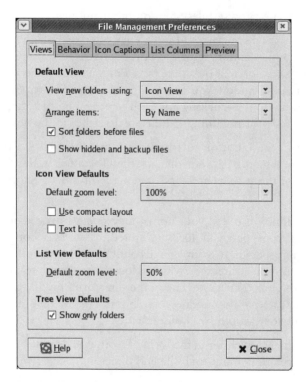

Figure 1-8   The Views tab of the File Management Preferences dialog box in Nautilus

In the Preferences dialog box, you can also review the Behavior tab, shown in Figure 1-9, to get a feel for what Nautilus can do with individual files. Each time you double-click a file, Nautilus tries to act on that file based on its contents. For example, if you double-click the icon or name of a text file, Nautilus shows the contents of that file. If you double-click a program, Nautilus starts that program. In the Behavior tab of the Preferences dialog box, you can adjust these actions to suit your preferences.

After changing to view a new subdirectory or double-clicking to view a file, you can return to the previous item you were viewing using the Back button on the toolbar, just as you might in a Web browser.

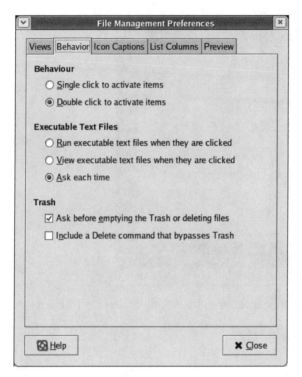

Figure 1-9 The Behavior tab of the File Management Preferences dialog box in Nautilus

TIP

You can perform many operations in Nautilus using keyboard shortcuts. For example, press F9 to view a side pane with information about any selected item, or press Alt+Left Arrow instead of clicking the Back button. Shortcuts are shown on the Nautilus menus and described in the Nautilus online help (which you can access by pressing F1).

When you right-click any file or directory in Nautilus, a context menu appears listing numerous things you can do with that file or directory. (See Figure 1-10.) Some of these options won't be familiar to you; they are explained later in this section and in later chapters. One option worth mentioning now, however, is the Properties item. Selecting this item opens a dialog box that shows you information about the selected file or directory. Figure 1-11 shows a Properties dialog box for a file.

As you learn more about the file system and about command-line utilities, return to a Nautilus window and see if you can perform the same operation using the graphical file manager. Knowing how to use multiple tools to perform a task can help you work more efficiently. Tips for doing some tasks in Nautilus are provided in the command-line section that follows.

Figure 1-10   A context menu appears after right-clicking an item in Nautilus

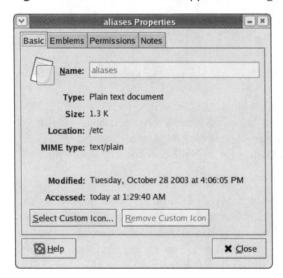

Figure 1-11   A Properties dialog box shows information about a file in Nautilus

Working at a Command Line

Although Linux has an increasing number of powerful graphical utilities such as Nautilus, most Linux system administrators would agree that you must be very comfortable working at a command line if you want to be truly proficient at managing a Linux system. Working at a command line requires you to memorize commands, but once you know the right commands, the command line is a much faster way to perform most tasks. In addition, some tasks simply cannot be done using a graphical interface.

In this section you learn about basic commands to move around in the file system. To try these commands, you can work at a console (text-mode login) or a terminal window within your graphical desktop.

Exploring Directories

When you first log in to Linux or open a terminal window, you are placed in your home directory, and a prompt appears, in this case *[nwells@london nwells]$*. You can enter the **pwd** command as shown below to display your **current working directory**, that is, the directory in which you are working. (The command name *pwd* stands for "print working directory.") The second line shows the system's response—the user's current working directory.

```
[nwells@inverness nwells]$ pwd
/home/nwells
```

Remember that Linux commands are case sensitive. Virtually all Linux commands—including all of the commands presented in this chapter—must be entered in lowercase letters. Entering the command PWD generates an error message.

The **cd** command changes the current working directory to a directory you specify. It does not, however, print anything on the screen—you see no feedback unless an error occurs. For example, if you are working in your home directory and want to change your current working directory to the /usr directory, you use this command:

```
[nwells@inverness nwells]$ cd /usr
```

Enter *cd* with no directory name. This always returns you to your home directory from whatever directory you are working in:

```
[nwells@inverness nwells]$ cd
```

As mentioned earlier, a double period indicates the parent directory of your current working directory. So the following command changes your current working directory to /home:

```
[nwells@inverness nwells]$ cd ..
```

In a Microsoft Windows command line, you can enter the command *cd..* without a space between *cd* and the two periods. This generates an error in Linux.

With this much background, you can explore the prompt used on the command line. It consists of four parts:

- Your user name ("nwells" in the previous examples)

- The name of the computer at which you are working ("inverness" in the previous examples). A name is assigned to your computer when Linux is installed; this part of the prompt typically does not change.

- The last directory name in your current working directory. (For example, if your current working directory is /home/abutler, the third item would be "abutler," and the prompt might be *[abutler@paris abutler]$*. But if you are working in the /usr/share/doc directory, the third item would be "doc," so the prompt might be *[abutler@paris doc]$*.

- The $ character. Whenever you are logged in as a regular user, a $ character appears. When you are logged in as the root user, a # character appears instead.

You can change the information provided in the prompt, but most system administrators don't. Now that you understand the prompt, the examples that follow will not show the entire prompt, but just a $ character (or a # character if you must be working as the root user for the example).

The **mkdir** command creates a new directory in the location you specify. For example, if you are in the directory /home/nwells, you can create a new subdirectory /home/nwells/documents using this command:

```
$ mkdir documents
```

If you are working in the /usr directory, you can create the /home/nwells/documents directory using the absolute path of the new directory:

```
$ mkdir /home/nwells/documents
```

In a Nautilus window, you can create a new subdirectory in the directory you are viewing by choosing Create Folder from the File menu, or by pressing Shift+Ctrl+N.

TIP

The **rmdir** command removes (deletes) an empty directory. If you try to delete a directory that contains files, you receive an error message. To remove entire directory trees, you can use the *rm -r* command, which removes everything inside a directory, including subdirectories. (Use this command with great care!)

In a Nautilus window, you can delete a directory by selecting it and pressing the Delete key.

TIP

The **ls** command lists the files in a directory. The *ls* command has dozens of options for displaying information about files and directories. One commonly used option is *-l* (a hyphen followed by lowercase letter "l"). Entering the command *ls -l* prints a long list of details about each file, such as when the file was created and how many bytes it contains.

You can include information on the command line after most Linux commands. Some pieces of information define what the command will operate on, such as a file name or directory name. These are called **parameters**. Some pieces of information alter how the command operates. These are called **options**, or command options. You will find in Linux documentation, however, that these two terms are used interchangeably. To understand the difference, consider two examples that apply to the *ls* command: The *-l* option (mentioned in the previous paragraph) controls what information the command displays. You can also include a parameter to control on which files the command operates. For example, the following command displays detailed information (via the *-l* option) on all files in the current directory that end with html (via the *html parameter).

```
$ ls -l *html
```

In Red Hat Linux, the *ll* command (lowercase LL, not one-one) displays a color-coded listing of directory contents with detailed information about each item in the directory. The information includes the size of files, the date the file or directory was created, and permission information that indicates who can access that item (you will learn more about the information provided by file listings in Chapter 4).

Information about the date and time when an event occurred is stored in the form of a **timestamp**. Linux maintains a set of timestamps for each file and directory that define when the file was created, when it was last modified, and when it was last accessed. The *touch* command updates a file's last accessed timestamp (that is, the date and time when the file was last accessed). If the file does not exist, it is created as an empty file.

For example, to create a new, empty file in your home directory, you could use these commands:

```
$ cd
$ touch test.doc
```

If you then use the *ls -l* command to look at the details of the file you just created, you see by the size and timestamp that it is in fact an empty file that was just created.

To make a copy of a file, use the *cp* command. You can use *cp* to copy a file within the same directory using a different file name, for example:

```
$ cp test.doc test.backup.doc
```

You can also copy a file to another directory using the same name. For example, the following command makes a copy of the report.doc file in the /tmp directory:

```
$ cp report.doc /tmp
```

To copy the file to a new directory with a new name, use a path with the new name. For example:

```
$ cp test.doc /tmp/test.backup.doc
```

In Microsoft Windows, you can use wildcards to match multiple file names. Linux has a more complex system that you will learn about in more detail in later chapters. For now, note that you can use (?) to match a single character, or (*) to match many characters, as you would with a wildcard in Microsoft Windows. For example, if your current working directory were /home/nwells/documents, the following command would copy all the files from /home/nwells/documents to /tmp/nwells:

```
$ cp * /tmp/nwells
```

You can use absolute and relative path names with any Linux command. For example, if your current working directory were /home/nwells/documents, the following command would copy all the files from that directory to /home/nwells (the parent directory of your current directory, as indicated by the ..):

```
$ cp * ..
```

> In a Nautilus window, you can copy one or more files that you have selected with your mouse by dragging and dropping them on a folder in another Nautilus window on your desktop. You can also right-click a file and choose Cut File or Copy File, then change directories, right-click again and choose Paste Files.

To delete a file, use the **rm** command (for *remove*). Be very careful using the *rm* command. When you delete a file using *rm*, the file cannot be undeleted as can files placed in a trash can or recycle bin on a graphical desktop. Linux graphical desktops provide a Trash icon. When you select an item in a Nautilus window and press the Delete key, the item is deleted by moving it to the Trash. You can double-click the Trash icon on your desktop to see (and restore if needed) any item that you have deleted using Nautilus. The *rm* command, however, does not use the trash can—it *permanently* deletes files.

In Linux the operations of moving and renaming a file are combined in one command, the **mv** command. The name *mv* is short for move; in essence, renaming a file is the same as moving it to a different file name. For example, if you have a file named report located in the /tmp directory, you can move it to the directory /home/nwells with this command:

```
$ mv /tmp/report.doc  /home/nwells
```

You can rename the file at the same time using a command such as this, which includes a new file name:

```
$ mv /tmp/test.doc  /home/nwells/test.backup
```

Using the *mv* command without a directory name as a parameter places the renamed file in the same directory as the original file. To move a file to a different directory, include the directory name and, optionally, a different file name.

> In Nautilus, you can move a file or directory to a new location by dragging it from one Nautilus window and dropping it in another. You can also right-click a file and choose Cut File, then change directories, right-click again and choose Paste Files. When using Nautilus to perform a move operation, you must rename the file separately by right-clicking and choosing the Rename option.

Viewing Files

Linux provides several utilities for viewing the contents of a file. The simplest of these is the *cat* command, which displays the contents of a file to the screen. For example, the following command displays the contents of the test file:

```
$ cat /etc/test
```

The *cat* command is also used to concatenate, or combine, multiple files into one larger file—that's where the name of the command comes from. The **zcat** command displays the contents of a compressed text file to the screen. If a file ends with the letters "gz", it has been compressed using the *gzip* command. To view the contents of a file that has been compressed with *gzip* without first uncompressing it, use the *zcat* command.

Most files do not fit on one screen, in which case the *cat* command works too quickly—you only see the last 20 or so lines of text in a file. To view a large file, use the **less** command, which displays the contents of a file one screenful at a time. You can use the arrow keys or Page Up and Page Down to move to different areas of the file. To move to the next screenful of text, press the spacebar. For example, the following command displays a large configuration file one screen at a time:

```
$ less /etc/termcap
```

Type *q* to exit the *less* command. The *less* command is similar to the **more** command, which is also used to display the contents of a file one screenful at a time. The *less* command has more features than the *more* command, but you can use either one to view the contents of files. The *less* and *more* commands are intended to display text files (with human-readable content).

You can use the **file** command to determine what a file contains. The *file* command tells you the type of data contained in a file. If you are not familiar with a particular file, use the *file* command to see what it contains before using the *less* or *more* command. For example, the following command shows the type of the indicated file, with the results appearing on the second line:

```
$ file /etc/printcap
/etc/printcap: ASCII English text
```

If you know that a particular file exists on your Linux system, but you cannot remember where it is, use the **slocate** command (for secure-locate) to find it. For example, suppose that to perform a certain task you need to edit a configuration file named services, but you cannot remember which directory it is stored in. Use this command to show all instances of "services" in a file name or directory name:

```
$ slocate services
```

If you cannot remember whether the file is called "services" or "serviced," use just part of the name:

```
$ slocate servi
```

Another command called *locate* provides the same functionality as *slocate*, but *slocate* is preferred because it only shows files that you have permission to access.

CAUTION

The *slocate* command shows you the entire path and file name for anything containing the text string you indicate. The more precise you can be, the shorter (and thus more helpful) is the list that *slocate* displays.

Before you can use *slocate*, the files and directories must be indexed. If you are working on a newly installed Linux system, or one that is not left on continuously, this index may not have been created. To create it, you must log in as root and execute the command **updatedb**.

NOTE

This section has described a few Linux commands you can use to manage files and directories from the command line. These commands and the other commands introduced in this chapter are summarized in the Command Summary near the end of the chapter. In the projects at the end of this chapter you can practice using these commands.

FINDING COMMAND HELP

This book introduces you to the most important topics and skills you need to know to work as a Linux system administrator. You can learn more details than there is room for in this book, and also explore additional Linux topics, using the resources described in this section.

Reading Linux Documentation

Because the developers of Linux and other free software projects were working entirely via the Internet, they shared descriptions of their software via electronic or online documentation. This documentation was typically incorporated into the project when it was distributed for everyone's use. Most Linux distributions include all of this documentation—thousands of pages of material that you can quickly access using a few simple commands.

When you read Linux documentation, remember that much of it was written by software developers. Because of that, much of the documentation for Linux software is written as if you already have read all of the *other* documentation on the system. You can find a wealth of useful detail, but as a newcomer to Linux, you should expect to read many things that you don't initially understand. Returning to material later will make everything clearer.

The Linux Documentation Project

The **Linux Documentation Project (LDP)** was begun by Matt Welsh in the early 1990s, when Linux was just becoming well known in technical circles. The LDP was one of the first efforts to document how Linux works and continues to provide Linux documentation today in a variety of formats. The LDP currently contains over 6000 pages of documentation, all of which is available online, free of charge, under a version of the GPL modified for use with documentation. The LDP consists of several types of documents. Some of these, such as the *Network Administrator's Guide* and the *Kernel Hacker's Guide*, are complete online reference manuals.

Initially, you will probably find the HOWTO documents to be the most useful part of the LDP. The **HOWTOs** cover specific topics, such as sharing a system between Windows XP and Linux, or maintaining network security. Most documents are written by one person with expertise in a topic. Documents called mini-HOWTOs focus on narrower subjects than do regular HOWTOs. HOWTO documents are usually written by software developers, but they are intended for readers who are not familiar with the topic being discussed.

The LDP and all of the HOWTO documents are included with many Linux distributions, though they are generally not installed by default because of their size. You can also read them on many Web sites.

TIP

A good place to begin researching the documentation available as part of the LDP is *www.tldp.org*.

Linux on the Internet

Linux was created on the Internet, and the Internet is still a great place to find out more about Linux. Every day, developers release new software, companies make announcements about Linux products, and various users provide new or revised information. When you have a challenging question, one effective method of finding an answer is to visit *www.google.com* and enter the key words of your question. For example, suppose you just acquired a new wireless networking card and want to know if Linux supports it. Entering something like "Linux driver D-Link DWL-2100AP" will probably locate several messages by Linux administrators discussing how to use this product. (If you're curious, Linux does support wireless networking, with new drivers becoming available regularly.) Table 1-3 lists some more general Web sites that might be useful as you explore the world of Linux.

Table 1-3   Linux-related Web Sites

Web site	Description
www.linuxjournal.com	A companion Web site to the monthly printed magazine; contains additional Linux links and information (mostly technically oriented)
www.linuxmagazine.com	A companion Web site to the monthly printed magazine; contains additional Linux links and information, both business and technically oriented

Table 1-3 Linux-related Web Sites (continued)

Web site	Description
www.linuxworld.com	A business-oriented online magazine (now with a printed version as well), containing interviews, links, technical reports, and other up-to-date information
www.slashdot.org	An eclectic collection of news items related to free software and other topics (such as Star Wars, new music technologies, cryptography legislation, etc.) of interest to free software developers
www.linuxhq.com	A collection of information about work on the Linux kernel, with useful links to many other sites and Linux resources
www.lwn.net	Linux Weekly News, a collection of news items related to Linux and other free software
www.linuxtoday.com	Recent news items on Linux and other free software
www.linuxgazette.com	Recent news items on Linux and other free software

The Web sites for each of the Linux distributions listed in Table 1-1 are also great resources for learning about Linux.

Documentation Included with Software Packages

Most of the software packages included with a Linux distribution provide at least some documentation. This documentation is installed on your system along with the software itself. You can normally view the documentation either in a text editor or a Web browser. In most distributions of Linux, the documentation is stored in the /usr/doc or /usr/share/doc subdirectory of the file system. Red Hat Linux stores documentation for each software package in a separate subdirectory of /usr/share/doc. Note, however, that the documents are of varying quality. Some software packages provide a single file with recent changes to the software; others provide a full manual in several formats.

Linux Command Information

As you can already sense, Linux includes many different commands, each with numerous options. It makes little sense to memorize all of the commands and options, because you only use a small percentage of them regularly. When you do need to use a new command or option, you can learn about it through the Linux command-specific information that is available online. This information is provided in two formats. You can access online manual pages (called **man pages**) for most Linux commands by using the ***man*** command.

For example, to learn all about the *ls* command, you can enter this command:

```
$ man ls
```

A lengthy document appears describing all the options available for *ls*. You can move around in this document using the arrow keys, Page Up, and Page Down. When you have finished reading, type *q* to exit the man page viewer. Each man page has a standard format. As with

1

many other parts of Linux, they may seem cryptic at first, but once you become familiar with them, you can easily locate the information you need for a command you want to use.

For some Linux commands, the definitive source of information is in a second format: an **info page**. You can view info pages using the *info* command. For example, you can also view details about the *ls* command using this command:

```
$ info ls
```

Info pages are not as widely used as man pages, though the info page format is more appealing in some ways (for example, info pages generally contain more examples, which are helpful for users learning a new command).

Chapter Summary

- An operating system provides an interface between the computer hardware and the applications run by the user.

- In its most basic form, an operating system manages the use of memory, CPU time, and other system resources. A complete operating system includes many other features to provide additional hardware support, a graphical environment, and utility programs.

- The Linux kernel, based in principle on UNIX technology (but not UNIX source code), was created by many talented individuals from around the world working under the leadership of Linus Torvalds, who continues to maintain the Linux kernel.

- The Free Software Foundation, led by Richard Stallman, created hundreds of software programs as part of its GNU Project. These are included with the Linux kernel in each copy of a complete Linux operating system distribution.

- The General Public License (GPL) is responsible in large part for the phenomenal growth of Linux in the last few years. It requires that source code be distributed with each copy of the Linux kernel (and many other free software projects). The so-called viral nature of the GPL means that anyone who changes part of the Linux kernel must also give away their work under the GPL.

- Various companies have created commercial products that are built around the Linux kernel and GNU software. These are called distributions.

- Linux offers important features such as stability, speed, security, flexibility, and low cost.

- A typical Linux installation requires about 1 GB of hard disk space, though much smaller and much larger installations are not uncommon. More RAM provides better performance because the Linux kernel can store frequently used information in memory for faster access.

- Several Linux certification programs are available from Red Hat Software, LPI, SAIR/GNU, and CompTIA. The Red Hat Certified Technician and Red Hat Certified Engineer programs require applicants to pass a hands-on exam.

❏ Red Hat Enterprise Linux is sold in several versions, such as WS, ES, and AS. Fedora is a separate project that is aimed at users who prefer a free software product rather than one with commercial support.

❏ Careers in Linux include system administrators, software developers, technical writers, industry analysts, and others.

❏ A system administrator occupies an important position of trust within an organization, but a good system administrator is nearly invisible to the people whose productivity he or she makes possible.

❏ Most users will rely on a graphical interface to log in and use Linux, though a text-only mode is also available. Commands can be entered and programs started at a command line or using numerous graphical utilities through a desktop interface such as GNOME or KDE.

❏ A graphical file manager called Nautilus provides a simple way to navigate the file system and perform most common file management tasks.

❏ Information in Linux is stored in a directory structure that begins with the root directory, /. Subdirectories and parent directories help organize large numbers of files. Commands such as *pwd*, *cd*, *mkdir*, and *rmdir* manage directories.

❏ Linux files and directories are organized in an inverted tree structure with a forward slash (/) representing the root (the top) of the tree. All Linux resources are accessed within directories; Linux does not use drive letters.

❏ Linux file names, directory names, and commands are case sensitive.

❏ An absolute or relative path can be used in a command that requires a path.

❏ Basic file management is done with commands such as *ls*, *cp*, *rm*, *mv*, *cat*, *less*, and *more*. You can learn more about any command by viewing its man page or info page.

❏ Linux files can include file extensions, but few Linux programs rely on file extensions to define what the file contains.

❏ Information about Linux is available online as part of the Linux Documentation Project (LDP), which includes many HOWTO documents on specific topics. Online documentation for Linux commands is included with every copy of Linux. Many publications and Web sites maintain daily news updates about what is happening in the world of Linux and free software.

COMMAND SUMMARY

Command	Description	Example
cat	Displays the contents of a file onscreen	cat /etc/printcap
cd	Changes to a different directory	cd /usr/share
cp	Copies a file to a new location or file name	cp report.doc report.backup
file	Displays a description of what a file contains or its purpose	file /etc/printcap
info	Displays the info page for a given command; similar to a man page	info ls
less	Displays the contents of a file on-screen, one screenful at a time	less /etc/termcap
ls	Lists the contents of a directory	ls -l
man	Displays the online manual page (the man page) for a given command	man slocate
mkdir	Makes (creates) a new directory	mkdir /tmp/documents
more	Displays the contents of a file onscreen, one screenful at a time	more /etc/termcap
mv	Renames a file or moves a file to a new location (possibly under a new name)	mv testfile testfile.old
pwd	Displays the current working directory	pwd
rm	Removes (deletes) a file	rm report.old
rmdir	Removes (erases) an empty directory	rmdir /tmp/documents
slocate	Displays matching file and directory names anywhere on the system	slocate services
touch	Creates a new, empty file, or updates the timestamp of an existing file	touch test
updatedb	Creates or updates the index of file and directory names used by the *slocate* command (must be run as root)	updatedb
zcat	Displays the contents of a compressed file onscreen	zcat /tmp/report.gz

KEY TERMS

absolute path — A complete description of how to access a desired subdirectory or file, specified from the root of the file system to the subdirectory or file. It must begin with a forward slash. *See also* relative path.

application — A program (such as a word processor or spreadsheet) that provides a service to a person using the computer, rather than simply managing the computer's resources.

binary code — Machine-readable instructions used to execute a program.

chief information officer (CIO) — The executive in an organization who determines how information systems are used within the organization to further its goals or mission effectively.

child directory — A subdirectory of a parent directory.

command-line interface (CLI) — A method of communicating with the operating system by entering textual commands at a prompt.

console — A text-only interface to the operating system, providing a command-line interface. Not part of a GUI.

copyleft — An ironic term that refers to the GNU General Public License (the GPL), signifying a radical departure from standard copyright.

current working directory — The directory in which you are working. Displayed using the *pwd* command.

desktop interface — *See* graphical user interface (GUI).

device drivers — Software that provides access to additional hardware, beyond core device support provided by the kernel.

end user — An individual who uses the computer systems in an organization to accomplish assigned tasks, but who often relies on a system administrator to keep those systems running smoothly.

file extension — The last part of a file name, traditionally the last three letters, separated from the rest of the file name by a period. Used in some cases to indicate the type of information the file contains, such as a document or graphic image of a particular format.

file manager — A graphical utility used to manage files and subdirectories. Nautilus in the GNOME desktop is one example. Konqueror is the default file manager in the KDE desktop.

forking — Starting a new free software project based on an existing project.

Free Software Foundation (FSF) — An organization founded by Richard Stallman to promote his ideals of freely available software and to create and distribute that software.

gcc — A C language compiler. Probably the best-known product of the GNU Project.

GNOME desktop (guh-NOME) — A graphical interface used by many Linux distributions, including Red Hat Linux.

GNU General Public License (GPL) — The free software license that Richard Stallman of the Free Software Foundation developed for the programs created by the GNU Project.

GNU Project — An effort by the Free Software Foundation to create a free UNIX-like operating system. Many of the programs in every Linux distribution come from the GNU Project.

graphical user interface (GUI) — Software that provides mouse-driven applications with menu bars, buttons, and so forth.

hard wired — Computer functionality that is arranged in the wires and other components that make up a computer. Hard-wired functionality cannot be easily altered.

help desk — A service in many organizations that assists end users in solving problems related to information technology.

home directory — An area of the file system in which a particular user is permitted to store data. Each regular user account has an associated home directory, named after the user account login name. These are typically subdirectories of the /home directory in Linux.

HOWTOs — Documents within the Linux Documentation Project that cover specific topics.

info page — A source of information for many Linux commands. Accessed using the *info* command. *See also* man page.

Information Systems (IS) department — A department within many organizations. IS staff are responsible for maintaining computer and information systems for other employees. (IS is called IT in some organizations.)

Information Technology (IT) department — *See also* Information Systems (IS) department.

KDE desktop — A graphical interface used by many Linux distributions.

kernel — The core of the operating system. The kernel interacts directly with the computer hardware and manages computer memory, the time allocated to each program running on a system, and other system resources.

LGPL (Library GPL) — A special version of the GNU General Public License intended to govern both free and commercial software use of software libraries.

Linux distribution — A Linux operating system product that includes the Linux kernel plus many software components, installation tools, documentation, and so forth.

Linux Documentation Project (LDP) — One of the first efforts to document how Linux is used. Started by Matt Welsh.

log in — To identify yourself to the operating system so that it knows that you are authorized to use the system, and which parts of the system to permit you to access.

man page — An online manual page for a Linux command. The man pages are accessed using the *man* command.

MIS (management of information systems or manager of information systems) — Another term for the IS or IT department or the staff who work in or manage that department.

multiprocessing – Operating with more than one CPU in a single computer (for example, a dual-Pentium system).

Nautilus — The graphical file manager provided with the GNOME desktop.

OpenSource — A trademarked name often used to refer to software licensed under the GPL.

operating system — Software that provides a set of core functionality for other programs to use in working with the computer hardware and interfacing with the user.

option — Information added to a command that determines how the command operates.

parameter — Information added to a command that defines what the command operates on, such as a file name or directory name.

parent directory — A directory that is above another directory, closer to the root of the file system.

path — A description of all the subdirectories in the file system hierarchy by which a particular subdirectory or file is accessed. Each part of the path—each subdirectory—is separated from others with a forward slash. *See also* relative path, absolute path.

public domain — Creative work (such as a software program) to which no one has a copyright ownership interest.

Red Hat Network (RHN) — A service provided via subscription by Red Hat Software using the Internet. This service automatically provides any security fixes, package upgrades, or other information needed to keep a Red Hat Linux system running smoothly and securely.

relative path — A description of how to access a desired subdirectory or file, specified relative to another location in the file system (typically the current working directory) rather than from the root of the file system (for which an absolute path is used). A relative path does not begin with a forward slash. *See also* absolute path.

SAGE (System Administrators Guild) — A professional organization for system administrators.

shell — A command interpreter that provides a command-line interface in a terminal window.

software — Instructions that control the physical computer components, but can be changed because they reside on a changeable media such as a hard disk.

software license — A legal definition of who can use a piece of software and how it can be used.

source code — A set of human-readable programming instructions used to create a piece of software.

Stallman, Richard — Founder of the Free Software Foundation and the GNU Project.

subdirectory — A directory that is contained within another directory, and thus further from the root of the file system.

system utilities — Programs that are used to manage a Linux system. *See also* utility programs.

terminal window — A command-line interface within a graphical desktop.

timestamp — A record of the date and time when an event occurred.

Torvalds, Linus — Originator of the Linux kernel; formerly a student in Helsinki, Finland.

total cost of ownership (TCO) — The sum of all costs involved in providing a technology solution, including components such as the initial cost of purchasing software and required hardware, support contracts, training for administrators, programmers, and end users, upgrade charges, and recovery costs if the technology fails unexpectedly.

UNIX — An operating system created at AT&T Bell Labs (now part of Lucent Technologies) about 30 years ago by Ken Thompson and Dennis Ritchie. UNIX is still widely used, and it provided the technical basis for Linux.

user account — A set of permissions to use the system, with an associated user name and password.

utility programs — Software that provides assistance in managing the hardware and operating system features (as opposed to doing other types of work such as word processing). *See also* system utilities.

X Window System — A graphical software environment used by almost all UNIX and Linux operating systems.

xterm window — A type of terminal window. Used generically to refer to a command-line window within a graphical desktop interface.

REVIEW QUESTIONS

1. An operating system does *not* do which of the following:
   a. Allocate system resources such as memory and CPU time.
   b. Initialize computer hardware so it can be used by software running on the computer.
   c. Keep track of multiple programs running at the same time.
   d. Provide word-processing features for users.

2. Name four career paths where a strong knowledge of Linux is useful.

3. Linus Torvalds began to create Linux because:
   a. He was hired as an operating system consultant by a major corporation.
   b. He wanted a powerful operating system but could not afford one.
   c. His professor required that each student create a basic operating system.
   d. He felt it would be a good career move.

4. The Free Software Foundation is dedicated to the idea that:
   a. No company should be able to charge money for any software.
   b. The real value of software is in customization, not in selling mass-produced copies.
   c. Richard Stallman's C compiler is the best in the world.
   d. Linux is an important development in operating systems.

5. The GNU Project is important to Linux because:
   a. It provides the majority of the system utilities used by Linux.
   b. GNU software is the only software compatible with Linux.
   c. The media attention generated by the GNU Project has made Linux popular.
   d. Richard Stallman is a strong supporter of the Linux movement.

6. The GPL includes all of the following facets *except*:
   a. GPL software must include source code.
   b. Modifications to GPL-licensed software must also be licensed under the GPL.
   c. Software that runs on a GPL operating system must be given away.
   d. A company cannot charge money for GPL-licensed software.

7. In general usage, the name "open source software" refers to:

   a. only programs that are licensed explicitly under the GPL

   b. programs that don't have source code included

   c. software that has source code included and follows a set of general principles espoused by the OpenSource consortium

   d. only programs released as part of the GNU Project

8. In the Linux kernel version 2.6.10, the second digit, 6, indicates:

   a. a major kernel release number

   b. a minor kernel release number for a stable kernel

   c. a minor kernel release number for a development kernel

   d. a patch release number

9. Version numbers for Linux distributions don't track Linux kernel version numbers because:

   a. Distributions include many components, so the vendor assigns a version number to the collection of software as a whole.

   b. Developers of the Linux kernel want to avoid having too close a tie with any single Linux vendor by using the same numbering scheme.

   c. Linux kernel versions change too quickly for standard retail cycles to keep up.

   d. Not all kernels are stable and no commercial distribution wants to create an image of poor stability.

10. HOWTO documents discuss a variety of specific subjects. They are written for:

    a. software developers

    b. journalists

    c. anyone new to the subject being discussed

    d. computer novices

11. The _____ directory is the beginning of the Linux directory structure—the top of the inverted tree.

    a. /

    b. /root

    c. /home

    d. /dev/hda

12. The *pwd* command is used to:

    a. Process writeable domains on the network.

    b. Control power used by a Linux system.

    c. Display the current working directory on the screen.

    d. List a summary of the writeable devices on the system.

1

13. The command *Ls -l* is invalid because:
    a. Linux commands cannot contain hyphens.
    b. Linux commands are case sensitive.
    c. *ls* is a script name, not a command.
    d. The *-l* option is not supported by the *ls* command.

14. Which task is not likely to be assigned to you as a system administrator?
    a. Develop a new cash register system using C programming.
    b. Install new hard disks in Linux servers.
    c. Teach new users how to access their e-mail accounts.
    d. Attend a conference on improving system security.

15. Linux file names can include:
    a. letters and digits, but not punctuation, or any special characters
    b. letters and digits, plus spaces
    c. letters, digits, with some punctuation, but no spaces
    d. letters, digits, punctuation, and many special characters

16. The *rm* command is used in Linux to:
    a. Remove special characters from a file name.
    b. Delete files from a hard disk.
    c. Remove case-sensitivity settings.
    d. Manage regular expressions.

17. A trash can facility on a Linux graphical desktop differs from the *rm* command in that:
    a. Files placed in the trash can are not deleted until the trash can is emptied, but files deleted by *rm* are deleted immediately.
    b. Files placed in the trash can are deleted immediately, but files deleted by *rm* are not truly erased until the system is restarted.
    c. The *rm* command overwrites data when files are deleted, but the trash can facility simply marks parts of the hard disk as available when the file stored in that space is deleted.
    d. Files can be placed in the trash can by any user, but only root can use the *rm* command.

18. Each answer contains several paths separated by semicolons. Which answer contains only absolute paths?

    a. ../home/abutler; /etc; documents

    b. /documents; share/doc; nwells/data

    c. /var/named; /etc/samba; /home/abutler

    d. /etc/sysconfig; printcap; ../../reports/

19. Within the Nautilus file manager, you can view the properties of a selected file or directory by:

    a. selecting Icon View from the Preferences View tab

    b. selecting List View for the folder in which the file or directory is located

    c. pressing F9

    d. right-clicking the file or directory and selecting the Properties item from the context menu

20. Within the Nautilus file manager, pressing Shift+Ctrl+N is analogous to which command?

    a. *mkdir*

    b. *rm -f*

    c. *ls -l*

    d. *cp* *

21. Which of the following commands is most likely to produce the following output on the screen? /home/abutler

    a. *cd*

    b. *cp* * */tmp*

    c. *pwd*

    d. *man ls*

22. You see in the output of *ls -l* an unrecognized file. You wonder what it contains. Your first step should be to use which command?

    a. *file*

    b. *cat*

    c. *less*

    d. *zcat*

23. If the *slocate* command fails to function as expected, it is likely because:

    a. You don't have permission to use it.

    b. The index of file and directory names has not been created using updatedb.

    c. The man page for *slocate* is not installed.

    d. You have entered the command in uppercase letters.

24. In Red Hat Linux, documentation files dedicated to each installed software package are stored:

    a. in the /usr/share/doc directory

    b. in the /documents directory

    c. as either man pages or info pages, but never both

    d. in compressed format

25. The Red Hat Enterprise Linux product line includes several versions such as

    a. WS, WA, WE

    b. WS, ES, and Fedora

    c. WS, ES, AS, and Professional Workstation

    d. Core 1 and Core 2

HANDS-ON PROJECTS

HANDS-ON PROJECTS

Project 1-1

In this project, you review Red Hat Software's Web site to learn about its products and certification programs. To complete this project, you should have a computer with access to the Internet and a functioning Web browser.

1. Start a Web browser. From the GNOME desktop in Red Hat Linux, you can start the **Mozilla** browser by clicking the icon with a globe on it, just to the right of the main menu button with the red hat on it.

2. Go to the site **www.redhat.com**.

3. Click the **Software** link on the home page.

4. Click links on the Software page (*www.redhat.com/software*) for **Enterprise Linux ES** and **Enterprise Linux AS**. What are the main differences between these two versions?

5. View the page on **Enterprise Linux AS**. What is the fastest response time provided by the available technical support options?

6. Explore the **Red Hat Network** and **Red Hat Application** pages to see what software and services are available to support Red Hat Enterprise Linux products.

7. Click the **Training** link at the top of the Web page.

8. Click the link on the left of the training page for the **RHCE/RHCT** Program.

9. Review the information in the table shown for the RHCT program. Click the link within the table for the **RH202** course. (This is actually the RHCT exam.) What is the cost of the exam? How long does the exam take to complete?

10. Review the cities in which the exam is available.

11. Back up one page and select the **RH302** course. (This is actually the RHCE exam.) Review the cities in which the exam is available, the cost of the exam, and how long it takes to complete.

12. Browse to *http://fedora.redhat.com*.

13. Locate the **FAQs** link and click it.

14. Does Red Hat Software provide formal technical support for the Fedora Project's Linux distribution?

Project 1-2

In this project, you look at some of the different Linux HOWTOs. To complete this project, you need a computer with access to the Internet and a functional Web browser.

1. Open your Web browser and connect to the Internet.

2. Go to the Linux Documentation Project at **www.tldp.org**.

3. Click the **HOWTOs** link, then click the **Alphabetical index** link to browse the titles of the HOWTO documents in HTML format.

4. Open up a HOWTO document that interests you. Review the table of contents. Note the author and the date of the last update to the HOWTO.

5. Read one section of the HOWTO. Return to the **Contents** page and select another section to review. Summarize the main points of the document.

6. Use the **Back** button on your browser to return to the **index** of HOWTO documents. Select a second HOWTO document to review. Note the date of the last update. Is a link provided so that you can contact the author to obtain more recent information?

Project 1-3

In this project, you use Linux commands to manage files and directories. To complete this activity you should have an installed Linux system with a valid user account.

1. Log in to Linux using your user account name and password.

2. If you logged in using a graphical login screen, open a terminal window by clicking on the icon in the lower-left corner of the desktop to open the main menu, then selecting **System Tools**, then **Terminal**. A terminal window opens.

1

3. Enter the **pwd** command to display your current working directory. Because you have just logged in, this should display your home directory.

4. Create a new subdirectory named "archive" within your home directory using the command **mkdir archive**.

5. Change to the new subdirectory you just created by entering **cd archive**.

6. Create a new file named "report" using this command: **touch report**.

7. Enter **ls –l** to view a detailed file listing of the files in the archive subdirectory. Can you see the size of the report file?

8. Change the name of the report file to "oldreport" using **mv report oldreport**.

9. Use the *ls* command to verify that the file report is no longer there—it has been renamed as oldreport.

10. Copy the oldreport file, making a second copy of the file in the same directory using the **cp oldreport oldreport2** command.

11. Move both of these files to your home directory using this command: **mv * ..**

12. Enter the **pwd** command to check that your current working directory is still the archive subdirectory of your home directory.

13. Use a relative path to remove one of the files from your home directory by entering **rm ../oldreport**.

14. List all the files in the current directory using the **ls** command.

15. Change back to your home directory using the **cd** command.

16. Because the archive subdirectory is empty, you can use the *rmdir* command to delete it by entering **rmdir archive**.

17. Use **ls –l** to check the contents of your home directory. You should see the old-report2 file with a size of zero.

18. Copy the termcap configuration file (its purpose is not relevant for this project) to your home directory and give it the name of an existing file by entering **cp /etc/termcap oldreport2**.

19. Use the **ls –l** command again. What happened?

20. Delete the file by entering **rm oldreport2**.

Project 1-4

In this project, you explore online documentation for a Linux command. To complete this activity you should have an installed Linux system with a valid user account. This project assumes you are working in a graphical desktop.

1. Log in to Linux using your user account name and password.

2. Open a terminal window by clicking on the icon in the lower-left corner of the desktop to open the main menu, then selecting **System Tools**, then **Terminal**. A terminal window opens.

3. Repeat Step 2 to open a second terminal window.

4. At the command prompt of the second window, enter **man ls** to view the man page for the *ls* command.

5. Press **Page Down** to skim the information in the *ls* manual page. What are some of the section headings that you note?

6. Search for the command options of the *ls* command. There are over 50 options. What do some of the options do?

7. Move to the top of the man page using either the **Page Up** key, the **up arrow**, or by pressing **1**, then **Shift+G**.

8. To search for the word color, press **/** and then type **color**, then press **Enter**. What do you find?

9. Switch to the other open terminal window by clicking anywhere inside the window.

10. Open the info page by entering **info ls**.

11. Use the arrow keys to scroll to the bottom of the page. What do you notice about this page?

12. Near the bottom of this info page, use the up and down arrow keys to place the cursor on the line * **Sorting the output::** Press **Enter**. What happens?

13. Press **Backspace** to return to the previous info page.

14. Type **q** to exit the info page viewer. You can enter the command *info info* to read more about how to control the info page viewer.

15. Change to the other open terminal window (containing the *ls* man page) by clicking anywhere in the window.

16. Exit the man page viewer by typing the **q** key.

17. Close the two terminal windows.

CASE PROJECTS

Evaluating Linux

Based on your enthusiasm and strong analytical skills, you have just been hired as a consultant by a major international consulting firm, McKinney and Co. Because you are interested in technology, your boss explains that you will be assigned to work on several information technology projects in the coming months. Although you are a junior consultant at the moment, your responsibilities weigh heavily on you. You realize that companies will spend millions of dollars based on your recommendations, and thousands of people will either lead highly productive lives or will soon be laid off based on how you enable their company to succeed.

Your first project assignment is with a small technology startup called PixelDust that sells digital photo services online. In talking with the president of the company, you determine that the company doesn't have a large budget for technology purchases, but that the company's entire reputation depends on having a successful online presence.

1. For the main Web server, your client is considering several platforms, including an IBM AIX system (a version of UNIX) running on an RS/6000 minicomputer, Windows XP running on a large Pentium system, and Linux, also running on a large Pentium system. You lean towards Linux, but the president hesitates because of concerns about the way Linux is developed. (She's just been reading about it in *BusinessWeek*.) She asks you to explain why Linux is more stable and secure than other systems, and how the company can run the new Web server on free software. Write a brief report summarizing your thoughts on the matter. What useful information might you find on the vendor Web sites listed in Table 1-1? What concerns might remain unresolved at this point?

2. The president of PixelDust has started to use Linux as the new Web server, and things are going well. Your manager at McKinney informs you that PixelDust has entered a new consulting agreement in which your team will create a new piece of software to add certain database features to their Web server. As you plan the project, you realize that much of what you need to do has already been done using free software. You are considering using this software to speed development of your project. What considerations will affect your decision? If you decide to use the free software and must make your own project available freely because of the GPL, what justification would you give PixelDust (who is paying you to write the software) and McKinney management? What concerns might both of these parties have? Under what circumstances do you feel that a piece of software should *not* use the GPL?

3. You have used Linux on a number of McKinney projects in the last few months. Do you anticipate problems in the future as Linux becomes more commercial and popular, with mainstream applications, advertising, etc.? How might this affect the attitude of free software developers? How would you feel about the increasing popularity of Linux if you were participating in Linux development? What could commercial Linux vendors do to help alleviate potential problems? What can you do as a consultant who relies on Linux?

2

EXPLORING THE DESKTOP

After reading this chapter and completing the exercises, you will be able to:

♦ Understand the graphical system used by Linux

♦ Configure basic features of the GNOME and KDE desktop interfaces

♦ Use graphical utilities such as editors, terminals, and browsers

♦ Use productivity applications such as e-mail, calendar, and word processing

In the previous chapter you learned about open source and free software development, which was the basis for the creation of the Linux kernel and the other components of the operating system. You also learned basic information about logging in to Linux and using a graphical file manager or command-line interface to explore the Linux file system.

In this chapter you explore the graphical interface in more detail. You begin by learning about the foundation of graphics in Linux, the X Window System. Then you learn about the desktop interfaces and how you can configure them. Finally, you will learn about numerous graphical applications that are part of most Linux distributions, including text editors, Web browsers, e-mail readers, and office productivity software such as word processors and spreadsheets.

LINUX GRAPHICAL DESKTOPS

A graphical display is optional in Linux, although most users working with Linux on their desktop choose to use a GUI. The foundation of the graphical display is called the X Window System. Other components, such as the GNOME desktop or a graphical application, rely on the X Window System. The interaction between these components is described later in this section.

Understanding the X Window System

As Microsoft Windows was establishing its place in the market during the mid-1980s, UNIX had already been in widespread use for years. It was extremely stable—millions of businesses around the world used UNIX. But it wasn't considered easy to use, or user friendly. A group working at the Massachusetts Institute of Technology (MIT) and Digital Equipment Corporation (DEC, now part of Hewlett-Packard through its acquisition of Compaq Computer Corporation) began working together on a graphical environment for UNIX. Their goals included making UNIX easier to use and encouraging the development of graphical standards among competing commercial versions of UNIX. This development process was dubbed **Project Athena**.

The work of Project Athena was eventually called the X Window System, with the assumption that X would be replaced with something more descriptive. But the X name stuck and is used to this day.

 The X Window System is sometimes called X Windows (which is considered an incorrect name) or just X (which is commonly used).

NOTE

The X Window System was released as public domain software in 1985. This allowed many UNIX vendors to begin creating products based on X, and it rapidly became the default graphical system for the entire UNIX market. The GPL (the license under which Linux was released) was not developed by Richard Stallman of the Free Software Foundation until 1992, so X was released under a different legal arrangement. By placing the software in the public domain, the developers (MIT and DEC) gave up their copyright to the software, leaving others free to create derivative works and copyright them. The result was a fragmented market, in which users could choose from various graphical systems based on the original work of Project Athena. Because the UNIX market was already fragmented and did not rely on the mass-market economies that are associated with Microsoft Windows, the availability of many varieties of X was not considered problematic.

In 1988 the Open Software Foundation, or OSF, took over work on Project Athena and continued working on newer, better versions of X. The not-for-profit OSF (now called the Open Group) continues to maintain X. Because X is public domain software, however, the source code is available to anyone. (For additional information, visit *www.x.org*.)

Although the Open Group managed development of the X Window System as public domain software, no version of X was freely available; it was included only as part of expensive UNIX systems from vendors such as IBM and Hewlett-Packard. These versions of X typically ran on expensive minicomputers such as the IBM RS/6000 and Hewlett-Packard PA-RISC-based systems.

The XFree86 Project was started as a nonprofit organization dedicated to creating a version of X for Intel-based versions of UNIX. The XFree86 Project software was welcomed by Linux developers because it provided the foundation for a graphical interface similar to that used by all other UNIX-like operating systems. X was soon incorporated into every mainstream Linux distribution. You can read more about the XFree86 Project at *www. xfree86.org*.

How the X Window System Functions

The Macintosh and Microsoft Windows graphical environments are successful because they run on widely available computer hardware. In particular, the developers of Microsoft Windows worked to ensure that Windows could use any popular video card; likewise, as Windows itself became hugely popular, video card manufacturers scrambled to make sure they created software to help Microsoft Windows function with their hardware.

Coming from UNIX roots, the developers of X took a different approach. Instead of embedding video card specifications in a driver, they designed a text-based configuration file that lets the user basically write the driver for any video card that comes on the market. For all this potential technological power, the result was that X was very difficult to configure on Linux.

Fortunately, recent developments by the XFree86 Project and by Linux vendors mean that virtually all video cards are now automatically configured by the Linux installation program. Later in this chapter you learn about using configuration utilities to set up or refine the graphical configuration.

Components of the X Window System

The developers of X used a clever design that has allowed X to continue as a viable technology more than 15 years after it was first released. This design separates control of the video card (sending signals to the computer hardware) from management of program information on the screen. The following list of components shows the modular nature of the X Window System design:

- An **X server** is the program that communicates with the video card, sending the most basic instructions on what images should appear on the screen. It is similar to a video card driver, but an X server also interacts with the keyboard and mouse used in a graphical environment. The X server relies on other components to tell it what to display and to process keyboard and mouse input.

- An **X client** is any graphical application, such as a graphical word processor, graphical configuration utility, or graphical game program. A graphical application in Linux does not directly control the screen display. Instead, the application (the X client) requests that the X server display something or collect keyboard and mouse input. The X server sends instructions on to the video card and collects keyboard and mouse input. By separating X server and X client functions, every X client doesn't need to know how to interact with every type of video card, keyboard, and mouse. The windows and dialog boxes associated with a graphical application are the output of the X server, as requested by the X client. X clients do not communicate directly with the video card, keyboard, or mouse.

- A **window manager** is a special-purpose graphical application (that is, a special-purpose X client). It controls the position and manipulation of the windows in a GUI. The window manager functions between regular user applications and the X server; each application doesn't need to implement window drawing and management features because the window manager takes care of those things. Virtually every graphical application uses the functionality provided by a window manager. The GNOME and KDE desktop interfaces include their own window managers.

- **Graphical libraries** are collections of programming functions that an X client can use to manage the elements of a graphical environment more efficiently. Some libraries are tied to a specific environment, such as KDE or GNOME; others are more widely used.

- The desktop interface is a graphical application that provides a comprehensive user interface, including menus, desktop icons, and usually several integrated applications. A desktop interface allows applications to work together better because they can make assumptions about the functionality of other programs. This permits features such as drag and drop, and copy and paste operations. GNOME and KDE are examples of desktop interfaces, but several others are available.

Figure 2-1 shows how the components of X can be arranged conceptually.

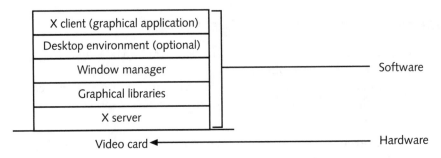

Figure 2-1 Components of the X Window System

2

NOTE

Reading about X clients and X servers, you may realize that the term "server" and "client" used in this situation have the opposite meanings that they normally do. That is, you normally think of the central place that runs a program as the server and the computer or program that the end-user is using as the client. The X Window System lets you separate client and server onto two different computers, so the terms can become even more confusing. In most situations, a server provides data in response to client requests for that data. Multiple remote clients can request data that is centrally located. When you use X, however, the servers (the part closest to each end-user) provide keyboard clicks and mouse movements to the clients, which are the applications being run in a central location.

As part of the Linux installation process, the XFree86 X server program is installed. Other Linux X servers are available from companies such as Xi Graphics (*www.xig.com*). Although the XFree86 X server is highly regarded, a commercial server may support video cards that the XFree86 server does not support; they may also provide higher performance (faster video) than XFree86 in some cases.

Because the X Window System separates the control of the video card (located in the X server) from the display presented to the user (by the window manager and desktop interface), the X Window System permits you to use different components at any "level" in the graphical system. For example, in addition to using different X servers, as just mentioned, you can use different window managers and different desktop interfaces.

The GNOME and KDE desktop interfaces each include a window manager. The window manager and the desktop are integrated so that you seldom work directly with the window manager unless you are configuring its features (as described in the next section).

A basic window manager that is available on most Linux distributions is called twm. twm does not include a desktop interface—instead, it provides only a minimal interface to help you launch other graphical applications. When only twm is running, you see a blank screen with a color pattern and a mouse pointer. Pressing a mouse button opens a menu from which you can start programs or execute other functions to control the graphical environment.

Some of the window managers available for Linux are described in the following list.

- *twm (Tab Window Manager)*: A classic UNIX window manager that has been used for many years, included with most versions of Linux, and installed as part of Red Hat Linux and Fedora

- *fvwm (Feeble Virtual Window Manager)*: Developed by Robert Nation, this program was the most common window manager for Linux until well-developed desktop interfaces became popular. It includes many of the same characteristics as twm, but requires only about half the memory required to run twm. The latest version of fvwm is called fvwm2. You can find more information about fvwm at *www.fvwm. org.*

- *wm2*: A minimal window manager requiring little memory and allowing little configuration

- *Window Maker and AfterStep*: Window managers that simulate the interface of the NeXT computer, though without the many applications that were included with the NeXT operating system

- *mwm (Motif Window Manager)*: A commercial window manager commonly included with commercial UNIX workstations. Before Linux desktops were popular, many window managers attempted to emulate this commercial window manager.

- *olwm (OpenLook Window Manager)*: A window manager that emulates the Open-Look style of interface created by Sun Microsystems, olwm is used on Linux primarily by developers who want to emulate the look and feel of a Sun UNIX workstation.

- *kwm*: The window manager used by KDE. kwm is rarely referred to by name in KDE; its many configuration options are integrated with the KDE preferences that control the desktop and the graphical login. (These options are shown on the Preferences submenu of the KDE main menu and discussed in the next section.)

Many graphical libraries are also available for X. A graphical library is installed on a Linux system just like any other application. But a graphical library is not started directly—it only provides tools for other applications. Two graphical libraries you should know about are the libraries associated with the GNOME and KDE desktops:

- The Qt library is the foundation of the KDE desktop, which is the most popular graphical environment used on Linux. (See *www.kde.org* for more information.)

- The GTK+ library was developed by Spencer Kimball and Peter Mattis at the University of California at Berkeley as the foundation of the GIMP graphics application. (The GIMP is a program similar to Adobe Photoshop.) Subsequently, GTK+ was used to create the GNOME desktop. (See *www.gnome.org* for more information.)

The default desktop interface in both Red Hat Linux and Fedora is GNOME. Unless you install *only* KDE, GNOME will be displayed after you log in to a newly installed system running Red Hat Linux or Fedora. (You can switch between installed desktop interfaces or window managers as described in the next section.)

Starting X

Nearly every commercially available Linux distribution is configured by default to display the graphical login screen described in Chapter 1, "Introducing Linux," after you start the system. If you prefer to work without the graphical interface, you can use the command line and just start the X Window System when you need to use a graphical program.

NOTE

More information about setting default start-up options is provided in Chapter 9, "Understanding System Initialization."

2

The standard command to start the X Window System from a command line is *startx*:

```
$ startx
```

This command automatically executes a number of other commands that start the X server and run the programs that make up the graphical environment that is configured on your system.

Desktop Interfaces

A desktop interface is a graphical environment that provides a collection of functions and utilities to make using a computer easier for those who do not have many commands memorized. In addition, some types of information may be much easier to work with in a graphical format. You can use a desktop interface to:

- Place icons on the screen's background (where no other windows are visible). Clicking on these icons starts applications or displays data files that the user commonly accesses.

- Manage multiple applications efficiently using multiple independent windows, toolbars, and keyboard controls.

- Use menus to access frequently used utilities and applications. You can customize these menus to meet your specific requirements.

- Use a collection of basic applications provided with the desktop, such as a text editor, calculator, calendar, note-taking application, audio CD player, and others.

- Use a convenient, integrated file management utility to view and manipulate files.

- Use applications created specifically for the desktop interface. These applications rely on a common set of functions that create a single look and feel for the environment, reduce the system resources required (because of shared functionality), and interact with other applications via drag-and-drop and cut-and-paste features.

Simple window managers such as fvwm include a few of the features listed above, but a desktop interface such as GNOME or KDE includes all of these features and is similar to the environment that users encounter on a Microsoft Windows or Apple Macintosh system. By using a desktop interface, a user who is unfamiliar with Linux or uncomfortable with computers can easily be taught to complete simple tasks without having specialized knowledge of the operating system (the type of knowledge you are learning in this book).

The KDE Interface

In 1996 Matthias Ettrich began creating a full-featured graphical environment for Linux. He dubbed the project the K Desktop Environment (KDE). KDE is now the most widely used desktop environment on Linux systems. When you install most Linux distributions (except Red Hat Linux or Fedora), KDE is installed by default with a complete set of KDE-compatible applications. These applications use the same graphical toolkit as the desktop itself and can thus share functionality such as common dialog boxes and drag-and-drop capability.

KDE includes a suite of applications for Internet access, system maintenance, personal productivity (organizers, calculators, music players), and many other basic tasks. KDE includes a set of icons at the bottom of the screen called the **Panel**. Clicking on an icon in the Panel starts an application. You can configure the Panel to include an icon for each of the applications that you commonly use. Each application that you start in KDE appears as a button in a separate taskbar or on the Panel. This is similar to the buttons that appear for each open application on the bottom of the screen in Microsoft Windows. You can switch between applications or open a minimized application using the corresponding button on the taskbar. A few standard icons are included on the KDE default desktop; each user can add others. Figure 2-2 shows a basic KDE desktop.

NOTE

The KDE desktop shown in Figure 2-2 is so similar to the GNOME desktop that you will be working with throughout this book that it may be difficult to see whether you are using GNOME or KDE. The appearance of items on the Panel and minor differences in the main menu can provide clues, but it may take some time for you to recognize these differences. (As two examples, the Search for Files item appears on the GNOME main menu, but not on the KDE main menu; also, an icon is included on the GNOME desktop for your home directory, but is not included by default on the KDE desktop.)

The GNOME Desktop

As KDE was first becoming popular, a group of developers within the Linux community became concerned that KDE was based on a graphical library that was not licensed using the GPL. The entire KDE project now uses an Open Source license, but because of this concern, a new desktop project based on the GPL was founded: the Gnu Object Model Environment (virtually always referred to as GNOME).

GNOME is a desktop interface very similar to KDE. It includes a Panel with an integrated taskbar (containing a button for each running application). Icons on the desktop let you start commonly used applications or data files. A main menu provides quick access to dozens of applications written to take advantage of the look and functionality of GNOME. The applications included with GNOME are similar to those provided with KDE. They include a powerful file manager, personal productivity applications, and system maintenance utilities.

2

Figure 2-2   The KDE desktop in Fedora

From the beginning, the GNOME project received encouragement and financial support from Red Hat Software. As a result, Red Hat Linux is one of the few major Linux distributions that installs GNOME by default. Because Red Hat is the largest Linux distributor, GNOME enjoys widespread support among Linux users.

In the following sections you learn more about some of the utilities and personal productivity applications that are included with GNOME and KDE. Keep in mind that Red Hat Software has worked to make the two desktop interfaces appear *very* similar. In Red Hat Linux and Fedora, both GNOME and KDE use a theme (these are described shortly) called Bluecurve. The Bluecurve theme is designed to look identical on both KDE and GNOME, so you can use either desktop comfortably without having to relearn where things are. If you use KDE on a different version of Linux (such as Debian or SUSE), the desktop may look different from the screens shown in this chapter (and throughout this book). The color selections, window outlines, and other features of the interface can be configured according to your preferences, as described shortly.

Also note that when you install Red Hat Linux or Fedora (see Chapter 8, "Installing Linux"), you can choose to install both GNOME and KDE. If you do this, GNOME will still be the default desktop interface, but KDE applications are also installed and can be executed from within GNOME.

The Graphical Login Screen

The graphical login screen that you see when you first turn on your Linux system is provided by a program called the X display manager. This program is called xdm; versions specific to KDE and GNOME are called kdm and gdm, respectively, though you won't see these terms as you work with the desktop interface—these are separate programs, and their configuration options are integrated with the configuration of the desktop interface itself.

When a user logs in using a graphical login screen, the display manager selects which programs to start based on the session chosen by the user. A **session** defines a set of graphical programs to run when a user logs in. For example, a session might be defined for the KDE or GNOME desktop, or to open just a single terminal window in a minimal window manager for troubleshooting. The label "Session" appears at the bottom of the graphical login screen in Red Hat Linux and Fedora. By clicking on that label, you can select which type of session you want to start when you log in.

Any time a user exits the graphical environment, the display manager is restarted automatically to provide the graphical login screen again. Thus the user never encounters a character-mode screen—a fact that can make new users much more comfortable with Linux.

Working with Graphical Windows

As in other graphical environments with which you may be familiar, you can use your mouse and keyboard to manipulate the graphical windows that are open on your graphical desktop in Linux.

Using your mouse, you can perform the following operations. (These descriptions assume you are using a default version of the GNOME desktop in Red Hat Linux or Fedora—the configuration of each of these can be changed according to your preferences.)

- The colored bar across the top of a window is called the title bar. Double-click the title bar to maximize the window so that it fills the entire screen. When you double-click the title bar of a window that has been maximized, the window returns to its former size.

- In the upper-right corner of each window (on the title bar) are three icons. Click the small "x" icon to close the window. Click the small square icon to the left of the "x" to maximize the window so that it fills all available space on the desktop. After you have maximized a window, you can click the same button again to return it to its former size. Click the horizontal bar next to the maximization icon to minimize the window—to make it disappear from the desktop and appear only as an item on the Panel at the bottom of the screen.

- Click the down-arrow icon on the left side of a window's title bar to open a window control menu. From that menu, you can select actions such as minimize, maximize, and resize. This menu is not associated with the application that is running in the window—it only controls the display of the window itself.

- Click and hold the left mouse button on the very corner of a window (not on the title bar) to resize that window. (Click on the very edge of the window—watch to see when the mouse pointer changes shape.) Release the mouse button when the window is the size you prefer.

2

- Click and hold the left mouse button on the title bar to move the window, dragging it to a new location on the desktop. Release the mouse button when the window is positioned where you want it.

X also has an internal "clipboard." Any time you click and drag to select text in a window, that text is copied to the clipboard. (Many applications such as text editors will also have a Copy feature on each of their Edit menus. This feature may act on a different internal clipboard.) If you switch to another window, you can paste information in the clipboard by either selecting the Paste item from the Edit menu (if it uses the default X clipboard) or by clicking the middle mouse button. If you have a mouse with only two buttons, press both mouse buttons at the same time to "emulate" the third, or middle, mouse button. If this feature has been enabled as part of your X configuration, you can use the copy-and-paste feature with any application, including those that don't have copy and paste functions built in. When you paste in such an application (by clicking both mouse buttons at once), the text is inserted as if it had been typed at the keyboard.

It's common to have multiple windows open at the same time on your desktop. The color of the title bar indicates which window has focus. The window with focus is the one that receives any keyboard input. In a default GNOME desktop, the window with focus has a blue title bar; others have gray title bars. You can switch the focus between open windows by holding down the Alt key and pressing Tab repeatedly, releasing both keys when the window you want is visible.

On most Linux desktop interfaces, including GNOME, you typically have four workspaces. These are sometimes called virtual desktops. A **workspace** is an empty background on which you can open application windows. By having four workspaces available, you can fill the background with different applications and easily move between them without minimizing and maximizing windows continuously. For example, you might open a Web browser on one workspace, an e-mail reader on another workspace, and a word processor on another. With each of these application windows maximized, you switch between workspaces to use the different applications.

In GNOME, a small set of four squares appears in the middle of the Panel on the bottom of the screen. This is the Workspace Switcher (see Figure 2-3). The Workspace Switcher includes an outline of any open windows on each workspace within the squares shown on the Panel. Click on one of the four squares on the Panel to switch your view to that workspace. You can also move any open window to any workspace using the items on the control menu of that window.

In addition to using your mouse to navigate among applications and manipulate open windows, many power users like to use keyboard shortcuts. Applications, such as Web browsers and word processors, support keyboard shortcuts for various operations. The desktop interface itself provides shortcuts as well. These may in some cases conflict with the keyboard shortcuts of an application you are using, in which case you need to change the configuration of the desktop interface to use the keyboard shortcut to control the desktop. A few useful keyboard shortcuts in GNOME are listed in Table 2-1.

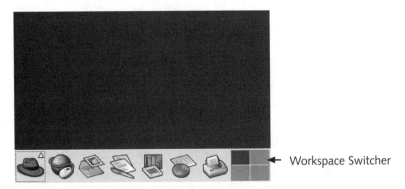

Figure 2-3   The Workspace Switcher on the GNOME Panel

Table 2-1   GNOME Keyboard Shortcuts

Keyboard shortcut	Description
Alt+Tab	Rotate focus among all windows
Ctrl+d	Exit from a command-line window, closing that window
PrtSc (Print Screen)	Copy the current screen to the desktop clipboard. You can then use the paste function in most graphical drawing tools to paste the screen image.
Alt+Left mouse button	Move the window; with Alt pressed, you can click anywhere in a window and drag it to a new location instead of clicking and dragging using the title bar
Alt+Right mouse button	Display the window control menu by clicking anywhere in a window except on its title bar
Ctrl+Alt+Backspace	Emergency exit from the X Window System. This immediately returns you to the graphical login prompt or to text mode. If you have any open windows with unsaved documents (such as a text editor), the information in those windows will be lost.
Alt+F1	Display the GNOME main menu
Alt+F4	Close the active window
Alt+F5	Return a maximized window to its previous size
Alt+F7	Move the active window; use the arrow keys to move the window (the current screen location is shown in the middle of the window), then press Enter when you're done moving
Alt+F8	Resize the active window; use the arrow keys to adjust the size (the current size is shown in the middle of the window), then press Enter when you're done resizing
Alt+F9	Minimize the current window
Alt+F10	Maximize the current window
F1	Open a window displaying the online help system

CONFIGURING **GNOME** AND **KDE**

GNOME and KDE are both highly configurable. In this section you learn about how the desktop configuration utilities are accessed and also explore a few example configuration changes.

Switching Between Desktop Interfaces

Although the default desktop interface in Red Hat Linux and Fedora is GNOME, many users like to have the option to select which interface they use. You can use the Desktop Switcher utility to select which desktop is displayed when you log in.

To use this utility, you enter the command *switchdesk* followed by the name of the desktop that you want to switch to (such as GNOME or KDE) in a terminal window. Remember, you can right-click your desktop and choose Open Terminal to open a terminal window. For example, this command changes your default desktop to KDE if you have installed the KDE software packages:

```
$ switchdesk KDE
```

A graphical version of this program called the Desktop Switcher (launched using the switchdesk-gui command) is also available, as shown in Figure 2-4. The corresponding software package is not installed by default, however, so you will need to install that package from your Fedora CDs—as described in Chapter 10, "Managing Software Packages and File Systems"—if you want to experiment with this program instead of using the command line version.

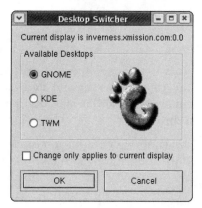

Figure 2-4   The Desktop Switcher utility, showing available desktop interfaces and window managers on a typical Fedora system

Each user on a Linux system can run the Desktop Switcher or *switchdesk* independently to select the desktop interface he or she prefers to use. When you select an available desktop in the Desktop Switcher or using *switchdesk* at the command line, you must exit the X Window

System and log in again for the change to take effect. To do this, log out using the last item on the GNOME main menu. When you log in again, the desktop you selected will be running.

If you experiment with a window manager such as tvm, you should plan to use the *switchdesk* command from a command line to change back to GNOME.

Saving Your Configuration Between Logins

Each time you log out, GNOME can note which application windows were open so that the next time you log in, the same applications are opened automatically. (But documents within those applications are not automatically loaded.) This is useful when you are working on numerous windows and need to log out for the day. Next time you log in, all of the terminal windows, browsers, and other applications that you opened from within GNOME are opened just as you left them.

To save your configuration between logins, select the Save current setup check box in the message box that appears when you choose Log Out on the GNOME menu. This check box is not selected by default because it takes additional time to log out and log in when application windows must be handled. You can change this setting so that your current setup is saved by default each time you log out. The next section describes how to alter this setting.

Configuring the Graphical Login Screen

You can set up the graphical login screen according to your preferences using the utilities provided in GNOME. Because the graphical login screen is used by all users on the system, you must be logged in as root or enter the root password before you are permitted to configure most parts of the graphical login screen.

To configure the graphical login screen, you select System Settings, then Login Screen on the GNOME main menu. (You can also run the *gdmsetup* command from a terminal window.) If you are not logged in as root (you should not typically be logged in as root), you must enter the root password before you can run this utility.

On the General tab of the GDM Setup utility (shown in Figure 2-5), you can select basic options such as whether a user should be logged in automatically as the system boots, or whether to log a user in automatically after a delay that you specify. Your choices depend, of course, on the level of convenience and security that your situation demands. For example, automatically logging in after 10 minutes of sitting idle can be very convenient, but it also presents a large security risk if you regularly leave your system unattended at work.

Not all of the configuration options for the graphical login prompt are accessible in the GDM Setup utility. You can also change configuration settings by editing the file /etc/X11/gdm/gdm.conf, though this is a fairly advanced operation.

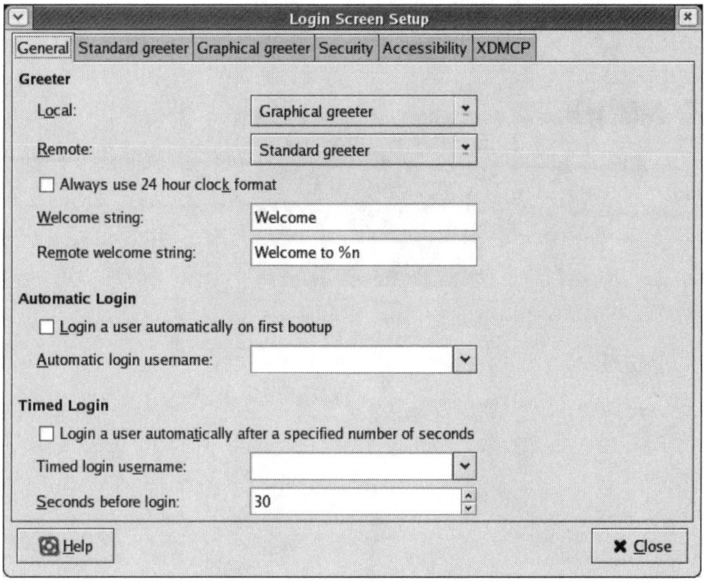

Figure 2-5 The GDM Setup utility

On the General tab, you can also select whether to use a standard greeter (login screen) or a graphical greeter for users logging in locally or remotely. Remote login is a powerful feature of the X Window System, but it is not discussed in detail in this book. Chapter 15, "Advanced Topics and Troubleshooting," contains some additional information. The Security and XDMCP tabs of this utility are also discussed further in Chapter 15, though it is helpful to at least review the Security tab at this point to see what options it offers; several of them may be helpful, such as allowing configuration of the graphical login screen from within the graphical login screen (i.e., before logging in successfully).

Separate tabs configure the standard and graphical greeter screens. The graphical greeter is used by default for local users (users sitting at the computer). On the Graphical greeter tab, you see a list of themes for the graphical login screen. A **theme** is a collection of colors, fonts, and images that give a display a certain look and feel. You can set up themes for other parts of the desktop interface, as described in the next section. In the Graphical greeter tab, you can select one of the installed themes from the list shown in Figure 2-6, or click the Install new theme button to add a theme to the list that you have downloaded from an Internet site or created yourself.

The **face browser** feature of the graphical login screen causes it to display a small graphic image for each user. If the theme you select for your graphical greeter includes a face browser, or if the face browser option is selected on the Standard greeter tab (under the Miscellaneous section in the bottom left of the window), then you can configure your own graphical image (your face, or whatever image you choose), by choosing Preferences, then Login Photo on the GNOME main menu.

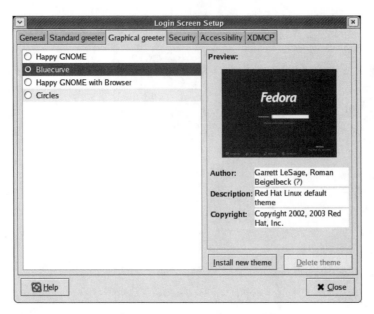

Figure 2-6   The Graphical greeter tab within the Login Screen Setup window

The Panel

As you've learned, the Panel is the bar across the bottom of the GNOME desktop interface. KDE includes a similar bar. The Panel is a separate application that displays the following:

- The main menu of the desktop interface

- The icons of programs you use frequently

- The Workspace Switcher

- A labeled button for each open window (you can click on any of the buttons to make that window active and visible)

- A date and time indicator

- Other informational items

When you right-click any icon on the Panel, a menu appears in which you can move the position of that item on the Panel, remove that item from the panel altogether, or view properties of the item (for example, see which application an icon opens). Figure 2-7 shows the Launcher Properties dialog box that appears when you right-click the Launcher icon on the Panel and select Properties.

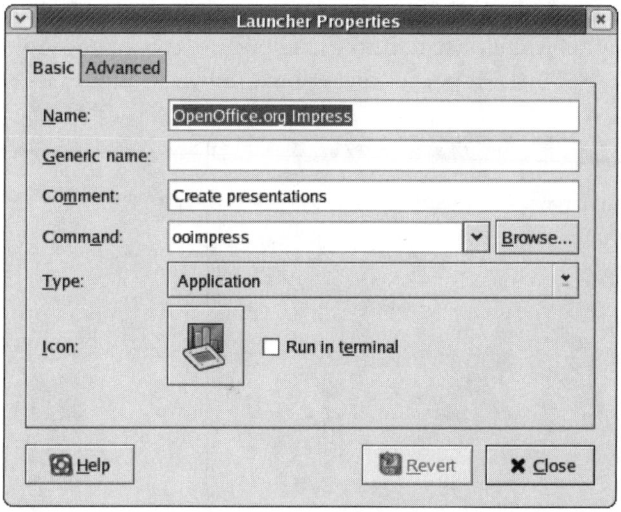

2

Figure 2-7   The Launcher Properties dialog box used to configure the Panel

When you right-click other parts of the Panel, the items displayed in the context menu correspond to the item you clicked. For example, if you right-click the Workspace Switcher, a Preferences item is included on the menu. Selecting that item opens the Workspace Switcher Preferences dialog box, shown in Figure 2-8. In this dialog box, you can set up features of the Workspace Switcher, including the number of workspaces provided and a label for each one.

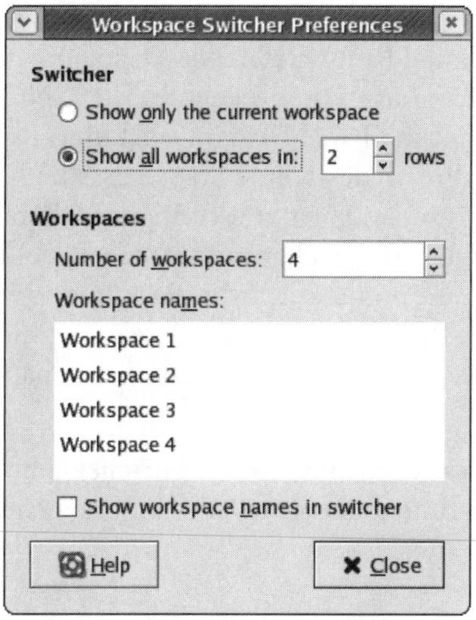

Figure 2-8   The Workspace Switcher Preferences dialog box

If you right-click on the date and time information, the context menu includes Copy time and Copy date, which copy the time or date into the clipboard as text, and Adjust Date & Time, which opens the Date/Time Properties dialog box, shown in Figure 2-9.

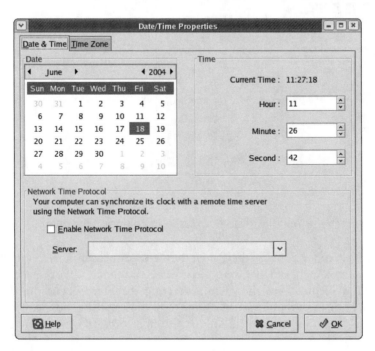

Figure 2-9   The Clock Preferences dialog box

Preferences for a few Panel options are set using the Panel Preferences dialog box, which you access by selecting Preferences, then More Preferences, then Panel on the GNOME main menu. You can configure additional properties of the Panel by right-clicking a blank area of the Panel and selecting Properties. The Panel Properties window appears. The General tab (see Figure 2-10) and Background tab (see Figure 2-11) let you configure where the Panel appears on the desktop, how large it is, and what the background of the Panel looks like, among other configuration options. For example, if you select the Background image field on the Background tab, you can then use the Browse button to select a graphic image to form the background of the Panel. (Some images, of course, make the information on the Panel quite hard to read.)

You can have multiple Panels on your desktop at the same time. Right-click a blank part of the Panel and choose New Panel from the context menu to add another Panel to your desktop.

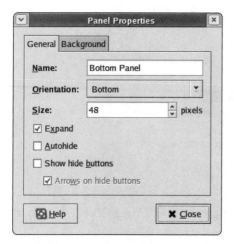

Figure 2-10   The General tab of the Panel Properties dialog box

Figure 2-11   The Background tab of the Panel Properties dialog box

On the default Panel or any Panel that you add to your desktop, you can add new items to the Panel by right-clicking and selecting Add to Panel. In the submenu that appears, you can select from a large number of tools such as a stock ticker or weather report (both under the Accessories submenu), a wireless link monitor, a volume control, or a battery charge-level indicator (for laptops), among others. You can also add an icon to start any item on the GNOME main menu. Just select the Launcher from menu submenu. This displays the entire GNOME main menu with all its submenus. But from this context menu, when you select an item, instead of starting that application, the Panel adds an icon so that clicking that icon will start the application you selected. Figure 2-12 shows the numerous menus that appear if you want to add a CD Player icon to the GNOME Panel.

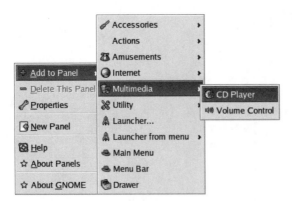

Figure 2-12   Cascading menus as they appear when adding a CD Player icon to the GNOME Panel

Configuring Other GNOME Features

You can configure many additional features of your desktop interface using items on the Preferences submenu of the GNOME main menu. For example:

- *Accessibility* changes preferences such as key repeat lengths, mouse actions, and other settings for physically challenged users.

- *Desktop Background* lets you select a background image for your desktop and how that image is displayed, such as tiled, centered, or scaled. (See Figure 2-13.) You can click Add Wallpaper to browse and find a new image to use as a desktop background.

- *CD and DVD* lets you determine how GNOME reacts when different types of new discs are inserted (audio CD, data CD, blank CD, or DVD).

- *Font* lets you select which typeface is used by default within applications, within the desktop itself, and within terminal windows. Example fonts are shown to help you select. (See Figure 2-14.)

- *Keyboard Shortcuts* lets you configure which key combinations control the operation of the desktop (if you don't like the default settings listed in Table 2-1 or want to add to them).

- *Menus and Toolbars* lets you define how menus and toolbars within GNOME-compatible applications are displayed. You can include text labels below icons on toolbars, and include small icons next to menu items (these are the default settings).

- *Mouse* lets you select a left-handed mouse (for users who place their mouse on the left side of their keyboard—right and left mouse buttons are then reversed from the default settings). You can also specify the delay used to define a double-click, as well as speed thresholds, and the appearance of mouse pointers. One interesting feature on the Cursors tab of the Mouse Preferences dialog box lets you display a pop-up

Figure 2-13   The Desktop Background Preferences dialog box

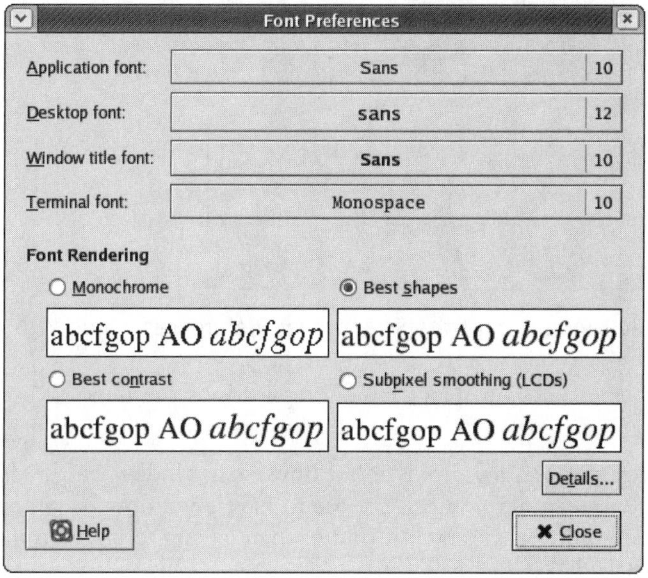

Figure 2-14   The Font Preferences dialog box

box that highlights the mouse pointer whenever the Control key is pressed. (This is very useful on a laptop used in a sunny room.)

- *Screensaver* lets you select among dozens of graphical screensavers, either selecting one or randomly rotating screensavers (choose in the Mode field of the Display Modes tab—see Figure 2-15). You select how long the computer sits idle before the screen saver is activated, how long each screensaver is used (if you are using the Random Screen Saver mode), and how long the computer sits idle before the screen is locked. If the Lock screen option is selected, the user must enter his or her password before the screensaver closes. (For each screen saver in the list on the left of the Screensaver Preferences window, you can select the Settings button to configure exactly how that screensaver operates.) The Advanced tab of the Screensaver Preferences window has several useful options to help you manage the power saving features of your monitor and determine how the screen saver operates.

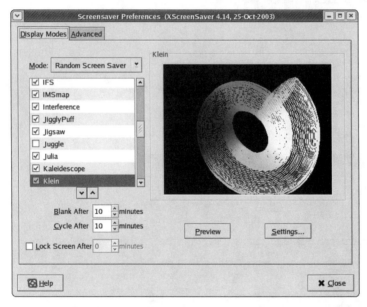

Figure 2-15   The Display Modes tab of the Screensaver Preferences window

- *Preferred Applications* lets you select which applications the desktop uses when it needs to access a terminal window, a text editor, or a Web browser.

- *Windows* lets you define a few items about how each window on the desktop can be controlled. For example, you can choose to have a window become active any time the mouse pointer passes over it (rather than having to click on the window or use Alt+Tab to make it active).

- *Theme* opens the Theme Preferences window, in which you can select the theme to use for your desktop. A desktop theme includes items such as the fonts used in menus and applications, the background image, the color or image used on the Panel, the graphical design outlining each window, and the standard icons used for items such as folders, graphics files, and Web pages. Figure 2-16 shows the Theme Preferences window. When you choose Theme Details in the Theme Preferences dialog box, you see a Theme Details dialog box in which you can select a specific style for controls, icons, and window borders (in the corresponding tabs—see Figure 2-17). As you select any item listed, the entire desktop changes immediately to reflect your selection. From the Theme Preferences dialog box, you can also select Install Theme to add a theme that you have downloaded or created.

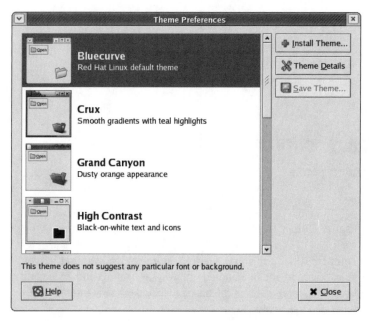

Figure 2-16   The Theme Preferences dialog box

Figure 2-17 The Theme Details dialog box

TIP

Desktop themes are a popular and powerful feature of GNOME that let you customize your environment in hundreds of ways. Creating and managing themes is discussed in more detail in the online help and in many Internet Linux resources mentioned in Chapter 1.

Besides selecting an item on the Preferences submenu, you can also access all of the configuration utilities described above by choosing Control Center on the Preferences menu. This opens a window with icons representing each configuration tool. You can then double-click on any item to open the corresponding preferences window. The Control Center showing all of the icons remains open. (See Figure 2-18.)

KDE includes very similar preference settings to those described here for GNOME. All can be accessed via the Control Center on the KDE main menu.

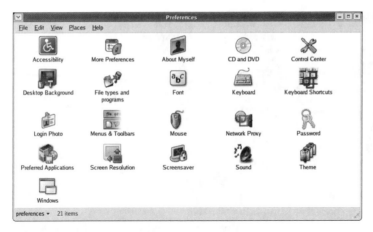

Figure 2-18   The GNOME Control Center window

CORE GRAPHICAL UTILITIES

In this section you learn about three key types of applications that are included with the GNOME and KDE desktop interfaces: a file manager, a text editor, and a Web browser. Remember as you work that graphical utilities are located in different submenus depending on which version of Linux you are using. The information provided here is based on Red Hat Linux and Fedora.

Configuring the Nautilus File Manager

In Chapter 1, you learned about the basic operation of the Nautilus file manager provided with GNOME. You can configure how Nautilus operates using the Preferences item on the Edit menu of Nautilus itself, or by selecting Preferences, More preferences, File management on the GNOME main menu. (The File types and programs item on the Preferences submenu also has related configuration options.)

The KDE desktop includes a powerful file manager called Konqueror that is similar to Nautilus.

NOTE

Within Nautilus, you can choose Backgrounds and Emblems on the Edit menu to open a window in which you select patterns and colors to apply to the background of the Nautilus window. You can click on the Patterns or Colors buttons to select a palette of items from which to choose. Click on any item in the Backgrounds and Emblems dialog box and drag it over to the Nautilus window, dropping it on the background of the window. The pattern or color fills the window. (See Figure 2-19.)

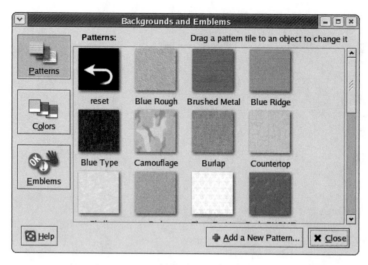

Figure 2-19 The Backgrounds and Emblems window used to configure the appearance of the Nautilus file manager

When you select the Emblems item in the Backgrounds and Emblems window, you can drag any of the icons and drop it on a folder or file icon in a Nautilus window. The emblem you selected is added to the icon for that folder or file. Figure 2-20 shows a folder with a standard folder icon and two other folders to which different emblems have been added. You can also right-click any icon and select the Properties item from the context menu. When the Properties window appears, choose the Emblems tab. On that tab, you can select or deselect any available emblems for that particular folder or file.

Figure 2-20 Folder icons in Nautilus; standard and with emblems added

You can open the File Management Preferences dialog box either by selecting Preferences from the Edit menu of Nautilus or by selecting File Management from the Preferences, More preferences submenu of the GNOME main menu. In the Views tab of this dialog box, shown in Figure 2-21, you can select default views that Nautilus uses, as well as how items are sorted and displayed. The Behavior tab contains similar options, including options that determine how Nautilus responds when you try to open a text file that contains programming instructions (a script file—see Chapter 14, "Writing Shell Scripts").

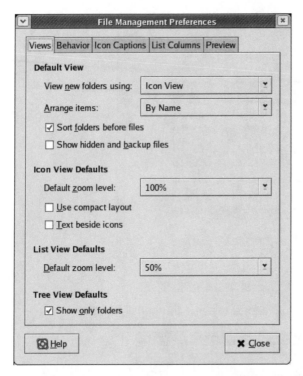

Figure 2-21   The File Management Preferences dialog box used to configure several aspects of the Nautilus file manager

The Preview tab lets you determine the contents of which files Nautilus will be able to display. For example, instead of just showing an icon indicating a graphic file, Nautilus can display a thumbnail version of the graphic itself. (See Figure 2-22.)

More complex configuration options are available by selecting File types and programs on the Preferences submenu of the GNOME main menu. In the File Types and Programs dialog box, shown in Figure 2-23, you can select a type of file, then review or define how GNOME operates on files of that type. For example, if you click on the arrow next to Images and double-click JPEG image, a window opens in which you can select the icon used to display all JPEG-format images, the programs to use to display these images if they are opened in Nautilus (using the Default action field of the Edit file type window), and several other features. You rarely need to modify anything in these windows, however, because GNOME includes hundreds of default settings that should handle virtually every file type you are likely to encounter.

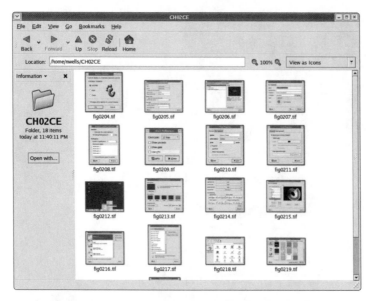

Figure 2-22   The Nautilus file manager displaying thumbnail images

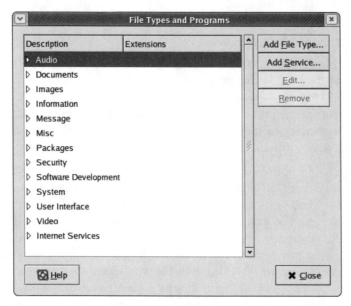

Figure 2-23   The File Types and Programs dialog box

Configuring the Use of Other Utilities

When you open a text file in Nautilus or double-click its icon on the GNOME desktop or in some other application, GNOME attempts to open the text file in the default text editor. As shown in Figure 2-24, you can set the default text editor in the Text Editor tab of the

Preferred Applications window (choose Preferred Applications on the Preferences submenu). By default, GNOME uses the gedit text editor, a graphical text editor that includes basic features and is very easy to use. You can also select other popular editors as the default, including vi (described in Chapter 3, "Using the Shell") or Emacs.

Figure 2-24   The Text Editor tab of the Preferred Applications dialog box

The Preferred Applications dialog box also lets you select a Web browser that GNOME opens whenever you select a Web page (an HTML document) on your desktop or within a Nautilus window. The standard Web browser is Mozilla—the open source version of the Netscape browser. You can install other browsers such as Opera or Lynx. If these have been prepared specifically for use in Red Hat Linux or Fedora, they may appear as options in the list box of the corresponding tabs of the Preferred Applications dialog box. If not, you need to provide the correct command for GNOME to use when starting that application.

POPULAR GRAPHICAL PROGRAMS

The previous sections have discussed how to configure your desktop interface and commonly used utilities such as the file manager and text editor. In this section you learn about several graphical personal productivity applications for Linux.

OpenOffice.org

OpenOffice.org is an office suite similar to Microsoft Office. OpenOffice.org is the official name of the application, though people refer to it casually as OpenOffice or OOo. OpenOffice.org began as StarOffice, an application suite developed by a German company called StarDivision, to compete with Microsoft Office. Sun Microsystems purchased StarDivision in 1999 and continued to upgrade the StarOffice product. They also started an Open Source project that became OpenOffice.org. You can purchase a copy of StarOffice from Sun for between $50 and $80 per user, or you can download OpenOffice.org for free at *www.openoffice.org*.

OpenOffice is an impressive office suite that includes the following applications:

- Writer, a full-featured word processor with paragraph styles, spell-checking, and thesaurus

- Calc, a spreadsheet with hundreds of built-in functions, plus pivot tables and charts

- Impress, a presentation tool that includes graphical and text capability as well as numerous templates

- Draw, a drawing tool that supports vector graphics (like Adobe Illustrator) and bitmapped graphics (like Adobe Photoshop or the GIMP, a Linux application)

- Database integration that permits users to interact with several different databases. Strong support is provided for MySQL, a popular Open Source database.

A few of the key features of these applications include:

- All applications are available for several operating systems (Linux, Solaris, Windows), so an organization can use the same office suite on multiple platforms. This makes system administration and user training simpler.

- Microsoft Office file formats are supported, so OpenOffice.org users can exchange files with colleagues who use Microsoft Office.

- Applications can also export in Adobe PDF and MacroMedia Flash formats.

- A macro recorder lets you record repetitive tasks.

- A development tool permits other companies to create add-on features that are integrated into OpenOffice.org menus.

- OpenOffice.org is available in over 30 languages, from Basque and Chinese to Arabic and Turkish.

Because OpenOffice.org is a large program (over 70 MB), you should install it from your Linux CDs if possible. For example, when you install Red Hat Linux or Fedora, you can choose to install OpenOffice.org as well. The various applications then appear on the Office submenu of your desktop.

OpenOffice.org Writer

To start the OpenOffice.org Writer word processor, choose Office, then OpenOffice.org Writer from the GNOME main menu, or click the fourth icon from the left on the default GNOME Panel. (From the left, the icons are for the main menu, a Web browser, an e-mail client, and then the word processor.)

The main window of Writer appears with toolbars above and to the left of the blank document, and a separate window listing paragraph styles. This window is called the Stylist—you can toggle display of the Stylist from the Format menu. As you enter text, you can click on a paragraph style in the list to set that entire paragraph to that style. For example, if you click Heading 1, the paragraph is changed to a large, bold font. Paragraph styles are also available in the toolbar just above the document window.

A convenient way to start a new document is to choose File, then AutoPilot, then select the type of document you want to create. A series of dialog boxes appears in which you enter information about the document you are creating; the document then appears in the editing window with your information correctly placed. Figure 2-25 shows one of the AutoPilot information windows used to create a fax.

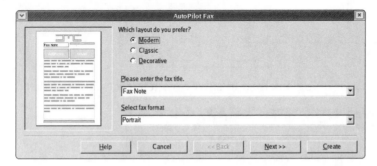

Figure 2-25   An AutoPilot dialog box used to create a new fax document in Writer

Exploring the Insert and Tools menus is a good way to get an idea of the features that Writer includes. For example, when you open the Insert menu, then select the Cross-reference item, you can select items in your document such as pages, footnotes, or bookmarks that you have placed and create a text reference to them that is automatically updated. You can also insert links to database information that you have imported into a text document, create variables, or use any of several other features. (See Figure 2-26.)

On the Tools menu, you see a list of writing tools including a spellchecker, a thesaurus, a hyphenation dictionary, autocorrect and autoformat (to fix common typos as you work), and outlining tools. By selecting items on this menu, you can also record macros or set up hundreds of preferences for how Writer operates using the Configure and Options dialog boxes (Figure 2-27 shows the Options dialog box).

OpenOffice.org Calc

The OpenOffice.org Calc program is a full-featured spreadsheet similar to Microsoft Excel. You can start it from the GNOME main menu or from a Panel icon, as you do with Writer.

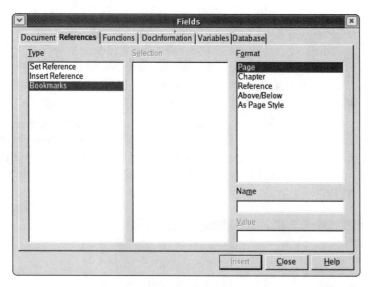

Figure 2-26   The Fields dialog box used to enter cross-reference data in Writer

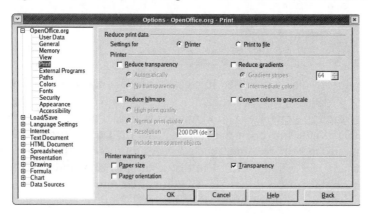

Figure 2-27   The Options dialog box in Writer

The main window of Calc opens with toolbars and a Cell Styles window that resemble those of Writer. (See Figure 2-28.) As you enter numbers and labels to create your spreadsheet, you can click a cell style to format that cell as a heading, a result, or according to other styles you set up (via the Style Catalog on the Format menu).

The main purpose of a spreadsheet is to process formulas. To try a simple example, enter a number in two different cells (use A1 and A2), then enter a formula such as "=A1+A2" in A3. More often, however, users rely on functions to calculate values in their spreadsheets. In Calc, you can select Function on the Insert menu to open the Functions AutoPilot. From this window, shown in Figure 2-29, you can select any of nearly 400 functions provided by Calc.

2

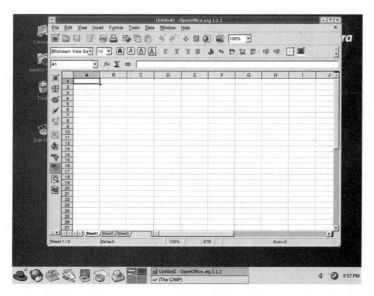

Figure 2-28 The main window of the OpenOffice.org Calc spreadsheet program

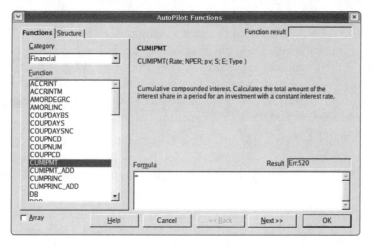

Figure 2-29 The Functions AutoPilot in the Calc spreadsheet

TIP

It's easier to select an appropriate function if you first select a category of functions, such as Database or Statistical from the Category field, so that a smaller number of functions is listed.

When you select a function from the Function list, a description of that function appears to the right of the Function list. When you have selected the function you need, click the Next button. A list of fields appears matching those required by the function you selected. You enter information in the fields (such as numbers, cell references, or other functions) and review the Result field to see if the function is working as you intended. When you have entered the information, click OK to close the AutoPilot and insert the function you have defined into the active cell.

Calc also has features such as a spellchecker, autocorrect, and the ability to record macros and import information from database sources. A specialized set of database-like features are provided on the Data menu.

Using E-mail Clients

If you use Linux as your main working environment, you probably need to use an e-mail reader (an e-mail client) on a regular basis. A default Linux installation provides several powerful graphical e-mail clients. In this section, you learn basic information about two of them: Evolution and Mozilla. Many other e-mail clients use similar designs, so that as you become more familiar with either of these two e-mail clients, you will be able to recognize and understand the features of other e-mail clients.

Evolution

Evolution is an e-mail client and calendar-scheduling program similar to Microsoft Outlook. Evolution was created by a company called Ximian, which is now owned by Novell (see *www.ximian.com*). You can start Evolution using the icon on the GNOME Panel (third from the left on the default Panel), or by choosing Evolution Email on the Internet submenu of the GNOME main menu. When you start Evolution the first time, it presents you with several setup windows to help you set up your e-mail account information. Having this information configured permits Evolution to contact your Internet service provider or other e-mail server to retrieve and send your e-mail messages.

When the first welcome window appears, click Forward to continue. In the Identity window, enter your full name and e-mail address. (See Figure 2-30.) You can also include a different Reply-To address, if you wish, and an organizational name. Click Forward to continue.

In the Receiving Mail window, you define an e-mail account. The option you select depends on where your e-mail messages are delivered and how they are stored. The most widely used system is probably the POP format, in which your e-mail messages are stored on the e-mail server of an ISP, and you retrieve them to your local system to read them. Check with your system administrator or ISP if you are uncertain about which item to select in the Server

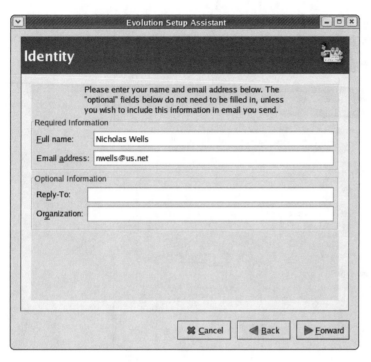

Figure 2-30   The Identity window used in Evolution as part of the new e-mail account setup procedure

Type field. The window changes based on the type you select. Figure 2-31 shows the window for configuring a POP e-mail account. Click Forward when you have completed the information in the window according to what your system administrator has provided. You may need to complete an additional page of configuration options as well, depending on the server type you selected. For example, POP e-mail accounts can specify how often to check the e-mail server for new messages, and whether to erase messages on the server when they are downloaded to Evolution. (If you are working at a remote site temporarily, for example, you might want to leave all messages on the e-mail server, reading them at the remote site but downloading them to your main working system when you return home.)

Figure 2-31   Configuring a POP e-mail account in Evolution

Next, you configure the Sending Mail window. (See Figure 2-32.) Again, your system administrator or ISP can provide the appropriate information for this window. Typically, you use an SMTP server type and a hostname such as mail or smtp followed by your domain name (or that of your ISP). For example, *mail.us.net* and *smtp.comcast.net* are two e-mail servers that users of those ISPs can use to send e-mail. As a precaution against spam (unwanted commercial e-mail), only registered users are permitted to send e-mail through most e-mail servers. In such cases, you are prompted for a password when you send messages as well as when you retrieve them. Click Forward when you have finished.

In the Account Management window, you can define a name for this account. Evolution lets you set up many e-mail accounts. The e-mail address is used by default as the account name, but you can enter anything in the Name field, such as "school e-mail," "family account," or "office—main account." When you click Forward, you see the Timezone window, in which you select your time zone. This lets Evolution correctly determine the time e-mail messages were sent and also what weather information to display. When you click Forward again, a Done window appears in which you can click Apply to close the Setup Assistant—after a moment the main window of Evolution appears, as shown in Figure 2-33. By default, the Summary window is displayed.

Figure 2-32   Configuring how e-mail messages are sent within Evolution

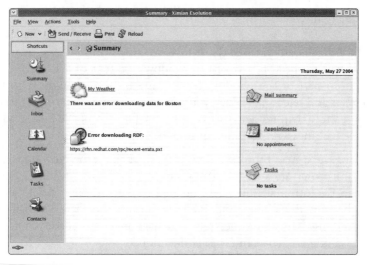

Figure 2-33   The main window of Evolution

The Summary window includes, by default, weather information, critical update notices for Red Hat Linux and Fedora, and a summary of e-mail, appointments, and tasks. Changing to the Calendar window (see Figure 2-34) or the Tasks window by clicking on the corresponding icon on the left of the Evolution window lets you manage appointments or lists of tasks. You can create categories of tasks, organized by priority, or create one-time or recurring appointments.

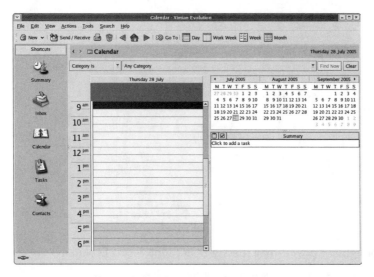

Figure 2-34   The Calendar window of Evolution

When you click the Inbox icon, you see the e-mail viewing window, as shown in Figure 2-35. Messages are listed in the top part of the window; the text of a selected message is displayed in the bottom part of the window. By clicking on the arrow next to the New button in the upper left and selecting Folder, you can create new e-mail folders to help you sort messages. Choose View, then Folder Bar to display the list of available folders so that you can drag and drop e-mail messages to different folders.

When you are viewing the e-mail Inbox window, you can click on the New button (not the arrow to the right of it) to create a new e-mail message. (See Figure 2-36.) Other buttons across the top of the Evolution window let you reply to, print, copy, delete, or forward messages, among other functions. The Send/Retrieve button checks the e-mail server for any new messages and also sends any messages that have been stored on your computer temporarily while awaiting an active Internet connection.

Mozilla E-mail

Mozilla is a Web browser, but it also includes a full-featured e-mail client that is similar to what you've just seen in Evolution. After you start Mozilla using the Panel icon showing a globe, or by choosing Internet, and then Mozilla Web Browser on the GNOME main menu, you can choose Window, then Mail & Newsgroups to open the Mozilla e-mail reader.

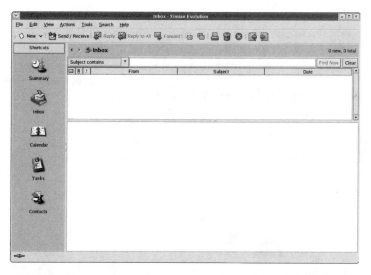

Figure 2-35   The e-mail management window of Evolution

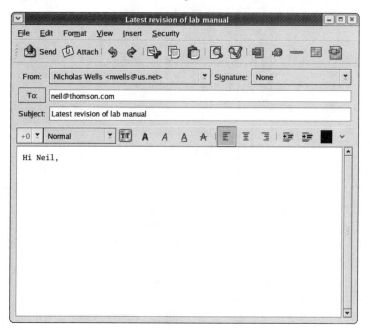

Figure 2-36   Creating a new e-mail message in Evolution

A New Account Setup Wizard appears. In this dialog box, select Email account and click Next. As with Evolution, you enter your name and e-mail address in the Identity window, then choose Next. POP is the default server type; enter the information requested, such as the incoming and outgoing server names. After you click Next, you are prompted in turn to enter a user name and an account name. You are prompted to enter a password as needed to access the retrieval and sending functions of the account you have defined. The Inbox window of Mozilla is shown in Figure 2-37. Folders are shown on the left, messages are listed in the top portion, and the text of a selected message is shown below. You can use the buttons on the toolbar or the menu items to manage your e-mail.

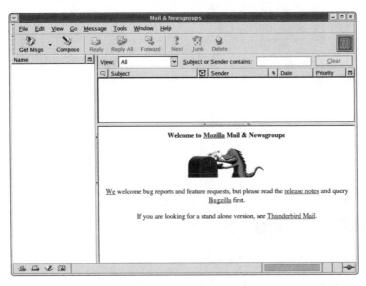

Figure 2-37   The e-mail management window in Mozilla

CHAPTER SUMMARY

- ❏ The X Window System is a powerful and flexible graphical environment that was developed at MIT. The XFree86 Project later created a version for Intel-based Linux and UNIX.

- ❏ Components of X include the X server that interacts with the video card, and the X client, a graphical application that uses the services of the X server. Commercial X servers are available for Linux. They add support for additional video cards and may provide higher performance.

- ❏ The terms "client" and "server" as used in the X Window System have opposite meanings compared to typical "client-server" computing. Within X, servers provide keyboard clicks and mouse movements instead of data, as a typical server does.

- ❏ A window manager or desktop interface provides the user interface to X. Older, basic window managers such as fvwm and twm are still in use, but most Linux systems rely on a full desktop interface such as KDE or GNOME.

- ❏ Graphical libraries make it easier to create new graphical applications by letting applications share programming code and system resources. Two of the most widely used graphical libraries are Qt (on which KDE is based) and GTK+ (on which GNOME is based).

2

❑ KDE and GNOME each provide a convenient desktop interface with icons, menus, and taskbars. They also include many graphical applications for configuring the desktop interface, managing system resources, and working with personal information.

❑ The graphical login prompt is provided by the xdm program, or the kdm or gdm program if KDE or GNOME is being used. These latter two programs can be graphically configured using utilities in KDE and GNOME.

❑ Graphical windows can be manipulated using mouse actions such as clicking and dragging or selecting icons on a window's title bar. Keyboard shortcuts are also supported for many window operations.

❑ Both KDE and GNOME include the ability to use multiple workspaces or virtual desktops in which different application windows can be open. This makes it easy to manage many open windows at the same time.

❑ GNOME and KDE can save the current state of the desktop interface and restore it the next time the same user logs in, so that applications and other windows are in the same position as when the user logged out.

❑ Hundreds of configuration options are provided for GNOME and KDE. These can be accessed via the Preferences submenu of the main menu, or by right-clicking various parts of the interface.

❑ GNOME and KDE include graphical utilities used for common system administration and management tasks. These include the Nautilus file manager in GNOME, the Konqueror file manager in KDE, simple text editors, Web browser, and terminal window programs. You can select the preferred program to use for each of these functions.

❑ OpenOffice.org is a full-featured office suite similar to Microsoft Office. It is included with most Linux distributions or can be downloaded for free. It includes Writer, Calc, Impress, and support for many database functions.

❑ Linux provides several e-mail readers. Evolution is similar to Microsoft Outlook and includes e-mail features, calendar features, task lists, and a contact manager. The Mozilla Web browser also includes a complete e-mail reader.

❑ To use either e-mail reader, you must first set up an e-mail account so that the e-mail reader knows where to locate messages and how to send new messages.

COMMAND SUMMARY

Command	Description	Example
gdmsetup	Starts a graphical utility used to configure the graphical login screen	gdmsetup
startx	Starts an X Window System session from the command line	startx
switchdesk	Starts a graphical utility used to switch between desktop interfaces installed on the system	switchdesk

KEY TERMS

face browser — A feature of the graphical login screen that causes it to display a small graphic image for each user.

graphical libraries — Collections of programming functions that an X client can use to create and manage the elements of a graphical environment more efficiently.

Panel — A bar displayed across the bottom of the GNOME or KDE desktop interface that includes icons for commonly used applications, a button to access the main menu, and other informational or management features.

Project Athena — The project sponsored by DEC and MIT to create a graphical environment or windowing system for UNIX.

session — A configuration that defines a set of graphical programs to run when a user logs in.

theme — A collection of colors, fonts, and images that give a display a certain look and feel.

window manager — A special-purpose graphical application (X client) that controls the position and manipulation of the windows within a graphical user interface.

workspace — An empty background on a desktop interface, where you can open application windows.

X client — A graphical application.

X server — The program that communicates with the video card to create images on the screen.

REVIEW QUESTIONS

1. The historical beginnings of the X Window System originated with:

   a. Project Athena

   b. early versions of Microsoft Windows

   c. the Apple Macintosh computer

   d. the XFree86 Project

2. Why might a person choose to purchase a commercial X server instead of using XFree86, which comes free with each copy of Linux?

3. Describe the function of an X server within the X Window System.

4. A(n) _____ is another name for any graphical application running in the X Window System.

   a. window manager

   b. X client

   c. X server

   d. Panel launcher

5. Name four window managers that can be used with the X Window System on Linux.

6. A window manager is best described as:

   a. a special-purpose X client that provides core graphical functionality for other X clients

   b. the management tool that administers the underlying X server

   c. the program that communicates directly with a video card in order to create windows on a computer's screen

   d. an optional component used to improve the appearance of some graphical applications

7. Name the two graphical libraries used by the two major desktop environments of Linux.

8. A graphical library is best described as:

   a. the functions that control the video card

   b. a collection of functions that any graphical program can use to create a common look and feel

   c. the configuration program used to set up X

   d. the X client that draws all windows and handles mouse and keyboard input

9. Choosing not to run X:

   a. is pointless because it runs in the background anyway

   b. can cause configuration problems on server-based systems

   c. saves the system resources that the X server and graphical programs would have consumed

   d. would be unreasonable on a Linux system used as an Internet server

10. The _____ command is normally used to start the X Window System if you are not using a graphical login.

    a. *xinit*

    b. *startx*

    c. *xdm*

    d. *xinitrc*

11. To minimize an active window in a GNOME desktop using default settings, you could either:

    a. Press Alt+F9 or select Minimize from the window control menu.

    b. Click the small "x" on the far right of the title bar or press Alt+F2.

    c. Click the small bar icon on the title bar or press F9.

    d. Double-click the title bar or press Alt+F9.

12. Describe the purpose of clicking and dragging to highlight text in one graphical window, then selecting another window and clicking both mouse buttons at the same time.

13. The Workspace Switcher in GNOME lets you:

    a. Save a record of open windows so that the next time you log in, the same windows and applications are opened automatically.

    b. Alter the position of the Panel on the desktop or add new icons to the Panel.

    c. Select a new desktop theme.

    d. Move between four desktop backgrounds, each of which can have different windows on it.

14. To enable the feature that saves your desktop setup each time you log out of GNOME, you would explore which item on the Preferences submenu?

    a. Panel

    b. CD and DVD

    c. Sessions

    d. Keyboard shortcuts

15. Describe the default action of the Alt+Tab and Alt+F1 key combinations in GNOME.

16. The Desktop Switcher utility lets you:

    a. Switch your desktop between GNOME and KDE.

    b. Switch your desktop between any installed window manager or desktop environment that the utility can locate on the system.

    c. Switch your desktop between GNOME and twm.

    d. Switch among different workspaces, just like the small squares displayed in the middle of the GNOME Panel.

17. Selecting a desktop theme lets you control:

    a. the look and feel of most aspects of your desktop interface

    b. how data CDs, audio CDs, blank CDs, or DVDs are handled when inserted into a drive on your Linux-based computer

    c. the language used by default for graphical applications

    d. the colors assigned to windows and buttons

18. Define an emblem as used in the Nautilus file manager.

19. When you select a text editor in the Preferred Application window of GNOME:

    a. You define which text editors are installed on the Linux system.

    b. You start that text editor with a text file from whichever window is active.

    c. You select the text editor that GNOME or Nautilus starts whenever you want to view a text file.

    d. You define how Web browsers within GNOME display text (non-HTML) documents.

20. OpenOffice.org consists of the following:

    a. word processor, project management, spreadsheet, database, and presentation software

    b. word processor, spreadsheet, and presentation software

    c. word processor, e-mail reader, calendar management, project management, spreadsheet, and database software

    d. word processor, spreadsheet, a drawing program, presentation software, and database tools

21. For which platforms is OpenOffice.org available?

22. Evolution is:

    a. a program that includes e-mail, calendar, task list, and contact management features, similar to Microsoft Outlook

    b. a component of the OpenOffice.org suite that provides e-mail and calendar functions

    c. the e-mail management window within the Mozilla Web browser

    d. available for download for a reasonable fee or purchased in many retail software outlets

23. When setting up a POP e-mail account, Evolution and Mozilla differ in that:

    a. One requires that you enter a valid e-mail address, the other uses only your user name.

    b. One supports leaving mail on the e-mail server, the other does not.

    c. One lets you enter passwords as part of the setup procedure, the other does not, but prompts you for passwords as needed.

    d. One is integrated with the GNOME main menu, the other is not.

24. List four features that Evolution provides via its Summary window or the standard icons on the left side of the Summary window.

25. Within the Nautilus file manager, the side pane is used to:

    a. Alert you to changes in configuration files.

    b. Display basic information about an object that has been selected in the left part of the window, including, for example, a thumbnail image of a graphic file, if so configured in the Preview tab of the File Management Preferences window.

    c. Display the name, creation date, last modified date, and contexts of any file selected in the left part of the window.

    d. Select how objects (files and directories) are displayed in the main part of the Nautilus window.

Hands-on Projects

HANDS-ON PROJECTS

Project 2-1

In this project, you experiment with manipulating windows on the GNOME desktop using your mouse and keyboard. To complete this project you should have Red Hat Linux or Fedora installed, and be running the GNOME desktop. The steps here assume that you are working at the system console. If you are using an X server to work remotely, the control key sequences (such as Alt+F1) may not work. This is especially true if you are using an X Server on a Microsoft Windows system.

1. Log in and wait for the GNOME Desktop to appear.

2. Press **Alt+F1**. The GNOME main menu appears. Choose **System Tools** on the main menu, then choose **Terminal**. A terminal window appears.

3. Press **Shift+Ctrl+N**. A new terminal window appears. Press the same keys again. A third window appears.

4. Click and drag the active (blue) title bar, moving it down to the bottom of the desktop so that it is not overlapping the other open windows.

5. Hold down the **Alt** key and press **Tab** twice. Release the **Alt** key. The first window you opened is now active.

2

6. Press **Alt+F10** to maximize this window.

7. Click the icon in the upper left of the maximized window (the far left end of the title bar) to display the window control menu. Choose **Move to Another Workspace**, then **Workspace 2** on the control menu.

8. Find the Workspace Switcher in the middle of the Panel along the bottom edge of the desktop. Click the upper-right box to activate workspace 2. Activate the maximized window by clicking anywhere in it. Press **Alt+F5** to return this window to its former size (unmaximized).

9. Notice the Workspace Switcher in the middle of the Panel. The upper-right box is shaded darker than the others, indicating that you are currently viewing that workspace (workspace 2, to which you just moved a terminal window).

10. In the upper-left workspace square on the Workspace Switcher, you see outlines of the other terminal window. Click that square to switch to workspace 1.

11. Click anywhere in the non-active terminal window to make that window active.

12. Minimize that window by pressing **Alt+F9**.

13. Find the buttons on the Panel that correspond to the windows on the workspace. What do you notice about the buttons? Click one of the buttons.

14. Click one of the terminal windows so that it is active. Press **Ctrl+d** to close that window.

15. Click the other terminal window. Press **Alt+F4** to close that window.

16. You can configure the Panel to include buttons for all workspaces, but by default, only windows on the currently viewed workspace are shown on the Panel. Click the upper-right square of the Workspace Switcher to display workspace 2.

17. Close the terminal window on workspace 2 in a different way than those listed in Steps 15 and 16. Log off your computer.

**HANDS-ON
PROJECTS**

Project 2-2

In this project, you configure some features of GNOME. To complete this project you should have Red Hat Linux or Fedora installed, running the GNOME desktop.

1. Log in and wait for the GNOME Desktop to appear.

2. On the GNOME main menu, choose **Preferences**, then **Windows**.

3. In the middle of the Window Preferences window, you see the option **Double-click titlebar to perform this action**. Suppose you are accustomed to the Microsoft Windows interface; make certain **Maximize** is selected in the list box, then click **Close** to close this window.

4. On the GNOME main menu, choose **Preferences**, then **Theme**.

5. Scroll down in the list of themes and click on the **Ocean Dream** theme. Notice how the borders of all windows and the buttons on the Panel immediately change.

6. Click the **Theme Details** button.

7. Click the **Icons** tab in the Theme Details window. Click the first item in the list, **Bluecurve**, to change all the icons back to their default setting (as they appear in the Bluecurve default theme). Notice how the icons on the Panel immediately change.

8. Change back to the **Controls** tab and click the **Metal** option in the list.

9. Click **Close** to close the Theme Details window. A Custom theme is listed at the top of the list in the Theme Preferences window. This theme represents your custom combination of elements that you have just selected from multiple preconfigured themes.

10. Choose **Save theme** in the Theme Preferences window to save a copy of this theme. In the Save Theme to Disk dialog box that appears, enter **Practice Theme** in the Theme name field and click **Save**. Your new theme is listed alphabetically in the Theme Preferences window.

11. Click on the Bluecurve theme to return to the default settings if you wish, then click **Close** to close the Theme Preferences window.

12. On the GNOME main menu, choose **Preferences**, then **Desktop Background**.

13. Click the Add Wallpaper button. A file browsing window appears.

14. You can browse to any location in your file system, but several background images are included with Red Hat Linux and Fedora in this directory (/usr/share/backgrounds/images). Double-click the **in_flight.jpg** filename. The file selection window closes, the background is changed, and the Desktop Background Preferences window shows the image you selected.

15. Find the Workspace Switcher on the Panel and click in the lower-right corner of it. This displays an empty desktop so you can see the image you selected without windows covering it. After reviewing the image, click in the upper left of the Workspace Switcher to return to where you can see the Desktop Background Preferences window.

16. If you didn't find a picture you liked, you might opt to have a colored background. Click on the **No Wallpaper** icon on the middle, far right of the Desktop Background Preferences window.

17. In the Desktop Colors field, choose **Horizontal Gradient**. Two color buttons show the two colors used to create the gradient. You can click on one or both to select a new color for the gradient.

18. To return to the default background, click **default.png**.

19. Click **Close** to close the Desktop Background Preferences window.

20. On the GNOME main menu, choose **Preferences**, then **Screensaver**.

2

21. Make sure the Display Modes tab is selected. In the Mode field, select **Only One Screen Saver**.

22. Spend a moment exploring the different screensavers (but not too long—there are nearly 200 to choose from). Select the **SBalls** screensaver for the moment.

23. Click the **Settings** button. A dialog box for configuring the SBalls screensaver appears.

24. Move the Speed slider to **Slow** and change the field below the Speed slider to **Plane**.

25. Click **OK** to close the configuration window and return to the Screensaver Preferences window.

26. Click the **Preview** button to see how the screensaver looks. After reviewing it, press **Esc** to exit from it.

27. If you want to improve the security of your system (by a small amount), click the **Lock Screen After** check box and select a number of minutes after which the screensaver locks the system. You must enter your Linux user password to exit the screensaver after it has locked the system.

28. Click **Close** to close the Screensaver Preferences window. Log off your computer.

HANDS-ON PROJECTS

Project 2-3

In this project, you work with the OpenOffice.org Writer program. To complete this project you should have Linux installed with the OpenOffice.org Writer program available.

1. Log in and wait for the desktop to appear.

2. Start OpenOffice.org Writer. If you are using Red Hat Linux or Fedora, you do this by choosing **Office**, then **OpenOffice.org Writer** on the GNOME main menu.

3. On the Writer menubar, choose **File**, then **AutoPilot**, then **Memo**.

4. In the AutoPilot Memo window, review the information shown, then click **Next**.

5. In the next window that appears, click the **Date** check box (don't worry that the date shown is incorrect—it is only there to let you choose the format of the date).

6. In the text entry field to the right of the Subject line check box, enter **Change to Travel Policy on Airline Ticket Purchases**. Click **Next** to continue.

7. Review the elements of the next window that appears. Uncheck the **Confidentiality level** check box, as you want everyone to see this memo. Click **Next** to continue.

8. Review the next window, then click **Next** to continue.

9. Click the **Create** button to create the Memo based on the information you have entered.

10. After a moment, the memo appears. If your system is not configured with your personal information, click the line after **From** at the top of the memo and enter your name.

11. Click the line after **To** at the top of the memo and enter **All employees**.

12. Triple-click on the line in the body of the memo labeled **[Please enter your text here]**. This selects the entire paragraph so that when you type, your message replaces this instruction.

13. Choose **Tools**, then **Spellcheck**. Note that **AutoSpellcheck** is activated by default. This feature underlines any unrecognized word with a wavy red line.

14. Type the following:

    effective immediately, all employes may travel in Business Class when business takes them overseas. please continue to seek the lowest fare possible.

15. Notice that as you type, Writer changes the first letter of each sentence to capitals (in the words Effective and Please). Also notice that the word "employes" is underlined with a wavy red line.

16. Press **F7** to start the spell-checking utility (or select Tools on the menubar, then choose Spellcheck, and then choose Check). After starting the spellchecker, a dialog box may appear asking if you want to start checking at the beginning of the document. Click **Yes**.

17. The Spellcheck dialog box appears, showing alternatives for "employes," which it has identified as an unrecognized word. The correct spelling is already selected in the Suggestions field, so press **Enter** or click **Replace** to continue.

18. A message box indicates when the spellcheck is complete. Click **OK** to close that message box.

19. Choose **File**, then **Page Preview** to see what your memo will look like when printed out. When you have finished reviewing the preview, choose **File**, then **Page Preview** again to return to the standard editing view.

20. Choose **File**, then **Exit** to exit Writer. When prompted to save or discard the file on which you have been working, you can choose **Discard**.

CASE PROJECTS

CASE PROJECTS

Exploring Desktop Utilities and Applications

1. You work for a small aerospace engineering firm that has about 2500 employees, all of whom use a computer for their daily work. As the system administrator for the firm, you are considering recommending a switch to Linux as the desktop platform for the engineering employees (about two-thirds of the workforce). Discuss what factors would guide your decision.

2

2. Either using a Linux system with both GNOME and KDE installed, or by exploring the information and screenshots provided on the Web sites *www.gnome.org* and *www. kde.org*, determine which desktop interface appeals to you more. Write a one-page summary of the features that influence your decision. Note in each case whether the feature is aesthetic (tied to the look and feel of the desktop) or functional (tied to the programs, utilities, or method of operation used by the desktop).

3. Obtain from wither your instructor or a friend one or more documents created with Microsoft Office. If you decide to locate documents by searching the Internet, try to get a word processor document (from Word) and another file created with either Excel (the spreadsheet) or PowerPoint (the presentation software). You may be able to find example documents on the Microsoft Web site, but be very careful about downloading documents from untrusted Web sites, as they may contain viruses that could infect your computers if they are opened on Microsoft Windows computers running Microsoft Office programs.

   Once you have obtained one or more sample files, open them using OpenOffice.org programs as described in this chapter. Note any problems you have. How well does OpenOffice seem to support Microsoft Office documents? How might your response to this question affect your decision in Case Project 1, above?

3

USING THE SHELL

After reading this chapter and completing the exercises, you will be able to:

♦ Use common features of the shell to work at the command line

♦ Manipulate variables in the shell to control your working environment

♦ Redirect data at the command line

♦ Edit text using the vi editor

♦ Print basic files from the command line

In the previous chapter you learned about the graphical environment in Linux, including how to configure basic features of the GNOME and KDE desktop interfaces, and how to use common utilities and personal productivity applications.

In this chapter you focus on the command line again. You learn how to enter commands more efficiently and execute multiple commands together using features of the shell.

One of the more complex parts of Linux is the vi text editor. In this chapter you learn the basic operation of that editor and why it is important that you learn to use it. Finally, you learn how to execute simple commands to print files from the command line.

Exploring the Bash Shell

As you learned in the first chapter, the command-line environment in Linux is controlled by a program called a shell. A shell is a **command interpreter**, meaning that the shell is simply a program that accepts input from the keyboard and uses that input to run commands or otherwise control the computer system. When you log in to Linux at a graphical login screen, no shell is started—there is no command interpreter running because there is no place for a user to enter commands at the keyboard. When you open a terminal window, a shell program is started to provide the interface (the command prompt) and interpret what you enter at the keyboard.

If you log in to Linux in text mode, a shell is started so that you have some method of controlling the system, as no graphical interface is being used. Part of the definition of each user account is the name of a login shell that is started when that user logs in at a text-mode console. Before you have logged in, however, many programs are running, but no shell is running. If you use a Linux-based computer as a server (for example, as an e-mail server), it may work for days or weeks without ever running a shell.

Working in a shell—either from a text-mode login console or in a terminal window on a graphical desktop—has the advantage of great flexibility: you can interact with any file that you have permission to access, you can start any program on the system, and you can use special features of the shell (described shortly) to work more efficiently. Some users prefer a graphical environment that requires less training to use. The capabilities that are immediately accessible in a graphical environment, however, are limited. For example, users of a graphical desktop can only start the programs that are included in menus and submenus, and they do not have access to hundreds of other programs that are part of a typical Linux system. Whether you need to use a shell or other way of interacting with the Linux kernel depends on the tasks you want to perform and the desktop environment you prefer.

The Shell Prompt

Figure 3-1 shows a standard shell prompt that appears after logging in to Linux using a text-mode login prompt or after starting a shell within a graphical environment. The **shell prompt** is a set of words or characters indicating that the shell is ready to accept commands that you enter. Recall from Chapter 1 that a default shell prompt looks like this example. The prompt you see depends on your user name (nwells here) and your host name (inverness here).

```
[nwells@inverness nwells]$
```

The last character of the shell prompt used in the standard Linux shell is a dollar sign, $. Other shells, described shortly, use different prompt characters, such as a percent sign, %. On all shells, when you log in as root (the superuser), the prompt character changes to a hash mark, #. This makes it easier for you to determine as you work whether you have root permission or not.

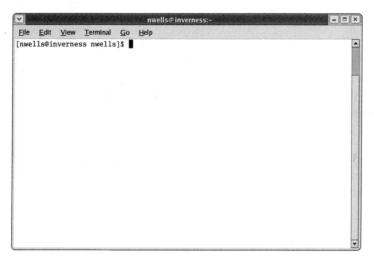

Figure 3-1   A standard shell prompt

CAUTION

You should not use the root account unless you are completing system administration tasks.

Sometimes a command that you have executed provides its own prompt where you can enter commands, similar to a shell environment. When you exit that program you return to the shell itself. Programs that provide their own prompt use a different character so you can tell that you are not working in the Linux shell. For example, when you run the *at* command (described in Chapter 6, "Managing Processes"), the prompt changes to a > character.

The Functions of a Shell

The purpose of a shell is to make it easy for users to run programs and work with files in Linux. That simple definition doesn't entirely capture the features of the shell, but it explains the basic rationale behind each shell's design.

A shell's primary purpose is to run programs. When you use the *ls* command to view the files in a directory, or use the *mv* command to rename a file, or use the *less* command to view a file, you are actually running a program that performs those tasks. The shell processes the information entered at the keyboard and uses it to start the program. In many cases, the information you enter on a command line includes parameters, such as the name of the file to copy and the location to copy it to. The shell passes these parameters to the program being started. For example, entering the following command at a shell prompt causes the shell to launch the *cp* command, handing it the two parameters report.doc and report.doc. bak. In this example, the *cp* command must decide what to do with the parameters, or return an error message if it cannot determine how to process the parameters.

```
$ cp report.doc report.doc.bak
$
```

NOTE   If a standard Linux command is completed without any errors, the shell prompt returns with no feedback at all. This is confusing at first, but it works well when you are creating scripts or commands that are to be automatically executed (the subject of Chapter 14, "Writing Shell Scripts"). The rule is that no news is good news.

If you enter the following command at a shell prompt, the shell tries to start a program called report.doc and hand that program the parameters report.doc.bak and cp. Because no program named report.doc exists, the shell (bash) returns an error message stating that it could not locate the requested command:

```
$ report.doc report.doc.bak cp
bash: report.doc: command not found
$
```

Besides the ability to start programs, the shell has many built-in features that help you work with files and commands on a Linux system. For example, from the shell, you can use keyboard shortcuts to enter long commands quickly, and you can control multiple programs that you have started from the shell prompt. In addition, you can define variables (assign numbers or strings to a name) to make your shell environment easier to use or to provide information (the values of variables) that other programs can access when needed.

A particularly important feature of a Linux shell is that it gives users the ability to write scripts that the shell can execute. A **script** is like a program or a macro. (A **macro** is a set of commands that can be executed by referring to the name of the macro.) A script is essentially a list of commands stored in a text file. Instead of entering each of these commands one by one at the command line, you can use a script to execute a series of commands automatically. You learn how to create your own shell scripts in Chapter 14.

Different Types of Shells

When UNIX was first created, its developers decided that the shell should be separate from the operating system. This meant that the shell could be changed without affecting the operating system. The shell has no special relationship to the Linux kernel—it is just like any other program, except its purpose is to start other programs. The original shell for UNIX, written by Stephen Bourne, is called the **Bourne shell**. The Bourne shell program is called sh (for "shell"). Although the Bourne shell is standard on all UNIX and Linux systems, it is an old program with limited functionality (it was first written nearly 30 years ago).

True to the foresight of the developers of UNIX, other developers altered or enhanced the Bourne shell to provide new functionality. These later-generation shells are used on UNIX and Linux systems today. Table 3-1 shows the commonly available shells for Linux.

Table 3-1 Linux Shells

Shell name	Program name	Description
Bourne shell	sh	The original UNIX shell. The sh program on Linux usually refers to the bash program. bash contains all sh functionality, plus interactive features such as history and tab completion (described later in this chapter) and shell programming via shell script files.
Bourne Again shell (**bash**)	bash	An enhanced and extended version of the Bourne shell created by the GNU Project for use on many UNIX-like operating systems. Commonly referred to as the bash shell, rather than by its full name; bash is the default Linux shell.
C shell	csh	A shell developed by Bill Joy in the 1970s. He focused on adding easy-to-use features for interactive work at the shell prompt. The C shell was the first to contain features such as history and tab completion (described later in this chapter); these features were later added to the bash shell and other shells as well. The C shell uses a more complex syntax for shell programming than the Bourne and bash shells. Because of this, it is not popular for shell programming, though its interactive features make it popular with users who are not creating shell programs.
TENEX/TOPS C shell (also called the **TC shell**)	tcsh	An enhancement of the C shell. This is the version of the C shell that is commonly used on Linux systems.
Korn shell	ksh	A proprietary (not freely available) shell written by David Korn. The Korn shell is a revision of the Bourne shell that includes the interactive features of the C shell but maintains the Bourne shell programming syntax, which is considered easier to use than C shell programming syntax.
Public domain Korn shell	pdksh	A version of the Korn shell that is freely available. (This shell is often accessed using the program named ksh on Linux systems.)
Z shell	zsh	A recently developed shell that combines Korn shell interactive features with the C shell programming style (for those who prefer the more complex syntax of the C shell).

3

The default shell for all Linux systems is bash. Users on a Linux system are normally content to use only the bash shell. Some experienced UNIX users, those who write a lot of shell scripts, or who need the features of another shell may use other shell programs. (The C shell and TC shell both use different shell programming methods than bash.)

Shells can be roughly divided into two groups based on the type of shell programming commands used. The two groups are:

- Those that follow the Bourne shell programming style (which is based on a very old programming language called ALGOL).

- Those that follow the C shell programming style (which is based on the widely used C programming language).

Further shell derivatives have combined features from different shells to make this grouping less distinct. For example, the Z shell includes many popular features of the bash shell but uses C shell-style programming. But the overall distinction between these two groups is still valid.

 Not all of the shells in Table 3-1 are installed by default or even included on the CD for all Linux distributions. Contact your Linux vendor or an Internet download site such as *www.freshmeat.net* or *rpmfind.net* to obtain a particular shell that is not included on your Linux CD.

In Linux, the shell started for each user is determined by the settings in the user account configuration file. Chapter 11, "Managing Users," describes how you can set up or modify this configuration file. If the shell you want to use is installed on the Linux system, changing to a new default shell is very easy using the *usermod* command described in Chapter 11. Each user on the system can select a preferred shell independent of all other users.

To immediately run a different shell that is installed on the Linux system you are using, enter the name of that shell program. For example, if you are working in the standard bash shell but you want to run the C shell instead, enter this command:

```
$ csh
```

Entering Commands

Modern shells such as bash and the Korn shell include features designed to simplify the process of entering commands and command parameters. Two of the most useful features are tab completion and command history.

Using Tab Completion

Tab completion is a shell feature that lets you enter part of a file or directory name, press the Tab key, and have the shell fill in the remainder of the name. Using tab completion makes it easier to enter long or complex directory paths and file names. This is helpful because Linux file names can be very long, and they sometimes include punctuation, multiple digits

3

or periods, and mixed uppercase and lowercase. Because tab completion is a feature of the shell, it works whenever you are entering text at a shell prompt, no matter which command you are entering. Anytime the shell determines that you are trying to enter a command name, a file name, or a directory name, you can use tab completion.

For example, suppose you want to use the *ls* command to display information about a configuration file in the /etc directory. You know that the name of the file you want to learn about is shown here (this file is installed by default on Fedora):

```
webalizer.conf.sample
```

To view information about this file, you change to the /etc directory and enter the *ls* command followed by the file name. But for this example, suppose you just enter the following:

```
$ cd /etc
$ ls web
```

To use tab completion at this point, you press the Tab key. The shell looks at the contents of the /etc directory for a file or subdirectory matching the letters you typed (web). If the shell finds a file name matching the letters you have entered, it fills in the remaining part of that file name. Immediately after pressing Tab, you see this at the command line:

```
$ ls webalizer.conf
```

The shell also beeps. In this case, the /etc directory contains two similar file names: webalizer.conf and webalizer.conf.sample. The shell fills in as much as it can, then beeps to indicate that there are multiple file names that begin with these letters. Press Tab twice in quick succession and the shell displays both of the matching file names:

```
$ ls webalizer.conf
webalizer.conf webalizer.conf.sample
$ ls webalizer.conf
```

Because you know that you want the second of these, you can enter the first character of the file you want, a period in this case:

```
$ ls webalizer.conf.
```

Now press Tab again and the shell fills in the full file name, webalizer.conf.sample, because that is the only file name beginning with webalizer.conf. in the directory.

NOTE
Depending on the situation in which you use tab completion, the shell tries to judge which items you want to access. For example, in some cases only executable files are compared to the text you enter.

When you first use tab completion, you may think it's more work than it's worth to keep pressing Tab and entering a few more letters if the file name is not unique. But after some practice, using tab completion to enter long file names or paths becomes an automatic response—much easier than typing the complete file or directory name.

TIP

When the first part of the name that you enter is a directory, tab completion fills in the directory name, ending with a forward slash. This means you can immediately begin typing the name of a subdirectory or file within that directory.

Using the History Feature

A second time-saving shell feature is the command history. The **command history** records each command that you enter at the shell prompt. You can quickly call up and repeat any command from this list without typing the command again. The list of recently entered commands is called the **history list**.

The simplest way to access the most recently executed command is to press the up arrow key at the command prompt. To execute the command after it is displayed, press Enter. Pressing the up arrow key repeatedly displays in turn each of the previously entered commands (the commands in the history list). Hold down the up arrow key to see dozens of commands flash by at the shell prompt (the full contents of the history list). Press the down arrow key to display commands farther down in the history list (those more recently entered).

When the command you want to repeat was entered some time ago, using the up arrow key to locate it in a large history list can be tedious. In this situation, the *history* command is useful. The **history** command displays the entire history list, which normally includes at least 1000 commands. The following shows the last few lines of a history list. (Of course, the commands and numbers in the history list on your system will differ from this sample output.)

```
33   who
34   vi /etc/passwd
35   gimp
36   cd /etc
37   cd X11/
38   cd xdm
39   more Xsession
40   rpm -qa |grep XFree
41   mount -t ext2 /dev/hda3 /mnt/openlinux/
42   mcopy /mnt/openlinux/etc/XF86Config-4 A:
43   file Xwrapper
44   umount /mnt/cdrom
45   type fvwm
46   exit
47   clear
48   mv ch05/ch04fig.zip ch04/
49   mv ch04/ch04fig.zip course_ch04/
50   cd course_ch04/
```

The length of the history list can make it difficult to quickly locate the command you want to reuse. You can use one of the following methods to locate a previously executed command:

- Use the history number.

- Use the beginning of a command.

- Search the history list.

The term "history number" refers to the number to the left of each item in the history list. For example, in the preceding history list, the first item has a history number of 33.

You can execute any of the commands in the history list by entering the number of that command prefixed by an exclamation point. An exclamation point is sometimes called a **bang** in UNIX and Linux. So to execute the most recent *mount* command in our example, you enter !41 (pronounced "bang forty-one").

The shell displays the command matching that number and immediately executes it. You don't need to view the history list before using this technique if you already know the number of the command you want to execute. But be aware that the numbers change as you enter new commands.

To use the command name to repeat a command, use an exclamation point followed by the first part of the command you want to repeat. In the sample *history* output shown, you could execute the most recent *mount* command using this command:

```
# !mou
```

When you execute this command, the shell searches for the most recent command that begins with the letters "mou" and executes it.

When executing a command from the history list using any of the three methods described, remember that the commands are executed from your current working directory, which may be different from the directory where they were originally executed. If a command does not include a full pathname, you might see unexpected results. Be especially careful when using the partial command name method to reexecute a command without checking the full text of the command.

You can also search the history list without reexecuting a command to see what the command parameters were or how you completed a task. This method requires the use of a pipe symbol (|) and the *grep* command, which are discussed later in this chapter and in Chapter 5, "Understanding Text Processing." To use this method, enter the *history* command, then a pipe symbol, then the *grep* command and the command name you want to locate. For example, in the sample *history* output shown previously, suppose you want to search for a *mount* command to see what parameters it contains. The following command displays all items in the history list that contain the *mount* command. You can then review the displayed output to learn about the previously executed command.

```
# history | grep mount
```

The bash shell supports additional techniques for executing commands. But the examples shown here for using tab completion and the *history* command should help you enter commands much more efficiently in Linux. To learn more about these features, review the online manual page for the bash shell by entering *man bash*.

The Shell Start-up Process

Several scripts are executed when you log in to Linux or start a new shell. These scripts initialize (or configure) various parts of your environment.

When a user first logs in to a Linux system, the script /etc/profile is executed. The **/etc/profile** script contains configuration information that applies to every user on the system. Each user's home directory can contain another start-up script called **.profile** (with an initial period). The .profile script in a user's home directory is also executed when the user logs in, but the .profile script is specific to a single user. Each user's home directory can contain a different .profile script. Only the root user can change the /etc/profile script; any user can change the .profile script in his or her home directory.

TIP

Any file name in Linux that begins with a period is a hidden file. This is less a security feature and more a convenience to keep files out of the way when they are seldom changed. To see a list of files that includes all hidden files, use the -a option with the *ls* command. Within your home directory, the command *ls -a* produces a long list of hidden configuration files.

On some systems, additional scripts are executed when a user logs in. For example, in Red Hat Linux, a set of scripts located in the /etc/profile.d directory is started by the /etc/profile script. The scripts in the /etc/profile.d directory add specific configuration information for many different Linux programs. Red Hat Linux also uses a file called .bash_profile rather than the standard .profile script in each user's home directory.

The profile scripts are executed when a user logs in; additional scripts are executed when a user starts a shell. Because a shell is started immediately when a user logs in at a text-mode screen, these additional scripts are generally executed immediately after the profile scripts. A user working in a graphical environment can start multiple bash shells without logging in to Linux again. When a new shell is started by a user who is already logged in, the additional scripts described next (such as /etc/bashrc) are executed; however, the profile scripts are not executed again.

Some Linux distributions, including Red Hat Linux, provide an /etc/bashrc script that is executed for all users on the system each time a bash shell is started. Other Linux distributions rely on the /etc/profile script for configuration settings that should apply to all users, though this script is only executed at the time a user logs in.

Each user's home directory contains a script called .bashrc. The **.bashrc** script is executed each time the user starts a bash shell. Any configuration information that a user wants to add to his or her environment can be placed in the .bashrc file. Additional scripts with similar names are sometimes used on a Linux distribution. Examples include the following:

- .bash_default, which is executed each time a bash shell is started
- .bash_login, which is executed each time a bash shell is started
- .bash_logout, which is executed each time a user closes a bash shell

You may find other scripts with similar names on your Linux distribution. In general, the names of these files describe when they are used. Consult your Linux vendor or try placing test commands in each file (see Chapter 14 for directions) if you are unsure of how the files are used. Figure 3-2 shows how a typical series of start-up scripts is executed when a user logs in to Linux.

```
/etc/profile ──▶ ~/.profile ──▶ /etc/bashrc ──▶ ~/.bashrc
                     or
              ~/.bash_profile
```

Figure 3-2   The process of executing start-up shell scripts

NOTE   Additional scripts are executed as part of the X Window System. For example, a user's home directory might contain a script file named .Xclients or .xinitrc that the X Window System checks for and executes as the graphical system is started. One key difference to note, however, is that when a user logs in or starts a shell, the systemwide script files (such as /etc/profile) are executed, *followed by* the corresponding file in the user's home directory. But when starting the X Window System, the system default files (such as /etc/X11/xinit/xinitrc) are executed *only if* corresponding files are not found in the user's home directory. Chapter 15, "Advanced Topics and Troubleshooting," describes these issues in more depth.

The scripts described here apply when a bash shell is started. Similar files are executed when a user chooses to work with a C shell, Korn shell, or other shell. For example, a user's home directory may contain a file called .cshrc or .kshrc. These scripts are executed each time a C shell or Korn shell is started, respectively. Because the script format is different for each type of shell, different script files are needed to initialize each shell. These configuration scripts can coexist in a user's home directory (and in the /etc directory, for systemwide configuration files), each one being executed only when the corresponding shell is started.

Using Aliases

An **alias** is a string of characters that is substituted for another string of characters at the shell prompt. The *alias* command lets you define how the shell will substitute one string of text for another string of text that you enter at a shell prompt. The general format of the *alias* command looks like this:

```
alias <string entered by user>=<string substituted by the shell>
```

For example, suppose that you are continually mistyping the *mount* command as *muont*. You could create an alias that corrects your typing error automatically:

```
alias muont=mount
```

With this alias in effect, each time you enter the string *muont* at the shell prompt, the shell replaces it with the string *mount*.

After you create an alias, each time you enter aliased text at a command prompt, the shell substitutes one string of characters for the other that you defined. You must be careful when you create an alias that uses an existing command name. For example, entering the command *alias more=less* would render the *more* command inoperative, because every time you entered *more*, the shell would substitute the string *less*. Many Linux distributions include a few aliases as part of the default configuration by placing them in the /etc/profile or /etc/bashrc script. To see a list of aliases that are in effect, enter the *alias* command without any text after it.

When the string substituted by the shell contains a space, it must be enclosed in quotation marks. For example:

```
alias ll="ls -la"
```

The *alias* command is useful in several circumstances, including those listed here:

- Aliases can shorten long commands. For example, if you regularly enter a command with many options, create an alias so you can enter that command with just two or three characters.

- Aliases can correct typing or spelling mistakes. For example, if you always enter *ruote* instead of *route*, you can create an alias that makes ruote=route. Aliases can help people new to Linux use the system without knowing all of the commands perfectly.

- Aliases can protect you from erasing or damaging files by automatically inserting options with commands that are used to delete files. For example, the command *alias cp="cp -i"* causes the shell always to execute the *cp* command with the *-i* option, which prevents overwriting files when copying.

- Aliases can add command names that you prefer to use, but that are not part of Linux by default. For example, you can use an alias to substitute the string *mv* for *rename*.

Of course, using aliases for these purposes won't help you master Linux commands, nor can it improve your typing skills. But used wisely, aliases can make tasks proceed more quickly as you work at a Linux command line.

TIP

Entering an alias command causes that alias to be active only as part of the current shell. If you decide on additional alias commands that you want to use regularly, add them to the .bashrc file in your home directory (or the startup file for whichever shell you are using, such as .pdkshrc) so that they are executed each time you start a shell.

Command-line Expansion

An alias is one example of how the shell substitutes something else for the text you enter on the command line. In fact, the shell can make many different substitutions, including the following:

- Aliases cause the shell to substitute one string of text for another.
- Variables (described in the next section) cause the shell to substitute the value of a variable for that variable's name.
- Command substitution causes the shell to execute one command and place the resulting output into the middle of another command.
- Special characters are interpreted by the shell to have a different meaning than the literal character.

Consider these examples, several of which use the *echo* command. The **echo** command writes text to the screen; it is often used in scripts (as discussed in Chapter 14). For each example, the output is shown after the command. The first example shows a standard *echo* command.

```
$ echo Your file has been processed

Your file has been processed
```

Now suppose you want to include the date in the output of the *echo* command. You can do that with command substitution. Enclose the command you want to execute in back quote characters or else between parentheses with a dollar sign in front.

```
$ echo Your file was processed on `date +%m/%d/%y`

Your file was processed on 07/15/05
```

The *date* command is first executed by the shell, then the output of that command is placed on the command line where the *date* command was.

The combination \n has special meaning to the shell. It indicates "newline" (sometimes called a carriage return). When the shell detects the \n combination, it interprets this as a single newline character. You use a special format on the command line to cause the shell to recognize the newline and similar special character combinations: enclose the combination in single quotes (not back quotes) and put a dollar sign in front of it:

```
$echo Text on line one$'\n'Text on line two
Text on line one
Text on line two
```

Another example of a special character that the shell recognizes is the semicolon. You use a semicolon to separate multiple commands. For example, the following combination of commands copies a file, then displays it using the *less* command:

```
$ cp /etc/bashrc /tmp; less /tmp/bashrc
```

You learned previously that you can use the ? and * wildcard characters to match multiple file names. When you enter an * on the command line, the shell actually substitutes all matching file names and passes them to the command you entered. For example, suppose you are working in a directory that has three files: file1, file2, and file3. When you enter this command:

```
$ cp file* /tmp
```

the shell examines the current working directory to see which file names match the pattern of file*. The resulting list of files is passed to the *cp* command. So the parameters passed to copy in this example would actually be:

```
file1 file2 file3 /tmp
```

Protecting Against Command-line Expansion

Although these examples show the power of command-line expansion performed by the shell, you might not always want to have the shell expand what you enter. For example, suppose you want to output the semicolon character using the *echo* command rather than have it create a compound command. Or suppose you needed the command you were executing to handle the * character rather than receiving a list of file names from the shell, as in the previous example of the *cp* command. In these and many similar cases, you want to avoid command-line expansion.

The shell provides three ways to protect against command-line expansion: escaping individual characters, single quoting, and double quoting.

The escape character in the shell is a backslash (\ ). When you include a backslash before a special character, that character is interpreted literally instead of as a special character. For example, suppose you want to output an asterisk. If you use this command:

```
$ echo *** Do not run this script while logged in as root! ***
```

the shell expands the *** to match every file in the current directory, so this command may list a lot of information you don't want. You can place a backslash in front of each asterisk to get the output you desire:

```
$ echo \*\*\* Do not run this script while logged in as root! \*\*\*
```

When you have multiple characters that you want to escape, you can enclose the entire expression in single quotes. This causes everything inside the single quotes to be interpreted literally:

```
$ echo ' *** Do not run this script while logged in as root! *** '
```

NOTE

Don't confuse the forward single quotes used to prevent command-line substitution (' ') with the reverse single quotes (back quotes) used to cause command substitution (' '). The forward single quote is usually located next to the Enter or Return key on the keyboard; the location of the reverse single quote varies, but may be located in the upper left, next to the number 1, or near either end of the spacebar.

A third form of protection against unwanted command-line substitution is the use of double quotes—standard quotation marks. Using these has nearly the same effect as single quotes, but some special characters are still interpreted by the shell rather than being used literally. When you use single quotes, everything between them is interpreted literally; when you use double-quotes, everything between them is interpreted literally *except* the following:

- $ Used to signal the start of a variable
- ' Used to signal the start of a command substitution
- \$ Used to output a $ character
- \' Used to output a ' character
- \" Used to output a " character
- \\ Used to output a \ character

So, for example, some parts of the following command are interpreted as special characters, and some parts are interpreted literally, as shown by the output:

```
$ echo "$USER has entered a \"value\" over \$500;
 this is not a valid entry."

James has entered a "value" over $500; this is not a valid entry.
```

Compare the above example to the output if single quotes were used instead of double quotes:

```
$ echo '$USER has entered a \"value\" over \$500;
 this is not a valid entry.'

$USER has entered a \"value\" over \$500;
 this is not a valid entry.
```

Figuring out exactly how the shell substitutes various characters in a complex command-line statement can be challenging, even for experienced system administrators. By experimenting with different combinations, you can learn how to get the results you are expecting. Although it doesn't have a lot of examples to guide you, a valuable reference is the man page for the bash shell. You can view this by entering the command *man bash*.

SHELL VARIABLES

A **shell variable**, as used in a Linux shell, is a name that can have a value assigned to it. The value can be a number or a string of text, though most variables used by the shell consist of text. Variables are typically created using all uppercase letters, though they don't have to be. (They are case sensitive, however, so be consistent in how you refer to a variable you have created.)

An **environment variable** is a variable that has typically been defined (assigned a value) as part of the process of initializing either the operating system or the particular shell in which a user is working. You can define other environment variables as needed. Any program (or any command executed at a command line) can access the values of environment variables as needed. Some environment variables are specific to each user on the system; others are the same for all users. For example, the value of the HOME environment variable is the path to a user's home directory and the USER environment variable has the value of the current user account name. But the OSTYPE environment variable holds the string "Linux," which is the same for all users on the system.

Many programs use environment variables to obtain information about your environment or about how a particular program should function. For example, a program might use the HOME variable to determine where to look for a user's data files. A program might also expect that certain environment variables have been set up specifically for the use of that program. For example, the documentation for a database program may state that before starting the program, you must define an environment variable named DB_DIR that defines the directory where the database files are located. If you execute the database program without first setting this environment variable, the program cannot function correctly. (The program would normally display an error message indicating the problem.) When programs need certain environment variables set, you should include a command to set those variables either in the systemwide start-up scripts or in a specific user's start-up scripts (if only one user runs the program in question).

You can use the *env* command to start a program with an environment variable setting that is not part of your current environment. The variable is only used for the program that you start. For example, suppose you want to execute a database program. The program requires that an environment variable called DB_DIR be set to the /data directory, but that variable isn't set in your environment, and you don't want to permanently set it because you are just experimenting with the database program. You can start the database program (assume it is called dbprogram) with the needed environment variable setting using this command. (You can follow the program name, dbprogram, with any options that the database program requires.)

```
$ env DB_DIR=/data dbprogram
```

The initialization scripts or start-up scripts that are run when Linux is started or when a user logs in create many environment variables and assign values to them. Each time a user starts a program, the environment of that new program is taken from (inherited from) the program that started it. When you open a shell within a graphical environment, the shell inherits all the environment variables of that graphical environment. If you start a program from the shell, that program inherits all of the environment variables from the shell.

The **set** command displays a list of all environment variables defined in your current environment. Sample output of the *set* command for a regular user (not root) on Red Hat Linux is shown below. Many variables listed by *set* are used by system processes with which you are not yet familiar, but you will recognize some of them. For example, the PWD variable contains the value of the current working directory. When you execute the *pwd* command, the value of this environment variable is displayed on the screen. When you use the *cd* command, the value of this variable is updated.

```
$ set
BASH=/bin/bash
BASH_VERSINFO=([0]="2" [1]="05b" [2]="0" [3]="1" [4]="release"
[5]="i386-redhat-linux-gnu")
BASH_VERSION='2.05b.0(1)-release'
COLORS=/etc/DIR_COLORS.xterm
COLORTERM=gnome-terminal
COLUMNS=80
DESKTOP_SESSION=default
DESKTOP_STARTUP_ID=
DIRSTACK=()
DISPLAY=:0.0
EUID=500
GDMSESSION=default
GNOME_DESKTOP_SESSION_ID=Default
GROUPS=()
GTK_RC_FILES=/etc/gtk/gtkrc:/home/nwells/.gtkrc-1.2-gnome2
G_BROKEN_FILENAMES=1
HISTFILE=/home/nwells/.bash_history
HISTFILESIZE=1000
HISTSIZE=1000
HOME=/home/nwells
HOSTNAME=localhost.localdomain
HOSTTYPE=i386
IFS=$' \t\n'
INPUTRC=/etc/inputrc
LAMHELPFILE=/etc/lam/lam-helpfile
LANG=en_US.UTF-8
LANGVAR=en_US.UTF-8
LESSOPEN='|/usr/bin/lesspipe.sh %s'
LINES=24
LOGNAME=nwells
LS_COLORS='no=00:fi=00:di=00;34:ln=00;36:pi=40;33:so=00;35:bd=40;
33;01:cd=40;33;01:or=01;05;37;41:mi=01;05;37;41:ex=00;32:*.
cmd=00;32:*.exe=00;32:*.com=00;32:*.btm=00;32:*.bat=00;32:*.
sh=00;32:*.csh=00;32:*.tar=00;31:*.tgz=00;31:*.arj=00;31:*.
taz=00;31:*.lzh=00;31:*.zip=00;31:*.z=00;31:*.Z=00;31:*.gz=00;31:
```

```
*.bz2=00;31:*.bz=00;31:*.tz=00;31:*.rpm=00;31:*.cpio=00;31:*.
jpg=00;35:*.gif=00;35:*.bmp=00;35:*.xbm=00;35:*.xpm=00;35:*.
png=00;35:*.tif=00;35:'
MACHTYPE=i386-redhat-linux-gnu
MAIL=/var/spool/mail/nwells
MAILCHECK=60
OLDPWD=/home/nwells
OPTERR=1
OPTIND=1
OSTYPE=linux-gnu
PATH=/usr/kerberos/bin:/usr/local/bin:/usr/bin:/bin:/usr/X11R6/
bin:/home/nwells/bin
PIPESTATUS=([0]="0")
PPID=1349
PROMPT_COMMAND='echo -ne "\033]0;${USER}@${HOSTNAME%%.*}:${PWD/
#$HOME/~}\007"'
PS1='[\u@\h \W]\$ '
PS2='> '
PS4='+ '
PVM_ROOT=/usr/share/pvm3
PVM_RSH=/usr/bin/rsh
PWD=/etc
QTDIR=/usr/lib/qt-3.1
SESSION_MANAGER=local/localhost.localdomain:/tmp/.ICE-unix/1206
SHELL=/bin/bash
SHELLOPTS=braceexpand:emacs:hashall:histexpand:history:
interactive-comments:monitor
SHLVL=2
SSH_AGENT_PID=1259
SSH_ASKPASS=/usr/libexec/openssh/gnome-ssh-askpass
SSH_AUTH_SOCK=/tmp/ssh-pNMW1206/agent.1206
SUPPORTED=en_US.UTF-8:en_US:en
TERM=xterm
UID=500
USER=nwells
WINDOWID=33554507
XAUTHORITY=/home/nwells/.Xauthority
XMODIFIERS=@im=none
XPVM_ROOT=/usr/share/pvm3/xpvm
_=set
i=/etc/profile.d/xpvm.sh
```

You can view the value of a single environment variable using the *echo* command. To see the value of an environment variable, execute *echo* followed by the environment variable name preceded by a dollar sign. The dollar sign is a special character that indicates to the shell that it should substitute the value of the variable at that point. For example, to print the value of the HOME variable to the screen, use the following command:

```
$ echo $HOME
```

The *export* command makes a newly created environment variable available to other programs run from that environment. For example, to define a new environment variable called db_data that your database program requires, and then make that variable available to other programs besides the shell itself (including the database program), use these two commands:

```
$ DB_DIR=/usr/local/db_data
$ export DB_DIR
```

The shell itself relies on many environment variables. The online manual page for the bash shell lists dozens of variables that the shell uses (or can use, if you set them) to control or select features of the shell. Two of these variables are described here as examples.

The **PATH** environment variable contains a list of directories on the Linux system that the shell searches each time a command is executed. When you enter a program name to be run at the shell prompt, the shell searches in each directory listed in the value of the PATH variable. If the program is not found in the first directory, the second is searched, and so forth. The command to view the value of PATH is *echo $PATH*. Sample output of this command on Red Hat Linux is shown here. (The value of PATH varies depending on whether you are logged in as root or as a regular user. The output here is for a regular user account.)

```
$ echo $PATH
/usr/kerberos/bin:/usr/local/bin:/usr/bin:/bin:/usr/X11R6/bin:/
home/nwells/bin
```

Suppose you want to execute a program, but the directory in which the program is located is not part of the PATH variable. You must provide the shell with the file's complete pathname. For example:

```
$ /tmp/downloads/screensaver-sample
```

If you simply enter *screensaver-sample* alone, the shell looks in the PATH directories and is unable to find the program. An interesting exercise is to press the Tab key twice on an empty shell prompt line. The shell attempts to use tab completion, but because you have entered no characters, the list of possible matches is very large—it includes all of the executable programs from every directory listed in the PATH variable. When you do this (press Tab twice), the shell requests confirmation with a message such as this one:

```
Display all 3636 possibilities? (y or n)
```

Pressing the "y" key for "yes" causes the shell to list all of the executable programs that it can find in the PATH directories.

Another environment variable used by the shell is PS1. This variable defines the shell prompt for bash. Note the default value:

```
$ echo $PS1

[\u@\h \W]\$
```

The \u, \h, and \W parameters refer to the user name, host name, and working directory, respectively. You can alter the shell prompt by changing the value of this variable. This is presented as Hands-On Project 3-1 at the end of this chapter.

DATA REDIRECTION

Most input and output operations in Linux are performed using standardized channels. Input normally comes from the keyboard and output normally goes to the screen. Channels of communication in Linux can be redirected, however, using **redirection** operators. The redirection feature gives you great flexibility in using Linux command-line utilities.

When a program expects input such as a line of text, it reads that information from the **standard input** channel (abbreviated **STDIN**). Normally, the STDIN data provided by the kernel comes from the keyboard. But you can redirect input so that the kernel hands the program data from a file or from another program instead of the keyboard.

Similarly, when a program generates output, it normally sends it to the **standard output** channel (abbreviated **STDOUT**) whenever it wants to display that information on the screen. The system normally writes anything sent to the STDOUT channel to your screen in the window from which the program was started. The STDOUT data can be redirected, however, so that anything a program sends to STDOUT is written directly to a file or sent to another program.

A third standard channel is called **standard error** (abbreviated **STDERR**). Error messages are written to standard error separately from STDOUT, in case STDOUT has been redirected. Of course, the output of STDERR can also be redirected to a new location such as an error log file.

A special tool for redirecting communication between programs is called a pipe. A **pipe** connects the output channel of one command to the input channel of another command. Pipes are used to connect the output of one application to the input of another application. Figure 3-3 shows how this works conceptually.

To see a pipe in action, consider two commands: *ls*, which lists the contents of a directory; and *sort*, which sorts all the lines in a file. The *ls* command normally writes output to the screen, whereas *sort* normally requires a file name as a parameter. But you can combine the *ls* and *sort* commands by entering the following at a Linux command prompt:

```
$ ls /etc | sort
```

The output of this *ls* command is not written to the screen. Instead, it is sent (piped) to the *sort* command. Although the *sort* command normally requires a file name, in this case it receives the names of the items to sort from the *ls* command. The result is that *sort* writes to the screen the lines from *ls*, sorted according to the first word in each line.

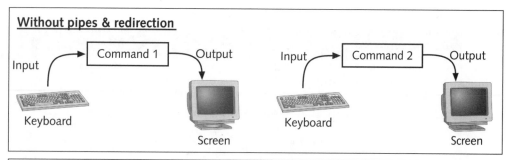

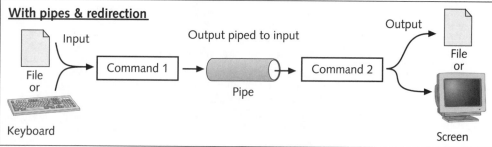

Figure 3-3   Connecting program output and input using pipes

Here is another example: The **wc** command is used to display the number of characters, words, and lines in a text file. You can provide a file name for *wc* to process, or you can pipe data into it from another command. In the following command, the *wc* command displays the number of characters, words, and lines in the output of the *ls* command (The number of lines show the number of items in the directory.)

```
$ ls /etc | wc
```

By combining the features of STDIN, STDOUT, and STDERR with the ability to redirect these communication channels and use pipes, each Linux utility can interact with other utilities and files to handle complex tasks for users and system administrators. Table 3-2 shows the special characters used on the Linux command line to instruct the shell to redirect communication between programs.

Table 3-2   Redirecting Input and Output

Symbol to use in a command statement	Description	Command-line example
> *filename*	Writes STDOUT output to the given file name	ls -l > savelisting
>> *filename*	Appends STDOUT output to the given file name (adding it to the end of any existing file contents)	cat newfile >> existing_file

Table 3-2 Redirecting Input and Output (continued)

Symbol to use in a command statement	Description	Command-line example
< *filename*	Sends data from the given file name as the STDIN, rather than reading from the keyboard	my_script < input_codes

<< *word*
text lines word
	Sends text lines as standard input, ending when *word* occurs. (EOF is a typical example of the code word chosen.) This is called a "here document" and is used in shell scripts to feed specific text to a program that reads from STDIN. See the bash man page for more details.	program << EOF
		   input line 1
		   input line 1
		   input line 1
		EOF

*program	program*	Creates a pipe between two programs, so that the STDOUT output from the command on the left of the pipe symbol is used as the STDIN input for the command on the right of the pipe symbol	ls	sort

A savvy system administrator knows command options and is comfortable combining basic utilities to provide all sorts of useful information by entering a single string of connected commands. Several examples of how this is done are shown here.

Suppose you have been working with a large data file. You are given a smaller set of information that you want to add to the larger file. You know that you can use the *cat* command to write the contents of any file to the screen (to STDOUT); using the append operator, you can add the small file to the end of the larger file:

```
$ cat small_file >> large_file
```

If you don't use the append operator, but use the basic redirection operator instead, the output from the *cat* command (the contents of small_file) creates a new file called large_file, overwriting the existing large_file:

```
$ cat small_file > large_file
```

Suppose now that you have a small file containing a list of name and address records. You want to sort those records, but you also want to see the sorted results on the screen. The **tee** command lets you redirect output to a file and also to the screen. For example, the following command displays the output of the *sort* command and also writes it to the file sorted_data.

```
$ sort data_file | tee sorted_data
```

You can have the *tee* command append data to the end of the named file by adding an *-a* option:

```
$ sort data_file | tee -a sorted_data
```

Next, suppose you want to e-mail the output of one or more commands to a user, either to another user on your system or to someone via the Internet. The ***mail*** command is a basic e-mail client that you can use from the command line to create an e-mail message (or to read messages, though it is not very user friendly for that task). The basic format of the *mail* command when used to send a message is:

```
mail -s "subject line" e-mail_address
```

After you type a command such as the one above and press Enter, you can enter the text of the message you want to send. When you press Ctrl+D to indicate that you have finished entering text, the message is sent. (You may have to press Enter once on the CC: line, depending on how your system is configured.) With that introduction, you can use a pipe to e-mail the output of any Linux command to someone. For example, the following command pipes the output of the *ps* command (listing all programs running on the system) to the *mail* command, e-mailing the output to the address nwells@comcast.net.

```
$ ps -aux | mail -s "ps output sample" nwells@comcast.net
```

Working with shell variables and performing complex redirection operations on the command line provides great flexibility as you configure a user's environment. But many parts of the Linux environment—and nearly all Linux programs—can or must be configured manually by editing text files. Although some effective graphical tools exist for performing these tasks, the skilled use of a text editor is one of the most basic abilities you must have as a system administrator. The next section describes how to use the most widely used Linux editor, vi.

EDITING TEXT WITH VI

The single most important utility for any system administrator is a text editor. This is because most of what happens on a Linux system is controlled by text configuration files. Graphical configuration utilities are sometimes available to assist with configuration, but a competent Linux system administrator can also modify the configuration files using any text editor. This provides the flexibility to update or repair a Linux system when special configuration utilities are unavailable.

Many different text editors are available for Linux. Some text editors are graphical, such as the gedit program in GNOME. You don't need special training to use a graphical text editor because a menu bar and dialog boxes guide you through any editing tasks you need to perform. The disadvantage of a graphical editor is that you must be using the X Window System. X may not be available either because you are managing a server across a network connection, or you have chosen not to install X on the Linux server itself. Whenever a graphical environment is not available, you can use a text-mode text editor.

Some widely used text-mode editors are listed here. Not all of them are included with every version of Linux, but several are probably available on the Linux system you are using.

- **vi**: The name stands for "visual editor," though you may wonder if this title is appropriate the first time you interact with vi: it doesn't provide any visual clues about how to use the editor's functions. This is the most widely used editor on UNIX and Linux systems. It is discussed in detail in this section. Different versions of vi, such as vim and elvis, are usually started with the command *vi*.

- **emacs**: This powerful editor provides macros, programming tools, customization, and hundreds of keyboard shortcuts. A graphical version called xemacs is available. emacs has a strong following among UNIX and Linux enthusiasts, but it is not as universally popular among system administrators as vi. emacs requires a large amount of hard disk space.

- **pico**: This simple editor includes onscreen information about the Control key sequences used to perform editing functions.

- *joe*: This is another simple text editor with onscreen command help feature.

vi is a very powerful program that is available on virtually every Linux system. Although vi is not easy to use, you must learn to use at least the basic features of vi in order to work as a Linux system administrator. This means you must memorize keystroke sequences and work without any onscreen prompts to guide you. Once you have learned a few commands, however, the patterns used to control vi start to emerge, and learning new commands becomes easier.

CAUTION   Because vi assumes you know what you're doing, you can easily overwrite important information if you edit real configuration files before you are comfortable with vi commands. Backing up files before editing them is a good precaution.

To start vi, enter the command *vi* at any Linux shell prompt. You can include the name of a file you want to edit after the program name, such as *vi /etc/profile*, or just enter *vi* to begin creating a new file. When you open a new file (or a small file), you see tilde characters (~) down the left side of the screen. These indicate lines that are not part of the file (because a new file is empty). Figure 3-4 shows vi after starting it with a small file to edit.

vi is a modal editor. In a **modal editor**, your keystrokes are interpreted differently depending on the mode you are working in. For example, if you are in command mode and press a key, the key is interpreted as a command; if you are in edit mode and press a key, the key is interpreted as data entry and is added to the document. vi has several modes. The most important ones for you to know immediately are:

- *Command mode*: Keystrokes are interpreted as commands to edit the file, such as deleting lines or searching for text.

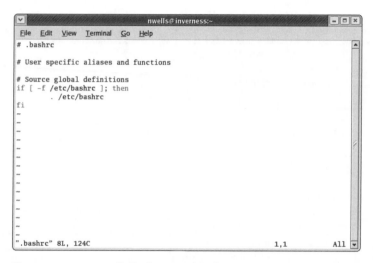

Figure 3-4 A small file being edited in vi

- *Insert mode*: Keystrokes are inserted into the document you are editing.

- *Replace mode*: Keystrokes are added into the document you are editing, overwriting any existing text at the place where you begin typing.

When you open vi, you begin in command mode. You can always return to command mode by pressing the Esc key. When you are in command mode, vi displays only the document you are editing. When you are in insert mode or replace mode, you see a message line at the bottom of the screen with the text "--INSERT--" or "--REPLACE--." (You'll learn how to switch between modes later in this section.)

NOTE

For many commands in vi you must enter multiple keystrokes. The following tables use the notation "Ctrl+X" to indicate "hold down the Control key while pressing the X key." The notation "1, Ctrl+g" indicates "press the 1 key, then hold down the Ctrl key while pressing the g key." All vi commands are case sensitive. The notation "Ctrl+g" indicates a lowercase "g". The notation "Ctrl+Shift+G" indicates an uppercase "G".

You can use the arrow keys and Page Up and Page Down to move around the screen as you edit a document. These keys normally work if you are in insert mode or replace mode. Table 3-3 shows additional commands you can use to move around a large document while you are in command mode.

Table 3-3   vi Commands Used for Moving around a Document in Command Mode

Keystroke	Description
j	Move the cursor one line down
k	Move the cursor one line up
h	Move the cursor one character left
l	Move the cursor one character right
w	Move the cursor one word forward
b	Move the cursor one word backward
Shift+G	Move to the last line of the file
1, Shift+G	Move to the first line of the file
10, Shift+G	Move to the tenth line of the file
Ctrl+g	Display a status line at the bottom of the screen to indicate the line number where the cursor is positioned and the name of the file being edited
H	Move the cursor to the top line of the screen
L	Move the cursor to the bottom line of the screen
0 (zero)	Move the cursor to the first character of the current line
$	Move the cursor to the last character of the current line

NOTE

If you are working on Linux over a network connection (for example, with a Microsoft Windows Telnet program), vi may not display text correctly. The first indication of a problem is usually that the arrow keys do not work correctly. You can still use the commands in Table 3-3 to move around the document, but you may want to investigate getting a better terminal program for the Windows system, such as PowerTerm Pro. (See *www.ericom.com.*) When you run vi in something besides a terminal window on GNOME or a text-mode console on your Linux system, you may need to reset the value of the TERM environment variable so that the shell can correctly interpret special characters used to control vi. The bash man page has more information about this topic.

In addition to moving from place to place in your document, you can change text in command mode. Table 3-4 shows a few common editing commands that you can use in vi's command mode. From the commands given here, you can deduce other similar commands. For example, if the command *10yy* copies 10 lines into the clipboard, the command *20yy* copies 20 lines into the clipboard. In vi, the storage area that you might call a clipboard is referred to as a buffer. You can use a basic buffer as you would a clipboard, but vi has many different buffers that you can refer to by name if you want to copy and move several blocks of text at the same time.

Table 3-4   Standard vi Editing Commands

Keystroke	Description
x	Delete one character to the right of the cursor
5x	Delete five characters to the right of the cursor
dw	Delete one word to the right of the cursor
5dw	Delete five words to the right of the cursor

Table 3-4   Standard vi Editing Commands (continued)

Keystroke	Description
dd	Delete the current line
D	Delete from the cursor position to the end of the current line
u	Undo the previous command (use repeatedly to undo several commands)
yy	Copy the current line into a buffer (the letter "y" refers to "yank," which is how vi refers to copying text to a buffer)
p	Put the line(s) from the standard buffer below the current line
J	Join the next line to the end of the current line (remove the end-of-line character at the end of the current line)
.	Repeat the last edit command

You can enter the insert or replace mode using several different commands, depending on where you want to begin entering text. Table 3-5 shows the most commonly used commands of this type. When you enter any of these commands (in command mode) you see the --INSERT-- or --REPLACE-- indicator at the bottom of the vi screen. Once you are in insert or replace mode, text that you enter appears in your document rather than being interpreted as a vi command.

Table 3-5   vi Commands to Enter Insert or Replace Mode

Keystroke	Description
i	Begin inserting text to the left of the current cursor position
a	Begin inserting text to the right of the current cursor position
I	Begin inserting text at the beginning of the current line
A	Begin inserting text at the end of the current line
o (the letter "o")	Insert a blank line after the line that the cursor is on, place the cursor on the new line, and begin inserting text
O	Insert a blank line above the line that the cursor is on, place the cursor on the new line, and begin inserting text
r	Replace one character with the next character entered
R	Enter replace mode; all text entered will overwrite existing text beginning at the current cursor position

All of the commands shown so far affect the document you are editing but do not display anything as you enter the command characters. Many vi commands do display the text that you enter, making it easier to enter these commands. Table 3-6 shows a few of these commands, as they would be entered in command mode. Most of them begin with a colon or a forward slash and are completed when you press Enter. After you enter the colon or forward slash, you see the characters of the command you enter at the bottom of the screen. For most of these commands, you must press Enter to indicate that you have finished entering the command.

Table 3-6 Additional vi Commands

Command	Description
:w \<Enter\>	Save the current document
: w *filename* \<Enter\>	Save the current document as *filename*
:q \<Enter\>	Exit vi
:q! \<Enter\>	Exit vi, discarding any changes to the current document
:wq \<Enter\>	Save the current document and exit vi
/*searchtext* \<Enter\>	Search for *searchtext*
/ \<Enter\>	Search again for the most recent *searchtext*
n	Search again for the most recent *searchtext*
:!*commandname* \<Enter\>	Execute *commandname* and return to vi

Although the commands in the preceding tables may seem too numerous to memorize, you will quickly become familiar with at least the basic commands required to add or delete text and then save your changes and exit from vi.

TIP

Use the command :h to see help within vi. After reading help, use the command :q to exit help and return to your document. Given the complexity of the help system in vi, an easier way to get some initial help can be to search for "vi command reference" on *www.google.com* and find a handy list of commands that you can print out for review.

PRINTING FROM THE COMMAND LINE

Chapter 12, "Configuring Networks," describes printing services in Linux in greater detail, but in this section, you learn how to quickly configure a printer that is attached to your parallel port, and then print files directly from the command line. Because many graphical applications do not let you control printing options precisely, it is a good idea to become familiar with the command-line printing utility.

Setting up a Printer

To set up a printer via the GNOME desktop interface, choose System Settings, then Printing. You must enter the root password when prompted in order to execute the Printer configuration utility. Once that utility has appeared (see Figure 3-5), press the New button to begin setting up a printer.

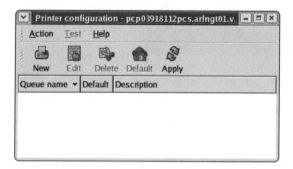

Figure 3-5 The main window of the Printer configuration utility in GNOME

After a few moments, the Add a new print queue window appears. A **print queue** in Linux is simply a printer definition—you use this utility to associate a physical printer with a named printer definition that Linux refers to as a print queue. Click Forward to begin the process. In the Name field, enter a name for the printer (see Figure 3-6). If you only have one printer, the default, "printer," is fine. If you have multiple devices or are working on a network with many printers, you might want to more creative. For example, you might name the print queue "hp4100" or "dave-print" to indicate which physical printer the print queue refers to. Enter a short description if you would like, then click Forward.

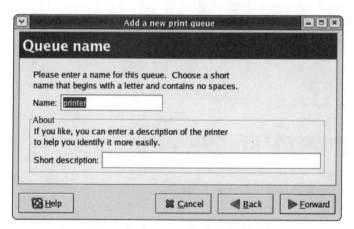

Figure 3-6 Defining a printer name in GNOME

For this example, assume you're configuring a printer that is connected to the parallel port of your Linux computer. (More complex examples involving networked printers are presented in Chapter 12.) The Select a queue type field lists Locally-connected, and the device corresponding to your parallel port is listed in the Queue type window as /dev/lp0 (see Figure 3-7). Click that device name, then click Forward.

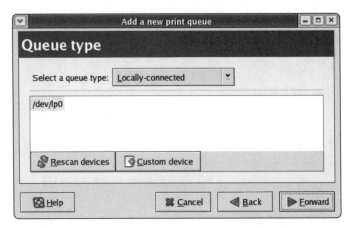

Figure 3-7   Selecting a queue type while defining a printer in GNOME

In the Printer model window, click the line labeled Generic and select the manufacturer of your printer from the list that appears. After a moment, all the models from that manufacturer that are explicitly supported by Linux are listed (see Figure 3-8). Select the appropriate one, then click Forward.

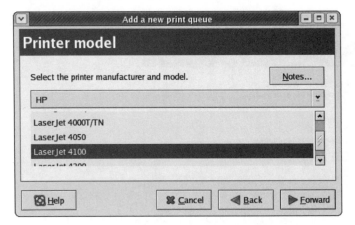

Figure 3-8   Selecting a printer model while defining a printer in GNOME

The final window is labeled "Finish, and create the new print queue." Review the information it contains, then click Finish. If you can, click Yes in the message box that appears so that the print queue is activated and a test page is printed. If the text page looks correct, you can respond to the message box that appears by clicking Yes. If you cannot print a text page, or the test page does not appear correctly formatted (for example, because a printer is not attached to your computer), then click No when prompted. You see the print queue, named "printer" or whatever you entered, listed in the main window (see Figure

3-9). Choose Action, Quit. If you are prompted by a message box, click Save to save your printer configuration. You are now ready to print documents.

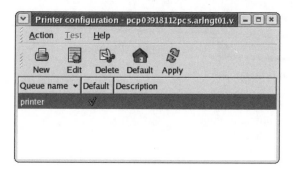

Figure 3-9   A newly defined printer

Printing from a Command Line

The command to print a file from the command line is **lpr**. You can print a file to the default printer using this command format:

```
$ lpr filename
```

 Another printing command, *lp*, has historically been a part of some UNIX systems, and is included as part of Linux. The options supported by *lp* are similar to those supported by *lpr*. See the man page of the *lp* command for further details if you have reason to use *lp* rather than *lpr*.

The *lpr* command uses a series of filters based on the type of file you print, so the same command works for PostScript files, PDF files, images, or plain text files, among others. The *lpr* command gets much more complicated when you want to control the print job more precisely instead of relying on the system defaults. Table 3-7 shows basic options that you can include with the *lpr* command to process a file in many different ways. (When you include one or more of these options on the command line, they apply to a specific print job, not to all print jobs sent to the printer. In Chapter 12 you learn more about how to control printing.)

Table 3-7   Basic Command Options for *lpr*

Option	Description	Example
-C	Set a priority class for the print job. Priorities range from A to Z. The default is A. Print jobs of a lower priority are printed after all print jobs of a higher priority.	lpr -C D stats.txt
-h	Don't use a banner or header page for this print job	lpr -h stats.txt

Table 3-7   Basic Command Options for *lpr* (continued)

Option	Description	Example
-J	Assign a name to this print job; the name appears on the banner page to help a user identify the print job.	lpr -J "Weekly statistics" stats. txt
-#	Specify the number of copies of the file to be printed; note that there is no space between the # option and the numeric value	lpr -#3 stats.txt
-m	Send an e-mail to the named user account if an error occurs during printing; if the user account is located on the same system, only the user's account name is needed, as in this example	lpr -m nwells stats.txt
-P	Specify a nondefault printer by name, when more than one printer has been defined; don't put a space between the P and the printer name	lpr -Phplj5 stats.txt

Many additional options may be supported as well, depending on the printing system you have installed. You can combine multiple *lpr* options on a single command line with the name of the file you want to print at the end of the command. If you regularly use multiple options, you should use the **lpoptions** command to "save" them so that each time you use *lpr*, the same set of options are applied to the command. For example, to set the media to legal and the banner page to confidential for all future print jobs, use this command:

```
$ lpoptions -P hplj -o media=legal -o job-sheets=confidential
```

You can create distinct instances of a printer that apply certain options, then print to that instance to use the options you have set. An **instance** is like a version of a printer definition with particular options set. For example, you could use the *lpoptions* command to create an instance of the hplj print queue called "briefs":

```
$ lpoptions -P hplj/briefs -o media=legal -o job-
sheets=confidential
```

Then you can print a file to that instance of hplj using this command:

```
$ lpr -P hplj/briefs williams.doc
```

You can also print a file using a pipe symbol (|), so that *lpr* gathers data from another program's output. For example, this command prints the output of the *sort* command to the default printer:

```
$ sort namelist | lpr
```

Using a pipe symbol to print, however, means that the print job has no distinct file name associated with it in the print job management tools that you will learn about later.

3

Chapter Summary

- A shell is a command interpreter that is used to start programs. It is not always running on Linux, but one or more shells may be started within a graphical desktop or after logging in from a console screen.

- Many shells are available, such as bash, the Korn shell, and the C shell. All shells are used primarily for starting other programs, including system administration utilities.

- Tab completion helps you quickly enter long file and directory names.

- The command history lets you quickly reenter a command that you have previously entered. The history is accessible by using the arrow keys, the *history* command, or the ! character at the command prompt.

- When a user logs in, certain shell scripts are executed; other scripts are executed each time a shell is started.

- Aliases within a shell cause the shell to replace text on a command-line entry with different text before trying to execute the command.

- The shell expands the text on the command line in several ways, including substituting variable values, performing command substitution, converting aliases, and so forth. Various characters have special meaning, such as the $ character, which is used to indicate the start of a variable.

- Command-line expansion can be prevented when appropriate using a backslash (the escape character), single quotes, or double quotes. A backslash escapes a single character. Single quotes cause the shell to ignore all special characters. Double quotes cause the shell to ignore most, but not all special characters.

- Environment variables store values that programs can access. You can view the value of an environment variable or set up a new environment variable from the shell prompt.

- Variables such as TERM and PATH define settings in the shell that allow programs to interact correctly. The *set* command displays all currently configured variables.

- Linux programs communicate by using channels of communication referred to as STDOUT, STDIN, and STDERR. The flow of data between programs can be changed using redirection operators on the command line. These operators can cause data to flow between programs and to or from files.

- Using redirection operators on the command line allows a system administrator to combine multiple simple commands into complex statements.

- Linux supports numerous text editors. The most widely available is vi, a powerful tool that requires you to memorize commands. Graphical editors are included on modern Linux desktops, but knowledge of vi remains a critical system administrator skill.

- vi is a modal editor—keystrokes are interpreted differently depending on the mode you are working in. Command mode and insert mode are the modes used most by new users of vi.

❏ After setting up a printer, you can print files from the command line using the *lpr* command.

COMMAND SUMMARY

Command	Description	Example
alias	Command within a shell that assigns a string of characters to a substitute string of characters	alias ll="ls -la"
echo	Prints text to the screen	echo "Hello"
env	Starts a program with an environment variable setting that is not part of your current environment	env DB_DIR=/data dbprogram
export	Makes a newly created environment variable available to other programs running in the same environment	export PS1="$"
history	Displays all of the stored commands in the history list	history
lpoptions	Sets one or more options for the *lpr* command so that they can more easily be used in the future	lpoptions -P hplj -o media=legal -o job-sheets=confidential
lpr	Prints a file or piped input (sends data to a print queue, from which it is sent to a printer)	lpr .bashrc
mail	Command-line utility used to send or read e-mail messages	mail -s "My bashrc file" nwells@comcast.net < ~/.bashrc
set	Displays a list of all environment variables defined in the current environment	set
tee	Sends output to both a file and the screen	sort data_file	tee sorted_data
vi	Starts the vi command-line text editor; Tables 3-3 to 3-6 show vi commands	vi /etc/webalizer.conf.sample
wc	Displays the number of characters, words, and lines in a text file	wc /usr/share/dict/linux.words

KEY TERMS

.bashrc — A configuration script that is executed each time the user starts a bash shell.

.profile — A configuration script that can be located in each user's home directory. A script that is executed each time any user on the system starts a bash shell. This script is not included by default on all Linux distributions, but can be created if needed.

/etc/profile — A script containing configuration information that applies to every user on the Linux system.

3

alias — A string of characters that the shell substitutes for another string of characters when a command is entered. Created in the shell using the *alias* command.

bang — In Linux jargon, an exclamation point character.

bash — Short for Bourne Again shell, an enhanced and extended version of the Bourne shell created by the GNU project for use on many UNIX-like operating systems. bash is the default Linux shell.

Bourne shell — The original shell for UNIX, written by Stephen Bourne.

C shell — A shell developed by Bill Joy in the 1970s. He focused on adding easy-to-use features for interactive work at the shell prompt. (Most of these features were later added to the bash shell as well.) The C shell is not popular for shell programming because its syntax is more complex than that of the Bourne, bash, and Korn shells.

command history — A feature of the shell that records in a list (the history list) each of the commands that you enter at the shell prompt.

command interpreter — A program that accepts input from the keyboard and uses that input to start commands or otherwise control the computer system.

emacs — A powerful editor that provides macros, programming tools, customization, and hundreds of keyboard shortcuts.

environment variable — Variable defined by the Linux shell so that all programs can access its value.

history list — A list that contains the most recently executed commands. (Normally at least 100 commands are included in the history list.)

instance — A version of a printer definition that has particular options set.

Korn shell — A revision of the Bourne shell that includes the interactive features of the C shell but that maintains the Bourne shell programming style. The Korn shell was written by David Korn.

macro — A set of commands that can be executed at one time by referring to the name of the macro.

modal editor — A text editor that uses multiple modes for editing text and entering commands to apply to that text.

PATH — An environment variable containing a list of directories on the Linux system that the shell searches each time a command is executed.

pico — A simple text editor that includes onscreen information about the Control key sequences used to perform editing functions.

pipe — A connection between two commands (indicated by the (|) character) that causes the output of one command to be used as the input of a second command.

print queue — A printer definition associated with a physical printer.

redirection — The act of changing either from where a Linux program receives its input or to where it sends its output.

script — A list of commands stored in a text file. Instead of entering each command one by one at the command line, a script automates the execution of a series of commands.

shell prompt — A set of words or characters indicating that the shell is ready to accept commands at the keyboard.

shell variable — A name used in a Linux shell that can have a value assigned to it.

standard error (STDERR) — The communication channel used by most Linux programs to send information about errors in program execution.

standard input (STDIN) — The communication channel used by most Linux programs to collect input (normally from the keyboard).

standard output (STDOUT) — The communication channel used by most Linux programs to write output (normally to the screen).

tab completion — A feature of the shell that lets you enter part of a file or directory name and have the shell fill in the remainder of the name.

TENEX/TOPS C shell (TC shell) — An enhancement of the C shell. This is the version of the C shell that is commonly used on Linux systems.

vi — (stands for "visual editor") The most widely used text editor on UNIX and Linux systems. Different versions of vi, such as vim and elvis, are usually launched with the command *vi*.

REVIEW QUESTIONS

1. The default shell used by Linux is:
   a. the Bourne shell
   b. The Bourne Again shell (bash)
   c. the TC shell
   d. the Z shell

2. When logged in as root, the shell prompt normally changes to display:
   a. %
   b. #
   c. the root directory
   d. $

3. The main function of a shell is to:
   a. track kernel resources for root
   b. provide a convenient programming environment
   c. complement desktop interfaces
   d. start programs

4. Name four different shells and briefly describe the differences between them.

5. Tab completion is useful when you need to:
   a. Repeat a previously used command.
   b. Reinitialize an environment variable.
   c. Enter long file names or directory names at the shell prompt.
   d. Create a brief shell program.

6. The *history* command is used to:
   a. Display a list of previously entered commands.
   b. Execute a previously used command.
   c. Change the environment variable controlling tab completion.
   d. Edit an existing text file.

7. Entering the command *!fr* would do the following in the bash shell:
   a. Cause an error because the command name is incomplete
   b. Reexecute the most recently executed command that began with "fr".
   c. Execute the *free* command to display system memory.
   d. Search for the pattern "fr" in the vi editor.

8. To have a command executed each time any user logs in to the Linux system, you place the command in which one of these files:
   a. /etc/profile
   b. /etc/.profile
   c. ~/.profile
   d. /etc/bashrc

9. If a directory contains the file names micron and microscope, and you enter micro and press Tab once, what happens?
   a. The shell prints all matching names, micron and microscope.
   b. The shell fills in the first alphabetical match, micron.
   c. The shell beeps.
   d. The micron command is executed.

10. Which of the following is a correctly formed alias for executing the *mv* command?
    a. *alias ren mv*
    b. *alias ren=mv -i*
    c. *alias mv=ren*
    d. *alias ren="mv -i"*

11. The command *echo $HOME* displays:
    a. the word HOME
    b. the current user's default shell
    c. the value of the HOME environment variable
    d. a prompt requesting a home directory path

12. Describe the contents of the PATH environment variable.

13. When the *export* command is used, an environment variable:

   a. Is available to other programs running in the same shell where export was executed

   b. Is available only to the shell itself

   c. Is not available to any program run by the same user

   d. Is available to all users on the system

14. Name at least three nongraphical text editors that may be included with a Linux distribution.

15. Knowledge of the vi editor is considered an essential skill because:

   a. Memorized vi commands correspond to other Linux command options.

   b. The vi editor is virtually always available to complete system administration tasks.

   c. Other editors are not as reliable or easy to use.

   d. The developer of vi also developed part of Linux.

16. Suppose you enter the command *vi my_file* and then press the following keys:

   ```
   itest<Esc>yyp:wq<Enter>
   ```

   Describe the result.

17. When you run a program called gather_data, it normally reads lines entered at the keyboard. If you use the command *gather_data < input_text* to run the program, which of the following occurs?

   a. The *gather_data* command is executed followed by the *input_text* command.

   b. The input that the gather_data program would normally read from the keyboard is taken from the input_text file instead.

   c. The input_text program runs first, collecting data, which is then passed through a pipe to the gather_data program.

   d. Both gather_data and input_text run as concurrent processes reading from the keyboard as STDIN.

18. A pipe is a method of connecting:

   a. processes with daemons

   b. the output channel of one program with the input channel of another program

   c. threads

   d. a deleted file name with that file's data as it resides on the hard disk

19. The command *ls | sort* causes which of the following to occur?
    a. The output of the *ls* command is sent to the *sort* command. The results are printed to the screen.
    b. It cannot be determined without information about the next command to be executed.
    c. The output of the *ls* command is written to a file named *sort*.
    d. The output of the *ls* command is filtered based on the options contained in the file named sort in the current working directory.

20. Using the *lpoptions* command, you can
    a. Configure a printer from the command line.
    b. Associate a set of *lpr* printing options with a name (called an instance) so that those options can be used more conveniently in the future.
    c. Check the status of existing print jobs to determine if any of the options assigned to those print jobs were not permitted by the printer configuration in effect at the time the print job was submitted.
    d. Set an environment variable that determines the default printer to use for the current user.

21. Which of these commands displays the current value of the USER environment variable?
    a. *echo "You are currently logged in as $USER."*
    b. *echo 'You are currently logged in as \$USER.'*
    c. *echo You are currently logged in as \$USER.*
    d. *echo 'You are currently logged in as "$USER".'*

22. How is the following text executed on a command line?
    ```
    echo 'This script has detected an error;
     please check your data.'; date; "Thank you."
    ```
    a. as two commands, followed by an error message
    b. as three commands
    c. as one command
    d. as two commands

23. How is the following text executed on a command line?

    ```
    echo "This script has detected an error\;
     please check your data."; date; "Thank you."
    ```

    a. as two commands, followed by an error message

    b. as three commands

    c. as one command

    d. as two commands

24. How is the following text executed on a command line?

    ```
    echo This script has detected an error.
     Please check your data.$'\n''date'$'\n'Thank you.
    ```

    a. It generates an error.

    b. as three lines of text, but generating an error

    c. as three lines of text

    d. It depends on the value assigned to the date variable.

25. Does the following text generate a shell error? Does it print the current date?

    ```
    echo 'This script has detected an error.
     Please check your data.$'\n''date'$'\n'Thank you.'
    ```

    a. It causes an error, but it also prints the date.

    b. It causes an error, and it does not print the date.

    c. It does not cause an error, nor does it print the date.

    d. It does not cause an error, but it does print the date.

HANDS-ON PROJECTS

Project 3-1

In this project, you use tab completion to explore the Linux file system and alter an environment variable within the shell. To complete this activity you should have a working Linux system with a valid user account. The file names described in this activity are taken from Red Hat Linux, but the steps should work on other Linux versions as well.

1. Log in to Linux using your user name and password.

2. If you are using a graphical environment, open a terminal window so you have a shell prompt.

3. Change to the directory /bin using the command **cd /bin**.

4. List the shells that are installed on the system using the command **ls *sh**. Can you recognize all of the shells listed?

5. Change to the directory /etc using the command **cd /etc**.

6. Type the command **ls –l host** but don't press Enter.

7. Press the **Tab** key twice. The first time you press Tab the shell beeps. The second time it displays a list of files in /etc that begin with host.

8. Type **s.** (including the period, so that the command line contains ls -l hosts.), but don't press Enter.

9. Press the **Tab** key twice. The shell beeps and then displays all the files in /etc that begin with hosts. (including the period). The list is shorter than the output of Step 7 because you added more characters to the search.

10. Type **a** and press **Tab**. The shell fills in the full file name so that the line reads ls -l hosts.allow.

11. Press **Enter** to complete the ls command that the Tab key finished filling in.

12. Change to your home directory by entering the command **cd**.

13. Enter the command **!ls** to execute the most recently used *ls* command, which you entered in Step 11. Why does the command display an error now?

14. Enter the command **echo $PS1** to display the format of the standard shell prompt.

15. Enter the command **man bash** to view the manual page for the bash shell.

16. Enter the text **/\\W** to search for the string \W, which is part of the PS1 value you saw in Step 14.

17. Use the arrow keys to review the list of parameters that you can use to redefine the PS1 environment variable. Locate the \d option.

18. Press **q** to exit the man page viewer.

19. Enter the command **export PS1="\d$PS1"**. What happened? What does the $PS1 at the end of the command indicate?

20. Enter the command **bash** to start a new shell. How does the shell prompt change? Why?

21. Enter the **exit** command to leave the new shell you started in Step 20. Then enter **exit** again to close the shell you have been working in since Step 2.

22. Open a new shell. What does the prompt look like? Why? Close the shell and log off.

Project 3-2

In this project, you work with the vi editor to make a change to a shell start-up script. To complete this project you should have a working Linux system with a valid user account.

1. Log in to Linux using your user name and password.

2. If you are using a graphical environment, open a terminal window so you have a shell prompt.

3. Enter the **pwd** command and check to make certain you are in your home directory.

4. Back up your .bashrc file before editing it: **cp .bashrc .bashrc.bak** (if you have trouble as you edit the file, you can exit from vi and restore your .bashrc file from the backup copy).

5. Enter **vi .bashrc** to display the .bashrc file in the text editor window.

6. Press **Shift+G** to move to the end of the file.

7. Press the **o** key to start inserting a new line of text.

8. Type the text **TEST_VAR="This is a test"** and press **Enter**.

9. On the next line type the text **export TEST_VAR** and press **Enter**.

10. On the next line type the text **alias tv="echo $TEST_VAR"**.

11. Press **Esc** to return vi to command mode.

12. Enter **:wq**, then press **Enter** to save the file and exit vi.

13. Enter **tv**. What is the result? Why?

14. Start a new shell by entering the command **bash**.

15. Enter **tv**. What is the result? Why?

16. Enter the **exit** command to exit the additional copy of bash that you started in Step 14.

17. Enter the command **vi .bashrc** to begin editing the same file as in previous steps.

18. Press the **j** and **k** keys as needed (or use the up and down arrow keys) until the cursor is located on the line containing TEST_VAR="This is a test".

19. Type **3**, then press **d** twice to delete the three lines that you entered.

If you make an error in editing this file, press "u" repeatedly to undo your editing changes.

TIP

20. Type **:wq** and press **Enter** to save the file and exit.

Project 3-3

In this project, you use the vi editor to create a new text file and modify it using many of the commands presented in this chapter. To complete this project you should have a working Linux system with a valid user account.

1. Log in to Linux using your user name and password.

2. If you are using a graphical environment, open a terminal window so you have a shell prompt.

3. Enter **vi assignment**.

4. Press **i** to enter insert mode.

5. Type this text and press **Enter**:

   I will not dip Jane's ponytail in the ink wells.

6. You are still in insert mode. Press **Esc** to change to command mode.

7. Use the arrow keys to move to the "J" in Jane.

8. Press **Shift+R** to enter replace mode.

9. Type **Meg**.

10. Press **Esc** to exit replace mode.

11. Move the cursor to the remaining "e" after Meg.

12. Press **x** to delete the "e".

13. Move the cursor to the "d" in dip.

14. Press **5dw** to delete five words to the right of the cursor.

15. Press **u** to undo that change.

16. Press **d$** to delete from the cursor to the end of the line.

17. Press **i** to enter insert mode. Press the spacebar.

18. Type **melt John's crayons on the radiator** but do not press Enter.

19. Press **Esc** to return to command mode.

20. Type **yy** to store the current line in the main buffer.

21. Type **1000p** to paste 1000 copies of the main buffer after the current line.

22. Press **Shift+G** to move the cursor to the last line of the file. Notice how the position indicator (on the bottom line of the display, on the right side of the window) changes to show the line number as 1001.

23. Press the letter **o** to change to insert mode on a new line below the current line.

24. Type your name.

25. Press **Esc** to return to command mode.

26. Type **:wq** and press **Enter** to save your file and exit vi. Close the shell and log off.

HANDS-ON PROJECTS

Project 3-4

In this project, you use redirection operators to change the default flow of information between programs and files. To complete this project you should have a working Linux system with a valid user account.

1. Log in to Linux using your user name and password.

2. If you are using a graphical environment, open a terminal window so you have a shell prompt.

3. Create two files, each containing one line of text using these commands:

   echo "Test file 1" > file1

   echo "Test file 2" > file2

4. View the contents of the first file you created, using this command:

   cat file1

5. Append the contents of file1 to file2, then view file2 by using the following commands:

   cat file1 >> file2

   cat file2

6. Execute the **ls** command for the /etc directory, sorting the resulting list of files and storing it in a file named etc_files in your home directory as shown:

   ls /etc | sort > etc_files

7. View the contents of the etc_files file by using the following command. Press **q** to exit the *less* command.

   cat etc_files | less

8. View the contents of the etc_files file again using this command:

   less etc_files

   The *less* program checks to see if there is input from the STDIN channel, as in Step 7. If so, *less* uses that input to operate on. If there is no input, then *less* checks for a file name on the command line that started the program, using the data in that file to operate on. Press **q** to exit the *less* command.

9. Execute the following command to list the contents of the /etc directory, sort it alphabetically, search for the string "conf" on each line (using the *grep* command), count how many lines are included in that list using the *wc* command, and write that count to the file conf_count.

ls /etc | sort | grep conf | wc >conf_count

Close the shell and log off. As Steps 6 and 9 illustrate, there is no limit to the number of redirection operators you can use at one time. As you learn more commands and experiment with how they can interact, you will find yourself using redirection operators regularly to combine the simple but basic commands of Linux to perform complex tasks.

CASE PROJECTS

CASE
PROJECTS

Using the Shell

McKinney & Co. has sent you to Las Vegas to consult on a project with a large travel agency, Global Worldwide Vistas. Global has Linux workstations for about 70 employees. The employees use the workstations to access several types of text-mode reservations systems. They also use a browser on the Linux systems to review Web sites related to travel and travel destinations, and to exchange e-mail with clients.

1. Jill, one of the more technically minded travel agents, approaches you with some requests and recommendations. It seems some of the programs used by the employees require that certain environment variables be set. Jill has been teaching employees how to set a variable at the command line before starting the programs in question, but she would like to have them set automatically so that users don't have to enter the values each time they start the program. How would you do this? Would it be more difficult or easier if every employee is running the program in question from a single central Linux server?

2. Thor, another travel agent, has taught himself how to use basic vi commands to create text files. He asks if you could install another text editor with better functionality. How do you respond? Do you see any reason not to grant this request? What factors play into your decision? What text editors or other programs might you consider setting up for Thor and the other employees?

3. Review the bash man page to locate the list of environment variables that the shell sets up by default, either for the use of programs run in the shell, or to control the shell itself. Comment on any that you find particularly interesting and how they might be helpful in your own system administration work.

4. The basics of command-line substitution and protection against substitution are described in this chapter. These topics are important both because understanding them permits system administrators to write complex and powerful commands (and scripts), and also because misunderstanding these two subjects is often the cause of seemingly intractable problems when writing scripts (see Chapter 14). To get a head start on becoming an expert in these topics, review the man page for the bash shell, studying more about how these features operate and what special characters bash uses to indicate various forms of substitution.

4

UNDERSTANDING USERS AND FILE SYSTEMS

After reading this chapter and completing the exercises, you will be able to:

♦ Create and manage user and group accounts

♦ View and set access permissions on files and directories

♦ Understand how file systems are configured and accessed

♦ Perform basic file compression and archiving tasks

In the previous chapter you learned more about using the Linux shell to start programs, including how to control special features of the shell such as aliases, command-line expansion, variables, and data redirection. You also experimented with the vi editor, a powerful tool that you will have many occasions to use.

In this chapter you learn how Linux relies on user accounts to control access to both the system itself and to files on the system. Users can also be formed into groups to help manage access; you learn about creating and managing both user accounts and group accounts in this chapter.

In addition, this chapter discusses file systems—the structured methods that Linux uses to record information in files and directories, typically on magnetic storage media such as a 3.5-inch disk or hard disk. You learn about types of file systems, how file information is arranged in a file system, how to control permission to access files, and how to work with basic compression and archiving utilities.

LINUX USERS AND GROUPS

To complete any operation in Linux, a person must first log in using a valid user account name and password. Setting up and maintaining these user accounts is an important part of the work of a system administrator. In general, the more user accounts you have on your Linux system, the more work is required to keep them all running smoothly. More users also means more security risks—thus proper management and tracking of user accounts is crucial to keeping the system running securely and efficiently.

NOTE When a remote user accesses your system through certain network services such as a Web server, they do not need to have a user account on your system. Instead, they use a Web browser to ask the Web server to perform a task. The Web server then completes the task via a user account designated for the use of the Web server program.

Types of User Accounts

You have already used your own user account and may have logged in using the root account on Linux. But Linux has many other preconfigured user accounts. These accounts serve special purposes on the system and have different characteristics compared to regular user accounts. The following sections discuss different types of user accounts in more detail.

The root Account

The administrative account (the **superuser**) on a Linux system is named **root**. This account is created when you install Linux. The root user can perform any operation on a Linux system. The root user on Linux is similar to the admin user on a NetWare server. Remember, there is also a root directory to the file system, designated by a forward slash (/).

NOTE The Linux root account is similar to the Administrator user account in Windows 2000/2003/XP. However, the Windows Administrator account does not have unrestricted access to all system files and resources; Windows 2000/2003/XP does not have a user account that is truly equivalent to the Linux root user.

Because the root user can perform any task on the system, *you should not log in as root for your normal work.* Even though you are the system administrator, root is not intended to be your main account. Always create a separate account (normally based on your name) and log in using this account for normal work. When you need to perform administrative tasks that require superuser privileges (such as creating new user accounts), change temporarily to the root user. When you have finished the task, return to your normal user account.

If you are working in the GNOME desktop, you can log in with your normal user account and still start any graphical administrative utility from the GNOME main menu. You are prompted to enter the root password if the utility can only be used by root. Figure 4-1 shows an example of the message box that appears when you are not logged in as root but try to start the graphical utility to manage users and groups (which is discussed later in this section).

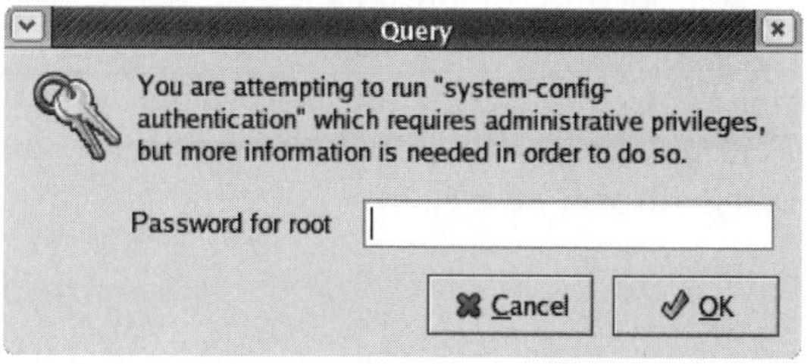

Figure 4-1 Entering the root password to run a restricted program

If you are working on the command line, you can temporarily change to the root user account using the *su* command. The *su* command (for substitute user) temporarily changes your access rights to those of another user. Unless you are already logged in as root, you must enter the password of the user whose access rights you want to assume.

If you type *su* without any parameters, you change to the root account. If you type *su* followed by a user name, you change to that user's access rights. This utility is sometimes used to assume the rights of another regular user, but more commonly it is used for the system administrator to become root for a time. (Normally, users should not have the password for any other user.) A hyphen after the *su* command causes the command to run login scripts and places you in the login directory of the user whose rights you are assuming. For example, to change to root access, you use the following command, entering the password when prompted (notice how the prompt changes when you become root):

```
$ su -
Password:
#
```

> **CAUTION**
>
> In some versions of Red Hat Linux, the path for administrative utilities is not added when you use *su* - to gain root access. To counter this problem (which is not present in Fedora), you may have to include the full path name to some utilities that only root can use—these are stored principally in /sbin.

If you omit the hyphen, you are not placed in the user's home directory. If you are logged in as root and use *su* to assume the access rights of another user (for example, to create files that have that user as owner), you are not prompted for a password when using *su*.

Regular Users

Regular user accounts are for users (actual people) who log in at a keyboard and use the Linux system. Although a regular account can be associated with a role in an organization (such as "manager" or "designer"), user accounts are commonly associated with named individuals. Regular user account names typically use a combination of first name or initial and last name or initial. User account names can be long, such as "Franklin Delano Roosevelt," but shorter names, such as "franklinr," are much more convenient.

It's common to define a standard method of converting real names to user names within an organization. This helps employees "guess" a person's e-mail address based on their name (if your e-mail address is your user name). For example, an administrator might consistently use a user's first name and last initial to create a user name. (Duplicate user names may require variations from any organizational standards you define.)

Special Users

In addition to the root user and the regular user accounts, Linux includes several default user accounts that Linux programs use. By using a special user account, these programs can control file permissions and ensure system security. Most special user accounts are created during the installation of Linux; others may be created by programs that you install.

The special user accounts on your system vary depending on the services you have installed. For example, if you have installed the PostgreSQL database package, your system contains a postgres user; otherwise, your system does not include this user. Although these user accounts are useful to specific programs, they do not have passwords or default shells defined. This means that a person cannot log in using these accounts.

Linux Groups

Linux lets you organize user accounts into groups. A **group** is a collection of user accounts that can be collectively granted access to files and directories (permission to access files and directories is the topic of the next section of this chapter). Assigning users to groups makes it easier to manage access to different areas of the system. For example, you might have a working directory where a group of employees are sharing documents for a project. By making all of these employees members of a Linux group, you can easily grant everyone permission to the project directory.

Each user in Linux is assigned to a primary group. The name of the user's primary group is stored with the user's account information. Users can also be members of many other groups. The members of each defined group are listed in the /etc/group file.

Some Linux systems, including Red Hat Linux, employ User Private Groups to increase system security. Under the **User Private Group** security model, the system creates a group with a single member for each new user account that is created. The new user is the only member of the group. When a user creates a file or directory, that user's private group is assigned as the group for the newly created file or directory; no other users have access to the file or directory by virtue of belonging to the same group as the user that created it. This prevents inadvertent security mishaps from making a user's files accessible to others that are part of the group assigned to a file.

To better understand the nature of groups, suppose you have created a new user account called "chrislee." Because your system employs User Private Groups, the primary group for this user is the group named chrislee. User chrislee is also assigned to the following groups: projectleads, salesteam, and hrcommittee. (See Figure 4-2.) Now suppose you want to give all members of the sales team access to a particular directory or group of files. You can just make salesteam the group assigned to the directory or files and grant group permissions according to the access that group members should have.

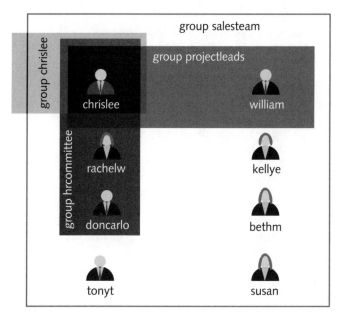

Figure 4-2   A user as a member of multiple groups

User and Group Files

User account information is stored in the file **/etc/passwd**. In earlier releases of Linux, password information for each user was also stored in this file, hence the file's name. Because of security problems in the past, password information is no longer stored in this file. Other information about each user is contained in the file, however. A sample /etc/passwd file from a new Red Hat Linux installation is shown on the next page, followed by a description of each of the file's colon-separated fields.

NOTE
The exact list of users created on a new Linux system depends on which version of Linux you are using and which features you have selected to install or activate.

```
root:x:0:0:root:/root:/bin/bash
bin:x:1:1:bin:/bin:/sbin/nologin
daemon:x:2:2:daemon:/sbin:/sbin/nologin
adm:x:3:4:adm:/var/adm:/sbin/nologin
lp:x:4:7:lp:/var/spool/lpd:/sbin/nologin
sync:x:5:0:sync:/sbin:/bin/sync
shutdown:x:6:0:shutdown:/sbin:/sbin/shutdown
halt:x:7:0:halt:/sbin:/sbin/halt
mail:x:8:12:mail:/var/spool/mail:/sbin/nologin
news:x:9:13:news:/var/spool/news:
uucp:x:10:14:uucp:/var/spool/uucp:/sbin/nologin
operator:x:11:0:operator:/root:/sbin/nologin
games:x:12:100:games:/usr/games:/sbin/nologin
gopher:x:13:30:gopher:/var/gopher:/sbin/nologin
ftp:x:14:50:FTP User:/var/ftp:/sbin/nologin
nobody:x:99:99:Nobody:/:/sbin/nologin
vcsa:x:69:69:virtual console memory owner:/dev:/sbin/nologin
mailnull:x:47:47::/var/spool/mqueue:/dev/null
rpm:x:37:37::/var/lib/rpm:/bin/bash
ntp:x:38:38::/etc/ntp:/sbin/nologin
rpc:x:32:32:Portmapper RPC user:/:/sbin/nologin
xfs:x:43:43:X Font Server:/etc/X11/fs:/bin/false
gdm:x:42:42::/var/gdm:/sbin/nologin
rpcuser:x:29:29:RPC Service User:/var/lib/nfs:/sbin/nologin
nfsnobody:x:65534:65534:Anonymous NFS User:/var/lib/nfs:/sbin/
nologin
nscd:x:28:28:NSCD Daemon:/:/bin/false
ident:x:98:98:pident user:/:/sbin/nologin
radvd:x:75:75:radvd user:/:/bin/false
apache:x:48:48:Apache:/var/www:/bin/false
squid:x:23:23::/var/spool/squid:/dev/null
johnl:x:500:500:John Lim:/home/johnl:/bin/bash
```

The following list describes the fields in each line of the output above. The last line of the file (the user johnl) is a regular user account that is used as an example.

- *User account name* (johnl): The name used by a person to log in to Linux. This field cannot contain uppercase letters or spaces.

- *Password* (x): The encrypted password for each user was formerly stored in this field. An *x* in this field indicates that the Shadow Password Suite is in use, in which case the encrypted password is stored in /etc/shadow. You will learn more about shadow passwords later in this section.

- *User ID number, or UID* (the first 500): A number from 0 to 65,535 that uniquely identifies this user on this Linux system. The number is arbitrary and normally is automatically assigned by the utility used to create a new user account. Numbers from 0 to 100 are reserved for special system uses (root always has a UID of 0). New regular user accounts commonly start with 500.

- *Group ID number, or GID* (the second 500): A number from 0 to 65,535 that uniquely identifies the primary group for this user account. The GID must correspond to a group defined in the /etc/group file (described shortly).

- *The user's real name* (John Lim): A complete name for the user. In the documentation, this is formally called the comment field. Spaces are permitted in this field. If the user account was created for a certain role in the organization, other text can be placed here instead, such as "Database Administrator."

- *Home directory* (/home/johnl): The location in the Linux file system that is used as the current working directory when the user first logs in. Whenever the user uses a tilde (~) on the command line, this directory is used. (For example, *cd* ~ changes your current directory to your home directory.)

- *Default shell* (/bin/bash): The program that runs automatically when the user logs in. The default setting for this field is /bin/bash, which runs the bash shell. If a user prefers a different shell (such as the Korn shell or C shell), this field can be changed to accommodate that. This field can also be used to start a nonshell program to restrict the user's actions.

Although you can edit the /etc/passwd file directly in a text editor, this is not a good idea if more than one system administrator might be working on the file over the network. In addition, small typing errors can make one or more user accounts inaccessible. Instead of a text editor, use the programs described in the following sections to update /etc/passwd. If you need to use a text editor to correct a problem in the file, use the special editing command **vipw**.

Groups on a Linux system are defined in the **/etc/group** file. You can edit this file if necessary using the command **vigr**. A part of the file in Red Hat Linux is shown here, with the fields in the file (again separated by colons on each line) described in the following list.

```
root:x:0:root
bin:x:1:root,bin,daemon
daemon:x:2:root,bin,daemon
sys:x:3:root,bin,adm
adm:x:4:root,adm,daemon
tty:x:5:
disk:x:6:root
lp:x:7:daemon,lp
. . .
ident:x:98:
radvd:x:75:
apache:x:48:
squid:x:23:
wine:x:66:
nwells:x:500:
rsolomon:x:501:
authors:x:502:rsolomon,nwells
```

- *The name of the group*: This field cannot contain uppercase letters or spaces. As with user names, shorter is often better; avoid names more than 10 or 12 letters long.

- *Group password*: This field is either blank or contains *x* (meaning the password is stored in another location). Group passwords allow a person who knows that group's password to temporarily assume that group's access rights using the ***newgrp*** command; this feature is rarely used.

- *Group ID (GID) number*: This number uniquely identifies the group. Group numbers are automatically assigned when you create a new group, though you can specify a number if you prefer.

- *Members of the group*: This field identifies members of the group. Note in the sample file that many groups do not have member users defined. A program may be able to assume the permissions of the group using system calls (programming instructions), but no user is part of the group by virtue of logging in. Some of the groups (such as sys and adm) have a comma-separated list of users as the last field. In addition to the two User Private Group items (for nwells and rsolomon in this sample file), a group named authors has been added to this default installation.

NOTE

Some UNIX systems employ a special group called **wheel**, which has special administrative powers; it is essentially a reduced version of the root account. On some systems a user must be a member of the wheel group in order to use the *su* command to change to the root account permissions. Although Linux includes a wheel group by default (with root as the only member), no special features or privileges apply to the wheel group in Linux.

Shadow Passwords

All programs and users may need to access the list of users stored in /etc/passwd. Each user's password used to be stored in this file as well, in an encrypted form. But if everyone could read the user names in the file, then everyone could also read the encrypted passwords. Having these passwords, even in this encrypted form, was a serious security breach that might have permitted unauthorized use of an account.

To protect against this problem, encrypted passwords are rarely stored in the /etc/passwd file. Instead, they are commonly stored in a file called **/etc/shadow**. Systems that use this file rely on the **Shadow Password Suite**, a collection of password-related programs that have been modified to recognize the /etc/shadow file. This file can only be read by the root user and certain utilities such as the login program.

Part of a sample /etc/shadow file follows. Fields on each line are separated by colons, as in the /etc/passwd file. The first field is a user account name that must correspond to a user account in /etc/passwd. The second field is the encrypted password text. Additional fields configure password security information for that user. For the many special user accounts, an asterisk in the second field indicates that the account has no password; no one can log in using that account.

```
ftp:*:10815:0:99999:7:::
nobody:*:10815:0:99999:7:::
gdm:!!:10815:0:99999:7:::
xfs:!!:10815:0:99999:7:::
nwells:$1$3gWKUouQ$L7XUsJWpIwtqLUoWlmVvN1:10816:0:99999:
    7:-1:    -1:134538436
rsolomon: 1J42Wuip3dYAh8$1pvNMAVK$UsrD6O90:10817:0:99999:
    7:-1:    -1:134538412
```

NOTE

Linux supports many password security features beyond shadow passwords. For more information, see *Guide to Linux Networking and Security* (Course Technology, ISBN 0-619-00094-5) Chapter 9.

Changing User Passwords

When logged in as root, you can change the password of any user account on the system. You use the *passwd* command to define or change a user's password. (This command has the same name as the /etc/passwd file.) When using this command as root, include the name of the user account whose password you want to define. You must enter the new password twice to be certain you have not made a typing error.

Suppose your system includes a user account lizw. To change her password, do the following:

1. Make sure you're logged in as root (typically by using the *su* command).

2. Enter the command *passwd lizw*. The following text then appears on the screen:

   ```
   Changing password for user lizw
   New password:
   ```

3. Type the new password for the Linux user account and press Enter. Nothing appears on screen as you type, so work carefully. The following text appears after you press Enter:
   ```
   Retype new password:
   ```

4. Type the new password a second time, exactly as you typed it the first time. This verifies that the password was entered as you intended to type it. When you press Enter the second time, the following text appears:
   ```
   passwd: all authentication tokens updated successfully
   ```

If you enter a password that is a poor choice (such as "password," the user name, or a simple word from the dictionary), you see a message stating BAD PASSWORD. Although this message should cause you to reconsider the password, the password is still changed. For a temporary password on new accounts, almost anything will do. Popular choices include the user's account name (lizw in this example), the word *password*, *change.me*, or something similar.

The standard procedure is for a system administrator to assign an initial password to a new account using the steps just given (or with a graphical user management utility). The administrator communicates the password to the new user, who should then immediately select a new password that is unknown to the root user or any other users.

The user can change his or her password using *passwd* without any parameters:

```
$ passwd
```

The root user can change any user's password; when a regular user changes his or her own password, different rules apply:

- The user must enter the current password for the account before entering a new password (twice).

- If a "bad password" is entered (such as a dictionary word), a warning message is displayed and the password is *not* changed.

As the system administrator, you must explain to users the importance of changing their passwords immediately after they begin using their account. Most system administrators feel that passwords should be changed monthly, even if the Linux system does not enforce frequent changes (as it can—see Chapter 11). This reduces the danger that someone will discover a user's password and be able to continue using it. Good passwords have these characteristics:

- They are at least five characters long, though a 7- to 10-character password is *much* more secure.

- They include digits or punctuation marks.

- They mix uppercase and lowercase letters in nonstandard ways.

- They are easy for the account owner to remember, but hard for anyone else to guess—even someone who knows the account owner well.

- They are not created from a simple manipulation of a word found in a dictionary or the name of a person or place.

A password that is hard to remember is probably hard for someone else to discover, but it doesn't help security much if the password is written on a note taped to the computer monitor.

CAUTION   As system administrator, you will deal with many different passwords. These include the root password, a personal account password, passwords for special administrative utilities, and passwords for other parts of your life, such as bank accounts, Web pages, and voice mail codes. If these passwords and codes are identical or similar, discovery of one of your passwords could jeopardize the security of many different areas of your work and personal life.

NOTE

You can alter the password security system used by Red Hat Linux by running the *authconfig* utility. This advanced security tool is described in *Guide to Linux Networking and Security* (Course Technology, ISBN 0-619-00094-5).

User Information Commands

4

Linux includes several commands to help you determine your current status while you are logged in. The **id** command shows your effective user ID (UID). For example, suppose you log in using a regular user account, jtaylor, whose user ID (in the /etc/passwd file) is 507. Then you use the *su* command to change to root. Your effective user ID is then 0 (for root). Then you use the *su* command to change to user cjones, whose user ID is 510. That is then your effective user ID. Your **effective UID** determines what access you are granted to files and directories. The output of the *id* command is shown here:

```
$ id
uid=500(nwells) gid=500(nwells) groups=500(nwells)
```

Even if you have changed users using the *su* command, you can always view the user name that you used to log in by executing the **logname** command. Another commonly used command that shows the user name of your currently effective UID is the **whoami** command. The **groups** command lists all of the groups that you are a member of.

You can use other commands to list which users are currently logged in and what they are doing. The **who** command lists all regular users on the system, with the location where they are logged in. The locations are terminal names; each terminal can be a terminal window, a console, or a network connection (via Ethernet or modem, for example). You will learn more about terminals in future chapters. The output of the *who* command is shown here:

```
$ who
root       tty3          Mar 26 10:33
nwells     :0            Mar 26 10:29
nwells     pts/1         Mar 26 10:30 (:0.0)
```

Additional information is provided by the **w** command, as shown below. In addition to the terminal where the user logged in, you see the time the person logged in, the program they are running (part of the name is often cut off, as in the output below), and information about the system resources the user is consuming. Totals on the first line of output indicate average load on the CPU and the number of users currently logged in. The man page describes in more detail the output of the *w* command. Any user can execute this command.

```
$ w
10:35:40  up 34 min,  3 users,  load average: 0.12, 0.16, 0.09
USER      TTY     FROM      LOGIN@   IDLE   JCPU   PCPU  WHAT
root      tty3    -         10:33am  1:44   0.01s  0.01s -bash
nwells    :0      -         10:29am  ?      0.00s  0.93s /usr/bin/gnome-
nwells    pts/1   :0.0      10:30am  0.00s  0.23s  1.65s gnome-terminal
```

FILE PERMISSIONS

Each file and each directory in Linux is assigned an owner—the **owner** is one of the users who has an account on the system. Each file and directory also has a group assigned to it—the group must be one of the groups named in the /etc/groups file. Linux determines who can access a file or directory based on who the owner is and which group is assigned to that object. **File permissions** define the access granted to a file or directory. (A directory is really a special type of file, so the term "file permissions" is typically applied to directories as well as files.) File permissions are also called the **access mode** of the file.

Three different permissions can be assigned, each represented by a single letter as indicated: read (r), write (w), and execute (x).

- **Read permission (r)**: Can read the contents of a file

- **Write permission (w)**: Can add or change information in a file or create new files in a directory

- **Execute permission (x)**: Can start a file as a program or see a file in a directory. For files, this permission is used only on programs or scripts that can be run as programs.

NOTE

Notice this unusual feature of the permissions assigned to directories: You can't see what files are in a directory (using the *ls* command), nor can you access any of those files—even if the file itself grants you permission—unless you have execute permission on the parent directory.

TIP

Linux file permissions provide adequate security to control access to files and directories, but they are not as detailed as those provided by other operating systems. The Linux 2.6 kernel supports an extended type of file permissions called Access Control Lists (ACLs). When using an ACL, you can specify permissions assigned to many individual users, rather than assigning permissions based only on three groups (owner, group, and all other users). ACLs are not yet used in standard Linux distributions, but will be in the near future.

Each of these three permissions can be assigned in three different ways:

- **User permissions** apply to the owner of a file or directory.

- **Group permissions** apply to members of the group assigned to a file or directory.

- **Other permissions** apply to all users on the Linux system who are not the owner of the file or directory in question and are not members of the group assigned to the file or directory.

Three permissions assigned to three sets of users create a total of nine permissions that can be assigned to any file or directory in Linux. These nine permissions are shown on the left side of the output of the *ls -l* command, as shown in the following example. (The far left character of the output is a type indicator, which is discussed in the next section.)

```
-rw-rw-r--   1 nwells  nwells      231723 Mar 19 09:14 file2
```

Although this list of characters can seem cryptic at first, only a few arrangements of permissions are commonly used. Table 4-1 describes the permission settings you are likely to see throughout Linux.

Table 4-1   Commonly Used File Permission Settings

Permissions	Description	Use
rwxr-xr-x	The owner can read, write (change), or execute the program; everyone else can read or execute it	For program files that everyone should be able to use, such as system utilities
rw-rw-r--	The owner and group members can alter the file, everyone (including the owner) can read the file	For data files to which everyone on the system should have access; these are the default permissions granted to a file that you create
r-x------	The owner can read and execute the program	For system utilities that only the owner (typically root) is permitted to execute
rw-r--r--	The owner can read and change the file; everyone else can read it	For configuration files. root can change the files, but all users need to read the configuration information

You can examine the permissions of a file or directory in a graphical desktop by right-clicking the object and choosing Properties from the context menu. Figure 4-3 shows the Permissions tab of the Properties dialog box for a file within the Nautilus file manager in GNOME. (The numbers shown on the Permissions tab are another method of representing permissions; this method is discussed later in this chapter.)

Changing Ownership

You can change the user and group assigned to a file or directory by using the ***chown*** command. But you can only use this command when logged in as root; regular users can't change ownership, even of files that they own. To use *chown*, type the command, followed by the user name and group (separated by a period or semicolon) that you want to assign to the file or directory, followed by the name of the file or directory. For example, the following command changes the owner of the file report.doc to jtaylor and the group assigned to that file to managers:

```
# chown jtaylor.managers report.doc
```

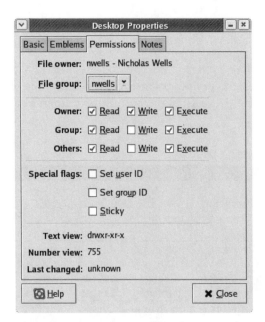

Figure 4-3   The Permissions tab of the Properties dialog box in Nautilus

You can also change just the owner of a file by leaving off the period and group name. The user and group that you assign to a file must already exist on the Linux system.

If you are logged in as root, you can use a graphical file manager to change the owner of a file. In Figure 4-3 you can see the owner and group listed; if you are logged in as root you can select a different user and group from drop-down lists. Note, however, that using the graphical interface you can only change the owner and group for one item at a time; using the *chown* command, you can change the ownership of many files and directories at once. For example, you could change the owner of every file in a directory (using * as a wildcard character that matches all files) with this command:

```
# chown jtaylor *
```

If you add the *-R* option to the *chown* command, the command is recursive, meaning that it changes the owner on any files in subdirectories of the current directory that match the file name given.

If you only want to change the group assigned to a file or directory, rather than the owner, use the ***chgrp*** command. It uses the same format as *chown*, but you only include a group name. For example, to assign the group managers to the file report.doc, but leave the owner unchanged, you use this command:

```
# chgrp managers report.doc
```

Changing File Permissions

You can change file permissions using the **chmod** (change mode) command. As a regular user, you can alter the permissions assigned to any file or directory that you own. If you are logged in as root, you can use *chmod* to change the permissions of any file or directory on the system.

To use the *chmod* command, include the type of permissions you want to change (user, group, or other, entered as u, g, or o), followed by a plus, minus, or equal sign to add, remove, or set all permissions, followed by the permissions you want to set (r, w, or x for read, write, or execute). For example, to add the write permission for other users to the file report.doc, use this command:

```
$ chmod o+w report.doc
```

Using a plus or minus sign in a *chmod* command adds or removes permissions from what is already assigned; using an equal sign sets specific permissions (overriding the previously assigned file permissions). For example, suppose the report.doc file has r-x permissions set for the group. The following command changes those permissions to rwx:

```
$ chmod g+w report.doc
```

But the following command changes the group permissions to be only rw, removing the x permission:

```
$ chmod g=rw report.doc
```

System administrators normally use a shortcut syntax with the *chmod* command. This alternative syntax is easier to use once you are familiar with it, but it's more challenging to learn. In this alternative syntax, each of the sets of three permissions (for user, group, and other) is represented by a number from 0 to 7. The three possible permissions (read, write, and execute) are assigned values of 4, 2, and 1, respectively. Now suppose that a system administrator wanted to grant read (4) and write (2) permission for the user, read (4) permission to the group, and no permissions to other users. The first digit used in *chmod* is for the user. In this case it is 6, the sum of 4 and 2. The second digit is for the group. In this case it is 4. The third digit is for other; here it is 0 (no permissions are granted). So the command looks like this (with the resulting permissions shown by *ls* after the *chmod* command):

```
$ chmod 640 report.doc
$ ls -l report.doc
-rw-r-----   1 nwells    nwells     45223 May 27 14:01 report.doc
```

Using the same method, if the system administrator wants to assign read (4), write (2), and execute (1) permissions to the user, and read (4) and execute (1) permissions to the group and to other users for a program file, the command looks like this (again with the results from *ls* shown after the *chmod* command):

```
$ chmod 755 program_file
$ ls -l program_file
-rwxr-xr-x    1 root      root       2177 May 29 14:01 program_file
```

Although this method may appear strange at first, you should become familiar with it; you will see it used often by experienced system administrators on all UNIX systems. You will also discover that only a few combinations of file permissions are commonly used. Some of these are shown in Table 4-2. Once you are familiar with the three-digit code for those commonly used sets of permissions, using the three digits is easier than entering all the letters with a plus, minus, or equal sign.

Table 4-2   Numeric Values of Commonly Used File Permissions

Permissions	Description	Numeric mode
rwxr-xr-x	The owner can read, write (change), or execute the program; everyone else can read or execute it	755
rw-rw-r--	The owner and group members can alter the file; everyone (including the owner) can read the file	664
r-x------	The owner can read and execute the program	500
rw-r--r--	The owner can read and change the file; everyone else can read it	644

Until those codes become familiar, a graphical environment such as GNOME or KDE provides an easy method of setting file permissions and seeing what the corresponding numeric code is. Within the Properties dialog box described previously, the Permissions tab includes check boxes in which you can activate or remove any of the nine permissions described in this section. Figure 4–3 shows the Permissions tab in the Properties dialog box of the Nautilus file manager. Note how the numeric and text-based indications of the file permissions are shown. Review these as you use the graphical interface to help you understand the different methods of representing Linux file permissions.

Default File Permissions

When the bash shell creates a new file because of actions you take at the command line (such as using the *touch* command or redirecting command output to a file), it creates the file with these permissions:

```
rw-rw-rw-
```

Other programs running in Linux may use other default settings, though these permissions are typical. The **umask** command defines a mask—a blocking mechanism—to stop certain permissions from being granted by default when files are created. The *umask* command is executed automatically when you log in to Linux. You can alter the permissions that can be assigned to a new file by executing the *umask* command again at any time. The *umask* command uses the same three-digit permission codes as the *chmod* command (4 for read, 2 for write, and 1 for execute), but they define permissions that are permitted on newly created files.

The value you give as a parameter to the *umask* command disables one or more of the existing default permissions. Using the *-S* option on *umask* is helpful because it shows which permissions are currently allowed on new files:

```
$ umask -S
```

If you enter this next command, all permissions are permitted on new files:

```
$ umask 000
```

If you enter the following command, no permissions at all are permitted for other on new files:

```
$ umask 007
```

In most cases, you have no need to change the default *umask* setting.

4

INTRODUCING THE FILE SYSTEM

In addition to creating and managing user accounts and assigning file permissions, managing the file system is a basic task for system administrators. In this section you learn basic information about file systems in Linux. More detailed information is provided in Chapter 8, "Installing Linux," and Chapter 10, "Managing Software Packages and File Systems."

Partitions and File Systems

A **partition** is a distinct area of a hard disk that has been prepared to store a particular type of data. For example, a computer that only contains Windows normally has only one partition on its hard disk. That partition is marked with a code indicating that the partition contains Windows data. Linux files are stored on a partition that is marked with a code used for Linux data.

You can think of a partition as an empty space on the disk with a label attached to it. Before a partition can hold information, it must be arranged based on the requirements of a particular file system type. A **file system** is an arrangement of information on a device such as a hard disk; the term is also used to refer to a particular partition or device on which Linux data is stored. For example, an administrator might refer to the file system contained on the first hard disk, saying "Our root file system is 24 gigabytes." The organization of a file system is composed of files and directories.

Figure 4-4 shows how three partitions might be arranged on a hard disk, with marks indicating the file system type and a file system format inside each partition. Linux typically uses one of two default file system types: ext3 (extended file system version 3, used by Red

Hat Linux, Fedora, and many others) or ReiserFS (used by SUSE, Lindows/Linspire, Gentoo, and a few others). The default file system type for older versions of DOS and Windows is called **FAT** (File Allocation Table). Windows NT and newer versions of Windows use **NTFS** (NT File System) or FAT32 (32-bit File Allocation Table). You will learn more about these file system types in Chapter 8.

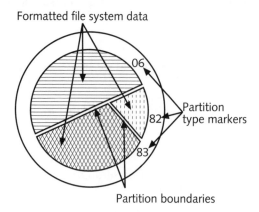

Figure 4-4   Partitions and file systems on a hard disk

When Linux is first installed, the installation program formats a partition to create a Linux file system. The system's files are then stored within that file system. You can see the status of all currently accessible file systems using the *df* command (display file systems). The output shows you the device on which the file system resides, the total storage space, the amount of free space, and other information.

```
$ df
Filesystem          1K-blocks       Used Available Use% Mounted on
/dev/hda1            6198404      342228   5541304   6% /
none                  257280           0    257280   0% /dev/shm
/dev/hdb1           10082852     5184900   4385764  55% /usr
/dev/hdb3          107086944     8204708  93442440   9% /mnt/winnt
```

The output of the *df* command is often easier to read if you use the *-h* option, which displays file system sizes and available space in MB and GB (with M or G) rather than in KB.

Inodes and Links

Within an ext2 or ext3 file system, a fixed number of entries are defined to hold information about files. Each of these entries is called an **inode** (pronounced eye-node). A file system typically contains more than enough inode entries for all the files you might possibly create on that file system. Each inode has an associated number and contains information such as the ID number for the owner and group assigned to the file, the file permissions of the file, the file size, the time the file was created, and numeric pointers to the areas of the hard disk that contain the file's data.

An inode controls the file to which it points, but it does not contain a file name. File names are stored separately. Each file name entry also includes an inode number, which is used to access the file via its associated inode. You can view the inode number associated with each file by using the *ls* command with the *-i* option.

A **file record** contains a file name and the inode number for that file; the file record is an indirect pointer to the file's data, through the inode. Every subdirectory is just a list of file records. Specifically, a **directory record** is a file that contains a list of files with corresponding inode numbers.

A **link** allows two or more file records to refer to the same physical data stored in a file system. For example, a link makes it possible for two users to have two different file names listed in their home directories, but actually be working with the same data when they edit those two files. Links are of two types: symbolic and hard.

A **symbolic link** (also called a soft link) is a file that refers to another file or directory, rather than containing data itself. For example, suppose several employees in a company want to work on the same file. The system administrator can place the file in a directory and then create a symbolic link in each user's home directory to access the real file. If the real file is /tmp/report.doc, the symbolic links might be /home/nwells/report.doc, /home/davis/report.doc, and /home/laura/report.doc.

Assuming the real file, /tmp/report.doc, has sufficient file permissions, all three users can access it by opening the respective files in their home directories. The file system follows the symbolic link to the file to which it points and opens that file. When users make changes after opening the file in their home directory, they are all changing the same file. Figure 4-5 illustrates a symbolic link.

Symbolic links are used when the same data must be accessed from two locations in the directory structure, or by two (or more) different names. Using a symbolic link takes only a few bytes of hard disk space—enough to store the file name to which the link refers. Symbolic links are commonly used in directories such as /lib and /usr/lib, where a system file must be referred to by several names in order for programs to find it.

To create a symbolic link, use the *ln* command with the *-s* option. The syntax of this command is:

```
ln -s <existing file> <symbolic link to be created>
```

For example, if you wanted to make a link from the /etc/profile file to your home directory under the name main_profile, use the following command:

```
$ ln -s /etc/profile /home/nwells/main_profile
```

In the command above, you might decide to use relative path names, depending on your current working directory.

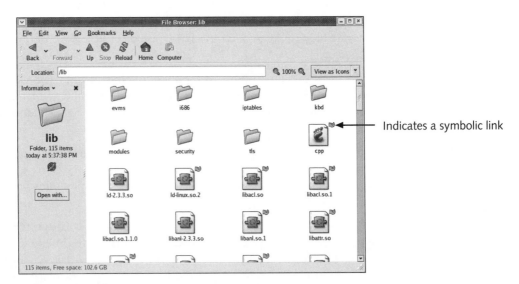

Indicates a symbolic link

Figure 4-5 A symbolic link

CAUTION
Don't confuse shell aliases and symbolic links. An alias causes the shell to substitute a different string in text that you enter. A symbolic link causes the file system to pass a request for one file to a different file in the directory structure.

In more technical terms, a symbolic link is a file record that includes a path and file name, but not an inode number. When a user refers to a symbolic link, Linux looks at the path and file name given in the symbolic link's file record. The file record for *that* path and file name includes an inode, which is used to access the file data for the symbolic link.

A **hard link** is a file record that includes a file name and inode, just like a regular file record. But a hard link refers to an inode that already has a file record pointing to it. The hard link is a second file record pointing to the same physical data. A single inode can have numerous file records (hard links) pointing to it. After a hard link is created, it is equal to the first file record that points to the same inode. If the first file record is deleted, the second file record (created as a hard link) is unaffected—it still refers to the same file data.

Both symbolic and hard links are used often in a Linux file system. Whenever you use the *ls -l* command, any symbolic links are indicated as extra file names in the right column of the output. An example of a symbolic link in Red Hat Linux is the *view* command. This output illustrates how you can use the *ls -l* command to show the *view* command:

```
$ ls -l /bin/view
lrwxrwxrwx  1  root root 2 Aug 12 13:36  /bin/view  -> vi
```

The arrow in the right column indicates that the file named view is a symbolic link to the file named vi (located in the same directory, because no path name is included). The letter *l* in the far left column of the screen output also indicates that the file is a symbolic link.

The number in the second column from the left (in this case, *1*) indicates the number of file records that refer to the same inode as this file record.

The zcat file name (also in Red Hat Linux) is an example of a hard link. The zcat file record refers to an inode to which two other file records also refer. The *ls -l* command again shows this:

```
$ ls -l /bin/zcat
-rwx-r-xr-x    3   root root   63555   Mar 25 13:28 /bin/zcat
```

In this sample screen output, the number 3 in the second column from the left indicates that the file record holding the file name zcat refers to an inode to which two other file records also refer (for a total of three).

Figure 4-6 illustrates the difference between a symbolic link and a hard link. In this figure, a programming language named Perl is stored in a file called perl5.6.1, where the 5.6.1 indicates a precise version number. Other file records also point to the same information (inode) using different file names. This allows users who might not know the precise version number to access the perl programming language file.

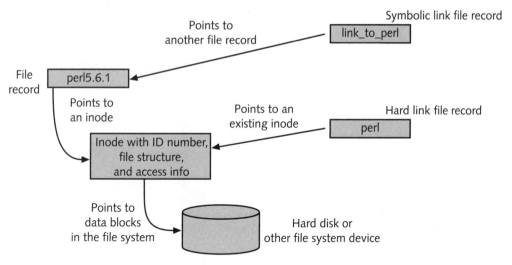

Figure 4-6 Comparing hard and symbolic links

File Types

Most of the files you have worked with so far have been standard data files, but you have also been introduced to other types of files, such as symbolic links. Because nearly everything in Linux is accessed using the file system, different types of files are used to perform different functions. Table 4-3 lists the seven types of files used by Linux. Several of these are used mainly by programs—you will not encounter them in your work at the command line and they are not discussed in more detail in this book.

Table 4-3 Linux File Types

File type	Symbol used in far left of *ls -l* output	Description
Regular file	-	Standard data files
Directory	d	A directory record, including subdirectories, which contains a list of file records and associated inodes or symbolic link pointer data
Link	l	A symbolic link (soft link) to another file record
Special file/ Character device	c	A character-oriented device such as a mouse or keyboard from which data is read or written one character at a time
Special file/ Block device	b	A block-oriented device such as a hard disk, from which data is read or written a block at a time (e.g., 512 characters at a time)
Socket	s	An interprocess socket, used to communicate between programs based on the file system permissions
Named pipe	p	Another way of communicating between programs, similar to a socket

You can learn numerous details about any file using the *stat* command. This command ties together a file name with an inode and shows you information such as the inode number, the device on which the file is stored, the most recent access time, and the assigned file permissions. Sample output is shown here:

```
$ stat /etc/profile
  File: 'profile'
  Size: 842         Blocks: 8          IO Block: 4096    regular file
Device: 301h/769d Inode: 225362        Links: 1
Access: (0644/-rw-r--r--)  Uid: (  0/  root)   Gid: (  0/  root)
Access: 2004-05-27 12:03:50.000000000 -0400
Modify: 2002-03-11 12:50:05.000000000 -0500
Change: 2004-04-29 04:46:47.000000000 -0400
```

Accessing Removable Media

Although most of the files that you use in Linux are available on the hard disk, you may need to work with CD-ROMs, 3.5-inch disks, or other removable media from time to time. In order to use any file system, including one located on a removable storage media, the file system must be mounted.

When you mount a file system, you instruct Linux how to access it—where it is located and what type of data it contains. Default information is stored for CD-ROM and 3.5-inch disks, so using them is straightforward. From the command line, you can use the *mount* command to mount a CD-ROM:

```
$ mount /mnt/cdrom
```

 CAUTION On many Linux systems, only root can mount file systems, including a CD-ROM or 3.5-inch disk. In Red Hat Linux, regular users are permitted to mount these removable media.

The /mnt/cdrom directory is a **mount point**—the path in the directory structure where you access the data in a file system. You use the *mount* command to make a new file system accessible via a mount point; you also use *mount* to list all of the file systems currently available to the system. Using the *mount* command without any parameters displays a list of the currently mounted file systems.

After executing the *mount* command above, you can access the data on the CD-ROM by changing to the /mnt/cdrom directory and using that directory as you would any other file on your system. When you insert a CD-ROM in many versions of Linux, you don't even have to execute the *mount* command—the graphical desktop detects that a CD-ROM has been inserted and automatically mounts it and possibly displays a window asking you how to proceed.

Removable disks are not detected automatically. Before trying to access a 3.5-inch disk, you can mount it using this command:

```
$ mount /mnt/floppy
```

After you have finished copying files to and from the floppy disk, or from a CD-ROM, you should not eject the disk—you cannot eject the CD-ROM—until you first unmount the media using the **umount** command (notice the command is *umount*, not *unmount*). Before you can unmount a file system, you must change to a directory that is not in that file system; if your working directory is /mnt/cdrom or one of its subdirectories, you cannot unmount the CD-ROM. These two examples show how you to unmount a CD-ROM or 3.5-inch disk:

```
$ umount /mnt/floppy
$ umount /mnt/cdrom
```

Another useful command for working with floppy disks is *fdformat*, which lets you format a 3.5-inch disk. On virtually every Linux-based PC, the 3.5-inch disk drive is accessed using the device name /dev/fd0. The *fdformat* command is used in the following manner:

```
$ fdformat  /dev/fd0
```

The man page of the *fdformat* command provides additional examples if this standard version of the command fails to locate and format a floppy disk.

Using find

Within a large file system, locating the file or directory you want to work with can be challenging. The **find** command helps you find objects matching exactly what you are looking for. The *find* command doesn't use a prebuilt index, as the *slocate* command does; it examines your file system at the time you run a command, so it may work more slowly than *slocate*. But it provides many more options than *slocate*.

The simplest use of *find* is to search for files that match a specific pattern and display them onscreen. In the following example, the path where the search should begin is /home; the name of the file to search for is report.doc, and the action to take with each matching file name is to display (print) the name onscreen (displaying to the screen is the default action, so the -print option shown here is not strictly necessary, but it illustrates the format for more complex *find* operations):

```
# find /home -name "report.doc" -print
```

NOTE

The *find* command uses full words as options, but is preceded by only a single hyphen instead of two.

The *find* options let you perform complex searches for information on your Linux system. For example, using a single (complex) *find* command, you can do any of the following tasks:

- Create an archive file of all the files that have been modified in the last 24 hours.
- Delete all files owned by a certain user on the Linux system.
- Create a list of all files that are larger than a certain size.
- Create a list of all files that have specific access permissions.
- Create a list of all files that do not have a valid owner.

In later chapters you will see *find* used in examples for such specific tasks as those listed here. For the moment, consider one more example of *find*. The following command searches the /tmp directory (and all its subdirectories) for files owned by user wilsonr that have the .jpg file extension and are larger than 50 KB. All matching file names are displayed onscreen and the files are immediately deleted.

```
# find /tmp -name "*jpg" -size 50k -user wilsonr -print -exec rm \{\} \;
```

Managing File Archives

System administrators often work with files that include compressed data or multiple files in an archival format. They do this to manage the data they are responsible for and as part of downloading and installing new software.

Compressing Files

Compressing files in Linux is a useful way to use less space for data that is rarely accessed, or to make files smaller before transmitting them over a network. You can compress any file in Linux using the *gzip* command. For example, to compress the file large.doc, use this command:

```
$ gzip large.doc
```

The preceding command transforms the file large.doc into a compressed file called large.doc.gz. The *gunzip* command uncompresses a file that you have compressed using *gzip*. For example, to uncompress the large.doc.gz file, use this command:

```
$ gunzip large.doc.gz
```

The resulting file is named large.doc.

How much the *gzip* program compresses a file depends on the type of data contained in the file. Text files and some types of graphics files may be compressed by 70 to 90%. That is, a file of 1 MB may be compressed to only 100 KB to 300 KB. Other types of data such as JPG graphics files or program files may only be compressed by 5 to 10% or less.

The *gzip* utility is the most commonly used compression tool on Linux systems, but it is not the only one available. Table 4-4 lists popular Linux compression utilities.

Table 4-4   Compression Utilities in Linux

Compress/ uncompress utility	Description
zip and *unzip*	Compresses multiple files into one file, much like a compressed tar archive. Compatible with pkzip and WinZip on other operating systems. Use this program to share files with users on non-Linux systems. Compressed files have the file extension .zip.
compress and *uncompress*	Provides poor compression compared to *gzip* (files are not as small when compressed with the *compress* command). It is an older utility supported on almost all UNIX systems. Compressed files have the extension .Z.
gzip and *gunzip*	Currently the most widely used compression utilities in Linux. Provides good compression. Compressed files have the extension .gz.

Table 4-4   Compression Utilities in Linux (continued)

Compress/ uncompress utility	Description
bzip2 and *bunzip2*	Provides excellent compression (creates very small files), but it is a newer utility that is not yet widely used. Limit your use to sharing files with those you know have bzip2. Compressed files have the extension .bz2.

Using tar and cpio for Archiving Files

A common format for transferring a group of files is called the tar archive. A **tar archive** is a single file that can contain other files, as well as the directory structure in which those files should be reassembled. You can create a tar archive (also called a tarball) using the ***tar*** command. (The command name comes from the term "tape-archive," because data used to be backed up solely on tape drives.) You typically give a tar archive a .tar file extension; when you include the compression options with the *tar* command, you typically use a .tgz or .tar.gz file extension. The resulting file is sometimes called a gzipped tarball.

A tar archive is an easy way to "dump" thousands of files onto a storage device such as a tape drive in order to make a backup copy of that data. Such tar archives are also a convenient way to send multiple files to another person—instead of attaching dozens of files to an e-mail message, you can create a tarball and attach just one. The tar archive is simply a collection of many files stored in a single file. One advantage of tar archives is that they are supported on virtually every UNIX and Linux system in the world, so they provide a convenient method of sharing files across the Internet. As you explore Internet sites containing Linux programs, you will see many tar archives.

When you download a tar archive or need to work with a tar archive that another person has given you, you can extract its contents using the *tar* command. For example, to extract the contents of an archive file named program.tgz, use this command (note that options for the *tar* command do not use a hyphen):

```
$ tar xvzf program.tgz
```

When you use the *tar* command to extract the contents of a tar archive, the tar archive remains intact. When you use the *gzip* or *gunzip* command to compress or uncompress a file, the original file is altered (compressed or uncompressed), and its name is changed accordingly.

TIP

The *tar* command and a similar command called ***cpio*** (for *copy in and out*) are used in Linux to create backups of files on the system. Sometimes other utilities rely on these programs in the background but use a graphical interface to make configuration and selection of backup options easier. Popular commercial backup utilities include features such as tracking tapes for you, keeping online indexes of each backup that you have performed, and automating schedules for unattended backup.

In addition to creating separate archive files, both *tar* and *cpio* can create an archive directly on a tape cartridge, 3.5-inch diskette, or other backup device without first creating a file on your hard disk.

The *tar* and *cpio* commands operate differently. With the *tar* command you must specify files to be included in a backup archive on the command line. By contrast, *cpio* always reads from the STDIN channel for the file names to include in an archive. The *tar* command writes data to a file name or device that you provide; the *cpio* command always writes data back to STDOUT. To compare these two methods of operation, consider the following two examples for creating a full backup of the /home directory. You can assume for this example that the device /dev/tape is configured as a tape drive. (Notice that you refer directly to a tape drive device; you do not mount it first.)

```
# tar cf /dev/tape /home
```

If you had a small set of files to archive, you could send the archive to a 3.5-inch disk:

```
# tar cf /dev/fd0 /boot
```

These two example commands use the *c* option of tar to create a new archive. The *f* option (for *filename*) followed by the device name indicates the location where the archived data will be stored. The last parameter, /home, indicates which files are to be archived. Because the parameter is a directory name, *tar* includes all files within that directory. A *cpio* command equivalent to the above *tar* command is:

```
# find /home -print | cpio -o > /dev/tape
```

This *cpio* command relies on the *find* command to generate a list of files (one file name per line) for *cpio* to back up. Those file names are sent to *cpio* using a pipe symbol because *cpio* reads the file names in from STDIN. The > redirection operator sends the archived files to the device /dev/tape. The *-o* option on *cpio* indicates that the archive is being output—that is, that data is being written out. A simpler example of *cpio* can archive the contents of a single directory to a local file using the *ls* command to generate the list of files to archive:

```
# ls | cpio -o > /tmp/archive.cpio
```

NOTE

You might have noticed that *tar* options do not normally include a preceding hyphen; those of the *cpio* command do.

The *v* option is normally added to both *tar* and *cpio* so that the output of the command is verbose, meaning that the command prints details of what it is doing to the screen. With that option added, the last example looks like this:

```
# ls | cpio -ov > /tmp/archive.cpio
```

You use a similar command with different options to extract files using *tar* or *cpio*. If you had created an archive on a 3.5-inch disk using *tar*, you restore the contents of the disk into the current directory using this command (with the *x* option standing for "extract" and the *v* option included to see verbose messages about command progress):

```
# tar xvf /dev/fd0
```

The *cpio* command uses the *-i* option for input, again extracting the contents of the backup media into the current directory. The *-d* option is also added here so that *cpio* creates subdirectories that existed in the data as required to re-create the original data organization. When using the *cpio* command with the *-i* option, *cpio* reads the STDIN channel to get the archived data; so the < redirection operator is used with the file name or archive device name.

```
# cpio -idv < /dev/fd0
```

These are very basic examples of *tar* and *cpio*. Each command supports dozens of options for features such as compressing files, preserving file attributes, controlling a tape device, setting timestamps on archived data, and many other things. You can review the man and info pages for each command to learn more.

Both *tar* and *cpio* rely on other Linux commands to help you create an incremental or multilevel backup. The most useful of these is the *find* command, mentioned in the previous section. For example, the following *find* command prints a list of all files in the /home directory (and its subdirectories) that have been modified in the last day by using the *-mtime* parameter with a value of 1:

```
# find /home -mtime 1 -print
```

By using the list of files generated by this command as the archive list for *cpio* or *tar*, you can easily create a backup with only recently modified files. The following two commands illustrate how to do this with either *cpio* or *tar*:

```
# find /home -mtime 1 -print | cpio -ov > /dev/tape
```

```
# tar cf /dev/tape ' find /home -mtime 1 -print'
```

The options available with the *find* command make it a powerful companion to *tar* and *cpio*. With *find* you can create a list of files owned by certain users, files modified or accessed within certain time limits, files with certain file permissions, or many other criteria.

CHAPTER SUMMARY

- User accounts form the basis of file system security in Linux. A person must have a valid user account to log in to Linux and access system resources.

- Linux includes multiple types of user accounts such as regular users, the root user, and special user accounts that are used only by utilities or other programs, but cannot be used to log in normally.

❑ You can change the user that you are working as (and thus your effective UID) using the *su* command. This is the normal method of gaining root privileges, as it is unsafe to work continuously as root.

❑ Each user can belong to multiple Linux groups, as defined in /etc/group. One group is the primary group for each user and is listed in that user's definition in /etc/passwd. User private groups assign one user to a group in order to improve file system security.

4

❑ Encrypted passwords are stored in the /etc/shadow file so that only root and a few special programs such as login can read this information. Access to encrypted passwords is a security hazard.

❑ The *passwd* command is used to change the password for a user account. Commands such as *id*, *w*, and *who* tell a user about the account currently in use, what other users are logged in, and to what groups the user belongs.

❑ Linux file security is controlled by nine permissions (three sets of three permissions each). The three permissions are read, write, and execute; the three sets of permissions are for the owner, for the assigned group, or for other users on the system. Only a few arrangements of these nine permissions are commonly used.

❑ The *chown* and *chgrp* commands alter the owner and assigned group of a file or directory. The *chmod* command, used with either character or numeric codes, alters the mode—the file permissions—of a file or directory.

❑ The *umask* command alters the default file permissions assigned to a newly created file or directory.

❑ File systems are organized collections of data that can be created within partitions on a hard disk. Within a Linux file system, inodes are data structures that contain information about all files stored on that file system.

❑ Hard and soft (symbolic) links refer directly and indirectly (respectively) to an inode, which in turn refers to the data contained in a file. The *ln* command is used to create both types of links.

❑ Linux uses the file system to access many types of data, including devices, pipes, and regular data files. The type of a file is indicated by a code letter in the far left of the *ls -l* output.

❑ Removable media must be mounted before they can be accessed within the Linux directory structure. They must also be unmounted before they can be safely removed. Default mount points make mounting CD-ROMs and floppy disks straightforward.

❑ The *find* command helps locate files with specified characteristics. It is a valuable tool because a typical Linux file system contains tens of thousands of files.

❑ Linux includes several utilities for compressing files. The most widely used is *gzip*, though the *bzip2* program provides better compression, and the zip format is compatible with other operating systems. Compression is also used as part of data backup and downloaded archive files.

❏ Downloaded archive files are typically created and accessed using the *tar* command. The *cpio* command is a newer utility that is used (along with *tar*) to create simple backup files in Linux.

❏ By using the *find* command with *tar* or *cpio*, complex file archives can be created with a single command.

COMMAND SUMMARY

Command	Description	Example
chgrp	Changes the group assigned to a file or directory; only root can use this command	chgrp managers report.doc
chmod	Changes the access mode (file permissions) of a file or directory, using either character codes or a numeric value	chmod g=rw report.doc
chown	Changes the owner and optionally the group assigned to a file or directory; only root can use this command	chown jtaylor.managers report.doc
cpio	Creates archives; also reads archive files created by the *tar* command	cpio -idv < /dev/fd0
df	Displays file system summary information such as device, mount point, percentage used, and total capacity	df -h
fdformat	Formats a 3.5-inch disk	fdformat /dev/fd0
find	Searches the file system for files matching given characteristics	find /home -name "report.doc" -print
groups	Lists all the groups of which the currently effective UID (current user) is a member	groups
gunzip	Uncompresses a file that has been compressed using *gzip*	gunzip archive.gz
gzip	Compresses files on a Linux system	gzip archive
id	Displays the currently effective UID, GID, and groups of which the effective UID is a member	id
ln	Creates a hard or symbolic (soft) link	ln -s /etc/profile /home/nwells/ main_profile
logname	Displays the user name used to log in to Linux (which may differ from the currently effective UID as displayed by the *whoami* or *id* commands)	logname

Command	Description	Example
mount	Makes a logical or physical device (such as a CD-ROM or 3.5-inch diskette) available as a file system in the Linux directory structure	mount /mnt/cdrom
newgrp	Temporarily changes the effective group of a logged in user analogous to the *su* command, but for group membership rather than user identity	newgrp managers
stat	Displays information about a file or directory taken from the corresponding inode, such as the file size, permissions, last access and modification times, and the device where the file is stored	stat /etc/profile
su	Changes your effective UID, taking on the identity of a different user than the one used to log in; (stands for substitute user)	su -
tar	Creates a single file that contains many other files, often compressed to save space	tar cvzf home_archive.tgz /home
umask	Blocks default file permissions that would otherwise be assigned when creating a new file or directory	umask -S
umount	Unmounts a file system that is currently accessible as part of the Linux directory structure	umount /mnt/cdrom
vigr	Safely edits the /etc/group file	vigr
vipw	Safely edits the /etc/passwd file	vipw
w	Lists all users currently logged in, with details about the programs each is running	w
who	Lists all users currently logged in, with details about from where each is logged in	who
whoami	Displays the currently effective UID	whoami

KEY TERMS

/etc/group — A configuration file in which group information (group names and membership lists) is stored.

/etc/passwd — A configuration file in which user account information is stored.

/etc/shadow — A configuration file in which encrypted user passwords and password configuration data are stored.

access mode — The file permissions assigned to a file or directory; the access permitted to that object.

directory record — A special type of file that contains the names and inode numbers of other files.

effective UID — The user ID that is used to determine what access to the file system a user is permitted. The *su* command changes the effective UID.

execute permission (x) — A file permission that allows a user to start a file as a program or see a file within a directory. Represented by the letter "x".

FAT (File Allocation Table) — The file system type used by older versions of DOS and Windows operating systems.

file permissions — Access rights that define the type of access a user has to a file or directory on the Linux system. Also called the access mode of a file or directory.

file record — A record within a Linux file system that contains a file name and an inode number or else, if a symbolic link, a file name and another file name to which the link refers.

file system — An organized collection of information on a storage device, typically a hard disk.

group — A named account that consists of a collection of users. Each member of a group has access to files owned by that group.

group permissions — A set of three file permissions (r, w, and x) that may be granted to members of the group assigned to a file or directory.

hard link — A file record that points to an inode that is already pointed to by at least one other file record.

inode — A data record, identified by a unique number within a file system, which contains detailed information about a set of data blocks commonly called a "file."

link — A file record that refers to the same physical file data as another file record. *See* symbolic link and hard link.

mount point — The path in the Linux directory structure where a file system is accessed.

NTFS (NT File System) — File system type used by recent versions of the Windows operating system such as Windows NT, 2000, 2003, and XP. Linux supports read access to this file system.

other permissions — A set of three file permissions (r, w, and x) that can be granted for all users on the Linux system who are not the owner of the file or directory in question and are not members of the group assigned to the file or directory.

owner — The user assigned to a file or directory, typically the user that created the object.

partition — A distinct area of a hard disk that has been prepared to store a particular type of data.

read permission (r) — A file permission that allows a user to read the contents of a file or browse the files in a directory. Represented by a letter "r".

root — The superuser, or administrative user account, on each Linux system.

Shadow Password Suite — A set of password-related utilities that implement a security system used to restrict access to encrypted password text in /etc/shadow.

superuser – The system administrative account; the root account.

symbolic link — A file that refers to another file name rather than directly to data in a file (via its inode). Also called a soft link.

tar archive — A file created by the *tar* command.

user permissions — A set of three file permissions (r, w, and x) that can be granted to the owner of a file or directory.

User Private Group — A security model that creates a new group containing one user when that user is first created.

wheel — A special system administrative group, not used officially in Linux.

write permission (w) — A file permission that allows a user to add or change information in a file or create files within a directory. Represented by a letter "w".

4

REVIEW QUESTIONS

1. Describe the effect of including a hyphen when executing the *su* command.

2. A user's primary group can be a User Private Group. True or False? Explain.

3. The /etc/passwd file does *not* contain which of the following fields:

    a. the name of the user account

    b. the file privileges for the user

    c. the user's default shell

    d. a UID and GID for the user

4. Explain the meaning of this line in the /etc/group file:
   webmasters:x:710:rthomas,cyang

5. To create or change a password on any user account, the following is used:

    a. the *useradd* utility

    b. the file /etc/shadow with a text editor

    c. the *passwd* command

    d. the UID and GID of the user

6. What does the fourth field in /etc/passwd contain?

7. Why should you not use a standard text editor to add users to /etc/passwd?

8. If you enter a new password for a user account that can be easily guessed, the message BAD PASSWORD appears and the password is:

    a. not updated unless you are root

    b. updated unless you are root

    c. only updated if you are logged in as a regular user

    d. updated if the password is not part of the dictionary of common words

9. A mounted file system is one that:
   a. has been included as part of the Linux directory structure
   b. has been correctly formatted for use in Linux
   c. allows any user to run programs located on it
   d. includes at least a root user account

10. The Shadow Password Suite enhances Linux security by:
    a. validating members of the wheel group as they log in
    b. hiding encrypted passwords in a file that only root can read
    c. checking that new passwords entered for users are not easily guessed
    d. stopping unauthorized users from accessing the root account

11. The *df* utility provides information about which one of the following?
    a. which users have mounted a file system
    b. the virtual memory usage as stored on all mounted file systems
    c. file system capacity, device name, and percentage used status
    d. per-directory usage and file system mount point

12. If you attempt to unmount a mounted file system and receive an error message, the most likely cause is:
    a. The file system was not mounted correctly in the first place.
    b. The *df* command is in the process of computing file system statistics.
    c. There is an error on the physical media that Linux cannot interpret.
    d. One or more users are working in a directory of the file system.

13. Describe the difference between an alias and a symbolic link.

14. Which command is used to create a symbolic link?
    a. *sh*
    b. *ln*
    c. *set*
    d. *sed*

15. The command *chmod 744 report.doc* grants _____ execute permission to the report.doc file.
    a. user (the file's owner)
    b. group (member of the assigned group)
    c. other users
    d. all users on the system

16. The owner and group assigned to a file are shown by which of the following commands?

    a. *chown*

    b. *ls -l*

    c. *newgrp*

    d. *id*

17. Execute permission on a file is required to:

    a. Start that file as a program.

    b. Create a directory with a matching name.

    c. Allow other users to read the file.

    d. Use the *su* command to view the contents of a restricted file.

18. The *tar* command creates archive files that are most often compressed by the _____ command:

    a. *bzip*

    b. *compress*

    c. *zip*

    d. *gzip*

19. The *tar* utility differs from the *cpio* utility in that:

    a. *cpio* always reads and writes to STDIN and STDOUT, and *tar* uses command-line parameters.

    b. *cpio* is a commercial utility, and *tar* is free software.

    c. *cpio* is widely used for Internet archive files, and *tar* is not.

    d. *cpio* is an older format that is not compatible with newer *tar* archives.

20. Describe why the *find* command is often used with *tar* or *cpio* for backups.

21. The _____ option causes the *tar* command to extract files from an archive file or device.

    a. *a*

    b. *x*

    c. *c*

    d. *e*

22. Describe how the *newgrp* command relates to the second field of each record in the /etc/group file.

4

23. The output of the *id* command includes:

    a. the effective UID, the effective GID, and a list of groups of which the effective UID user is a member

    b. a list of all terminals on which the current user is working

    c. the user name used to log in

    d. the effective UID and the effective GID

24. If the far left column in the output of the *ls -l* command shows the character "s" you would know that the object on that line was a:

    a. regular file with *su*-based superuser access

    b. special block device file

    c. special character device file

    d. socket

25. Which utility typically provides the highest compression ratio (makes the smallest compressed file from a given data file)?

    a. *zip*

    b. *bzip2*

    c. *compress*

    d. *gzip*

HANDS-ON PROJECTS

HANDS-ON PROJECTS

Project 4-1

In this project, you use the *su* command and various user information commands to see how the effective UID can change. To complete this project, you need to have both a regular user account and root access to your Linux system.

1. Log in to Linux using your regular user account.

2. If you logged in using a graphical login window, open a command-line window.

3. At the $ prompt, enter the **id** command to see your currently effective UID.

4. Create a file named newfile in your home directory by typing **touch newfile**.

5. Use the *ls* command to view the owner and group assigned to this file by entering **ls -l newfile**. What do you see?

6. Enter **su** (without a hyphen) to change to the root account, and supply the root password when prompted.

7. Use the **id** command again to see how your effective UID has changed.

8. Enter **logname**. What do you see?

9. Create another new file called newfile2 by entering **touch newfile2**.

10. Enter **ls –l newfile2** to view the user and group assigned to this file. What do you see?

11. Assuming you are working in a terminal window, press **Shift+Ctrl+N** to open an additional terminal window.

12. In one of those windows, enter **w** to see who is logged in. What do you notice?

13. Change back to the window in which you are working as root. (Press Alt+Tab until the correct window appears or click the appropriate button in the Panel.)

14. Press **Ctrl+D**. You exit from the *su* command and return to working as your regular user.

15. Verify your identity using **whoami**.

16. Close each of the terminal windows by pressing **Ctrl+D** repeatedly (while each window has focus).

Project 4-2

In this project, you view and change file permissions using the command line and graphical interfaces. You also test the *umask* command. To complete this project, you need a Linux system with a regular user account.

1. Log in to Linux using your regular user account.

2. If you logged in using a graphical login window, open a command-line window.

3. Create a new file called xyz by typing **touch xyz** at the $ prompt.

4. Enter **ls –l xyz** to view the permissions and owner/group for this file.

5. Enter **ls –i xyz** to view the inode number of the file.

6. Use **stat xyz** to view information stored in the inode associated with this file.

   Notice that the numeric mode and character representation of file permissions are both shown, as are the owner, group, inode number, and other information.

7. Enter **chmod o+w xyz** to change the permissions of the file.

8. Check the permissions with **ls –l xyz**.

9. Use the **chmod 700 xyz** to change permissions again.

10. Check the permissions by using **ls –l xyz**.

11. Assuming you are working in a graphical desktop, double-click the Home directory icon on your desktop. (In GNOME, for example, this icon would be labeled something like "jtaylor's home.")

12. Find the xyz file in the Nautilus window that appears. Right-click the icon for that file and click **Properties** on the context menu that appears.

13. Change to the **Permissions** tab. Study the information presented in this tab.

14. Click several of the permissions check boxes and notice how the numeric mode changes in the bottom half of the dialog box.

15. When you have finished viewing this information, close the dialog box, and exit Nautilus.

16. At the command line, view the current *umask* setting by typing **umask**. What does this setting permit or not permit?

17. Enter **umask 077** so that no permissions are ever granted to Group or Other when a new file is created.

18. To test this, type **touch abc** and thus create another new file called abc, and then check its permissions by typing **ls –l abc**.

19. Change the *umask* setting back to the default by typing **umask 002**.

20. Enter **chown root abc** to change the owner of this file to root. What do you notice?

21. Erase your test files by entering **rm abc xyz**.

Project 4-3

In this project, you experiment with the *tar* command to create a simple data archive file and then extract the contents of that file into another directory. To complete this activity you should have a working Linux system with root access.

1. Log in to Linux using your regular user account.

2. If you logged in using a graphical login window, open a command-line window.

3. Use the **su** command to change to root. Enter the root password when prompted.

4. Change to the /etc/init.d directory by entering

   ```
   cd /etc/init.d
   ```

5. Review the file names and file permissions for the various configuration files in this directory by entering

   ```
   ls -l | less
   ```

6. Press **q** to exit the *less* command when you have finished reviewing the output of the *ls* command. Create a tar archive of the configuration files in the /etc/init.d directory by entering

   ```
   tar cf /tmp/testing.tar /etc/init.d/*
   ```

   Because you are including the path name to both the testing.tar archive file and the directory containing the information you want to archive, you can execute this command from any location on the system.

7. Enter a similar command, this time including the *v* option, as in

```
tar cvf /tmp/testing2.tar /etc/init.d/*
```

After you execute this command, you see a list of all the files in the /etc/init.d directory appear on the screen as each is added to the archive file.

8. Change to your home directory (/root) by entering the **cd** command.

9. Use the **ls** command to examine the contents of your home directory. Make certain you do not have a file called network in your home directory. (You shouldn't, but if you do from a previous exercise, rename it to something else to complete this project.)

10. Use the *x* option of the *tar* command to extract a single file from the tar archive that you just created, by entering

```
tar xvf /tmp/testing2.tar etc/init.d/network
```

The file is placed in your current directory. Because of the *v* option the file name is printed to the screen as it is extracted.

11. Use the **ls** command to review the contents of your home directory. Do you see a file called network? Look for a directory called etc.

12. Enter **cd etc/init.d** (without an initial forward slash) to change to the etc/init.d subdirectory of the /root directory. The *tar* command created the subdirectory in which the requested file was located, starting with your current directory when you issued the command to extract the file from the archive.

13. Use the **ls** command again to see the network file in the etc/init.d subdirectory of your home directory.

14. Close the command-line window and log out.

HANDS-ON PROJECTS

Project 4-4

In this project, you experiment with the *cpio* archive utility. To complete this activity you must have a working Linux system with root access. The directory names used as examples assume you are running Red Hat Linux, but the commands work on any version of Linux.

1. Log in to Linux using your regular user account.

2. If you logged in using a graphical login window, open a command-line window.

3. Use the **su** command to change to root. Enter the root password when prompted.

4. Create a cpio archive of a small subdirectory using the following command:

```
find /usr/share/doc/pam-0.77/ -print | cpio -oVH ustar >
~/archive.cpio
```

5. Look in the man page for *cpio* to find what the *V* and *H* options do.

6. Use the following *tar* command to view the contents of the archive you created:

   tar tvf ~/archive.cpio | less

7. Notice that the full directory path for each file is included. What information is included for each file besides the file name? Press **q** to exit the *less* command when you have finished reviewing the output of the *ls* command.

8. What option could you use to change the ownership stored with each file? (See the *cpio* man page.)

9. Determine the size of the subdirectory you archived by typing **du /usr/share/doc/p* | grep 77$**.

10. View the size of the cpio archive file by entering **ls –l ~/archive.cpio**.

11. How do these two compare?

12. Add another directory to the archive file using this command:

    **find /usr/share/doc/bash-2.05b/ -print | cpio -oAVH
    ustar -O ~/archive.cpio**

13. View the *cpio* man page again to determine what the *A* and *O* options are used for.

14. Check the size of the archive file now by entering **ls –l ~/archive.cpio**.

15. Compress the archive file by typing **gzip ~/archive.cpio**. Enter the **ls-l** command and note the size of the compressed archive file.

16. Uncompress the archive so you can work with it by entering

    gunzip ~/archive.cpio.gz

    Many tape drives and backup utilities automatically compress data that is not compressed, so storing the *cpio* file directly to a tape cartridge without using *gzip* would not take up as much space as the uncompressed file takes up on your hard disk.

17. Delete one of the files that you archived from its original location (confirm the deletion when prompted) by entering

    rm /usr/share/doc/bash-2.05b/CHANGES

18. Extract the backed up version of that file from your cpio archive by entering

    cpio --extract /usr/share/doc/bash-2.05b/CHANGES < ~/archive.cpio

19. Make certain the file is back by entering

    ls /usr/share/doc/bash-2.05b/CHANGES

20. Delete your archive file (confirm the deletion when prompted) by entering

    rm ~/archive.cpio

21. Close the command-line window and log out.

CASE PROJECTS

File Compression, Permissions and Archiving

Your most recent McKinney & Co. consulting project involves archiving large quantities of data in compressed form and granting certain users access to the archived data. You need to do some research to answer questions that have come up.

4

1. Review the list of compression tools available in Linux (see Table 4-4. All of these are included in Red Hat Linux and Fedora. Test each of these utilities by compressing a set of text files, program files, and image files. (You can use the find command to locate some of each on your system.) Determine the average compression ratio for each (what percentage of the original size the compressed file occupies). Also note the speed of compression by entering the *date* command immediately before and after each test. (You may need to work with large files to make the timing data reasonably easy to gather.)

2. Experiment with the *touch* and *umask* commands to determine what you think are the optimal default file permissions to be granted on newly created archive files in different circumstances. Create a grid outlining different settings and the default permissions to be used, with the *umask* command to implement each one.

3. Research the *find* man page to create a single *find* command that lists all files within the /usr/bin directory that have file permissions set to 755 and have more than three hard links to them. The *find* command should print out to STDOUT (the screen) the last access time, size in 1K blocks, and the file name of each matching file, with each of these three items being separated by a tab. Keep in mind the information in Chapter 3, "Using the Shell," about preventing command-line expansion so that the parameters you enter are passed intact to the *find* command rather than being expanded by the shell.

5

UNDERSTANDING TEXT PROCESSING

> ### After reading this chapter and completing the exercises, you will be able to:
>
> ♦ Use regular expressions in a variety of circumstances
> ♦ Manipulate text files in complex ways using multiple command-line utilities
> ♦ Use advanced features of the vi editor
> ♦ Use the *sed* and *awk* text processing utilities

In the previous chapter you learned how access to Linux files and directories is controlled by user and group accounts, and how specific permissions to a file or directory can be managed using command-line and graphical utilities. You also learned some basic information about file systems in Linux, including mounting removable media and understanding inodes and hard and symbolic links.

In this chapter you learn more about working with utilities on the command line in order to process the output of commands or data stored in text files. The foundation for many of these tasks is learning how to write regular expressions; you'll learn about these powerful techniques to define patterns in Linux. You then learn how to use these techniques with additional command-line utilities, within the vi editor, and within the special programs *sed* and *awk*.

REGULAR EXPRESSIONS

System administration tasks frequently involve patterns of information. These patterns might apply to file names, information on a Web server, information within database files, or in many other locations and situations. In Chapters 1 and 3 you saw that Linux can use a * character as a wildcard to match any file name. This is a feature common to many computer systems. The * character is actually just one part of a much more powerful system for defining patterns called "regular expressions." A **regular expression** is a flexible way to encode many types of complex patterns. You can use a regular expression to define a pattern in many situations: as a parameter to most Linux commands, within the vi editor, and within programming languages, including shell scripts (which you will learn about in Chapter 14, "Writing Shell Scripts").

Regular expressions are used for text—the output of commands or plaintext stored in files. They are not really useful for binary files. But much of your work in Linux involves text, whether you are parsing the output of commands, searching configuration files, creating shell scripts, or wading through lengthy documentation on a new program.

As a simple example of the power of regular expressions, a single regular expression can describe each of the patterns in the following sentences:

- Lines containing the word "President" or "president" (uppercase or lowercase "P")
- File names with the digits "18" followed by any other digits
- Text at the beginning of a line that starts with "Cruise" or "cruise" and includes the word "ship" later in the same line
- File names that end with TIFF, TIF, Tif, Tiff, tif, or tiff

You may already have experience using wildcards to describe file names. For example, you can refer to all files ending with the .doc extension by using the wildcard expression *.doc. The * character has special meaning as a wildcard. Regular expressions operate in the same way; they can be as simple as *.doc, but they can also include more complicated statements because they can include many characters that have special meanings. Table 5-1 lists some special characters that you can include in a regular expression. Mastering regular expressions is very useful for a Linux system administrator—with a few keystrokes you can perform tasks that would otherwise require complex programs or seem impossible to automate.

Table 5-1 Common Regular Expressions in Linux

Expression syntax	Meaning of syntax
*	Match zero or more characters
. or ?	Match zero or one character
+	Match one or more characters of the preceding pattern
^	Match text at the beginning of a line

Table 5-1 Common Regular Expressions in Linux (continued)

Expression syntax	Meaning of syntax
$	Match text at the end of a line
[abc]	Match one of the characters in brackets
[^abc]	Exclude all of the characters in brackets
\	Escapes the special meaning of the character that follows it
		(the pipe symbol) Separates alternative choices
{n}	Matches n occurrences of the preceding pattern
{n,}	Matches at least n occurrences of the preceding pattern
{n,m}	Matches at least n occurrences, but not more than m occurrences of the preceding pattern

The acceptable syntax for a regular expression—and the meaning of some special characters used in them—varies in small but important ways depending on where you are using the expression. Within a shell script, as a parameter to some utilities, within vi, and in other places, you must watch for slight variations in meaning. It's best to test your regular expressions in a way that lets you undo the results (or try them again) as you learn exactly what effect different special characters have. The documentation for different utilities, of course, describes how regular expressions are processed. Once you are familiar with the basic functioning of a regular expression, understanding variations between programs is straightforward.

Walking through a few more examples will help you understand the cryptic descriptions in Table 5-1 and see how regular expressions are constructed. Notice first of all how the same character can have different meanings in different positions. For example, the ^ character generally means "tie this pattern to the beginning of a line," but when placed inside brackets, the ^ means "not" and serves to exclude all characters within the brackets.

Suppose you have a directory full of image files. The name of each file is "reunion" followed by a number. The files are numbered from 00 to 45 (reunion00 to reunion45). You can use several regular expressions to match all of those files in a command such as *ls*, *zip*, or *gimp* (an image editing program):

```
reunion*
```

matches them all. But if some of the files were saved with a capital "R", this doesn't match them all. You can use this:

```
*union*
```

but it's less precise. For example, if you had other files in the same directory with names that included "union," it would match them as well. A more precise pattern is:

```
[Rr]eunion*
```

This matches only files starting with "R" or "r", followed by "eunion," followed by any text. Suppose that you only want to include the first twenty images in the pattern. You use this regular expression:

```
[Rr]eunion[01][0-9]
```

This matches only files that have a 0 or 1 in the first position after "reunion" (or "Reunion"), and files with any digit 0 to 9 in the second position. So files reunion00 to reunion19 match.

If these files have a file extension such as .jpg or .tif, you want to include that in the regular expression. The following matches all 45 files and assumes they have a file extension as well.

```
[Rr]eunion[0-9][0-9].jpg
```

A more compact way to express the previous example uses curly braces to indicate repetition of a pattern. Notice that we have [0-9] repeated above. To specify that we want only files with two digits after the word "reunion," we use this expression:

```
[Rr]eunion[0-9]{2}.jpg
```

Now suppose that your files are named reunion-a through reunion-z. You could match all of these with this expression:

```
reunion-[a-z].jpg
```

You can use ranges such as 0-9, a-z, and A-Z in any regular expression. If you had mixed up lowercase and capital letters, you might need to revise the above expression to match both:

```
reunion-[a-zA-Z].jpg
```

If you had multiple letters after the word reunion, you could precisely control how many were matched using a set of curly braces. If you want to match all of these files *except* reunion-d.jpg, you use this expression:

```
reunion-[^d].jpg
```

Next, suppose that multiple individuals were saving the image files and used slightly different names. Some use the word "reunion," but others use "reun", and one person just uses "r". You can match all of these by using a pipe symbol (|) within brackets. Normally, a set of characters in square brackets matches just one character (any one of the characters in brackets), but when a pipe symbol is used, the expression matches alternate sets of characters:

```
r[union|un|]-[a-zA-Z].jpg
```

Notice that the last pipe symbol in the first set of square brackets has nothing after it, because it matches file names such as r-b and r-c.

The examples given here don't include the (^) or ($) characters, because those are not useful when matching file names on the command line. Later in this chapter, you'll see multiple examples of these used with other regular expression characters to find patterns within text files. As you can imagine, regular expressions can become very complex, and every character of the expression is important. Check your work and test your expressions as you learn how they operate in different circumstances.

Manipulating Files

In this section you learn about command-line utilities that are useful for searching, sorting, reorganizing, and otherwise working with text files. These commands are often used in combination, connected on a single command line by pipe symbols; they also commonly rely on regular expressions, either to select on which files to operate, to select text within the output of a previously executed command, or to match text within a text file. The descriptions in this section use documentation or configuration files on your Linux system to explore the features of each command, but you can use them for any text file you need to process.

NOTE

Files created by word-processing or office suite programs such as OpenOffice. org, Word, or Excel are not text files. They contain many special codes that might interfere with processing using the commands described in this section. You can typically export data from these word-processing programs in a text format (using the Save As command, for example). This may make the data accessible for the analysis that you want to do. You may even be able to later import the text information back into the program (formatting information is typically lost). Web pages are written in HTML, which is a text format, so the utilities here may be useful in processing them.

Searching for Patterns with grep

You have already learned how to use the *locate* and *find* commands to locate a file with specific characteristics. To search the contents of files, however, you should use the **grep** command. *grep* can rapidly scan files for a pattern that you specify, printing out the lines of text that contain text matching the pattern. You can then take further action on these matching lines of text by using a pipe to connect *grep* with other filtering commands.

As a simple example of *grep*, suppose you want to see which shell is used by a certain user account, wilsonr. Rather than opening a user management tool (as discussed in Chapter 11, "Managing Users") or looking at the /etc/passwd file in a text editor, you can enter this command and immediately see the line of /etc/passwd that contains the information you need:

```
$ grep wilson /etc/passwd
wilsonr:x:564:564::/home/wilsonr:/bin/csh
```

The last item in the output line indicates that the current default shell for user wilsonr is the C shell (csh). Note that the *grep* command searches only for wilson, not for wilsonr. If multiple user names on the system include the string wilson, *grep* displays a matching line for each one. As a system administrator, you learn when to take shortcuts—on a system with few users, the search pattern "wil" might have worked as well as "wilson." Because anyone can read the /etc/passwd file, you can try this *grep* example using your own user name as well.

Use the *grep* command to search within text files, not within binary-format data such as program executables and image files.

TIP

Consider another example: suppose you have a directory full of text files and you want to see all occurrences of a string pattern that includes ThomasCorp. The following command lists all of those occurrences, showing the file name containing the string and the complete line of text containing the string:

```
$ grep Thomas[cC]orp  *txt
```

If the regular expression you use with a *grep* command includes characters that the shell might try to expand, you should escape them with a backslash. For example, if you want to search for a dollar amount using *grep*, you can't include $ on the command line or the shell will interpret it as a variable and replace it with a value. Instead, you use \$ to pass a "$" character for *grep* to search for.

CAUTION

The first parameter—Thomas[cC]orp—is a regular expression defining what text *grep* looks for. When using the *grep* command, an asterisk is never needed at the beginning or end of the string pattern (such as ThomasCorp*), because *grep* locates the string wherever it occurs. The above example of *grep* finds instances of the following strings:

- Thomascorp
- ThomasCorporation
- ThomasCorps

But these strings are not found:

- Thomas Corporation
- Thomas corporation
- Thomas Nast

The second parameter to *grep* is also a regular expression. It defines which files to search. The asterisk in the command indicates that all files in the current directory that end with "txt" should be searched. The shell expands that parameter so that all matching files are handed to *grep* to search.

The results of the *grep* command might include lines such as these:

- Annual_report.txt: As news of ThomasCorporation reaches customers around the world, we are pleased to. . .
- memo0518.txt: that Rachel and I think Thomascorp should be looking seriously at acquiring an interest in. . .
- meetingsummary.txt: Discussed needs of ThomasCorp to diversify plastics manufacturing capacity for. . .

The *grep* command is often used at the end of a pipe, so that *grep* is searching the output of another command instead of a file. For example, you could pipe the output of the *locate* command through *grep* to refine a search. Suppose you want to search among all .tif graphics files on the system for your airframe image, but you can't remember the exact file name you used (perhaps airframe.tif, airframes.tif, old_air_frame.tif, or something similar). You can use a command such as this:

```
$ locate tif | grep frame
```

In cases such as this, *grep* uses only a single parameter—the pattern to search for. Rather than include a file name to define the text to be searched, the output of the *locate* command is searched. The results are printed to STDOUT—the screen.

Examining File Contents

Linux includes many commands to tell you about a file. You have learned about some of these already, such as the *file* command, which tells you what type of data a file contains. In this section you learn about commands that examine the contents of files in more detail.

The **head** and **tail** commands display the first few lines and last few lines of a file, respectively. By default, *head* prints the first 10 lines of a file, and *tail* prints the last 10 lines of a file. Both print the output to STDOUT, which you can redirect as needed. To change the number of lines produced as output, add the *-n* option to either the *head* or *tail* command. For example, to output the last 20 lines of a file named README, use this command:

```
$ tail -n 20 README
```

The *tail* command includes a feature that lets you see lines as they are added to a file. When you use the *-f* option, *tail* displays the last 10 lines of the file, but it doesn't return you to a command prompt—instead, it "follows" the file, printing new lines as they are added to the file by other programs. This is very useful for tracking a log file. For example, suppose you are not certain if your USB device is being detected when you plug it in. (A USB device might be a scanner, hard disk, or digital camera, for example.) The system log file, /var/log/messages, displays messages from the Linux kernel as it detects any new devices. So to see if your USB device is being detected, you can enter the following command, then insert your USB device, and watch the screen to see if new messages appear at the end of the file. Figure 5-1 shows example output from this command (your output will vary depending on what is running on your system at the moment).

```
$ tail -f /var/log/messages
```

The messages are written to the file by another program, but the *tail* command watches for them and writes them to STDOUT. When you want to end the *tail* command (stop following the file), press Ctrl+C.

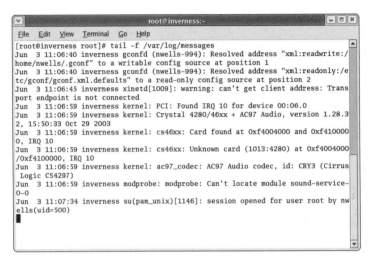

Figure 5-1   The output of the *tail –f* command

You can count the number of characters, words, and lines in a file using the **wc** command (for word count). When you enter this command with a file name, the output includes three numbers and the file name. If you use a regular expression with the command, you see statistics for each matching file. For example, if you enter this command, you see counts for each HTML file in the current directory:

```
$ wc *html
1050    7742    62670    index.html
453     3298    21054    products.html
```

The example lines above illustrate how *wc* displays information: the numbers shown are the number of lines, the number of words, and the number of characters. You can use options on the command line to display only some of this information.

The commands discussed in this chapter are intended to help you process text files, but sometimes you need to learn something about a binary file or other data file. The ***strings*** command extracts text strings from a file that includes binary and other nontext data. This is useful when you need to see text strings stored in a binary file, or strip off noncharacter information from a special-format data file. When you do this, you may see a lot of information that is not useful to you, but this command provides a convenient way to check for information that may not be otherwise available. Figure 5-2 shows the output of a *strings* command examining the contents of a system library file.

TIP

If you use the *strings* command to extract data from a word processor file, such as a Word file, be aware that word processors often store modifications in the middle of the file. For example, if the user changed a line of text in a document file, both the original line and the changed line may appear when you use *strings*.

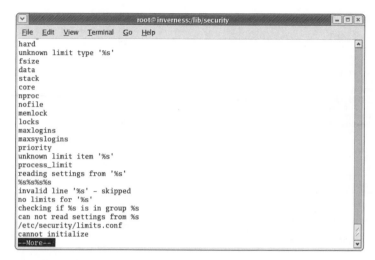

Figure 5-2   Sample output of the *strings* command

Manipulating Text Files

At times you want to modify part of a text file by adding, removing, or altering data in the file based on complex rules or patterns. This kind of modification is called **filtering**. While some powerful text editors such as vi or Emacs can perform many filtering operations, many system administration tasks are easier if you use command-line programs to filter text files. This is especially true when you want to automate a filtering operation using a shell script, in which case an interactive text editor is inappropriate.

Linux provides many commands for filtering text files. A simple example is the *sort* command. You can use the ***sort*** command to sort all of the lines in a text file, writing them out in alphabetical order or according to an option you provide to the command. The simple example here prints a list of all users on a Linux system, sorted by the user name. Figure 5-3 shows the output of this command; your output will vary depending on the user accounts on your system:

```
$ sort /etc/passwd   | more
```

Other options for the *sort* command allow you to merge and sort the contents of multiple files, sort based on different fields within each line of a file, or check whether a file is already sorted.

When you are sorting files, you may want to remove duplicate lines. The ***uniq*** command does this. For example, if you have a file containing names and addresses, the following commands sort that file and remove any duplicate entries. The results are written to a new file. (Without the final redirection to a file, the *uniq* command writes them all to STDOUT so they are displayed on a screen.)

```
$ sort addresses | uniq > addresses_sorted
```

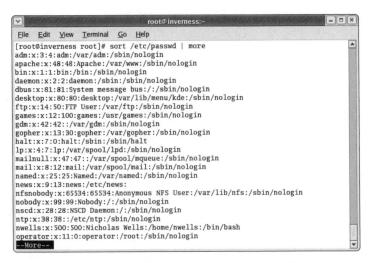

Figure 5-3   The output of a simple *sort* command

When you have multiple versions of a file, Linux provides several commands that help you see differences in those versions. These commands are most frequently used for programming—to see what changes have been made to source code—but they are also useful for configuration files, Web pages, and documentation.

The *diff* command is the most widely used of these comparison commands. When you include two file names on the *diff* command line, it displays the differences between the two files. The output format of *diff* is strange when you first see it, but it is a standard format that is understood by thousands of programmers and system administrators. Suppose, for example, that you made a backup copy of a configuration file called smb.conf and then edited the original (this file controls the Samba server, which is not discussed in this book). If you changed the workgroup name in that file and added a comment describing the change you made (a good practice), the following *diff* command would show your changes:

```
$ diff oldsmb.conf smb.conf
18c18,19
<       workgroup = MYGROUP
---
> #Changed MYGROUP to HOME on 5-23-05
>       workgroup = HOME
```

The first line of the output indicates the line numbers where the difference was found—lines 18 and 19. Lines starting with < indicate lines that were not found in the second file; lines starting with > indicate lines that were not found in the first file. Another way to think of this is that if the second file listed on the command line is the more recent file, the < and > indicate lines that have been removed and inserted, respectively, when compared to the older file. The output of the *diff* command can be handy to review manually, but it is also used by many programming commands to automatically make changes to source code files using the *patch* command. This operation is discussed in more detail in Chapter 13, "System and Kernel Management."

The ***cmp*** command gives a quick check whether two files are identical. If they are not, the command displays the line number and byte number in the file where the first difference occurs. The ***comm*** command is used to compare sorted files to see if they differ at all. By adding the *-3* option, the *comm* command only lists lines that differ between the two sorted files:

```
$ comm -3 addresses newaddresses
```

Although most of us use an e-mail reader or word processor to compose messages or letters, there are many other times when we would like our work checked for spelling errors. The *ispell* spell checker uses a large dictionary to examine a text file, prompting you with suggestions whenever a word in the file is not found in the dictionary. Though *ispell* is very useful, an improved spell checker called *aspell* is currently available as well. On Red Hat Linux, no documentation (such as a man page or info page) is provided for *ispell*; *aspell* documentation is provided in the directory /usr/share/doc/aspell.

To start *ispell*, give it the name of the file you want to spell check:

```
$ ispell /usr/share/doc/bash-2.05b/article.txt
```

The *ispell* program uses the entire terminal window. The top portion shows you the word that *ispell* has located that it doesn't recognize; the bottom portion shows you a list of alternative choices. Numbered choices are words that *ispell* suggests you use to replace the word it doesn't recognize; a few letter choices indicate options to control *ispell* operations. (See Figure 5-4.) Table 5-2 shows the commands you can use as you work in *ispell*.

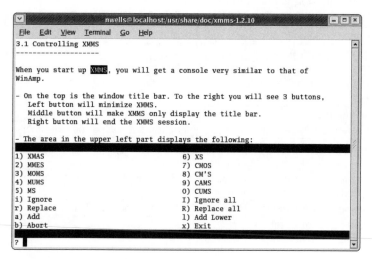

Figure 5-4 The *ispell* editing window

Table 5-2   Command Keys within *ispell*

Command key	Description
Numbers	Change the unrecognized word selected by *ispell* to be the word next to the number you press
r	Change to an editing mode in which you enter the word you want to replace the unrecognized word
R (uppercase)	Change to an editing mode and replace all occurrences of the word with the text you enter
i	Ignore the unrecognized word (don't make any changes to the file)
I (uppercase)	Ignore this and all future occurrences of the word in the document
a	Add the word to the dictionary that *ispell* uses—you use this for a word that is common in many of your documents but that isn't in the main dictionary
x	Exit from *ispell*

Another set of filtering commands treats each line of a text file as a collection of fields separated by spaces, commas, or any character you specify. For example, suppose you have a text file in which each line has a name, address, phone number, and e-mail address, all separated by semicolons. You can use a single Linux command to extract the name and phone number from each line and place them in a separate file. Table 5–3 describes some useful text-filtering commands in Linux. You can learn more about a specific command by reviewing its man page.

Table 5-3   Linux Text-filtering Commands

Command	Description
cut	Remove sections (fields) from each line of a file
expand	Convert tabs to spaces
fmt	Format text files (standardize spaces, set a line width, indent lines, etc.)
join	Merge lines from two different files based on a matching field within the files
nl	Add line numbers to each line of a file
od	Display the contents of a file in a numeric format, such as hexadecimal
paste	Merge lines from two files
split	Split a single file into two or more smaller files
tac	Reverse the lines in a file (outputing the last line of the file first); notice that this command is the reverse of *cat*
tr	Transpose all occurrences of one character with another character
unexpand	Convert spaces to tabs

Using sed and awk

More complex commands for altering text include a complete programming syntax to define how to filter a text file. An example of these complex filtering programs is *sed*. The *awk* command is generally used for formatting output. It is described in the section that follows.

Filtering and Editing Text with sed

The **sed** command (for "stream editor") processes each line in a text file according to a series of command-line options (the options can be stored in a separate file if they are lengthy). Instead of using commands such as those in Table 5–3 to transpose characters, print out fields within each line, or format output, you can use *sed* to process one or more text-processing commands.

The following sample *sed* command prints to the screen all lines of the /tmp/names file that contain the text "lincoln." You would probably want to pipe this output to another command or redirect it to a file, though the basic command is shown alone here:

```
$ sed -n '/lincoln/p' /tmp/names
```

The command used by *sed* is enclosed in single quotes. The pattern between the two forward slashes ("lincoln" in the above example) is a regular expression. By default, the *sed* command prints each line to STDOUT (the screen); the *p* in this command makes that explicit, with the *-n* option causing *sed* to print only the lines that match the pattern.. As another *sed* example, the following command prints to the screen all lines of the /tmp/ names file *except* those containing "lincoln." (The *d* indicates "delete matching lines from the output.")

```
$ sed '/lincoln/d' /tmp/names
```

The next example shows how to replace all occurrences of the pattern "lincoln" in a file called /tmp/names with the string "Abraham Lincoln." Notice how this method of specifying a search-and-replace operation matches the syntax you learned for vi.

```
$ sed 's/lincoln/Abraham Lincoln/' /tmp/names
```

The more general syntax of the substitution command in *sed* looks like this:

```
/pattern1/s/pattern2/pattern3/g
```

This means that *sed* watches for lines containing pattern1. Within any line containing pattern1, *sed* replaces occurrences of pattern2 with pattern3. By default, however, the substitution command only replaces the first occurrence of pattern2 on each line. The *g* option at the end of the command causes *sed* to replace all occurrences (globally) on each line. The next example shows the substitution command.

If you want to perform multiple operations with *sed*, you can execute them all from the command line, or you can place them in a file and then give *sed* the name of the file containing the commands. For example, suppose you regularly need to reduce the "Latinisms" in a colleague's writing. You want to execute the following *sed* commands to filter the text file:

```
s/etc\./and so forth/g
s/i\.e\./that is/g
s/e\.g\./for example/g
```

To perform all three actions at once, you use the *-e* option, like this:

```
$ sed -e s/etc\./and so forth/g -e s/i\.e\./that is/g -e s/e\.
g\./for example/g  news-article
```

You can also place the three lines shown in a file as a *sed* script. If your *sed* script file is named "nolatin," and you want to apply this script to a file called news-article, you use this command:

```
$ sed -f nolatin news-article > new_news-article
```

As you saw in *vi*, you can add line number ranges in front of most *sed* commands. For example, if you only want to replace "lincoln" with "Abraham Lincoln" in lines 100 to 500 of a file, you use this command (the default line range is 1,$ to specify the entire file):

```
$ sed '100,500s/lincoln/Abraham Lincoln/' /tmp/names
```

When you use a regular expression in a *sed* command to match a complex pattern, you might want to use the matching text as part of what you substitute. You can use the (&) operator to do this. The (&) operator within a *sed* command refers to the text that matches pattern2 in the syntax description given. Suppose, for example, that you are processing a file that contains numbers intended as dollar amounts, but the dollar sign isn't used in the file. You can search for numbers meant as dollar amounts using a regular expression, such as this one:

```
/[0-9]*\.[0-9][0-9]/
```

To insert a dollar sign before each matching expression, you use this *sed* expression:

```
s/[0-9]*\.[0-9][0-9]/\$&/g
```

Suppose you have a file named my_letter that contains this text:

```
David has picked 45 bushels of apples, which we hope to sell at
8.50 per bushel.
That is better than last year's price of 7.50 per bushel, but
not as much as the 9.00 we had
hoped for. Still, given the 8.25 per bushel that our
competitors have been getting,
we can't complain.
```

Then you used the following command:

```
$ sed 's/[0-9]*\.[0-9][0-9]/\$&/g' my_letter > new_letter
```

The contents of the new_letter file would look like this:

```
David has picked 45 bushels of apples, which we hope to sell at
$8.50 per bushel.
That is better than last year's price of $7.
50 per bushel, but not as much as the $9.00 we had
hoped for. Still, given the $8.
25 per bushel that our competitors have been getting,
we can't complain.
```

Notice that the number 45 is not affected because it doesn't match the format in the regular expression (with a period followed by two digits). You can try this without the *g* at the end of the command to see that the 9.00 figure is not affected (only the fist matching pattern on the line is changed).

sed is often useful as part of a pipeline of Linux commands, much like you would use other text-processing command such as *grep* or *sort*. *sed* has the advantage of letting you perform automatic substitutions within a line of text, and combining many operations to be performed on a single file. The output of other Linux commands is often the text on which you want to use a *sed* command. For example, you can process the output of commands such as *df*, *ls -l*, and others that you will learn about in later chapters.

In the info page for *sed* you can learn about commands to append, insert, and change text in many additional ways.

Formatting with awk

The **awk** command is similar to *sed* in some ways. It processes text, extracting parts of a file and formatting the text according to information you provide on a command line or in a script file. But although *sed* is generally used to edit a stream of text line by line, *awk* is more often used to format output based on fields within a line of text. A good example would be the output of the *ls* command, or a text file containing address and phone number information. Often you can perform the same functions with either *sed* or *awk*; once you become familiar with each command, you can decide which command to use for different system administration tasks that arise.

TIP

If you are curious, the *awk* utility uses the Awk programming language. The name of this computer language is taken from the last names of the three men who wrote the original version of the program: Aho, Kernighan, and Weinberger (they are always listed in this order, though the name of the program is awk and not akw).

In *awk*, each field on a line is normally separated by **whitespace**, meaning a series of one or more spaces or one or more tabs. You can change which character *awk* uses to separate fields. For example, you might have a file where each line contains a name and an e-mail address, separated by a comma. In that case you would want to define the field separator for your *awk* command to be a comma so that *awk* could correctly separate the two pieces of information on each line of the file.

Once *awk* separates fields on a line of text it is processing, the first field is referred to by $1, the second by $2, the third by $3, and so forth. The basic format for *awk* commands looks like this:

```
/pattern/ { actions }
```

You can have multiple actions for one pattern, and you can have multiple lines such as this one, to match different patterns in a file. *awk* tries to match each pattern to each line of the file, performing the actions on that line if the pattern is found. If you want to have some actions performed only once—either before processing any lines in the text files or after processing all lines—you can use the BEGIN and END keywords instead of a pattern. For example, if your *awk* script includes the following line, *awk* prints a welcome message just one time, before starting to process each line of text in the files you hand to *awk* to be processed.

```
BEGIN { print "The address filter has started." ; }
```

Some examples of using *awk* can help you see its power. Suppose you are working with output from the *ls -l* command, part of which looks something like this:

```
-rw-rw-r--   1 syoung   users      878786 Mar 19 10:20 fig-1.tif
-rw-rw-r--   1 ycho     users      878786 Mar 19 10:22 fig-2.tif
-rw-rw-r--   1 nwells   users      279532 Mar 19 10:23 fig-3.tif
-rw-rw-r--   1 nwells   users      471570 Mar 19 10:23 fig-4.tif
-rw-rw-r--   1 nwells   users      471570 Mar 19 10:23 fig-5.tif
```

You can see that the first field of each line is the file type and file permissions, the second is the number of hard links, the third is the file owner, the fourth is the assigned group, and so forth. Each line includes nine fields (the timestamp is separated into three fields by whitespace).

You can use *awk* to print out only the owner and file name fields of each line using this command. This example uses no pattern, just an action. The semicolon indicates the end of the action; you can include multiple actions if needed.

```
$ ls -l | awk '{ print $3, $9 ; }'
```

You can include a regular expression (a pattern) to select which lines *awk* includes in the output. For example, to select only symbolic links from the output of *ls -l*, you use this command:

```
$ ls -l | awk '/^l/ {print $3, $9 ; }'
```

The above sample output doesn't include any symbolic links, but you can also select only those files owned by ycho, printing just the file name of each one:

```
$ ls -l | awk '/ycho/ {print $9 ; }'
```

Of course, there are other ways to perform these two tasks, such as using *ls* to list symbolic links or *find* to list files with a certain owner. Using more complex *awk* commands lets you use variables, make comparisons, and perform other complex functions that are very similar to those that you will learn about in Chapter 14, "Writing Shell Scripts."

To use a variable or comparison in an *awk* command, you put it at the beginning of the command, instead of a pattern. For example, suppose you want to examine the output of the *ls* command, displaying only those lines where a file has more than three symbolic links. The number of links is the second field of the output of *ls -l*, so you can use a comparison operator in *awk* to only print lines where the second field is more than three. Rather than only printing some of the fields, in this case you want to print the entire line. To do that, you can use the $0 variable, which refers to the entire line of text that *awk* is processing:

```
$ ls -l | awk ' $2 > 3 {print $0 ; }'
```

When you are processing a large file, you often want to use more than one *awk* command. You want to examine each line for different patterns or comparisons and take different action depending on the result. You can create an *awk* script file that has multiple commands, then execute *awk* with the file name containing multiple *awk* commands:

```
$ awk -f awk_command_list text_file
```

When you use multiple *awk* commands—in a script file or on the command line—to process a large text file, it can take some time for *awk* to process each line of text using each command in your script. For example, suppose you are performing several comparisons, with substitutions such as these:

```
$2 > 9 {print $0, "OVER 9" ; }
$2 > 7 {print $0, "OVER 7" ; }
$2 > 5 {print $0, "OVER 5" ; }
$2 > 3 {print $0, "OVER 3" ; }
```

In this case, any line that matches the first comparison also matches the next three comparisons, resulting in the line being printed multiple times and wasting processing time. The solution to this problem is the next command in *awk*. When you have multiple *awk* commands that are used to process a single file, you know that if one command is used (either the pattern matches or the comparison is true), then you don't want any other commands processed for the current line of text. For the previous example, you want to use the *next* command to alter the lines like this, so that if a line matches the first comparison, none of the other commands are applied to that line.

```
$2 > 9 {print $0, "OVER 9" ; next;  }
$2 > 7 {print $0, "OVER 7" ; next;  }
$2 > 5 {print $0, "OVER 5" ; next;  }
$2 > 3 {print $0, "OVER 3" ;  }
```

Project 5-4 at the end of this chapter shows a complete example of how you can use *awk* to process the output of a Linux command.

MORE ADVANCED TEXT EDITING

In Chapter 3, "Using the Shell," you learned about using the *vi* editor to create and modify text files. With the information you have learned in this chapter, you are well prepared to use some of the more advanced features of vi. This section describes several additional features of vi, including those that involve searching for patterns using regular expressions.

File Operations in vi

You can open vi at the command line without entering a file name. In that case, you begin working on an empty, unnamed file. When you are ready to save your work, you press Esc (if you are not already in command mode), then Enter :w, then a space, then the file name you want to give to the text file you are creating. When you press Enter, the file is saved and you can continue working in vi. If you start editing an existing file in vi by entering the file name at the command line when starting vi, you can always write the file to disk by entering :w in command mode. In fact, if you start editing a file and want to change the name of that file, you can also use :w *file name*.

 Remember that all commands in vi, both standard commands and those that appear on the bottom of the screen (such as those that begin with a colon), are case-sensitive.

CAUTION

If you need to insert another file into the file you are editing, enter :r *file name* in command mode. The file you name is inserted at that point in the current file. You can always press "u" to undo the insertion.

When you use the :w command to write the file you are editing, the system may indicate to vi that you cannot write the file—that is, that you cannot update it. This may be because the file is owned by another user and you only have read permission (not write permission), or because the file does not have write permission set, even though you own it. vi informs you of this when you use the :w command. You can try to override the warning—saving the file even though you normally would not be able to by entering :w! in command mode. This causes vi to save the file if you are working as root or if you are working as a regular user and own the file you are editing.

Similarly, when you use the *:q* command to exit from vi, vi warns you if you have made changes to the file but have not saved them (you haven't used *:w*). In this case you have several options:

- Enter *:wq* in command mode to write the file (save it) and quit (exit from vi) at the same time.

- Press ZZ in command mode. This operates just like entering *:wq* but is a bit quicker. Be careful about getting in too much of a habit of using ZZ, however, because sometimes you don't really want to save changes you might have made!

- Enter *:q!* to override the safety feature and quit vi without saving your work—discarding your changes.

Screen Repositioning

In addition to the arrow keys (along with the h, j, k, and l keys, which imitate arrow keys in command mode), and Page Up and Page Down, vi supports many additional methods of positioning your cursor within the text of a file you are editing. These are especially useful when you are editing (or just viewing) a very large text file.

In Figure 5-5, notice the 92,20 in the bottom-right corner of the screen. These numbers indicate the line number and cursor position on the line, respectively. You can watch them change as you move around in a file.

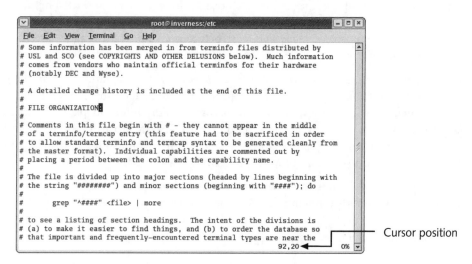

Figure 5-5 Cursor position information in vi

When you are editing a file containing documentation, you can use parentheses and curly braces to move forward or backward by one sentence or paragraph at a time. For example, if you press) repeatedly, the cursor jumps forward to the end of each sentence in the text. Pressing } repeatedly jumps the cursor forward by a paragraph at a time. The (and { keys move the cursor backward.

The Ctrl+F and Ctrl+B key combinations move you one screen forward and backwards, respectively. Pressing Shift+G can take you to any line in the file. When you are in command mode, type the line number you want to go to, then press Shift+G. A common use of this is to return to the top of your file by pressing 1, Shift+G rather than pressing Page Up repeatedly to reach the top of the file. Pressing Ctrl+g displays a line at the bottom of the screen showing the current file name and line number.

As you become more familiar with a file you are editing, you may want to use marks. A **mark** is like a bookmark—it "saves your place" within a text file. The mark is not written in the file, but it is remembered by vi as you edit. After you place a mark, you can use that mark to return to a place in your file, or to perform editing functions. vi supports 36 marks, which you can refer to using the 26 letters of the alphabet and the digits 0 to 9. To insert a mark at your current line while you are in command mode, press m followed by the mark you want to set. For example, to set mark "a" to be at your current line, press ma while in command mode.

After you have set one or more marks, you can refer to them using the single forward quote. For example, to jump to the "a" mark, press 'a in command mode. The single quote generally refers to your previous position in the file, so pressing the single quotation mark twice (") moves you to the place you were before pressing 'a. Pressing (") repeatedly flips you between those two locations in your file.

Many times, vi is used by programmers to create or review programs written in a language such as C++. vi can help you examine program source code by jumping automatically between matching parentheses, brackets, or braces. Anytime you place the cursor on a parenthesis, bracket, or curly brace (opening or closing), you can press % to jump to the matching item. vi tracks all intervening sets of parentheses and so forth, which can be a real challenge to do yourself in a complex program.

Another useful key combination when working with programming source code is Shift+J, which joins two lines (removing the newline character at the end of the current line).

More Line-editing Commands

Many of the commands you enter in vi are not displayed as you enter them. For example, when you press *dd*, a line is deleted, but you don't see the letters "dd" on the screen. Other commands *do* appear on screen. These commands typically start with either a colon or a forward slash. Examples of colon-initiated commands are the *:w* and *:q* commands that you have already seen. When you enter a colon in the command mode of vi, you switch to the line-editing method of entering a command—the command that you enter is displayed on the last line of your window.

You can enter :*h* to view the vi help file. Within the help file, you can find references (which are actually hyperlinks) to other help files. When the cursor is on one of these references, you can press Ctrl+] to jump to that file. Press Ctrl+T to return back to your previous place (like pressing the Back button in your Web browser). When viewing the help file, enter :*q* to exit and return to working on your own file.

To search forward from your current cursor position, press the forward slash while in command mode. The slash appears on the bottom line. Enter the pattern you want to search for, then press Enter. You can use a regular expression as the search pattern; the position indicators that tie a pattern to the beginning or ending of a line are useful when searching in vi. For example, to search for the word "configuration" occurring at the beginning of a line, starting with either lowercase or capital "C", you press / then type ^[cConfiguration] and press Enter. You are then moved to the first occurrence that matches the regular expression you entered; other matches are highlighted on the screen.

To move to the next matching occurrence of a pattern you entered, press the n key (in command mode).

You can also search backward from the current cursor position by pressing ? in command mode instead of / before entering the search pattern. Whether you use / or ? to enter the search pattern, you can also press N to search backward for other occurrences of the pattern (without reentering the regular expression).

More complex than just searching for a pattern are the search-and-replace operations you can perform in vi. These are initiated using a colon (:) and take the following general form:

`:line-number-range s/search-pattern/replacement text/flags`

Although this is a bit more complicated that your average word processor, it's also a lot more powerful and flexible (and usually a lot faster).

The line number range lets you perform this task (or many others you will learn about as you study vi) only on a part of a file. Because it's normal to perform an operation on an entire file, however, you often use the range 1,$, which means "from line 1 to the last line of the file." The s// combination indicates a search-and-replace operation. Though it may not seem intuitive, you will at least find it familiar—you'll see the same technique used in other programs later in this chapter, as well as other situations you might encounter, such as the Perl programming language. **Perl** is a programming language that developers use to create scripts for working on text files and completing other complex tasks.

The only flag you should know immediately is the g flag, for global. Without this flag, the replacement only occurs once per line. With the g flag, all instances in the range you indicate are affected.

As a basic example, suppose you want to replace "configure" with "Configure" anytime "configure" occurs at the beginning of a line. You enter the following (the g flag is not needed here because when a pattern is tied to the beginning of a line, it can only occur once per line):

```
:1,$ s/^configure/Configure/
```

If you make a mistake, remember that you can press u to undo your edit.

Anytime you are working in vi, you can execute another Linux command as if you were at the shell prompt. This is sometimes called **shelling out**. To do this, type *:!* followed by the command you want to enter. For example, suppose you are editing a file and realize you need to check the exact file name within the /etc/samba directory. To do this, enter the following:

```
:!ls /etc/samba
```

The directory listing appears on the screen, followed by a message to press Enter to continue. When you press Enter, the output disappears and you return to vi. Note that you cannot use tab completion or regular expressions when you enter a command within vi.

Setting vi Options

Numerous features of vi are controlled by configuration settings that you can view and change using the *set* command. To view all of the options currently set in vi, enter the following:

```
:set all
```

Figure 5-6 shows sample output from this command. Press the spacebar multiple times to see all the screens of settings. After all are displayed, you return to the document you are editing. Use *:set* without the word *all* displays all options that the current user has set. This is a shorter list; it includes items set automatically as part of your start-up scripts.

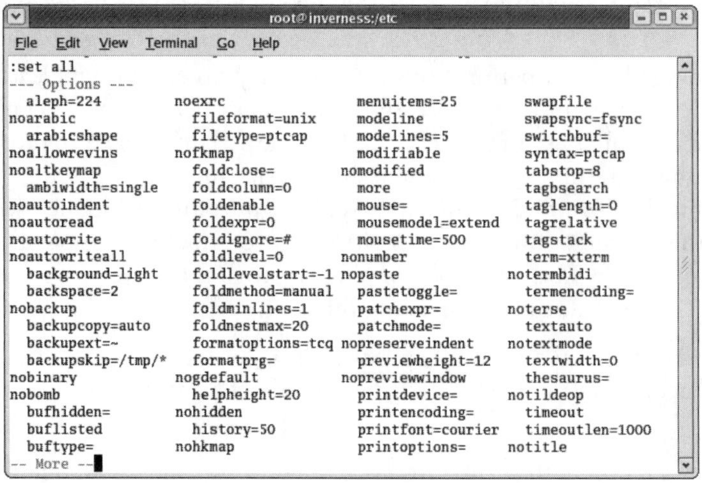

Figure 5-6   The *set* options in vi

You can set any option using that option's full name or a two-letter abbreviation for the option. For example, to turn on line numbering so that a number is displayed next to each line in your file, enter the following:

`:set nu`

To turn that option off again, enter:

`:set nonumber`

As you become a more advanced user of vi, you might discover several options that you want to have set or unset each time you use vi. You can automate those settings in two ways. First, you can define an environment variable called EXINIT that contains the *set* command you want executed each time you start vi. For example, suppose you want to include line numbers but turn off the "smart indent" feature, which automatically indents text on new lines based on the indent of previous lines (this can be a real timesaver when creating a computer program). You could enter the following line in the .bash_profile script in your home directory so that it executes each time you start a shell:

`EXINIT='set nu nosmartindent'`

5

vi then executes this command each time vi is started, establishing your preferred settings. Notice that you can enter multiple items after a *set* command—you can do this within vi as well.

The second method of defining vi settings is to place them in a file called **.exrc**. vi checks for this file as well as the EXINIT variable each time it is started. The .exrc file overrides information in the EXINIT variable. By placing settings in an .exrc file, you can control vi settings differently in different directories. For example, if you have a directory containing documentation files, you might want different vi options than in a directory containing HTML Web pages or programming source code. vi has settings to make working with each type of file easier, such as the ability to highlight keywords in HTML or a programming language. In this situation, you can create an .exrc file in each directory that contains different settings. vi can then apply those settings when loading a file from that directory. A sample .exrc file might look like this:

```
set nu
set nosmartindent
```

Summary of vi Commands

You are probably getting a sense now of how powerful vi is—and how complex it can be to use. But patterns should also begin emerging as you work with it. For example, you have learned that the d key is used as part of a delete command; the) key can refer to the end of a sentence, and the $ character sometimes refers to the end of a file. You have also seen examples in Chapter 3 (Table 3-4) of adding a number to the beginning of a command to execute it multiple times. You can combine these elements to perform just the task you want. For example:

- Pressing d$ deletes from the current position to the end of the line
- Pressing d) deletes from the current position to the end of the sentence
- Pressing 3d) deletes the next three sentences

Table 5-4 summarizes the additional vi commands presented in this chapter. Refer to this table in conjunction with Chapter 3, Tables 3-3 through 3-6, to become familiar with vi.

Table 5-4   Additional vi Commands

Command	Description
:w!	Save a file, even if the file permissions do not permit writing (if you have the ability because you are the file owner or are working as root)
:q!	Quit vi, discarding any changes that have been made to the file but not saved
:r file name	Insert another file into the current file
:w file name	Save the current file under a different name
:wq	Save the current file under the current name and exit vi; equivalent to pressing ZZ
( )	Move backward or forward by one sentence
{ }	Move backward or forward by one paragraph
Ctrl+F	Move forward one screen (normally about 25 lines)
Ctrl+B	Move backward one screen (normally about 25 lines)
1, Shift+G	Go to line 1 in the file; enter any line number before pressing Shift+G to jump to that line
Shift+G	Go to the end of the file; this is equivalent to pressing $, Shift+G
Ctrl+g	Display the current file name and line number at the bottom of the vi window
ma	Set a mark labeled internally as "a" at the current line; any character or digit can be used to define up to 36 different marks
'a	Jump to the line labeled internally with mark "a"
"	Jump to the previous cursor position; press (") repeatedly to flip between two positions
%	When the cursor is placed on a (, [, or {, this command jumps to a matching element (opening jumps to closing; closing jumps to opening)
J	Join the next line to the end of the current line, removing the newline character at the end of the current line
:h	View the vi help file
Ctrl+]	Follow a hyperlink within the help files
Ctrl+T	Return to a previous document after following a hyperlink (within the vi help files)
/	Start searching for a pattern from the current position forward
?	Start searching for a pattern from the current position backward
n	Jump to the next occurrence of the most recent search pattern entered using / or ?

Table 5-4   Additional vi Commands (continued)

Command	Description
N	Jump to the previous occurrence of the most recent search pattern entered using / or ?
:1,$ s/Configure/ configure/g	Within the line range of 1 to the end of the file, search for the pattern "Configure" and replace it with the text "configure" for all occurrences on each line (the g flag indicating a global replace)
:!*command*	Execute a Linux command
:set nu	Set line numbers on; undo with *:set nonumbers*; use *:set all* to view all current settings; use the EXINIT environment variable or an .exrc file to configure vi settings automatically

5

CHAPTER SUMMARY

- Regular expressions are used in many places in Linux to define patterns of information. They can be used as part of nearly all command-line utilities and within many programs such as the vi editor.

- Regular expressions use special characters such as *, ?, ^, $, and \ to indicate special meanings when defining patterns. Special characters can be escaped using a backslash so that they are interpreted without special meaning.

- The *grep* command is used to search within text files or the output of another command (via a redirection pipe) for lines of text containing a pattern that has been defined using a regular expression.

- Many Linux commands help you learn about the contents of files by displaying part of the file or determining data about the file, such as how many words it contains.

- Data in files can be manipulated using commands such as *sort* and *uniq*, as well as numerous other commands that examine, format, extract, or modify parts of a text file.

- The *ispell* utility provides a way to spell check text files.

- The *sed* and *awk* commands support a complex scripting language that includes regular expressions. Much of the syntax in *sed* and *awk* is similar to that used in other command-line utilities or in programs such as vi.

- In vi you can use complex combinations of commands to reposition the cursor within text. These include matching parentheses, moving by sentence or paragraph, or jumping to a specific line number or user-defined mark in the file.

- The vi editor supports search and-replace operations using a syntax such as *sed*, with regular expressions defining the pattern to search for.

- From within vi, a user can shell out to execute any Linux command by typing :! *command_name*.

❏ The *set* command within vi defines the editor settings. These settings can be automatically set for each user by including information in a EXINIT environment variable or by placing *set* commands in an .exrc file within any directory where text files are located.

COMMAND SUMMARY

Command	Description	Example
awk	Used to create scripts for working on text files and completing other complex tasks; based on the Awk programming language	ls -l l awk '{print $3,$9}'
cmp	Determines whether two files are identical. If they are not identical, the position of the first difference is displayed. No other information is provided.	cmp addresses newaddresses
comm	Determines if two sorted files are identical	comm -3 addresses newaddresses
diff	Determines differences between two text files, showing those differences in a standardized (somewhat cryptic) format that is used by other commands to manage source code and perform other system administration tasks	diff oldsmb.conf smb.conf
grep	Searches for patterns of information within a text file or command output	grep wilson /etc/passwd
head	Displays the first few lines of a text file (10 lines by default)	head /etc/passwd
sed	Processes each line in a text file according to a series of commands provided by the user	sed -n '/lincoln/p' /tmp/names
sort	Sorts all of the lines in a text file, writing them out in alphabetical order or according to options provided to the command	sort /etc/passwd
strings	Extracts human-readable text strings from a binary or other non-readable data file	strings /bin/ls
tail	Displays the last few lines of a text file (10 lines by default). In "follow" mode the command continues to display new lines as they are added to the end of a text file	tail -f /var/log/messages
uniq	Removes duplicate lines from a sorted text file	sort addresses l uniq > addresses_sorted

Command	Description	Example
vi	Starts the vi command-line editor; see Tables 3-3 to 3-6 in Chapter 3 for basic commands; Table 5-4 presents additional commands	vi /etc/profile
wc	Displays the number of characters, words, and lines within a text file	wc /usr/share/dict/linux.words

5

KEY TERMS

.exrc — A configuration file for vi, which can be stored in any directory. Any vi settings stored in this file are applied when vi is used to edit any text file in the same directory.

filtering — The process of adding, removing, or altering data in the text file based on complex rules or patterns.

mark — A place holder within a text file being edited in vi. Similar to a bookmark on the Web. Setting a mark lets you immediately return to that spot in the file.

Perl — A programming language that developers use to create scripts for working on text files and completing other complex tasks.

regular expression — A format that uses characters with special meanings (such as * or ^) to define patterns of characters or digits within Linux programs.

shell out — To start a program as if working at the Linux command line (the shell) from within another program (such as the vi editor).

whitespace — A series of one or more spaces or one or more tabs.

REVIEW QUESTIONS

1. A regular expression is used to:

   a. Define a list of programs that a shell can execute.

   b. Assign values to variables.

   c. Define a potentially complex pattern of characters or digits.

   d. Build file names with specialized file extensions.

2. The regular expression [cC]hapter0[12345]* does *not* match which of the following files?

   a. chapter01

   b. Chapter03.doc

   c. Chapter1.doc

   d. Chapter02

3. Which of the following regular expressions matches the text "Reunion-2004"?
    a. [Rr]eunion[0-9][0-9][0-9][0-9]
    b. [Rr]eunion-{4}[0-9]
    c. Reunion-[0-9]{4}
    d. [Rr]eunion[0-9][0-9]

4. The *grep* command is *not* useful for which of the following?
    a. searching for all file names that match a pattern
    b. determining which directories are currently in use
    c. finding lines of text that contain a certain word
    d. locating specific information in the output of another command

5. Searching documents created by word-processing programs is not an appropriate use of the *grep* command because:
    a. Word-processing documents are typically larger than the type of file that *grep* was designed to process.
    b. Other Linux commands cannot be used with word-processing documents; therefore, using *grep* with those documents is of limited usefulness.
    c. Using *grep* interferes with the formatting information stored in those files.
    d. Word-processing documents contain nonreadable codes (nontext information).

6. If you execute a *grep* command without providing the name of one or more files to search, you should:
    a. Provide input using a pipe from another utility.
    b. Be certain to specify a regular expression that defines the pattern to search for.
    c. Using the regular expression provided as part of the *grep* command, rely on the shell to determine which stream of data is used.
    d. Expect an error message.

7. You need to track the output of a text file in real time as lines are added to that file by another program. Which command do you use?
    a. *head -f*
    b. *tail -f*
    c. *awk {print $last}*
    d. *| grep $*

8. Several commands are available in Linux that let you compare two or more files to determine how they differ. One of these programs in particular is widely used by programmers and system administrators and is a tool commonly used for assisting with modified source code on Linux systems. Which is it?
    a. *diff*
    b. *cmp*

c. *tac*

d. *comm*

9. Which of the following features is *not* supported by default in *ispell*?

   a. adding new words to the *ispell* dictionary that are commonly found in your documents but that are not in the default dictionary

   b. seeing a list of suggestion words to correct the spelling of a word that *ispell* does not recognize, then selecting one of those words to insert in the document by pressing a single key

   c. easily skipping words that *ispell* thinks are misspelled but that you don't want to alter in your text file

   d. entering a new spelling for a word that was misspelled, but for which the correct spelling was *not* provided as a suggestion, and having that correct spelling be automatically inserted each time the word is misspelled in the rest of the document

10. The *wc* command displays:

    a. the number of lines, words, and characters in a file

    b. the owner of a file

    c. a specific field within each line of a file

    d. text matching a search string within a file

11. Name five programs that can be used to filter text files in Linux.

12. The command *ls | sort* causes which of the following to occur?

    a. The output of the *ls* command is sent to the *sort* command. The results are printed to the screen.

    b. It cannot be determined without information about the next command to be executed.

    c. The output of the *ls* command is written to a file named sort.

    d. The output of the *ls* command is filtered based on the regular expression contained in the file sort.

13. When you run a program called *gather_data*, it normally reads text as a user enters it at the keyboard. If you use the command *gather_data < input_text* to run the program, which of the following occurs?

    a. The *gather_data* command is executed followed by the *input_text* command.

    b. The input that the *gather_data* program normally reads from the keyboard is taken from the input_text file instead.

    c. The *input_text* program runs first, collecting data, which is then passed through a pipe to the *gather_data* program.

    d. Both *gather_data* and *input_text* run concurrently, reading from the keyboard as STDIN.

14. Which independent Linux command replaces tabs in a text file with a fixed number of spaces?

    a. *tabs*

    b. *unexpand*

    c. *expand*

    d. d.:1,$ s/\t/ /g

15. The name of a script file can be provided to *sed* or *awk* on the command line using which command-line option?

    a. -f

    b. */file name/*

    c. '*file name*'

    d. {*file name*}

16. Using a ! along with a standard *write* command in vi causes the editor to:

    a. Attempt to write the file despite a file permission that does not by itself permit writing the file, though this can only be done if the person editing the file is the owner of that file or is working as root.

    b. Exit from the editor after writing the revised file to disk.

    c. Display the *write* command at the bottom of the vi window instead of simply executing it.

    d. Store settings in a separate file in the directory where the file currently being edited is located.

17. Which of the following creates a mark at the current line within vi so that you can quickly jump to that line in the file?

    a. :*mb*

    b. '*a*

    c. *mv*

    d. *yy*

18. The vi editor checks for an environment variable and for a hidden initialization file in the directory in which a file being edited is stored. These are called, respectively:

    a. SET, .virc

    b. EXINIT, .exrc

    c. $VI, initrd

    d. EX, .bash_vi

19. Describe the meaning of *1,$* as a range operator at the beginning of a search and replace command within vi.

20. Describe the difference between the following four search commands in vi: / ? *n N*

HANDS-ON PROJECTS

Project 5-1

In this project, you use several basic filtering commands to modify a text file. To complete this project you should have a working Linux system with a valid user account. This project should work on any version of Linux with a standard utility set.

1. Log in to Linux using your user name and password.

2. If you are using a graphical environment, open a terminal window so you have a shell prompt.

3. Use the following command to copy the /etc/passwd file to your home directory as a test file named data1 (we use this file because it has lines that are separated into fields):

   ```
   cp /etc/passwd ~/data1
   ```

4. Make sure you are working in your home directory by typing:

   ```
   cd
   ```

5. Use this command to look at your working file to see how it is organized and formatted:

   ```
   less data1
   ```

6. Each line in this file is divided into fields using a colon. Press **q** to exit the *less* command. Now use the *cut* command as shown below to extract from each line the first and seventh fields (the user name and associated default shell):

   ```
   cut -d : -f  1,7 data1 > data2
   ```

7. Review the contents of data2 using the *less* command as shown here:

   ```
   less data2
   ```

8. Press **q** to exit the *less* command. Convert the colon (:) character between the remaining two fields of each line of data2 to a tab character using the *tr* command as shown here and store the result in data3:

   ```
   tr ":" "\t" < data2 > data3
   ```

9. Use the following command to sort the lines in the data3 file into alphabetical order and store the result in data4:

   ```
   sort data3 > data4
   ```

10. You decide that you should have sorted the file in the opposite order. Reverse all the lines in the data4 file using the *tac* command as shown below, and store the results in data5:

    ```
    tac data4 > data5
    ```

5

11. Use the following command to add a line number to the beginning of each line in the data5 file and store the result in data6.

```
nl data5 > data6
```

12. Use the following *less* command to review the results of these commands:

```
less data6
```

13. Press **q** to exit the *less* command.

14. Starting with the data1 file you copied in Step 3, perform all of these filtering operations again on single command line using pipes as shown below, sorting the result in data_new:

```
cut -d : -f  1,7 data1 | tr ":" "\t" | sort | nl | tac >
data_new
```

Project 5-2

In this project, you practice using regular expressions and redirecting input and output in various ways. To complete this project, you need any working Linux system with a regular user account. The file location given for the sample file (linux.words) is based on Red Hat Linux and may differ in other Linux distributions, but you can use *locate* to find that file on most other versions of Linux.

1. Log in to Linux using your user name and password.

2. If you are using a graphical environment, open a terminal window so you have a shell prompt.

3. Linux uses a dictionary of about 45,000 words to check new passwords, refusing them if the newly entered password or a simple variant of it is in the dictionary. Copy this dictionary file to your home directory as a working file using the following command:

```
cp /usr/share/dict/linux.words ~/words
```

4. Each word is on a separate line in the words file. Use *grep* to search for all words that begin with "w" by using this command:

```
grep ^w words
```

5. Use the following command to pipe the result through *less* so you can page through it. Press **q** to exit *less* when you have finished looking through the output.

```
grep ^w words | less
```

6. Find all words that end with "w" by using the following command:

```
grep w$ words
```

7. Use the following command to find all words that begin with "w" and end with "w". In this pattern, the period (.) matches any single character, and the * means to match the previous character zero or more times.

```
grep ^w.*w$ words
```

8. Use the *-c* option as shown below to count how many words begin with "s". How many are there? (This actually displays the number of lines matching the pattern; because each line of this file contains a single word, the result here also gives you the number of matching words.)

```
grep -c ^s words
```

9. How many words start with either "st" or "sm"? (Use a single command to determine the answer.)

10. If the *grep* command you enter does not find a file to search listed on the command line, it tries to search STDIN. You can enter data directly at the keyboard or pipe another source of data to *grep*. Use the following command to send the output of the *cat* command as STDIN. No file name is specified for *grep*, so it reads the STDIN provided by *cat*.

```
cat words | grep ^w | less
```

11. You can also specify a file to use as STDIN without using *cat*.

```
grep w$ < words
```

In this case, the command looks very similar to the command without redirection (*grep w$ words*), because *grep* tries to use a file name first, then relies on STDIN. Some programs always look to STDIN for their input, in which case you could *only* use the < *words* method to pass that data as input to the program.

**HANDS-ON
PROJECTS**

Project 5-3

In this project, you practice using the *sed* command. This project uses the httpd.conf configuration file, which is installed by default on most Linux systems. On Red Hat Linux and Fedora, it is located in /etc/httpd/conf, as the project describes. On other versions of Linux, you may need to find it in a different directory for Step 2. The contents of the file should work well in any case. Some aspects of Web server configuration are mentioned in the project simply to provide reasons for the text-processing operations, but you are not expected to learn these.

1. Log in to Linux using your user name and password and open a terminal window.

2. Use the following command to copy the Web server configuration file, httpd.conf, to your home directory as a working copy for this project.

```
cp /etc/httpd/conf/httpd.conf ~
```

3. Use the following *less* command to browse through this configuration file to get an idea of what it contains. Lines beginning with # are comments.

```
less ~/httpd.conf
```

4. Press **q** to exit the *less* command.

5. Suppose you are running a Web server on a system with very little memory. You want to remove all the comments from the httpd.conf configuration file. Try this *sed* command:

```
sed '/^#/d' httpd.conf |less
```

6. Press **q** to exit the *less* command after reviewing the output. You see that the *sed* command removed all of the comments, but left all of the blank lines. Though it makes the configuration file harder to read, you want to remove everything except the actual configuration parameters. Each one starts with a letter or a "<" character. Use this *sed* command:

```
sed -n '/^[A-Za-z\>]/p' httpd.conf > httpd2.conf
```

7. To check your understanding of regular expressions and *sed*, describe the purpose of each character between the single quotes in the *sed* command in Step 6.

8. The configuration file includes statements defining icons for a Web server to use for different file types. These statements begin with the AddIcon keyword. You have moved the icons to a different directory than the default, so you need to change the /icons directory name to be /newicons for each line with the AddIcon keyword. Use this *sed* command to modify the previous version of the configuration file:

```
sed -n '/^AddIcon/s/\/icons/\/newicons/p' httpd2.conf |less
```

9. Press **q** to exit the *less* command after reviewing the output. What do you notice about the output of this command? Try this one:

```
sed '/^AddIcon/s/\/icons/\/newicons/p' httpd2.conf |less
```

10. Press **q** to exit the *less* command after reviewing the output. Suppose you noticed that some of the AddIcon lines had not been changed because they were misspelled as AddIcan. This *sed* command changes those as well:

```
sed '/^AddIc[oa]n/s/\/icons/\/newicons/p' httpd2.conf |less
```

11. Press **q** to exit the *less* command after reviewing the output. Web servers have configuration information that lets them work with multiple languages. This is configured in part by the AddLanguage lines, which include file extensions to define different languages (such as .ru for Russian). Suppose that the standard has changed and you need to insert the characters ".int" in front of each AddLanguage file extension. You use this *sed* command:

```
sed '/^AddLanguage/s/\.[a-z][a-z]/\.int_&/p' http2.conf |less
```

12. Press **q** to exit the *less* command after reviewing the output. What problem do you notice on the AddLanguage line containing the .cs extension?

13. Try this command to fix the problem:

```
sed m'/^AddLanguage/s/\.[a-z][a-z]/\.int&/gp' http2.conf
|less
```

14. Press **q** to exit the *less* command after reviewing the output.

15. Delete the two working files from this project, pressing **y** if prompted to confirm the deletions:

```
rm httpd.conf httpd2.conf
```

**HANDS-ON
PROJECTS**

Project 5-4

In this project, you use the *awk* command to process the output of various Linux commands. To complete this project, you need any working Linux system with a regular user account.

1. Log in to Linux and open a terminal window.

2. Execute the *df* as shown command to see what the output looks like on your system. The output varies based on what file systems you are using. Notice that the output probably includes a swap partition and may include networked file systems.

```
df
```

3. Suppose you want to use *awk* to display only the lines of output from *df* that are regular local file systems. Each of these starts with a device name such as /dev/hda1, so you could use a regular expression that matched an initial forward slash. Try this command:

```
df | awk '/^\// { print ; }'
```

4. Although this isolates the regular file systems, it may still give you more information than you want in some cases. Suppose you just want to see the available space and the mount point for each regular file system. Try this command:

```
df | awk '/^\// { print $4, $6 ; }'
```

5. Next, suppose you want to only print a line for regular file systems that have less than 300 MB of storage space remaining. 300 MB is represented by 300000 in the Available column of the *df* output (field $4). Try this command:

```
df | awk '$4 < 300000 { print $4, $6 ; }'
```

(The results you see depend on the status of your file systems. Adjust the number in the command (300000) so that you see at least one output line. You might want to use the > comparison operator instead of the < comparison operator if you have large file systems.)

6. You can use multiple patterns or comparisons in a single *awk* command using the && operator. This means that both of the conditions you specify must be matched. In the following command, a line must start with a / character and also have field $4 less than 300000 or the line is not printed (the parentheses are not strictly needed, but help make complex statements easier to read):

```
df | awk '/^\// && ($4 < 300000) { print $4, $6 ; }'
```

7. You learned in this chapter that you can change the default field separator that *awk* uses. One way to do this is by setting the MYFS shell variable. You can also specify the field separator on the command line when starting *awk*. For example, to work with the /etc/passwd file, you need to set the field separator to a colon. Use this command to display the user name and default shell for each user account. Notice that there are no patterns to match or comparisons to make because you want to print the first and seventh fields from every line:

```
awk -F: '{print $1, $7 ; }' /etc/passwd
```

8. In many versions of Linux (including Red Hat Linux and Fedora), regular user accounts have a UID of 500 or above. To display only information about regular user accounts, try this command:

```
awk -F: '$3 >= 500 {print $1, $7 ; }' /etc/passwd
```

9. If you want to use multiple comparisons or checks with *awk*, you can do it in several ways. You can create a script file, as Chapter 14 describes. You can also enter multiple lines at the command prompt. Type the following and press Enter:

```
ls -l /lib | awk '
```

10. A > prompt appears, showing that the shell knows you are not finished entering a command (because of the opening single quote). Enter each of the following lines. After you press Enter on the last of these lines, the shell recognizes that you have finished and processes everything you have entered:

```
BEGIN {print "OWNER   INFO       FILE" ;}
/^l/  {print $3, "-SYM LINK-", $9 ; }
/^d/  {print $3, "-DIRECTORY-", $9 ; }
$5 > 1000000  {print $3, "-BIG FILE!-", $9 ; }
' | less
```

11. In the previous example, each line of the file is processed by each of the three lines in your *awk* command (the three lines after the line with BEGIN). You can also use pipelines with multiple *awk* commands. For example, suppose you want to include only some lines from the output of *df*, and then perform a comparison on those lines. To remove the lines, try this command again, as you used in Step 4:

```
df | awk '/^\// { print $4, $6 ; }'
```

12. Suppose your goal is not to print information for all regular file systems, but only for those that have more than 90% of their storage used. To begin, you use *awk* to remove all nonregular file systems:

```
df | awk '/^\// { print ; }'
```

13. Next, you want to remove the "%" character so that you can numerically compare the percentage used on each file system with your threshold of 90%. The *sed* command works well for this task because it doesn't involve fields within each line. Try this combined command:

```
df | awk '/^\// { print ; }' | sed 's/\%//'
```

14. Next, you want to compare the fifth field of the output with 90. If that field is above 90, you may need to work with the file system to create more storage space. Use *awk* to examine the fifth field and print a message if a warning is appropriate (type everything on one line and let it wrap around to the next line as you type):

```
df | awk '/^\// { print ; }' | sed 's/\%//' | awk '$5 >90
{print "WARNING: CHECK", $6 ;}'
```

15. Because your file systems are probably not over 90% used, you probably saw no output from the previous command. Press the **up arrow** key and use the **left arrow** key to edit the previous command you entered, changing the 90 to **10**, then press **Enter** again. This lets you test that the command works. You can then change the number to **90** and create a command such as this that is automatically run every hour and e-mails a warning to a system administrator when necessary.

CASE PROJECTS

CASE PROJECTS

Text Processing and Database Files

1. In your most recent consulting assignment, you are working for a government agency that provides weather data to citizens (its "customers"). They have asked for your assistance collating information from their numerous weather information sources to help provide customized information for different customers as those customers request data via a Web page. As you study the setup at the agency, you notice that several databases are being used in an uncoordinated way:

   □ One database contains a list of locations for which weather data is available.

   □ A second database contains a list of weather sources, with the locations for which that source has weather data listed as fields on the same line as the source name.

   □ A third database contains names of other Web sites that have information about weather or travel resources for different locations; the location is listed after the Web address on the same line.

Employees at the agency have been culling bits of information from the databases manually in order to send e-mails to customers when they ask for an update or for travel-related information about the location for which they check the weather regularly. The agency employees want to implement an automated database solution that e-mails weather and travel updates to each user, but they worry it will take you quite a while to put such a system in place. It wouldn't take you long of course, but to show them how well placed their confidence in you is, you decide to produce some lists for them using basic text-filtering commands.

Assume that all the database information is stored as text files and that each record contains all information on a single line.

Describe the commands you will use to combine data from three databases to generate output containing one location, the sources for weather at that location, and the Web pages for travel information on that location.

2. Search online at a site such as google.com for a command reference chart for vi. Use that chart and the tables in Chapter 3 and this chapter to create your own vi reference chart to glance at as you edit files using vi.

3. Study the documentation for *vi*, *bash*, and *grep*. Write a brief report outlining the differences in how these three programs handle regular expressions.

6

MANAGING PROCESSES

After reading this chapter and completing the exercises, you will be able to:

♦ Define processes as used by the Linux kernel

♦ View and control running processes using command-line and graphical utilities

♦ Understand and manage how memory is used by Linux processes

♦ Schedule delayed execution of processes

In the previous chapter you learned how to work with text files using a variety of command-line utilities. Some of these utilities are simple, such as the *wc* command to provide a word count of a file; others are very complex, such as the *sed* and *awk* programs, which support complex syntax in separate script files. You also learned about configuring settings and performing some more advanced operations in the vi editor. Some of these resembled in syntax the operations you can perform using *sed*, *awk*, *grep*, or some of the other utilities. A common thread running through the discussion of text processing was the importance of using regular expressions to define patterns of text on which the utility or editor would operate.

In this chapter you learn about processes—programs—on Linux. Because a typical Linux system has dozens or hundreds of processes running at the same time, learning to manage those processes is a critical system administration skill. You will learn about different techniques for starting processes, how to view status information about processes that are currently running, and which utilities you can use to control and alter the status of processes. Part of this management includes learning how to schedule the execution of processes for a later time, so that you don't have to be sitting at your computer in order to start a task at a certain time.

DEFINING PROCESSES

In casual conversation about Linux, a process is nothing but a program running on Linux. But to better understand how Linux operates, and how you can manage its resources, you should also be familiar with a more technically correct definition.

The Linux Multitasking Model

A Linux **process** is a program that is running on the system. It can be started either from a command line, a graphical desktop, the kernel itself, or by another process. The kernel maintains a collection of information about that program, including the most recent part of the program that was executed, where it stores its data, what resources it is trying to use, and so forth. By maintaining this information about all processes that are running on Linux, the kernel can maintain efficiency and security.

As you know, Linux is a multitasking operating system. It can run many processes at the same time. Of course, a single microprocessor can really only perform one task at a time. To "multitask," the Linux kernel lets a process have a **time slice**—a few microseconds—to do its work. Then the kernel "pauses" that process and lets another process work for a few microseconds. Time slicing is common to all operating systems that don't have multiple microprocessors. By carefully controlling what each process is allowed to do, and by enforcing such things as file permissions, the Linux kernel is able to keep each process from having bad effects on other processes. For example, the kernel prevents one process from accessing system memory allocated to a different process. Although you will learn more about the Linux kernel in Chapter 13, "System and Kernel Management," you can sense from this discussion that much of what the kernel does is schedule the activities of different processes and maintain the integrity of system resource allocation (such as system memory and access to file systems).

Creating Processes

When Linux is first started, the kernel starts a process called init. (Chapter 9, "Understanding System Initialization," is devoted to discussing the startup sequence and initialization.) Every process on Linux is assigned a **process ID (PID)**, which is a unique number identifying a process with the Linux kernel. The init process is assigned a process ID number of 1. The init program then starts other processes, which in turn start other processes. Every process running on Linux is a "descendant" of the init process. For example, init starts a graphical login screen, which starts a graphical desktop, which starts a terminal window, which starts a bash shell, in which you enter a command. Later in this chapter you will learn commands that show you the hierarchy of processes going back to init.

To create a new process in Linux, a program **forks**. Forking creates another process that might be related to the parent process in any of several ways. For example, one process might start another process and return to what it was doing, or it might wait for the process it started to finish all of its tasks and exit.

When a process ends, it is said to exit. When a process exits, the information about that process that the kernel was maintaining is discarded, and all the resources that the kernel had allocated to that process are released, so they can be allocated to other processes.

Note that the information that the kernel maintains about a process is different from the process itself or the data it maintains. For example, if you start the *ls* command in a shell, the kernel maintains information about the *ls* command as a process. But the command itself—the executable programming code that makes up the *ls* utility—is located separately in memory, as is the data that the *ls* command might need to work with the file listings it is creating.

6

Process States

The state of each process running on Linux is carefully watched by the kernel. You can view these states using the utilities described in the next section. Possible states include:

- *Running*: The process is executing, though it must wait for its assigned time slices and must pause for a few microseconds between steps in its execution.

- *Sleeping*: The process is waiting for something to happen that doesn't depend on the kernel giving it another time slice. For example, it might be waiting on some input from a device. When a process is sleeping, it doesn't consume any CPU processing time, though it still has memory allocated to it by the kernel and the program itself.

- *Stopped*: The process has been halted before it exited normally; this is typically only seen when you are debugging programs that you are writing.

- *Zombie*: A zombie process is a process that is no longer active—the program itself has been closed, for example—but the Linux kernel is still maintaining information about the process and allocating resources to it. The kernel regularly clears out any zombie processes and frees up their resources.

Swap Space

Sometimes the kernel needs to allocate more resources in the form of system memory than the system actually has. In this situation, the kernel copies some information from memory to the **swap space**—typically a separate hard disk partition called a swap partition. Swap space is also called **virtual memory** because it acts like memory: it holds programs and data used by the Linux kernel in a way that acts like an extension of the system's RAM. As you view information on processes, you can see which are **swapped out**. When the kernel does this, the process cannot run until it is swapped in again. On a very busy system or a system without sufficient system memory, processes are continuously being swapped in and out as their state changes. **Thrashing** occurs when the kernel spends so much time moving processes to and from the swap space that the kernel and the processes bog down and work inefficiently. You might even notice this if you hear your disk drive working (or see a status light indicating disk activity) for a long time while you wait for a response from the system. When this happens, you should add more memory or shut down some of the processes.

In Chapter 8, "Installing Linux," you will learn more about swap space as you install Linux.

MANAGING LINUX PROCESSES

In this section you learn about how to view information about Linux processes and then control the status of those processes as needed to manage the resources of your Linux system.

Starting Processes from the Shell

Although you might spend a lot of time working in Linux using a graphical desktop, there will also be times when you want to start multiple programs at the same time while working in a terminal window or text-mode console. For example, you might start a system administration utility that is not included on the graphical menus, but then also view a man page or start the vi editor to work with a configuration file. Linux shells include many tools for managing processes that you start from a command line.

Because the default shell for Linux is bash, commands described in this section apply to the bash shell. Similar features are available in other shells such as *ksh*, *csh*, *tcsh*, and *zsh*.

When you start a program, that program takes control of the command line where you are working. The parent process pauses to wait for the new process to finish. For example, if you enter the command:

```
$ man ls
```

the man page for *ls* appears, and you no longer see a prompt where you can enter additional commands. Some commands don't display screen output like the man page viewer, but they still leave you without an active prompt to enter additional commands. For example, if you use the following command to start the GIMP graphical program from a terminal window, the command prompt does not reappear until you either close the graphical program or press Ctrl+c to close it from the terminal window. While the graphical program is running, the shell is effectively "busy" running the command you entered.

```
$ gimp
```

If you type an ampersand (&) after the name of a command, the shell forks a new process without pausing itself. This is called placing the process in the background. In other words, both the program you start and the shell itself continue to operate—the shell is not "busy" running it any longer. This means you can start another command immediately. For example, if you are working in a graphical command-line window and enter the command:

```
$ gimp &
```

the GIMP graphical program appears, but the command prompt also reappears in the terminal window, so you can enter other commands in the same shell where you started GIMP. Multiple processes started from a single shell are called jobs. A **job** is a process that is associated with a shell. The *jobs* command lists all jobs or processes that are running as descendants of the current shell. (These could also be called **child processes** of the shell.)

You can use the Ctrl+z key combination to suspend a job that the shell is busy running. For example, if you had started GIMP without an ampersand, you could press Ctrl+z to suspend GIMP, returning you to an active shell prompt. Then you use the *bg* command to run the suspended program in the background.

A suspended job is not ended—it does not exit. But it stops running normally—its status changes to stopped while it waits for further instructions before resuming normal execution. The *jobs* command lists processes that are currently suspended.

The output of the *jobs* command includes a job number assigned by the shell. The process ID number assigned by the Linux kernel is not shown by the *jobs* command. When a job is suspended, you can either place it in the background (restart it without displaying output to the current console) or place it in the foreground (allow it to take control of the screen again). To place a job in the foreground, use the *fg* command. You specify a job number (given by the *jobs* command) in order to recall a job to the foreground.

The following procedure uses the *gedit* graphical editor to illustrate how to use *bg* and *fg*:

1. Open a Linux command line within a graphical environment.

2. Start the *gedit* program:

   ```
   $ gedit
   ```

   This command runs in the foreground and occupies the command line so you can't enter other commands.

3. Click on the command line window to make it active, then press Ctrl+z to pause the foreground command (*gedit*).

4. Enter the *jobs* command. You see *gedit* listed, probably as job number 1.

5. *gedit* is currently paused or suspended. Resume it as a background process by entering this command:

   ```
   $ bg %1
   ```

   The command line is now free to run other programs.

6. Enter the command *man ls*. The man page for the *ls* command appears.

7. Press Ctrl+z to pause the *man* command.

8. Enter the command *man ps*. The man page for the *ps* command appears.

9. Press Ctrl+z to pause the second *man* command.

10. Enter the command *jobs*. You see output showing both *man* commands and the *gedit* command.

11. Note the job number of the first *man* command. Enter the command *fg %2*. (Use the number for the first *man* command in place of 2 if necessary.) The *ls* man page appears again.

12. Press *q* to end the *man ls* command.

13. Enter the *jobs* command again. You see that the *man ls* command is no longer listed.

Some commands (including the *man* command) are only used to display information. Starting a man page with an ampersand or using *bg* while viewing a man page automatically suspends the command. It only runs when in the foreground.

In the next section, you will learn how to find the process ID (PID) number of a running process. You can use this number instead of the job number when executing *fg* or *bg*. The PID might be useful both because it is unique for the whole system (where the job number is unique only within a single shell) and the PID can be determined automatically in many cases, so that two commands are not required (one to determine the PID and one to act on it). To use the PID, include the PID without the percentage sign that you use with the job number. For example, suppose a process you have started is job number 3 in the current shell and has a PID of 725. You can bring the process to the foreground with either of these commands:

```
$ fg %3
$ fg 725
```

Using Virtual Consoles

As you learned in Chapter 2, "Exploring the Desktop," you can open multiple command-line windows within a graphical environment. You can also use virtual consoles in Linux to work in multiple text-mode sessions at the same time. A **virtual console** is simply one type of login screen. You can access the Linux virtual consoles by pressing a combination of keys on your keyboard. Having multiple virtual consoles allows you to start multiple text-based login sessions on the same computer.

Networked Linux systems allow many users to log in using a network connection. Virtual consoles provide the same type of login functionality without a network connection—from a single keyboard.

When Linux starts running, it might start a graphical login screen—this is the norm for most systems. But it also starts multiple virtual consoles that are simply waiting for someone to log in. The virtual consoles are assigned to the function keys, typically F1 through F6. (Some systems might have more than six consoles, but six is standard.) The graphical environment (X) runs as virtual console F7.

If you logged in using a text-mode console instead of the graphical login screen, you start working in the first virtual console. You access the second virtual console by pressing Alt+F2. This displays a new login prompt, where you can log in using any valid user name and password. Any commands that you start from this virtual console run independently of those on other virtual consoles. Each console starts a separate copy of the bash shell, so the *jobs* command only lists jobs started in one virtual console, even if you have logged in using the same user name.

NOTE

If you are sitting at a console (the actual Linux system, rather than accessing Linux remotely over a network), you can switch between a graphical desktop and a text-mode virtual console by pressing Ctrl+Alt+F1 for the first virtual console, Ctrl+Alt+F2 for the second, and so on, to Ctrl+Alt+F6 for the sixth virtual console. Once you are viewing a text-mode virtual console, use Alt+Fx to change to a different virtual console. To switch back to your graphical desktop, press Alt+F7.

Learning about Processes via the Command Line

The **ps** command lists the processes that are currently running on your Linux system. The process list can be brief, or it can contain a great deal of information. By adding options to the *ps* command, you can control which pieces of information are included in the listing of processes and how that information is organized. The basic format of the *ps* command uses no parameters and produces a listing of programs that you have started in your current shell (this is generally a short list, as shown here):

```
$ ps
PID      TTY       TIME       CMD
576      tty1      00:00:00   login
584      tty1      00:00:00   bash
741      tty1      00:00:00   ps
```

In this list, the first field is the PID (process ID). You must refer to this number when using several commands that manage processes. The second field shows the terminal that the process is using for output (*tty1* is the first text-mode console screen). The third field shows the CPU time that the process has used so far. The fourth field shows the command that started the process.

Adding options to *ps* causes it to include information such as the user that started the process (the process owner), the process priority (discussed shortly), the process' current status (such as paused or running), and the PID number of the parent process (the process that started this one). The *a* and *x* options show you the processes started by all users, the processes started by the system at boot time, or other processes that have no controlling terminal (tty).

The output of *ps* with the *a* and *x* options is much longer than the output of *ps* alone. It includes all of the daemons that are running in the background as you work on Linux. A **daemon** is a background process that doesn't have any screen output but waits for certain system activity and then acts on it. For example, multiple login commands running on other virtual consoles, the Web server (called httpd), the system logging daemon, and possibly many other daemons and components of a graphical desktop are all included in a typical listing. By adding the *u* option, you can see information about how each process is using your Linux system. The first few lines of *ps* with these three options are shown here (*less* is used because the listing is several screens long):

```
$ ps aux | less
USER      PID   %CPU %MEM  VMZ    RSS TTY STAT START   TIME COMMAND
bin       381   0.0  0.9   840    300 ?   S    13:32   0:00 rpc.portmap
daemon    451   0.0  1.9   1156   596 ?   S    13:32   0:00 lpd
daemon    471   0.0  1.0   828    324 ?   S    13:32   0:00 atd
nobody    845   0.0  2.5   1384   784 ?   S    13:32   0:00 httpd -f
nobody    846   0.0  2.5   1384   784 ?   S    13:32   0:00 httpd -f
root        1   0.0  1.0   828    332 ?   S    13:31   0:04 init
root        2   0.0  0.0     0      0 ?   SW   13:31   0:00 (kflushd)
root        3   0.0  0.0     0      0 ?   SW   13:31   0:00 (kpiod)
```

Some of the output of the *ps aux* command will not make sense until you learn more about memory management, the topic of the next section in this chapter.

NOTE

The first line of the output contains column headings that indicate which user started the process, the percentage of CPU time and memory used by the process, the terminal on which the process is running, current status, and other information. Again, to manage a process, you want to note the PID of the process in the second column from the left.

You can use the *f* option to display the relationship between different processes, showing which processes start other processes. As described in the previous subsection, the init process is always the first process in this list. A partial listing based on the *a*, *x*, and *f* options is shown here:

```
$ ps axf
PID TTY      STAT TIME COMMAND
  1 ?        S    0:04 init
  2 ?        SW   0:00 [kflushd]
  3 ?        SW   0:00 [kpiod]
535          S    0:00 sendmail: accepting connections: p
550 ?        S    0:00 gpm -t ps/2
564 ?        S    0:00 httpd
```

```
568 ?      S     0:00 \_ httpd
571 ?      S     0:00 \_ httpd
577 ?      S     0:00 \_ httpd
594 ?      S     0:00 xfs
638 tty2   S     0:00 login — root
664 tty2   S     0:00  \_ -bash
676 tty2   T     0:00     \_ man ls
677 tty2   T     0:00     |   \_ sh -c /bin/gunzip
678 tty2   T     0:00     |       \_ /bin/gunzip
679 tty2   T     0:00     |       \_ /usr/bin/less -is
680 tty2   T     0:00     \_ top
686 tty2   R     0:00     \_ ps axf
639 tty3   S     0:00 /sbin/mingetty tty3
642 tty6   S     0:00 /sbin/mingetty tty6
644 ?      S     0:00 update (bdflush)
```

The processes are presented in a tree diagram. For example, process ID (PID) 638 (see the left column of the output above) is the *login* command, where a user has logged in as root. The login process started a bash shell (the next line in the output, process 664). The root user started several commands within the shell, including *man ls* (PID 676) and the *ps* command (PID 686). The *man* command started other commands to uncompress the man page file. Many processes were started by the Linux kernel when the system was started. These processes appear without any tree structure.

Each process has a parent process—that is, the process that started it. A parent process can have many child processes.

To manage your system effectively, you often need to display detailed information about specific processes. The *ps* command has many options that let you select which processes are included in the command output. It also has options to let you select what information is displayed about each of those processes. Table 6-1 lists *ps* options for selecting which processes to display.

NOTE

It might be helpful to think of a large spreadsheet with every process on a separate row, and every piece of information about the process in a separate column. The *ps* options in Table 6-1 let you choose which rows to display. The *ps* options in Tables 6-2 and 6-3 let you choose which columns to display. You can combine both types of options in one *ps* command to see exactly the information you need.

Table 6-1   *ps* Options Used to Select Processes to Display

Option	Description
-A	Selects all processes on the system
T	Selects all processes running in the current terminal
x	Selects all processes that were not started normally from a terminal (this list includes system initialization scripts and network services)

Table 6-1   *ps* Options Used to Select Processes to Display (continued)

Option	Description
r	Restricts output to running processes (those that are not sleeping); this option is used in conjunction with another selection option
-C	Selects processes by the command used to start the process; to use this option, you need to follow it with the name of the command
-p	Selects processes by PID number; to view information on a single process, enter its PID number as a value after the option
--user	Selects processes by user name; to use this option, type the user name after the option
--group	Selects all processes belonging to users who are members of the group named after the option

For example, while logged in as root (note the # prompt) you could use the following command to list all processes owned by user jtaylor:

```
# ps --user jtaylor
```

You can select which pieces of information (sometimes called fields) *ps* displays for each process by adding command-line options such as those shown in Table 6–2. Many of the unfamiliar terms in the Description column (such as "nice level") are discussed later in this chapter. A few are used only for special troubleshooting or programming tasks—refer to the *ps* man page for more information on these.

Table 6-2   Process Information Fields Available from *ps*

Display code (column heading in ps output)	Description	Command-line option
PID	Process ID	pid
PGID	Process group ID	pgid
SID	Session ID	sess
TTY	Controlling terminal	tty
TPGID	Process group ID of the owner of the terminal running the process	tpgid
USER	Owner of the process	user
PRI	Time left of a possible timeslice allocated to the process	pri
NICE	Nice level	nice
PLCY	Scheduling policy	plcy
RPRI	Real-time priority	rpri
MAJFLT	Number of major faults loading information from a file system	majflt
MINFLT	Number of minor faults (with no disk access involved)	minflt
TRS	Size of the text used by the program (in KB)	trs
DRS	Size of the data used by the program (in KB)	drs

Table 6-2   Process Information Fields Available from *ps* (continued)

Display code (column heading in ps output)	Description	Command-line option
SIZE	Virtual image size of the process (in KB)	size
SWAP	Space used on swap device by this process (in KB)	swap
RSS	Kilobytes of the program resident in memory	rss
SHARE	Shared memory size in KB	share
DT	Number of pages of information that are dirty (not yet updated to hard disk)	dt
STAT	State of the process	stat
FLAGS	Process flags	f
WCHAN	Kernel function at the point where the process is sleeping	wchan
UID	User ID of the owner of this process	uid
%WCPU	Weighted percentage of CPU time consumed	wpcpu
%CPU	Percentage of CPU used since last update	pcpu
%MEM	Percentage of memory used	pmem
START	Time that the process was started	start
TIME	Total amount of CPU time (cumulative) that the process has used since it was started	time
COMM	Command line that started the process (abbreviated)	comm
CMDLINE	Command line that started the process (complete)	cmd

To specify a field from Table 6-2, use the arguments in the right column of the table with the *o* option. For example, to display processes owned by jtaylor and display just the command line and PID for each of those processes (option *comm* in Table 6-2), use this command:

```
# ps -user jtaylor o "comm pid"
```

Instead of listing the exact fields you want, you normally use one of the options in Table 6-3. These options each define a collection of related fields.

Table 6-3   Combinations of Process Information Fields Available from ps

Command-line option	Description
i	Show fields related to controlling jobs in a shell
s	Show fields related to signals that each process handles
u	Show fields that define how the owner of each process is using system resources
v	Show fields detailing how each process is using virtual memory

Table 6-3 Combinations of Process Information Fields Available from ps (continued)

Command-line option	Description
l	Show numerous fields considered by system administrators to be of interest in tracking processes but not otherwise related (as the above groupings for job control, virtual memory, and so forth, are groups of related fields)
o *or* --format	User-defined format (display all of the fields listed after the option; each field to be included in the output is defined by using a code from the right column of Table 6-2)

As a system administrator, you must manage numerous processes started by many users. You need to track how these processes consume system resources—particularly CPU time and memory. The %CPU and TIME fields of the *ps* command output are especially useful in tracking how processes use CPU time.

The %CPU field compares the amount of CPU time used by a process with the total time elapsed since the previous computation of the %CPU field, in the form of a percentage. The Linux kernel tracks a small slice of time (such as one second) and then determines for how much of that one second a process was using the CPU. That computation creates a percentage used for the %CPU field of the *ps* command output. The %CPU field does not show the average amount of CPU time used by the process since it was started. The %WCPU field is weighted to show a 30-second average of the percentage of CPU time used by a process. This field is more helpful for showing the overall usage pattern for a process.

The TIME field provides a cumulative measure of the amount of CPU time consumed by a process. Processes that have been running since the system was started may still have a TIME value of 0:00 because they are background processes with very little activity to monitor—they spend most of their time sleeping, waiting for some event to occur such as relevant network traffic. But some processes that are only recently started may show a large TIME value (for example, 5:30 to indicate five and a half minutes), indicating that they are using a lot of the CPU's time. The START field tells you when a process began running. When a process has a large TIME value after running for only a short time, you might need to change the priority of that process to prevent it from slowing down other processes. The section "Controlling Processes" describes how to do this.

Viewing Process Information in /proc

The **/proc file system** is a collection of information about the Linux kernel that you access as if it were actually data files stored in subdirectories of /proc. Chapter 15 describes the information in this file system in more detail, but one area relevant to this section is that /proc contains detailed information about each process running on Linux. This information is updated from moment to moment, as the status of a process changes. The *ps* command and the *top* command (described in the next section) both use information from /proc to generate their listings.

Before you can access information in /proc regarding a specific process, you need to find the process's PID number using the *ps* command.

Suppose that, using the *ps* command, you discover the PID for a particular process is 1066. You can then look for information about the process in the directory /proc/1066. Most of this information is difficult to use directly because it consists of numbers without explanations—you use administrative utilities such as *ps* to display this process data in a meaningful way. One part of the process data that is readable, however, is the cmdline file, which tells you the command used to start the process. This command shows the line entered to start process 1066 (the result indicates that *gedit* is used to start the process):

```
# cat /proc/1066/cmdline
gedit
```

You can explore other subdirectories of a process information directory such as /proc/1066 on your Linux system to see what types of process-related information is available.

Viewing Processor Usage with top

The *top* utility displays a list of running processes arranged by how much CPU time each is using. The process that is consuming the greatest amount of CPU time is shown at the top of the list, and the output of *top* is updated regularly (every five seconds by default, but you can configure the update interval).

You can run *top* and leave it on your screen to watch the activity of different processes and see which are using a lot of CPU time. If one process begins to take more than its fair share of CPU time (in your judgment as system administrator), you can take corrective action, as explained later in this section.

top is normally started without any options, like this:

```
$ top
```

When you start *top*, it takes over the text window that you are working in. You cannot run *top* in the background (using the symbol & after the command), because *top* sends its output immediately to the screen. You can, however, use redirection (such as the > operator) to send the output of *top* to a file. Figure 6-1 shows *top* in a terminal window. Table 6-4 in the next section describes several keyboard controls you can use within *top*.

TIP

You might see the *top* command itself in the output of *top*. When the *top* program is listed near the top of the output, you can be sure that the system is not under a heavy load.

Controlling Processes

You can use the *jobs*, *fg*, and *bg* commands to control processes (jobs) that were started within a single shell. Using the **kill** command, you can control any process on the system. The name of this command is somewhat unfortunate: although it is often used to kill, or end, processes,

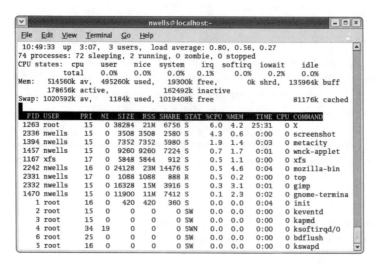

Figure 6-1 The *top* utility

it actually sends signals to processes. Some of those signals end the process; others serve different purposes, such as suspending a process or causing a program to reread its configuration file.

You must be logged in as root to control processes that you didn't start. Notice how most of the example commands in this section begin with the # prompt.

NOTE

Signals are messages that can be sent between processes. About 30 different signals are available, but most of these are not used regularly. Each signal has a name and a number associated with it. To see a list of all the signals, use the *kill* command with the -l option (for *list*):

```
$ kill -l
```

When writing a program, a software developer decides to which signals the program responds. Some programs only respond to one or two signals. Others may respond to more signals, depending on the purpose of the program. For example, a program designed to control your computer in the event of a power failure responds to the signal from a power supply indicating that the main power is out. Other programs wouldn't respond to this signal.

Almost all programs respond to the SIGTERM signal (signal number 15). This signal requests that the program end. Another special signal is SIGKILL (signal number 9). The SIGKILL signal is not handled by the program itself. Instead, if you send a SIGKILL using the *kill* command, the signal is handled by the Linux kernel, which shuts down the indicated process. Any unsaved data in a program is lost when SIGKILL is used to end a process. You should use SIGTERM (rather than SIGKILL) to shut down processes, because SIGTERM requests that a program close itself, giving the program a chance to clean up its work, close any open files, and so forth, before ending. When you use SIGKILL, the process is cut off before it can do any of those things. SIGKILL is very useful, however, when a process is not responding to SIGTERM.

Because you can always stop any process by sending it the SIGKILL signal, a renegade program virtually never crashes the Linux kernel. The only potential problem you might encounter is when a program malfunction causes the screen, mouse, and keyboard to become unusable so that you can't actually run the *kill* command. In such cases you can sometimes log in to the system over the network and kill the process that is malfunctioning, so you still don't have to restart Linux.

As an example of using the *kill* command to send a signal, suppose a user on your Linux system had started a program called *myeditor*. The program has stopped responding to user commands (it is "locked up"), but it still appears on the screen. You can use *ps* in another terminal window to see the state of the process:

```
# ps ax | grep myeditor
```

The output of this command shows you the PID number for the *myeditor* program. Using this information, you can send a signal to the process. (Here we assume you are logged in as root; the user that started *myeditor* could also use the *kill* command to send a signal):

```
# kill -15 1482
```

This command sends a request to *myeditor* to close. The command can also be written using the name of the signal:

```
# kill -SIGTERM 1482
```

If the program does not respond to the request to terminate (it still appears in the output of *ps ax* and on the screen), you can send a SIGKILL signal that causes the Linux kernel to end the process immediately:

```
# kill -9 1482
```

A special form of the kill command is **killall**. This command sends a signal to all processes started by a given command. This is particularly useful when a program is starting copies of itself faster than you can locate the PIDs and use *kill* to shut them down. For example, if the *myeditor* program were behaving that way, you could use this command:

```
# killall -9 myeditor
```

Be careful not to use *killall* when multiple copies of a program are running and you only want to end one of them. In that case, use *kill* with the appropriate PID.

CAUTION

Changing Process Priorities

Each process is automatically assigned a **priority** when it is started. This priority determines how much CPU time is granted to the process as the kernel allocates time slices among all processes. Normally, all processes have the same priority—that is, all processes are assigned an equal time slice. Another name for the priority of a process is **nice level**. The idea behind the name "nice" is that if a user on the system decides a certain program is not time sensitive, the user can make the program "nicer" to other users' programs by giving up some of its CPU time. The system administrator can make any process nicer, whether the user who started it is feeling generous or not.

TIP PRI in the *ps* command output is short for *Priority*, but this field actually indicates how a process is using the CPU time allocated to it. Notice that this field changes regularly for a given process as the process works, using CPU time at different moments.

The NICE or NI field in the output of the *ps* and *top* commands indicates the nice level, or priority level, assigned to a process. The nice level is a fixed value assigned to a process. This value determines whether a process receives extra CPU processing time or less CPU processing time compared to other processes running on the system. You can change the nice level to alter the relative priority of a process.

The standard nice level is 0, which indicates that a process has equal priority with all other processes that have not had their nice level altered. Any user can raise the nice level of a process that he or she has started (and thus owns), making it nicer to other programs. The highest nice level, which makes a program run the slowest, is 20. The root user can make any process nicer, but root can also make programs less nice by lowering their nice level. The root user can lower the nice level of a process to -20, which gives that process a lot of extra CPU time. This might be necessary, for example, if the root user is trying to do an emergency backup of data without completely interrupting users' work.

You can alter the priority of a process using the *nice* and *renice* commands. You use the **nice** command to start a process and assign it nonstandard priority at the same time. If you use the *nice* command with just the name of the program to start, *nice* starts the program with a nice level 10 higher than the default (of zero). You can also specify a nice level as an option. For example, to start a script named *analyze* with a nice level of 5, use this command:

```
$ nice -5 analyze
```

If you are logged in as root, you can also start a command with a negative nice value to give it more processor time than it would have by default:

```
$ nice --15 analyze
```

The **renice** command changes the nice level of a process that is already running. To use *renice*, you must know the PID of the process you want to affect. The root user can perform more complex tasks using *renice*. These tasks require additional information such as the user ID (UID) of the owner of a process.

As a first example, suppose you start a complex script named *analyze*. After starting the script, you decide you can wait for the results of the script until you return from lunch, allowing other users' programs to run more efficiently. You can change the nice level of the process by using the PID of the running script with the *renice* command. For example, if the PID of the analyze script is 1776, this *renice* command changes the running script's priority to 10 so that it takes longer to complete.

```
# renice +10 1776
```

Suppose next that as the system administrator you discover that a certain user, jtaylor, is running several computationally intensive programs that are slowing down system response for other users. After checking with this user, you learn that the programs are a valid use of the system resources, but they are not time critical. To make things run more smoothly for other users, you raise the nice level of all processes run by jtaylor so they run more slowly. This command changes the priority of all running processes owned by jtaylor to 5:

```
# renice +5 -u jtaylor
```

NOTE   Changing the priority level of a process using *nice* or *renice* affects how much CPU time the process is allocated, but it does not affect other factors that might have an even greater impact on how fast a program operates. Two prime examples are hard disk access and network speed, neither of which the CPU can speed up.

Controlling Processes within top

As you view process information using *top*, you can use a number of keyboard options to control both the display of information and the status of Linux processes. You can, for example, *renice* a process by pressing the *r* key and entering the PID of the process followed by a new nice level. For example, suppose the first few lines of the process list in *top* look like this:

```
PID   USER      PRI NI SIZE RSS   SHARE STAT LIB %CPU  %MEM  TIME   COMMAND
1066  jtaylor   17  0  1012 1012  820   R    0   4.7   3.2   0:00   analyze
1     root      0   0  100  52    36    S    0   0.0   0.1   0:04   init
2     root      0   0  0    0     0     SW   0   0.0   0.0   0:00   kflushd
3     root      0   0  0    0     0     SW   0   0.0   0.0   0:00   kpiod
4     root      0   0  0    0     0     SW   0   0.0   0.0   0:00   kswapd
```

To change the nice level of process 1066 (the *analyze* command, as indicated by the far-right column), you follow these steps:

1. Press the *r* key. A message appears above the process list asking you to enter the PID of the process to be reniced.

2. You enter the PID of the process (1066 in this example).

3. A message appears asking you for the new value to assign to this process. For this example, the nice level is being raised to 10; it could also be lowered from 0 to a negative number if you are running as root. Enter 10.

4. Watch the NI column of the process listing to see the nice level value change. Because of the higher nice level, the process moves down in the process list after a moment as its CPU usage decreases (unless the system has nothing else competing for CPU time, in which case the process list might not change much).

As you are viewing the output of the *top* command, you can use the keys listed in Table 6-4 to control *top*. Other command options for *top* can be specified on the command line when you first start the utility. These options control sorting information in *top*, displaying or hiding certain information fields, and changing how some fields (such as %CPU) are calculated. See the man page for the *top* command for further details.

Table 6-4   Interactive Commands in *top*

Description	Press this key	Notes
Update the process list display immediately	Spacebar	
Show a help screen with a command listing	h *or* ?	
Kill a process	k	You will be prompted for the PID
Change the number of processes included in the display	n *or* #	You will be prompted for the number of processes to include
Quit the *top* program	q	
Renice a process	r	You will be prompted for the PID and new nice level
Change the automatic update interval	s	You will be prompted for a value (in seconds) for the update interval

Using Graphical Process Management Tools

Several graphical process management tools are available for Linux. This section briefly describes where to find some of those tools and how to use them.

The **KDE System Guard** utility graphically displays a process list and lets you interact with that list to rearrange or kill processes. You can start this program by entering *ksysguard* from a command line within your desktop.

NOTE

If you execute the command *kpm*, a minimal version of the KDE System Guard appears in which you can manage processes but not other parts of the system, as shown in the figures of KDE System Guard.

Figure 6-2 shows the KDE System Guard window with the Process Table tab selected. If you choose All Processes from the list box at the bottom of the window you see a listing similar to the output of the *ps aux* command. Check the Tree check box to see output resembling *ps* with the *f* option, with parent-child relationships between processes shown.

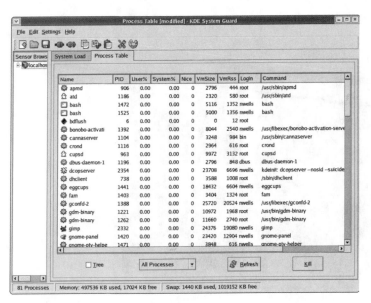

Figure 6-2   The KDE System Guard utility Process Table tab

TIP   Within the KDE System Guard, click any column heading to sort the process list using that column.

The process list in the KDE System Guard is also similar to the output of the *top* command. Fields of information are shown for each process. The list is updated every few seconds. You can click on the list box below the process list to select which processes are displayed. This is equivalent to using one of the selection options in Table 6-1. You can also click the Refresh button to update the process information if it's not updating quickly enough for you. After you click a process to select it, you can click the Kill button below the list to end that process. You can also right-click a process to do any of the following:

- Change which information fields are displayed for all processes.
- Select certain processes from the list.
- Send a signal to a process (remember, SIGTERM and SIGKILL are the signals commonly used to stop a program).
- Renice a process. When you choose this item, a dialog box appears in which you use a slide control to adjust the nice level of the process (moving the slider to the left for a lower nice level yields a higher priority and faster running process).

Figure 6-3 shows the KDE System Guard with the System Load tab selected. Notice also the sensor browser information on the left side of the window. You can use these parts of the utility to manage other parts of the system, including managing system memory and virtual memory (as discussed in the next section of this chapter).

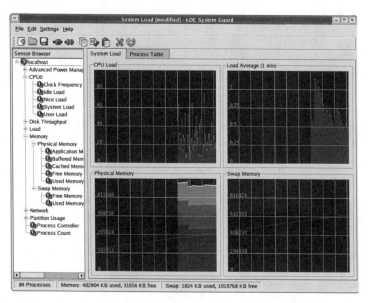

Figure 6-3   The KDE System Guard utility System Load tab

If you're using the GNOME desktop, you can use the **GNOME System Monitor** to manage processes graphically. To start this utility, choose System Tools, then System Monitor on the GNOME main menu, or enter the command *gnome-system-monitor*. Figure 6-4 shows the main window of the GNOME System Monitor with the Process Listing tab selected.

In this window you can select which processes to display (All Processes are selected by default). Choose the More Info button to display information fields for the selected process. An End process button lets you kill any selected process. You can right-click any process and select Change Priority to set the nice level for that process.

If you kill a process that has child processes, those child processes will also exit in most cases.

CAUTION

The Resource Monitor tab, shown in Figure 6-5, displays the current load on the CPU as well as memory usage information.

In addition to the KDE System Guard and GNOME System Monitor, you can install another program called GKrellM that lets you view system status information on your desktop continuously. This program is not installed by default, but you can add this software package from your Fedora CD-ROMs. (Chapter 10, "Managing Software Packages and File Systems," describes how to install additional software packages on your system.) The GKrellM program doesn't list individual processes, but it presents summary CPU load information, plus data about disk usage, memory usage, battery status (on a laptop) and other system information. You can start this program by entering *gkrellm* in a terminal window or

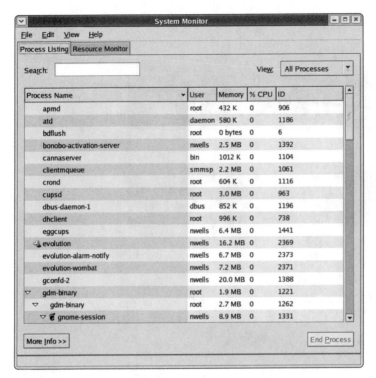

Figure 6-4   The GNOME System Monitor utility

by selecting System Tools, More System Tools, and then GKrellM System Monitor from the GNOME main menu (after installing the package from your Fedora CD-ROMs). Figure 6-6 shows this utility. Right-click any portion of the utility to open a configuration window in which you can configure that part of the utility.

As another helpful option for tracking how busy the CPU is, you can place an applet on the GNOME Panel that shows a graph of the CPU load, updated every few seconds. To activate this applet, right-click an empty part of the GNOME Panel, click Add to Panel, then Utility, then System Monitor.

Actively Monitoring the CPU Load

You have learned about several tools for viewing process information and updating the status of one or more processes. But how can you apply that knowledge to manage your Linux system effectively?

Many system administrators begin by keeping a CPU load monitor visible on their Panel as they work. When the CPU load is consistently high, you can begin checking for processes that might need attention. As you start working on a new Linux system, you can judge from user comments what load level on the CPU monitor equates to slow response times for users

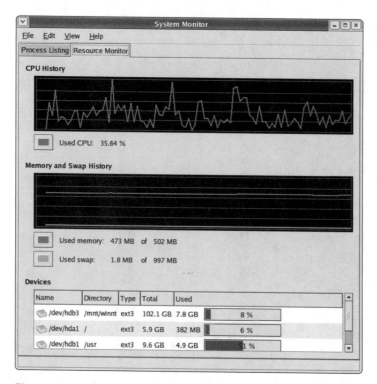

Figure 6-5   The GNOME System Monitor utility Resource Monitor tab

based on the programs they are running. A very fast CPU can tolerate a high load level and still deliver acceptable response times.

When you decide to investigate the cause of a high load, begin by using *top* or one of the graphical utilities to see if a single process is using a high percentage of CPU time. A "runaway process" started by a user might be the cause of the heavy load. In this case, you can change the priority of the process, talk to the user who started the process, and kill the process if necessary. As you become more familiar with the normal load on your system, you will be able to tell from a small load graphic on your Panel when a single process has suddenly run wild (for example, because of incoming network traffic or a programming bug).

When many legitimate processes are causing the heavy CPU load, the *ps* and *top* command options (or the graphical utilities) can help you determine whether one set of programs (such as the Web server), one type of program (such as shell scripts), or one user's programs are causing the heavy load. In each case, when you know the details, you can take corrective action by renicing a set of processes based on the command name or the user name.

Figure 6-6   The GKrellM System Monitor window

TIP   Even if you can't immediately fix a system with a slow response, consider explaining the situation to end-users. Leaving end-users uninformed is one of the fastest ways to lose their support, and most people will be quite accommodating as long as they know you understand their concerns and are working on the problem.

In some situations, everything might appear to be normal, with no processes taking undue CPU time and no troublesome applications, yet the system might nevertheless be very busy. When this situation persists for several days or weeks (depending on the IT strategy of your organization), you need to increase your system capacity. As a rule, you will always need more of everything in the future. Tracking CPU usage and taking action to correct errant processes simply lets you delay spending money on additional computing power until you really need it. To this end, you can reduce the CPU load in several ways. Here are a few ideas:

- Raise the nice level of numerous user processes so that they are not all competing at the same level. Of course, users will complain about the slowness of the system unless the CPU is fast enough to run their applications adequately. You must determine the importance of various tasks and then judge the performance levels that are allowable for different users and tasks. Maybe your Web server is critical because it generates sales, but users won't notice if their word processors run a bit slower. Or maybe the Web server just provides information, while users run important macros in their word processors. You must determine which processes are most critical.

- On systems with this capability, you can add a second microprocessor. (Check which version of Linux you are using—Red Hat Enterprise Linux AS supports multiple processors, but the WS and ES versions do not. The Linux kernel itself might or might not be configured for multiprocessor support on your distribution.) Adding processors significantly reduces the load on your server, but it might be expensive and might require that you upgrade Linux to use a kernel with multiprocessing enabled.

- Move some tasks to a different computer. You might have an older system that is too slow to handle many user accounts, but works effectively as an e-mail server. Removing the e-mail server functions from your main server can reduce the load enough to let users' programs run more quickly.

- Add memory. This often reduces the CPU load on a busy system because the CPU spends less time moving data to and from the swap space. System administrators accustomed to Linux are proud that it can run well with 64 MB of memory, but a system with 2 GB of RAM has distinct advantages.

- Use higher-performance peripherals. Many systems seem slow because the CPU is waiting on a component such as a network connection or a slow hard disk. Upgrading these components can increase overall system throughput dramatically.

MANAGING MEMORY

The previous section described how to track and manage the way processes use the system's CPU. This section describes how to manage other key system resources: physical memory (RAM) and virtual memory (swap space). More RAM always leads to better performance on a busy system, because the Linux kernel and Linux programs can only interact with information stored in RAM. Information stored on a hard disk (even on a swap partition—in virtual memory) must be loaded into RAM before it can be manipulated or presented to a user.

One aspect of managing memory is noting how the numerous applications running on a Linux system can share memory to make more efficient use of this limited resource. Although this is chiefly decided by developers who write the programs you run, understanding how shared libraries work can help you manage applications on your system.

Understanding Shared Libraries

A Linux system includes a large number of files that contain programming code but are not part of any program that you execute at the command line. These files are programming libraries. A **library** contains prewritten functionality that any program can use. The developer that creates the library publishes a list of what each part of the library does, and how other programs can interact with it. For example, Linux includes libraries to access files, to create network connections, to display text, and hundreds of other functions. By relying on libraries, programmers can create new applications in a fraction of the time, with fewer errors, and with more standardized options compared to writing the entire system themselves.

TIP   A library in Linux is similar to a DLL in Microsoft Windows. DLL stands for dynamically linked library, though most of the DLLs you encounter when you work with Microsoft Windows applications are those that are used only by a specific application.

6

When you run a program that was created using a library, the library must either be installed on your system or included within the program itself. These two categories define the relationship between a library and program that uses it:

- **Statically linked applications** include library functions in the main program. They require no additional library files on the Linux system. Each copy of an application loads into system memory a duplicate copy of all the library functions it uses.

- **Dynamically linked applications** assume that any needed library files are available on the Linux system. The library functionality is not included with the program itself. Dynamically linked applications use **shared libraries**. This means that several applications can use a single copy of a library that has been loaded into memory. (This also means that if the correct libraries are not loaded on the Linux system, a dynamically linked application cannot run.)

Running multiple applications that are dynamically linked to the same libraries requires less memory than running multiple statically linked applications. If you load one application and its attendant libraries, then load a second application that is dynamically linked to those same libraries, the libraries are not loaded a second time. Instead, the second application "shares" the libraries with the first application. If 10 applications are using one shared library, the library still only loads into memory once, rather than 10 times. Dynamically linked applications save a great deal of memory in situations where applications use the same libraries.

Most Linux applications are dynamically linked to use a set of shared libraries that are installed on a Linux system by default. For example, if you run numerous graphical applications in the GNOME desktop, most of the functionality of each application is contained in libraries shared by all GNOME applications.

You can use the *ldd* command to list all the libraries that a program requires. For example, use this command to see the libraries used by the *ls* command (you must always use the full path of the program as a parameter):

```
$ ldd /bin/ls
```

Understanding Paged Memory

You learned earlier in this chapter that when the Linux kernel doesn't have enough memory to hold all the processes it is managing, it temporarily copies information to the swap space while it uses memory for other tasks. Then it copies the information back from the swap space to continue working on the first task.

The natural assumption when you learn about Linux swap space is that the kernel moves one application at a time to or from swap space. In fact, however, information is transferred to and from swap space in smaller units, known as pages. A **page** of memory is a block of 4 KB of RAM.

 NOTE You will see references to an *application* being swapped. It's fine to use this expression if you understand that the kernel does not really swap complete applications; it swaps enough pages from the application's memory to create the amount of free space needed by other processes.

When one application requires additional RAM that is not available, the Linux kernel locates another application that is sleeping, stopped, or waiting for some event to occur (such as a floppy disk to respond). The kernel then moves data from pages of memory in the second application's memory space to the swap space. The kernel moves only enough data to free the amount of memory needed by the first application. The copied data might be taken from the middle of the inactive application's memory. The kernel keeps track of which pages of memory are moved to swap space and makes the freed memory available to the first application.

When a program that was inactive becomes active again, the kernel moves the swapped data back from swap space to the same memory pages from which they were taken. Because the memory is restored by the kernel before the application becomes active again, the application cannot tell that its memory was used by another application for a time.

Swapping individual pages of memory (rather than complete applications) dramatically improves the performance of Linux on heavily loaded servers. If Linux swapped complete applications (rather than individual memory pages), system resources might be wasted copying a very large application to swap space when only a small percentage of its memory was needed by another program.

Tracking Memory Usage

The *free* command displays information about both RAM and virtual memory.

```
# free
          total        used      free      shared    buffers  cached
Mem:    191260       182144    9116      0         28840    49196
-/+ buffers/cache:   104108    87152
Swap:  265064        0         265064
```

All the information displayed by *free* is in kilobytes. You can use command-line switches to change the display to bytes or megabytes. The columns of information in the output of *free* are described here:

- The *Mem* line refers to physical memory (RAM).

- The *-/+ buffers/cache* line refers to RAM that is allocated to data stored by applications or data cached from the hard disk.

- The *Swap* line refers to swap space (located on your swap partition).

- The *total* column indicates the total amount of memory available to Linux. The sample output shows a small system with about 192 MB of RAM and 256 MB of swap space.

- The *used* column indicates how much of the total memory is currently in use for both RAM and swap space.

- The *free* column indicates how much space is free for both RAM and swap space.

- The *shared* column is no longer used by the Linux kernel, but it is maintained for compatibility with older programs that expect this information to be provided by the kernel. You should ignore this number.

- The *buffers* column indicates the amount of memory dedicated to buffers. A **buffer** is memory used by an application for data storage. (For example, an application such as a spreadsheet uses buffers to hold documents as you edit them.)

- The *cached* column indicates memory used to store data from the hard disk, on the assumption that it might be needed by an application. If few applications are running, Linux uses most of the available RAM as a disk cache to improve performance. As more applications are started, less memory is used for disk caching.

The first few times you see the output of *free*, the numbers won't mean much. With experience, you will come to understand what Linux is doing by reviewing these numbers. Some indicators to watch for in the output of *free* include the following:

- If the last line of the *free* column (the *Swap* line) is small, you are in danger of running out of both physical and virtual memory. If this happens, the kernel will crash. As you get closer to running out of memory, performance decreases significantly.

- If many applications are running at the same time on a system without much RAM, the system is subject to thrashing. Thrashing wears out the hard disk and significantly decreases application performance. Thrashing indicates that an application has gone haywire or that you need more RAM.

- The first line of the *free* column on the *Mem* line is normally very small. This is because Linux tries to use all available RAM for caching hard disk information. If more applications are started, less information is cached. If the *Mem* line of the *free* column shows a value near zero, you can still start several applications without using swap space. Check the value of the *cache* column to see how much memory might be available for additional applications.

Several fields of *ps* command output also provide information about memory usage:

- The %MEM field shows the percentage of available system memory that the process is using.

- The STAT field (for Status) shows whether the application is sleeping (indicated by an S). Pages from a sleeping application can be swapped to hard disk if memory is needed for another process. The STAT field shows a W if pages from a process have been swapped to hard disk. The command line used to start a process (the COMMAND field) is enclosed in square brackets if pages from a process have been swapped to hard disk.

- The RSS (Resident Set Size) field shows the amount of RAM currently used by the process. This value is given in kilobytes.

Viewing Virtual Memory Information

The general state of the swap space (the virtual memory) on your system is shown by the *free* command and by both graphs and numeric displays in the utilities described in this section, such as the KDE System Guard and the GNOME System Monitor.

You can also use the **vmstat** command to view detailed information about how swap space is being used. The output of the *vmstat* command is cryptic until you become familiar with the abbreviated labels for the fields that it displays. When *vmstat* is run as a regular command, its output is based on information averaged over time since the system was started. You can also run *vmstat* as you would *top*, with the display updated every few seconds. In this case the information is computed since the last update rather than since the system was booted. To run *vmstat* as a regular command, simply enter *vmstat*. Sample output is shown here:

```
# vmstat
procs    memory                      swap      io        system      cpu
 r  b    swpd    free   buff  cache   si   so   bi   bo   in   cs   us sy wa id
 0  0       0 308620  13628 107396    0    0   77   21  111   73    2  1  0 97
```

The fields displayed in the output of *vmstat* are explained in the following lists. Under the *procs* main heading:

- *r*: Number of processes waiting for run time
- *b*: Number of processes in uninterruptible sleep

Under the *memory* main heading you see fields that mirror the output of *free*:

- *swpd*: Amount of virtual memory used (KB)
- *free*: Amount of free RAM (also called idle memory) (KB)
- *buff*: Amount of RAM used as buffers (KB)
- *cache*: Amount of RAM used to cache hard disk data (KB)

Under the *swap* main heading:

- *si*: Speed as data is swapped into RAM from disk (average, in KB per second)
- *so*: Speed as data is swapped out to disk from RAM (average, in KB per second)

Under the *io* main heading:

- *bi*: Speed as data is sent to a block device (the hard disk), measured in blocks per second
- *bo*: Speed as data is received from a block device (in blocks per second)

Under the *system* main heading:

- *in*: Number of interrupts per second, including the clock
- *cs*: Number of context switches (changes between active processes) per second

Under the *cpu* main heading, each item indicates a percentage of total CPU time for four areas:

- *us*: User time, devoted to functions not within the kernel
- *sy*: System time, devoted to functions within the kernel
- *wa*: Idle time, waiting for I/O (such as information coming from a hard disk)
- *id*: Idle time, when the CPU is waiting for something to do

To run the *vmstat* command in interactive mode as you would *top*, so that its output is periodically updated, include a number after the command to indicate the delay between updates. For example, the following command displays an updated line of information every two seconds:

```
$ vmstat 2
```

The information provided by *vmstat* is useful for locating bottlenecks on your system related to hard disk performance, lack of sufficient memory, or problems with specific applications.

SCHEDULING PROCESSES

Up to this point, when you have started processes you have either selected an item from a menu or entered a command in a terminal window. Linux also lets you define a task and have it execute automatically, either when you are doing other work on the system or when you are away from the system (such as in the middle of the night).

The **at** command lets you define one or more commands to be executed at some future time. The **crontab** command lets you define one or more commands to be executed repeatedly at intervals that you designate. The *at* command relies on a background process called *atd*; the *crontab* command relies on a background process called *crond*. Each of these background processes checks once per minute to see whether any scheduled tasks should be executed.

A scheduled task is often called a job (just as a process executed in a shell can be called a job). The terms *at* **job** and *cron* **job** refer to commands or scripts that you have scheduled to be executed at a specific time using the *at* or *cron* commands, as described in the sections that follow.

Automating One-time Tasks

Sometimes you want to perform a task automatically at some future time. For example:

- You need to start a backup operation after all employees have left for the evening.

- You want to start a large database query during lunch, but you need to leave the office early.

- You need to remind several users on the network (and yourself) of a 3:00 meeting.

In each of these cases, you can use the *at* command to schedule the task for future execution.

Using the at Command

To automate a task with the *at* command, you can either enter commands directly at the command line, or you can list them in a file. For complex tasks that require several commands, it's best to list them in a file so you can review them carefully before scheduling them using the *at* command.

After you create a list of commands to execute in a file, you can schedule execution using this syntax:

```
at -f <filename> <time specification>
```

For example, suppose you created a file called usage_report containing the following lines:

```
logger Starting du to create disk usage report on /home
du /home > /var/log/du_report
logger Completed disk usage report
```

If you want these commands to execute at 11:30 p.m., you would enter this command:

```
$ at -f usage_report 23:30
```

 When you give a file name to the *at* command, each of the lines in that file will be executed as if you had entered it at the shell prompt.

NOTE

The *atd* daemon will check once per minute for any jobs that have been scheduled using the *at* command. At 11:30 p.m., the job scheduled by the command above will be executed. Any results from the command (that is, text that would normally be written to the screen) are e-mailed to the user who scheduled the *at* job. In this example, the commands in usage_report do not generate any screen output—it has been redirected to a file.

The time specification in the *at* command is very flexible. You can include a standard 24-hour format, such as 23:30 in the previous example; you can also include items such as the words "now," "minutes," "hours," "days," or "months." You can include the words "today," "tomorrow," "noon," "midnight," and even "teatime" (4:00 p.m.). Table 6-5 shows several examples of specifying a time with the *at* command.

Table 6-5   Example Time Specifications Using the *at* Command

Time specification	Description
at -f file now + 5 minutes	Execute the commands in file five minutes after the *at* command is entered
at -f file 4pm + 5 days	Execute the commands in file at 4:00 p.m., five days from now
at -f file noon Jul 31	Execute the commands in file at noon on July 31
at -f file 10am 08/15/05	Execute the commands in file at 10:00 a.m. on 15 August 2005
at -f file 5:15 tomorrow	Execute the commands in file at 5:15 a.m. tomorrow

Here are some points to remember about specifying times within the *at* command:

- Each item in the time specification is separated by a space.
- You cannot combine multiple phrases (such as "4 hours" and "25 minutes").
- When you use the word "now," it should be the first word of the time specification.
- When a specific clock time is used (such as 11:00), the command file is processed the next time the system clock reaches the indicated time. For example, if it is currently 9:00 a.m. and you want to schedule a task for 11:00 a.m. tomorrow, you must indicate *tomorrow* in the time specification or the task is executed at 11:00 a.m. today (because 11:00 a.m. has not occurred yet today).
- If the *at* command cannot understand the time specification, you see a message stating "Garbled time," and the command is not accepted for processing.

When you enter an *at* command with a valid file name and a valid time specification, you see a message such as the one shown here:

```
warning: commands will be executed using /bin/sh
job 9 at 2005-10-21 05:15
```

The job number and the time displayed depend on the state of your Linux system. This message reminds you that the commands in the file will be executed using the /bin/sh program. (On most Linux systems this is another name for the bash shell.) It also indicates the exact date and time when the commands will be executed.

Using at Interactively

To use the *at* command as shown in the preceding section, you must prepare a file containing the commands you want to execute. If you prefer, you can enter commands at the shell prompt instead of preparing a separate file in advance. The only disadvantage of entering commands interactively is that you cannot alter a command after it has been edited; you have to cancel the *at* job and reenter it.

To use the *at* command interactively, simply omit the *-f filename* portion of the *at* syntax. For example, enter a command such as this:

```
# at now + 5 hours
```

When you press Enter after typing such a command, you see a special prompt: *at>*. At this prompt you enter the command that you want the *atd* daemon to execute (5 hours from now, in this example). You can enter shell scripting commands, as described in Chapter 14, "Writing Shell Scripts."

After entering all the commands that you want the *atd* daemon to execute, you indicate that you have finished by pressing Ctrl+d. This key combination sends a special character that signifies the end of your input. You see <EOT> on the last line containing the *at>* prompt, followed by a message indicating the job number and time that the *atd* daemon will execute the command.

When you enter a series of commands at the *at>* prompt, any results that would have been displayed onscreen when the commands are executed are e-mailed to you, just as they are when you specify a command file using the *-f* parameter. The e-mail message that the *atd* daemon sends you has a subject such as "Output from your job 11," where the number at the end of the message is the job number assigned by *at* when you finished entering commands at the *at>* prompt.

TIP

Your Linux system must be turned on at the time an *at* job is scheduled to run. For example, if you schedule an *at* job to run in four hours, but your computer is not turned on in four hours, the command is not executed then (obviously), nor will it be executed when the system is turned on again. The *atd* daemon does not check for commands that should have been executed previously but were not.

Sometimes you want the output from a command to appear onscreen instead of being e-mailed to you. For example, if you need to send yourself a reminder, having it sent to your e-mail won't be much help. If you remember to check for the e-mail message, you'll remember the event of which you were to be reminded. As an alternative, you can use the *tty* command to send output from a command to the terminal in which you are currently logged in. The **tty** command returns the name of the terminal device to which you are currently working. For example, if you have logged in on the first virtual console of a Linux system and you enter the command *tty*, you see the device name /dev/tty1 displayed onscreen. You can use the output of this command to redirect output of a command that you submit to the *at* command. For example, suppose you submitted an *at* job as follows (notice that the *tty* command at the end of this command is enclosed in single backward quotation marks; you press Ctrl+d on the second > prompt to end the *at* command):

```
$ at 3:45
> echo Go to your 401k meeting in conference room 6! > `tty`
>
$
```

When the *atd* daemon processes this line, the *tty* command is executed first, and the output from the *tty* command (such as /dev/tty1) is substituted for the `tty` text. The *echo* command then sends the line of text to the terminal where you are working (such as /dev/tty1). Any error messages will still be sent to standard output (and thus e-mailed to you). You can also redirect the Standard Error (STDERR) channel using this format:

```
echo Go to your 401k meeting in conference room 6! 2>&1 > `tty`
```

The Standard Error channel is channel number 2. The above statement redirects channel 2 to channel 1, which is Standard Output. Standard Output is then redirected to the device name given by the *tty* command: the device to which you are logged in.

NOTE

If you are working in multiple graphical terminal windows, the *tty* command might not allow the *atd* daemon to send the output to the precise window in which you are working.

Using the batch Command

A command similar to the *at* command, and which also relies on the *atd* daemon, is the *batch* command. Rather than running commands at a specified time, the **batch** command runs your commands when the system load average drops below 0.8. (You can see the system load by using the *top* command.) If you enter multiple commands at the same time using the *batch* command, to avoid overloading the system the *batch* command only starts one command at a time. The *batch* command is useful for times when you want to run a CPU–intensive or time-consuming program but the system is currently very busy with other tasks. In this case, you can use the *batch* command to enter the name of the program you want to run. As soon as the system is no longer so busy, the command is executed. As with the *at* command, the results of commands run by *batch* are e-mailed to you.

For example, suppose you need to start a time-consuming task such as reconfiguring the Linux kernel using the *make* command (as described in the next section). You can enter the *batch* command as shown below. Notice that no time parameters are included; the commands run as soon as the system load permits. You can include the *-f* option with the *batch* command, or just use the command name and then enter commands at the *at*> prompt, as you would when using the *at* command.

```
# batch
at> cd /usr/src/linux
at> make dep; make clean; make bzImage
at><EOT>
```

As with the *at* command, you press Ctrl+d when you have finished entering the commands you want *batch* to process. As soon as the load on the system is small enough, *batch* executes the commands you entered.

Automating Recurring Tasks

You can use the *crontab* command to execute commands automatically at regular intervals. You might use *crontab* when you need to regularly:

- Create a list of files that have not been accessed in a long time to check whether they can be deleted or archived.

- Create a backup copy of all active files (those recently accessed).

- Compile a list of all directories on the system, sorted by size, to help you identify areas that are using a lot of hard disk space.

- Remove core files or other unused files that are using a lot of hard disk space.

- Delete files in the /tmp directory that have not been used recently.

- Rotate log files to keep them from becoming too large.

- Run security scanning software (for example, check e-mail attachments for viruses or search system log files for multiple login failures).

- Store the results of the *ps* or *df* command to make a snapshot of the system's state at different times.

Many Linux distributions include a simple method of automating tasks that doesn't require you to use the *crontab* command. In Red Hat Linux, the /etc directory contains subdirectories named cron.hourly, cron.daily, cron.weekly, and cron.monthly. You can place a file in any of these subdirectories. The commands in that file are executed hourly, daily, weekly, or monthly, depending in which directory you place the script. This does not let you specify a precise time for your script, but most system administration tasks don't require a precise execution time.

The files you place in the cron-related subdirectories of /etc can be either shell scripts or lists of commands as you used with the *at* command.

TIP

You can also create your own *crontab* commands to execute commands at more precise times, or when your system doesn't provide a method like Red Hat Linux for automating tasks using specific crontab directories. Every Linux system should include an /etc/crontab file, which illustrates the format of a standard entry for the *crontab* command. The /etc/crontab file in Red Hat Linux is shown here. This example file uses a special script called *run-parts* that is provided with Red Hat Linux and Fedora.

```
SHELL=/bin/bash
PATH=/sbin:/bin:/usr/sbin:/usr/bin
MAILTO=root
HOME=/

# run-parts
01 * * * * root run-parts /etc/cron.hourly
02 4 * * * root run-parts /etc/cron.daily
22 4 * * 0 root run-parts /etc/cron.weekly
42 4 1 * * root run-parts /etc/cron.monthly
```

In this /etc/crontab file:

- The SHELL variable defines which shell the *crond* daemon uses to execute the commands and scripts listed in the file.

- The MAILTO variable defines which user on the Linux system receives an e-mail message containing the output from all *cron* jobs defined in the file.

- The HOME and PATH variables define a working directory and the directories where system commands are located. These variables are used by all commands and scripts listed in this file (and hence by all scripts in the cron.daily through cron.monthly subdirectories).

- The lines that end with the names of the subdirectories (such as cron.daily) include the user name root. All of the *cron* jobs that you place in the cron.daily and related directories are executed via the root user account. They are executed by an administrative utility called run-parts, which is only used within this file.

If you want to specify an automated task more precisely than just placing a script in a directory such as /etc/cron.daily, you can create your own *cron* job similar to those listed in /etc/crontab. The flexibility of *crontab* can make it challenging to use, however.

The /etc/crontab file in Red Hat Linux and Fedora includes numbers and asterisks that define when the commands on that line (run-parts for most of /etc/crontab) are executed. Each crontab specification begins with five fields, described here as they appear on each crontab line from left to right (see also Figure 6-7):

- *Minute of the hour*: This field can range from 0 to 59.

- *Hour of the day*: This field can range from 0 to 23.

- *Day of the month*: This field can range from 0 to 31, but be careful about using the days 29, 30, or 31: nothing will happen in the month of February; and nothing will happen in February, April, June, September, or November if you use 31.

- *Month of the year*: This field can range from 0 to 12. You can also use the first three letters of a month's name (in upper- or lowercase).

- *Day of the week*: This field can range from 0 to 7 (0 and 7 are both Sunday; 1 is Monday). You can also use the first three letters of a day's name (in upper- or lowercase).

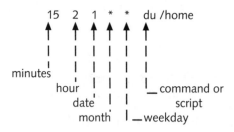

Figure 6-7 An example *crontab* specification for the first day of every month at 2:15 am

The *crond* daemon examines all five of these fields once per minute. If all five fields match the current time, *crond* executes the command on that line. Using an asterisk in a field means "execute this command no matter what the current value of this field is." For the command to be executed, all five fields must match the current time and date. For example, based on the following time specification, *crond* runs the command on this line at 10 minutes after every hour, every day. The specification is not limited by certain days of the week or month.

```
10 * * * * du /home > /tmp/disk_usage
```

NOTE If you do not include a user name after the time specification, *crond* executes the command as whichever user submits the *cron* job. Only root should bother including a user name, as regular users can't submit a job to be run as another user.

Based on the following time specification, *crond* runs the command on this line on the first day of every month at 2:15 in the morning:

```
15 2 1 * * du /home > /tmp/disk_usage
```

Any field can contain multiple values, either separated by commas (without spaces after the commas) or defined by ranges with a hyphen separating them. For example, this time specification causes *cron* to execute the command on this line on the 1st, 10th, and 20th of every month at 1:00 a.m.:

```
0  1 1,10,20 * * du /home > /tmp/disk_usage
```

TIP To view examples and learn more about forming complex time specifications for use with *crontab*, view the man page for the crontab configuration file by entering *man 5 crontab*.

To use *crontab* to submit your own *cron* jobs, you create a file that has a time specification and a command to execute. Unlike the *at* command, you must create a file containing this information; you cannot enter *cron* job commands interactively. Suppose, for example, that you wanted to run the *du* command on /home and sort the results every morning at 1:00 a.m. You do this by following these steps:

1. Create a text file containing the time specification and the command you want to execute. For this example, the file contains the following line (you need to submit this *cron* job as root so that the *du* command can access all home directories):

   ```
   0 1 * * *  du /home | sort > /root/disk_usage
   ```

2. Submit the file to the *crond* daemon using the *crontab* command. If the file you created in Step 1 were called du_nightly, the command would look like this:
   ```
   # crontab du_nightly
   ```

Notice that the command shown in Step 1 fits on a single line.

If you need to perform more complex tasks, you can create two files: a shell script and a *cron* job specification. You cannot use multiple command lines within a single *cron* job specification.

Suppose, for example, that you had developed a series of shell scripts that check the security of the Linux system by reviewing log files, checking network activity, and watching user login activity. If the script that performed all of these activities were called secure_system, you could run that script every morning at 1:30 a.m. by adding this line to your du_nightly file before submitting the file using the *crontab* command:

```
30 1 * * * /sbin/secure_system
```

The full path name of the script is included so that the *crond* daemon is able to locate the script when it attempts to execute this job.

In the /etc/crontab file shown previously, you saw environment variables at the beginning of the file. You can also include environment variables in *crontab* specification files that you create. For example, suppose you want the du_nightly *cron* job to be executed via the root user account so that it can access all home directories, but you want an e-mail message sent to your regular user account so you won't have to log in as root to read the message. To do this, you can include a MAILTO variable at the top of the du_nightly file. The du_nightly file now looks like this:

```
MAILTO=nwells
0 1 * * *  du /home | sort > /root/disk_usage
30 1 * * * /sbin/secure_system
```

You can learn about other environment variables supported by the *crontab* command in the *crontab* man page. You can also use the *-u* option to submit a *cron* job as another user if you are logged in as root. For example, you could submit the du_nightly job as user jtaylor using this command:

```
# crontab -u jtaylor du_nightly
```

Managing Automated Tasks

After you have submitted commands for future execution using *at* or *crontab*, you can view what commands are waiting to be executed and delete them if necessary. You must be logged in as root to manage *at* jobs and *cron* jobs that you did not submit. The root user can submit jobs as any user (using the *-u* option shown previously) and can also view or modify jobs submitted by any user on the system.

Checking the Status of Jobs

The two daemons *atd* and *crond* are started when you boot Linux using standard service scripts in /etc/rc.d/init.d. You can use those scripts to stop and restart the daemons if needed, but because these daemons carefully check the dates on files to see when new *cron* jobs have been submitted, you should never need to restart the daemons.

All of the commands that you submit using *at* or *crontab* are stored in a subdirectory of /var/spool. Jobs submitted using *at* are stored in the /var/spool/at directory; jobs submitted using *crontab* are stored in the /var/spool/cron directory. The two types of jobs are stored differently, however. Jobs for the *atd* daemon contain all the environment variables and related information that the shell needs to execute the *at* job, independent of any other process. *cron* jobs store a more limited amount of information because they are executed in an environment that the *crond* daemon defines for the user who submitted the *cron* job.

Suppose you enter a single *du* command using the *at* command. When you enter this command, it might appear onscreen like this:

```
# at now + 10 minutes
at> du /home > /tmp/du_save
at> <EOT>
```

If you view the contents of the /var/spool/at directory, you see a strange file name such as a0000d00f08407. This file name is generated automatically by the *at* command. Looking at the contents of this file, you can see a number of environment variables. These variables record the state of the shell in which the command was entered via the *at* command. This allows the same shell environment to be duplicated when the command is executed at a later time. The last line of the file is the command that is actually executed at the specified time.

The information in the /var/spool/at directory does not, however, indicate the time when the command will be executed. Because of the complicated format of these files and their interaction with the *atd* daemon, you should not directly modify files in the /var/spool/at directory. Instead, use the *atq* and *atrm* commands to manage *at* jobs that are awaiting execution.

The *atq* command lists all queued *at* jobs—jobs awaiting execution by *atd*. For each job, this command lists a job number and the date and time when the job will be executed:

```
# atq
6     2005-08-15 10:00 a root
9     2005-12-21 05:15 a root
12    2005-12-31 11:45 p root
```

TIP

You can also use the *at* command with the *-l* option (for *list*) to see the same output as the *atq* command.

6

Use the ***atrm*** command to cancel a command that you have submitted using *at*. You can also use the *-d* option (delete) with the *at* command to remove a job from the list of pending *at* jobs. To use either *atrm* or *at -d*, you must include the job number. You obtain the job number using *atq* or *at -l*. For example, to remove job 11, you can use either of these commands:

```
# atrm 11
# at -d 11
```

You can use a similar set of commands to manage *cron* jobs. To begin with, you'll notice that files stored in /var/spool/cron are different from files stored in /var/spool/at. The /var/spool/cron directory contains a single file for each user who has submitted jobs using *crontab*. For example, if you have submitted a job using *crontab* while logged in as root, the file /var/spool/cron/root exists. If you submitted a job using *crontab* while logged in as jtaylor, the file /var/spool/cron/jtaylor exists. The file in /var/spool/cron that is named for your user name contains a composite of all *cron* jobs that you have submitted. For example, when you have submitted a single *cron* job, the file looks something like this:

```
# DO NOT EDIT THIS FILE - edit the master and reinstall.
# (secure_cron installed on Mon Oct 20 18:12:16 2005)
# (Cron version — $Id: crontab.c,v 2.13 1994/01/17 03:20:37
# vixie Exp $)
30 1 * * * /sbin/security_scan
```

As with the contents of the /var/spool/at directory, you should not directly edit a *crontab* file in /var/spool/cron. Instead, use the options provided by the *crontab* command, as summarized here:

- *crontab -l* lists *cron* jobs for your user account.

- *crontab -r* removes your *crontab* file. Use this option carefully, as it removes the entire file; any *cron* jobs you have submitted are lost.

- *crontab -e* opens your *crontab* file in a text editor, so you can make changes in the times or commands defined for your *cron* jobs. It's important that you use the *-e* option on the *crontab* command rather than using a regular editor session (such as vi /var/spool/cron/jtaylor) to change your *crontab* file. Using *crontab -e* prevents file-locking conflicts that can cause problems with the *crond* daemon.

Controlling Access to at and crontab

The default settings on most Linux systems allow any user to submit commands for future execution using either *at* or *crontab*. You can restrict access to *at* and *crontab* so that only certain users can use these commands. The files that enforce this control are:

- /etc/cron.allow: Contains user names (one per line) that are allowed to use the *crontab* command

- /etc/cron.deny: Contains user names (one per line) that are not allowed to use the *crontab* command

- /etc/at.allow: Contains user names (one per line) that are allowed to use the *at* command

- /etc/at.deny: Contains user names (one per line) that are not allowed to use the *at* command

TIP   On some Linux systems, the files listed above might be located in the /var/spool/cron and /var/spool/at subdirectories, in which case they are named simply allow and deny.

On most Linux systems, none of these four files exists, meaning that any user can use both *at* and *crontab*. (On some systems, however, having none of these files can mean that only root can use *at* and *crontab*.) When you attempt to use the *at* or *crontab* command, the command checks the permission files in the following order:

- If the /etc/cron.allow file exists, a user must be listed in that file to use the *crontab* command. The same rule applies to /etc/at.allow for the *at* command.

- If the cron.allow (or at.allow) file does not exist, but the cron.deny file does exist, any user listed in cron.deny (or at.deny) cannot use the *crontab* command (or the *at* command).

By controlling access to the *at* and *crontab* commands on a busy Linux system, you can make it more difficult for regular users to consume system resources when you need to do system administration work or schedule business-critical tasks.

CHAPTER SUMMARY

❏ Linux is a multiprocessing operating system. Each process is managed by the Linux kernel, which can allocate resources to a process and end a process if necessary. CPU time is allocated in time slices.

❏ New processes are created by forking an existing process. Processes in Linux have parent-child relationships.

❏ The state of each process is tracked by the kernel and can be viewed using command-line or graphical utilities. If a process is not active, the kernel can move part of its data to swap space, which acts as virtual memory to allow more processes to be managed at the same time.

❏ Multiple processes can be started from a single shell. Starting a process with an ampersand runs the program in the background.

❏ Within a shell, the *jobs* command manages multiple processes started in that shell. You can also place jobs in the foreground or background using the *fg* and *bg* commands.

❏ Virtual consoles let you log in at multiple independent text-mode screens.

❏ The *ps* command can display many different fields of information about each process, as determined by command-line options, including parent-child relationships between processes. You can also select which processes to display using command-line options.

❏ The *kill* command sends signals to processes or to the Linux kernel when necessary to end a process.

❏ You can view process information within the /proc file system or using a number of utilities, such as *ps* and *top*.

❏ Each process in Linux is assigned a priority, called a nice level. You can raise the nice level to make a process run slower (be nicer to other processes). The root user can change the priority of any process; other users can raise the nice level of processes they have started.

❏ The *nice* and *renice* commands set a process's nice level; other command-line and graphical programs also let you change a process's nice level.

❏ The *top* command lists processes according to how much CPU time they are using. The output of *top* is updated every few seconds. *top* can also be used to control processes by sending them signals.

❏ KDE System Guard and the GNOME System Monitor are two useful graphical process management utilities. Each displays many fields of information about each process and can be used to send signals to a process.

❏ Many system administrators like to display a CPU load monitor on the Panel of their desktop so they can keep an eye on system load.

❏ Shared libraries let many Linux programs access the same programming functionality without loading it into memory multiple times.

❑ Dynamically linked applications use shared libraries; statically linked applications have a copy of the programming libraries they need built into the application itself.

❑ The *free* and *vmstat* commands display information about RAM and virtual memory usage.

❑ A system without sufficient RAM can experience thrashing as applications are repeatedly moved to and from swap space.

❑ The *at* command schedules a task for execution by *atd* at some future point. The task can be defined using a file name containing one or more commands, or by entering the specific commands directly.

❑ Tasks scheduled using *at* can be managed using the *atq* and *atrm* commands. The ability to use *at* to schedule tasks can be managed using at.allow and at.deny files in /etc.

❑ The *batch* command accepts tasks for future execution without a fixed time. They are executed when the system is not busy.

❑ The *crontab* command schedules tasks that are to be executed on a regular basis, such as daily or weekly. A complex but flexible time specification indicates when the task should be executed. The *crontab -e* command lets you edit all tasks for users that have been scheduled for regular execution.

COMMAND SUMMARY

Command	Description	Example
at	Lets you enter one or more commands to be executed once at some future time by the *atd* daemon (see Table 6-5 for example time specifications)	at 5:00 report_script
atq	Lists each of the jobs awaiting execution by *atd*, including a job number and the date and time when the job will be executed	atq
atrm	Deletes (removes) a job from the queue used by *atd* to execute commands	atrm 14
batch	Executes scheduled tasks when the system load average drops below 0.8	batch
bg	Places a job (process) in the background (either by suspending it or by preventing its output from appearing in the current shell's terminal window), thus allowing the shell prompt to become active again	bg
crontab	Lets you enter one or more commands to be executed repeatedly by the *crond* daemon at intervals that you designate	crontab du_script
fg	Brings a job (process) running in a shell to the foreground so that the job controls the shell's terminal window	fg %4

Command	Description	Example
free	Displays the amount of free and used memory (physical and virtual), with basic information about how that memory is being used	free
jobs	Lists jobs (processes) started in the current shell environment	jobs
kill	Sends signals to processes, often to end them via a SIGTERM or SIGKILL signal	kill -9 1433
killall	Sends signals to all processes that match a command name rather than a PID (as used with *kill*)	killall vim
ldd	List all the libraries that a program requires	ldd /bin/ls
nice	Sets the nice level of a Linux process as it is being started	nice -5 analyze
ps	Displays the processes currently running on the system (See Tables 6-1, 6-2, and 6-3 for a list of command options)	ps aux
renice	Changes the nice level of a Linux process that is already running	renice +10 1776
top	Shows the most CPU-intensive processes running on Linux at a given moment, along with related information for those processes (See Table 6-4 for keyboard controls within *top*)	top
tty	Returns the name of the terminal device in which you are currently working	tty
vmstat	Displays detailed usage information for the swap file system (plus basic information about RAM usage)	vmstat

6

KEY TERMS

/proc file system — A collection of information about the Linux kernel and other system resources that you access as a file system.

at **job** — A command or script that you have scheduled to be executed at a specific time in the future using the *at* command.

buffer — Memory used by an application for data storage.

child process — A process that was started by another process. All processes are child processes of the init process, some further removed than others.

cron **job** — A command or script that you have scheduled to be executed repeatedly at specific times in the future.

daemon — A background process that typically doesn't have any screen output but waits for certain system activity and then acts on it.

dynamically linked applications — Linux programs that do not include within themselves the library functions that they require to operate. The libraries must be installed (as shared libraries) on the Linux system on which the applications are executed.

fork — Method used to create a new process in Linux by starting it from within an existing process.

GNOME System Monitor — A graphical utility for the GNOME desktop that is used to monitor and control processes running on Linux.

jobs — Within a shell, processes that have been started as child processes of that shell.

KDE System Guard — A graphical utility that displays a process list and lets you interact with that list to rearrange or kill processes.

library — A file containing prewritten programming functionality that any program can use.

nice level — The priority level assigned to a Linux process, which determines how much CPU time the process is allocated compared to other processes.

page — A block of 4 KB of memory. A page is the unit of memory in which the Linux kernel moves data to and from swap space.

priority — In the context of process management, a value assigned to a process running on Linux that determines how much CPU time is granted to the process. Also called the nice level.

process — A program that has been started via the Linux kernel and about which data is maintained by the kernel for purposes of controlling that program and allocated system resources (especially CPU time and system memory).

process ID (PID) — A number from 1 to about 65,000, assigned to each process by the Linux kernel when that process is first started. The PID is used in many utilities to define which process can be affected by the utility.

shared library — A single copy of a function library that has been loaded into memory for use by multiple dynamically linked applications.

signal — A message (one of a fixed set defined by the Linux kernel) that can be sent to any process and responded to according to how that program is written.

statically linked applications — Linux programs that include library functions in the program itself so that they are not dependent on the libraries loaded on the Linux system.

swap out — The act by the Linux kernel of copying data occupying a portion of RAM to the swap space so that the RAM can be used by another application for a time.

swap space — Storage space—typically on a hard disk—that the Linux kernel uses as extra memory when RAM is insufficient or a process is inactive. Also called virtual memory.

time slice — An allocation of CPU time assigned to a process by the Linux kernel. Used to implement multitasking.

thrashing — Excessive movement of processes between RAM and swap space, resulting in reduced system performance and excessive wear on the hard disk.

virtual console — A separate login screen that you access by pressing a combination of keys on your keyboard. It allows you to start multiple text-based login sessions on the same computer.

virtual memory — *See* swap space.

REVIEW QUESTIONS

1. The command *ps -A xo comm* displays the following information:

   a. The command is invalid; it displays an error message.

   b. All processes started by the user who executes the *ps* command, with a standard set of fields pertaining to that user

   c. All processes running on the system; a revised nice value is requested for each one that matches the string *comm*.

   d. All processes running on the system, including those with no controlling terminal, with the command-line field displayed for each one

2. The _____ field in the *ps* command output defines how much cumulative CPU time a process has used since it was started.

   a. TIME

   b. %CPU

   c. RSS

   d. START

3. The CMDLINE field of the *ps* command output displays:

   a. The command used to start the *ps* command (including all *ps* command options applied to the current output)

   b. The command line used to start the process shown on each line

   c. The last signal sent to control the process on each line

   d. The equivalent output from the *vmstat* command

4. Which of the following commands is invalid if run by a regular user?

   a. *renice -10 1035*

   b. *renice 10 1035*

   c. *vmstat 5*

   d. *renice 5 1035*

5. Which of these programs does not allow you to change the nice level of a running process?

   a. GNOME System Monitor

   b. *free*

   c. KDE System Guard

   d. *top*

6

6. To update the process data displayed by the *top* command, you press which key?

   a. r

   b. spacebar

   c. u

   d. n

7. Dynamically linked applications are preferred for their better memory usage unless:

   a. Statically linked applications are also available.

   b. Multiple users need to run the same application at the same time.

   c. The necessary libraries to run the application are not installed on the Linux system.

   d. The *free* command indicates that only virtual memory is available.

8. Thrashing occurs when:

   a. An excessive amount of information is moved to and from the swap partition in a short time.

   b. The *top* and *ps* commands both try to access process information at the same time.

   c. Physical and virtual memory are deadlocked over where program data should be stored.

   d. Multiple bottlenecks limit the speed of a Linux system.

9. The command *vmstat 4* does which of the following?

   a. Lists information on the process with PID of 4 if it is located in virtual memory.

   b. Sets the default nice level for virtual memory processes to 4.

   c. Displays continuous updates of the virtual memory status on a new line every four seconds.

   d. Starts four instances of the virtual memory management module.

10. How can you switch between multiple virtual consoles in text and graphical environments?

11. Describe at least four fields of information provided by the command *ps auxf*.

12. By starting multiple jobs from one shell, you can:

   a. Conserve resources for each process you start.

   b. Prevent the swap space from thrashing.

   c. Manage those jobs with the *jobs*, *fg*, and *bg* commands.

   d. Kill any unneeded process quickly.

13. Briefly explain the difference in time specification formats for the *at* and *crontab* commands.

14. The background processes that manage commands submitted using *at* and *cron* are:

     a. /etc/cron.allow and /etc/cron.deny

     b. *crond* and bash

     c. *atd* and *crond*

     d. *init.d* and *xconfig*

15. When using the *at* command interactively to enter commands scheduled for future execution, you indicate that you have finished entering commands by pressing:

     a. Ctrl+d

     b. Ctrl+c

     c. Esc

     d. Ctrl+x

16. The *batch* command is used to schedule jobs so that:

     a. Jobs from *at* and *crontab* are not executed at the same time.

     b. Commands used in a DOS environment can be executed by Linux.

     c. The system will not be overloaded with scheduled tasks.

     d. Regular users can schedule tasks.

17. A simple method for root to schedule recurring system administration tasks is to:

     a. Use the *at* command in interactive mode.

     b. Add a script to a directory such as /etc/cron.daily or /etc/cron.weekly.

     c. Create a graphical program using Python with Tk extensions.

     d. Debug existing shell scripts on the system.

18. The output of a *cron* job is normally sent via _____ to the user who submitted the *cron* job or to the user defined by the _____ variable within the file containing the *cron* job.

     a. e-mail, MAILTO

     b. e-mail, USERLOG

     c. tty, MAILTO

     d. standard output, USERLOG

19. Name, in order from left to right, the fields of the *crontab* time specification, giving the range of valid numeric values for each one.

20. Output from a command executed as part of a *cron* job cannot be redirected to a file using standard redirection operators because the environment in which the *cron* job was created is unlikely to exist when the job is executed. True or False?

21. The _____ file can include a user name in order to deny that user access to the *crontab* command.

    a. /etc/cron.allow

    b. /etc/cron.deny

    c. /usr/local/bin/deny

    d. /etc/at.deny

22. Name the two separate commands that can be used instead of *at -l* and *at -d*.

23. All processes in Linux, except the init process (PID 1) are created:

    a. using standard command-line parameters or scripts

    b. when another process forks

    c. using *at*, *batch*, or *cron*, supported by *atd* and *crond*

    d. whether or not swap space is currently available, as shown by *vmstat*

24. A zombie process is one that:

    a. does not respond to the keyboard or to mouse controls

    b. is not a child process of the current working environment

    c. is not associated with any open terminal window

    d. is no longer in existence, though the Linux kernel still maintains information as if it were

25. Describe why you should try SIGTERM before using SIGKILL.

HANDS-ON PROJECTS

**HANDS-ON
PROJECTS**

Project 6-1

In this project, you explore how signals sent with the *kill* command interact with running processes. To complete this project you should have an installed Linux system with root access.

1. Log in as root and open a command-line window.

2. Switch to the third virtual console by pressing **Ctrl+Alt+F3** if you are working in a graphical environment or **Alt+F3** if you are working in text mode.

3. Log in to virtual console 3 using a regular user account.

4. View a man page in virtual console 3 by using this command:

    ```
    $ man mount
    ```

5. Switch back to where you logged in for Step 1 by pressing either **Alt+F1** or **Alt+F7**. Log in as root.

6. Review a structured list of processes running on Linux and locate the processes running on tty3 (look under the TTY column for tty3):

   # **ps axf | less**

7. For each, note the PID (on the far left) and the command name (on the far right). Also notice the tree structure in which they are shown.

8. Press **q** to exit the *less* command. Use the *kill* command with the appropriate PID to request that the *man* command running on the third virtual console close (the PID you use depends on what you observed in the previous step):

   # **kill -15 1114**

9. Switch to virtual console 3. What result do you see?

10. Start a new *man* command:

    $ **man mount**

11. Switch back to your original console.

12. Execute the same *ps* command and note the same information for tty3:

    # **ps axf | less**

13. Has the PID of the *man* command changed?

14. Within the output of the previous *ps* command, find the *login* command that appears to be the parent of the processes running on tty3 (it probably lists ? as its TTY). Note the PID of that *login* process.

15. Press **q** to exit the *less* command. Kill the login process on that terminal:

    # **kill -SIGTERM [PID]**

16. Switch to virtual console 3. What result do you see and what do you conclude?

17. Switch back to your original virtual console, and log out.

HANDS-ON PROJECTS

Project 6-2

In this project, you use the GNOME System Monitor to explore different ways of viewing process information. The tasks shown in this activity could also be done using the *ps* command on any Linux command line, but the graphical interface provides a good way to interact with a large amount of system information without requiring you to memorize numerous command options. To complete this project you need Red Hat Linux installed with the GNOME desktop.

1. Log in to Linux and start the GNOME desktop if necessary.

2. Start a program that you can monitor. On the GNOME main menu, choose **Accessories**, then **Calculator**.

3. Start the GNOME System Monitor by clicking **System Tools**, and then clicking **System Monitor** on the GNOME main menu. The main window of the System Monitor utility appears.

4. In the **View** list box above the list of processes, make sure that **My Processes** is selected, to list only processes with your user name as owner.

5. Open the Preferences dialog box by clicking **Preferences** on the Edit menu.

6. Scroll down the **Process Fields** list in the Preferences dialog box.

7. Check the **Nice** box so that the nice level of each process is shown. Click **Close** to close the Preferences dialog box.

8. The calculator that you started in Step 2 is called *gcalctool*. Locate that process in the list and right-click on it.

9. Click **Change Priority** in the pop-up menu that appears.

10. In the Change Priority dialog box, raise the nice level of that process to 20 with the slider bar and click **Change Priority**. You see the new nice value in the Nice field. The field displays 19 because internally, nice values are represented from –19 to +19.

11. Right-click on **gcalctool** again and click **Memory Maps**.

12. Review the list of libraries on which the calculator application relies. Without trying to understand everything in the dialog box, review the information to see what parts appear familiar.

13. Close the dialog box and exit the GNOME System Monitor. Close the Calculator application and log out.

HANDS-ON PROJECTS

Project 6-3

In this project, you track the status of the virtual memory (swap space) as you work with several applications. Normally you do not track virtual memory this carefully as you personally work with applications. Instead, you have the easier job of watching the system-monitoring tools while other users are working with programs. To complete this project you should have an installed Linux system. The Mozilla browser is used in the steps that follow, but you can substitute any large program on your system.

1. Log in to your Linux system and start the graphical system.

2. Open a command-line window.

3. Enter this *vmstat* command to display in interactive mode an updated status line once every two seconds:

   ```
   $ vmstat 2
   ```

4. Open the Mozilla Web browser by clicking the icon next to the GNOME main menu icon on the Panel, or by clicking **Internet**, then **Web Browser** on the GNOME main menu.

5. Watch the values in the *vmstat* output change as the browser program starts. Which fields do you see changing?

6. Open a second terminal emulator window and enter the following command to see the physical and virtual memory information, updated once every two seconds:

   ```
   $ free -s 2
   ```

7. Start another large program, such as a second copy of Mozilla, or one of the OpenOffice.org or KOffice applications (all are located on the GNOME main menu under the Office submenu).

8. Watch the values in the output of the *free* command change. Do the values in *vmstat* change as well? What additional information can you see in the *vmstat* output? If you opened a second copy of Mozilla or Netscape, how do the shared libraries used by the two copies of the same program affect the memory usage when you started a second copy? (Recall from Project 6-2 that you can use GNOME system monitor to view information about the shared libraries used by the Mozilla process.)

9. Click one of the command-line windows (where you are running *vmstat* or *free*) to activate the window. Then press **Ctrl+c** to end the output of the command displayed in that window. Enter the command **top** and review the output to see which processes are currently swapped out (stored on the swap partition). The letter W in the STAT column indicates that a process is swapped out.

10. As you read the output of these system administration tools, what can you conclude about how these tools affect system performance? What comments would you make about the value of using graphical system-monitoring tools such as those mentioned in this chapter?

11. Close all open windows and log out.

Project 6-4

In this project, you submit a job for future execution using the *at* command. This project uses shell scripting commands that are not discussed until Chapter 14, but they provide a good example of how *at* can be used to perform a task at a later time. To complete this project you must have Linux installed with a regular user account.

1. Log in to Linux using your regular user name and password.

2. If you are using a graphical environment, open a command-line window.

3. Enter the **at** command with a time designation as follows:

   ```
   $ at now + 15 minutes
   ```

4. At the at> prompt, enter this loop command:

   ```
   at> for i in /etc/*conf
   ```

5. Enter the **do** command at the next at> prompt.

6. Enter **wc –w $i** at the next at> prompt.

7. Enter **done** at the next at> prompt. Your screen should now look like this:

```
$ at now + 15 minutes
at> for i in /etc/*conf
at> do
at> wc -w $i
at> done
at>
```

8. Press **Ctrl+d** to finish entering the commands you want to automate. What message do you see? What time is specified? Is it a relative time or an absolute time based on the time specification that you entered?

9. Enter the **atq** command. What information do you see about the job you just entered? Note the job number of your *at* job.

10. If you wish, use *atrm* to remove the job from the *at* queue, using the job number given by the *atq* command. For example:

```
$ atrm 15
```

11. If you decided not to remove the *at* job you entered, what will happen at the time given by the *at* command (when you finished the entry with Ctrl+d)? Wait 15 minutes and then use a mail reader (such as mail, elm, pine, or Netscape) to view the output of your *at* job as an e-mail message.

12. Close all open windows and log out.

HANDS-ON PROJECTS

Project 6-5

In this project, you submit a job for future execution using *crontab*. To complete this project you must have Linux installed with a regular user account and root access. (If you don't have root access, you won't be able to complete all the steps.)

1. Log in to Linux using your regular user name and password.

2. If you are using a graphical environment, open a command-line window.

3. Start vi or another text editor and create a file in your home directory called du_job that contains this single line:

```
30 2 * * * du /home > /tmp/du_output
```

Save the file and close the text editor.

4. Describe the time specification that you entered in the du_job file.

5. What problem could occur with the command entered in the du_job file because you are working as a regular user?

6. Submit the file you created as a new *cron* job:

```
$ crontab du_job
```

7. Review the contents of the crontab file for your regular user account:

```
$ crontab -l
```

8. What do you see? How does it relate to the information you entered in the du_job file? Can you see an indication of the file name du_job and when it was submitted using *crontab*?

9. Enter **su** to change to the root account.

10. Enter the root password when requested.

11. Open a text editor to create a new file called /etc/cron.deny.

12. Enter a single line in the new cron.deny file that includes the regular user account name that you used to log in, in Step 1. For example, the file might include a single line like this:

```
jtaylor
```

13. Save the text you entered and exit the text editor.

14. Switch from the root account back to a regular user account:

```
# exit
```

15. Enter **crontab -r** to remove the crontab file for your regular user account. What happens? Why?

16. Enter **su** to change back to the root account, entering the root password when prompted.

17. Enter a command such as this one to erase the crontab file for the regular user account (substitute your own regular user account name):

```
# crontab -u jtaylor -r
```

18. Remove the cron.deny file so that in the future all user accounts have access to the *crontab* command (unless you prefer to restrict it for some reason on this Linux system):

```
# rm /etc/cron.deny
```

19. Enter **exit** to log out of the root account.

20. Close all open windows and log out.

CASE PROJECTS

Running Cron Jobs and Understanding Processes

The Starwood movie studio has asked for your help. The computer graphics specialists creating their next feature film want to automate some of their CPU-intensive graphics commands so they can schedule them to run during lunch or after hours. You set up the /etc/cron.allow file to permit this, but after a few days, it becomes obvious that your training session was not sufficient:

1. One of the *cron* jobs submitted by a user looks like this:

   ```
   * * * * 1-5 grep html 'ls -r /' > ~/Webpages
   ```

   Describe what this command does and explain why it is causing problems for every user on the system.

2. Rewrite the *cron* time specification to execute the command every morning at 3:34 a.m.

3. Play with the *ldd* command to see which shared libraries are used by some of the programs that you use. View the *ldd* man page to get started. Check the shared libraries for both some command-line utilities and some graphical programs.

4. At the command line, explore the contents of the /proc directory to see what information is provided for each process and how the information in different directories relates to what is provided by utilities like *ps* and *top*. Use the *cat* command to view the contents of files in subdirectories of /proc.

7

USING NETWORK CLIENTS

> **After reading this chapter and completing the exercises, you will be able to:**
>
> ♦ Log in to a Linux system over a network connection
> ♦ Use command-line tools for common network services such as FTP and the Web
> ♦ Perform simple network diagnostic checks

In the previous chapter you learned about managing processes on Linux using a variety of command-line and graphical utilities. You learned about different techniques for starting processes, how to view status information about processes that are currently running, and which utilities you can use to control and alter the status of processes. You also learned how to schedule the execution of processes for a later time, so that you don't have to be sitting at your computer in order to start a task at a certain time.

In this chapter you learn about basic network clients that you can use as a system administrator to access a system across a network connection. Several methods are presented, including those that are secure and recommended, and those that may be widely used but are highly unprotected. You also learn about popular network data services such as FTP and the Web that you can use to update your system or locate new software that you need. To help you effectively access remote connections and utilize network data services, you also learn about simple network diagnostic tools that can help you identify—and sometimes fix—networking problems.

REMOTE LOGIN

When you log in to Linux at a text-mode console or the graphical login prompt, the Linux kernel starts a shell or a graphical desktop that you use to communicate with the kernel and start other programs to do your work. Because networking is integrated into the kernel, you can easily log in across a network and perform virtually the same work as if you were seated in front of the Linux system.

When you access another computer using a program, such as a Web browser, you are communicating with a Web server on the other computer. That Web server program controls what you can do remotely—it permits you to download certain files (Web pages), but it does not permit you to run any program you choose on the remote computer.

Several other programs that run on Linux *will* permit you to do just this. A program running on a Linux system listens for connections over the network. This type of program is called a **server**. It serves up information to another program based on requests made by that other program. The program making the requests is called a **client**. Figure 7-1 illustrates the relationship between client and server.

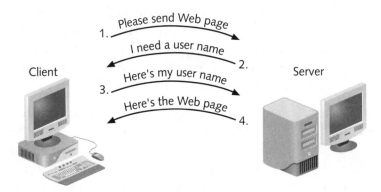

Figure 7-1   Client/server interaction to retrieve a Web page

When a client attempts to make such a connection to a server, the server must determine if the client is permitted to connect, and then it must determine what actions the client may perform based on such factors as what security information is provided by the client.

Linux supports several methods of client/server communication that let you execute commands on Linux over a network as if you were sitting in front of the Linux computer. The three principal methods are described in this section. *As you learn about them, remember the warnings noted here!*

- **Telnet** is the most basic remote login capability. It is widely supported and requires no special security configuration. It is not set up by default on Red Hat Linux, however, because it is completely unprotected. This means that all of the information communicated between two computers (the client and server), including your password when you log in, is visible to any user on the network who knows how to use simple networking tools (which are included with Linux). *You should only use Telnet when you trust every computer on your network with all the information on your system.*

- The **r-utilities** (r for "remote") were designed to let you access remote computers in order to run programs, transfer files, or perform other functions within a trusted network environment. This set of utilities is designed for convenience, not security. They can be very useful when you have user accounts on multiple systems in a single local network (a LAN). *You should only use r-utilities when you are working behind a strong firewall and trust everyone else on your network.*

- **Secure Shell (SSH)** is similar to Telnet, but the software package includes other programs similar to the r-utilities. The SSH program uses encryption so that everything transmitted over the network is unreadable to other users. *You should try to use SSH for all remote commands.* Even when you trust other users on the system, using SSH is a better choice, though it can require a little more configuration than Telnet or the r-utilities.

The Telnet Remote Login Utility

Telnet is a terminal emulation program. It allows you to log in to a remote computer as if you were sitting at that computer's keyboard. Once you are logged in, you can view any files that your user account permits you to view. You can also execute any command, including changing or deleting files, or restarting the system.

To use Telnet, you must have a Telnet client that requests a connection to a computer and a Telnet server that accepts and manages that connection. The Telnet client program is installed by default on Red Hat Linux and most other Linux systems. If you have access to a remote computer on which a Telnet server program is running, you can access it via the *telnet* command by entering the host name of the remote system:

```
$ telnet paris.mydomain.org
```

If a connection can be made—that is, if a Telnet server on that host accepts your request for a connection—then you are prompted to enter a user name and password. Once logged in, you see a command prompt as if you were sitting at the remote computer.

NOTE

When you start using Telnet or SSH, you understand better the purpose of the default command-line prompt in Linux. The host name is included so that you can tell which computer processes the commands that you enter.

After you have logged in, when you enter a command, that command is executed on the remote computer. For example, if you enter *ls*, you see a listing of your home directory on the remote computer, not on the computer where you are working. Telnet is not designed to transfer any information between computers except your keystrokes as you type, and the characters that are displayed on the screen.

Many companies that use text-based programs such as database management tools, retail sales software, or office management applications (such as a doctor's office) may run their software on Linux (as the server) but have Microsoft Windows clients access the program via Telnet. This allows office workers to use Windows programs *and* the Linux program.

If you want to try a Telnet session using Microsoft Windows as the client, start the text-mode Telnet program that is included with most versions of Windows. Other Telnet programs for Windows are also available for free download. A popular choice is the PuTTY program, available at *www.chiark.greenend.org.uk/~sgtatham/putty/download.html*. It supports Telnet as well as the *ssh* and *rsync* commands described later in this chapter.

To use a graphical Telnet program, you generally need to know the following information:

- The remote host to which you want to connect. For this field you can enter a host name such as *paris.mydomain.org* or an IP address such as 192.168.100.43.

- The port number to which you want to connect. By default, the Telnet port—23—is used.

- The type of terminal that you want the software to emulate. A standard choice is a **VT100** terminal. Hundreds of terminal models exist, but VT100 is the most widely supported.

- User name and password. You normally must enter a user name and password, which is sent to the remote host (the server) as part of your login. A graphical Telnet program typically lets you save this information, so you don't have to enter it each time you connect to the same remote host. Figure 7-2 shows a Telnet session being started in Windows. (Depending on your version of Windows, the program may differ slightly from that shown in the figure.)

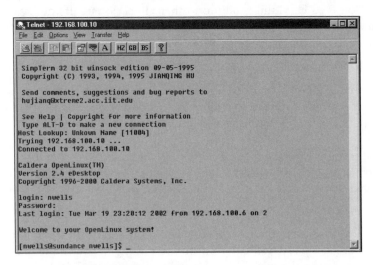

Figure 7-2   The Windows Telnet program with a session in progress

The Telnet server program, *telnetd*, is available for Linux, but is not running by default on Red Hat Linux because of the serious security hazards it presents. You can start this server program as described in Chapter 9, "Understanding System Initialization."

Using r-Utilities for Remote Execution

The r–utilities are not used much anymore, though they can be very useful if you are working with multiple computers in a trusted network. The r–utilities are most effective when you can set up a configuration file on multiple computers where you have a user account. You can then perform many functions across the network without even entering a password. This is convenient, but it is also why they are not used much.

Although the r–utilities assume that you have an account on a remote system that matches your user name on the local host, you also can specify a different login name to use on the remote host. A simple configuration file on the remote host lists the names of hosts and users who are allowed to run r–utilities using that user's account. The r–utilities and their functions are presented in Table 7–1.

Table 7-1 Common r-utilities

Utility name	Description
rwho	Lists the users that are logged in on all hosts attached to the local network that have the r-utilities networking features activated
ruptime	Lists all hosts attached to the local network (that are using r-utilities) with the uptime for each (how long that system has been running since the system was restarted)
rlogin	Logs in to a remote host; very similar to Telnet, but uses the r-utilities authentication methods described in this section
rsh	Executes a command on a remote computer without logging in (a command is executed but you never see a login prompt from the remote computer)
rcp	Copies files between different computers (the local computer and a remote computer or between two remote computers)

NOTE

The r-utilities rely on Remote Procedure Call (RPC) networking, which is managed in Red Hat Linux by the *portmap* network service. This service is typically installed and running by default.

A few examples can illustrate how the r-utilities are used and how to configure them. For any of these examples to work on your network, the remote computer must be configured to permit r-utilities connections. On a Red Hat Linux system, you can do this by editing the file /etc/xinetd.d/rlogin or /etc/xinetd.d/rsh, locating the line "disable = yes" and changing it to read "disable = no". (If you edit this file, you must restart the *xinetd* program using the *service* command, as discussed in Chapter 9, before the changes take effect.) These changes permit the *in.rshd* and *in.rlogind* server programs to accept connections from an authorized client.

NOTE

On some Linux systems, the r-utilities are not set up; you may have to install additional software packages.

Suppose you have a user account named nwells on host stockholm and a user account named nicholas on host oslo. (You could use full domain names and access hosts on different network segments, but considering the security hazards of these utilities, it's best to stay close to home.) Assume that the following conditions are in place:

- r-utilities networking support (*rpc*) is enabled on both client and server.
- The r-utilities server programs (such as *in.rlogind*) are installed on the server as described above.
- The r-utilities client utilities (such as *rlogin*) are installed on the client.
- You have a valid user name and password for an account on the server.

Now whenever you are logged in to stockholm, you can enter the **rlogin** command with the *-l* option to specify the account name on oslo that you want to use. You are prompted for the password to that account. An initial exchange looks like this:

```
[nwells@stockholm nwells] $ rlogin -l nicholas oslo
password:
[nicholas@oslo nicholas] $
```

Once logged in to oslo, you can enter commands and otherwise act as if you were sitting in front of oslo. You enter the *exit* command to terminate the *rlogin* session.

While *rlogin* is great when you need to work with interactive programs on a remote host, you can use the **rsh** command to execute a program on a remote host without logging in, or **rcp** to copy files between two hosts.

You could continue to use the *-l* option and enter a password with every command, but these utilities offer convenience—and security risks. You can set up a configuration file on oslo that allows you to run *rsh* and *rcp* without ever entering a password. If you have root access to oslo, you can create a file called **/etc/hosts.equiv** that contains all the hosts and user names that are permitted to access this system (oslo) using r-utilities. As an individual user you can create a hidden file in your home directory called **.rhosts** containing a list of hosts and user names that you want to permit to access your account without a password. A sample .rhosts file on oslo might look like this:

```
stockholm nwells
helsinki wells
```

With this file in place, this next section reviews a couple of additional examples showing what you can do with the *rsh* and *rcp* commands. While logged in to stockholm, you can display a list of the processes running on oslo without ever "logging in" to oslo by using this command:

```
$ rsh oslo ps aux
```

The output from this command is displayed on stockholm's screen. If you want to store the results in a file on oslo, the command would include a redirection operator enclosed in single quotes so that your local shell doesn't interpret it and create the file on stockholm:

```
$ rsh oslo ps aux '>' processlist
```

The *rcp* command lets you copy files between any two computers that are running the r–utilities. You simply include the host name as part of the file specification. For example, while logged in to stockholm, you can copy a file named processlist from oslo to stockholm using this command:

```
$ rcp  oslo:processlist  /home/nwells/
```

You can also copy between two other computers (not the one you are sitting at). For example, while logged in at stockholm, you could copy a file from oslo to helsinki with this command (assuming the .rhosts files on both oslo and helsinki include the stockholm host name with nwells as the user name):

```
$ rcp  oslo:processlist  helsinki:/temp/processlist_backup
```

Secure Shell (SSH)

The simplest description of Secure Shell (SSH) is that it is an encrypted version of Telnet—it lets you access a remote host the same way Telnet does, but without the danger that everyone on the network can see what you are transmitting. Everything sent by SSH is encoded so that only the authorized recipient can read it. This simple explanation, however, hides the power of SSH: unlike Telnet, SSH can act as a complete networking toolkit.

For example, protocols such as FTP and remote sessions of the X Window System are completely unprotected. However, you can start an SSH session and tie an FTP or X session to it, so that all traffic for the FTP or X connection is transmitted using SSH—and is completely encrypted.

Like other Linux Internet services, **ssh** consists of a client utility (*ssh* or *slogin*) and a server program (*sshd*). In addition, the SSH package includes utilities such as *scp*, which acts like *rcp*, letting you copy files between any two computers on your network with full encryption. SSH is available as a commercial product—see *www.ssh.com*. Linux distributions rely on the free version of SSH, called **OpenSSH**—see *www.openssh.org*. OpenSSH is installed by default on many Linux systems, including Red Hat Linux.

SSH is just one part of secure network communications. Other tools such as IPsec and Cryptographic IP Encapsulation (CIPE) also play a role, though they are beyond the scope of this book.

TIP

The OpenSSH implementation of SSH is used on most Linux distributions. On Red Hat Linux it is installed by default as five separate software packages: openssh, openssh-clients, openssh-server, openssh-askpass, and openssh-askpass-gnome. The OpenSSH programs have lengthy man pages that describe both the technology of the programs and the options that each supports. In particular, the *ssh* and *sshd* man pages are useful.

OpenSSH was originally written for the OpenBSD operating system and is now available for many variants of UNIX, Linux, Windows, Macintosh, Java, PalmOS, and others. This means that you can communicate securely between any of these operating systems using SSH.

NOTE

SSH can authenticate a connection in several ways. (To **authenticate** is to prove to a computer that a person or program is in fact who it claims to be.) The least secure method, which is not discussed here, relies on the r-utilities files, such as /etc/hosts.equiv and ~/.rhosts. (You won't see these files unless you've configured the r-utilities.) The SSH documentation recommends against using the r-utilities method for the reasons just discussed. The second alternative is to rely on user passwords. While using passwords is much better than the *rhosts* method or an unencrypted Telnet session, it still doesn't provide public key authentication of the session. Public key encryption is the third and best way to use SSH. **Public key encryption** is a method of encrypting (encoding) information that can establish a secure connection without sending a key (think "password") over the network connection in a way that compromises the security of the connection.

To use SSH with password authentication, make certain that the *sshd* daemon is running on the system to which you want to connect. The *sshd* daemon is configured in the file /etc/ssh/sshd_config. The default configuration in Red Hat Linux should work fine to get you started. To check the status of the *sshd* server program, use the following command on the server while logged in as root:

```
# service sshd status
```

If the server is ready to accept client connections, you should be able to use the following command on the client to connect to *sshd* on the server:

```
$ ssh -l username server
```

The *-l* option indicates the user account ("l" is for "login name") on the server that you want to use to connect. Because the server doesn't know anything about the client at this point, you receive a warning that the server doesn't have a host key for the client. If you are not overly worried about sophisticated security attacks, this shouldn't concern you; you can enter the word "yes" to proceed. You are then prompted for the password of the user name you entered on the server you entered. At that point you are logged in to the remote system (the system running *sshd*).

To use public key encryption in OpenSSH, you must first set up cryptographic key pairs. A key pair includes a public key, which you distribute to others, and a private key, which is never revealed. By using your public and private keys, plus the public and private keys of another user account, the connection is established without ever sending either private key over the network. The *sshd* server stores a key pair in the directory /etc/ssh. For example, the file ssh_host_rsa_key.pub contains a public key. To create a key pair for your own user account, you must use the *ssh-keygen* program and specify a key type of either RSA or DSA using the *-t* option. (RSA and DSA are two types of encryption supported by *ssh*.) The default key length is 1024 bits, but you can alter that length with the *-b* option (many other options are supported as well—see the man page for *ssh-keygen*). A sample command to set up your own key pair looks like this:

```
$ ssh-keygen -t rsa -b 2048
```

After a few moments, the key pair is generated and you are prompted for the file in which the key pair should be saved. If you accept the default by pressing Enter, your private key is stored in ~/.ssh/id_rsa and your public key is stored in ~/.ssh/id_rsa.pub. You must also enter a passphrase (twice) to protect this key pair. You may choose to press Enter to leave the key pair unprotected by a passphrase; you can then create scripts that use *ssh* without pausing to request your passphrase. This decision depends on who else is using your computer and how you intend to use *ssh* to access your accounts on remote systems.

Once you have a key pair generated on one account, you should place the public key from that account in the authorized_keys file on each system where you want to log in using *ssh*. For example, suppose you have an account named alvarez on your principal computer (call it stockholm). You also have an account named sarah on a second computer (call it oslo) that you want to have secure access to using *ssh*. You could follow these two steps to facilitate that: While logged in on stockholm as alvarez, use *ssh-keygen* to generate a key pair; next, using any method you choose (*scp*, FTP, *rcp*, e-mail, or floppy disk), copy the file /home/alvarez/.ssh/id_rsa.pub on stockholm to the file /home/sarah/.ssh/authorized_keys on oslo. (This assumes that you used a key type of RSA; if you used DSA, the file name is id_dsa.pub.)

If you have only these two accounts, the authorized_keys file does not already exist, and you can copy the key file using a command such as this from stockholm:

```
$ scp -l sarah ~/.ssh/id_rsa.pub system2:~/.ssh/authorized_keys
```

To complete this command you enter your password for the sarah account on oslo. If you have multiple accounts and had already created an authorized_keys file, you can add another key to the end of the authorized_keys file using a command such as this one (recall that the >> operator appends data to the end of an existing file):

```
$ ssh -l sarah system2 cat ~/.ssh/id_rsa.pub >> system2:~/.ssh/
authorized_keys
```

Once you have the public key from one account listed as an authorized user on another account, you can use *ssh* to log in or *scp* to copy files without entering a password. The keys are exchanged in the background to verify your identity.

If you intend to use the SSH suite on a number of systems, review the **ssh-agent** command. This command provides useful tools for managing key pairs and authentication among multiple SSH-capable systems.

NOTE

DATA SERVICES

In Chapter 2, "Exploring the Desktop," you learned about some popular e-mail clients used in Linux. You have also used Web browsers such as Mozilla, which is an open source browser that is included with virtually every Linux distribution. In this section you learn about other tools for accessing the Web and e-mail, and about other network-based data services.

Accessing the Web

Lynx is a text-based browser that lets you access Web sites when you are working on a system that doesn't have a graphical interface. It is also very fast, partly because it doesn't try to download any flashing advertising banners. Lynx supports fill-in-forms but can choke on complex tables, Java, and many other advanced features. Lynx is not installed by default, but you can add it to your system by changing to root, inserting Fedora CD 1 and entering this command:

```
# rpm -Uvh /mnt/cdrom/Fedora/RPMS/lynx*
```

Lynx is a small program compared to the other Linux browsers covered in this section, and it can be run from any command-line window. Figure 7-3 shows a Lynx screen. Compared to graphical browsers, Lynx keyboard commands take more practice to use effectively, but again, using the program to navigate Web pages becomes very fast once you are comfortable with Lynx.

To start Lynx, enter *lynx* on any command line, followed by a Web page address. For example:

```
$ lynx www.yahoo.com
```

or

```
$ lynx http://www.yahoo.com
```

Use the up and down arrow keys to move between links on the Web page. When a link you want to jump to is selected, use the right arrow to go there (like clicking on it in a graphical browser). Use the left arrow key like the back arrow in a graphical browser. To move between screens of text without reference to links on the page, use Page Up and Page Down.

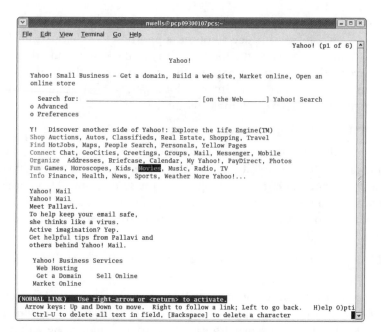

Figure 7-3   The Lynx text-based Web browser

Many other keys for different browser functions are displayed at the bottom of the Lynx screen. To exit Lynx you can use the q key (then confirm with y) or just press Ctrl+c.

You can also download pages automatically with Lynx, almost as if you were opening a local HTML-formatted text file. To do this, use the *-dump* option. This causes Lynx to act as a command-line utility, printing the HTML code from the page to STDOUT instead of displaying it as a formatted page. For example, the following command saves the indicated page in the file nasa_home_page.html:

```
$ lynx -dump http://www.nasa.gov/lb/home/index.html > nasa_home_
page.html
```

You can combine the *–dump* Lynx option with other commands such as *grep* to search the contents of Web pages or compare versions of a Web page to see if updates have been made.

Downloading Web Pages

If you need to access a lot of Web pages from the command line, you should also become familiar with the ***wget*** command. This command lets you download Web pages much like the *lynx -d* method, but *wget* is designed specifically for command-line downloading of Web pages rather than interactive viewing.

To download a Web page, use this basic format:

```
$ wget http://www.gnu.org/philosophy/philosophy.html
```

The real power of *wget* is shown by the options it supports. Suppose, for example, that you want to download a Web page but include all of the supporting files that permit the file to be displayed locally (without accessing the Internet). To do this, you can add the *-p* option. The *-k* option converts all links on the page so that they refer to the files that *wget* has downloaded to your system rather than to Internet locations. So after using this command, you can view the named HTML page completely offline:

```
$ wget -k -p http://www.gnu.org/philosophy/philosophy.html
```

If you need to download a large Web page, you can start *wget* in the background by ending with an ampersand (as you learned in Chapter 4, "Understanding Users and File Systems"). The program continues running even if you log out of the system (it still stores the files in your home directory). If your connection is slow or subject to interruption, you can include the *-t* option to indicate how many times *wget* should retry the connection to be certain it gets all parts of the Web page:

```
$ wget -t 40 -k -p http://www.gnu.org/philosophy/philosophy.
html  &
```

In some cases, you want to examine not only the Web page itself, but the information sent by the Web server, so that you can better understand what the server is doing. Multiple lines of information (called headers) are sent with each Web page. You can view these or save them to a file with the *-S* or *-s* option, respectively.

The most powerful feature of *wget* is its ability to download recursively. A **recursive** procedure is a procedure that can repeat itself indefinitely. In this context, a recursive download means that *wget* can download the Web page you indicate, plus all pages referred to on that page (all the linked pages), plus all the pages linked to from those pages, and so forth. You can limit the number of recursive levels using the *-r* option to turn on recursive downloads and the *-l* option to set the number of levels of recursion to use. For example, including the options *-r -l 3* downloads three levels of Web pages. Using the options listed below, you can let *wget* try to collect all the Web pages on a site. The *wget* utility is able to convert links to use them locally (on your system), and perform other adjustments to make the pages work correctly on your system.

This process of copying an entire Web site or FTP site is called **mirroring**. Mirroring is an important tool for many FTP sites—in order to lighten the load on an FTP server (these are discussed in the next section), a system administrator finds another trusted site to mirror the information. This permits users to access the same information from multiple locations, reducing the bandwidth requirements on each and providing better service for users of the site. Web sites are not typically mirrored for the same reason, but many times a user or administrator likes to mirror a Web site. There are several reasons this can be useful:

- To read the site's pages without having an active Internet connection
- To study how the entire site is organized in order to learn Web design techniques
- To analyze the information on the site using Linux text-processing tools

- To cache the information on a local server in order to reduce the network load when users at your location regularly download pages from a certain Web site

To mirror an entire Web site, you can use the following *wget* command:

```
$ wget -m -k -K -E http://www.gnu.org/ -o /tmp/gnu_site_log  &
```

The *-m* option sets mirroring, which turns on recursive downloading; the *-k* and *-K* options convert links for use on your local system; the *-E* option forces an .html ending on downloaded pages, which is useful when the server is providing pages using .asp or another format less commonly used by Linux; the *-o* option defines a log file where progress and any errors generated by *wget* are written. (Table 7-2 summarizes the basic *wget* options described in this section.)

Table 7-2 Basic *wget* Options

wget command-line option	Description
-p	Download all supporting files to permit local display of a Web page referred to on the *wget* command line
-k	Convert links in a downloaded Web page so that they refer to the downloaded supporting files (such as images)
-t 40	Retry the download the stated number of times if the download of the Web page (or supporting files) is interrupted for any reason (such as a poor Internet connection)
-S	View Web page header information as the page and other files are downloaded
-s	Save downloaded Web page header information to a file
-r	Use recursive downloads (download the named Web page and also all pages linked to by that page); used with the -l option
-l 3	Set the number of levels for recursive downloads; used with the -r option
-E	Force an .html ending on downloaded files so that they are processed correctly by a standard Linux Web browser
-m	Mirror a Web site using a recursive download of Web pages
-o logfile	Define a log file where information about the download is stored for later review

You can use the *cron* feature that you learned about in Chapter 6, "Managing Processes," to automatically update the mirror of a Web site or FTP site with a command such as the example just given. Some Web site administrators may not like the idea of your mirroring their site, though they are providing the site for public use. If you are concerned about this, you can add the *--random-wait* option to your *wget* command. This option causes *wget* to pause for a random amount of time between 0 and about 2 seconds between each page so that statistical analysis of a server's Web logs won't indicate that someone is using a program like *wget* to mirror the site.

Notice that the URLs given in the *wget* examples include the http:// protocol designator. You can also use the ftp:// designator to have *wget* download files from FTP sites, or even mirror an FTP site. The man page for *wget* includes numerous options specific to FTP sites.

When using *wget*, KGet, or similar programs, remember that downloading large numbers of files from the Web can quickly consume a lot of hard disk space. Also remember that you must observe copyright laws for the material you **CAUTION** download—just because you can access information does not mean you have permission to use the information in any way you choose. Read the legal notices on Web sites containing information that you want to repost or use in some way besides to read yourself.

If you want to download Web pages but don't have needs as complex as *wget* can support, consider the **KGet** graphical utility for downloading Web pages. This utility, part of the KDE desktop, lets you enter one or more URLs and have them downloaded to your system in the background while you do other work. This is very useful when you have a slow network connection—you can download all the files needed to efficiently view a Web site without waiting for each file to load as you are viewing it. Figure 7-4 shows the KGet interface. If you have installed this program on Red Hat Linux, you can start it by selecting Internet, then More Internet Applications, then KGet on the GNOME main menu.

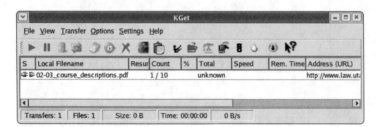

Figure 7-4 The KGet graphical Web page download manager

Although it is less useful than *wget* for most users, you can also use the **fetchmail** command-line utility to download e-mail messages from a POP or IMAP-based e-mail server. Once downloaded to your local system, you can use **NOTE** a text-based e-mail reader such as elm, pine, or mail, or else a graphical e-mail reader such as Evolution or Mozilla (see Chapter 2) to view and send e-mail messages.

Using rsync

If you regularly need to mirror large amounts of information between two or more computers, you should also learn how to use the *rsync* utility. This utility is not designed specifically for mirroring Web or FTP sites, though it could be used for that if you had sufficient access permissions on both systems. Instead, it is intended for situations where you have a collection of files (such as software development files or documentation) that you want to keep updated on two or more systems. The *rsync* program uses SSH to transport files between systems, but after the first time files are copied to a remote system, *rsync* checks the remote files to see what changes need to be updated.

For example, suppose you have a collection of hundreds of documentation files (something like the /usr/share/doc subdirectory in Red Hat Linux). You have copied that collection of files to another server where users access the documentation. But you continue to add files and edit documents on your system. When you use *rsync* to update the remote server, only the changes that you have made are sent to the remote system, rather than sending the entire collection each time you want to update it. This means you can update the collection of files regularly (for example, every morning at 2:15 a.m.), without wasting network bandwidth or computer time with files that are already at the remote location. Some setup is required to use *rsync*, and it supports hundreds of options, but as a simple example, consider this command, which updates the files on oslo (the system on which the *rsync* command is executed) with any changes that have been made to the original files stored on stockholm. Compression is used (the -*z* option) to reduce the amount of data sent over the network; recursion is used to update all files within the named directory:

```
# rsync -avz stockholm:docs/  /data/docs
```

Accessing FTP Servers

The **File Transfer Protocol (FTP)** is a standard method used to move files between computers on the Internet. Although you will often download files for your Linux systems using the Web, FTP servers are a very useful resource. In fact, Web pages often include download links that use FTP. For example, if a Web page includes a link such as this one, clicking on the link causes your Web browser to use FTP to download the file:

ftp://ftp.xmission.com/pub/linux/ppp_conf-v1.1.tar.gz

FTP servers can be used in two ways. First, most publicly visible FTP servers support anonymous access. That is, they are intended for members of the public to log in using a standard "guest" account and download (or sometimes upload) files. To use an FTP server in this way, you must log in using the user name *anonymous* or *ftp*. For your password, you enter your e-mail address. When you access such a site using your Web browser, the browser provides this login information automatically in the background, then displays information from the anonymous FTP site. For example, if you enter the URL *ftp://ftp.ibiblio.org/pub/Linux* in your Web browser, you see the listing that appears in Figure 7-5. You can click on a file to download it or a subdirectory to browse into that directory.

The first level of virtually all anonymous FTP servers includes a pub subdirectory, which is used to hold "public" files. Start your browsing by changing to this subdirectory.

TIP

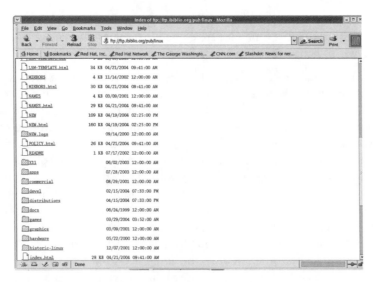

Figure 7-5 An FTP site viewed in a Web browser

A second method of accessing an FTP server is by using your user name and password on the server. The administrator of the FTP server must permit this type of connection, as it poses certain security risks. When you log in, you are placed in your home directory instead of in the "anonymous" user area. Using a Web browser, you can access an FTP server on which you have an account using a URL like this one (where nwells is the user account name on the FTP server):

ftp://nwells@ftp.xmission.com/pub

The Web browser starts the connection and prompts you for a password to pass on to the FTP server. You then see the contents of your home directory in the Web browser window.

Although Web browsers can function as clients to retrieve information from FTP servers, a graphical FTP client is usually a better choice if you have a number of files with which to work. When you browse an FTP site using a Web browser, the browser might disconnect from the FTP server after each link that you select (for example, when you enter a new subdirectory). This is an inefficient way to use FTP. Also, using most Web browsers, you can only download one file at a time.

Several graphical FTP clients are available. One impressive program is IglooFTP Pro, which you can download from *www.iglooftp.com* (click the Linux link to access the correct version). Another strong program is gFTP, which you can install by changing to root, inserting Fedora CD 2, and entering this command:

```
# rpm -Uvh /mnt/cdrom/Fedora/RPMS/gftp*
```

In Red Hat Linux, you can start the gFTP program by selecting Internet, then More Internet Applications, then gFTP on the GNOME main menu. In the gFTP window, you enter the host name of the computer you want to access (or an IP address if you don't have a host name). The port, user name, and password are used, so you can leave those fields blank unless you are connecting to a server on which you have a user name and password (rather than using anonymous FTP access).

To initiate a connection, click the icon with two computers pictured in the upper left of the window under the menu bar. The great advantage of using a graphical FTP client (and note that gFTP can actually access data using multiple protocols, including HTTP) is that you can see all the available files on your system and a remote system, easily change directories, and drag and drop files to manage downloads that involve large numbers of files. Figure 7-6 shows gFTP with the local file system on the left part of the window and a remote file system (an FTP site) on the right side. You can select one or more directories or files on the right side and drag them to the left side to download files. Press the Ctrl key while clicking on each item to select multiple items before dragging them. If you have permission to upload files (for example, if you have a regular user account on the FTP server), you can drag and drop files from the left side to the right side to upload them. Of course, you can also use the menu items to perform these same operations.

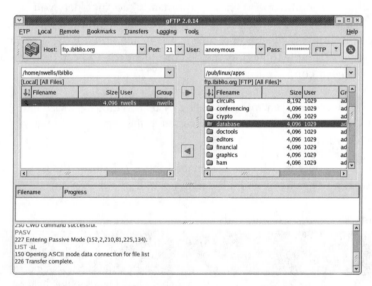

Figure 7-6 Using gFTP for easier FTP downloads

Although both Web browsers and graphical FTP clients are handy, you should also be familiar with the basic text-mode FTP client so that you can download files when a graphical interface is not available.

All the FTP clients described here—graphical, Web browsers, and text-mode programs—communicate with an FTP server without encrypting the user name and password. If you are using a regular user account to access files via FTP, this can pose a serious security threat. In this case, you should use *ssh* to connect to your FTP server.

The standard text-mode utility for FTP access is the *ftp* program. You normally start this program with the name of an FTP server that you want to access, entering the appropriate user name and password when prompted, for example:

```
$ ftp ftp.ibiblio.org
```

When you start the *ftp* program, the prompt changes to ftp>. At the ftp> prompt you can enter some commands similar to those used in a Linux shell. For example, you use *cd* to change to a different working directory, and *ls* to list files in a directory. If you are working with a regular user account on the FTP server (rather than relying on anonymous FTP access), you can also use commands such as *rm*, *rmdir*, *mkdir*, and *cp* to work with files stored on the FTP server.

The *ftp* program can transfer files in text mode or binary mode. You should always perform transfers in binary mode because text mode corrupts any program files that you download (such as new Linux software packages). To set *ftp* for binary mode, enter the *bin* command.

To download a file using *ftp*, use the *get* command; to upload a file (if you have permission to do so), use the *put* command. These commands do not let you use regular expressions—you must specify a single file. You can use the *mget* and *mput* commands to download or upload multiple files with one command. When you use these commands, *ftp* prompts you to confirm each file to be downloaded or uploaded. You can turn this behavior off or on using the *prompt* command.

To exit the *ftp* program, you enter the *bye* command. Table 7-3 shows the most commonly used commands within the text-mode FTP client, *ftp*.

Table 7-3   Commonly Used *ftp* Commands

Command within the *ftp* program	Description
bin	Turn on binary mode. This mode may be set by default but should be used for all downloads and uploads. The alternative mode, ASCII, corrupts binary files (such as programs or images).
bye	Exit the *ftp* program.
cp	Copy a file from one location to another on the FTP server; normally requires regular user access to the FTP server (not just anonymous access).
get *filename*	Download a file (cannot be used with a regular expression).
ls	List files contained in the current directory on the FTP server.
mget *expression*	Download multiple files using a regular expression (such as *.tgz).

Table 7-3   Commonly Used *ftp* Commands (continued)

Command within the *ftp* program	Description
mkdir	Create a new directory on the FTP server; normally requires regular user access to the FTP server (not just anonymous access).
mput *expression*	Upload multiple files using a regular expression (such as *.html).
prompt	Turn on or off prompting for download or upload of individual files when using *mget* or *mput* commands.
put *filename*	Upload a file (cannot be used with a regular expression).
rm	Remove (delete) a file on the FTP server; normally requires regular user access to the FTP server (not just anonymous access).
rmdir	Remove a directory on the FTP server; normally requires regular user access to the FTP server (not just anonymous access).

Many Linux administrators prefer the **ncftp** program to the *ftp* program. The *ncftp* program has a cleaner user interface and can be easier to use. All of the commands just mentioned function in the same way, but *ncftp* also provides features such as tab completion of file names (like the bash shell), progress indicators for downloads, and restarting downloads when one is interrupted. You can experiment with both *ftp* and *ncftp* to see which you prefer.

The *ncftp* software package includes two other utilities, **ncftpget** and **ncftpput**, that are similar in function to the *wget* utility. Both are intended for noninteractive downloading and uploading in shell scripts or other automated situations. Of course, *wget* can also perform FTP downloads, but *ncftpget* is another tool that might provide just the features you need.

NETWORKING AND NETWORK DIAGNOSTIC TOOLS

As you work with networking tools such as those discussed in this chapter, you will occasionally have trouble accessing the network. By understanding some basics of networking and using a few standard utilities, you can often solve basic networking problems.

Introduction to Networking

The core of networking in Linux is the **Internet Protocol (IP)**. This protocol uses various types of networking hardware to send packets of information across a network. The networking hardware may be **Ethernet** (the most widely used type of networking hardware), or token ring, or a wireless method such as 802.11b.

Each computer that uses IP must have an address assigned to it. An **IP address** allows computers to locate each other on the network. Many techniques are used to move packets of information efficiently through networks to reach their correct destination. The general term for this process is **routing**. Routing is only necessary when you have multiple networks that need to communicate. On any network that is connected to other networks, at least one computer is designated as the gateway. A **gateway** or **router** is a computer that is attached to multiple networks (for example, it may have two Ethernet network cards), and through which a computer on one network can reach other networks.

An IP address is represented as a series of four numbers, each from 0 to 255. For example, one IP address is 198.60.70.5. An IP address also has a **network mask** associated with it. A network mask looks like an IP address in form, but serves a different function: the mask helps the system route packets correctly between multiple networks. A standard mask is 255.255.255.0.

Many different protocols use IP to communicate. The most widely known is the **Transmission Control Protocol (TCP)**. TCP provides a stable connection between two computers for such things as Web browsing or FTP file downloads. The expression "TCP/IP" refers to TCP using IP as a foundation for communication—the two protocols work together, each doing part of the work. Many other protocols also use IP as a foundation for network communication.

You don't normally refer to IP addresses, of course. Instead, you use domain names such as *www.course.com*. A domain name must be converted to an IP address before a utility can access the computer you're trying to reach. This conversion is done using a protocol called the **Domain Name System (DNS)**. A program such as a Web browser contacts a **DNS server**, provides a domain name and is informed of the corresponding IP address in return.

Because all IP addresses must be unique, you cannot simply pick an address and start using it. When you configure networking on your system, you must either enter an IP address provided by your system administrator or by your Internet service provider, or else you can specify that the system should automatically obtain an IP address. To automatically obtain an IP address—along with a network mask, the IP address of a gateway, the IP address of a DNS server, and even a host name if needed—a computer can use the **Dynamic Host Configuration Protocol (DHCP)** to request an IP address. If a **DHCP server** is located on the same network, it sees the request and provides an IP address and other information. The computer that receives the IP address can then communicate as a separate entity on the network.

Networking is such a core part of most users' experience with Linux that your system is probably already set up to access the Internet or at least other systems on a local network. You can enter the *ifconfig* command (for interface configuration) to view the active networking interfaces. Typically, you see two network interfaces on a Linux client. One is the local interface, abbreviated *lo*. This is an internal networking tool that is often called the loopback interface. It always has the IP address of 127.0.0.1. The second is the Ethernet interface, which is abbreviated as *eth0* (a second Ethernet card would be *eth1*). Sample output from the *ifconfig* command is shown here:

```
eth0      Link encap:Ethernet  HWaddr 00:01:02:76:FC:69
          inet addr:192.168.8.18 Bcast:192.168.8.255 Mask:255.
          255.255.0
          UP BROADCAST RUNNING MULTICAST  MTU:1500  Metric:1
```

```
          RX packets:6 errors:0 dropped:0 overruns:0 frame:0
          TX packets:40 errors:0 dropped:0 overruns:0 carrier:0
          collisions:0 txqueuelen:1000
          RX bytes:890 (890.0 b)  TX bytes:3376 (3.2 Kb)
          Interrupt:11 Base address:0x1080

lo        Link encap:Local Loopback
          inet addr:127.0.0.1  Mask:255.0.0.0
          UP LOOPBACK RUNNING  MTU:16436  Metric:1
          RX packets:3037 errors:0 dropped:0 overruns:0 frame:0
          TX packets:3037 errors:0 dropped:0 overruns:
          0 carrier:0
          collisions:0 txqueuelen:0
          RX bytes:2779522 (2.6 Mb)  TX bytes:2779522 (2.6 Mb)
```

In the output above, note the *eth0* and *lo* sections. The IP address assigned to each interface is labeled *inet addr* on the second line of the corresponding section. The *ifconfig* command used alone lists the active network interfaces. This utility is used with numerous parameters to set up the interfaces, though this is done behind the scenes when you start Linux. (Chapter 9 describes this process in some detail.)

You can also use graphical tools to set up or alter your network configuration. The prime tool in Red Hat Linux is redhat-config-network, which you can run by selecting System Settings, then Network on the GNOME main menu. Chapter 12, "Configuring Networks," discusses networking utilities and configuration in much greater detail, though you will also be exposed to the basics of this process in Chapter 8, "Installing Linux."

Using ping for System Testing

When your network connections do not appear to be working, the simplest tool for diagnosing the problem is *ping*. The **ping** utility sends a diagnostic data packet to the computer you specify. If the other computer can be reached across the network, you know that the network connectivity between the two systems is working.

 TIP
The word "ping" is used as a verb: "I'll ping the DNS server and see if it responds." System administrators also apply "ping" as a more general verb meaning to contact people: "Did you ping Jim to see if he's coming to lunch?"

To use *ping*, include the host name or address of the host that you want to contact. For example:

```
$ ping 198.60.22.20
```

The *ping* command sends a series of 64-byte packets to the host with the IP address 198.60.22.20. If the host is reachable via whatever routers are between you and it, the IP stack on that host responds with a message saying "I'm here," and your system prints a message on your screen to show that the remote host is "alive." Another packet is sent every second until you stop the *ping* program. The resulting output looks like this:

```
PING 198.60.22.20 from 64.24.90.213 : 56(84) bytes of data.
64 bytes from 198.60.22.20: icmp_seq=0 ttl=244 time=319.537 msec
64 bytes from 198.60.22.20: icmp_seq=1 ttl=244 time=299.984 msec
64 bytes from 198.60.22.20: icmp_seq=2 ttl=244 time=299.994 msec
64 bytes from 198.60.22.20: icmp_seq=3 ttl=244 time=300.008 msec
64 bytes from 198.60.22.20: icmp_seq=4 ttl=244 time=280.005 msec
64 bytes from 198.60.22.20: icmp_seq=5 ttl=244 time=280.006 msec
64 bytes from 198.60.22.20: icmp_seq=6 ttl=244 time=279.998 msec
--- 198.60.22.20 ping statistics ---
7 packets transmitted, 7 packets received, 0% packet loss
round-trip min/avg/max/mdev = 279.998/291.298/319.537/10.805 ms
```

When you press Ctrl+c to end the *ping* program, it calculates the statistics that are printed at the end of the listing. It's common to use a series of *ping* commands to test networking. By using these commands in the order given here, you can identify at what point a problem has occurred on your network.

NOTE   The *ping* command on a Windows system sends four echo packets and then stops. In Linux, *ping* continues until you press Ctrl+c.

- First, ping 127.0.0.1 to check that the internal networking stacks are functioning and that networking is enabled in the Linux kernel. If this does not work, networking has not been activated on your system.

- Next, ping your own IP address to check that your networking card is configured correctly. You can view the output of the *ifconfig* command to locate the assigned IP address of your Ethernet or other networking interface.

- Next, ping the IP address of another host on your local network segment to check that your Ethernet card and cable are functioning correctly. (You may have to ask a neighbor what his or her IP address is, or use the address of the gateway if you know it.)

- Next, ping the IP address of a host on another network close by to check that the default gateway or basic routing instructions are correctly configured. If this does not work, the problem is with your routing or gateway.

- Next, ping an IP address beyond your organization (such as a Web server on the Internet) to check that distant routers are able to work with those in your organization in getting traffic to and from the Internet or other distant networks.

- Finally, ping a host name (such as *www.cisco.com*). This demonstrates that your DNS server (or other name resolution system) is working correctly, as well as the other networking protocols mentioned.

You can also use *ping* with a host name:

```
$ ping ftp.xmission.com
```

A good practice when testing your network is to begin by pinging your own host name to see that it can be **resolved** (converted into an IP address). Then *ping* the host name for another host on your local network, then of a distant host or Internet site. If none of the host name pings works, but the *ping* command does respond when you use an IP address, then you know that your system is not able to convert domain names into IP addresses because it cannot reach a functioning DNS server.

The basic idea with these *ping* operations is to ping to hosts further and further away from your system. If something stops working, you know where the error occurred. For example, if you can ping other hosts within your local network segment but not on any other segments, you know that your packet cannot get outside the local segment.

CAUTION

A warning is in order regarding pinging Internet sites: Because several types of security attacks rely on the *ping* command, some systems are configured to completely ignore ping packets. This means that when you ping some servers on the Internet, you will see no response even though the network connection works fine!

One example of a ping-based security attack is the "flood ping," which sends many *ping* commands in rapid succession from multiple hosts, overwhelming the server that tries to respond to them. Another example is the "ping of death," in which a single *ping* command with a very large payload is sent to a server; the payload overflows the memory space allocated for *ping* packets and corrupts other parts of the server's memory.

To avoid wasted time because of systems that don't respond to *ping*, find a few Internet sites (universities are a good bet) that do respond, then use those sites for your occasional *ping* tests.

Notice now the parts of the *ping* output from the listing shown previously. They include:

- The number of bytes sent in the packet. You can change this using a parameter of *ping*, should you ever need to.

- The host name (if you included one) and IP address of the host you are pinging.

- A sequence number, starting with 0. The number counts up by 1 until you press Ctrl+c to end *ping*.

- The Time to Live (ttl) of the *ping* packet. This is the number of routers that the packet can pass through before being discarded. The default here—224—is quite high, indicating that you *really* want to reach the host.

- The time elapsed between sending the *ping* packet and having it returned. In this example you see a time of about 280 milliseconds (shown as msecs). On fast connections, you often see times below 100 milliseconds; try pinging within your local network and you'll often see times in the teens. Note that *ping* waits one second between each packet sent, even though the response comes back in much less time.

- The statistics shown after you press Ctrl+c include minimum, maximum, and average time to get a response, plus the number of packets for which no response was received (typically zero percent if you reached the host without problems).

The *ping* command has numerous command-line options that let you set such parameters as the number of packets to send before automatically stopping, the time to wait between each packet (the default is one second), the size of packet to send (the default is 64 bytes), and other specialized features that are useful for debugging routing problems. For example, the *-R* option lists all of the intervening routers that your *ping* packet passed through to reach the destination host. (This is similar to the *traceroute* command described next.)

Using traceroute to Examine Routing Patterns

When the information provided by *ping* is not enough to help you figure out a networking problem, *traceroute* is another utility you can try. The **traceroute** command carefully tracks each router (each hop) between you and a destination host. This lets you see exactly where the packets are going and how long each hop takes. Sample output from the command *traceroute 198.60.22.77* is shown here:

```
 1   192.168.100.5 (192.168.100.5)  2.922 ms   9.798 ms   19.928 ms
 2   wdc2-dial7.popsite.net (64.24.80.232)  219.817 ms   199.408 ms   199.944 ms
 3   wdc2-dial7.popsite.net (64.24.80.232)  199.930 ms   209.430 ms   199.942 ms
 4   wdc2-core1.popsite.net (64.24.80.225)  199.995 ms   199.461 ms   199.923 ms
 5   wdc1-core1-p1-0.starnetusa.net (64.24.80.1)  200.004 ms   199.437 ms   189.952 ms
 6   wdc3-core1-pos2-0.starnetusa.net (216.126.145.122)  199.987 ms   199.401 ms   199.952 ms
 7   jsy1-core1-a3-0-2.starnetusa.net (216.126.145.105)  220.021 ms   949.325 ms   900.048 ms
 8   chi1-core1-s4-0.starnetusa.net (216.126.145.113)  1619.974 ms   3579.417 ms  *
 9   * sjc1-core1-a3-0-2.starnetusa.net (216.126.146.18)  2045.692 ms   319.424 ms
10   pao1-core1-p6-0.starnetusa.net (216.126.145.97)  360.012 ms   319.415 ms   339.969 ms
11   xmission-paix.xmission.com (198.32.176.42)  289.961 ms   1049.435 ms   949.921 ms
12   xmission-paix.xmission.com (204.228.132.29)  819.957 ms   309.562 ms   309.941 ms
13   core-border.xmission.com (166.70.4.10)  309.973 ms   309.580 ms   309.887 ms
14   ftp.xmission.com (198.60.22.77)  309.989 ms   319.627 ms   309.934 ms
```

Each line is numbered. In this example, it took fourteen hops to get from our system to the server *ftp.xmission.com*. The IP address is shown for each router along the way, along with a host name for that machine if *traceroute* can find one. Three timing values are shown after the IP address for each router. *traceroute* sends three "probe packets" and shows the length of time that each took to respond. If an asterisk (*) appears in the listing, the router did not respond within the default time limit of five seconds. *traceroute* tries a maximum of 30 hops to reach a destination, though you can change that number using a command-line parameter.

traceroute lets you move step by step through the Internet to reach the host in which you are interested. Because not all systems follow standard practices, some lines of the *traceroute* output may contain nothing but three asterisks. In most cases, however, *traceroute* is a very useful tool for diagnosing problems such as the following:

- Where a packet stops. You try to reach a certain host, but because of bad routing information, it reaches a certain point on the Internet and doesn't go any further. The output of *traceroute* shows you the last router reached by the packet.

- Where a packet slows down. Your connectivity to a certain site seems unusually slow. *traceroute* indicates the time to receive a response from each router. The one that takes an inordinate amount of time to respond deserves special attention.

Other problems are possible, of course, but these are two common uses for *traceroute*. Command-line options in *traceroute* include setting the maximum number of routers to try and limiting the time to wait for each response.

A basic graphical interface for *traceroute* is provided in Red Hat Linux and Fedora by the My traceroute program. You can start this program by entering the command *xmtr*. After you provide the name of the host you want to reach, this program provides the same information as the command-line program, but in a graphical window. Figure 7-7 shows this utility.

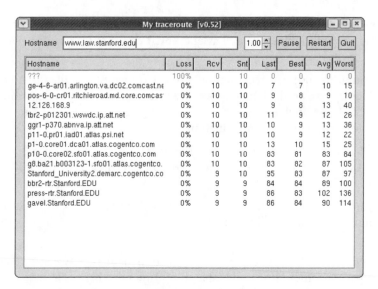

Figure 7-7   The My traceroute graphical utility

CHAPTER SUMMARY

☐ You can remotely access a Linux system using several different tools and protocols. When doing this, one system acts as a server—providing data, and another acts as a client—making requests for data.

☐ Three well-known methods of accessing Linux systems remotely are Telnet, the r-utilities, and the SSH suite of utilities. The first two are considered unprotected and highly vulnerable and should not be used except for convenience on networks that are completely trusted.

☐ Telnet provides a login prompt as if you were seated in front of the remote computer that you are accessing.

☐ The r-utilities let you access a remote system without even entering a password, if appropriate files are configured on the remote system. Commands within the r-utilities include *rsh* and *rlogin* for Telnet-like remote access, and *rcp* for copying files between two systems, similar to the *cp* command.

☐ The hosts.equiv configuration file lets the r-utilities function without using passwords. The r-utilities do require the RPC networking (via the *portmap* function), and support from various server programs.

☐ The Secure Shell protocol (SSH), implemented in the OpenSSH package, provides an encrypted replacement for Telnet, as well as encrypted communications for many other protocols.

☐ SSH can communicate using three methods: based on r-utilities files (which is not recommended), using passwords (which is better), or using public key encryption (which is best by far). SSH uses public key encryption to communicate between computer systems without exchanging secret information.

☐ Many command-line utilities are provided in Linux to download Web pages and access FTP sites. The Lynx browser is a text-mode Web browser that provides fast access to simple Web pages.

☐ The *wget* program is a powerful utility that can download an entire Web site for local browsing. A simpler program that provides basic functionality similar to *wget* is the KGet graphical utility.

☐ The *rsync* program is used to synchronize a collection of files between two or more computers. It supports compression and is able to update only changes in transferred files.

☐ FTP servers can be accessed using most Web browsers. Both anonymous and regular user accounts can be accessed in this way.

☐ Graphical FTP clients are more convenient than Web browsers when performing anything more than very basic downloads. gFTP and IglooFTP Pro are two examples of graphical FTP clients.

❑ The text-based *ftp* and *ncftp* programs let you interact with an FTP server at the command line, downloading or uploading files and otherwise managing files on the FTP server based on the permissions that your user account has been granted.

❑ Networking in Linux is based on the Internet Protocol (IP); it is most often used with the TCP protocol. To use IP, a computer must have an IP address and additional configuration information.

❑ IP addresses can be assigned explicitly by the person configuring a system, or they can be obtained dynamically using DHCP.

❑ Computers communicate across multiple networks by relying on routing information and sending data packets through routers or gateways. Ethernet is the most widely used type of networking hardware.

❑ Commonly used host names and domain names are converted to IP addresses by DNS servers. A client must request that a DNS server resolve a domain name before it can access the computer to which the name refers.

❑ The *ifconfig* utility displays network interfaces in Linux. Many graphical utilities are available to configure networking, including the redhat-config-network utility.

❑ The *ping* command sends a test packet to a network location to determine if that location is reachable over the network. Though this is a very useful network testing tool, some systems (including many Web servers) do not respond to the *ping* command.

❑ By pinging locations that are further and further away, you can locate the point at which network connectivity breaks down.

❑ The *traceroute* command provides additional information beyond *ping* by showing the computers (the routers) that a data packet traverses between your system and the system you want to reach. The information provided by *traceroute* helps troubleshoot problems related to slow connections or inability to connect to a remote host.

COMMAND SUMMARY

Command	Description	Example
fetchmail	Retrieves e-mail messages from an e-mail server using protocols such as POP and stores them locally for viewing by a text-mode or graphical e-mail reader	fetchmail -u brent mail.us.net
ftp	Starts the *ftp* text-mode utility for downloading and managing files on an FTP server (Table 7-3 lists commonly used commands with the *ftp* program)	ftp ftp.ibiblio.org
ifconfig	Displays currently configured network interfaces or configures new network interfaces	ifconfig

Command	Description	Example
kget	Starts the KGet graphical utility used to manage downloads of Web pages	kget &
lynx	Starts the Lynx text-mode Web browser	lynx www.yahoo.com
ncftp	A more advanced version of the *ftp* utility	ncftp ftp.ibiblio.org
ncftpget	A utility for noninteractive downloading from FTP sites.	ncftpget ftp://ftp.ncftp.com/pub/ncftp/ncftp.tar.Z
ncftpput	A utility for non-interactive uploading to FTP sites	ncftpput -R pikachu.nintendo.co.jp /incoming /tmp/stuff
ping	Sends data packets between systems for network testing	ping www.cisco.com
rcp	Allows a user to copy files between two hosts. Either or both of the hosts can be remote to the host on which *rcp* is executed	rcp oslo:processlist /home/nwells/
rlogin	Allows a user to log in to another host, much like the *telnet* command	rlogin oslo
rsh	Allows a user to execute a command on a remote host without logging in to that host	rsh oslo ps aux
rsync	Synchronizes a set of files that is stored on two or more systems and needs to be kept consistent as changes are made to the files	rsync -avz stockholm:docs/ /data/docs
ssh	Provides secure network connectivity through encryption with the SSH protocol; a more secure equivalent to *telnet*	ssh -l sarah system2
telnet	Allows a user to log in to a remote computer as if sitting at that computer's keyboard; not secure	telnet paris.mydomain.org
traceroute	Lists each router (each hop) that a packet passes through between a source host and a destination host	traceroute 198.60.22.77
wget	Downloads files from Web or FTP servers, storing them locally for later review (Table 7-2 contains a list of commonly used *wget* options)	wget -k -p http://www.gnu.org/philosophy/philosophy.html

KEY TERMS

.rhosts — A file stored within a user's home directory to determine who is allowed to access that user's account via r-utilities commands such as *rsh* and *rcp*. *See also* /etc/hosts.equiv.

/etc/hosts.equiv — A systemwide database of remote hosts and user names that are permitted to access the host using r-utilities. *See also* .rhosts.

authenticate — To prove to a computer that a person or program is in fact who it claims to be.

client — A program or computer that is requesting information or service from another program or computer. *See also* server.

DHCP server — A computer that responds to requests from hosts on a network, providing them with an IP address and other network configuration information.

DNS server — A server that responds to requests from clients needing a domain name converted to (resolved to) an IP address.

Domain Name System (DNS) — The protocol used to convert domain names such as *www.course.com* into IP addresses such as 198.60.22.5.

Dynamic Host Configuration Protocol (DHCP) — The protocol used by clients and DHCP servers to provide an IP address and other network configuration data to computers on a network. *See also* DHCP server.

Ethernet — The most widely used type of networking hardware.

File Transfer Protocol (FTP) — Protocol designed for transferring files between a server and one or more client computers.

gateway — A computer attached to two or more networks such that computers on one network can reach other networks by sending data packets to the gateway computer.

Internet Protocol (IP) — Protocol used for all network communication in Linux. Used in conjunction with other protocols such as TCP.

IP address — A numeric address such as 198.60.45.5 that is uniquely associated with one computer on the network.

KGet — Graphical utility used to manage downloads of Web pages.

Lynx — A text-mode Web browser.

mirroring — Making a copy of a Web site, FTP site, or other collection of files, typically across a network connection.

network mask — A numeric code that resembles an IP address. Used to correctly route data packets between different networks.

OpenSSH — The free version of SSH utilities included in most Linux distributions.

public key encryption — A method of encrypting information using a public and private key, such that the private key is never sent over the network.

recursive — To repeat a procedure on successive sets of data or levels.

resolve — To convert a domain name into an IP address using the DNS protocol.

router — A computer connected to two or more networks that transfers data packets between those networks to reach their correct destination. Also called a gateway.

routing — The process of determining where to send data packets on a network based on factors such as the sender's IP address and network mask.

r-utilities (for "remote utilities") — Programs that allow a user to access remote hosts to run programs, transfer files, or perform other functions within a trusted network.

Secure Shell (SSH) — A protocol that provides network connectivity equivalent to an encrypted version of Telnet, plus additional support to allow encryption of other protocols.

server — A computer or program that provides data or a service to another program or computer. *See also* client.

ssh-agent — A part of the SSH suite that helps manage key pairs and authentication among multiple SSH-capable systems.

Telnet — A terminal emulation program that allows a user to log in to a remote computer as if sitting at that computer's keyboard.

Transmission Control Protocol (TCP) — A protocol that works with the Internet Protocol (IP) to provide stable connections for data transfer services such as the Web or FTP.

VT100 — The most widely supported dumb terminal standard.

REVIEW QUESTIONS

1. Name three types of remote connectivity supported by Linux and explain why one is preferred over the other two.

2. One advantage of Telnet is that:
   a. It provides a secure connection between any two Internet hosts.
   b. It provides a graphical interface for easier use.
   c. It can be used on many different platforms, including Linux and Windows.
   d. Other protocols such as FTP can use Telnet for greater stability.

3. Name three utilities that are part of the r-utilities suite and explain what each does.

4. The *rcp* program is able to copy files between:
   a. two remote systems
   b. the local system and a remote system that has .rhosts configured
   c. any recursive directories
   d. any two computers that are configured to use the r-utilities programs

5. Name the three types of authentication that SSH can use to connect to a remote system. Which is preferred as the most secure?

6. Which utility is used to prepare a set of keys needed to use public key encryption within SSH?
   a. *sshd*
   b. *ssh-keygen*
   c. *ssh-agent*
   d. *slogin*

7. Why might you need to use the *-l* option with the *ssh* command?

8. If you use the *ssh* command without first creating and storing a key pair on the remote host:
   a. You are prompted for a password to aid authentication.
   b. The *sshd* program does not permit a connection.
   c. Only the unsecured r-utilities method of authentication can be used.
   d. The standard configuration of *sshd* automatically generates a key pair and sends it back to the client.

9. If you have installed and configured r-utilities, then including a host and user name in your .rhosts file allows a person using the *rcp* command on another host to:

    a. Copy files to or from your home directory without entering a password.

    b. Also use *rlogin* without entering a password.

    c. Execute the command if /etc/host.equiv also lists the remote host.

    d. View the output of the *rlogind* daemon.

10. SSH is commonly used in place of Telnet because:

    a. SSH provides a secure communications channel that is much more immune to security attacks.

    b. Telnet patents do not expire for several more years.

    c. SSH is strictly open source and Telnet is not.

    d. SSH protocols use a more robust encryption algorithm than that used by Telnet.

11. When using Telnet you might refer to VT100 because it is:

    a. a standard protocol designation used by Telnet

    b. the port used by default to connect to the Telnet server

    c. the most commonly used terminal emulation standard

    d. the speed at which terminal emulation connections are typically handled

12. Telnet is considered dangerous because:

    a. It provides access to networking stacks, to which only the root user should have access.

    b. It transmits data—including passwords—without encrypting them, so anyone on the network can see them by using special software.

    c. It causes an increased number of Ethernet collisions by ramping up network traffic with broadcast messages to the local network segment.

    d. It requires that a user provide a password to gain access to a remote system.

13. When using the *wget* command, you should include the *http://* designation to download a Web page so that:

    a. The program knows which protocol to use when accessing the server.

    b. The program can convert Web links for local access.

    c. The entire Web site is downloaded.

    d. *ncftp* is not used in the background.

14. Suppose you want to mirror a Web site to your local computer in order to study the information it contains. You intend to update the mirror once each month to view changes in the Web pages on the site. You are concerned that the Web site administrator will block access if he realizes you are mirroring the entire site instead of using a regular browser to access it. In order to reduce the chance that the *wget* program creates suspicion, you can:

    a. Use the *-k* option with *wget* so that information from the remote Web site is converted for use locally.

    b. Use *traceroute* to see how packets are reaching the Web server.

    c. Use the *--random-wait* option with *wget*.

    d. Use the *-m* option with *wget* so that mirroring is enabled.

15. The *rsync* program is best suited for:

    a. synchronizing collections of files such as software development files

    b. mirroring FTP sites

    c. mirroring Web sites

    d. downloading large collections of e-mails

16. On a publicly available anonymous FTP server, the first level subdirectory that you should go to when locating files to download is virtually always:

    a. /anonymous

    b. /ftp

    c. /bin

    d. /pub

17. A graphical FTP client can be more convenient than a text-mode FTP client such as *ncftp* because:

    a. The graphical program lets you perform standard file operations on a remote server when you are logged in to the FTP server using a regular user account.

    b. The graphical program lets you see lists of files locally and remotely and drag and drop multiple files between systems.

    c. *ncftp* doesn't support features such as tab completion of file names.

    d. The graphical programs are always installed by default and text-mode programs might not be available on some systems.

18. The *ncftp* package includes a utility that is similar in functionality to *wget*. This utility is called:

    a. *ncftpget*

    b. *ncftpput*

    c. *mget*

    d. *kget*

19. If an IP address is not assigned explicitly when networking is configured, one must be obtained automatically from a server on the network using_____ .

    a. DHCP

    b. a local gateway

    c. TCP

    d. DNS

20. The process of *resolving* a domain name:

    a. determines which router should be used to access the computer to which the domain name refers

    b. determines the IP address associated with that domain name by contacting a DNS server

    c. uses the *ifconfig* command to view the network interface through which a domain name was last accessed

    d. uses the *traceroute* command to see how the domain name was reached

21. *ping* is used to test networking connections by:

    a. trying to contact systems that are progressively further from your host to see if any networking problems occur

    b. flooding the network with traffic to see if it has sufficient bandwidth

    c. testing whether remote servers are configured to respond to ping packets

    d. noting the route that packets take when a system responds that it is active

22. *traceroute* is a useful troubleshooting tool because:

    a. All data sent by *traceroute* is fully encrypted, so it can be used safely on untrusted networks.

    b. It reports all routing information known by each system it contacts.

    c. It reports each router that a packet passes through to a remote computer, along with the time needed to reach that router.

    d. It uses TCP to report errors generated by the IP stack of intermittent routers that may be misconfigured and that slow down packets as they traverse large networks.

23. If you cannot ping a host on your local network using that system's IP address, you probably wouldn't bother checking:

    a. whether you could ping a host on the Internet

    b. the cable connections on your own computer

    c. whether you could ping your own system's IP address

    d. whether you could ping that system using its domain name or host name

24. Which of the following is *not* included in the output of the *traceroute* command?

    a. the time required to reach each router

    b. the domain name of each router used to reach the destination

7

   c. the IP address of each router used to reach the destination

   d. the size of the test packet sent by *traceroute*

25. A DHCP server can provide what information to a host on the network in response to a DHCP client request?

   a. only an IP address

   b. an IP address, a network mask, a gateway address, a DNS server address, and a host name, among other things

   c. an IP address and a DNS server address

   d. only the network mask and a gateway address

HANDS-ON PROJECTS

HANDS-ON PROJECTS

Project 7-1

In this project, you configure a key pair and use the *ssh* command. You should work as partners with another student or colleague. The two systems mentioned in the steps are your system (you are user1 in the commands that follow) and your partner's system (he or she is user2—substitute appropriate user names where user1 and user2 appear in the steps). To complete this project, you should have two Linux systems with OpenSSH packages installed. (These are installed by default on Red Hat Linux.)

1. Log in as a regular user on the first system, referred to as system1 in the commands that follow. If necessary, open a command-line window.

2. Generate a key pair for your regular user account:

```
$ ssh-keygen -t rsa -b 2048
```

Press **Enter** to accept the default file name for the key, then press **Enter** twice when prompted for a passphrase.

3. Copy the public key you just generated to the list of authorized keys for the other user you are working with.

```
$ scp ~/.ssh/id_rsa.pub user2@system2:/home/user2/.ssh/
authorized_keys
```

You must enter the password for user2 to complete this command. If necessary, type **yes** when asked if you want to continue.

4. If user2 already has keys listed in the authorized_keys file, this command overwrites them by creating a new authorized_keys file. To prevent that from happening, copy the keys to a separate file on system2 (for example, you could save them in a file called saved_key). Then append that file to the authorized_keys file using this command on system2:

```
$ cat saved_key >> /home/user2/.ssh/authorized_keys
```

5. Now try to log in to system2 from system1 using the *ssh* command.

   ```
   $ ssh system2
   ```

   Why doesn't this work as expected?

6. Try this command to log in:

   ```
   $ ssh -l user2 system2
   ```

7. Assuming that you don't always want to enter the login name on the remote system (or that you work with several systems and can't keep track of multiple user names), review the man page for *ssh* to determine how you can set up the ~/.ssh/config file so that you don't have to include the *-l user2* parameter when executing *ssh*. What line would you use in the config file?

8. Close all windows and log out.

HANDS-ON PROJECTS

Project 7-2

For this project, you need a running Linux system with root access and Internet access. Beginning with Step 3, think about what the successful completion of each step indicates about your network. To complete the last few steps (as indicated) you need to have your instructor's permission, as these steps may create a heavy load on your network.

1. Log in to Linux using a regular user account.

2. If you are working in a graphical desktop, open a command-line window. Use the **su –** command to change to root access. (If you forget the hyphen, you will not have a complete root environment and will not be able to access the needed commands.)

3. Run the **ifconfig** command to view your networking devices. Check that you have both **lo** and **eth0** devices configured. This indicates that you have networking activated and a working Ethernet card. On some systems, a different type of networking device may be shown, such as *tr0* for a token ring card.

4. Use **ping 127.0.0.1** to ping your loopback device. This indicates that networking is correctly configured. If *ifconfig* shows the *lo* interface, this step is virtually certain to succeed. Press **Ctrl+c** to exit the *ping* command.

5. Ping your own IP address, which you saw in the output of the *ifconfig* command in Step 3 (look at the eth0 interface). This indicates that your Ethernet card has a valid IP address.

6. If you are working in a classroom or computer lab, ask your neighbor for his or her IP address, then ping their host. This indicates that the cabling between systems is intact and that nothing is interfering with packets leaving your computer.

7. Using the **–f** option, for flood, ping your neighbor again. This option sends pings as fast as possible. Each period that is printed on your screen after you execute this command indicates one dropped packet (because the host being pinged cannot

respond quickly enough). This gives a rough indication of your network speed, but also indicates how someone with a fast network connection could cause trouble by using ping.

8. Have the neighbor you are pinging try to complete a networking task such as opening a browser window and downloading a Web page from the Internet. The flood ping places a heavy load on the network and should be used with caution. This is why some system administrators block pings.

9. Close all windows and log out.

**HANDS-ON
PROJECTS**

Project 7-3

To complete this project, you need a functioning Linux system with the Lynx browser installed (on some systems it is not installed by default). You should also have Internet access and permission to write files on the local system. You do not need root access.

1. Log in to Linux and open a command-line window.

2. Lynx has several dozen command-line options controlling its functions. Start the Lynx browser with the *-dump* option to dump the referenced Web page to STDOUT. Include a redirection operator to store the Web page to a file. Here is an example, but you can choose any URL you wish:

   ```
   lynx -dump http://www.gnu.org/philosophy/philosophy.html >  ~/
   gnu_philosophy.html
   ```

3. Use *-dump* again, but instead of storing the results to a file, pipe them through another Linux command. For example, search for a specific word with *grep*. Here is one example that searches the home page of the FreshMeat Open Source developer site for the word "wget." If an update to the *wget* package is listed on the FreshMeat home page, a line of text is printed on your screen; otherwise, nothing appears:

   ```
   lynx -dump http://www.freshmeat.net | grep wget
   ```

4. Start Lynx again with the following URL:

   ```
   lynx www.yahoo.com
   ```

5. Use **Page Up** and **Page Down** to look through the document.

6. Press the / (forward slash) key to initiate a search. Type the word **movies**.

7. Press **Enter** or the **Right Arrow** key to jump to the selected Movies link on this Web page. (If you see a question asking whether a cookie from the selected Web site can be stored on your system, select Yes.)

8. After scanning the page, press the **Left Arrow** to move back to the previous page (like the Back button in a graphical browser).

9. Press **Ctrl+c** to exit Lynx.

10. Use *wget* to download part of the Free Software Foundation Web site to your local system. Depending on the speed of your network connection, you may want to reduce the recursion level option (*-l*) from 3 to 2.

```
wget -p -k -r -l 3 http://www.gnu.org/ -o gnu_log &
```

11. Use a graphical Web browser to access the Web pages you have downloaded using **wget**.

12. Close all windows and log out.

CASE PROJECTS

7

CASE PROJECTS

Working with Network Clients and Connections

You are researching a project to provide space science information for schools in your area. Someone has suggested that you copy the NASA Web site to one of the school district's local servers. Students often access the NASA site, but it is very busy and sometimes slow.

1. Briefly explore the site *www.nasa.gov*. What concerns would you have about mirroring that site? How might you overcome some of those concerns given the goals stated for mirroring the site?

2. One of the largest FTP sites is *ftp.ibiblio.org*. The school would also like to mirror this site for the convenience of users. How do your concerns about doing this compare to your concerns in Question 1?

3. Would you use *rsync*, *wget*, or another tool to mirror part of the *ibiblio.org* FTP site? Look on sites such as *freshmeat.net* and *sourceforge.net* to locate other possible tools to help you maintain a large FTP site mirror.

4. As you work with FTP in your organization, you are concerned that all the information transmitted using FTP is unprotected—someone with basic networking knowledge can see all the data as it traverses the network. You decide to use *ssh* to encrypt this FTP data. Review the man page of *ssh* and *sshd*, as well as documentation provided on *www.openssh.org*, to see how you can use *ssh* to create a secure communications channel for the *ncftp* program.

INSTALLING LINUX

After reading this chapter and completing the exercises, you will be able to:

♦ Learn about the hardware components of your computer system

♦ Configure hard disk space to hold a new Linux installation

♦ Install Linux

♦ Automate installation of multiple systems

In the previous chapter you learned about basic network clients that you can use as a system administrator to access a system across a network connection. Several methods were presented, including Telnet, r-utilities, and the Secure Shell (SSH). You also learned about command-line and graphical utilities for accessing network data services such as FTP and the Web; these tools permit automated downloading of Web information as well as downloading numerous Web or FTP sites simultaneously. To help you effectively access remote connections and utilize network data services, you also learned basic information about networking and saw the *ping* and *traceroute* network diagnostic utilities.

In this chapter you learn how to prepare for and then install a new Linux operating system. To this point, you have been working on a system that another person installed. You now have enough background to understand the issues surrounding a new Linux installation. This chapter discusses those issues—including hardware compatibility, preparing your hard disk, and creating dual-boot systems—then it walks you through an actual installation of Red Hat Software's Fedora Linux (the product included with this book). After you install the new system, you learn about postinstallation configuration issues. Finally, you will learn about utilities that let you perform similar installations on multiple systems, or perform installations without needing to enter any information during the installation.

REVIEWING YOUR COMPUTER'S HARDWARE

Most of the computer systems that you have used or purchased yourself probably had an operating system already installed. You didn't have to think about how the operating system ended up on the computer's hard disk or how it was configured to use components such as the mouse, the video display capabilities, and the keyboard.

Although you can purchase computers with Linux preinstalled, you can learn a great deal about your computer system and about how Linux operates by installing the operating system yourself.

Before you install Linux, you must plan your installation to make effective use of your hardware and prevent problems from occurring in the midst of the installation. To plan your installation, you must gather information about your computer hardware so that you can answer questions that arise during the installation process. You also must determine the best way to organize Linux on your computer—you will learn later in this chapter about completing both of these tasks.

Although the information in this chapter is useful for installing Linux on a single computer, it is even more important to understand installation planning issues when you install Linux on multiple computers, or on a large server with multiple hard disks and advanced hardware components.

You will soon discover that Linux is quite easy to install, especially on newer computers, about which Linux can automatically determine much of the needed information about your system. But the more you know about how the installation process functions, the better you can deal with problems that arise, and the more flexibility you will have when complex installation scenarios present themselves.

Understanding Computer Hardware

As you have already seen with regard to hard disks, Linux treats your computer hardware as a collection of devices. Information is stored on a hard disk device, output is written to a video card device, input is read from a keyboard device, and so forth. Linux must be configured to use all of the devices on your computer system to function correctly. Sometimes the task of configuring your hardware is a challenge, although normally you don't need to do much at all.

NOTE

Linux can be used on many types of computers, including those that use different types of microprocessors (CPUs), such as Alpha, SPARC, PowerPC, and Xeon. The discussion in this chapter is devoted solely to computers using Pentium-level Intel and Intel-compatible microprocessors—in other words, standard PCs.

Different types of hardware devices communicate with the operating system in different ways. This means that you may need to gather an array of information about your computer system before you can install Linux. The section "Creating a System Inventory," later in this chapter, explains how to locate the information you need. Because Linux installation programs have become so automated, gathering hardware information for your computer may be more an exercise than a necessity, but the background material provided in this section will help you in many situations where hardware questions arise.

You should begin by learning a few common terms that describe your computer hardware. Space or capacity on a computer system is measured in bytes. A **byte** is enough space to store one character. Each byte is typically composed of eight bits. A **bit** stands for *b*inary d*i*git; it can hold a value of either one or zero. Eight bits together—a byte—represent a numeric code that corresponds to a character.

Because computers store many characters, space is commonly measured in **megabytes**, abbreviated as **MB**. One megabyte is 1,048,576 bytes, or enough space to store roughly 1 million characters. Another common term is **gigabyte**, abbreviated as **GB**. One gigabyte is 1024 MB, or roughly enough space to store 1 billion characters. For comparison, this chapter has about 120,000 characters in it. A 400-page novel can contain about 600,000 characters, or less than 1 MB.

Storing Information

The electronic memory of a computer is called **random access memory**, or **RAM**. Information in RAM is only available when the computer is turned on. When you turn the computer off, everything stored in RAM is lost. RAM is normally measured in MB, with most newer computers having from 128 MB to 512 MB of RAM. Computers used as servers may have 1–4 GB of RAM.

Another electronic component in a computer is called **read-only memory**, or **ROM**. ROM stores instructions controlling how the computer starts up and how the computer's devices are configured. Like RAM, ROM is stored on a computer chip, but information in ROM is not lost when the computer is turned off; it is permanent, or nonvolatile. One of the key things stored in ROM is the **Basic Input/Output System**, or **BIOS**, which provides instructions to the operating system for using the devices on the computer. The BIOS itself cannot be changed—it is permanent. But the computer also contains a special type of RAM that stores parameters to control parts of the computer configuration. You may hear this special storage referred to by its technical name, **CMOS RAM**. CMOS RAM depends on a tiny battery to maintain configuration data when the computer is turned off. You can change settings in the CMOS RAM using a utility that is part of the BIOS. Information stored in CMOS RAM by the BIOS utility might include the setting for the computer's clock, information about the structure of each disk drive, a start-up password, and many other details.

TIP

CMOS RAM is an acronym for Complementary Metal Oxide Silicon Random Access Memory. It is usually pronounced "sea-moss-ram." This term describes the technique used to manufacture these memory chips.

You can usually access a menu to view and reconfigure settings related to the BIOS by pressing a key or key sequence while the computer is starting. To find out which key, watch the screen when you turn your computer on. You should see a message such as "Press Del for Setup." You then have a few seconds during the system start-up to press the specified key, at which point the computer displays the BIOS configuration menus rather than starting the operating system. You rarely need to change your BIOS settings before installing Linux. (The exception is that you may need to change the order in which the BIOS tries to start from devices—CD-ROM, removable disk, and so on—based on how you decide to start the installation program.)

The hard disk is a magnetic storage space for data such as the operating system and data files that you create. You can think of magnetic storage as being like the stripe on the back of a credit card, except that a hard disk in a typical new computer holds billions of characters (40 GB to 250 GB of data). Hard disk storage is not permanent; you can make changes to information on the hard disk. But it is also nonvolatile—storage on the hard disk remains intact when the computer is turned off. When you turn on your computer, the instructions stored in ROM (the BIOS) load information from the hard disk into RAM for regular operations. When the computer is switched off, the information in RAM is discarded, but the data on the hard disk remains, ready to be reloaded the next time the computer is turned on. Table 8-1 highlights the differences between RAM, ROM (where the BIOS is stored), and the hard disk.

Table 8-1 Computer Storage Components

Component	Permanent (cannot be changed by a computer user)	Volatile (disappears when the power is turned off)
RAM	No	Yes
ROM	Yes	No
Hard disk space	No	No

A computer can have multiple hard disks. Each one is configured as a separate device. In an operating system such as Windows, two disk drives are called C: and D:. In Linux, the naming scheme is different. Hard disks that are attached to the computer using an IDE interface are identified as /dev/hda for the first hard disk, /dev/hdb for the second, /dev/hdc for the third, and /dev/hdd for the fourth.

Hard disks that use a SCSI interface use a similar pattern of names, but with the letters "sd" instead of "hd." For example, the first SCSI hard disk is /dev/sda. Hard disks that use a USB interface are also accessed via a SCSI device name in Linux.

You use these same device names to refer to a CD-ROM drive that is attached to the IDE or SCSI controller card on the system. For example, the CD-ROM drive is often the third IDE device (that is, the first device on the second IDE controller). Thus, the CD-ROM can be accessed by referring to /dev/hdc (though /dev/cdrom is the more commonly used term). The Linux installation program normally locates the CD-ROM containing installation files without any input from you.

When you see a reference to Windows in this chapter, the reference applies to all versions of Windows (95, 98, ME, NT, 2000, XP) unless otherwise noted.

TIP

Communicating with Devices

8

Many computer devices communicate with the microprocessor and software programs via interrupt requests. An **interrupt request**, or **IRQ**, is a numbered signal that a device sends to the operating system to request service. A PC has only 16 IRQs, numbered from 0 to 15. Newer devices that use the Plug and Play (PnP) standard automatically communicate the correct IRQ number to Linux; to configure some devices, especially older devices, you might have to determine which IRQ the device uses and specify it for Linux. Later in this chapter you will learn how to determine the IRQ used by a device. For newer devices, the BIOS and the device negotiate configuration information. Linux then learns about the device by querying the BIOS.

Once a device sends an IRQ signal to the processor, the device and the CPU can communicate data and status information between them. This is done using two methods: direct memory access and port-mapped input/output.

A **direct memory access (DMA) channel** allows a device to read and write directly to the computer's RAM, rather than asking the microprocessor to perform that action for the device. DMA allows a device such as a sound card to read and write information to memory much more quickly than if the microprocessor were involved in each data transaction.

Only a few devices, such as sound cards, use DMA. Most devices use **port-mapped input/output (port-mapped I/O)**—a technique that uses a separate range of memory addresses devoted to device access as a place for a device to send and receive data. Essentially, each device-specific address works like a post office box. The device places data in a specific location called an **I/O port**; software programs retrieve the data from that location using special CPU commands and also place new data there. The device can then retrieve the data placed by the software. For a device to use port-mapped I/O, it must have a port number assigned to it. Most devices can use several different ports, so you can configure your computer to avoid a conflict between two devices that try to use the same ports. A few devices, including sound cards, use both a DMA channel and an I/O port, but this is unusual.

As you learn about networking in Linux, you will see references to networking port numbers. These are much more commonly discussed than the I/O ports you are learning about here.

NOTE

To refer to the I/O port for a device, you use a special numbering system because of the way bytes store information. You may have heard of binary numbers, in which everything is represented by zeros and ones (recall that each bit stores a single binary digit: a zero or a one). Another numbering system used with computer hardware is called hexadecimal. **Hexadecimal** numbering is a base 16 counting system. It uses the letters *A* through *F* (usually capitalized) to count the numbers 10 through 15. Using hexadecimal (often called **hex**) numbers is strange at first. For now, remember that when you encounter strange numbers that contain letters, they are simply hexadecimal numbers. Be certain to write them down carefully and enter them in Linux using the format that you see them in, including all the letters.

Hexadecimal numbers are often written with a prefix of 0x to identify them as base 16 numbers. For example, you might see the number 0x220 used as an I/O port address. The 0x indicates that this is a hexadecimal number. You don't need to convert it to a normal (decimal, or base 10) number. Just use it in Linux as it is written.

The range of IRQ numbers from 0 to 15 can be represented by single hexadecimal digits. The possible IRQ numbers in hex are 0, 1, 2, 3, 4, 5, 6, 7, 8, 9, A, B, C, D, E, F.

TIP

Hard Disk Devices

The hard disk in a computer must communicate with the microprocessor using an electronic interface that controls how data is sent and received. Several interfaces are used for hard disks in PCs: IDE/ATA (integrated drive electronics/advanced technology attachment), SCSI (small computer systems interface), USB (Universal Serial Bus), Serial-ATA (a newer high-speed interface), and FireWire (also referred to as IEEE-1394). You may be familiar with other storage formats, such as CompactFlash and SecureDigital memory cards that can be used as hard disks. Although these devices store information like a hard disk, they must use a reader of some sort that communicates with the computer using one of the technologies just listed.

IDE is a low-cost, easy-to-manage interface used on virtually all new computers to connect hard disks and CD-ROMs to the CPU. Standard new PCs always include one IDE hard disk. An **IDE controller** is a device that handles communication between the hard disk and the microprocessor. The IDE controller is normally integrated into the system board rather than being a separate expansion card. To use an IDE controller card to connect to the CPU, the hard disk must be compatible with the IDE interface. Such hard disks are referred to as IDE hard disks. Each IDE controller can be connected to two IDE devices, such as hard disks and CD-ROM drives. Many computers come with two IDE controllers. Figure 8-1 shows how two IDE controllers, each with a separate cable, can be connected to hard disk and CD-ROM devices.

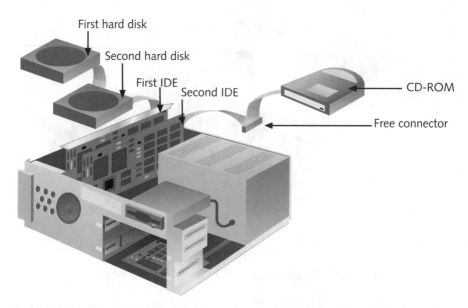

First hard disk

Second hard disk

First IDE

Second IDE

CD-ROM

Free connector

Figure 8-1   Hard disk and CD-ROM devices on multiple IDE interfaces

In reviewing hardware on newer computers, you will see references to EIDE, IDE-U, UltraIDE, and ATA-100. These terms all refer to IDE-compatible devices. The latest versions of IDE (such as UltraIDE) improve the speed and configuration flexibility of the IDE interface. All of these should be supported by Linux. When reviewing the specifications for an IDE hard disk, note that faster models have a rotational speed of 7200 rpm; slower models have a rotational speed of 5400 rpm but are less expensive.

The newer Serial-ATA standard is different from the enhanced IDE controllers that are standard in newer PCs, but Serial-ATA is also supported by Linux. Some add-on IDE controller cards, however, provide support for more than the standard four IDE devices. Some of these add-on controllers are not supported by Linux.

SCSI is a high-performance interface used to connect many types of devices to a computer. SCSI is designed for higher performance than IDE. A single SCSI controller can support up to 15 devices, and performance doesn't degrade as new devices are added, as it does on an IDE controller. But SCSI devices are much more expensive than IDE devices, and with the growing popularity of USB, SCSI is seen infrequently in desktop PCs. SCSI devices include hard disks, scanners, plotters, tape backup drives, and other devices. As with IDE, a SCSI controller card provides the connection between SCSI-compatible devices and the CPU of the computer. A single SCSI controller card can connect up to 15 devices, each linked by a cable, as illustrated in Figure 8-2.

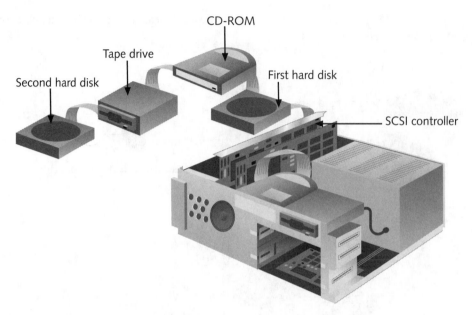

Figure 8-2 Multiple SCSI devices are linked together by cables

The **USB** interface is used for everything from scanners and digital cameras to hard disks and DVD drives. Support for USB is very good in recent versions of Linux, especially because the kernel can automatically detect a USB device after it is plugged in and make it immediately available. Although USB support is typically set up by default (as in the Fedora Linux you install later in this chapter), you can also refer to *www.linux-usb.org* to learn more about support for USB in Linux.

Supported Linux Hardware

Linux works with thousands of different hardware devices, from very old proprietary CD-ROM drives to the latest high-speed networking cards. But not all devices work with Linux. Although Linux is growing in popularity, not all device manufacturers provide software to support their products on Linux. Instead, they sometimes rely on the free software community to create that software, often based on technical information provided by the manufacturer. As a result, if no free software developer has taken an interest in supporting a hardware product that you need, that product might not be supported in Linux. In fact, the newer the hardware device, the less likely that Linux supports it, because Linux developers haven't had time to obtain specifications and create a device driver since the product was released. The exceptions are products from the relatively few companies that actively support the Linux platform.

NOTE

The software used to support a hardware device in Linux is usually called a driver, or **device driver**. You must have the appropriate driver in order to use any hardware device, including something as simple as a keyboard. Many device drivers are standardized and included by default in Linux; only a few devices require special efforts to locate driver software.

This overstates the problem, however, as nearly all hardware devices you might be interested in are supported by Linux. The list of hardware that Linux supports is much too long to include in this book. But before starting a Linux installation, it is a good idea to check on the Web site of a Linux vendor to see if the hardware that you want to include on your Linux system is supported.

One of the most comprehensive sites for exploring Linux hardware compatibility is located at *http://hardware.redhat.com*. Although this site is run by Red Hat Software, the information that you find here applies to all Linux distributions. This is true because hardware support is provided through the Linux kernel, and all versions of Linux rely on essentially the same kernel. A sample Web page showing information on this hardware compatibility site is shown in Figure 8-3.

8

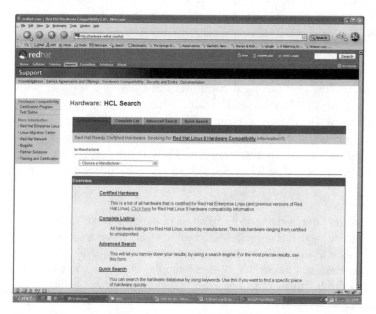

Figure 8-3   Linux hardware compatibility information on the Red Hat Software Web site

Understanding Networking

In Chapter 7, "Using Network Clients," you learned basic information about networking. This section provides more details on networking concepts. If your system administrator has set up a DHCP server on your network, however, configuring networking when you install Linux is easy: you just specify an option such as "Use DHCP" or "Use Dynamic Configuration."

If you do not have a DHCP server on your network and you plan on using Linux on a network, you need to define basic networking parameters when you install Linux. Even if you are using DHCP for your first installation, a basic knowledge of networking concepts is critical for your work as a Linux system administrator.

To communicate with each other effectively, computer systems use networking protocols. A **protocol** is an organized pattern of signals or words. Linux networking involves many different protocols, some of which you saw in Chapter 7. One protocol provides basic communication between network adapters (hardware in the computer that provides an interface between the computer and the network). Another lets Web browsers communicate with Web servers. Altogether, Linux supports dozens of networking protocols, each one designed for a different purpose. Some of the most important protocols are discussed in the following sections.

IP Networking

Recall that to configure networking, each computer must have a unique IP address, either assigned explicitly or from a DHCP server. IP addresses are used all over the world, but if any two users have identical IP addresses, their networks can malfunction. To avoid these problems, you must only use an IP address that has been assigned to the computer on which you install Linux. Typically, if you are not relying on DHCP, your instructor or your Internet service provider (ISP) assigns you an IP address from a range of addresses that they have been assigned.

NOTE

A newer version of IP called IPv6 (for version 6), or IPng (for Next Generation) is also available, though it is not widely used yet. IPv6 addresses are four times as large as regular IP addresses (which are sometimes called IPv4, for version 4). Having larger addresses means that IPv6 can support many more networked devices. IPv6 also has many other advanced features to improve the Internet. IPv6 is an advanced topic that is not discussed in this book, but Linux fully supports IPv6 networking. You can learn more about it by visiting *www.6bone. net*.

All of the IP addresses on a single network are related; for example, their first three numbers may be the same. Several special IP addresses are associated with setting up Linux networking so that packets can be passed around the network. These special IP addresses are:

- A network mask that tells the networking system in Linux how to identify IP numbers that are part of the local network, as opposed to IP numbers that are assigned to computers outside the local network.

- A **network address** that identifies the local network of which the computer is a part. This address is used to determine how data is routed to its intended destination.

- A **broadcast address** that identifies a special IP (Internet Protocol) address that sends a packet of data to all computers on the local network.

- A gateway address that identifies the computer that can send packets of data outside the local network, to the Internet, or to other networks in an organization.

Most Linux installation programs calculate default values of the above addresses if you enter an assigned IP address. If you rely on a DHCP server, it provides all of these values. Check the values on screen as you install Linux and be certain they match the information provided by your system administrator or instructor. If you received only an IP address, accept the default values that the installation program provides.

Domain Names and Host Names

A name assigned to an organization for use in identifying a collection of their computers is called a **domain name**. Some examples of domain names are *ibm.com*, *linux.org*, and *nasa.gov*. Domain names within a large organization may be longer than this. For example, within IBM, you may find domains called *marketing.ibm.com*, *sales.ibm.com*, and *research.ibm.com*. The last word of a domain name is always one of the standard top-level (most generalized) domain names. Table 8-2 shows a few of the top-level domains you are likely to see. Not all of the top-level domain names are listed, because each nation has a separate top-level domain name. Also, other top-level domain names are occasionally added, such as .info and .biz. You can learn more about current domain names by visiting *www.iana.net*.

Table 8-2 Top-level Domains

Name	Description
.com	Commercial/business entities
.org	Noncommercial organizations
.net	Organizations whose work relates to the Internet
.edu	Educational institutions, usually colleges and universities in the United States
.gov	U.S. government organizations
.mil	U.S. military organizations
.us	Top-level domain for networks in the United States; used mostly for local governments and schools
.de	Top-level domain of Germany (Deutschland)
.uk	Top-level domain of the United Kingdom

Domain Name System (DNS)

For the computers on your local network, you may decide to maintain a file that lists each host name and the corresponding IP address of that computer. This is convenient for small networks, but quickly becomes unmanageable as the network grows in size. Even on a small network, making a change in one host name means you must update the configuration file on every computer on the network.

A better approach for large networks and the Internet as a whole is the Domain Name System (DNS), a network service devoted to the task of mapping human-readable domain names and host names to the IP addresses of specific networks and computers. A DNS server is the computer that actually performs this conversion. The process works like this: When you enter the address *www.ibm.com* in a Web browser, the browser sends a network packet to a DNS server asking for the IP address of *www.ibm.com*. Once that address is returned by the DNS server, the Web browser can establish a connection to the IBM Web server using the IP address.

When you configure networking as you install Linux, you must either provide the IP address of a DNS server, or rely on DHCP to provide one for you. This allows your Linux system to use DNS to convert host names and domain names into IP addresses.

Creating a Shared System

You can install Linux on a system that already uses another operating system, such as Windows XP. This allows you to experiment with Linux and take advantage of its features while still using another operating system to support other needs, such as running applications that are not available for Linux. A system with more than one operating system installed is called a **dual-boot system** (even if it has more than two operating systems).

An alternative method of trying out Linux is to use a **live CD** version of Linux. This type of Linux distribution boots from a CD-ROM and uses system memory (RAM) as storage, but it never writes any information to your hard disk. When you shut down your computer and remove the Linux CD, you return to the operating system that is installed on your hard disk. Of course, you cannot experiment will all aspects of Linux using a live CD version. Important system administration tasks such as managing file systems and virtual memory are not possible when you are not using the hard disk. The best-known live CD version of Linux is Knoppix (*www.knoppix.com*).

If you decide to create a dual-boot system, a program called a **boot manager** lets you select an operating system each time you boot the computer. Two popular boot managers used by Linux distributions are **GRUB** and **LILO (Linux Loader)**. Installing a Linux boot manager is part of every Linux installation.

To create a dual-boot system, you must decide where on the computer's hard disks each operating system will reside. Two basic options are available:

- Store each operating system on a separate hard disk.

- Store multiple operating systems on a single hard disk.

Storing each operating system on a separate hard disk makes installation straightforward. During the installation, you indicate on which hard disk Linux should be installed. If you are using an external hard disk, including a USB or FireWire hard disk, this can be very convenient.

Storing multiple operating systems on a single hard disk is a much more complicated process. You must first decide how much space you need for each operating system. The first operating system installed on the computer (often a version of Microsoft Windows) probably takes up a lot of space already. You can determine the amount of hard disk space used on a Windows system as follows:

1. Double-click the My Computer icon on the Windows Desktop.

2. Right-click the icon for the hard disk. (This normally has a name, followed by (C:), to indicate that it is drive C:.) A context menu opens.

3. Click Properties. The Properties dialog box opens.

4. View the information on the General tab of the Properties dialog box, which is shown in Figure 8-4. This window shows the amount of used space and free space.

5. Click Cancel to close the Properties dialog box.

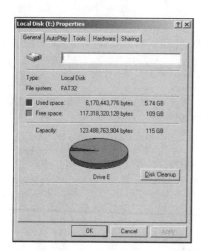

Figure 8-4   Hard disk information in the Windows Properties dialog box

Once you know how much space is available on the hard disk where Windows is stored, you can decide how much of the available free space you can use for your Linux operating system.

As with other operating systems, the exact components you need to install depend on what you intend to do with Linux. The more components you add, the more space you need on the hard disk. Each Linux distribution offers different standard installation options. Usually you can select a standard installation (such as Desktop or Server), or you can select more precisely which software packages you want to install. If you are familiar with Linux software, you may want to specify one or more packages to install; otherwise, you should simply indicate a general type of installation, such as a Desktop or Server system.

The sizes of a few standard options that you might see as you install different Linux distributions are shown in Table 8-3. Most distributions inform you of the amount of disk space needed as you select different options.

Table 8-3   Typical Linux Installation Options

Type of installation	Typical hard disk space required	Comments
Server installation without graphics support	300–600 MB	A server system doesn't require graphical support, which saves hard disk space. The amount of space required depends on which network services are provided (for example, e-mail server, Web server, file server, etc.). For many servers, you should also calculate the amount of hard disk space needed for data storage (such as Web pages or e-mail messages). Other servers (DNS) require very little hard disk space.
Standard desktop/ workstation installation with graphics and common utilities	600–900 MB	If you do not intend to use your system as a server, a workstation installation is a good choice. It includes a graphical desktop, some networking capabilities, common utilities, and documentation.
Developer's workstation	700 MB–1.3 GB	A developer typically uses a standard graphical workstation but adds many packages to aid in software development.
Complete installation	1.3 GB–6+ GB	A "complete installation" combines all packages for a graphical workstation, a developer, a network server, and more. It typically does not install *all* packages in the distribution, however, because some are experimental, or highly specialized, or conflict with each other (that is, you can choose one or the other but not both). If you have plenty of hard disk space, a complete installation is a nice way to make nearly everything available that you might want to use as you explore Linux.

In addition to space for the operating system, as shown in Table 8-3, you must add the hard disk space you want to have available *after* installing Linux. That space will be used for data files. These include user documents, e-mail messages, Web pages, graphics files, database archives, or system maintenance data.

A basic guideline for new Linux users is to have a minimum of 1.5 GB of free hard disk space to comfortably perform a workstation installation with enough disk space left to experiment with your system. If you have 6 GB or more of free hard disk space, you can usually perform a complete installation with plenty of space for experimentation and working with data files. If you want to use Linux as your desktop system, you may want to plan on more disk space depending on what you do on your system. For example, if you store a lot of digital music or digital photos, you need more space than if you simply read e-mail and create standard business documents using a word processor.

Graphical Systems

For years, the most challenging part of installing Linux was configuring the video hardware to provide a graphical interface. Fortunately, current installation programs automatically detect what video card you have installed and configure it without any input from you.

TIP The one exception to easy graphical configuration is when you install Linux on a laptop. In that case, you may want to consult the Web site *www.linux-laptop. net* to see how Linux experts who own the same model of laptop as you have managed to get Linux running properly.

Despite the easy steps for installation, it is a good idea to understand some video card concepts for those times when the installation doesn't go as smoothly as planned. Video cards are inherently a challenging topic because very few standards exist—every vendor tries to create something newer and better using proprietary technology that requires special software for each new product. And although some video card vendors are dedicated to supporting Linux, most leave the Linux market on its own, providing occasional technical assistance.

Creating a System Inventory

The Linux installation program (described in the next section) will probably detect all of your hardware and proceed without a hitch. While working as a system administrator, however, you are sure to encounter a few system components that Linux doesn't recognize. The information in this section helps you learn about your computer system in anticipation of those times. The more you understand about your hardware, the better you can help the installation proceed smoothly by answering questions and locating any additional software that Linux needs to support your hardware.

Finding the Manuals

Most computer systems include some type of printed manual that describes how to set up and use the system. Unfortunately, this documentation is usually filed in some forgotten corner. Although manuals seem to be getting smaller every year, yours probably contains at least a few key specifications for your system. If you can locate your computer's manual, do the following:

- Look in the index under the name of any hardware component that you want to learn more about.

- Check the table of contents for a section named "Specifications" or "Troubleshooting."

- Review the first few pages of the section on setting up the system. It may contain other details about the hardware.

Most computers come with separate manuals for each component; each of these manuals is provided by a different manufacturer. (Sometimes these manuals are tucked inside a sleeve with a CD-ROM full of software for the device.) Look for separate manuals on the following items:

- Main system (the CPU)

- Monitor

- Mouse

- Video card

- Modem

- CD-ROM drive

- Sound card

If you can't locate the printed manuals, try going online. Visit the Web site for the manufacturer of the component. Search under Products, Technical Support, or a related topic. Locating technical information on a huge Web site can be time consuming, but this information is generally free. A sample Web page showing the specifications for a Toshiba laptop is shown in Figure 8-5.

Reviewing BIOS Settings

Sometimes you can find information that is not evident in the printed or online documentation by reviewing the BIOS of the computer itself. Different systems use various methods of accessing the BIOS configuration menus, where you can learn about system status and devices. An onscreen message normally explains how to enter the Setup or BIOS information screen when you first boot the computer. Depending on your system, you might be asked to press F2, Del, Esc, or some other key or combination of keys to enter the BIOS menus. Review the system documentation if you don't see a message explaining how to enter the BIOS menus.

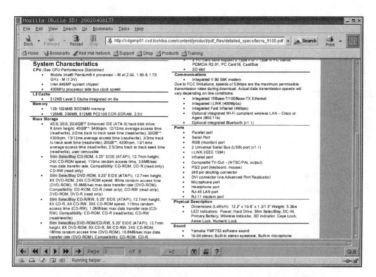

Figure 8-5   A sample Web-based specifications sheet

The exact steps for exploring the BIOS menus are not given here because each manufacturer uses a different interface for configuring the BIOS. A sample screen for BIOS configuration is shown in Figure 8-6.

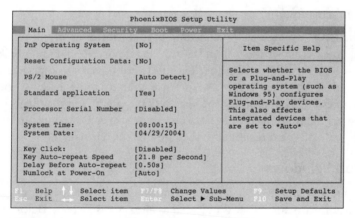

Figure 8-6   BIOS configuration menus

Keep the following points in mind as you examine the BIOS menus for hardware information:

- Most BIOS configurations include a number of options that are not relevant to installing Linux. These include things such as the time to wait before entering low-power mode and whether to include a power-on password. You can ignore these options and focus on locating information about devices you need to configure in Linux.

- Different levels of information may be provided in different menus. The details you need for a complex Linux configuration are more likely found in the Advanced portion of the BIOS configuration. Most users don't need to know this information to use a system that is already up and running.

- You can make changes to the settings in the BIOS and save them as you exit the BIOS setup utility. Don't do this unless you have studied the system documentation and are familiar with the features you are altering. Watch carefully as you exit the BIOS menus to make sure you do not accidentally choose a Save and Exit option unless you intend to. If you make changes, write down the settings that you alter so that you can change them back to their original values if the computer doesn't function as expected.

You should find the following information as you review your BIOS settings:

- Amount of RAM on the system

- Hard disk interface type and size of each hard disk

- Serial ports available on the system and the IRQ used by each one

- IRQ numbers used by other devices that might conflict with devices such as a sound card or network adapter (You usually can't see the IRQ used by these devices in the BIOS menus.)

- SCSI card make and model

- USB port information

Without accessing the BIOS, you can use a related method for locating system information: simply watch the screen carefully as the system starts. Many devices—including SCSI cards, video cards, and add-on IDE cards—will print identification messages to the screen as they are initialized at system start time. Some also prompt you to press a key during their initialization process to enter a setup utility specific to that device. You may have to power the system off and on several times to read the messages, but you can often gain much useful information from these small "advertisements" that are printed on screen.

Studying Microsoft Windows

If your computer is already running a Microsoft Windows operating system, you can take advantage of the device information that Windows has already discovered. Before installing Linux, you can start your computer in Microsoft Windows and write down all the configuration information you might need to use when installing Linux.

On newer versions of Microsoft Windows, such as Windows XP Professional, you can use the System Information utility to explore detailed information about your computer hardware. On the Start menu, choose All Programs, then Accessories, then System Tools, then System Information. In the left side of the window that appears, you can select which type of hardware you want to learn about. Details appear on the right, as shown in Figure 8-7.

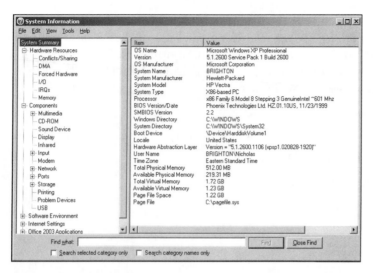

Figure 8-7 The System Information utility in Microsoft Windows XP Professional

Device information is also available on any version of Microsoft Windows via Control Panel. You can open Control Panel by clicking Start, then Control Panel (or Start, then Settings, then Control Panel in some versions of Windows). You can also double-click the My Computer icon on the Desktop, and then click Control Panel (it may be hidden on some systems). The Windows Control Panel (shown in Classic view) is shown in Figure 8-8. The icons on each Microsoft Windows system vary slightly based on the hardware and software that you have installed; so your screen is likely different from the figure.

Figure 8-8 The Microsoft Windows Control Panel

Different versions of Windows (such as 98, NT, XP, ME, and 2000) arrange information differently in Control Panel. You can explore several of the Control Panel sections by double-clicking icons that appear to have useful information. For example, you might try double-clicking one or more of the following Control Panel icons (not every icon is available on every version of Windows):

- Devices
- Display, via the Settings tab (choose the Display Type or Advanced Settings button)
- Multimedia, via the Devices tab
- Network, via the Adapters tab
- Ports
- Printers
- SCSI Adapters
- System

In the various lists of devices, you might be able to see the manufacturer and model name in some cases. Within some Windows dialog boxes, you can further research your system's hardware by selecting a hardware device and choosing the Properties button at the bottom of the dialog box or by selecting Properties from a right-click context menu.

You can also use Windows to find details about your networking configuration. Because a computer cannot run both Windows and Linux at the same time, you can normally use the same networking information for Linux that you use for Windows.

Within Windows Control Panel, the Network icon opens a dialog box in which network configuration details are displayed. The Identification tab in the Network dialog box includes a Computer name field with a name for your system. This name is associated with Windows networking, but you may want to use this as your host name when you install Linux. Ask your system administrator for advice.

Within some versions of Windows, the Configuration tab of the Network dialog box lists many different Windows networking components. One item is labeled TCP/IP, followed by the name of your networking device (this is usually an Ethernet networking adapter). Figure 8-9 shows the Network dialog box. The TCP/IP item is normally at the end of the list of network components (it does not appear in the figure).

With the TCP/IP item selected in the Configuration tab, click the Properties button. This opens the TCP/IP Properties dialog box. In this dialog box you can collect the following information:

- On the IP Address tab, you see the IP Address field and the Subnet Mask field (which refers to the Network Mask field as described previously). The Obtain an IP address automatically option indicates that the Windows system uses DHCP. If this option is selected in Windows, you can select DHCP for networking when you install Linux.

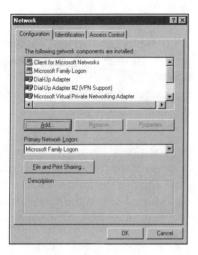

Figure 8-9 The Configuration tab of the Network dialog box in Microsoft Windows

- On the Gateway tab, the Installed gateways item provides the IP address that you should use as the gateway address when installing Linux.

- On the DNS Configuration tab, the DNS Server Search Order list contains at least one IP address. If multiple addresses are shown, you should write them all down. The Host and Domain names above the DNS Server Search Order list are the host name and domain name used for Windows networking. Unless directed otherwise, you should use these as the host name and domain name when you install Linux. If the Disable DNS option is selected, the information in this dialog box may not be valid, or it may not be shown as described. In this case, ask your system administrator or ISP for the DNS-related information mentioned here.

On newer versions of Microsoft Windows, you can find the IP address information used by Windows by entering the command *ipconfig* in a command-line window. (Don't confuse this with the Linux command, *ifconfig*). To see information graphically, choose Network Connections (in the Classic view of Control Panel), or Network and Internet Connections, then Network Connections (in the Category view of Control Panel). When the Network Connections window appears, right-click the Local Area Connection and choose Properties. In the General tab of the Properties dialog box, you should see an item in the list called Internet Protocol (TCP/IP). Click this item, then click the Properties button below the list of items. In the dialog box that appears, you see that your system obtains a network configuration automatically, or you see the IP address and DNS server information that you can use when configuring Linux.

Exit all of the Windows dialog boxes described here by choosing the Cancel button. This way you won't accidentally alter your Windows settings and cause problems with your hardware or networking configurations.

CAUTION

Asking Networking Questions

If you are not relying on DHCP to automatically configure networking, the only way to obtain the correct network settings is to ask the person (or organization) that assigns those settings. For instance, you cannot simply choose a network address, nor is the network address of your gateway or other servers something that you can guess. You need to ask the authority who originally set up your network connection—that is, you need to consult your instructor, system administrator, or ISP.

In some cases, you are allowed to select a host name for your Linux installation. You can choose any brief name that you want for the host name. System administrators often use a pattern of names for setting up multiple computers, such as the names of animals, cities, foods, colors, or something similar. The names are arbitrary, but you must provide the name to the person who manages the DNS name server on your network so that e-mail and other services can be directed to your computer.

CONFIGURING DISK SPACE

You must install Linux in a dedicated partition on the hard disk. Recall from Chapter 4, "Understanding Users and File Systems," that a partition is a distinct area of a hard disk that has been prepared to store a particular type of data. For example, a computer that only contains Windows normally has only one partition on its hard disk. That partition is marked as containing Windows data. To install Linux you must prepare another partition that is marked as containing Linux data.

You must create a Linux partition whether you plan to establish a dual-boot system or install only Linux on your computer. For a dual-boot system with two operating systems sharing one hard disk, you must prepare space for Linux before starting the installation program. For other installations, you can use the Linux installation program to prepare the hard disk partitions.

TIP

As mentioned previously, specialized versions of Linux such as the Knoppix distribution run directly from a CD without ever being installed on your hard disk. Other versions of Linux run entirely within a single file on a Microsoft Windows system. These products are fun to play with but are not something a working system administrator would rely on for a server or workstation. Visit *www.distrowatch.com* to learn more about the wide variety of Linux distributions available.

Figure 8-10 shows how three partitions might be arranged on a hard disk, with marks indicating the file system type and a file system format inside each partition. Most versions of Linux use ext3 (extended file system version 3) as a default file system type. The default file system type for older versions of DOS and Windows is called **FAT** (file allocation table) or FAT16. Windows NT, 2000, and XP use either **NTFS** (NT file system) or **FAT32** (file allocation table, 32-bit).

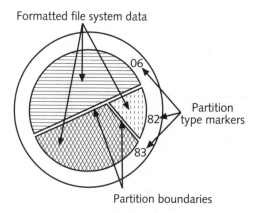

Formatted file system data

Partition
type markers

Partition boundaries

Figure 8-10   Partitions and file systems on a hard disk

Because of limitations in how hard disks were designed years ago, each hard disk can have only four partitions. These are called **primary partitions** and are numbered 1 through 4. To avoid the limitation of four primary partitions, you can set up multiple **logical partitions** within a single primary partition. Logical partitions are numbered beginning with 5. A logical partition is the same as a primary partition as far as your operating system is concerned, but the software used to configure your hard disk must set up logical partitions differently than primary partitions.

Some Linux distributions such as Red Hat Linux use logical partitions by default so that a complex Linux installation on a large hard disk doesn't use all the available partitions.

Among all of the partitions on a hard disk, one can be marked as the **active partition**, or the bootable partition. If you haven't modified the default settings, the BIOS passes control to the operating system stored on this partition.

In the next section, you will learn about the tools you can use during the installation process to create Linux partitions. To use these tools, you must have free space available on your hard disk. The information that follows will help you understand how to use the partitioning tools in the installation and how to create free space on a hard disk that is initially used only for Microsoft Windows.

Booting the System

When you turn on a computer, the BIOS initializes the devices on the system, then passes control to whatever program is located on a small area of the first hard disk called the **Master Boot Record**, or **MBR**. The MBR contains a small program that decides how to start an operating system. Normally, the MBR does this by passing control to the program located on the boot record of the active partition. The **boot record** is a small area on each partition that contains a boot manager program to start the operating system on that partition. For partitions containing Linux, the boot record contains a copy of GRUB, LILO, or a commercial boot manager.

The Linux boot manager can be stored on either the MBR or on the boot record of the active partition. The boot manager on a Linux partition can include instructions that pass control to another partition, such as a partition containing a Windows operating system. This creates a dual-boot system in which you choose which operating system to start each time you turn on the computer.

Figure 8-11 shows how a hard disk is arranged to include an MBR and a boot record on multiple partitions, with one partition being marked as active. Sometimes the boot record is called the boot sector, or the root sector, of the partition.

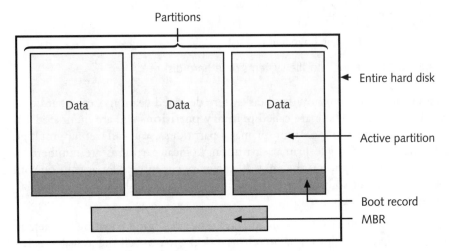

Figure 8-11 A hard disk with an MBR and boot records on each partition

Hard Disk Geometry

The operating system stored on a hard disk arranges information according to the file system used on that partition. Each operating system has a default file system. But the hard disk itself is designed to store information according to the physical characteristics of the hard disk. Sometimes you need to know about the disk drive layout to configure the system properly.

A hard disk is composed of multiple flat platters that hold magnetic data. These platters are stacked together, with small devices moving between the platters to read the data on each platter. Each concentric circle on a platter is called a **track**. When you format a hard disk, each track is divided into multiple sectors. A **sector** is a unit of data storage on a hard disk. Normally a sector contains 512 bytes. Sectors are often grouped together into larger units called clusters or blocks. A default hard disk **block** in Linux is a unit of hard disk space that contains 1024 bytes, or two sectors. Figure 8-12 shows a single platter of a hard disk with the tracks, sectors, and blocks illustrated.

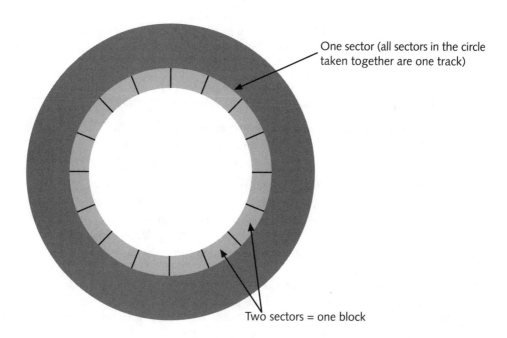

One sector (all sectors in the circle taken together are one track)

Two sectors = one block

Figure 8-12   Tracks, blocks, and sectors on a hard disk platter

Taken together, all of the tracks at the same position on each platter are called a **cylinder**. If you imagine a cylinder being inserted through a stack of platters, all of the tracks that the cylinder intersects as it passes through the platters are collectively called a cylinder. Figure 8-13 illustrates this concept.

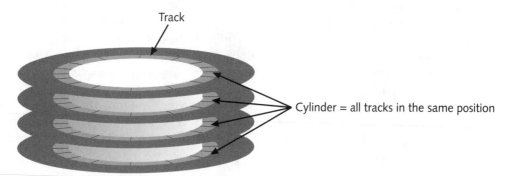

Track

Cylinder = all tracks in the same position

Figure 8-13   A cylinder on a hard disk

Figures 8-12 and 8-13 illustrate the concepts behind hard disk layout, but they are somewhat deceptive. A hard disk often has over 1000 cylinders, or concentric tracks, on each platter.

This is an important point. Hard disks with many cylinders can cause installation problems for Linux if you are using a computer with a very old BIOS. The installation program warns you of any potential problems.

Swap Partitions

The Linux operating system and the files that you create in Linux are stored on an ext3 partition. In addition to this partition, you should create a separate partition used as a swap partition for the Linux kernel's virtual memory, as described in Chapter 4.

Using a separate partition controlled by the Linux kernel allows the virtual memory feature to work very quickly, without interfering with other hard disk operations that read from or write to the Linux partition where regular data files are stored. A swap partition is normally from 64 MB to 1 GB in size, though it can be smaller or larger depending on how much hard disk space you have and how busy the Linux system will be.

TIP If you have multiple hard disks in your system, configure your swap partition to be on a different hard disk than the bulk of your data files. This allows more efficient access to virtual memory and data files because each can be accessed independently instead of waiting for one another.

You create a swap partition just as you create a regular Linux partition, using the tools provided with the installation program. A basic guideline for the size of the swap partition is that it should be twice the size of your RAM; if you have 256 MB of RAM, you should have a swap partition of about 512 MB.

Preparing a Shared Hard Disk

To create a dual-boot system running Linux and Microsoft Windows (or another operating system), you must have a separate hard disk on which Linux will be installed, or else you must use some of the hard disk space currently occupied by Windows to install Linux. If you choose the latter approach, you must use a utility to "shrink" the Windows partition to allow free space for Linux. This is sometimes done by splitting a single Windows partition into two Windows partitions, the second being empty. Then you can reconfigure that empty partition for use by Linux. Fedora Linux does not include a disk partitioning utility, as it is intended mainly for users who will be using exclusively Linux. But several utilities are available to help with this task. Remember that you only need one of these utilities if you are creating a dual-boot system. The Linux installation program itself will create Linux partitions for you.

- **FIPS** is a free utility that is included with some Linux distributions. You can download FIPS from *www.igd.fhg.de/~aschaefe/fips/*. Its use is described in this section. FIPS is fairly reliable, but it has not been updated since 1998. As a result, it does not work with NTFS partitions (the default file system on Windows 2000/2003 and Windows XP).

- The **parted** partition editor. This is another free utility, but it also cannot work with NTFS partitions. (See *www.gnu.org/software/parted* for more information or to download this program.)

- PartitionMagic, available from Symantec (*www.symantec.com*), is a popular commercial product that provides a graphical interface to create new partitions, and helps you back up data before altering the hard disk. It also functions with NTFS, so you can use it to share a single hard disk between Linux and newer versions of Windows.

- QtParted is a graphical partition editor intended to be a clone of PartitionMagic. QtParted is not yet stable, however, so you should use it with great care. Information is available at *http://qtparted.sourceforge.net/*.

CAUTION

Before using any program that modifies your partition information, you should back up any important data on your Microsoft Windows system by copying it to disks, tape, or to a network server.

8

The FIPS program is a text-mode program that is included with some Linux distributions, usually in a separate directory called /utils, /dostools, or something similar.

Before using FIPS or most other partitioning utilities, you should arrange all the data on your Windows partition so that it is grouped together. This leaves a contiguous area of free space at one end of the hard disk. To accomplish this, you must defragment the Windows system. **Defragmenting** is a procedure that arranges each file on your hard disk so that all parts of the file are next to each other (as opposed to the parts of a file being fragmented, or spread across the entire hard disk). When you defragment a Windows system, all of the files are placed at the beginning of the hard disk. Figure 8-14 shows conceptually how a Windows partition is arranged before and after the defragmenting operation.

CAUTION

On some Windows systems, defragmenting the hard disk leaves a few blocks of data spread throughout the disk, even though *most* files are defragmented. Depending on the position of these blocks, you may not be able to use FIPS to create a large enough empty partition to install Linux. In this case, you need to rely on more advanced software than FIPS to create a dual-boot system, even for an older version of Windows. Consider using the PartitionMagic product mentioned previously.

NOTE

Defragmenting is also called optimizing a hard disk, because some operating systems (such as Windows) work much more efficiently (optimally) if you defragment your hard disk on a regular basis. Linux hard disks are not subject to fragmentation because Linux arranges data differently than Windows.

Most versions of Windows include a utility for defragmenting your Windows partitions. The steps to defragment a Windows partition vary based on the version of Windows you are

Before defragmenting   After defragmenting

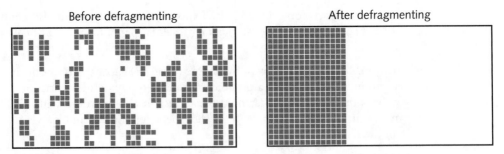

Figure 8-14 Conceptual representation of a partition before and after defragmentation

using. The following procedure for Windows XP should get you started (but remember that FIPS cannot split a Windows XP partition):

1. Double-click the My Computer icon on your Windows desktop.

2. Locate the hard disk on which you will later install Linux (this is normally C: in Windows).

3. Right-click the icon for that hard disk. A context menu appears.

4. Click Properties. The Properties dialog box for the selected hard drive opens.

5. Click the Tools tab to display the options shown in Figure 8-15. Click the second item on the Tools tab to open the Defragment utility.

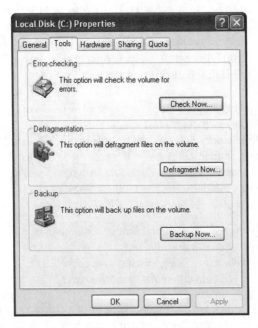

Figure 8-15 The Tools tab in the Properties dialog box for a hard disk in Windows XP

6. Select the drive letter for the file system you want to defragment.

7. Click Analyze (near the bottom of the screen). After a few moments, you see a message box that informs you of the condition of this file system.

8. If the message box indicates that the file system needs to be defragmented, click Defragment in the message box. The defragmentation process begins.

   If the message box indicates that the file system does not need to be defragmented, you can click Close in the message box, then exit the defragmentation program. You may still decide, however, to click Defragment, because this process can move data to the beginning of your Windows file system and may provide more space to create a Linux partition.

Defragmenting a large hard disk can take several hours. If you are working on a version of Windows before Windows XP, you may need to restart Windows in Safe Mode before running the defragmentation utility. Figure 8-16 shows the defragmentation program running.

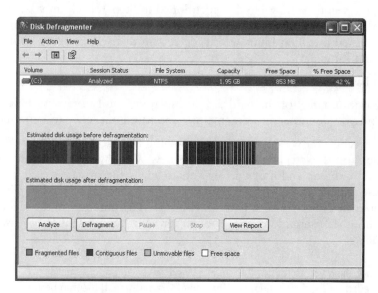

Figure 8-16   The Disk Defragmenter window in Windows XP

With the free space arranged on your Windows partition, you can run the FIPS program to split an older Windows partition (such as Windows 98) into two pieces. To run FIPS, follow these steps:

1. Obtain two 3.5-inch disks.

2. Start Windows and copy the FIPS program from Fedora CD 1 to one of the removable disks. The program is located at \dosutils\fips.exe.

If you are using another version of Linux, the location on your Linux CD will vary, but the program name is typically still fips.exe.

3. Click the Start button in Windows, click Shut Down or Turn Off Computer (depending on the version of Windows you are using). Then click Restart.

4. As the system restarts, press the F8 key to start Windows in Safe Mode.

5. When Windows has restarted, open the Start menu, select All Programs, then Accessories, then Command Prompt to open a command-line window.

6. At the C:\ prompt, start the FIPS program using the command *fips* preceded by the drive letter for your removable disk drive (for example, *A:\fips*).

   FIPS must be run in Windows' Safe Mode to avoid conflicting with other programs. Because the CD-ROM drive is normally not available in Safe Mode, you must copy the FIPS program to a removable disk.

7. Read the messages on screen, and then press a key to continue.

8. Using the second removable disk mentioned in Step 1, back up your disk information by following the instructions on screen. (Keep this disk until you have finished installing Linux and made certain that you can start both Windows and Linux.)

9. If you have multiple hard disks, select the one you want FIPS to alter.

10. The partition table for the hard disk is displayed. You can review this information, but you don't need to do anything about it. Press a key to continue.

11. FIPS presents you with two numbers showing the size of the current Windows partition (on the left) and the size of the new Windows partition (on the right). Use the up and down arrow keys to adjust the space on each partition. Because you are changing the point at which the partition will be split in two, one number goes up as the other goes down. The number on the right (shown in MB) should be large enough for your Linux partition *and* swap partition.

NOTE

FIPS will not allow you to reduce the original Windows partition to a smaller size than is needed for the data residing on that Windows partition. If the number on the left for the size of the original Windows partition will not go low enough to allow space for Linux when the second Windows partition is deleted, you have not effectively moved all the data to the front of the Windows partition. Or the Windows partition may simply be too full to store Linux on the same computer.

12. Press Enter to accept your settings.

13. The partition table is displayed again as it will appear when updated by FIPS. If you are comfortable with the sizes shown, press C to confirm that you want to write this information to the hard disk. You can press Ctrl+C to exit FIPS without making any changes to your hard disk.

14. Restart your computer normally so that the updated hard disk information is reread into your system.

After using FIPS, you should have a smaller Windows partition containing the Windows operating system and your Windows data; you also have a second Windows partition that contains no data. During the Linux installation you delete this second, empty Windows partition and configure the resulting free space on the hard disk into the Linux partition and Linux swap partition.

INSTALLING LINUX

This section describes how to install Red Hat Software's Fedora Linux. The information you will learn as you complete the installation is applicable to virtually all versions of Linux, though each distribution arranges its installation programs a bit differently, and a few installations may ask highly technical questions during the installation that are not covered here. (Generally, the more flexible an installation program, the more knowledge you must have to complete it.) Project 8-2 at the end of the chapter walks you through a complete installation of Fedora Linux from the CDs included with this book.

NOTE If you are preparing to take the Red Hat Certified Technician Exam, note that it is based on the Red Hat Enterprise Linux product rather than the Fedora Linux that is included with this book. The installation of Red Hat Enterprise Linux, however, is practically identical to the installation of Fedora. A few software packages are different in the two products (as are the color schemes), but the main difference lies in the product update and technical support options, as described in Chapter 1, and more fully on *www.redhat.com*.

Linux Distributions

People like having favorites: one person insists that Ford trucks are better; another buys only Chevrolet. One person always drinks Coke; another chooses Pepsi every time. The differences between products may be slight, but the loyalty they inspire is not. Linux users often have similar feelings about the version or distribution they have chosen. One person insists that Debian Linux is the only reasonable choice; another uses Red Hat/Fedora or SUSE exclusively.

Although having a favorite is fine, remember that Linux distributions are very similar to each other technically. Each one takes the Linux kernel from the same location on the Internet, and each uses the same set of supporting utilities. The organization or individual creating a distribution often has a specific goal that determines which parts of the distribution are highlighted, or what additional items are added to the basic Linux software. For example, some distributions focus on ease of use, others on security, others on completeness; still others focus on a particular technical purpose, such as creating the perfect e-mail server.

TIP   Software engineers at Red Hat Software have back-ported features from more recent kernels (2.6) into older kernels (2.4) that are still shipped with Red Hat products. This is sometimes confusing, and has annoyed a few Linux developers, but it relates only to advanced or specialized features that will not affect your work as a beginning system administrator.

Table 1-1 (in Chapter 1) names several of the better-known distributions. These distributions differ based on their installation program, the software that each installs by default, where they store configuration files, and other factors.

Fedora Linux is included with this book. Fedora Linux is based on Red Hat Linux and forms the technology core for Red Hat Enterprise Linux. Although many other excellent distributions are available, Red Hat has been a stable, long-term participant in the Linux market.

If you are interesting in using another version of Linux, you can obtain a copy by downloading it or purchasing it, either in a low-cost CD package (visit *www.cheapbytes.com* or *www.linuxcentral.com*), or in a full retail package (visit your local computer store or *www.cdw.com*).

An Overview of Linux Installation

Installing an operating system on a computer is different from installing an application such as a word processor. When you install an application, the existing operating system provides a foundation for the installation process. When you install a new operating system, only the hardware is available—no other software can assist the installation program. The new operating system must somehow initialize itself sufficiently to install itself on the computer.

When you start a Linux installation program, the general procedure runs like this:

1. A user starts the installation program by starting the computer from a Linux CD or removable disk.

2. The installation program runs a copy of Linux within the computer's RAM.

3. The installation program determines where the files for the installation are located, either by asking the user or automatically probing the system.

4. The installation program determines where the Linux operating system should be installed, again, by either asking the user or by automatically probing the system for available space. A **target hard disk partition** (the target partition) is the location on the system's hard disk where Linux will be installed.

5. The user answers questions posed by the installation program about which software packages should be installed and how core system services should be configured. (For example, the user creates an administrator password and enters the network addresses to use.)

6. The installation program copies the Linux software packages from the **installation source** (the set of files from which Linux is installed) to the target partition.

7. The user answers a few remaining questions about initial system configuration.

8. The installation program configures the system based on the user's input and installs a boot manager so Linux can be started.

9. The user starts the newly installed Linux operating system, either by pressing a key or restarting the computer.

Installation Source Options

The procedures in this book assume that you are installing Linux from a CD-ROM. But Linux supports other installation methods. If your installation source files are stored on another medium or in another location, you can specify this as you begin the installation program. The most common installation sources are:

- *CD-ROM*: Use files from the CD-ROM drive attached to the system on which you are installing Linux.

- *Hard disk*: Use files stored on a hard disk within the system on which you are installing Linux. This must be a hard disk partition or hard disk that is distinct from the location where Linux will be installed. A system administrator copies files from a Linux CD-ROM or downloads files from an Internet site, storing them on a hard disk for convenience or to overcome technical problems that make other installation methods impractical.

- *Network installation*: Use files that are located on a server connected to the same network as the computer on which you are installing Linux. Depending on the version of Linux you are installing, you may be able to connect to the server on which the files are located using any of the following network protocols: FTP (a standard Internet format); SMB (used by Microsoft Windows servers); NFS (the Network File System protocol, commonly available on all Linux and UNIX systems). Performing a network installation requires additional configuration on the server that provides the installation source, but this method allows a system administrator to install multiple Linux systems from a single networked copy of the installation source.

To perform a network installation, you must prepare another computer so it can provide the installation data. Setting up a network file server to do this is beyond the scope of this book, but many versions of Linux (including Fedora) support network installations. Additional information on network configuration and network services is provided in Chapter 12, "Configuring Networks."

Options for Starting the Installation

When you turn on a computer, the BIOS checks the status of the system and then passes control to one of the disk drives, depending on how it is configured. Normally, it first checks whether a removable disk is inserted; on newer computers, the CD-ROM/DVD drive or a USB drive may also be checked. If neither contains a bootable disk, control passes to the program contained in the Master Boot Record (MBR) of the first hard disk.

To start the Linux installation program, you must pass control directly to the Linux installation program located on either a floppy disk or a CD-ROM, so that the BIOS never passes control to the MBR and starts an operating system that is already installed. You can do this by creating a boot disk from a data file provided on the Linux CD-ROM. A **boot disk** is a removable disk that can start up your computer and initialize the installation program. Most users can rely on newer computers that have bootable CD-ROM drives. A **bootable CD-ROM drive** is a drive that can start an operating system (or other program) directly from a CD-ROM.

Most Linux products (including Fedora Linux) provide a bootable CD-ROM. To see if your CD-ROM drive is bootable, try inserting the installation or first Linux CD-ROM into the CD-ROM drive and then restarting the computer. If the installation program appears on screen, your CD-ROM drive is bootable.

TIP   If the installation program does not start from the installation CD-ROM, your CD-ROM drive may still be bootable, but the BIOS is configured to try to start an operating system from the hard disk before checking the CD-ROM drive. You can change the order in which devices are checked at start time by reconfiguring the BIOS as described previously.

If you can't start the Linux CD-ROM, you typically must create a boot disk (also called an **install disk** by some vendors). The first Linux CD-ROM in your distribution normally contains a copy of a boot disk in the form of a disk image. A **disk image** is a single file that contains an exact copy of a floppy disk. The easiest way to create the boot disk is to copy the disk image from the CD to a removable disk using the rawwritewin program in Windows, or the *dd* utility on an existing Linux system. You can download the rawwritewin program from *http://uranus.it.swin.edu.au/~jn/linux/rawwrite.htm*.

Fedora Linux does not include utilities needed to install on older systems—it provides the ability to boot directly from CD or DVD, and a very large disk image that you can copy to a keychain-style USB drive, then boot from that drive, if your BIOS supports that option. This USB boot image is located in the /images directory of CD 1 and is called diskboot.img. On older versions of Fedora and many other versions of Linux, you will find a file of a similar name that is intended to be copied to a 1.44 MB removable disk. Copying this file to a removable disk creates a boot disk that you can use to start the installation. On some older computers, the drivers needed to access hardware during the installation are not included in the bootdisk.img file. If you have trouble during the installation, you might need to create disks from the other images in the images subdirectory. Because Fedora only boots from CD, DVD, or a USB drive, no additional disk images are needed—everything fits on the single large images used to boot from these devices.

The /images subdirectory also includes a boot.iso file. This is a CD-ROM image file that you can use to create a bootable CD.

The Installation Process

In most cases, installing Linux proceeds to completion without any problems; many users don't even bother to read any documentation before beginning, they simply start from a Linux CD and answer a few questions posed on screen. This section describes what is happening behind the scenes and how your answers to onscreen questions affect the final Linux system.

Projects 8-3 and 8-4 at the end of this chapter provide step-by-step instructions for installing Fedora.

Answering Initial Questions

After you have started the installation program from a bootable CD-ROM, DVD, USB device, or removable drive, you need to answer questions about how you will interact with the installation program. For example, you must choose a keyboard layout and a language for the installation. Depending on the version of Linux you are using, you might also be asked about your mouse, time zone, video card, or other details before selecting an installation source and target partition.

In many versions of Linux, you can back up to change your answer to previously asked questions until the installation program begins writing data to the hard disk. You can also simply turn off your computer if you choose to abandon the installation before anything is written to the hard disk; any data that was previously stored on your hard disk remains unaffected.

Preparing Hard Disk Partitions

In the previous section, you learned that you must divide a hard disk partition containing Microsoft Windows so that Linux could be installed on the same computer. In this section you learn how to use that free space, or free space on any hard disk, to prepare for installing Linux.

Within the Linux installation program, you configure partitions on which Linux is stored. You must set up a swap partition and one or more data partitions. To set up partitions, you edit the **partition table**, a small data table stored on the hard disk that defines the size and file system type for each partition on the hard disk.

NOTE

If you are not creating a dual-boot system, some installation programs (including Fedora Linux) set up partitions for you automatically. This time, to help you learn about Linux, you should perform this task manually.

Most Linux vendors provide a graphical interface in which you can configure partitions. In Chapter 10, "Managing Software Packages and File Systems," you will learn about a powerful text–mode utility called *fdisk* (for *fixed disk*, meaning a hard disk). You can use the *fdisk* utility within some installation programs to create and configure partitions, but in this chapter we focus on using graphical tools.

Recall that to refer to hard disks in Linux, you use a device name within the file system structure: the first IDE hard disk is /dev/hda; the second is /dev/hdb. To refer to one partition, you can add a partition number after the device name. For example, the first partition on the second IDE hard disk is represented as /dev/hdb1. SCSI or USB devices use a similar pattern of names, but with the letters "sd" instead of "hd." For example, the first SCSI hard disk is /dev/sda. The second partition on the second SCSI hard disk is /dev/sdb2.

TIP

You use these same device names to refer to a CD-ROM drive that is attached to the IDE or SCSI controller card on the system. For example, the CD-ROM drive is often the third IDE device (that is, the first device on the second IDE controller). Thus, the CD-ROM can be accessed by referring to /dev/hdc. (CD-ROMs do not have multiple partitions as hard disks do.) The Linux installation program normally locates the CD-ROM containing installation files without any input from you.

Deciding on Mount Points

In Windows, you might have two hard disks that are accessed as C: and D:. Linux does not use drive letters to refer to storage devices. Instead, different devices are accessed using subdirectories of a single directory structure. Linux defines a mount point for different file systems or storage devices. A **mount point** is a subdirectory through which a set of data is accessed. As you install Linux, you may decide to create separate partitions for different parts of your file system, or to store different information on separate hard disks. Deciding how to arrange information on partitions and hard disks is an important part of installing large or complex Linux systems.

To complete the installation, you must specify a mount point for the new Linux file system. That is, you must define which hard disk device corresponds to the directory where Linux is installed. The beginning point for every Linux file system is the root directory, /. So, for example, you could define during your installation that the "/" directory should correspond to the /dev/hda1 partition; the Linux file system is created and all Linux files installed on that partition.

You might also specify that directories such as /home or /usr are to be stored on a separate partition or a separate hard disk. Arranging data in different ways can improve access speed, make it easier to back up data, make it easier to upgrade the operating system or share data between operating systems, or simply use a variety of storage devices that you have available. The /boot directory is a special directory that contains the Linux kernel in Fedora Linux. To start up correctly on some hardware, this directory needs to be stored on a separate (small) partition. The installation program informs you if this is the case for your system.

In addition to the mount points for data directories just described, you must specify the partition to use for swap space (the swap partition). This partition is not visible in the directory structure because it is only used directly by the kernel as virtual memory.

For your first Linux installation, you can plan to select only a swap partition and a partition for the / directory. All operating system files are then installed on a single partition. You can experiment with more complex multiple-partition installations after you have learned more about Linux.

Choosing What to Install

Each Linux distribution includes thousands of different programs, such as the Linux kernel, the Apache Web server, GNU Project utilities, programming languages, compilers, graphical systems, games, and so forth. When installing Linux, you must decide which of these components to install. The amount of flexibility you have in deciding what you install varies by distribution.

Some distributions group the many possible components into a few different installation types. The **installation type** you choose determines which Linux software is installed; the right installation type for your system depends on how the system will be used. For example, you might have a choice of installing a minimal system (which includes only the most basic components), installing a standard system (which includes the components the average user is most likely to use), or installing everything from the CD. Often, however, you have more options regarding which software components you want to install.

Most Linux systems gather many related files into a single software package. For example, all Linux products provide the Apache Web server, which is made up of dozens of files, as a software package. A **software package** is a single file that contains all the files needed to install and use an application or group of related applications. Special data formats are used to store many files in a software package. The **Red Hat Package Manager (rpm)** is the most popular data storage format for creating software packages; it is used by many different distributions. Another well-known software package format comes from the Debian distribution. Packages stored using this format use a .deb file extension and are managed using the *dpkg* utility.

You will learn more about the rpm format in Chapter 10. Typical Linux products include between 400 and 2500 software packages. To simplify matters, these packages are grouped into functional categories such as text processing, networking utilities, or software development tools. Some Linux installations employ further generalizations based on a broad usage category for the Linux system. For example, a single selection such as Web server installation or Desktop system might define all of the categories, software packages, and files to install. During the installation you can specify which sets of packages or which type of system you want to install. Different Linux distributions allow different levels of detail in this selection process. Figure 8-17 illustrates conceptually the variety of groupings, from general installation types to specific files.

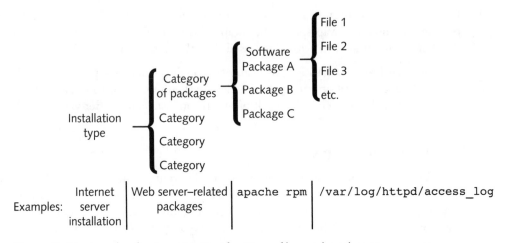

Figure 8-17   Levels of categorization for Linux files and packages

Fedora Linux provides three installation types, plus a Custom installation option. When you select Custom, you are presented with about 30 package groups from which you can select what you want to install. Table 8-4 shows the package groups that Fedora Linux provides during a Custom installation. It is recommended that you install those package groups shown with an asterisk (*) in the left column. These packages total about 3.4 GB. If you don't have this much space available, eliminate all items in the Development section as well as the Office/Productivity item. This reduces the installation size to about 2.0 GB.

Table 8-4   Package Groups in Fedora Linux

Package group	Comments
Desktops	
*X Window System	The foundation for all graphical applications in Linux; required to use the GNOME or KDE desktop
*GNOME	The GNOME desktop interface
*KDE	The KDE desktop interface

Table 8-4 Package Groups in Fedora Linux (continued)

Package group	Comments
Applications	
*Editors	Text editors; recommended
Engineering and Scientific	Engineering and scientific applications, such as scientific calculators and graphing programs
*Graphical Internet	Graphical Web browsers, e-mail readers, and similar tools; recommended
*Text-based Internet	Text-based Web browsers, e-mail readers, and similar tools; recommended to complete Chapter 7
*Office/ Productivity	Office suites, contact manager (Evolution) and other personal productivity applications. Recommended if space is available. This item adds 350 MB to the install size.
*Sound and Video	Utilities to listen to sound and music (including music CDs), view video clips, and in some cases, edit sound and music files
Authoring and Publishing	High-end tools for working in specialized document formats
*Graphics	Graphical editing tools such as the GIMP (a program similar to Adobe Photoshop)
Games and Entertainment	Dozens of strategy, card, and action/arcade games, as well as desktop diversions
Servers	
*Server Configuration Tools	Red Hat Software's graphical configuration tools; recommended
*Web Server	Apache Web server; recommended if you intend to experiment with server functionality
Mail Server	Various e-mail servers
*Windows File Server	The Samba Windows-compatible file and print server. Permits Linux to act as a file and print server on a Windows network. Recommended if you intend to experiment with server functionality or use Linux for network-based installation using the SMB protocol.
DNS Name Server	The BIND name server
*FTP Server	The FTP server; recommended if you intend to experiment with server functionality or use Linux for network-based installation using the FTP protocol
SQL Database Server	A complete client/server database
News Server	A newsgroup server
*Network Servers	Various small server programs, including the DHCP server; recommended if you intend to experiment with server functionality

8

Table 8-4 Package Groups in Fedora Linux (continued)

Package group	Comments
Development	
*Development Tools	Software development tools such as compilers and debugging utilities. Use this item if you intend to download source code and compile it on your system. Tools for specific types of development follow—select any that apply to the type of development you intend to do (the types of programs you intend to download as source code). All five items in this section add about 900 MB to the installation size.
*Kernel Development	Linux kernel source code and configuration utilities; the Development Tools item and this item are needed to complete all tasks outlined in Chapter 13, "System and Kernel Management"
*X Software Development	Tools and libraries for graphical software development and compiling graphical programs from source code
*GNOME Software Development	Tools and libraries for software development (and compiling from source code) of programs that rely on elements of the GNOME desktop
*KDE Software Development	Tools and libraries for software development (and compiling from source code) of programs that rely on elements of the KDE desktop
System	
*Administrative Tools	System administration tools; recommended
*System Tools	Additional system administration tools; recommended
*Printing Support	Servers and utilities to permit printing from Linux applications; recommended
Miscellaneous	
Everything	Install all software packages that do not conflict with one another. This includes more packages than all of the other items in this table. When this item is selected, all other items are unavailable. Install size for this option is approximately 6.2 GB.
Minimal	Install only enough packages to create a basic working Linux system. When this item is selected, all other items are unavailable. Install size for this option is 510 MB.

TIP   Fedora Linux also allows you to select individual packages to install, but choosing among hundreds of packages takes more effort than most people want to invest during the installation process. You'll find it is usually much easier to install package groups when installing Linux. Then you can easily add or remove individual software packages after completing the installation.

User Accounts

The Linux installation process creates the root user account. During installation, you must specify a password for the root account. Choose this password carefully and guard against anyone discovering it. Because the root account is so powerful, you should only use it to complete system administration work. Either during or immediately after installing Linux, you should also create a regular user account for nonsystem administration work. You need to choose a brief user name (such as thomasj, jane, or rms). You must also enter the user's full name and a password for that user account.

Configuring the Boot Manager

During the Linux installation you may have the option of installing the Linux boot manager in one of several locations. The option you select depends on how you have configured any other operating systems on the computer. A generally safe choice is to accept the option that is presented as a default by the installation program. This option is selected based on what the installation program finds on your hard disks. The following list explains some reasons for choosing each of the possible locations for the boot manager:

- *The Master Boot Record*: Placing the boot manager on the MBR ensures that Linux boots correctly after a new installation because control passes directly from the BIOS to the Linux boot manager. However, if you have other operating systems installed on the same computer, you must configure the Linux boot manager to start them.

- *The boot sector of the partition on which Linux is being installed*: If the MBR is intact, this is the preferred location for the Linux boot manager. Control passes from the BIOS to the MBR, then to the Linux boot manager, so long as the Linux partition is marked as the active partition (this is done by the installation program). The Linux boot manager can pass control to a boot manager on a different partition to start other operating systems as needed.

- *A floppy disk*: This allows you to keep the MBR intact and leave another partition (such as one containing Windows) as the active partition. To start Linux, you must insert the removable disk on which you have installed the Linux boot manager. This can add a small measure of security or ease of use, depending on who will be using your system. But it also takes much longer to start the system, which is an issue if you are restarting regularly in a testing environment.

After you have installed Linux, you can restart your computer and begin using the operating system.

KICKSTART INSTALLATIONS

The descriptions in the previous section outline a basic Linux installation. They do, of course, cover a lot of information that you are not likely to *need* to complete a Linux installation—most of the time, you can simply click Next repeatedly and the installation proceeds without any problems.

But there are other times when you need other features beyond those outlined in the previous section or presented in Project 8-2 at the end of the chapter. Some of these, such as setting up a network installation server and preparing multidisk file systems are left to later chapters. This section describes one advanced feature: using Red Hat's Kickstart tool.

Kickstart is a method of automating installation selections so that you can reinstall a system, or install multiple identical systems, without entering all the information discussed in Project 8-2. Instead, the installation program relies on a configuration file that contains all of the settings to complete the installation.

The basic process for using Kickstart is as follows:

1. Create a **kickstart configuration file** using the graphical Kickstart Configuration utility or else use the kickstart configuration file created when you installed Linux (this is the safer choice when first using Kickstart).

2. Copy the kickstart configuration file onto a removable disk under the name ks.cfg.

3. Insert the Fedora CD and boot the Linux installation program on the system where you want to use the kickstart configuration file to control the installation.

4. At the first screen, instead of just pressing Enter to start the installation program, enter the text *linux ks=floppy* and press Enter.

5. The kickstart configuration file is read and used to control all aspects of the installation that are defined in that file. Assuming the configuration file is complete, the system restarts when the installation is complete, without any intervention on your part.

Reviewing the Kickstart Configuration File

When you complete an installation in Project 8-2, a kickstart configuration file is created based on the choices you made during that process. The file is /root/anaconda-ks.cfg. You can follow the steps just given and use that file to immediately experiment with Kickstart, but it's a good idea to review the contents of the file first. Project 8-4 uses this file as the basis of a Kickstart installation.

The contents of the file for one system are shown here for reference. Note that this file is different from the file on your system because each system uses different partitions, has different hardware, and requires different software packages be installed. You can use any text editor to view the kickstart configuration file on your system.

Although you may not have installed Linux yourself yet, someone installed your system. If you have root access, you can use any text editor to view the existing kickstart configuration file. Try entering this command in a graphical terminal window:*gedit /root/anaconda-ks.cfg*. You should see something similar to the following:

```
# Kickstart file automatically generated by anaconda.

install
cdrom
lang en_US.UTF-8
langsupport --default en_US.UTF-8 en_US.UTF-8
keyboard us
mouse genericwheelps/2 --device psaux
xconfig --card "Matrox Millennium G200" --videoram 8192 --
hsync 31-64 --vsync 60-60 --resolution 1024x768 --depth 24 --
startxonboot --defaultdesktop gnome
network --device eth0 --bootproto dhcp --hostname inverness.
xmission.com
rootpw --iscrypted $1$OO.JLHNk$ykhkMOJSwuAmbq8kc0U3i1
firewall --enabled --port=http:tcp --port=ftp:tcp --port=ssh:tcp
authconfig --enableshadow --enablemd5
timezone --utc America/New_York
bootloader --location=mbr --append hdc=ide-scsi rhgb
# The following is the partition information you requested
# Note that any partitions you deleted are not expressed
# here so unless you clear all partitions first, this is
# not guaranteed to work
#clearpart --linux
#part / --fstype ext3 --size=100 --grow
#part swap --onpart hdb2
#part /usr --fstype ext3 --onpart hdb1

%packages
@ kde-software-development
@ office
@ kde-desktop
@ network-server
@ web-server
@ x-software-development
@ server-cfg
@ dialup
@ sound-and-video
@ editors
@ admin-tools
@ system-tools
@ base-x
@ gnome-desktop
@ gnome-software-development
@ graphics
@ ftp-server
@ kernel-development
@ smb-server
@ development-tools
@ printing
@ text-internet
```

```
@ graphical-internet
kernel
grub

%post
```

Using the Graphical Configuration Tool

You can create a kickstart configuration file from scratch in any text editor, or you can use the graphical Kickstart Configurator tool. To start this tool in GNOME, choose System Tools, then Kickstart. From a command line, enter *system-config-kickstart* while logged in as root.

You can explore this utility without being logged in as root, but you cannot access the /root/anaconda-ks.cfg file generated during the installation of Fedora unless you are logged in as root. Because this file makes a good working sample, it is helpful to be logged in as root.

The Kickstart Configurator window is shown in Figure 8-18. This utility is divided into several topics, which you can select by choosing an item on the left side of the window. Each topic corresponds to a section of the installation process that you have been studying.

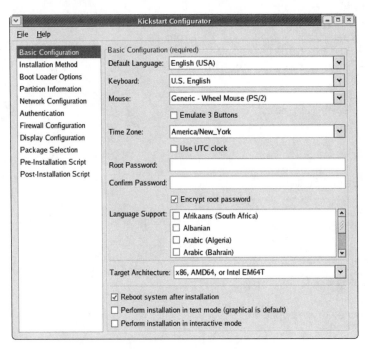

Figure 8-18   The Kickstart Configurator

This utility functions as a tool to create a kickstart configuration file. You can use the Open File item on the File menu to work with an existing kickstart configuration file. You can see what the file you are defining looks like at any time by choosing Preview on the File menu. When you finish using the utility, choose Save File on the File menu to create the ks.cfg file. That file is what you must copy to a boot disk and use to control the installation process.

You do not need to define every option in Kickstart Configuration (or in a kickstart configuration file) in order for Kickstart to control an installation. You are prompted for any critical items that are undefined when Kickstart Configurator creates a file for you; for options that are not defined, the installation program simply uses a default setting. For more information about any of the topics in Kickstart Configurator, you can choose Contents on the Help menu.

CHAPTER SUMMARY

8

- Most Linux installation programs can detect a computer's hardware for you, but understanding computer hardware helps you when a Linux install doesn't proceed smoothly.

- Components of a computer are called devices in Linux. Each is controlled by software called a driver.

- Memory and hard disk space are measured in bytes, typically in megabytes or gigabytes.

- Devices communicate with the CPU of a computer using interrupts, direct memory access, or port-mapped input/output. Sometimes information about these techniques must be provided to the Linux kernel to correctly use a device.

- Linux supports thousands of hardware components (devices). It is a good idea to research the specific devices you want to use to see if they are supported.

- To use Linux networking, you must assign an IP address to your computer or else have a DHCP server available to provide dynamic network configuration.

- Other networking information may be required, such as a network mask and the IP address of a gateway system. A system administrator, instructor, or ISP can provide this information.

- Protocols define how devices and parts of an operating system communicate with each other. Linux uses many different protocols.

- You can compile a detailed system inventory by referring to the computer documentation, a vendor's Web site, or by checking computer settings in Windows (if it is already installed on the computer where Linux will be installed).

- Hard disks are composed of platters, each divided into tracks and sectors. Tracks on multiple platters that are vertically aligned are called a cylinder. Cylinders are used to define partitions.

- You can use Linux on the same computer as another operating system by setting up a dual-boot system. Each time you boot such a system, you select which operating system to start.

❑ If you intend to create a dual-boot system, you must prepare the hard disk before you start to install Linux. You create partitions for the Linux file system and swap partition using a utility such as parted, FIPS, or PartitionMagic.

❑ The BIOS controls the boot process by passing control to the MBR, which in turn can contain a Linux boot manager such as GRUB or LILO, or it can pass control on to the boot record of the active partition.

❑ Many Linux distributions are available, each with a slightly different technical focus and often with different end users as its primary customers. Vendors of commercial distributions try to distinguish their products by offering documentation, technical support, additional software packages, or related services.

❑ Linux installations are started by a boot disk or bootable CD-ROM, DVD, or USB device. A user defines the source of the Linux files and the target partition where they will be stored. The user also answers a number of questions during the installation process to define exactly what software will be installed and how it will be configured.

❑ Attractive graphical installation programs are standard in commercial versions of Linux. On many systems a complete Linux installation takes only about 15 minutes plus the time required to copy files to your hard disk.

❑ You can install Linux from a CD-ROM, from files stored on a hard disk, or across a network connection. The CD-ROM option is most widely used except when Linux is installed on a large number of systems at the same time, in which case a network install is most likely.

❑ The various components of Linux are sometimes arranged on different hard disk partitions to make system administration tasks easier. You can configure these partitions within the Linux installation program.

❑ Installation programs generally provide multiple installation types that let you define the sorts of programs you want to install as part of Linux. For example, server, graphical workstation, or software development station might define different sets of applications that are installed with the basic operating system.

❑ Software packages are managed using special file formats such as the Red Hat Package Manager format (rpm).

❑ Installing multiple identical systems or reinstalling the same system multiple times can be done more easily using the Kickstart method, which uses a configuration file to hold all installation selections.

❑ A Kickstart installation uses a text configuration file called ks.cfg. This file is stored on the boot disk. It can be created manually or using the Kickstart Configurator graphical utility.

Command Summary

No new Linux commands were introduced in this chapter.

KEY TERMS

active partition — The bootable partition; the partition that the MBR passes control to if the MBR does not itself contain a boot manager.

BIOS (Basic Input/Output System) — Information stored in ROM that provides instructions to the operating system for using the devices on a computer.

bit — A binary digit; a bit can hold a value of either one or zero.

block — A unit of hard disk space; typically one that contains 1024 bytes, or two sectors.

boot disk — A removable disk that can start an operating system, especially one that starts a Linux installation program.

boot manager — A program that lets you start one or more operating systems each time you start a computer. (Examples include GRUB and LILO.)

boot record — A small area on each partition that contains a program to start the operating system on that partition.

bootable CD-ROM drive — A CD-ROM drive that can start an operating system (or other program) directly from a CD without accessing the hard disk. (This feature of the CD-ROM drive must be enabled by the BIOS.)

broadcast address — An IP address that sends a packet of data to all computers on a network.

byte — Storage space sufficient to store one character; eight bits.

CMOS RAM — A special memory chip in which computer configuration details are stored. The data is maintained by a tiny battery and is modified as needed using a BIOS utility.

cylinder — A set of tracks at the same location on all the platters of a hard disk.

defragment — A procedure that arranges each file so that the parts of the file are next to each other on the hard disk; places all sectors composing a file into contiguous disk locations.

device driver — Software used to communicate with or control a hardware component.

direct memory access (DMA) channel — A communication method within a computer that allows a device to read and write directly to the computer's RAM, without going through the microprocessor first.

disk image — A single file that contains an exact copy of a floppy disk.

domain name — A name assigned to a collection of computers on a network.

dual-boot system — A computer that allows a user to choose which operating system to start each time the computer is started.

FAT — (file allocation table) The file system type used by older versions of Windows (such as Windows 3.1).

FAT32 — (file allocation table, 32-bit) The file system type used by some versions of Windows (such as Windows 98).

FIPS — A program that creates two separate partitions from an existing Windows partition. Used to create an empty partition that can be deleted and the resulting free space used for installing Linux. Can not be used with the NTFS file system (Windows NT, 2000, XP, or Server 2003).

8

gigabyte (GB) — A measure of space on computers equal to 1024 megabytes, or roughly enough space to store 1 billion characters.

GRUB — A Linux boot manager; used by default on Red Hat Linux and Fedora distributions.

hexadecimal (hex) — A numbering system using base 16. Hex uses 0 to 9, plus the letters A through F (usually capitalized) to count the numbers 10 through 15.

I/O ports — Special addresses (resembling memory addresses) used by a device for port-mapped I/O.

IDE — A low-cost, easy-to-manage interface used by most computers to connect hard disks and CD-ROM drives to the CPU.

IDE controller — A hardware component used to communicate between an IDE-compatible hard disk or other IDE device and the microprocessor.

install disk — A disk used to start the Linux installation program on some distributions of Linux. See *boot disk*.

installation source — The set of files from which Linux is installed. These files are normally stored on a Linux CD-ROM.

installation type — A specification indicating which Linux software to install; the appropriate installation type depends on how the Linux system will be used.

interrupt request (IRQ) — A numbered signal that a device sends to the operating system to request service.

Kickstart — A method of controlling the installation of Red Hat Linux or Fedora using a prebuilt configuration file instead of responding to questions at the keyboard during the installation.

kickstart configuration file — The text file used to control a Kickstart installation, named ks.cfg.

LILO (Linux Loader) — A Linux boot manager.

live CD — A CD-ROM containing a Linux distribution that can be run in computer memory and using the data on the CD-ROM, without ever performing a traditional Linux installation. No information is ever written to the hard disk.

logical partition — A hard disk partition that exists within one of the four partitions that a hard disk can traditionally manage. Logical partitions are numbered beginning with 5. See also *primary partition*.

Master Boot Record (MBR) — A small area on the first hard disk that contains a program to decide how to start an operating system. Control passes from the BIOS to the program in the MBR when a computer is first booted.

megabyte (MB) — A measure of space on computers equal to 1,048,576 bytes, or enough space to store roughly 1 million characters.

mount point — A subdirectory through which a set of data such as a hard disk partition is accessed.

network address — An address that identifies the local network of which a computer is a part. This address is used to determine how data is routed to its intended destination.

NTFS (NT file system) — The default file system type for Windows NT, Windows 2000, Windows XP, and Windows Server 2003.

parted — A free partition-editing tool that can be used to change partition sizes, including changing the size of an older Windows partition to make room for Linux. Comparable to the FIPS utility, but more powerful and more recently updated.

partition table — Information on a hard disk that defines the size and file system type of each partition on that hard disk.

port-mapped input/output (port-mapped I/O) — A device communication technique that uses a separate range of memory addresses called I/O ports as a place for a device to send and receive data. Essentially, each device-specific port address works like a post office box.

primary partition — One of the four partitions that traditional hard disk electronics can effectively manage. See also *logical partition*.

protocol — An organized pattern of signals or words used to communicate efficiently.

random access memory (RAM) — Volatile electronic storage within a computer.

read-only memory (ROM) — Nonvolatile electronic storage within a computer. Used to store information about how the computer starts and how the devices in the computer are configured.

Red Hat Package Manager (rpm) — A data storage format for software packages.

SCSI — A high-performance interface used by many types of devices to connect to a computer.

sector — A unit of data storage on a hard disk. Normally a sector contains 512 bytes.

software package — A single file that contains all the files needed to install and use an application or group of related applications. Special data formats are used to store many files in a single software package.

target hard disk partition — The location on the system's hard disk where Linux is installed. Also known as *target partition*.

track — One of many concentric circles of data storage area on each platter of a hard disk.

USB (Universal Serial Bus) — A method of connecting peripherals, including storage drives, to a computer. USB devices are typically attached via an external cable.

8

REVIEW QUESTIONS

1. A byte is enough space to store:

   a. one character

   b. one hexadecimal digit

   c. one sector

   d. one megabyte

2. When you see a value in gigabytes, it probably refers to:

    a. an IRQ number

    b. a monitor refresh rate

    c. hard disk size

    d. RAM size

3. Which of the following cannot be changed by a user?

    a. magnetic data on a hard disk

    b. electronic storage in RAM

    c. the configuration settings in the BIOS

    d. the BIOS stored in ROM

4. Which of the following is *not* part of the communications scheme between devices and the CPU?

    a. IRQ

    b. FIPS

    c. I/O ports

    d. DMA channel

5. The _____ numbering system is often used to refer to information about computer hardware.

    a. hexadecimal

    b. MBR

    c. binary

    d. SCSI

6. Which of the following is *not* a valid hexadecimal digit?

    a. E

    b. D

    c. A

    d. H

7. The _____ interface is a high-cost, high-performance method of connecting hard disks to a computer.

    a. LILO

    b. SCSI

    c. IDE

    d. MBR

8. Which is *not* a valid IP address?

   a. 0.0.0.0

   b. 12.456.27.198

   c. 207.198.27.1

   d. 10.10.255.255

9. Name four items of information about the network that may be required to complete a Linux installation.

10. By using DHCP, a Linux system can:

   a. Convert a domain name to an IP address.

   b. Pass packets outside the local network to the Internet.

   c. Send broadcast messages to all computers on the network.

   d. Obtain an IP address from a server on the network.

11. Name four methods of obtaining system hardware specifications prior to installing Linux.

12. The Windows _____ can provide many hardware details about a computer.

   a. Search dialog box

   b. FIPS program

   c. Start menu

   d. Control Panel

13. Assuming a Windows system is using TCP/IP networking, which networking information is not included in any Windows dialog boxes accessible through Control Panel?

   a. the IP address of the system

   b. the IP address of one or more DNS servers

   c. the IP address of the NFS server to use for installation

   d. the IP address of one or more gateway servers

14. Explain why you must receive an IP address assignment rather than simply choosing one you like (as you may be able to do with a host name).

15. A file system resides within a:

   a. partition

   b. track

   c. block

   d. sector

8

16. DMA is one method of device communication, but most devices communicate with the CPU using special addresses called:

    a. channels

    b. ports

    c. active partitions

    d. blocks

17. The parted or FIPS program is used to:

    a. Split a single Windows partition into two Windows partitions.

    b. Create a partition marked for the ext2 file system.

    c. Combine two Windows partitions into a single Windows partition.

    d. Resize ext2, ext3, or Linux swap partitions once Windows data has been successfully defragmented.

18. When a file system is defragmented, the files are arranged so that:

    a. They are alphabetical in the directory structure.

    b. All parts of a file are next to each other on the hard disk.

    c. Compatible files are next to each other on the hard disk.

    d. Linux can easily use the files from Windows.

19. The installation program included with a Linux distribution is usually created by:

    a. the company, or vendor, that sells the Linux distribution

    b. the team of developers that created the kernel

    c. the Gnu project of the Free Software Foundation

    d. Linus Torvalds

20. Explain why installing a new Linux system is different from installing an application such as a spreadsheet or a database package.

21. The target hard disk partition is where:

    a. a dual-boot Windows system resides

    b. the Linux operating system will be installed

    c. backup data must be stored for Linux to access it

    d. the Linux installation program is stored

22. Possible locations for the installation source data do *not* include which of the following:

    a. the target hard disk partition

    b. a local CD-ROM

    c. a local hard disk

    d. a networked server using the SMB protocol

23. When you turn on a computer, _____ sends control to the MBR of the first hard disk, or to another device such as a bootable CD-ROM drive or a floppy drive.

    a. Linux

    b. the `fdisk` utility

    c. the boot manager

    d. the BIOS

24. The boot disk is not needed if:

    a. You are using DHCP for the Linux installation.

    b. You have a bootable CD-ROM drive.

    c. You are using a network-based installation.

    d. You have already created two partitions using FIPS.

25. In which circumstance do you need a boot disk to start the Linux installation program?

    a. when the computer does not have a bootable CD-ROM drive or similar device

    b. when installing on a laptop

    c. when the hard disk has become corrupted

    d. when installing from a network installation source

26. Name the utility used in Windows to copy a disk image to a removable disk.

27. The device name /dev/hda3 refers to:

    a. the third partition on the first IDE hard disk

    b. the third partition on the first SCSI hard disk

    c. the third IDE hard disk

    d. the swap partition stored on a boot disk

28. Name three reasons why you might place different parts of the Linux file system on different hard disk partitions.

29. The partition table is located on the hard disk and contains:

    a. a list of Linux device names for everything on the system

    b. boot parameters to help Linux locate and correctly use the different hardware

    c. a copy of the boot manager

    d. a data table with the size and type of each partition on the hard disk

8

30. The surest way to have the Linux boot manager correctly start Linux is to install it on:

    a. the MBR

    b. the boot sector of the active partition

    c. a networked server

    d. the installation source partition

HANDS-ON PROJECTS

Project 8-1

In this project, you use Windows Control Panel to learn about your computer system. To complete this activity you need a computer with Windows installed. You can complete this activity as an exercise even if you do not install Linux on the same computer later on. The steps here apply to Microsoft Windows XP. If you are using an older version (such as Windows 95), you need to experiment and explore the options provided in your Control Panel.

1. Click **Start**, then click **My Computer** on the Windows Desktop. The My Computer window opens.

2. Click **Control Panel** under the Other Places heading.

3. Double-click **System** in the Control Panel window. The System Properties dialog box opens. (If you are working in the Category view of Control Panel, click the **Performance and Maintenance** icon, then the **System** icon.)

4. You see the General tab. On that tab, locate the amount of system memory in your computer. Convert this number to MB if it is displayed in another form (such as KB).

5. Change to the **Hardware** tab of the System Properties dialog box.

6. Click **Device Manager**. Scroll down to the item labeled Ports (COM & LPT) and click the **+** (plus symbol) to the left of that item.

7. Double-click the item **Communications Port (COM1)**. You see a dialog box describing how the COM1 serial port is configured to transmit and receive data.

8. Click the **Resources** tab. You see the I/O port address (labeled I/O Range) and the Interrupt Request Line (IRQ) currently used by this serial port.

    A serial port can nearly always use default values for the I/O port address and IRQ, so you rarely change these fields. But you can see here how a device can use different values for these parameters if needed to avoid a conflict with other devices on the computer.

9. Click **Cancel** to close the Communications Port (COM1) Properties dialog box. Chose **File**, then **Exit** to close the Device Manager. Click **Cancel** to close the System Properties dialog box.

10. Double-click the **Display** icon in Control Panel. (If you are using Category view, click the **Back** button, then click **Appearances and Themes**, then click **Display**.)

11. Click the **Settings** tab in the Display Properties dialog box.

12. Notice the number of colors and the resolution of your current Windows display. Linux can operate at the same level, or perhaps better (higher resolution or more colors), depending on what hardware you have on your computer.

13. Click the **Advanced** button in the lower right of the dialog box. The information shown depends on the type of video hardware installed in your computer. In many cases, an Adapter tab is available that contains detailed information about your video card, including the manufacturer, model name, and amount of video memory installed.

14. Use the **Cancel** button(s) to close all open dialog boxes so that you see only Control Panel again. Close the Control Panel.

HANDS-ON PROJECTS

Project 8-2

In this project, you install the Fedora distribution. To complete this activity you should have an Intel- or compatible-based computer with a bootable CD-ROM drive. The computer should have a minimum of 32 MB of memory (Red Hat Software lists 256 MB as the minimum for Red Hat Enterprise Linux, but a minimal installation does not require that much memory). The installation requires between 510 MB and 6.3 GB of hard disk space. The packages groups marked in Table 8-4 require about 3.4 GB of hard disk space. See the notes in Table 8-4 if you do not have this much hard disk space available.

Installing Linux is the most involved project in this book. Because so many variations exist in available computer hardware, the steps you have to follow may differ slightly from the steps given in this project. Every effort has been made to alert you to important variations and prepare you to answer any questions that come up.

These steps assume that you are installing Linux on a desktop computer (not a laptop), on an IDE hard disk, and that you do not need additional special hardware drivers (though comments are provided regarding such drivers).

1. Insert the Fedora CD 1 in your CD-ROM drive and turn on your computer.

2. After a few moments, a welcome screen appears.

   a. Press **Enter** to immediately start the installation in graphics mode.

   b. If you have previously had trouble with the graphics mode, type the word **text** and press **Enter**.

   c. If you tried the installation previously and the system appeared to crash during the start-up phase, you can try entering **linux noprobe** and pressing **Enter**. This prevents the installation program from probing hardware, which causes problems on a few systems.

3. Assuming that you pressed **Enter** without typing any text or simply waited, the system pauses for several moments, then probes your video card and monitor. After a few moments, the graphical installation program begins and you see the CD Found screen shown in Figure 8-19. (To reach this first screen after pressing Enter in Step 2, may take as much as four full minutes, depending on your computer's speed.)

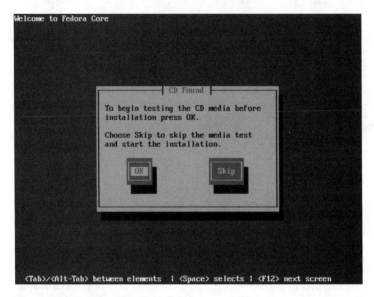

Figure 8-19 The CD Found screen

4. Because many people download Fedora or purchase CDs from download service companies, you have the option of validating your Fedora CDs in this first screen. This process takes several minutes—if you have not had problems with your CDs, you can use the **Tab** key to select Skip and press **Enter** to continue.

If you are installing across a network, you do not see this screen. Instead, you need to enter information about how to access the installation sources on your local network. For example, you need to enter the IP address of the server where the files are located.

5. After the CD is tested (or when you skip that step), the first graphical installation screen appears.

On the left side of the screen you see help text. You can review this area at any time during the installation to see detailed information on the choices presented at that point in the installation. A Release Notes button also has late-breaking information about the product that you should review.

On the lower-right side of the screen are two buttons labeled Back and Next. You use these buttons to navigate through the installation program, choosing Next to proceed to the following screen or Back if you wish to return to a previous screen to make a change or review something.

If you are using the text mode installation program instead of the graphical installation (which is the focus of these steps), you see the Back and Next buttons. You can navigate between buttons using the Tab key.

If you are using the graphical installation program but your mouse does not work (it normally works immediately), you can use the Tab and Enter keys to choose the Next button; the fourth screen of the Installation program lets you configure your mouse correctly.

6. Choose the **Next** button to continue past the Welcome screen. The Language Selection window appears with a list of language options. Click on a different language than U.S. English if appropriate and then choose **Next**. The language changes immediately to match your selection.

7. The Keyboard Configuration window appears. If you are using a non-U.S. keyboard or a special keyboard such as a Microsoft Natural keyboard, select the appropriate items for your keyboard. Choose **Next** to continue.

8. The Mouse Configuration window appears. (Figure 8-20.) Your mouse is probably already working, but you can select your model from the list shown if it was not correctly auto-detected and highlighted. If the mouse model you select uses a serial port interface, you can then select the appropriate serial port in the box below the list of mouse models. The list includes both the Linux device name (on the right) and the better-known port name (on the left). Click on the appropriate line to select it.

You may want to also select the Emulate 3 buttons check box at the bottom of this window. Some functions in Linux use the middle button of a three-button mouse. If you are using a two-button mouse, checking this box causes Linux to act is if you pressed a middle mouse button anytime you press both mouse buttons at the same time. Click **Next** to continue.

If your mouse was not working when you first saw the Mouse Configuration window, it should begin working when you click Next. If it does not, use the back button on the following screen to return to the Mouse Configuration screen and reconfigure your mouse.

NOTE   Depending on the type of monitor you are using, you may see a Monitor Configuration window after the Mouse Configuration window. Review the information on this screen, but in virtually all cases, the default information shown is acceptable and you can simply click **Next** to continue.

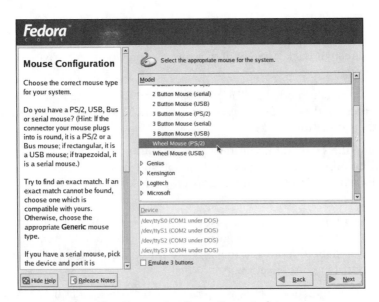

Figure 8-20   The Mouse Configuration window

9. If you are installing Fedora on a system where Fedora has already been installed, the Upgrade Examine window appears. Although you could select the Upgrade an existing installation option, choose the Install Fedora Core option to perform a complete installation from scratch. Click **Next** to continue.

10. The Installation Type window appears. (See Figure 8-21.) Selecting Personal Desktop, Workstation, or Server makes the installation simpler. But to help you learn more, select **Custom** so that you will be shown a list of package groups to select from later on. Click **Next** to continue.

11. The Disk Partitioning Setup window appears. (See Figure 8-22.) This window tells you that the installation program can automatically set up partitions on your system or let you determine manually how Linux will be installed. If you were installing Linux on a new computer or one with no valuable data on its hard disks, the automatic option makes installation very easy. But once again, to learn more, select the second item, **Manually partition with Disk Druid**. Then click **Next** to continue.

12. The Disk Setup window appears. The top part of the screen shows a representation of your hard disk as a horizontal bar divided into labeled partitions. The bottom part of the screen lists partitions by their Linux device names (such as /dev/hda1) and also gives their sizes, partition type, and other information. Between these two areas of the window are buttons you can use to set up partitions.

    a. If you feel at any time that you have become confused or selected the wrong thing, click the Reset button. The partition table will be reread from the hard disk. Nothing is written to the hard disk until you click the Next button and confirm your partition changes.

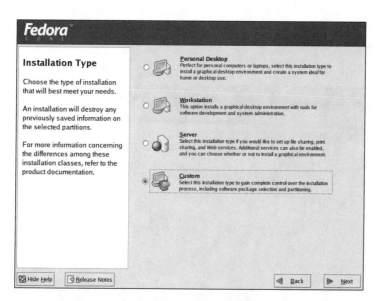

Figure 8-21   The Installation Type window

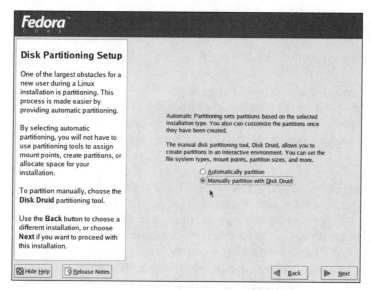

Figure 8-22   The Disk Partitioning Setup window

b. If you have an empty Windows partition that you intend to use for Linux, click on that partition in the list and click Delete to remove it from the partition table.

c. Once you have sufficient free space on your hard disk, click the **New** button. A dialog box appears in which you define the partition. (See Figure 8-23.) Choose **swap** from the File System Type drop-down list. In the Size field, enter a size in megabytes for the swap partition (this should be from about 128 MB to 1 GB). Make certain that **Fixed size** is selected in the Additional Size Options section of the dialog box. Click **OK** to add this partition to the new partition table you are defining.

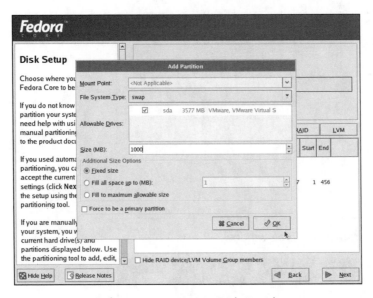

Figure 8-23   Defining a partition in Disk Druid

d. Click **New** again. A dialog box appears. Enter **/** in the Mount Point field or select it from the drop-down list. Choose **ext3** from the File System Type drop-down list. You can enter a size if you prefer, but you might want to just choose Fill to maximum allowable size in the Additional Size Options section. Click **OK** to add this partition.

When you click OK, the installation program analyzes the partition you have created for the root file system. If that partition might not function correctly with your BIOS, you see a warning message stating that the partition "may not meet booting constraints for your architecture. Creation of a boot disk is highly encouraged." You can then select either Modify Partition or Continue. If you select Modify Partition, create a separate, small partition (85 MB) for the /boot subdirectory that is located near the beginning of the hard disk (with smaller cylinder numbers). Then you can create a second, larger partition for the root file system, /. If you select Continue instead of Modify Partition, you should be sure to create a boot disk later in the installation process. If booting Linux directly from your hard disk fails because the BIOS cannot work with your Linux partitions, you can still boot the system from the boot disk.

NOTE

You must have at least two partitions to install Linux: a swap partition and a Linux partition for the root file system (/).

NOTE

e. If you want to make a change in your new partition structure, use the Edit or Delete buttons, then use New again to re-create the partition definition. The diagram at the top of the window illustrates the partitions as you create them. Click **Next** to continue.

f. Depending on your preexisting hard disk configuration, you might see a dialog box listing the partitions that will be formatting during the installation of Linux. If such a dialog box appears, verify that these partitions are *not* partitions that contain information you want to retain (such as on an existing Windows partition). Then click **Yes** to confirm use of the partitions.

13. The Boot Loader Configuration window appears. You should accept the default selections in this window and simply click **Next** to continue unless told differently by an instructor or system administrator.

If you are using this system for both Linux and Windows, you can click the Add button to add a boot option. You must assign a name and define the partition where the other operating system is stored. (See Figure 8-24.)

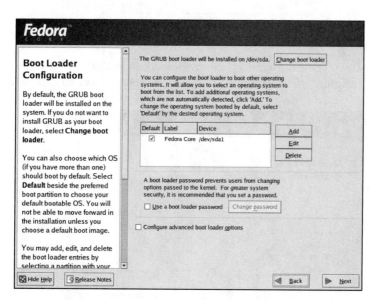

Figure 8-24   Adding an operating system to the boot loader configuration

You can also select Configure advanced boot loader options to select which part of the hard disk the boot manager is installed on. You can explore this option (see Figure 8-25), but should not need to alter the default setting the installation program selects. After reviewing the available options, click **Next** to continue.

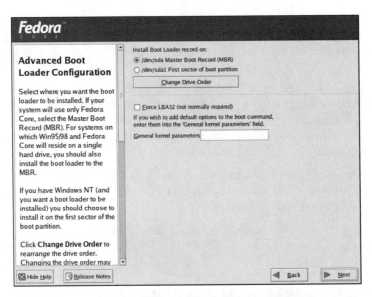

Figure 8-25   Selecting where to install the boot loader

14. The Network Configuration window appears. (See Figure 8-26.) If you are relying on DHCP for assigning network information, simply click **Next** to continue.

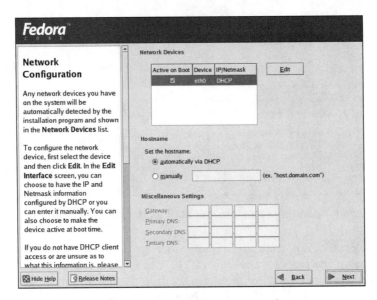

Figure 8-26   The Network Configuration window

If you have been given a host name for your computer, select **manually** under the Set the hostname field and enter the host name.

If you have been given an IP address, click the **Edit** button, deselect the Configure using DHCP check box, then enter the information you were given in the dialog box (see Figure 8-27). Click **OK** to continue, then enter any other information you were given in the Miscellaneous Settings area. Then click **Next** to continue.

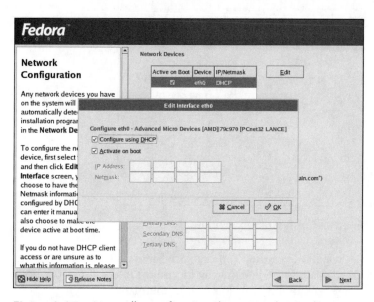

Figure 8-27   Manually configuring the network interface

15. The Firewall Configuration window appears. (See Figure 8-28.) The items on this window are important but are beyond the scope of this book. This project assumes you are working in a lab environment, but for safety's sake, make certain that Enable firewall is selected. Then select the first three boxes, WWW, FTP, and SSH. Click **Next** to continue.

16. The Additional Language Support window appears. In this window you can choose to install documentation and interface text (for dialog boxes and menus) for a number of languages beyond the English that is installed by default. Check the box next to any of these that you wish to install, but note that each one takes up many megabytes of hard disk space. If you do select additional languages, you should also select the default language for your installation from the drop-down list at the top of the window (it only lists languages that you have checked below). Click **Next** to continue.

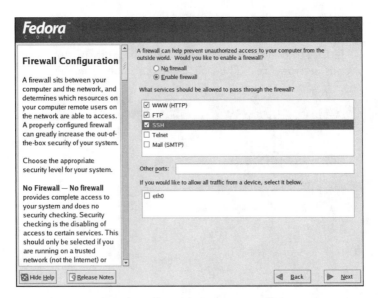

Figure 8-28   The Firewall Configuration window

17. The Time Zone Selection window appears. (See Figure 8-29.) Begin by selecting the time zone where you are located, either by locating it in the list at the bottom half of the screen or by clicking on your location in the map.

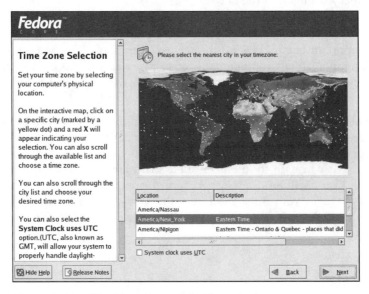

Figure 8-29   The Time Zone Selection window

If you are running only Linux on your computer, you should select the System clock uses UTC check box. Computers that also have Windows installed should not use this option.

Click **Next** to continue.

18. The Set Root Password window appears. Select a password for the root account, then enter that password in the Root Password and Confirm text fields. Click **Next** to continue.

19. The Package Group Selection window appears. (See Figure 8-30.) This window appears as the result of selecting Custom for your installation choice. Package groups are listed as shown in Table 8-4. Select the packages that you want to install. (Those recommended for this book are marked with an asterisk in the left column of Table 8-4.)

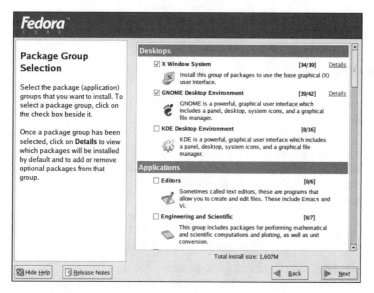

Figure 8-30   The Package Group Selection window

The total hard disk space required to install the packages you have selected is shown below the list of package groups. Anytime you select a package group, the number to the right of that item changes. For example, it might change from "0/42" to "39/42." This means that when the group is not selected, zero packages from that group will be installed. When you first select it, 39 of 42 packages in that group will be installed. You can click the Details link to the right of the package group name to display a list of all the packages in that group. In this dialog box (shown in Figure 8-31), you can select or deselect specific packages. Unless you are familiar with specific package names, you should only select package groups, rather than individual packages, but it is instructive to review the details dialog boxes.

Click **Next** to continue.

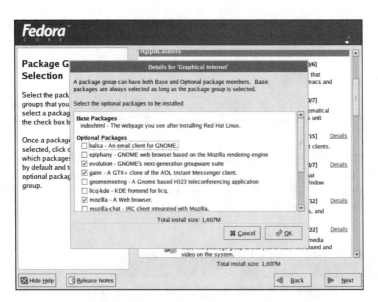

Figure 8-31 Viewing a detailed list of packages

20. The About to Install screen appears. If you are ready to begin the installation, click **Next** to continue.

If you fear you may have made a selection during the installation that will erase existing data on your computer, you can simply turn your computer off at this point. Nothing has been changed on your hard disk until you press Next on the About to Install window.

21. If you are installing from CDs, a message informs you which CDs are required based on the packages that you selected to install. Click **Continue** to go on.

22. Several messages appear as the installation program works, then the Installing Packages window appears (see Figure 8-32). This window includes a progress bar at the bottom indicating the progress of the installation. The name of each software package is listed below as it is installed. This screen will remain visible for 10 to 60 minutes as all packages are installed. (The time required for installing packages depends on the speed of your CPU and your CD-ROM drive.) When prompted, insert the requested CD in the CD-ROM drive, then click **OK**.

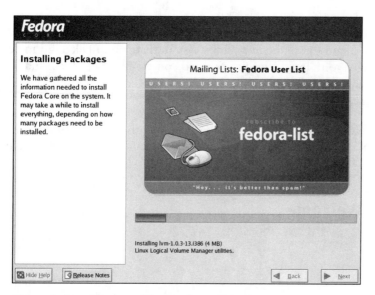

Figure 8-32 The Installing Packages window

23. The Congratulations window appears. (See Figure 8-33.) Remove the CD-ROM and click **Reboot** to start the newly installed copy of Linux.

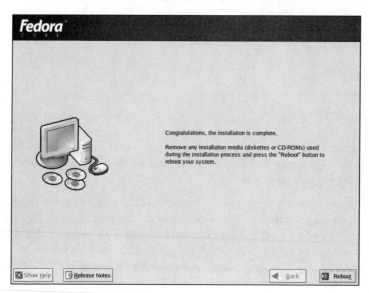

Figure 8-33 The Congratulations window

Several aspects of configuring the newly installed system are performed after the system is restarted. These are described in Project 8-3.

Project 8-3

In this project, you begin to use the new Linux system that you installed in Project 8-2. To complete this activity you should have just finished completing Project 8-2 and be ready to work on your newly installed system.

1. Remove any CDs from the computer.

2. If your computer is not already on from restarting at the end of Project 8-2, turn it on and wait a few moments. The Welcome screen shown in Figure 8-34 appears. Click **Next** to continue.

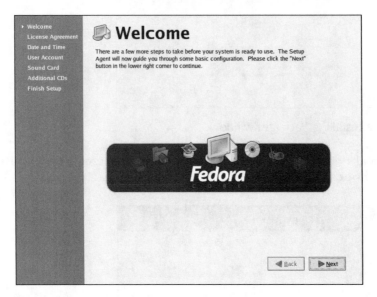

Figure 8-34   The Welcome window

3. The License Agreement window appears. Review the text of the license. If you are comfortable with its terms, select the **Yes, I agree to the License Agreement** button and click **Next** to continue.

4. The Date and Time window appears (see Figure 8-35). In the **Date** section, select the current date. In the **Time** section, select the current time using a **24**-hour clock (1:00 p.m. is 13:00, and so forth). The **Network Time Protocol** section lets you define a network server that can provide highly accurate time updates. Unless you have been given this information or have researched an appropriate server yourself (see *www.ntp.org*), leave this section blank. Click **Next** to continue. If necessary, select the the resolution and color depth that you wish to use in the screen that appears, then click **Next** again.

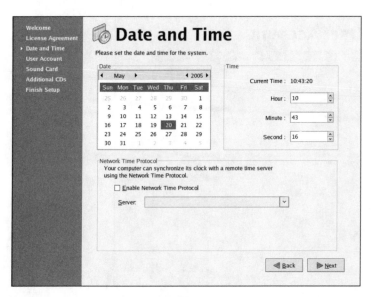

Figure 8-35   Defining the date and time

5. The User Account window appears, as shown in Figure 8-36. Enter a user name for the account in the **Username** field (for example, jthomas or jamest); enter your complete name in the **Full Name** field (for example, James Thomas); enter a password for this account in the **Password** and **Confirm Password** fields. Click **Next** to continue

   In Chapter 10 you will learn how to set up additional user accounts.

6. If Linux is able to detect a sound card on your system, the Sound Card window appears, as shown in Figure 8-37. (If no sound card is detected, skip to Step 9.) The details of your sound card are listed. Click the **Play test sound** button to test the sound.

7. Click Yes or No in the sound test dialog box based on what you hear. If you click No, you are informed that your sound card will not function in Linux. Click OK to close that dialog box.

8. Click **Next** in the Sound Card window to continue.

9. The Additional CDs window appears. It is unlikely that you need to add software packages using this screen, but if you do, click the Install button and follow the onscreen instructions. Otherwise, click **Next** to continue.

10. The Finish Setup window appears. Click **Next** to continue. After a few moments, you see the graphical login prompt indicating that you can log in to Linux and begin using your newly installed system.

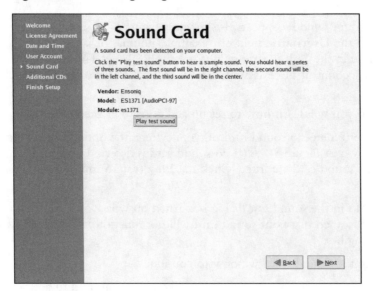

Figure 8-36   Creating a regular user account

Figure 8-37   Testing the sound card configuration

**HANDS-ON
PROJECTS**

Project 8-4

In this project, you install Fedora using the Kickstart feature. To complete this activity, you should have a completely installed Fedora or Red Hat Linux system. (For example, if you have just completed Projects 8-2 and 8-3, you are ready to complete this project.) You also need root access to the installed Linux system (be certain you know the root password).

Finally, you must have a standard formatted removable disk (the disk should not have been formatted with the ext2 file system). The steps shown here use the Fedora installation CD-ROMs that accompany this book and require that you have a bootable CD-ROM drive.

CAUTION

Reinstalling Linux using this procedure erases any data on your Linux partitions. It also erases the regular user account created as part of a standard installation (via Projects 8-2 and 8-3). You need a system administrator or instructor to create a regular user account after completing this project (or you can turn to Chapter 11, "Managing Users," to see how to create a basic user account using the *useradd* command).

1. Start Linux and log in as root. If you are working in a graphical desktop, open a command-line window.

2. Insert the disk into the removable disk drive.

3. Use the following command to copy the kickstart configuration file that was created during the standard installation (in Projects 8-2 and 8-3) to the disk. The name must be changed to fit the name expected by the installation program for a kickstart configuration file.

mcopy /root/anaconda-ks.cfg A:ks.cfg

You can use the Kickstart Configurator program to create or modify this file, but using the file created during the installation ensures that the file will work properly.

4. Insert your Fedora CD-1 in your CD-ROM drive. Eject the disk so that your computer does not try to start from the disk, but instead starts from the Fedora CD.

5. Restart your computer.

6. After a moment, the initial start screen appears. Insert the floppy disk into the floppy drive. Start the Kickstart installation by defining where the kickstart file is located. Enter this text at the boot prompt:

linux ks=floppy

NOTE

The exact windows that appear during this procedure depend on your hardware and the choices made during the standard installation that created the kickstart configuration file. The steps shown here reflect a fairly standard installation. If other screens appear besides those noted, refer to Project 8-2 for comments on how to respond to those screens. Additional configuration information can be included in a kickstart configuration file to eliminate the screens that appear in this project, but comparing this project to Projects 8-2 and 8-3 gives a good idea of how a Kickstart-based installation can simplify the system administrator's task.

8

7. After a couple of minutes, the Disk Partitioning Setup window appears, as shown in Figure 8-22. Make certain that **Automatically partition** is selected and choose **Next**.

8. The Automatic Partitioning window appears. Select **Remove all Linux partitions on this system**. (If you do not have any other operating systems sharing this computer with Linux, you can also select Remove all partitions on this system.)

9. Make certain the **Review (and modify if needed) the partitions created** check box is not checked. By leaving this unchecked, you avoid an additional step during the installation, but you would only do this if you were not worried about destroying information on any partitions of this computer.

10. Click **Next** to continue. Click **Yes** in the message box that appears to confirm that you want the partitions created as configured in the kickstart configuration file. The installation process begins. This process takes from 10 minutes to 60 minutes, depending on the speed of your hardware.

11. When the installation process is completed, click **Reboot**.

12. After a few moments, the graphical login screen appears. You can log in as root and begin using the system normally (you should have a system administrator or instructor create a regular user account so that you don't have to use the root account every time you log in.)

Case Projects

CASE
PROJECTS

Preparing to Install Linux

Your next consulting assignment is to help a company called PixelDust upgrade the Web servers they use for their online digital photo services.

1. The Web servers need much more hard disk space to work efficiently in the coming 12–18 months. Go online and research available hard disks. Determine whether IDE, SCSI, or USB drives are a better choice for this project. What effect do cost, ability to upgrade later (scalability), Linux support, and reliability have on your decision?

2. Having decided on a type of hard drive, you now must determine how much hard disk space to add to the servers. You learn that each of the photos that PixelDust processes averages 0.8 MB. They have 560 current customers and process an average of three new photos a week for each one. They also anticipate obtaining 50 new customers per week during the coming year, each of which will process the same number of photos. If PixelDust wants to add hard disk space that will be sufficient for the next 12 months, with a 15% safety margin (that much extra space), how much hard disk space do you need to provide? How might your answer alter your decision to Question 1 above?

3. PixelDust is wondering about the possibility of using some older computers they have found on sale as part of their collection of Web servers. What concerns might

you have about using them? How do you determine if you could, in fact, use them?

Other consulting proposals have arrived on your desk recently:

4. One potential client manages a group of resorts known collectively as the Lakewood Resorts. Lakewood Resorts has recently started to expand its operations by promoting its resorts to vacationers around the country. To support this expansion, they have installed a call center with about 100 computers to handle incoming requests for information and reservations. Each computer is staffed by a representative who can answer questions and make reservations or send out a resort brochure. You propose that all of the computers run Linux and be connected to a large reservations computer located in another office. You and your technical staff will install Linux on all of the systems. Based on the options you learned in this chapter, would you use a local CD-ROM drive to install each system or place the installation source files on a networked server? Explain the reasons for your choice. Describe in detail the additional features (beyond those discussed explicitly in the chapter) you would like to see in a Linux distribution or installation program to support your work on this project. Visit the Web sites of several Linux vendors, and see what features you can find that fit your criteria. How important would having these features be for a project like this? What if you had to install Linux on 2500 computers?

5. You are also trying to decide which Linux distribution you would use for the Lakewood project. What technical or nontechnical features are important to you as you prepare your plan to install Linux on the call center's computers? Given the standard cost range of Linux distributions mentioned in the chapter, how important is the cost of the Linux product in making your decision?

6. Suppose all the call center's computers already have Microsoft Windows installed. You have been asked to make each one a dual-boot system, so that representatives can use Windows software occasionally if necessary. Does this request change the Linux product you would choose? Would you recommend this model to Lakewood? Conduct research on the Internet or through Linux vendors to locate commercial Windows software to help you install (or prepare to install) the Linux systems. Assuming that the Linux systems were already installed and you were later asked to add Windows to each system, how would your arrangement of the Linux partitions (and possibly multiple mount points) affect your ability to make the requested change to the systems? Are some possible future needs too costly to prepare for now?

8

UNDERSTANDING SYSTEM
INITIALIZATION

After reading this chapter and completing the exercises, you will be able to:

♦ Describe how standard PC hardware starts an operating system

♦ Configure how the LILO or GRUB boot loader starts the Linux kernel

♦ Configure the *init* program and the scripts used to start system services

♦ Manage system services after start-up

In the previous chapter you learned how to prepare for and then install a new Linux operating system. You learned about hardware compatibility, preparing your hard disk, and creating dual-boot systems. You then walked through an actual installation of Fedora and learned how to complete numerous postinstallation configuration options.

In this chapter you learn about how the Linux kernel is initialized and what processes are begun as the system is started. You learn about the scripts and commands that control those core processes and how you can modify the default configuration used to start your Linux system.

HARDWARE INITIALIZATION

The phrase "booting a computer" comes from the word "bootstrapping," or "pulling yourself up by your bootstraps." The computer must get itself started from scratch. The CPU immediately has "control" when you turn on a computer's power, but the CPU needs instructions to follow. The basic process for bootstrapping is for the CPU to begin executing commands in the BIOS (and stored in various other hardware components); the BIOS to pass control to a boot loader; and the boot loader to pass control to the Linux kernel. Once the kernel is running, it must perform various steps before it can run regular programs.

NOTE

The phrase "pass control" means that one program can load another program into memory and tell the CPU to start executing that program instead of itself.

Becoming more familiar with some of these steps can help you manage your systems and understand various features of the Linux kernel. Here is a more detailed outline of what happens after you start a PC-type computer:

1. The CPU (for example, the Intel Pentium IV processor) initializes itself and begins sending out signals to control other parts of the computer.

2. The BIOS performs a power-on self test (POST), during which it checks memory and other hardware, such as detecting the type of storage devices that are attached to the system. During the POST phase, if any errors are found, the system beeps a number of times, with the number of beeps corresponding to the hardware problem discovered. This lets you diagnose the problem when you don't yet have a screen display visible because the video card has not been activated.

3. The BIOS sends a signal to the SCSI controller card (if one is installed), telling it to initialize itself. SCSI controllers usually contain their own BIOS. As the main system BIOS activates the SCSI controller, the SCSI BIOS determines how the system sees the devices attached to the SCSI controller. You can configure the SCSI BIOS by pressing a key during the SCSI BIOS initialization sequence (a message on the screen tells you when and what key to press).

4. Other hardware components, such as special IDE cards, USB expansion cards, or network cards, may be instructed to initialize themselves. During Steps 3, 4, and 5, you may see messages on the screen indicating that you can press a key to enter a setup menu of some type. In that menu, you can control how that device operates. Chapter 8, "Installing Linux," discussed the BIOS setup menus. Similar menus may be available for other devices as well.

5. Based on its configuration (which you can typically alter), the BIOS determines which devices to search for an operating system. It may start with the 3.5-inch disk drive, then check the CD-ROM drive, then the first IDE hard disk. Some systems permit you to boot from a USB device or from information transmitted over a network. In this step, the BIOS loads a boot loader into memory and passes control to that program. At that point, the BIOS is no longer controlling the computer.

Figure 9-1 illustrates the steps of initializing system hardware. Notice how the last step of Figure 9-1 meshes with the first step in Figure 9-2.

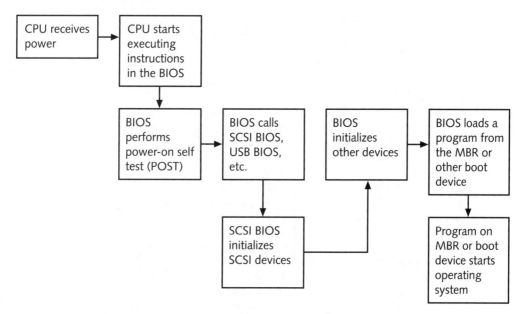

Figure 9-1   Initializing system hardware at boot time

The Boot Loader

The BIOS isn't particular about what program it starts. It looks in a certain location for an executable program, loads what it finds into memory, and passes control to that program so that it can send instructions to the CPU. In some cases, the BIOS actually loads the first part of an operating system (such as a Linux kernel). This is done for some Linux systems that run from a 3.5-inch disk. In nearly all cases, however, the BIOS loads a small program called a boot loader or boot manager, as you learned in Chapter 8. The two boot loaders commonly used on Linux systems are called LILO (Linux Loader) and GRUB (Grand Unified Boot Loader). GRUB is a more advanced program and is the default on most systems. Both are discussed in the next section.

The BIOS looks for an executable program in the first sector of the 3.5-inch disk or CD-ROM. If it doesn't find a bootable disk or bootable CD-ROM, it typically checks the first sector of the first IDE hard disk. This location is called the Master Boot Record (MBR).

Traditionally, the MBR contained a very small program that examined the partition table to determine which partition was marked as the active partition, then loaded the first sector of that partition and passed control to that program. Things have become more complicated, but that basic scenario is still accurate. The process the computer uses to load an operating system, as discussed briefly in Chapter 8, is illustrated in Figure 9-2 and discussed in more detail in the paragraphs that follow.

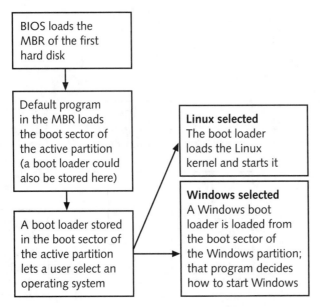

Figure 9-2 A typical process for booting an operating system stored on a hard disk

Because modern PCs can run many different operating systems, a boot loader lets you control which of many operating systems is started each time you turn on your computer. As discussed in Chapter 8, the boot loader can be stored on the MBR, or it can be stored on the boot record of any partition. If the MBR has not been altered to contain a boot loader, but instead simply points to the active partition, then the boot loader must be contained on the boot record of that partition or it will never be found.

Because boot loaders can be located in several places, you can use **chained boot loaders**. This means that when one boot loader passes control to another program, it is actually passing control to another boot loader instead of an operating system. Consider this example of chaining boot loaders: Suppose you have a computer with two large hard disks, each containing several partitions. The first hard disk has several versions of Linux installed; the second hard disk has several versions of Microsoft Windows installed. You could then install a boot loader on the MBR that contained the following choices:

- Windows operating systems
- Linux operating systems

If a person starting the computer selects the first choice, the boot loader passes control to the boot record of the first partition of the second hard disk. That boot record contains another boot loader that presents the following choices:

- Windows XP Professional
- Windows 2000
- Windows 98

Based on the selection made at this menu, the second boot loader passes control to one of the partitions on the second hard disk to start the selected operating system.

If the person selected the second choice at the first boot loader menu, the boot loader can pass control to the boot record of one of the partitions on the first hard disk. That boot loader might have a menu listing several versions of Linux that can be started.

If you have been using Windows-based computers, you probably think of the operating system kernel as some hidden component, separate from the rest of the file system. It is hidden in Windows, but in Linux, the kernel is just a regular file, normally stored in the /boot subdirectory. When a boot loader starts the Linux kernel, it simply loads the kernel file into memory and passes control to it. (You learn more details about that complex step shortly.) The kernel then uses a certain partition as its root file system.

Because of this simple structure, system administrators often experiment with multiple Linux kernels, booting different kernels to try different hardware configurations or different kernel features. A boot loader can easily be configured to start five different "operating systems" that are actually five different kernels stored in the same subdirectory of a single partition. All those kernels are configured to use that partition as their root file system.

TIP

The kernel is normally a file named vmlinuz in the /boot directory.

You can also use a boot loader to start different versions of Linux—such as SUSE, Red Hat, Debian, and Slackware—that you have installed on separate partitions.

After booting a version of Linux, you can use the **_uname_** command to display information about the kernel to see exactly which version you are using. This is very helpful when you have multiple versions of Linux on the same system. This command displays the full version number of the current kernel:

```
$ uname -a
```

The following command displays the timestamp of the kernel, showing when it was compiled. This is helpful when you are modifying your kernel by adding patches or recompiling (as discussed in Chapter 13, "System and Kernel Management").

```
$ uname -v
```

Starting the Kernel

Once the boot loader finds a Linux kernel to start, it loads the first part of the kernel and passes control to it. That initial piece of the kernel loads the rest of the kernel into memory and uncompresses it. You often see an onscreen message indicating that the kernel is being loaded and then uncompressed.

When the entire kernel is loaded and uncompressed, the kernel initializes system memory and begins examining hardware components so it can communicate with them. For example, the kernel initializes the PCI bus, sets up network protocols, and initializes device drivers so it can communicate with the corresponding devices. Finally, the kernel determines the arrangement of hard disks and mounts file systems.

As the kernel performs all of these tasks, it writes messages to the screen. You see these messages scroll by as each piece of hardware is located and initialized. When this process is complete and you have logged in to Linux, you can execute the *dmesg* command to view the messages stored by the kernel during the boot process. The *dmesg* command displays the contents of the **kernel ring buffer**, an area of memory where messages from the kernel are stored. If the memory space fills up, the oldest messages are discarded. If you don't use the *dmesg* command right after you start the computer, the *dmesg* command may display only messages that the kernel generated after the hardware was initialized. In that case, you can view the contents of the file /var/log/dmesg with *less* or a text editor. This file stores the contents of the kernel ring buffer immediately after starting the system. Figure 9-3 shows an example of how this information appears.

On Red Hat Linux or Fedora systems, additional messages generated during system start-up are stored in the file /var/log/boot.log.

TIP

Using Boot Parameters

When the boot loader starts a Linux kernel, it can pass information to that kernel, much like you can pass options or parameters to a command-line utility. These **boot parameters** are codes that instruct Linux how to operate or how to access parts of the computer system's hardware.

```
                            root@inverness:/var/log
File   Edit   View   Terminal   Go   Help
ACPI: BOOT (v001 PTLTD  $SBFTBL$ 0x00000001  LTP 0x00000001) @ 0x1ffffbd9
ACPI: DSDT (v001      HP HolmesHZ 0x00000001 MSFT 0x01000007) @ 0x00000000
Kernel command line: ro root=LABEL=/ hdc=ide-scsi rhgb
ide_setup: hdc=ide-scsi
Initializing CPU#0
Detected 601.368 MHz processor.
Console: colour VGA+ 80x25
Calibrating delay loop... 1199.30 BogoMIPS
Memory: 514264k/524224k available (1503k kernel code, 9572k reserved, 1110k data, 136k init, 0
k highmem)
Dentry cache hash table entries: 65536 (order: 7, 524288 bytes)
Inode cache hash table entries: 32768 (order: 6, 262144 bytes)
Mount cache hash table entries: 512 (order: 0, 4096 bytes)
Buffer cache hash table entries: 32768 (order: 5, 131072 bytes)
Page-cache hash table entries: 131072 (order: 7, 524288 bytes)
CPU: L1 I cache: 16K, L1 D cache: 16K
CPU: L2 cache: 256K
Intel machine check architecture supported.
Intel machine check reporting enabled on CPU#0.
CPU:     After generic, caps: 0383f9ff 00000000 00000000 00000000
CPU:            Common caps: 0383f9ff 00000000 00000000 00000000
CPU: Intel Pentium III (Coppermine) stepping 03
Enabling fast FPU save and restore... done.
Enabling unmasked SIMD FPU exception support... done.
Checking 'hlt' instruction... OK.
POSIX conformance testing by UNIFIX
mtrr: v1.40 (20010327) Richard Gooch (rgooch@atnf.csiro.au)
mtrr: detected mtrr type: Intel
ACPI: Subsystem revision 20031002
ACPI: Interpreter disabled.
PCI: PCI BIOS revision 2.10 entry at 0xfd9a3, last bus=1
PCI: Using configuration type 1
PCI: Probing PCI hardware
:
```

Figure 9-3   Kernel messages stored in /var/log/dmesg after system start-up; viewable after start-up using the *dmesg* command

If you are using the GRUB boot loader, press "a" when you see a list of operating system choices. This lets you type a boot parameter before starting Linux. If you are using LILO, enter the name of the system you want to start, then a space, then the boot parameters to pass to the Linux kernel.

NOTE

In LILO you can press the Tab key to see a list of names for the available operating systems. GRUB lists the choices for you automatically.

You can use boot parameters to activate features of Linux. For example, by using the boot parameter *single*, you start Linux in a special single-user maintenance mode:

```
linux single
```

Another example is the *mem=* boot parameter. The kernel has trouble recognizing the correct amount of system memory on some systems with more than 64 MB of RAM. (Recall that the *free* command shows you how much memory the kernel is aware of.) You can use the *mem=* boot parameter to tell Linux how much memory you really have. (Note that if you tell the kernel that you have more memory than you really have, it will eventually crash trying to access the nonexistent memory.) For example, if your system has 512 MB of RAM, you can start Linux with this command:

```
linux mem=512M
```

Multiple formats are supported for the *mem=* parameter, and you can include multiple parameters at one time. The Linux kernel supports dozens of boot parameters, though you are unlikely to need most of them unless you are working with high-end or unusual hardware, or need to use a special feature temporarily. To see a complete list of boot parameters, enter the command *man bootparam*.

CONFIGURING BOOT LOADERS

When you install Linux, a boot loader is configured for you. As you learned in Chapter 8, the installation programs for Red Hat Linux and Fedora permit you to add other operating systems to the boot loader configuration so that you can still start those operating systems after installing Linux on a dual-boot system.

The configuration files created by the installation program let you examine how a boot loader operates. Unless you install other operating systems or create new versions of the Linux kernel, you shouldn't need to change the boot loader configuration. Some system administrators, however, rely on GRUB or a commercial boot loader to manage a dozen operating systems on a single computer.

Chapter 13, "System and Kernel Management," discusses how you can update the boot loader configuration after installing or creating a new version of the Linux kernel.

TIP

Using LILO

The LILO boot loader is simpler than GRUB, with fewer features and fewer configuration options. The standard configuration file for LILO is /etc/lilo.conf. On Fedora and Red Hat systems, a file called /etc/lilo.conf.anaconda is created as a sample configuration file, though LILO is not used by default.

To use LILO after installing Linux, you create a configuration file describing the operating systems that you want LILO to be able to start. You then must run the *lilo* command, which examines the lilo.conf file and stores the appropriate information in the MBR or in the boot record that you have indicated. (You also must run this command anytime you make a change to the lilo.conf file.) Because the *lilo* command examines the exact location of the Linux kernel in your file system, if you make any changes to the Linux kernel file (such as adding an update to it), you must run the *lilo* command again so that LILO can boot that kernel. (GRUB does not require this step.)

You must be logged in as root to make any changes to the files discussed in this section.

NOTE

A sample lilo.conf file is shown here:

```
boot = /dev/hda
delay = 10
image = /boot/vmlinuz
     root = /dev/hda1
     label = linux
     read-only
other = /dev/hda3
     label = windows
```

Because LILO is designed for booting Linux kernels, each version of Linux is referred to as a **boot image**. Other operating systems use the term "other" and must have their own "start-up code." The lilo.conf file shown above has two lines that apply to the entire file, followed by two sections, one that boots a Linux kernel located on the first partition, and a second that passes control to a Windows operating system located on the third partition. The lines of the configuration file are examined in more depth here:

- *boot = /dev/hda*: This line tells the *lilo* command where to store the boot loader. This example refers to the MBR. If the device name /dev/hda2 were used, the boot loader would be stored on the boot record of the second partition.

- *delay = 10*: This line determines how long LILO waits until it starts an operating system. LILO typically prints a prompt like this example and waits for the user to either press Enter to start the default (first listed) operating system, or else enter the name of one of the systems (as defined by the two *label* = lines). After 10 seconds, LILO starts the default operating system without any input from the user.

- *image = /boot/vmlinuz*: This line defines a Linux kernel that LILO lists as an option to boot to. The */boot/vmlinuz* refers to a file in the /boot subdirectory. When you execute the *lilo* command, it stores the exact location of the kernel image on the disk within the MBR or boot record so that it can start it at boot time. The three indented lines that follow this line define information about the Linux kernel. *root = /dev/hda1* defines the partition that the kernel should be told to use as its root file system. *label = linux* defines the name that LILO will use to refer to this image. This text is displayed when a user presses the Tab key after seeing the boot prompt displayed by LILO. The user can then enter this text to select this operating system. The *read-only* line indicates that the file system should be mounted in a read-only mode. This is typically done in order to check the integrity of the file system; it is then remounted in read–write mode for normal use.

- *other = /dev/hda3*: This line defines a non-Linux operating system. The label indicated (*windows*) defines the text that LILO will use to refer to this operating system. If a user selects this item, LILO passes control to the boot record of the third partition on the first IDE hard disk (*dev/hda3*).

Using GRUB

The GRUB boot loader is installed by default when many versions of Linux are installed. If you want to add GRUB to a system that is using a different boot loader, you first create a GRUB configuration file and then use the ***grub-install*** program to copy GRUB to the appropriate location. For example, to copy GRUB to the boot sector of the second partition of the first SCSI hard disk, you use this command:

```
# grub-install /dev/sda2
```

The configuration file for GRUB (the default boot manager in Red Hat Linux) is /boot/grub/grub.conf. This file is quite similar in layout and syntax to the lilo.conf file. A sample GRUB configuration file for a dual-boot Linux system is shown here (without comments that the file includes):

```
default=0
timeout=10
splashimage=(hd0,1)/boot/grub/splash.xpm.gz
title Red Hat Linux (2.4.18-3)
        root (hd0,1)
        kernel /boot/vmlinuz-2.4.18-3 ro root=/dev/hda2
        initrd /boot/initrd-2.4.18-3.img
title DOS
        rootnoverify (hd0,0)
        chainloader +1
```

The grub.conf file includes global configuration details as well as a configuration for one or more operating systems. The lines of this sample file are described here. Complete information about using GRUB is available by entering *info grub*.

- *default=0*: This line defines which of the defined operating systems are started automatically if the user does not make a selection. The first option (Red Hat Linux in this case) is numbered 0.

- *timeout=10*: This line defines how long GRUB waits for user input before starting the default operating system.

- *splashimage=...*: This line defines a graphic image that GRUB displays at start-up. The *.xpm* file extension refers to a very simple graphical file format. To see (or alter) this image, enter the following command within GNOME: *gimp /boot/grub/splash.xpm.gz*.

- *title Red Hat Linux...*: This line assigns a text label to an operating system choice. Red Hat products include the kernel version number so you can identify which version you will be running, though the text can be anything you choose. The next three indented lines define how GRUB can start that operating system. The root line defines the root partition to use for this operating system (the second partition (the first is number 0) of the first hard disk—GRUB does not distinguish between IDE and SCSI disk drives). The kernel line defines the kernel file that should be booted, with the boot parameters that it uses (*ro* and *root=/dev/hda2* to define the partition for the root file system). The *initrd* line defines a special file that GRUB loads first to help get the kernel loaded.

- *title DOS*: This line assigns a text label to an operating system choice. The two indented lines that follow define a root working partition for GRUB (the MBR in this case). In this case, the *rootnoverify* indicates that GRUB should not try to understand what is contained on the partition indicated (because it's not an operating system that GRUB works with directly), but instead assume that a chained boot loader is present on the first sector of that partition, and pass control to it when this operating system is selected.

The grub.conf configuration file is used to define the menu options (and splash screen) presented when you start your computer. You can also install GRUB on the MBR of a computer without using any configuration file by running the *grub* command as root and using the *setup* command within GRUB's interactive shell. Figure 9-4 shows the GRUB shell after executing the *help* command to list all the commands that GRUB supports.

9

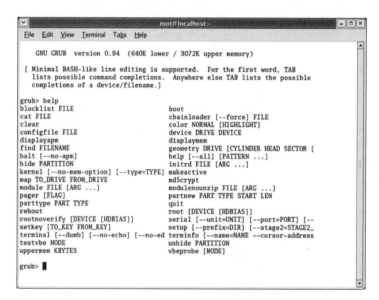

Figure 9-4 The GRUB shell, listing all GRUB commands

If you install GRUB in this way, then the next time you start your computer, instead of starting an operating system, you will see a GRUB shell prompt. At that point, you can enter a command to start the operating system that you select. Using a configuration file simplifies the use of GRUB.

When you start your system after installing Red Hat Linux or Fedora, you see a menu that lists operating systems that GRUB can start. At that point you can also start using the GRUB shell to control your system more precisely or modify the GRUB configuration. Just press "c" while viewing the list of options.

INIT AND ITS SCRIPTS

After the Linux kernel is loaded and has initialized the system's hardware components, it starts a program called *init*. The ***init* program** is a master control program that starts many other programs, such as the program that provides a login prompt. The *init* program also runs many scripts that initialize the system services you have installed. Many of these system services are network servers, such as an FTP server or Web server. Other services manage system logging, or various aspects of security or user management. These services operate in the background, watching for activity that they need to handle. A background process that behaves in this way is often called a daemon.

The *init* program is controlled by the /etc/inittab configuration file. This file contains pointers to the scripts that *init* runs to initialize the Linux system each time it is turned on. The /etc/inittab file is different in each version of Linux, but after reviewing the file on one system, you should be able to recognize features on other Linux systems. Most of the files referred to in /etc/inittab are in the /etc/rc.d subdirectory on Red Hat Linux and Fedora. Three main configuration files located in /etc/rc.d are listed here.

- *rc.sysinit*: The main system initialization script for Red Hat Linux and Fedora. It includes commands for setting up how the keyboard is used, which environment variables are needed, and many other hardware-specific configuration details that are not handled by the Linux kernel.

- *rc*: Script that starts system services such as networking, printing, automated script execution, and many others. The specific services that are started depend on how the system is configured. The *rc* script is used to set up services according to run level, as described in the next section.

- *rc.local*: Script executed after other initialization scripts. It is initially empty (it has only a few comments but no commands). You can place commands in *rc.local* that you want to have executed each time the system is turned on.

Understanding Run Levels

A **run level** is a numbered mode of operation in which a preconfigured set of services is activated. Table 9-1 shows the run levels used by Red Hat Linux and Fedora; many other versions of Linux use very similar settings.

Table 9-1   Run Levels in Linux

Run level	Name	Description
0	Halt	Shuts down all services when the system will not be restarted
1	Single-user mode	Used for system maintenance. Does not require logging in with a user name and password—operates as root. Does not provide networking capabilities.
2	Multiuser mode without networking enabled	Rarely used except for system maintenance or testing
3	Regular multiuser networking mode	Standard multiuser text-mode operation; non-graphical systems (such as network servers) use this mode for normal operation
4	-	Not used
5	Graphical login	Identical to run level 3 except a graphical login is used
6	Reboot	Shuts down all services so the system can be restarted

9

The run level that the *init* program starts when Linux is booted is defined in the /etc/inittab file. For a typical Red Hat Linux or Fedora system, the default run level is 5, indicating that the system should start in multiuser mode, with networking enabled, using a graphical login screen.

The *id:* line in /etc/inittab defines the default run level used by *init*. You can change the 5 to a 3 and restart your computer to see how a nongraphical login appears. The last line in the /etc/inittab file, beginning with an *x:*, defines the program that *init* starts to provide the graphical login screen.

By using the **init** or **telinit** command (they are equivalent), you can tell the *init* program to change to a different run level. This is commonly done only to restart or halt the system. For example, entering this command restarts the system:

```
# telinit 6
```

You learned in Chapter 6, "Managing Processes," about virtual consoles. Each is defined in /etc/inittab. Six lines similar to this line appear in /etc/inittab:

```
1:2345:respawn:/sbin/mingetty tty1
```

This line tells *init* that it should start the *mingetty* program, which provides a login prompt. This program is handed the parameter *tty1*, the first virtual console. The *init* program respawns (restarts) the *mingetty* program if it exits, so the virtual console stays active. The first 1 is simply a label; the second set of numbers, 2345, indicates the run levels for which this line will be used—everything except the special purpose levels, 0, 1, and 6. Project 9-3 describes how you can edit the /etc/inittab file to add an additional virtual console.

When you make a change in the /etc/inittab file, execute the command *telinit q* to cause *init* to reread its configuration file and activate the changes. Be sure to back up /etc/inittab and make changes carefully!

NOTE

Understanding rc Scripts

After running the *rc.sysinit* script, the *init* program starts the *rc* script located in the /etc/rc.d directory with a parameter that includes the run level to use. The *rc* script then starts the appropriate system services based on the selected run level.

Each run level is associated with a subdirectory. These subdirectories are located in the /etc/rc.d directory. For example, the directories /etc/rc.d/rc5.d and /etc/rc.d/rc6.d include files that control which system services are used in run levels 5 and 6, respectively. The run-level subdirectories contain files that indicate which services are to be started or stopped when operating Linux in that run level.

Each file in the run-level directories begins with a K or an S, followed by a two-digit number. The number indicates the order in which services are started or stopped. Services that begin with a K are stopped (killed); services that begin with an S are started. The files included in the run-level directories depend on which services you have installed on your Linux system. A typical listing for the /etc/rc.d/rc5.d directory is shown here:

K01yum	K70bcm5820	S28autofs
K05saslauthd	K74ntpd	S40smartd
K15httpd	K74ypserv	S44acpid
K20nfs	K74ypxfrd	S55cups
K24irda	S00microcode_ctl	S55sshd
K25squid	S05kudzu	S56rawdevices
K34yppasswdd	S08iptables	S56xinetd
K35smb	S09isdn	S80sendmail
K35vncserver	S10network	S85gpm
K35winbind	S12syslog	S90crond
K36lisa	S13irqbalance	S90xfs
K45named	S13portmap	S95anacron
K50snmpd	S14nfslock	S95atd
K50snmptrapd	S20random	S97messagebus
K50tux	S24pcmcia	S97rhnsd
K50vsftpd	S25netfs	S99local
K70aep1000	S26apmd	

The first S item (in the middle column, with the lowest number, 00) is for the *microcode_ctl* service, which applies any needed patches (microcode) to the CPU. Next, the *kudzu* service (number 05) starts, checking for new hardware on the system; next, the *rc* script starts *iptables* (number 08). Many other services are started as well, ending with the local service, which runs the *rc.local* script. The items that start with K in this directory indicate services that are installed on the system, but which are not active, either because they are not needed or because they have not been configured for use.

The /etc/rc.d/rc0.d directory contains a similar list of services, but with K instead of S before most of the file names, because run level 0 is used to shut down the system. A few services related to stopping the system begin with S in the run level 0 directory. For run levels 0 and 6 (shutdown and restart, respectively), the numbers are in approximately the reverse order: the first services (network access, for example) form a foundation for the entire system and are therefore the last services to be stopped.

The initialization of services in each run level includes another complication. The files you see in the run-level subdirectories are not regular files—they are symbolic links to scripts that stop and start the services. Looking at an example should clarify the point. If you use the *ls -l* command to see a long listing of the files in the /etc/rc.d/rc5.d subdirectory, you see that the S10network file is actually a symbolic link that points to /etc/rc.d/init.d/network. Because the file (the link) in the /etc/rc.d/rc5.d subdirectory contains a leading S, the *rc* script executes this script with the word "start" after it. Thus, the *rc* script actually executes this command to start the network service:

```
/etc/rc.d/init.d/network start
```

 NOTE The scripts in /etc/rc.d/init.d are installed as part of the software package that they control. You do not need to create—and should not modify—these scripts. The exception is when you are using a service that was not installed using a complete software package (as discussed in Chapter 10, "Managing Software Packages and File Systems.") In that case, you cannot use the structures discussed in this section to control the service, but need to make an entry in the *rc.local* script (or a similar start-up script) or start the service manually from the command line.

Figure 9-5 shows how the initialization components described in this section relate to each other. Each file in the various run-level directories operates in the same manner as the S10network link just described. All of them point to scripts stored in the /etc/rc.d/init.d directory. The scripts in this directory provide an organized method of starting and stopping system services.

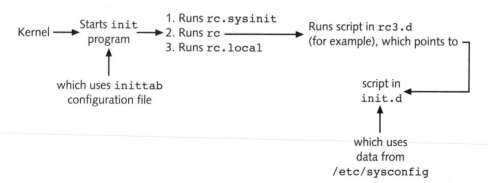

Figure 9-5 The Linux initialization process

The system initialization process described in this section is known as System V ("system five") initialization. It is based on the model used for years by the System V version of UNIX.

CONTROLLING SERVICES

Many of the services listed in the run-level directories relate to networking, which is not discussed in detail in this book. But the concept of system initialization is important because these scripts make it easy for you to change almost anything on a Linux system (short of using a new Linux kernel) without restarting the computer. For example, suppose you had reconfigured your printing system (as described in Chapter 12, "Configuring Networks"). Rather than restart the system to have your changes take effect, you could call on the scripts that manage the printing function by executing these two commands to reinitialize printing:

```
# /etc/rc.d/init.d/lpd stop
# /etc/rc.d/init.d/lpd start
```

Red Hat Linux and a few other Linux systems support this combined command:

```
# /etc/rc.d/init.d/lpd restart
```

Virtually all Linux network services—and many others—use this system.

Managing Services

The *service* command lets you perform this task without referring to the directory names. As long as you know the name of the service you want to control (as listed in the /etc/rc.d/init.d directory), you can use the *service* command to control that service. Just include the service name and the action to be taken. The following example restarts the printing service:

```
# service lpd restart
```

Similarly, suppose you have just finished configuring a DNS name server on your system. The service is initially not activated. To start it, use this command:

```
# service named start
```

If you have made changes in the DNS server configuration and need it to reread its configuration files, enter this command:

```
# service named restart
```

Another common use of the *service* command is simply to see the current state of a service:

```
# service named status
```

Using the *service* command only changes the current state of the service. You can also use the **chkconfig** command to alter the files in the run-level directories so that a service is started or stopped each time the system is started. To use this program, you specify the service you want to configure and *on* or *off* to indicate that the service should be activated or not activated. By default, the utility alters the settings for run levels 2, 3, 4, and 5. You can include a *--level* option to define other run levels to be affected. For example, if you want the *named* DNS server to be activated when you start your system, you would use this command:

```
# chkconfig named on
```

You must know the name of the service you want to configure as it appears in the /etc/rc.d/init.d subdirectory in order to use *service* or *chkconfig*.

Managing Services Graphically

You can also use a graphical utility to configure system services. Red Hat Linux and Fedora include the Service Configuration utility. You can start this program within GNOME by choosing System Settings, then Server Settings, then Services on the main menu. Or, you can enter *serviceconf* in a command-line window. The main window of this program lists the services that are available on your system (as determined by the contents of /etc/rc.d/init.d). Those that are active (have an "S" for the current run level) are shown with a check mark next to them). You can change the configuration of a service by selecting a run level from the Edit Runlevel menu (3, 4, and 5 are supported), and then placing check marks next to services you want to activate. Click the Save button below the menu bar to store the changes you have made to the system configuration.

CAUTION   Do not remove check marks from services that are active by default unless you understand what the service does. Many unfamiliar services provide important background functionality.

Although not as convenient as the command line for most administrators, the Service Configuration utility is a helpful way to learn about the services installed on your system. By selecting a service on the left side of the window, you can see a description of that service and status information about the service. For example, Figure 9-6 shows the *iptables* service selected. This service manages firewall functionality. The status section of the window displays the current firewall settings that *iptables* is using.

After selecting any service on the left side of the Service Configuration window, you can use the Start, Stop, and Restart buttons below the menu bar to manage that service.

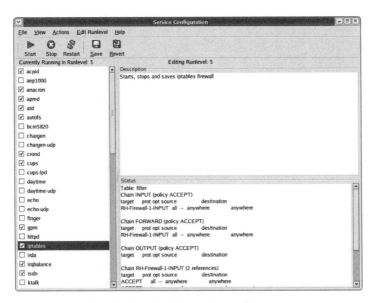

Figure 9-6   The Service Configuration utility

Configuring System Services

The initialization scripts in /etc/rc.d/init.d are provided when you install Linux. If you install a new software package for an Internet server or a system service or daemon, a script is typically placed in the correct directory and configured to activate the service at start-up time.

The initialization scripts in /etc/rc.d/init.d typically use configuration information located in the /etc/sysconfig directory and its subdirectories. The files in /etc/sysconfig are named for services, with each file containing name-value pairs that define configuration options for that service. For example, the /etc/sysconfig/network file on a Fedora system might look like this:

```
NETWORKING=yes
HOSTNAME=incline.xmission.com
GATEWAY=192.168.100.5
```

These lines are used by the script */etc/rc.d/init.d/network* to control how networking is set up. (Information on specific network device configurations, such as IP addresses for Ethernet cards, is located in the network-scripts subdirectory of /etc/sysconfig.)

You can edit the files in /etc/sysconfig directly, but because the content of these files is often not intuitive, you can avoid configuration problems by relying on utilities designed to configure specific services, when available, as described in other areas of this book. For example, you can use the *system-config-network* utility to configure the /etc/sysconfig/

network file and the files within /etc/sysconfig/network-scripts, and the *system-config-securitylevel* utility alters the /etc/sysconfig/system-config-securitylevel file based on your firewall selections.

Although a file in /etc/sysconfig can configure the system service script in /etc/rc.d/init.d, the service itself often has another set of configuration files in the /etc directory. For example, a file called /etc/sysconfig/httpd can define parameters for starting up a Web server using the /etc/rc.d/init.d/httpd script, but the Web server itself is configured using the file /etc/httpd/conf/httpd.conf. You learn about these other configuration files as you explore specific services in detail (for example, Chapter 12, "Configuring Networks," describes Linux printing, which is configured using several files in /etc).

Shutting Down Linux

As you have used the GNOME or KDE desktop interface, you have selected a menu item to shut down your computer. You now know enough about the Linux initialization process to understand why you cannot simply turn off your Linux system: dozens of system services are running in the background, even if you are not working with a program on your desktop. Because Linux processes cache hard disk data in memory, turning off a Linux computer without shutting it down in an orderly way can cause data loss.

A big improvement in recent years has been the addition of a journaling file system to Linux: the ext3 file system. A **journaling file system** tracks each disk operation to be certain that it is either completed or not done at all. A journal is kept that permits the operating system to "back out" of a disk operation if it is not completed successfully. Using a journaling file system means that, although you may still lose data if your computer suddenly loses power, your file systems are unlikely to ever be corrupted by that power loss. This also saves a great deal of time when restarting a system that has been unexpectedly shut down. Restarting a large server that has lost power can require hours as the operating system checks the integrity of large file systems. With journaling, the operating system can instead rely on the journals that were kept of each disk transaction. You will learn more about these disk integrity checks and managing the ext3 file system in Chapter 10, "Managing Software Packages and File Systems."

An orderly or methodical shutdown of Linux is also called a **graceful shutdown**. This means that all Linux services are stopped and all data is written to disk. You can then safely restart or turn off the computer. When you gracefully shut down your system, the kernel changes to run level 0 or 6 so that all services are stopped and other processes can exit gracefully. You can shut down Linux gracefully by:

- Entering the *reboot* command. The ***reboot*** command shuts down all services by changing to run level 6, then restarts your computer.

- Entering the *halt* command. The ***halt*** command shuts down all services by changing to run level 0, then stops the computer with the message "System halted." When you see this message on the screen, you can safely turn off your computer.

- Entering the *shutdown* command. The **shutdown** command takes a parameter that indicates how long to wait before shutting down the system and a parameter to indicate whether the system should be restarted or halted. For example, to halt the system beginning in five minutes, use the command *shutdown -h 5*. To restart the system in three minutes, use the command *shutdown -r 3*.

- Pressing Ctrl+Alt+Del. This executes a shutdown command that immediately restarts the system. (The exact shutdown command that the system executes when you press Ctrl+Alt+Del is configured in the /etc/inittab file.)

- Entering the command *telinit 0* to halt the system, or the command *telinit 6* to restart the system (shutting down all services first in both cases).

If you are working in a graphical desktop, you can use the Log Out item on the main menu of GNOME or KDE. This item opens a dialog box in which you can choose to log out, shut down the system, or restart the system. If you choose Log Out, the graphical login screen appears after a few moments so that the system is secure and you (or another user) can log in. You can also choose to restart or shut down the system from the graphical login prompt.

NOTE Although it's important to know how to shut down Linux, many Linux systems are left running for weeks or months (or years) between reboots. Unless you are working on a machine in a computer lab, or you need to change to a new kernel, or install new hardware, you can leave the system running a very long time. (Ask your instructor or lab manager if systems should be turned off before you leave each day.)

On servers or multiuser Linux systems, only the system administrator should be allowed to shut down the system. By using boot parameters or starting the system from a 3.5-inch disk, a user can disrupt the system's security during a reboot. A system administrator should watch for evidence of unauthorized reboots to be certain that nothing improper has been done to the system. In Chapter 13 you learn how to read system log files where information is stored about system reboots.

CHAPTER SUMMARY

- The CPU, BIOS, and other hardware components of a computer must initialize themselves before attempting to load any operating system. These components may have setup menus that permit you to set configuration options.

- After initialization, the BIOS attempts to load a program—a boot loader or an operating system—from a device such as a removable disk, CD-ROM, or hard disk.

- If the BIOS attempts to load information from the hard disk, it loads the Master Boot Record and passes control to the program it finds there.

❑ A boot loader is typically the first software loaded on a Linux system. The purpose of the boot loader is to load the Linux kernel or pass control to another boot loader or operating system.

❑ Multiple boot loaders can be installed on one system and chained together to accomplish specific configuration goals. Care must be taken so that all installed operating systems can be booted.

❑ Two boot loaders are commonly used on Linux systems. LILO is an older program; GRUB is a newer boot loader with many additional features. GRUB is the default boot loader for Red Hat Linux, Fedora, and many other versions of Linux.

❑ The boot loader can be contained in the MBR or in a boot record of any partition. In the latter case, control must be passed to the boot record by another program (such as another boot loader stored in the MBR).

❑ Messages generated by the kernel after it starts are stored in the kernel ring buffer. These can be viewed using the *dmesg* command.

❑ When starting a Linux kernel, the boot loader can pass parameters to the Linux kernel that instruct it how to operate or how to work with specific hardware components.

❑ LILO and GRUB are each configured using text configuration files stored in the /boot directory. The *lilo* command must be run after making any changes to the lilo.conf file.

❑ The grub.conf file is optional; if provided (the default setting), it creates a selection menu at boot time; if not provided, the GRUB command-line interface appears at boot time. From that interface, a user can select which operating system to start.

❑ Both lilo.conf and grub.conf include global parameters and sections that define how to start one or more operating systems.

❑ The *init* program is the first process started by the Linux kernel. It runs several scripts that start numerous daemons. These scripts are located in the /etc/rc.d subdirectory on most Linux systems.

❑ A run level is a mode of operation that defines what processes are started at boot time. Run level 5 is the normal, graphical mode in which Linux is used on a desktop system.

❑ Scripts start or stop services based on the settings in a run-level directory. Symbolic links begin with either a K to stop a service or S to start a service in that run level.

❑ The *service* command alters the current status of a service; the *chkconfig* command changes the permanent status of a service as configured for one or more run levels. The Service Configuration utility (*serviceconf*) lets you perform similar tasks in a graphical window.

❑ Many of the service scripts located in /etc/rc.d/init.d rely on information in a configuration file. These files are located in /etc/sysconfig. Other configuration files are used as well.

❑ To avoid data loss, you must gracefully shut down Linux using a command such as *reboot*, *halt*, or *shutdown*.

COMMAND SUMMARY

Command	Description	Example
chkconfig	Configures which services are started by default when you boot Linux; modifies the contents of run-level directories such as /etc/rc.d/rc5.d	chkconfig named on
dmesg	Used to view the kernel ring buffer; often used to view messages stored by the kernel during the boot process	dmesg
grub-install	Installs the GRUB boot loader	grub-install /dev/sda2
halt	Used to switch to run level 0 in order to shut down all services and then stop the computer with the message "System halted"	halt
init	Manages the *init* program in order to, for example, switch the system to a different run level or reread the /etc/inittab configuration file	init q
reboot	Switches to run level 6 in order to shut down all services and then restart the computer	reboot
service	Changes the current state of a system service by executing a script located in the /etc/rc.d/init.d subdirectory; used with a service name and a parameter such as *stop*, *start*, or *restart*	service network restart
shutdown	Shuts down Linux gracefully	shutdown -r 5
telinit	Switches the system to a different run level or reloads the /etc/inittab file after it has been modified (using the *q* option)	telinit q
uname	Displays information about the operating system, including the kernel version	uname -v

KEY TERMS

boot image — A Linux kernel which can be started by a boot loader.

boot parameter — A parameter provided to a boot loader, which is in turn passed to the Linux kernel at boot time in order to control how the kernel operates or to assist the kernel in working with hardware components.

chained boot loaders — Multiple boot loaders that refer to each other, located at different positions on one or more hard disks in a single computer, such as on the MBR, and on one or more boot records of distinct partitions.

graceful shutdown — The technique used to stop all Linux services and shut down all file access in an orderly way before turning off or restarting the computer.

init **program** — A master control program that starts many other processes on the system, such as those providing a login prompt. The first process started after the Linux kernel is loaded and initialized.

journaling file system — A file system that tracks each disk operation to be certain that it is either completed or not done at all. A journal is kept that permits the operating system to "back out" of a disk operation if it is not completed successfully. Linux supports several journaling file systems, including the ext3 file system, which is used by default.

kernel ring buffer — A memory area within the Linux kernel where some kernel messages are stored. When the buffer is full, the oldest message in the buffer is discarded as new messages are written. The contents of the buffer can be viewed using the *dmesg* command.

run level — A mode of operation that defines which Linux system services are activated.

REVIEW QUESTIONS

9

1. Which of the following occurs first when a computer is booted?

   a. The BIOS displays a setup menu of configuration options.

   b. The kernel starts the *init* program.

   c. The BIOS loads the MBR.

   d. The CPU starts executing commands found in the BIOS.

2. On newer computers, the BIOS can typically boot from which of the following devices?

   a. hard disks, CD-ROM drives, removable disks, a network connection, or USB devices

   b. hard disks or CD-ROM drives

   c. hard disks, CD-ROM drives, or removable disks, and USB devices

   d. hard disks or a network connection

3. When using LILO rather than GRUB, you must do which of the following after making a configuration change in order for the change to be effective the next time you boot Linux?

   a. Nothing; changes are effective as soon as they are made in the configuration file.

   b. Run the *lilo* command as root.

   c. Use the LILO shell to update the MBR or boot record of the appropriate partition.

   d. Use a graphical utility to check that all operating systems installed on the computer can still be booted by LILO.

4. Assuming a standard configuration, the BIOS looks first in which of the following locations on a hard disk when trying to find a boot loader or operating system?

a. the MBR (the first sector of the first IDE hard disk)

b. the boot record of the active partition on the first IDE hard disk

c. the boot record of the first partition on the first IDE hard disk

d. the partition referred to as the default image by the boot loader, no matter where it is located

5. In order to use chained boot loaders, you must be certain that:

a. At least three different operating systems are correctly installed on the computer

b. You use GRUB rather than LILO as the first boot loader in the chain.

c. The first boot loader can be found by the BIOS, and each operating system can be reached via one of the chained boot loaders.

d. The MBR contains the first boot loader, and each operating system is stored on an active partition.

6. The Linux kernel is a file having a name that starts with _____ and typically stored in the _____ subdirectory.

a. vmlinuz, /boot

b. vmlinuz, /etc/rc.d/inittab

c. inittab, /boot

d. grub.conf, /boot/grub

7. Which feature is part of GRUB but not LILO?

a. including non-Linux operating systems in the list of bootable systems

b. altering the boot manager configuration at boot time, while the boot manager is actually running

c. handling boot parameters to alter Linux kernel functions

d. providing a text configuration file that a system administrator can review within the Linux file system

8. Describe the output of the *uname* command.

9. The GRUB boot manager can be reconfigured directly as you boot your system, but is also controlled by this configuration file:

a. a./boot/grub.conf

b. /etc/boot

c. c./boot.conf

d. /boot/grub/grub.conf

10. Which of the following statements about boot parameters is accurate?

   a. They are passed to the Linux kernel by the boot loader.

   b. They are used only to help the kernel configure hardware settings.

   c. They are supported by GRUB but not by LILO.

   d. They must be included in the appropriate GRUB or LILO configuration file.

11. The scripts in /etc/rc.d/init.d are provided by:

   a. the system administrator who installs Linux

   b. the *rc* script, which runs before any of the init.d scripts

   c. the software package that installs the service that the script controls

   d. the kernel itself

12. Explain the difference between the configuration data stored in files within the /etc/sysconfig directory and service-specific configuration data stored in other subdirectories of /etc.

13. The _____ utility displays kernel hardware configuration messages from the system boot process.

   a. *init*

   b. *sysconfig*

   c. *dmesg*

   d. *uname*

14. The *init* program relies on the following configuration file:

   a. /etc/lilo.conf

   b. /etc/inittab

   c. /etc/rc.d/init.d/inittab

   d. /etc/rc.d/rc

15. Name the two run levels normally used to run a Linux-based computer, and describe the difference between those two run levels.

16. The files in /etc/rc.d/init.d can be used to:

   a. Automatically insert kernel modules.

   b. Stop and restart most standard services in Linux.

   c. Reconfigure the boot manager.

   d. Set default file permissions for the root user.

17. Name three commands that can be used to begin a graceful shutdown of Linux.

18. A boot loader can be configured to boot multiple Linux kernels that use the same partition as their root file system. True or False?

19. The timeout= parameter in a GRUB configuration and the delay= parameter in a LILO configuration both refer to:

    a. the average time needed to start the default operating system

    b. how long the BIOS waits before looking for the next chained boot loader

    c. how long the boot loader waits for the kernel to load before restarting the system under the assumption that an error has occurred

    d. how long the boot loader waits for user input before booting the default operating system

20. The *service* command is used to:

    a. View or change the current status of a service via a script located in /etc/rc.d/init.d.

    b. Change the boot-up status of a service that is controlled via a script located in /etc/rc.d/init.d.

    c. Modify settings stored in files within the /etc/sysconfig subdirectory.

    d. Display the current status of any daemon running on the system.

21. The *chkconfig* command is used to:

    a. View or change the current status of a service via a script located in /etc/rc.d/init.d.

    b. Change the boot-up status of a service that is controlled via a script located in /etc/rc.d/init.d.

    c. Modify settings stored in files within the /etc/sysconfig subdirectory.

    d. Display the current status of any daemon running on the system.

22. Name the graphical configuration utility provided with Red Hat Linux and Fedora that can be used in place of the command-line utilities *service* and *chkconfig*.

23. If a journaling file system prevents partially written information from causing a corrupted file system in Linux, why is it still important to use graceful shutdown techniques rather than just turning off the system power?

24. Which command is typically executed when the Ctrl+Alt+Del key combination is pressed, and where is that command configured?

25. What is the command you use to cause the *init* program to reread its configuration file after you have made changes to it?

HANDS-ON PROJECTS

Project 9-1

In this project, you learn about the Linux kernel running on your system. To complete this project you should have an installed Linux system.

1. Log in to Linux.

2. If you logged in using a graphical login screen, open a terminal window. Use the **su** command to change to root access.

3. Enter the command **uname –r** to see which version of the Linux kernel is running on the computer. What kernel version are you running?

4. Enter the command **uname –v** to see the timestamp of the Linux kernel.

5. Enter the command **cat /proc/version**. How does the information displayed compare to the output of the *uname* command? Compare this output with the output of the *uname -a* command.

6. Review the contents of the grub.conf file by entering the command **less /boot/grub/grub.conf**.

7. Locate the indented line in the file that begins with "kernel," and note the directory and file name to which it refers.

   Do you see any boot parameters on the kernel line?

8. Press **q** to exit the *less* command.

9. Enter the command **cd /boot** to change to the directory where the kernel is located.

10. Enter the **ls –l** command to see the files in the boot directory. Can you locate the file named in the kernel line grub.conf? That file is the Linux kernel. How large is the file? Why? What is the real kernel size?

11. Enter the command **dmesg | less** to review the kernel boot messages. What parts of the system hardware do you recognize in the output? How might this output help you manage the system's hardware?

12. Press **q** to exit the *less* command.

13. Close all open windows and log out of Linux.

Project 9-2

In this project, you review the initialization process for your Linux system. To complete this project you should have an installed Linux system.

1. Log in to Linux. (Don't use the root account, even if you have that password.)

2. If you logged in using a graphical login screen, open a terminal window.

3. Enter the command **cat /etc/sysconfig/network**. What configuration options do you recognize in the output?

4. Change to the rc.d initialization directory: **cd /etc/rc.d**.

5. Enter the **ls** command. What file names do you recognize from the discussion in the chapter?

6. List the files in the init.d subdirectory: **ls init.d**. Can you recognize any network or other services that match the names of the files in this directory?

7. List the files in the rc5.d subdirectory: **ls rc5.d**. How do the files in this directory correspond to those in the init.d subdirectory?

8. Change to the init.d subdirectory: **cd init.d**.

9. View the *syslog* script using the *ls -l* command: **ls -l syslog**. Notice the file permissions assigned to the script. Who is permitted to read the script? (The syslog script controls the system logging programs described in Chapter 10.)

10. Execute the syslog script using the command **./syslog restart**. Wait a few moments, watching the messages that appear on screen. Press **Ctrl+c** to stop the script if you tire of waiting for it, since it may take several minutes for the command prompt to return. What can you conclude about the file permissions allowing everyone to read the script?

11. Use the *less* command to look at the contents of the script: **less syslog**. You can learn a lot about creating scripts by reviewing existing scripts on the system. (Chapter 14, "Writing Shell Scripts," describes how to create your own scripts.) Press **q** to exit the *less* command.

12. Change back to your home directory using the command **cd** with no parameters. (This always returns you to your home directory.)

13. Enter **pwd** to verify that you are in fact in your home directory.

14. Close all open windows and log out of Linux.

HANDS-ON PROJECTS

Project 9-3

In this project, you modify the *init* program's configuration file to add an additional virtual console to your system. To complete this project you should have an installed Linux system with root access.

1. Log in to Linux using your regular user account.

2. If you logged in using a graphical login screen, open a terminal window.

3. Change to root access by entering **su –** and the root password when prompted.

4. Make a backup copy of the init program's configuration file: **cp /etc/inittab /etc/inittab.backup**

5. Open a text editor with the inittab file: **vi /etc/inittab**

6. Near the end of the file, locate the line that reads: 6:2345:respawn:/sbin/mingetty tty6

7. Copy that line just below where you originally find it (in vi, press **yyp** to do this).

8. Edit the copy (the second of the identical lines) so that both sixes are eights: **8**:2345:respawn:/sbin/mingetty tty**8**

9. Save the inittab file and exit your text editor.

10. Test which virtual consoles are currently configured on your system by pressing **Ctrl+Alt+F1**, then press **Alt+F2**, **Alt+F3**, etc. Each one will look identical, so it will not appear that the screen is changing, but you can log in to each virtual console if you wish to. (If you press Alt+F7, you switch back to the graphical desktop.)

11. Press **Alt+F8**. Notice that there is no login prompt.

12. Switch back to the graphical desktop or any virtual console where you are logged in.

13. Cause *init* to reread the inittab file so that your changes are activated: **telinit q**

14. Press **Alt+F8** or **Ctrl+Alt+F8** to switch to virtual console 8. Notice that you now have a login prompt on that console.

15. Return to your working terminal by pressing **Alt+F7**.

16. Edit /etc/inittab and remove the line you added.

17. Cause *init* to reread the /etc/initab file again: **telinit q**

18. Close all open windows and log out of Linux.

HANDS-ON PROJECTS

Project 9-4

In this project, you start the system in single-user mode to change the password for root when it has been lost or forgotten. To complete this project you should have an installed Linux system with root access. These steps assume you are using the GRUB boot loader. A similar procedure is used with LILO.

1. Log in to Linux using your regular user account and open a command-line window.

2. Reboot the system by entering **reboot** in the command window.

3. Watch the screen carefully. When the Fedora boot screen appears that lists the operating system, you would normally press Enter to start Linux immediately. If you did nothing, Linux would start automatically after a few seconds. For this project, press **a**.

4. A string of boot parameters appears on screen. The exact parameters you see depend on the hardware you have installed Linux on. Press the **spacebar**, then **s** to add another boot parameter. Then press **Enter**. The *s* parameter indicates that Linux should boot into run level 1: single user mode.

9

5. Watch as the system boots. Note that the system takes less time to boot because it starts fewer services than normal. After a few moments, you see a text-mode command line at the bottom of the screen. You can now work in Linux, though neither multiple virtual terminals nor networking are available. Note that you never entered a password.

6. Enter **whoami** to discover which user account you are working as.

7. Enter the **passwd** command to change the root password.

8. Enter a new password for root as prompted. Repeat the entry as prompted. The root password has now been changed.

9. Enter **exit** to exit from single-user mode. You immediately see messages as the system changes to run level 5. After a few moments, the graphical login screen appears.

Case Projects

Booting the System and Managing Services

1. Reboot your computer several times and make a list of all the setup menus that you see mentioned. Enter each one and explore the options that it permits you to set up. Note the order in which different hardware components have their turn at initialization. Do you see any configuration options that you might want to change? Do you see any that you think might affect the performance or security of your Linux system?

2. In Hands-On Project 9-4, you started the system in single-user mode to reset the root password. Summarize in a one-page report what single-user mode does, what security hazards it presents in a Linux lab, and how you might use what you have learned about hardware configuration to safeguard against those hazards. Review the man page for the boot loader you have installed (LILO or GRUB) and add comments about how the boot loader can be configured to protect against these or similar security problems.

3. The method of starting and managing services using multiple scripts in /etc/rc.d/ init.d (or a similarly named directory) is called System V initialization, after the System V UNIX systems in which the model was first used. What advantages and disadvantages do you see in using this method? Use the Internet or other sources to research other UNIX-related operating systems that use different methods to control daemons. In particular, you might look at the BSD version of UNIX (you can start with *www.freebsd.org* or *www.netbsd.org*). What other methods do you see and how do they compare in your eyes?

4. Reviewing one of the previous case projects that you've completed, or a situation that you face in your work, examine the list of services included in the run level 3 directory (typically /etc/rc.d/rc3.d) and determine which ones to eliminate for the system to run with the minimal number of services. Use *chkconfig* to configure your system (take careful notes on what you change), then change the /etc/inittab file to start in run level 3 by default and restart the system. Explore differences compared to the default installation, then return the system to its previous state.

9

MANAGING SOFTWARE PACKAGES AND FILE SYSTEMS

After reading this chapter and completing the exercises, you will be able to:

♦ Manage software packages that use the rpm format

♦ Use Red Hat Network to update a Red Hat Linux or Fedora installation

♦ Manage and install new file systems

In the previous chapter you learned how the Linux kernel is initialized and what processes are started as the system is booted. You learned about the scripts and commands that control those core processes and how you can modify the default configuration used to start up your Linux system. You also learned how to shut down a Linux system using command-line utilities.

In this chapter you learn about software packages: how you can download, install, and manage applications that have been created using a special format for easy administration. Part of that installation and management often involves upgrading existing software packages on your Linux system. This can sometimes be done using an automatic update tool such as Red Hat Network, which is discussed in this chapter. Finally, you learn more about file systems, including more details about managing partitions, setting up mounting options, and creating new file systems when you add devices to your computer.

MANAGING PACKAGES

In Chapter 8, "Installing Linux," you learned that Linux groups related files into packages for easier management. In this section you learn more about how to manage these software packages. A **software package** is a single file that contains all the files needed to install and use an application or group of related applications. Special data formats are used to store many files in a software package along with information about how the package should be installed and how it can be used.

The **Red Hat Package Manager** format (abbreviated as **rpm**) is the most popular data storage format for creating software packages; it is used by many different distributions and is discussed in more detail in this section. Other formats are also used by various Linux distributions. The Slackware distribution, for example, relies on standard compressed tar archives (which have the .tar.gz or .tgz file extension).

Another well-known software package format is the Debian package format, used by the Debian Linux distribution. Packages stored using this format have a .deb file extension. You can use the *dselect* utility to manage Debian package in a menu-driven, text-mode interface. The deselect utility is a front end to the command-line utility, *dpkg*, which is analogous to the *rpm* command discussed in more detail later in this section. Rather than use the *dpkg* command for all package interaction, however, the *dpkg-reconfigure* command is used to alter the settings of a package once it has been installed.

A useful utility included with Debian Linux is the *alien* utility. This utility can convert between the .tgz, Debian, and Red Hat packaging formats, allowing you to install the package in a format that is not standard on your system. (Of course, the location of some files included in the package can still be inappropriate for your system.)

Managing Packages Graphically

When you installed Linux, you had the option of selecting a custom installation. If you did so, you were able to select which types of packages were installed. You can use a graphical utility in Red Hat Linux or Fedora to change what is installed using a view very similar to what you used during the installation process. After experimenting with this utility, you will learn about the command-line utility behind the graphical program.

A fairly complete installation of Fedora Linux that used 2.9 GB of hard disk space contained 768 individual software packages.

To start the graphical utility, enter *system-config-packages* in a terminal window. You must enter the root password to use this program. The window that appears resembles the selection screen used when you installed Red Hat Linux or Fedora (see Figure 10-1). In this window, you can select the check box next to any of the categories of packages to add packages from that category.

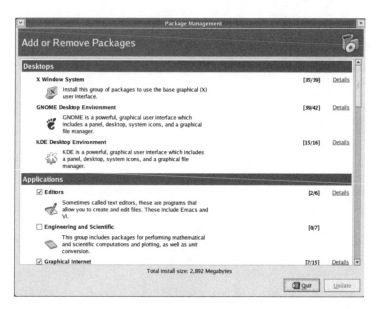

Figure 10-1   The main window of *system-config-packages*

NOTE   Not all features of the installation program are represented in the *system-config-packages* utility. For example, you cannot select Minimal or Everything. You also cannot uninstall the GNOME or KDE desktop, as that would make the utility itself unable to function. To make major changes such as these, you can use the command-line utility described in the next section, or else reinstall Linux with different options.

To the right of each category is a Details link. By selecting this link, a window opens listing the individual software packages that are included in that category. Not all of these packages are installed by default when you select the check box next to a category. For example, when you select Editors, only three of seven packages in that category are installed by default. If you select the Details link, you can then check the box next to other packages in that category that you want to have installed. (See Figure 10-2.)

When you have gone through all the different categories and selected the other packages that you want to install, you click Update in the main window of the utility. This causes the utility to prepare to install all of the packages you have selected, including any other packages that are needed in order to install those you selected. A dialog box informs you when this process is completed, and you can click Continue to begin the installation. You should have the Red Hat Linux or Fedora CDs (or the files from the CDs) available to continue. You are prompted to install the appropriate CDs as needed.

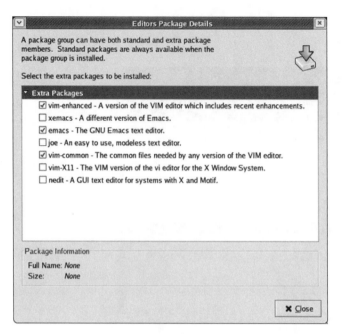

Figure 10-2 Selecting other packages to install within *system-config-packages*

Using rpm to Manage Software Packages

The *system-config-packages* utility and other graphical package management tools you can find for Linux rely on command-line utilities to perform their operations in the background. By knowing about those utilities, you can better manage the software installed on your system.

The **rpm** command-line utility maintains a database listing all the software packages installed on your system, with lists of the files included in each package, which packages are dependent on which other packages, and other information. You can query this database to learn about what software is installed, what version of a software package you are using, who created the package, and so forth. You can also use the *rpm* command to install new software packages or erase software packages from the system.

The name of a package file as you see it on your CD-ROM includes version information. An example file name would be gedit-2.4.0-3.i386.rpm. The version of the *gedit* text editor is 2.4.0, the release code for the package is 3, the platform it was created for is the i386 (Intel PCs), and the format of the file is rpm. After the package is installed on your system, however, you should refer to it by the package name, without the version information. The corresponding package name for the previous example would be simply *gedit*. You will see both of these used in the subsequent examples.

The hundreds of options supported by the *rpm* command fall into several categories:

- Use the *-q* option to query the database and learn about packages (either installed packages or those not yet installed).

- Use the *-i* or *-U* option to install or upgrade a package when you have a new rpm file you want to add to your system.

- Use the *-e* option to erase (uninstall) an rpm package from your system.

These options can be used in combination. For example, to query the rpm database for a list of all files included in a package, you combine the *-q* option with the *-l* option:

```
$ rpm -ql setup
```

To see a list of all the packages installed on your system, use the *-q* and *-a* options:

```
$ rpm -qa
```

The *-q* and *-a* options are often used together with the *grep* command to search for a package when you are unsure of the exact name or whether the package is installed. For example, if you wanted to see what Web server-related packages were installed, and you knew that the Web server program was httpd, you might use a command such as this one to see a list of all package names that include the string "http":

```
$ rpm -qa | grep http
```

If you see a file on your system and need to know of which package it is a part, use the *-q* option with the *-f* option (you must use the complete path of the file you want to learn about).

```
$ rpm -qf /etc/services
```

You can install new rpm files either from your Linux CD-ROM or you can download them from the Internet. Suppose that you have downloaded an updated rpm file for the Z shell from rpmfind.net. The file you have downloaded to the /tmp directory is called zsh-4.2.0-1.i386.rpm. You want to install it on your system. This command would do that:

```
# rpm -Uvh /tmp/zsh-4.2.0-1.i386.rpm
```

NOTE

You can use *rpm* to query information about packages when logged in as any user, but only root can install, upgrade, or delete packages.

If you have downloaded a collection of packages that need to be installed together, you can use a regular expression to specify the package names. The *rpm* utility examines each matching package name and determines the correct order in which the packages need to be installed. For example, suppose you had not installed the *gimp* image manipulation program previously, but want to now. This program consists of five different packages (for documentation, extensions, and so forth). If you had downloaded all five packages into a directory or located all five on a CD-ROM, you could install them all, in the correct order, with this command:

```
# rpm -Uvh gimp*
```

The *-U* option in the previous examples upgrades the named package or packages. This is a safer way of installing packages, in case you already have a newer version of the package installed. The *-v* option displays detailed messages in case of problems, and the *-h* option displays a series of hash marks (#####) on the screen to show you that the installation is progressing.

TIP

Each rpm file can include a digital signature that indicates the person or organization that created the package. When you download an rpm from the Internet, there is a small chance that someone might have altered the original file in some way. By checking that the digital signature on the rpm file matches the signature of the person or organization that created the package, you can greatly improve the security of your systems.

In order to determine whether it recognizes the digital signature on an rpm file, the *rpm* utility maintains an internal database of keys. A key is part of the encryption information that is used to digitally sign an rpm file. If you installed Fedora, several relevant keys are located at /usr/share/rhn. You can import them into the rpm database using these commands (while logged in as root):

```
# rpm --import /usr/share/rhn/RPM-GPG-KEY
# rpm --import /usr/share/rhn/RPM-GPG-KEY-fedora
# rpm --import /usr/share/rhn/RPM-GPG-KEY-fedora-test
```

Other keys are available from Linux vendors or individuals who create important software packages for Linux (such as the Apache Web server or Linux kernel updates). Once you have the relevant keys in your rpm database, you can check the digital signature of any rpm file to see if the *rpm* utility recognizes the signature on the file. Use this command:

```
# rpm --checksig -v packagefilename
```

After you have installed a package, you can use the *rpm* command to verify that the files installed on your system match what the software package contains. To do this, use the *-V* option. To use this option, you should have the rpm file on your system (provide the file name in the *rpm* command) and also have the package installed on your system.

```
# rpm -V /tmp/zsh-4.2.0-1.i386.rpm
```

The *rpm* command informs you of any discrepancies between the package and what is installed on your system.

An rpm file is a collection of many files. When you install Linux, the data from the rpm files is copied from your Linux CD-ROM or other installation media to your Linux-based hard disk. The rpm package files themselves are not copied; if they were, you would actually have two copies of each package: the installed files and the uninstalled package.

This means that if you erase a package file from your system (the file with the rpm file extension), you must locate the rpm file again on your Linux CD or on a Web site in order to reinstall that package. An example of the *-e* (erase) option is shown here:

```
# rpm -e zsh
```

The *rpm* command includes dozens of more complex options, which you can review by entering the *rpm* command with no options or viewing the rpm man page.

UPDATING THE SYSTEM AUTOMATICALLY

A commonly used feature of Microsoft Windows is the Windows Update client, which automatically locates and downloads updates to the operating system and informs you that they are ready to install. Red Hat Linux uses a very similar model to download upgrades or security fixes for key operating system packages installed on your system. These might include security fixes for network clients, updates to core system utilities, and updates to the kernel itself. This is all done using the **Red Hat Network**. You can subscribe to the Red Hat Network service, or, depending on the version of Red Hat Linux that you purchased, you may be entitled to an annual subscription as part of your purchase. Individuals can use basic Red Hat Network functionality for free, just by registering.

The Red Hat Network uses an icon on the Panel in GNOME or KDE to indicate its status. The icon is a check mark in a blue circle (indicating everything is OK or you haven't registered yet) or a flashing exclamation point in a red circle (indicating that you need to install updates). You can add the icon to your Panel if it's not there (or has been removed) by clicking System Tools on the GNOME main menu, and then choosing Red Hat Network Alert icon. Figure 10-3 shows this icon on the Panel.

 ← Red Hat Network Alert icon

Figure 10-3   The Red Hat Network Alert icon on the GNOME Panel

If you have not registered for the Red Hat Network, you can double-click the Network Alert icon on the Panel. The service will see that you are not registered and a message box appears that includes a button you can click to begin the registration process using the Internet.

By right-clicking the Alert icon, you can select from options to configure how the Red Hat Network service is used for your system, or start the ***up2date*** utility that lets you actually manage updated software packages. When you right-click and choose Configuration, a series of configuration windows appear. The first is shown in Figure 10-4. The main purpose of this tool is to let you read the terms of use for Red Hat Network and to enter a proxy or authentication information if needed to access Red Hat Network from your location. (These are usually not necessary.)

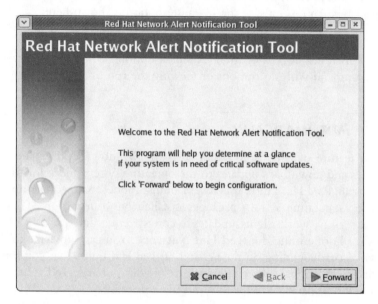

Figure 10-4   Starting to configure the Red Hat Network service for your system

To configure the overall settings for Red Hat Network, choose System Tools, then Red Hat Network on the GNOME main menu. A window with three tabs appears. The General tab is shown in Figure 10-5. In this tab, you see the name of the Red Hat Network server that the program will periodically check for updates. Click Refresh to update from the Internet the list of servers available for updates. You can use the fields below the server name if you must connect to Web servers through a proxy; you can provide the proxy server name and any user name and password that you must use to access the proxy server.

On the Retrieval/Installation tab, shown in Figure 10-6, you define what the Red Hat Network utility does with software package updates after they are retrieved from Red Hat Software. In the Package Retrieval Options section, you can specify that packages are not installed or upgraded after being downloaded (the default is to install them). Also by default, however, packages are not upgraded if you have made changes to the default configuration file. This avoids overwriting your configurations. Such packages are stored in the Package storage directory named at the bottom of the window, from which you can install them yourself after backing up any modified configuration files. You can also choose to download the source code rpm as well as the binary RPM. Typically only developers want to download these packages.

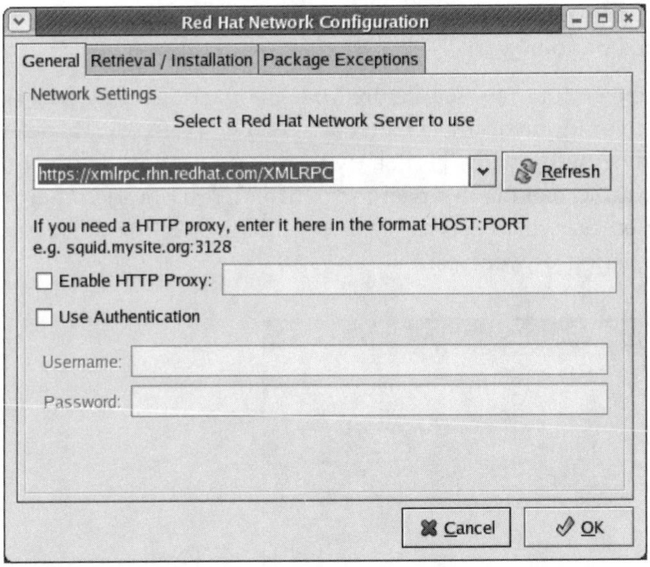

Figure 10-5   The General tab of the Red Hat Network Configuration tool

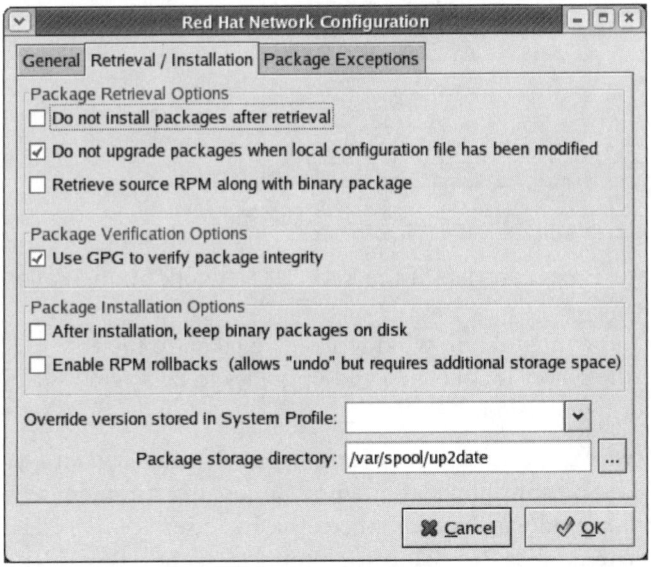

Figure 10-6   The Retrieval / Installation tab of the Red Hat Network Configuration tool

By default, all packages are verified using GPG—this is essentially the same as using the *--checksig* option on the *rpm* command as discussed in the previous section. Finally, in the Package Installation Options section of this tab, you can select to have the rpm files saved after installation (this takes extra disk space, of course—the default is to erase them after they have been installed). And you can enable rpm rollbacks, also at the cost of additional disk space. Rollbacks are useful if you are experimenting with a Linux system and are concerned that updates might interrupt your work.

Finally, in the Package Exceptions tab (see Figure 10-7), you can identify packages or files that you don't want to have automatically updated by Red Hat Network. By default, the list includes only packages beginning with "kernel," with the assumption that you don't want your kernel upgraded without making that decision yourself. You can add other packages or even individual files based on which services you consider critical or don't want to have altered without explicit action on your part.

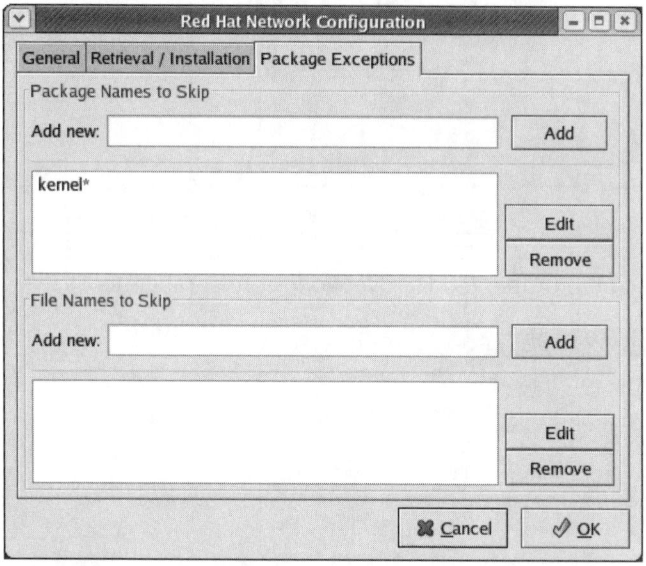

Figure 10-7   The Package Exceptions tab of the Red Hat Network Configuration tool

When you click OK in this configuration window, you are taken to the Red Hat Network update windows, where the server is contacted and upgrades to packages installed on your system are identified and downloaded.

The basic Red Hat Network service described here is part of a larger Red Hat Network architecture that Red Hat Software provides at an extra cost to customers who purchase Red Hat Enterprise Linux products. In addition to the basic service, Red Hat Software highlights the **Management** and **Provisioning** products within Red Hat Network's offering.

By purchasing access to these services, you can add capabilities such as those in the following list to help keep your systems secure and up to date. The great advantage in these pay services is the ability to work with multiple Linux servers through a single interface, rather than trying to log in to multiple systems, collect data about what is installed or needing upgrading, and then coordinating it from a central location. Red Hat Network automates all of these functions:

- Manage upgrades across multiple systems, with timed deployment and different upgrade models and permissions assigned to the administrators of different Linux servers.

- Compare what is installed on one system against a default system profile or against another Linux system.

- Build systems from "bare metal" using a preconfigured set of packages and configuration files (only available through the Provisioning product).

- Use rollback features to maintain multiple levels of status so that you can take a system back to any point in time (only available through the Provisioning product).

- Provide complete automated updates for all applications rather than just critical operating system files (only available through the Provisioning product).

TIP

For more information on the technology and products behind Red Hat Network, visit *www.redhat.com/software/rhn/*.

10

Managing software packages, either directly or through an update system such as Red Hat Network, is only a part of managing files in Linux. In the next section, you learn more about the underlying structure and utilities you can rely on to manage entire file systems in Linux.

UNDERSTANDING THE FILE SYSTEM

When you installed Linux, the installed program created a root file system in which the operating system files were stored. The root file system may have been created on several partitions—for example, one for the /boot directory, one for the /home directory, one for the /usr directory, and another as the root directory, /. Linux uses ext3 or a similar file system as the default file system type for these partitions. After installation is completed, you might need to modify or add new Linux partitions or hard disks, or you might need to access data stored using non-Linux file system types. This section discusses how Linux file systems are constructed, how to create and manage Linux file systems, and how to access other types of file systems.

Reviewing File System Types

You learned in Chapter 4, "Understanding Users and File Systems," that a file system is a collection of data structured in a certain way so that it can be efficiently accessed. A file system must include information about the data it is storing in order to permit efficient access. For example, you have learned about inodes and using the *stat* command to view inode information and other details about an existing file. Each inode contains information about a single file in the file system. The file system arranges inodes on the storage media to provide efficient access to that information, as well as to the data the inode refers to. The ext2 and ext3 file systems include a collection of information about the file system as a whole called the **superblock**. The superblock contains details such as the size of each block on the file system, the volume label, the date of the last integrity check, the amount of space reserved for the root user, and several other pieces of information. A duplicate copy of the superblock is stored at dozens of locations in a large file system. If a complete copy of the superblock cannot be found, the file system cannot be accessed.

The ext2 and ext3 file systems do not place files one after another, filling up each area of a hard disk in order. Instead, they place files at various points located throughout the entire area of the file system. This permits a file to grow in size without being as likely to be broken into pieces because it "runs into" space taken by another file. This means that the fragmentation problem of some other file systems, such as FAT, FAT32, and NTFS, is not present in ext2 and ext3 file systems—you never need to defragment your Linux file system.

The ext3 file system is just like the ext2 file system except that ext3 is a journaling file system: it stores information about each disk operation so that if an error occurs (such as the system being shut down), the file system does not become corrupted. This journaling adds a small amount of overhead, but is much better than risking file system corruption.

Two other journaling file systems are available for Linux. The Reiser file system (typically called **ReiserFS**), is the default file system on the SUSE, Lindows/Linspire, Gentoo, and other Linux distributions. ReiserFS is in many ways similar to ext3, but uses a method of deciding where to place files that is reputed to be more efficient, leading to faster access times, especially when dealing with large numbers of files (such as a million files in a single directory). A good technical description of ReiserFS is available at *www.namesys.com/v4/v4.html*.

Another journaling file system available for Linux is called the **Journaling File System (JFS)**. This file system was developed by IBM and is now distributed under the GPL—the same license as Linux itself. JFS was designed for IBM enterprise servers. It currently ships as part of most commercial Linux distributions. You can learn more about JFS by visiting *http://oss.software.ibm.com/developerworks/opensource/jfs/*.

The Linux kernel uses a **virtual file system** model. This is a method of accessing data that separates the file system type from the operation a program wants to perform. Virtually all programs want to perform the same types of operations on a file system: display the contents of a directory, open a file, read from a file, write to a file, and so on. When a program requests that the Linux kernel perform one of these operations, the kernel determines the type of the file system for which the operation has been requested. The kernel then has the driver for the appropriate file system type perform the operation. This model means that Linux can support any new file system type for which a driver is available. Dozens of file system types are supported, though Linux itself relies on those mentioned here for hard disk storage of regular files. Later in this section you will see how to work with different file system types.

When you start Linux, the kernel uses several specialized file systems as a way to access different types of system data. You learned about the proc file system, which provides information about the kernel when you view parts of the /proc subdirectory. Table 10-1 shows a number of file systems that Linux can use in a standard system. Some of these are located within system memory; others are stored on the hard disk (within an ext3 file system, for example), but are accessed using different utilities to provide a special service of some kind.

Table 10-1   File Systems Used within Linux

File system type	Mount point	Description
binfmt_misc	/proc/sys/fs/binfmt_misc	File system used to register different types of programs (older Linux, newer Linux, Java, DOS, Windows) so that the Linux kernel can automatically execute them when a program of that type is given on the command line
devpts	/dev/pts	File system used by the kernel to interact with pseudoterminals (programs running in graphical environments and certain other situations)
proc	/proc	Provides up-to-date information about the kernel and all processes running on Linux
root	/	Serves as the base of a running Linux system; the root file system cannot be unmounted unless you first shut down Linux
swap	No mount point; a special file system used by the Linux kernel	Used to create virtual memory, allowing the Linux kernel to work as if the amount of system memory available is the sum of RAM and all swap space
tmpfs	/dev/shm	File system used by programs for accessing shared memory resources
usbdevfs	/proc/bus/usb	File system used to access USB devices

You previously used the *mount* command to make a new file system such as a removable disk or CD-ROM drive accessible within Linux. Each file system must be mounted so that the kernel is aware of it and can prepare the correct resources to access information stored on that file system. When you execute the *mount* command without any parameters, you see a list of the currently mounted file systems. Here is one example:

```
$ mount
/dev/hda2 on / type ext3 (rw)
none on /proc type proc (rw)
usbdevfs on /proc/bus/usb type usbdevfs (rw)
none on /dev/pts type devpts (rw,gid=5,mode=620)
none on /dev/shm type tmpfs (rw)
/dev/hdb2 on /usr type ext3 (rw)
none on /proc/sys/fs/binfmt_misc type binfmt_misc (rw)
/dev/fd0 on /mnt/floppy type vfat (rw,nosuid,nodev)
```

The output of the *mount* command includes unlabeled fields, from left to right, as described in the following list:

- The device where the file system is located (such as /dev/hda2 on the first line of the output above, which refers to a hard disk partition)

- The mount point for the file system (the path in the directory structure where the file system can be accessed, such as / on the first line of the output above)

- The type of the file system (preceded by the word "type"); this indicates the format of data stored on the file system (ext3 is the type on the first line above)

- The options that apply to the file system (described later in the chapter); the options on the first line of the output above are rw, indicating that the file system is mounted for both reading and writing of data

Managing Linux file systems is critical to running an efficient Linux system. Although file systems as a rule don't require much day-to-day maintenance, the more people using a Linux system and the more crucial the data stored on that system, the more important it becomes to watch over and maintain the file systems. (In this regard, pay special attention to backing up your file systems, as discussed in Chapter 13, "System and Kernel Management.")

TIP

A useful method of interacting with removable disks that *does not* require you to first mount the disk is to use the ***mdir***, ***mdel***, and ***mcopy*** commands. These commands mirror the old MS-DOS commands *dir*, *del*, and *copy*. These commands mount the removable disk in the background and use "old fashioned" drive letters on the command line. For example, to see the contents of a removable disk, insert the disk and enter *mdir A:*. To copy a file from your home directory to the disk, enter *mcopy ~/myfile A:*. These commands are all part of the mtools package, which is installed by default on Red Hat Linux and Fedora.

Checking File System Status

One of the very rare times when the Linux kernel crashes is when the root file system becomes full. Likewise, if the space where users' files are stored becomes full, users are not be able to complete their work.

The *df* command you learned in Chapter 4 displays space usage information for each file system that is currently mounted. (*df* only displays information for regular file systems, not the special file systems such as the swap partition and /proc.) In the following sample output from *df*, the first two file systems are dangerously full:

```
$ df
File system   1k-blocks    Used       Available    Use%    Mounted on
/dev/hda4     956173       895614     11160        99%     /
/dev/hda3     1018329      901074     64643        93%     /opt
sundance:/a   2017438      1210459    806979       60%     /a
```

The fields output by the *df* command, from left to right, are described in the following list:

- The device where the file system is stored; this is normally either a hard disk device name or a networked location (as in the last line of the sample output, which indicates a remote file system on the host named sundance)

- The number of 1 KB blocks on the device. This indicates the file system's overall size. For example, in the sample output, the size of the three devices currently mounted are approximately 1 GB, 1 GB, and 2 GB, respectively.

- The number of 1 KB blocks that are used on the device

- The number of 1 KB blocks that are free on the device

- The percentage of capacity reached so far (percentage full) for the device

- The mount point for this device

For large file systems, changing the default size display can make reading the output of *df* much easier. For example, to display the file system size and available space in megabytes, use this command:

$ df -B M

To display the data in gigabytes, use this command:

$ df -B G

If a file system is becoming full, you probably won't have the luxury of shutting down the Linux system while you figure out what to do. The busier your Linux system, the quicker a file system can fill up as multiple users download files, create new documents, and back up existing files.

Executing the *df* command on a large ISP server resembles the following example. After reviewing this output, you should be able to see why larger systems require more careful maintenance procedures to keep them running smoothly.

File system	1024-blocks	Used	Available	Capacity	Mounted on
/dev/dsk/c0t3d0s0	229610	110187	119423	48%	/
/dev/dsk/c0t3d0s6	306954	245175	61779	80%	/usr
/dev/dsk/c0t0d0s0	5783718	3378119	2405599	58%	/var
/dev/dsk/c0t1d0s7	2663048	1983612	679436	75%	/space1
/dev/dsk/c0t1d0s6	533992	232744	301248	44%	/usr/local
nfs.isp.com:/home	69837128	42182931	27654197	60%	/home
mail.isp.com:/var/mail	10766840	8172635	2594205	76%	/var/mail

If you see that a file system is nearing 100% of capacity, you can immediately free space by performing one of the actions in the following list. Remember, however, that you must free space in the directories where the file system is mounted. For example, if you have a separate partition mounted as the /home directory and that partition is almost full, you must free space in /home or its subdirectories. Freeing space in /tmp doesn't help.

- Look for large or numerous files in the /tmp directory that can be deleted (if it's part of the file system that is becoming full).

- Look for large or numerous files in the /var subdirectories, especially in /var/tmp/ and /var/spool/.

- Move the system log file (/var/log/messages) to another file system that isn't as full. (See Chapter 13 for more information on managing log files.)

- See if any of the user subdirectories are using an unusually large amount of disk space. (Remember that you can use the *find* command with a user name to determine if one user has consumed an inordinate amount of disk space.)

- Consider deleting unused archive files that are backed up or even applications that you can reinstall later when space is not critically short.

Although you need to be very careful as you delete files, you might have to act quickly to respond to an overly full file system. The *du* (disk usage) utility can be a big help. The **du** utility lists the size of a directory and all its subdirectories. A few sample lines from the output of *du* are shown here:

```
# du /home/lizo
22      ./public_html
2228    ./Public/shell_programming
2229    ./Public
2       ./Desktop/Autostart
2       ./Desktop/Trash
8       ./Desktop/Templates
13      /Desktop
1       /.kde/share/apps/kfm/tmp
1       /.kde/share/apps/kfm/bookmarks
6       /.kde/share/apps/kfm
1       /.kde/share/apps/kppp/Rules
1       /.kde/share/apps/kppp/Log
3       /.kde/share/apps/kppp
10      /.kde/share/apps
15      /.kde/share/config
1       /.kde/share/icons/mini
2       /.kde/share/icons
1       /.kde/share/applnk
1       /.kde/share/mimelnk
30      /.kde/share
31      /.kde
1       /archive
2337    /home/lizo
```

The number at the far left indicates how many 1 KB blocks are used by the subdirectory. Every subdirectory is shown separately, with totals for the parent directory. For example, the line showing 13 KB for the /Desktop directory includes the sum of the /Desktop/Autostart directory, the /Desktop/Trash directory, and the /Desktop/ Templates directory, as well as any files located in the Desktop directory itself. By looking at the last line, you can see how much space is used by the entire directory tree. More importantly, if you need to manage how space is used on a file system, you can see which subdirectories are consuming space, even if they are buried deep in the directory structure.

As with the *df* command, you can change the display of *du* so that megabytes or even gigabytes are displayed. The man page has complete details, but an example of displaying size in megabytes instead of kilobytes is shown here. Note that both *df* and *du* round up, so a directory with only a few small files is listed as 1 MB in size. The final line of *du* output shows the most accurate information in this situation, as the actual sizes (not the rounded up amounts) are used to complete each directory total.

```
$ du -B M /home/lizo
```

Suppose you wanted to see if any single home directory consumed more than 100 MB of space. The default output of the *du* command is given in KB, so you calculate that 100 MB is equal to roughly 100,000 KB of space. The following commands change you to the /home subdirectory and then list any directories containing over 100 MB of data:

```
# cd /home
# du | grep ^.....[0-9]
```

If any line of the output of *du* starts with a number with more than five digits, *grep* displays that line, showing you the oversized subdirectory. The output of the above command might look like this:

```
172529    ./nwells/images/NASA_mars/
110218    ./nwells/database/archive/
121749    ./rsolomon/doc/HTML/
```

Running *du* on the root directory of a large system can take some time (and slow down everyone else's work). Any directory that contains thousands of files or hundreds of subdirectories requires some time for the *du* command to process.

To avoid drains on the system, consider using the *du* command in the middle of the night to update a file containing the output of *du*. Then you can quickly search that file for overly large directories—directories that may require your attention if space becomes scarce.

In addition to the *df* and *du* commands, you can use various graphical tools and system administration scripts to check the status of file systems. For example, on the GNOME main menu, you can choose System Tools, then Hardware Browser (or enter *hwbrowser* at a command line). When the Hardware Browser opens, click the Hard Drives item on the left side of the main window. If you have installed KDE, you can also use the KDiskFree program. From the GNOME main menu, choose System Tools, then More System Tools, then KDiskFree (or enter *kdf* at a command line).

File System Attributes

The ext3 file system assigns a set of attributes to each file. These attributes are not displayed by the *ls* command, nor are they often used, but they can be very helpful in some circumstances.

Use the **lsattr** command to list the attributes of files in a directory. By default, most files have no attributes set. You can use the **chattr** command to change the attributes of one or more files. To use this command, determine the code letter for the attributes you want to add or remove from a file. Use a plus sign (+) or minus sign (−), respectively, to add or remove those attributes. To assign the entire set of attributes for a file, use an equals sign. (The use of (+), (−), and (=) for *chattr* is very similar to their use as part of the *chmod* command.) You can add the -R option to make your action recursive to the contents of all subdirectories in the named directory if you are setting attributes for multiple files. The possible attribute values are listed in Table 10-2. Note carefully which are supported and which are not yet supported.

Table 10-2 File Attributes in Linux

° File attribute code letter	Description
A	Do not update the *atime* field of a file's inode when the file is accessed; this reduces the disk activity on laptops
a	The file can only be appended to—no part of the file can be overwritten; only root can set this attribute on a file
c	The file is automatically compressed by the kernel before being written to disk (this attribute is not yet supported and has no effect)
D	Used for directories; write changes to files in this directory immediately instead of waiting for the disk cache to fill up; this reduces the efficiency of disk operations but also reduces the chance that a change is not written to disk in case of a system failure.
d	Skip this file when using certain commands to back up the system
E	Indicates that a compression error has occurred. This attribute cannot be changed with *chattr*, but is displayed by *lsattr*. It is used by developers working on kernel compression features.
I	Indicates that a directory has been indexed in a particular way (using hashed trees); this attribute may not be set or reset using *chattr*, but is displayed by *lsattr*
i	The file is immutable. It cannot be modified, deleted, appended to, or renamed. No link can be created to this file. Only root can set or clear this attribute.
j	Use journaling for the file. If you are using ext3, all files use journaling by default, so this attribute is not needed. Only root can set or clear this attribute.
s	Safe delete this file; when the file is deleted, its contents are all written as zeros, rather than simply marking its space as free
S	Write changes to this file immediately to disk; the equivalent for a file of the D attribute on a directory
T	A special purpose directory attribute used by the Orlov block allocator algorithm

Table 10-2 File Attributes in Linux (continued)

File attribute code letter	Description
t	Extra data at the end of this file (that would fill only part of a disk block) will not be merged with similar partial-block data from other files). This feature is called tail-merging. It is not yet supported by ext3, but this attribute will be needed when support is fully implemented.
u	When the file is deleted, save its content so it can be undeleted later if needed (this attribute is not yet supported)
X	Used by developers working on kernel compression; it cannot be changed using *chattr*, but it is displayed by *lsattr*
Z	Used by developers working on kernel compression; it cannot be changed using *chattr*, but it is displayed by *lsattr*

For example, to change the attributes of a file named timesheet to be immutable (unchangeable), you can use this command:

```
# chattr +i timesheet
```

To cause all files in a directory and its subdirectories to not have their *atime* field updated when they are accessed, you can use this command:

```
# chattr -R +A *
```

Checking File Systems

The *fsck* utility (usually pronounced FIZZ-check) checks the integrity of your file systems, making certain that each inode is correctly linked to a file, that the blocks of each file can be found, and so forth. The *fsck* utility can also repair minor file system problems. *fsck* is a front end that uses checking programs specific to the file system type that you want to check. For example, if you run *fsck* on a standard ext3 file system, *fsck* uses the program fsck.ext2 to check the file system (ext2 and ext3 are so similar that the same program is used for both).

In older Linux systems, the *fsck* program was run automatically after a file system had been mounted a certain number of times (20 was the default). That is no longer the case, and *fsck* does not check your file systems unless you explicitly start it yourself. It's a good idea to do this every few months on a busy system to make certain no hard disk errors are creeping in. The challenge is that *fsck* must be run on a file system that is not mounted. In order to check your root Linux file system, you must start your computer from a removable disk and run *fsck*. Conversely, if you have multiple data partitions (for example, a separate partition for the /home directory), you might be able to unmount and check that file system when users are unlikely to need access to it.

NOTE Creating a removable disk that you can use for this type of system check or other troubleshooting needs is described in Chapter 15, "Advanced Topics and Troubleshooting."

To use *fsck*, you simply supply the device name you want to have checked. For example:

```
# fsck /dev/hda1
```

If you don't supply a device name, *fsck* tries to check all of the file systems listed in the /etc/fstab file, which is described later in this section. The superblock of an ext3 file system maintains information about how many times the file system has been mounted since it was last checked by *fsck* and the last date and time it was checked.

Creating New File Systems

As a Linux system grows, it often requires additional storage space. As you will learn in Chapter 13, you can use backup systems to remove unused information and store it on compact disc, streaming tape, or other devices. Nevertheless, the amount of "live" storage needed often grows to exceed an administrator's original expectations. In fact, part of planning a Linux system in an organization is knowing in advance what steps to take when the system must be expanded. If these steps are outlined in advance, a system administrator is less likely to make choices that create obstacles to efficient system upgrades later on.

Adding a file system generally means adding a hard disk device to your system and making that hard disk available to Linux by formatting and mounting it. This is done for the root file system as part of the Linux installation process. But in that case, the installation utility takes care of most of the details. In this section you will learn how to set up additional file systems stored on a hard disk, CD-ROM, or other devices.

You can install new file systems that are permanent (loaded each time you start Linux) or temporary (loaded only occasionally, as needed). File systems can be stored on a device with removable media (such as a cartridge) or fixed media (such as a hard disk).

To install a new hard disk or other peripheral device, consult your hardware manual. Once the hard disk or other device is installed, you can use the Linux *fdisk* command described in the next section to examine its partitions, creating new Linux partitions as needed. Before any hard disk can be used as a native Linux file system, it must have Linux partitions defined.

Using the fdisk Utility

Almost all file system devices use either an IDE or SCSI interface to communicate with your computer (this includes file systems stored on USB hard disks, which use the SCSI device names in Linux, such as /dev/sda4).

To manage partitions in Linux after the operating system is installed, you typically must use the *fdisk* utility. This text-mode utility is not hard to use, but it can make new users nervous because it modifies hard disk partitions, and a small error can make everything on the hard disk inaccessible. Just remember that nothing you do in *fdisk* is written to the partition table until you exit *fdisk*. Your modifications to the partition table are only effective when you write the changes to disk with the *w* command to exit *fdisk*.

Suppose you have just installed a second IDE hard disk on your Linux system. You could begin using *fdisk* to set up partitions on that hard disk with the following command (notice that no partition number is given; *fdisk* is operating on the entire hard disk device):

```
# fdisk  /dev/hdb
```

Table 10-3 lists the single-character commands in *fdisk* that you are most likely to need.

Table 10-3   *fdisk* Commands

Command	Description
m	Lists all *fdisk* commands
p	Displays the current partition table
n	Begins defining a new partition
t	Defines the file system type marker on an existing partition
d	Deletes a partition currently existing in the partition table
b	Sets a selected partition as active (bootable)
w	Writes to disk any changes made to the partition table within *fdisk*, then exits *fdisk*
q	Quits *fdisk*, abandoning any edits to the partition table

Figure 10-8 shows sample output from the *p* command in *fdisk*, showing how partition information appears onscreen. The steps that follow show how you can define a Linux partition on a newly installed hard disk.

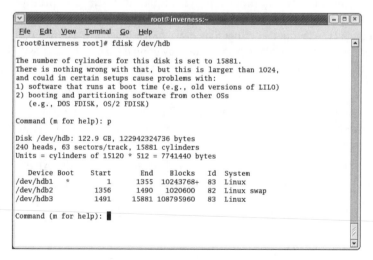

Figure 10-8   Sample output from the *fdisk* command

10

1. Start *fdisk* with the device name of the new hard disk:

   ```
   fdisk /dev/hdb
   ```

2. Type *p* to list the partitions currently defined on the hard disk. (On a new hard disk there may be none.)

3. If you are using an old hard disk that contains existing partition data, enter *d*, followed by the partition number when prompted, to delete each partition on the hard disk. (Remember, you're only deleting the definition from a memory copy of the partition table; you can press Ctrl+c to exit *fdisk* if you become uncertain of what you're doing.)

4. Enter *n* to begin creating a new partition.

5. Enter *p* for primary partition. (You can create more than four partitions on a hard disk using extended, or logical, partitions, but you shouldn't need to do this.)

6. Enter a partition number for the partition you are creating. For this value, enter the next free partition on the hard disk. On a brand new hard disk, the number you enter should be 1.

7. Begin to define the size of the new partition by entering its first cylinder as requested. The range of available cylinders on the hard disk is listed in parentheses, like this:

   ```
   First cylinder (1-1526, default 1):
   ```

8. Finish defining the size of the partition. To do this you can enter either a size, or a cylinder number. Example sizes you can enter are *+900M* for a 900 MB partition, or *+4G* for a 4 GB partition. To use the entire hard disk as a single partition, enter the last cylinder number displayed in the *fdisk* prompt.

NOTE If you specify a cylinder number rather than a size to finish defining a partition, you can learn the actual size of the partition only by using the *p* command to list the partitions and the size of each.

9. Specify the partition type by entering *t*. The partition type informs any operating system that looks at the partition table in what format the data is stored on the partition.

10. Enter the type code for a Linux native partition, which is 83. (At this point you can enter *l* (lowercase letter "L"), for "list," to see a listing of partition type codes, which is interesting to review.)

NOTE   When you create partitions for a new Linux system, you also create a partition of type 82 as Linux swap space. You also want to use the *a* command to define one of the partitions as active (bootable). The bootable partition is shown with an asterisk in the output of the *p* command. When creating Linux partitions on additional hard disks, none of the partitions needs to be marked as active because none is the location from which the system boots.

11. Use the *p* command to see how the partitions are now defined.

12. If you are satisfied with the partition configuration, write the partition table to the hard disk and exit *fdisk* by entering *w* for write.

If you do not want to write the new partition table to the hard disk (you prefer to abandon your work within *fdisk*), enter *q* to quit *fdisk*.

Formatting File Systems

Once you have marked a partition as containing a certain type of data (Linux, type 83), you must format the partition using an appropriate file system. As an analogy, think of a file cabinet. Marking a partition is like placing a label on a file drawer. Formatting a partition is like filling the drawer with labeled file folders. The drawer is then ready to have data filed in a useful way.

To create a new ext2 or ext3 file system, use ***mke2fs*** (for "make ext2 file system"). This command formats the partition, erasing all information on it, and organizes space for data to be recorded so that the partition can be used by Linux. Because you normally want to create an ext3 file system, use the *-j* option to add journaling. Include the device name for the partition that you created using *fdisk*:

```
# mke2fs -j /dev/sdb2
```

If you want to create a JFS or ReiserFS file system instead of an ext3 file system, you use either ***mkfs.jfs* or *mkreiserfs*** instead of *mke2fs*. These utilities are located in the jfsutils and reiserfs–utils packages, respectively, which are not installed by default in Fedora using the options recommended in Chapter 8. Both utilities are used in a manner similar to *mke2fs*:

```
# mkfs.jfs /dev/sdb2
# mkreiserfs /dev/sdb2
```

TIP   You can type *mk* and press Tab twice while logged in as root to see all of the related file system commands.

When creating a file system using any of these commands, you can add options to control how the file system is formatted. For example, you can alter the default block size, change the number of inodes allocated in the file system, add a volume label, reserve a percentage of the file system for root, or set other options that are outlined in the man page for each of these commands.

NOTE If you are using RAID or a volume management system, as discussed in Chapter 8, "Installing Linux," you may be interested in additional formatting options beyond those mentioned here. See the man pages as well for information about using these specialized file systems.

When you format a file system, you see many lines of output on the screen as the program lists all of the structure information that is being written to the device. In any case, formatting even a large hard disk is quite fast. On a fast Pentium system, using *mke2fs* to create a 40 GB file system takes only a couple of minutes.

You can use the ***fdformat*** command to format 3.5-inch disks. The format includes the device name of the floppy drive:

```
# fdformat /dev/fd0
```

In addition, a graphical removable disk formatter, ***gfloppy***, can be started by choosing System Tools, then Floppy Formatter on the GNOME main menu. (See Figure 10-9.)

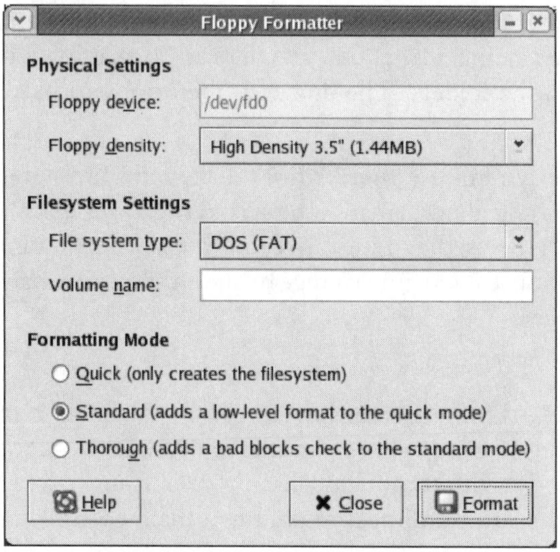

Floppy Formatter

Physical Settings

Floppy de_v_ice: /dev/fd0

Floppy _d_ensity: High Density 3.5" (1.44MB)

Filesystem Settings

File system _t_ype: DOS (FAT)

Volume _n_ame:

Formatting Mode

○ _Q_uick (only creates the filesystem)

◉ _S_tandard (adds a low-level format to the quick mode)

○ Thoro_u_gh (adds a bad blocks check to the standard mode)

[Help]   [✗ _C_lose]   [_F_ormat]

Figure 10-9 The *gfloppy* Floppy Formatter

After formatting an ext3 file system using *mke2fs*, you can use the ***tune2fs*** utility to examine the superblock of the file system and make minor changes to the file system parameters. Not all file system parameters can be altered using *tune2fs*. For example, you cannot change the block size used by the file system without reformatting the file system.

Use *tune2fs* with the *-l* option (for "list") to show the superblock of a file system:

```
# tune2fs -l /dev/hda1 | less
```

Although the default settings are sufficient for most system administrators, understanding how file systems are constructed and how you can view and alter their characteristics can help you troubleshoot disk problems and use disk storage more efficiently as your Linux systems become larger and more complex.

> A utility designed solely for software developers and advanced system administrators is the **debugfs** utility. (This utility is used for ext2 and ext3 filesystems; the **debugreiserfs** utility is used for ReiserFS file systems.) With *debugfs*, you can modify inodes, change the links between file names and inodes, and perform other advanced maintenance operations that require a full understanding of the structure of the file system. Use caution when experimenting with this utility.

Mounting New File Systems

After you have formatted a file system, you can mount it as part of the Linux directory structure and begin storing data on it. To access a file system, you use the *mount* command, indicating the device on which the file system is stored and a directory (a mount point) where the file system should be made accessible in the directory structure. When you previously mounted removable disks or CD-ROMs, you used only the mount point, like this:

```
# mount /mnt/cdrom
```

This was possible because the Linux system was able to determine the other needed parameters to use that file system. When you create a new file system, you must supply all the needed information. For example, if you formatted a new hard disk as a document archive for your office, you could create a directory called /archive, then mount the new file system so it is accessible at that point. These two commands accomplish that:

```
# mkdir /archive
# mount -t ext3 /dev/sdb2 /archive
```

This *mount* command says: mount a file system of type ext3 located on the device /dev/sdb2, and make it accessible at the directory /archive.

Now when you go to the /archive directory, you see a subdirectory called lost+found. The lost+found directory is placed in the beginning of all new ext2 and ext3 file systems. This directory is initially empty, but when you use *fsck*, files might be created in the lost+found directory. You very rarely see anything in this directory, but nevertheless don't delete the directory. The presence of the lost+found directory indicates that the new file system has been mounted successfully.

A file system cannot be in use when you unmount it. If any users on the Linux system are working with a file on the file system, or if any user's current working directory is located within that file system, the *umount* command fails, indicating that the file system is busy. The Linux kernel stores information about each mounted file system that includes the number of files currently being accessed. All users must stop using files on the file system and change their current working directory to a location outside the file system before you can unmount that file system.

10

NOTE   When removable media such as CD-ROMs are mounted, the Eject function of the drive is disabled until the device is unmounted. This is not true of removable disk drives, which means it is possible for a user to eject a removable disk while it is still mounted. This can cause minor problems, or even result in lost data. For example, files will still be marked as open even though they cannot be accessed.

Using Networked File Systems

Although a complete discussion of networked file systems is beyond the scope of this book, you should be aware that many Linux networks use these file systems to share data transparently over the network. Additional information is provided in Chapter 15, "Advanced Topics and Troubleshooting."

NOTE   A more complete discussion of networked filed systems is included in Chapter 5 of *Guide to Linux Networking and Security* (Course Technology 2003, ISBN 0-619-00094-5).

You already know that you can use a Web browser, an FTP client, or various command-line utilities to access data located on another computer. You can also use the *mount* command to make a directory on another computer appear as part of your local file system. This is similar to the idea of "mapping a network drive" in Microsoft Windows, where you assign a Windows share to a drive letter. Because Linux doesn't use drive letters, you might guess that you mount a networked file system to a subdirectory where it can be accessed.

Networked file systems in Linux are normally accessed using either the Network File System (NFS) or Server Message Block (SMB) protocols. A system administrator might tell you, for example, that you have access to a networked file system via NFS that is located on the server named glasgow in the directory /doc_archive. You decide to mount that file system on your computer in the subdirectory /glasgow_docs, which you have already created using *mkdir*. You can then mount the networked file system using this command, entering the password given to you by the administrator if prompted (a password is usually not needed):

```
# mount -t nfs glasgow:/doc_archive /glasgow_docs
```

Automating File System Mounting

As a system administrator, you want to automate everything that you can so that your time is free for tasks that require new analysis and problem-solving skills. As you saw earlier, several types of file systems are mounted automatically when you start Linux. New file systems that you create from additional hard disks or other devices can also be automatically mounted at boot time.

The key to automounting file systems is the **/etc/fstab** configuration file. This file contains one line for each file system that you want to have automounted when Linux boots. It also contains a line for file systems that you want to mount after booting Linux without providing all of the file system information in the *mount* command (as you did when mounting a CD-ROM or removable disk). A default fstab configuration file for Fedora is shown here (the exact values depend on where you have installed Linux on your system):

```
LABEL=/        /              ext3      defaults                    1 1
none           /dev/pts       devpts    gid=5,mode=620              0 0
none           /proc          proc      defaults                    0 0
none           /dev/shm       tmpfs     defaults                    0 0
LABEL=/usr     /usr           ext3      defaults                    1 2
/dev/hda3      swap           swap      defaults                    0 0
/dev/cdrom     /mnt/cdrom     iso9660   noauto,owner,kudzu,ro       0 0
/dev/cdrom1    /mnt/cdrom1    iso9660   noauto,owner,kudzu,ro       0 0
/dev/fd0       /mnt/floppy    auto      noauto,owner,kudzu          0 0
```

The fields of this configuration file, from left to right, are described in the following list:

- The device where the file system is located or, if LABEL is used, the volume label on the hard disk to use for this file system. The label can provide a shortcut reference to a partition; you can have the label point to a different partition without needing to edit the fstab file.

- The mount point in the directory structure where the device is accessed after being mounted. Each file system has a mount point directory except the swap space, which is used only by the Linux kernel.

- The file system type iso9660 is the CD-ROM standard; proc and swap are examples of special file system types.

- Options that apply when this file system is mounted. You will learn more about these options later in this section.

- Whether the file system can respond to the *dump* command (which is not used much any more). A *1* (number one) in this field indicates that the *dump* command can be used to print information on the structure of the file system. Only ext2 or ext3 partitions should have this field set to 1.

- The order used to check file systems when Linux is booted. Each time Linux starts, it checks the status of file systems in fstab before mounting them. The root file system should be numbered 1; other ext2 or ext3 file systems should be numbered 2. If 0 is used, the file system is not checked. All file systems that are not automounted can have 0 in this field.

The options used to mount file systems are an effective way to increase security and ease system administration work. The options that you can use on a line within /etc/fstab depend on the type of file system being mounted. For example, many options can be used for NFS (network-mounted) file systems that are not applicable to other types of file systems. Useful options are described in Table 10-4.

10

Table 10-4 Option Field Settings for the *mount* Command

Mount option	Description
async	Specifies that all reads and writes to the file system should be asynchronous—in other words, that information is buffered (stored in memory) to improve access speed
auto	Specifies that the file system should be automatically mounted at boot time or when the mount command is used with the -a option
dev	Designates the file system as a special device in the /dev directory
exec	Permits programs stored on the file system to be executed
noauto	Indicates that this file system should not be automatically mounted; instead, the file system must be mounted by an explicit mount command
noexec	Indicates that programs stored on the file system cannot be executed
nouser	Specifies that no regular users can mount the file system; instead, only root can mount it
ro	Mounts the file system as read-only, which means no data can be written to it
rw	Mounts the file system as read/write—the standard mode in which data can be written to the file system
suid	Allows special user ID permissions to be used on this file system
user	Allows a regular user to mount the file system; this is useful if you are running a desktop Linux system and don't want to switch to the root user account to mount a removable disk or CD-ROM
users	Functions the same as the user option except that any user can unmount the device
defaults	Includes the options rw, suid, dev, exec, auto, nouser, and async

Additional options are described in the man page for the *mount* command.

You can add options when executing a *mount* command, rather than relying on the options within /etc/fstab. If you do, as shown in this example command, the options given on the command line override any listed in /etc/fstab.

```
# mount -t ext3 -o defaults /dev/sdb2 /archive
```

Consider two examples when you would add a line to /etc/fstab to automate file system mounting. Suppose you had set up a large SCSI hard disk to hold a database application. You want the database file system to be mounted automatically when you start Linux. Users should not be able to run programs off the database file system. For this situation, the fstab line might look like:

```
/dev/sdb2  /opt/db  ext3  defaults,noexec  1  2
```

As a second example, suppose you are using Linux as your desktop workstation and have installed a new DVD drive. The device shouldn't be mounted at boot time because you don't normally keep a DVD disk in the drive, but you want to be able to mount the device without changing to the root user account. You also want to protect any writeable DVD disks from having any data damaged. You might use this line in the fstab file:

```
/dev/hdd /mnt/dvd  iso9660  ro,noauto,user  0 0
```

Once you have the fstab file set up, you can use the *mount* command with only the device name or mount point. The *mount* command looks in the fstab file for all of the additional information needed to mount the file system. This is why you can mount a CD-ROM with only the name of the mount point:

```
# mount /mnt/cdrom
```

No additional information is needed on the command line because *mount* retrieves everything else from the fstab file. If you use the *mount* command without sufficient information (and the information is not contained in the fstab file), *mount* displays an error message and the file system is not mounted.

Using the autofs Mounting Service

You sometimes will want users to be able to access a file system without having it mounted continuously. At the same time, you may not want users to be able to (or have to) mount a file system when they need to access it. The solution to this dilemma is the **autofs** service. This service is a daemon that watches for users to change directories into a directory that is configured as an autofs mount point. When a user enters that directory, the autofs daemon mounts the needed file system in the background so that the user can access data on it.

The autofs service is operated by a script in the /etc/rc.d/init.d directory, so you can use the *service* and *chkconfig* commands to manage it. By default, no file systems are automounted by autofs, but you can configure as many automounting file systems as you need. You should configure the file /etc/auto.master with a list of all mount points that autofs should watch for users to enter. For example, if you want autofs to mount a file system whenever a user enters /misc, add this line to the /etc/auto.master file:

```
/misc      /etc/auto.misc
```

You then must create a file called /etc/auto.misc that contains the options to use when autofs mounts a file system to /misc. These basically mirror the options contained in the /etc/fstab file; they are described in the man pages for autofs, automount, and auto.master.

After making changes to the /etc/auto.master file, you must restart the autofs server so that it knows about the mount points it should watch for. Use this command the first time you add an entry to /etc/auto.master:

```
# service autofs start
```

Use this command if you add more mount points or remove mount points from the file /etc/auto.master:

```
# service autofs reload
```

Managing Swap Space

The swap space that you set up when you installed Linux is a special file system that you don't directly manage—only the kernel accesses that space, and it is only used while the system is running. That is, nothing in swap space is reused the next time the system is started.

You can, however, affect the performance of your system by making certain that you have sufficient swap space and that the swap space is located efficiently. For example, if you have multiple hard disks, having the swap space on a separate hard disk from where commonly used data is stored lets both hard drives work at the same time, increasing the speed of the system. Conversely, if you have the swap space on the same hard drive with all of your data, the hard disk must "take turns" accessing the swap space for the kernel and the data partitions for your programs. Many system administrators use multiple swap partitions on large systems to give the kernel plenty of fast-access disk storage. Some even focus on things such as locating the swap partition near the center of each hard disk, where average access times are shorter.

If you decide to add a swap partition to your system, you can use the *mkswap* command to format a partition that you have set up using *fdisk* (and marked as type 82). This is similar to using the *mke2fs* command to format an ext2 or ext3 partition. Just use a command such as this one to format the partition as swap space:

```
# mkswap /dev/hda2
```

Once you have formatted a partition as swap space, you can add a line to /etc/fstab to tell Linux how to activate the swap space at boot time. The example file shown previously includes this line:

```
/dev/hda3     swap     swap     defaults     0 0
```

Swap space is activated by the *swapon* command within the system initialization scripts in /etc/rc.d.

You can also create swap space as a special file within another file system. This is much less efficient, but makes an interesting exercise. You create a swap file in Project 10-3.

Setting Quotas on Disk Usage

Another way you can manage file systems is by imposing a limit on the amount of hard disk space that any user or group can use. These limits are called **disk quotas**. For example, if you have defined a quota of 100 MB for a user and that user tries to create a new file (of which he is the owner) after using 100 MB of disk space, the system does not permit him to create that file.

Setting up quotas requires four steps:

1. Enable quotas on a file system by including the **usrquota** or **grpquota** option when the file system is mounted (for example, include it within the /etc/fstab file).

2. Use the *edquota* command to establish a quota for one or more users or groups.

3. Activate the quota system using the *quotaon* command.

4. Review current disk usage for a file system using the *repquota* command, or for a particular user or group using the *quota* command.

Quotas are not often used in business offices (except perhaps on e-mail servers), but may be very helpful in schools or other institutions where many users share a Linux system. You can learn more about disk quotas by reviewing the man pages for the commands described in this section.

A similar feature lets you impose additional limits on the actions of users. The *ulimit* command is part of the bash shell. By adding this command to a user's startup script (for example, in /home/nwells/.profile), you can limit the system resources that the user can access from that shell. Resources that you can control via the *ulimit* command include the number of processes running concurrently, the amount of virtual memory used, the amount of file system storage consumed, and the number of seconds of CPU time that can be used.

To see the current state of these values use this command:

```
$ ulimit -a
```

You can change your own values using additional *ulimit* commands, so this method is not appropriate to restrict the activities of advanced users, but it is sufficient to set basic resource limits for regular users. As an example, the following command sets a limit on the file system space that can be consumed (new files created) by the shell to one megabyte (1024 blocks):

```
$ ulimit -f 1024
```

Using disk quotas and the *ulimit* command is a type of file system accounting. These features let you control and monitor usage of file system resources by users.

CHAPTER SUMMARY

- Software packages are single files that contain all the files and instructions needed to install an application or collection of utilities. The most popular formats for software packages on Linux are the Red Hat Package Manager format (which use .rpm file extensions) and the Debian package format (which use .deb file extensions).

- The *dpkg* utility is used to manage Debian packages via the command line.

- The *system-config-packages* utility is used to manage rpm packages graphically on Red Hat Linux or Fedora systems. The *rpm* command is used to manage rpm packages via the command line. It includes options to verify, query, install, and erase packages. The *rpm* command maintains a database of information about the packages that are currently installed.

❑ The Red Hat Network service permits automatic updating of operating system files over the Internet for Red Hat Linux and Fedora distributions. This service is managed through the *up2date* graphical utility and an icon on the GNOME Panel.

❑ Advanced services of Red Hat Network are available for a fee and provide updating services suitable for large organizations with many Linux servers that need to be managed collectively.

❑ Linux supports many file systems types by using a virtual file system model. Popular journaling file systems used by default on Linux include ext3, ReiserFS, and JFS.

❑ Information about an ext3 file system is stored in the superblock. You can view or alter the superblock parameters using the *tune2fs* command.

❑ The *mount* command attempts to use information stored in /etc/fstab to determine how to mount a file system if all the needed parameters are not supplied on the command line.

❑ The /etc/fstab file contains a list of all file systems that the system mounts at boot time, as well as those that might be mounted later on.

❑ The *df* and *du* commands are helpful in watching how disk space is being used on a busy Linux system. The *df* command displays information for an entire file system; *du* displays the disk space used by directories.

❑ Each file and directory can be assigned attributes such as "immutable." Most of these are not used regularly, but they are viewed and set with *lsattr* and *chattr*, respectively.

❑ The *fsck* utility examines a file system to see that its contents have not been corrupted. If errors are found, *fsck* can also repair them.

❑ You can add new file systems to Linux by setting up partitions using the *fdisk* utility, then formatting the newly created partition using *mke2fs* or a similar utility. New file systems can be manually mounted directly using the *mount* command, or they can be listed in /etc/fstab with options that cause them to be mounted automatically each time the system is started.

❑ The *fdisk* utility configures partition data on a hard disk. It should be used with great care.

❑ Linux supports networked file systems using protocols such as NFS and SMB. These are accessed using the *mount* command and a server name as a parameter.

❑ The autofs service, once configured using /etc/auto.master, can automatically mount file systems whenever a user enters a named directory that is a mount point for a file system not yet mounted.

❑ Swap space is created much like regular file systems, using the *mkswap* and *swapon* commands, though it is used only by the kernel.

❑ Disk quotas are configured using the *edquota* command for any file system on which the usrquota or grpquota options have been specified. These quotas restrict how much disk space a user is permitted to consume. The *ulimit* command, a part of the bash shell, also allows you to limit the system resources that users can access.

Command Summary

Command	Description	Example
alien	Installs or converts a software package to a different format, such as an rpm-format package to a Debian-format package	alien --to-deb gimp-1.1.7-3.i386.rpm
chattr	Changes the attributes assigned to a file or directory (see also lsattr)	chattr +i timesheet.doc
debugfs	Debugs low-level file system details for an ext2 or ext3 file system using an interactive shell	debugfs /dev/hdb1
debugreiserfs	Debugs low-level file system details for a ReiserFS file system using an interactive shell	debugreiserfs /dev/hdb1
df	Displays space usage information for each file system that is currently mounted	df
dpkg	Manages packages created using the Debian package format	dpkg --install gimp_1.1.7-2_i386.deb
dpkg-reconfigure	Changes the configuration of a Debian-format software package that is already installed on the system	dpkg-reconfigure gimp
dselect	A text-based, menu-driven front end used to manage Debian format software packages; relies on the dpkg command-line utility	dselect
du	Displays disk space usage for all files in a directory and its subdirectories	du /home
edquota	Edits the disk space quota assigned to a user	edquota
fdformat	Formats a removable disk	fdformat /dev/fd0
fdisk	Interactive utility used to view and alter hard disk partitions	fdisk /dev/hdb
fsck	Checks the integrity of a file system, optionally repairing errors it finds	fsck /dev/hda2
gfloppy	Graphical program used to format removable disks	gfloppy
lsattr	Lists the attributes assigned to a file or directory	lsattr *
mcopy	Copies a file between a Linux file system and an unmounted DOS-format removable disk	mcopy ~/my_file A:
mdel	Deletes a file located on an unmounted DOS-format removable disk	mdel A:my_file.doc

10

Command	Description	Example
mdir	Lists the contents of an unmounted DOS-format removable disk	mdir A:
mke2fs	Formats (makes) an ext2 or ext3 file system within an existing partition that is marked as type 83	mke2fs -j /dev/hdb3
mkfs.jfs	Formats (makes) a JFS file system within an existing partition that is marked as type 83	mkfs.jfs /dev/hdb3
mkreiserfs	Formats (makes) a ReiserFS file system within an existing partition that is marked as type 83	mkreiserfs /dev/hdb3
mkswap	Formats (makes) as swap space an existing partition that is marked as type 82 (or a file)	mkswap /dev/hda4
quotaon	Causes file systems configured with usrquota or grpquota options to begin tracking and enforcing disk space quotas	quotaon
system-config-packages	Graphical utility used to manage rpm-format packages in Red Hat Linux and Fedora	system-config-packages
repquota	Reports the disk usage for each user on a file system	repquota /dev/hda1
rpm	Manages rpm-format software packages and the system database that tracks what packages are installed	rpm -q gedit
swapon	Activates a formatted swap partition or swap file	swapon
tune2fs	Displays or changes parameters within the superblock of an ext2 or ext3 file system	tune2fs /dev/hda2
ulimit	Imposes resource limits on users working within a shell, restricting such items as the number of processes that can be run or the amount of file system storage that can be used	ulimit -f 1024
up2date	Uses the Red Hat Network service to download operating system packages that have been upgraded; only available on Red Hat Linux or Fedora systems	up2date

KEY TERMS

/etc/fstab — A configuration file that contains a file system table with devices, mount points, file system types, and options. Used by the *mount* command.

autofs — A system service that watches for users to enter configured mount points and then automatically mounts the corresponding file system. Managed via the autofs script in /etc/rc.d/init.d. Configured using the /etc/auto.master file.

disk quotas — Limits assigned to each user or group that restrict the total amount of space that the user or group can consume on a file system.

grpquota — Option that can be used within the /etc/fstab file that causes a file system to track disk space quotas for each group. Used in conjunction with the *quotaon* and *edquota* commands.

Journaling File System (JFS) — A high-performance journaling file system developed by IBM and available on most Linux systems.

Management — A middle level of Red Hat Network functionality (available for a fee). Permits additional upgrade services, such as comparing two systems to see if they have the same packages installed.

Provisioning — The highest level of Red Hat Network functionality (available for a fee). Permits additional upgrade services, such as upgrading applications as well as operating system files, and upgrading multiple systems simultaneously from "bare metal."

Red Hat Network — A service provided by Red Hat Software to automatically update systems using Red Hat Linux or Fedora. Two advanced levels of service (for which Red Hat Software charges a fee) are called Management and Provisioning.

Red Hat Package Manager (rpm) — A software package format developed by Red Hat Software and used by numerous Linux distributions.

ReiserFS — A file system type that provides high performance and journaling. Used by default on several Linux systems, including SUSE and Gentoo.

software package — A collection of multiple files, along with descriptive information, security data, and installation instructions. Permits a user to install or upgrade an application or set of utilities with a single command. The Red Hat Package Manager (rpm) format and the Debian format are the two widely used software package formats on Linux.

superblock — A record containing detailed status information about an ext2 or ext3 file system. Stored at multiple locations on each ext2 or ext3 file system. Viewed or altered with *tune2fs*.

usrquota — Option that can be used within the /etc/fstab file that causes a file system to track disk space quotas for each user. Used in conjunction with the *quotaon* and *edquota* commands.

virtual file system — A method used by the Linux kernel to generalize access by programs to file data so that the kernel can support multiple, modularized file system types.

REVIEW QUESTIONS

1. Name the two widely used software package formats for Linux, with the file extension used for each type and the command-line utility used to manage each.

2. Within the *system-config-packages* utility, selecting details and checking a package name:

   a. causes that package to immediately be installed

   b. verifies whether that package is currently installed correctly

   c. marks the package as one that will be installed after the Update button is selected after other categories of packages have also been reviewed for possible changes

   d. has no effect as this utility only reflects the choices made during a custom installation.

3. Which option of the *rpm* command is used to verify the cryptographic signature so you know for certain the person or organization that created a given rpm file?

   a. *--checksig* or *-K*

   b. *-V*

   c. *-qa*

   d. *-Uvh*

4. If you know the name of a package, you can see a list of all the files contained in that package using this command:

   a. *rpm -qf packagename*

   b. *rpm -Uvh packagename*

   c. *rpm -ql packagename*

   d. *rpm -e packagename*

5. If you have an rpm-format file stored on your system, and then you use the rpm command to install that software package, the rpm file will no longer be on your system. True or False?

6. When querying an installed package using the *-q* option, you use
   _____ ; when installing an rpm file using the *-U* option, you use
   _____ .

   a. the name of the package alone; the complete file name with all version numbers and file extensions

   b. the name of the package alone; the name of the package alone

   c. the name of the package with all version numbers and file extensions; the complete file name as it appears in an *ls* listing

   d. the name of the package alone; the -h option as well to check for incompatibilities during the installation process

7. The command *rpm -q packagename* does the following:

   a. determines whether *packagename* is installed on the system

   b. locates *packagename* on a CD-ROM

   c. erases *packagename* if it is currently installed

   d. summarizes the disk quota for users of *packagename*

8. The volume label for a file system is:

   a. changed using *fsck*

   b. viewed using *mke2fs*

   c. stored in /etc/fstab

   d. stored in the superblock

9. Defragmentation, the process of collecting all parts of a file into one contiguous part of a hard disk:

   a. is performed in Linux using the *fsck* utility

   b. is not needed in Linux because of the way ext2, ext3, and other Linux file systems arrange files

   c. should be performed as part of each boot up, though it is typically done automatically by the /etc/rc.d/ startup scripts

   d. causes data loss if performed on an ext3 file system

10. The Linux kernel is able to support multiple file systems types because it uses:

    a. a virtual file system that separates standard disk operations from the drivers that perform those operations

    b. the /etc/fstab file to list the file system type of file system to be mounted

    c. the management and provisioning aspects of Red Hat Network

    d. virtual memory in either a swap partition or a swap file

11. Which piece of information is *not* provided in the output when the *mount* command is entered with no parameters or options?

    a. the mount point for each mounted file system

    b. the file system type for each mounted file system

    c. the size of each mounted file system

    d. the options with which each mounted file system was mounted, as defined in the /etc/fstab file or in the *mount* command, if the file system was mounted manually (without reference to etc/fstab)

10

12. Which of the following lists contains only commands used to learn about the status of file systems?

    a. *df, du, fsck, tune2fs, mount*

    b. *df, du, tune2fs, mount, mke2fs, fdisk*

    c. *fsck, tune2fs, mount, swapon*

    d. *df, du, mount, rpm, dpkg*

13. The _____ command is used to display the attributes assigned to a file or directory.

    a. *dmesg*

    b. *lsattr*

    c. *chmod*

    d. *chattr*

14. Name two attributes that are currently supported by the ext3 file system and two attributes that are not yet supported or are used only for developers at this time.

15. The Linux command used to format a Linux ext3 hard disk partition is:

    a. *mke2fs*

    b. *fdisk*

    c. *fsck*

    d. Linux does not use formatted partitions.

16. Disk quotas let you manage how much disk space a user consumes, but they must be first enabled:

    a. on a group-by-group basis using standard file permission settings

    b. within the startup scripts in a user's home directory

    c. on the file system where you want the quota to apply (in /etc/fstab)

    d. by adding an option to the /etc/passwd file for each affected user

17. A mounted file system is defined as one that:

    a. has been included as part of the Linux directory structure

    b. has been correctly formatted using a supported Linux file system type

    c. allows any user to run programs located on it

    d. includes at least a root user account

18. The *fdisk* utility is used to:

    a. format Linux partitions

    b. configure the boot loader

    c. establish partitions of the correct type to hold a Linux file system

    d. configure swap space

19. The *df* utility provides information about which one of the following?

    a. which users have mounted a file system

    b. the virtual memory usage as stored on all mounted file systems

    c. file system capacity, device name, and percentage used status for each mounted file system

    d. per-directory usage and file system mount point

20. Describe the effect of the *defaults* option in a configuration line of the /etc/fstab file.

21. Describe the main advantage of having swap space located on a hard disk separate from the Linux data partitions.

22. If you attempt to unmount a mounted file system and receive an error message, the most likely cause is:

    a. The file system was not mounted correctly in the first place.

    b. The *df* command is in the process of computing file system statistics.

    c. An error exists on the physical media that Linux cannot interpret.

    d. One or more users are working in the file system.

23. The autofs service is used to:

    a. Permit users to access file systems that are not mounted by automatically mounting them when the user enters a configured directory (mount point).

    b. Automatically run *fsck* on each file system at appropriate intervals to avoid propagating corrupted file system data.

    c. Help *df* and *du* process disk usage data.

    d. Provide disk quota services for any file system for which the *usrquota* or *grpquota* option is set.

24. Virtual memory space to be used by the kernel must be located on a single separate partition, which can be located either on the same hard disk or a different hard disk from the root file system. True or False?

25. Which command is used to establish a quota for a user when disk space quotas have been enabled for a file system?

    a. *usrquota*

    b. *quotaon*

    c. *repquota*

    d. *edquota*

10

HANDS-ON PROJECTS

HANDS-ON PROJECTS

Project 10-1

In this project, you explore the rpm package database on your system. To complete this project you should have an installed Linux system running Red Hat Linux or Fedora. You need root access to complete this project because you use the *redhat-config-packages* command; the second part of the project, in which you use the *rpm* command-line utility to query the package database, does not require that you be logged in as root.

1. Log in to Linux and open a command-line window. Change to root access using the **su –** command. (Don't forget the hyphen after *su* or you will not have automatic access to all administrative utilities.)

2. Enter the command **system-config-packages** to start the graphical package management tool.

3. After the utility starts up, scroll down until you see the Office/Productivity category and click on the Details link to the right of that label.

4. Review the list of packages shown. Only some of these are selected by default if you selected this category during the installation of Linux. Check one of the packages that sounds interesting to you that was not checked when you first opened the dialog box.

5. Click the **Close** button at the bottom of the dialog box.

6. Click the **Update** button at the bottom of the main window of the utility.

7. After a moment, a message box appears telling you that all packages you have selected to be added (just one in this case) have been prepared. Click **Continue**.

8. The program begins trying to install the package. After a moment, it prompts you for the appropriate CD-ROM on which it expects to find the new packages to be installed. Click **Cancel** to cancel this updating process and exit from the utility.

9. At the command line, use the *rpm* command to determine if the zsh package (the Z shell, an enhanced version of the bash shell) is installed on your system:

   ```
   $ rpm -q zsh
   ```

10. Use a similar command to determine if bash is installed. Note the version number of the shell:

    ```
    $ rpm -q bash
    ```

11. List all of the files included in the bash package, using the *less* command so that you can scroll up and down the list using the arrow keys. Based on their location in the file system, what are most of the files included with this package?

```
$ rpm -ql bash | less
```

12. Type **q** to return to the command prompt. Search for all the installed shells on your system. Each shell typically includes the characters "sh," so try searching for all packages that include those characters. What shells can you spot among the output of the command?

```
$ rpm -qa | grep sh
```

13. Suppose you have seen the file /etc/profile and want to know which package contains that file. View that information with this command:

```
$ rpm -qf /etc/profile
```

14. View package information for the setup package:

```
$ rpm -qi setup
```

15. Exit the command-line window you are using. Log out of Linux.

Project 10-2

In this project, you practice accessing file systems in Linux. To complete this project you should have an installed Linux system with root access and a formatted removable disk. The configuration of directories in the project is based on Red Hat Linux and Fedora, but most Linux systems are identical to what is described here.

1. Log in to Linux and open a command-line window. Use **su –** to change to root access.

2. Insert a removable disk in the drive of your computer.

3. Mount the disk:

```
mount /mnt/floppy
```

4. Copy a file to the disk:

```
cp /etc/login.defs /mnt/floppy
```

5. List the contents of the disk:

```
ls /mnt/floppy
```

6. Unmount the disk:

```
umount /mnt/floppy
```

7. Try to list the contents of the disk again:

```
ls /mnt/floppy
```

Why doesn't the file appear?

8. Review the line in /etc/fstab that lets you mount this file system without specifying a device name:

`grep floppy /etc/fstab`

9. What options are applied when the removable disk is mounted? Look up each option in the man page for *mount*.

NOTE One of the options you may see in the output of Step 8 is "kudzu." This utility automatically manages added or changed hardware in Red Hat and Fedora systems. You rarely interact directly with kudzu. Its inclusion as one of the options in /etc/fstab indicates that kudzu will manage adding or removing that device from /etc/fstab as a relevant device is detected. You can read more in the man page for kudzu.

10. Note the file system type in the output of Step 8. Use the **tune2fs** command to view the superblock of the floppy file system. What result do you see? Why?

11. Remove the floppy disk and log out of Linux

Project 10-3

HANDS-ON PROJECTS

In this project, you create a swap file. To complete this project you should have an installed Linux system with root access.

1. Log in to Linux and open a command-line window. Use **su –** to change to root access.

2. Use the **df** command to view the state of your file systems. Do you see the swap partition that was created during the installation of Linux?

3. View the contents of the /etc/fstab file to locate the partition currently used for swap space (if more than one is used, select any of them). Make a note of the partition device name (such as /dev/hda2—the exact device will vary depending on how your system was installed).

`grep swap /etc/fstab`

4. Use *fdisk* to determine the size of your swap partition:

a. Start *fdisk* with the appropriate hard disk device, for example (note that no partition number is included, because fdisk works with the entire hard disk):

`fdisk /dev/hda`

b. List the partitions on the hard disk by typing **p** and pressing Enter.

c. Note the size of your swap partition in the output of the *p* command in *fdisk*.

d. Exit *fdisk* by pressing **Ctrl+c**.

5. Create a file full of zeros in the root directory to use as an experimental 64 MB swap file.

`dd if=/dev/zero of=/swap bs=1024 count=65536`

6. Format the swap file you just created:

```
mkswap /swap
```

7. Edit the /etc/fstab file in a text editor:

```
vi /etc/fstab
```

8. Add this line to the end of the /etc/fstab file:

```
/swap       swap       swap       defaults       0 0
```

9. Save the /etc/fstab file and exit the text editor.

10. Activate all swap space listed in the /etc/fstab file (including your newly added entry):

```
swapon -a
```

11. Your original swap partition and the experimental swap file are now both available to the kernel as swap space. To see evidence of this, display the kernel's swap space table using this command:

```
cat /proc/swaps
```

12. Edit the /etc/fstab file again and remove the extra line you added to the swap file. Would you expect this step to immediately affect the current state of the swap space?

13. Turn off the experimental swap file:

```
swapoff /swap
```

14. Delete the swap file, confirming the deletion when prompted:

```
rm /swap
```

15. Log out of Linux.

CASE PROJECTS

CASE PROJECTS

Designing File Systems

Your employer, McKinney & Co. has been awarded a contract to help with a foreign assistance project. You have been asked to lead the project and, hearing that it was near some beautiful beaches, you have graciously turned over your current project to a colleague and accepted this challenging new assignment. Your task is to help the Ministry of Justice of the Government of Cylonica place all of their supreme court cases and various other legal materials online. One of the first technical aspects of the project is designing the file systems on which the data will reside.

1. The legal data consists of statutes (laws) and court cases, and is never altered once it is loaded. Several hundred GB of data are anticipated as part of the final project. Legal researchers can add their own notes to cases, creating a personal database of study items. Several background applications are used to manage the databases,

10

execute searches, index newly loaded material, and interact with users (chat, e-mail to the Minister's office, and so on). Several hundred users are expected to begin using the system as soon as it is completed; usage will increase as more people become aware of it.

2. Design the layout of the file systems for the Linux server on which this system will reside. Show how you would set up partitions or separate hard disks and devices to accommodate each of the needs mentioned above. Prepare sample entries for an fstab file showing the options that you would likely use for each mounted file system. Include information about how you would configure the swap space on the devices you choose to use.

3. An international conference in England had generated substantially more interest in the legal research site than was expected. You notice one day that the *df* command shows one file system at more than 95% capacity. Describe some steps you might take to remedy this problem. How would your actions vary depending on which of the file systems was at 95%?

4. After completing this project and returning home, you learn that a typhoon has raged through Cylonica. The resulting power fluctuations caused one of the hard disks to crash. Your plan included regular backups, of course. What factors in the file system arrangement you designed make it easier to get the system running again?

11

MANAGING USERS

After reading this chapter and completing the exercises, you will be able to:

♦ Create and manage user accounts

♦ Manage complex file permissions

♦ Review advanced user security issues

In the previous chapter you learned about software packages: how you can download, install, and manage applications that have been created using a special format for easy administration. Because part of that installation and management often involves upgrading existing software packages on your Linux system, you also learned about an automatic update tool called Red Hat Network. Finally, you learned more about file systems, including managing partitions, setting mount options, and creating new file systems when you add devices to your computer.

In this chapter, you learn more about managing user accounts on your system. This involves basic operations such as creating a new account and making changes to that account. It also involves managing unusual changes to accounts involving special file permissions and using remote user databases. Finally, this chapter discusses policy considerations that can help you determine how to manage large numbers of end-users.

CREATING AND MANAGING USER ACCOUNTS

To complete any operation in Linux, a person must first log in using a valid user account name and password. Setting up and maintaining these user accounts is an important part of the work of a system administrator. In Chapter 3, "Using the Shell," you learned how to manage the initialization files for a user account, such as .profile and .bashrc. In Chapter 4, "Understanding Users and File Systems," you learned where user account information is stored. In this section you learn how to create new accounts and make changes in those accounts. In general, the process of creating new user accounts runs like this, though the exact steps you need to perform vary depending on the number of users you are creating, the system configuration in which you are working, and other factors:

1. Add default files that you want to be part of every user's home directory to the /etc/skel directory (the functioning of this directory is described later in this chapter).

2. Create a home directory for all users. Typically, this is /home, which is installed by default on most Linux systems, but you can also create subdirectories for groups of user accounts, such as /home/CS185 and /home/CS110.

3. Configure default settings to be used for all users, either in /etc/login.defs or in /etc/default/useradd (as discussed later in this chapter).

4. Create groups so that you can assign membership to user accounts that you create.

5. Create a user account for each person using either command-line or graphical utilities, as described in this section.

6. Create a valid password for each user and give the user that password so he or she can begin using the account.

In general, the more user accounts you have on your Linux system, the more time you will spend managing them. More users also means more security risks—thus proper management and tracking of user accounts is crucial to keeping the system secure.

Managing User Accounts Graphically

Recall that each line in the /etc/passwd file contains fields defining a new user account. An example line might look like this one:

```
johnl:x:500:500:John Lim:/home/johnl:/bin/bash
```

The fields include (from left to right): the user name, a password (or an x to indicate that the shadow password system is used), a UID, a GID, a comment field (used for the full name on regular user accounts), the user's home directory, and the user's default shell.

You have learned about the *vipw* command that you can use to edit the /etc/passwd file directly to define a new user account. After adding a line to /etc/passwd, you need to use the *passwd* command to define a password, then create the home directory and add any default files you want to include for that user. The new user can then log in and begin using the system. There are, however, better ways to create user accounts, especially when you have dozens or hundreds of accounts to create on a new system.

You can use any of several different utilities to create new user accounts. If you are working in a graphical desktop, you might prefer using a graphical tool; if you need to create many user accounts, a command-line utility can be much more efficient, especially because it can be used within a script. (As you read Chapter 14, "Writing Shell Scripts," think about how you could use a script and a data file to automatically create user accounts using the utilities you learn about in this section.)

 TIP   Although many utilities are available to create and manage user accounts, few utilities let you access all possible user account configuration options. Become familiar with the limitations of the tools you use so you know when to use something else to complete a complex or unusual task.

Most commercial versions of Linux include at least one graphical utility for creating and managing user accounts. SUSE Linux, for example, includes the YaST administration program, which includes tools to create and manage user accounts. Some distributions rely on the freely downloadable Webmin program (see *www.webmin.com*) with its user and group management module.

11

Red Hat Linux and Fedora include the ***system-config-users*** utility, which you can start from any graphical terminal window. By default, this utility shows you all user accounts on the system (the entire contents of the /etc/passwd file). In most cases, you don't want to work with all user accounts, but just those regular user accounts that represent real individuals or roles in your organization. To change the display to only include those users, open the Preferences menu and select Filter system users and groups. Figure 11-1 shows the system-config-users program with only regular users listed.

If you have a large number of regular user accounts on your system, you can enter a regular expression in the Search filter field and click Apply filter to display only matching user names. For example, if you knew you wanted to edit user account Thomas, but you had a list of 1200 user names in the window, you can enter "tho*" in the Search filter field, click Apply filter, and the window is updated to display only user names starting with "tho," which would probably be a very small number, permitting you to very quickly locate the account you needed on screen. To view all users again, delete all text from the Search filter field and click Apply filter again.

All of the information from the /etc/passwd file is shown in columns in this window (except the encrypted password). You can use this utility to edit each of these fields, as well as the password information stored in /etc/shadow.

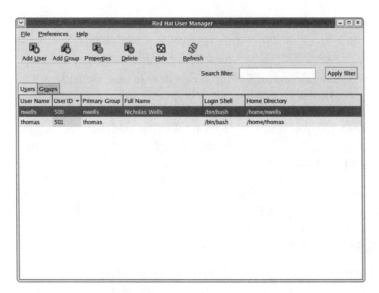

Figure 11-1   The main window of system-config-users

Editing User Information

To begin editing a user, double-click a user name or click a user name and then click the Properties button above the list of users. The dialog box shown in Figure 11-2 appears, in which you can change the information in each field of each tab. Most of the fields in the User Data tab refer to information stored in /etc/passwd. You can alter the following information:

- *User Name*: Change the user name only with great care. Many parts of Linux, such as file permissions, are tied to the user ID, which you cannot change using this utility. But some things, such as a user's e-mail address and the name of the user's home directory, are tied to the user name. This field cannot contain spaces or special characters. Most system administrators keep user names to about 10 characters or less. Although they can be longer, long user names tend to be more work for the user and can interfere with some operations.

- *Full Name*: This is the information stored in the comment field of /etc/passwd. Most administrators store the full name of the user or else a description of the role of the account (such as Print Server Administrator). This field can be up to 255 characters in length.

- *Password* and *Confirm Password*: These fields let you set a password for the user. Although you can reset passwords using this utility, you should also tell users to change their password as soon as possible so that they are not using a standard password issued by the system administrator.

- *Home Directory*: You should not change this field unless you have moved all home directories to a new location or have changed the user name.

■ *Login Shell:* The utility includes a drop-down list that shows all available shells on the system that you can choose from.

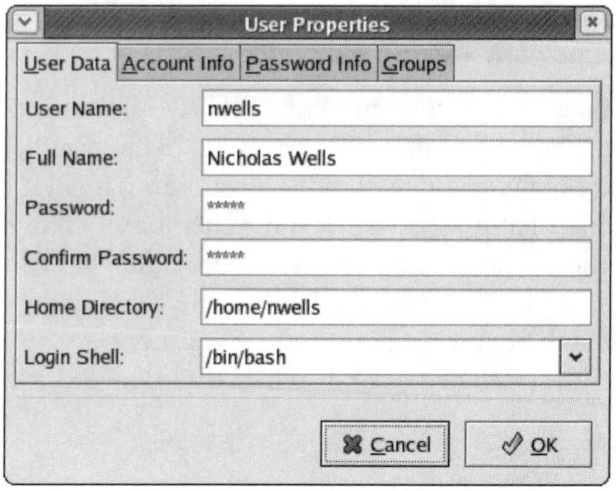

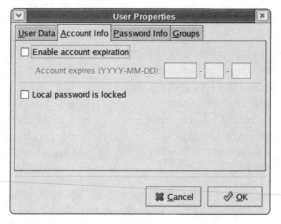

Figure 11-2   The User Data tab: Editing a user account in system-config-users

On the Account Info tab, shown in Figure 11-3, you can enable account expiration and lock the local password. If you enable account expiration, you enter a year, month, and day when the account expires. There are several methods you can use to disable an account if a problem occurs with an employee in an organization (these are discussed in the next subsection); the account expiration feature is used for such things as when a student's account on a school system expires at the end of the semester, or a ISP subscriber whose account expires at the end of the month, but whose expiration date is updated each time a new payment is received.

Figure 11-3   The Account Info tab: Editing a user account in system-config-users

When the Local password is locked check box is selected, the password cannot be changed by the user. This is useful when you have a user whose passwords are synchronized between multiple systems or whose user information is part of a larger shared network database. By preventing the user from changing the password on the account, you can maintain the user's ability to work across multiple systems with a single password.

The Password Info tab is shown in Figure 11-4. The top line of this tab shows you when the user last changed his or her password. You also can enable password expiration here. Having passwords that expire is a very good security practice, though most users hate it. It means that every once in a while, they must think of a new password and remember it. This sometimes causes users to simply write down the current password on a sticky note next to their desk, which defeats the purpose of requiring new passwords. With some training, however, you can help users understand the benefits of expiring passwords: if another person has discovered someone's password, their unauthorized access ends when the password is changed.

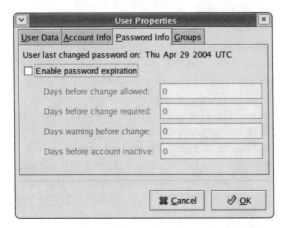

Figure 11-4   The Password Info tab: Editing a user account in system-config-users

Many security experts recommend that passwords expire every 30 to 60 days. The day after requiring a new password, some users simply try to change back to their preferred password, so the Days before change allowed field lets you prevent them from changing it again until a certain period has elapsed. The Days before change required field is the expiration time (perhaps 30 to 60 days). The Days warning before change field provides a warning when a user logs in that their password is soon to expire. The Days before account inactive determines how long after the account expires before the user can no longer use the expired password to log in to the system. All of this information is stored in the /etc/shadow file.

As an example of how to use these fields, suppose you want to set up your system so that users must change their password every 60 days (about eight and a half weeks). You don't mind if they change it any time after about six weeks, but you want to start reminding them to change it in the last week. They can have three days of what are sometimes called "grace logins" using the expired password before their account is unavailable. To set this up, you enter 45 in the Days before change allowed field, 60 in the Days before change required field, 7 in the Days warning before change field, and 3 in the Days before account inactive field.

NOTE

Most administrators want to give a few days of grace logins. If a user's account becomes inaccessible because of an expired password, it means extra work for the system administrator to set up a new password to reenable the account.

The Groups tab of the User Properties dialog box is shown in Figure 11-5. In this tab, all of the groups defined on the system in the /etc/group file are listed twice: once in a list with a check box next to each group name, and once in a drop-down list as part of the Primary Group field. As you have learned, each user is assigned a primary group. The group ID of that group is included in that user's record in /etc/passwd, and that group is assigned as the group for any files that the user creates.

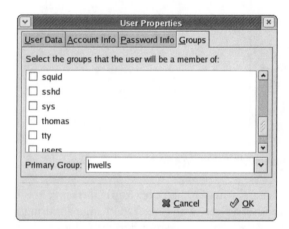

Figure 11-5   The Groups tab: Editing a user account in system-config-users

Some Linux distributions, including Red Hat Linux and Fedora, use the User Private Group model in which a user's primary group is a group with the same name as the user, that contains only that user as a member. Other Linux distributions place all users in a group named "users" or something similar.

After reviewing the user's primary group (which was assigned at the time the user account was created), you can give the user membership in other groups by checking any of the boxes in the upper part of the tab. For example, suppose a user is assigned to work on a new project and needs access to a different set of files on the system. You might use this utility to uncheck the group that the user has finished working with and check the new group name, so that the user becomes a member of that group and has access to the project files.

After you have reviewed information and made any necessary changes in the User Properties dialog box, click OK to close the dialog box.

Creating a New User

In the system-config-users utility, you can create a new user account by clicking the Add User button just below the menu bar. The dialog box shown in Figure 11-6 appears. In this dialog box, you enter a user name, full name, and a password (twice). For most users, you can then click OK and the user account is created. On rare occasions you might select a nonstandard shell in the Login Shell field.

Figure 11-6   Creating a new user in system-config-users

The settings used to create a new user are stored in the **/etc/login.defs** file. You can review this file in any text editor, but in most cases you won't need to change anything in this file. Comments in the file describe the settings, which correspond to the fields you learned about for editing a user account in the previous subsection.

By default, the utility creates a home directory for you based on the user name you enter. (For example, if you create an account called amoffett, the home directory will be /home/amoffett.) The utility also creates a user private group for the user and assigns that group as the user's primary group. (For example, a group named amoffett with only that user as a member.) After the user account is created, you can use the Edit feature of the utility to make the user a member of other groups. You can also specify the User ID (UID) manually, but this is not recommended unless you are trying to repair an account that was previously used and had a specific UID. Otherwise, you risk having two user accounts with the same UID, which causes numerous problems with the file system.

Having matching UIDs on multiple systems is important when using the r-utilities to remotely access networked resources, but these services are not secure and their use is discouraged for most networks.

When you have finished filling in the fields, click OK to create the new user account.

Creating a New Group

Creating a new group is more straightforward than creating a new user. Click the Add Group button, then enter a group name in the Group Name field (see Figure 11-7). As with users, you should not try to specify a group ID manually unless you have a good reason, such as trying to restore access to files that have a certain GID already assigned. Click OK to create the new group.

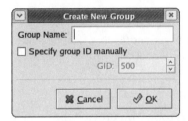

Figure 11-7   Creating a new group in system-config-users

You can view all groups on the system by switching the main window to the Groups tab, then double-click any group name to edit the member list for that group.

Deleting a User

You can easily delete a user account in system-config-users by selecting the user name on the Users tab and then clicking the Delete button below the menu bar. A dialog box prompts you to confirm that you want to delete the account and whether you want to also delete the user's home directory.

System administrators are of two minds about deleting accounts. Some feel that deleting the account is the best way to keep the system "clean." They think that removing the user's account from /etc/passwd and /etc/shadow, and removing the user's home directory frees up storage space for others.

Another group of system administrators thinks that deleting user accounts can cause more trouble than just disabling them permanently. They may delete or archive the user's home directory from the command line (using a command such as *tar*), but leave the user's account in /etc/passwd intact. The reason for this is to prevent problems like the following from occurring:

- A new user is created with the same user name as the deleted user, and e-mail intended for the previous user is dropped in the e-mail box of the new user.

- A new user is created with the same UID as the previous user and some files remained from the previous user that have that UID listed as the owner. The new user with the same UID will have access to those files (effectively, he or she will own them).

You can think about these issues and decide for yourself whether to delete user accounts or simply disable them (as described shortly).

Creating New Users at the Command Line

The basic command-line utility for creating new users is **useradd**. With this utility you can create new accounts using many different options, and even automate user creation in scripts.

On some Linux systems, including Red Hat Linux and Fedora, a command named *adduser* is available. This is simply a symbolic link to the *useradd* command.

To add a user with *useradd*, you must be logged in as root. You provide the name of the new user account as a parameter. For example, to add a new account called rsolomon, you use this command:

```
# useradd rsolomon
```

System defaults are used to create the account and a home directory. These system defaults are stored in the /etc/login.defs file and in the /etc/default/useradd file.

You can add options to the *useradd* command to override the system default settings or include more user information as part of the account configuration. For example, if you want to include the user's full name in the comment field (generally a good idea), you can use the -*c* option. The -*g* option defines a primary group for the new user. A command incorporating these two options looks like this:

```
# useradd -g sales -c "Raley Solomon" rsolomon
```

Values that include spaces, such as "Raley Solomon" in the above example, must be enclosed in quotation marks so the *useradd* command does not interpret the part after the space (Solomon) as a command parameter.

Table 11-1 shows options you can use when executing *useradd*.

Table 11-1 *useradd* Command Options

Option	Description	Example
-c	Defines a user's full name or other comment for this account	useradd -c "Jose Carrera" josec
-d	Specifies the home directory path (useful mostly for special user accounts that use a nonstandard home directory location)	useradd -d /usr/home/ josec
-e	Specifies the date this user account expires (and is disabled automatically); used for temporary accounts	useradd -e 03/15/01 josec
-f	Specifies the number of days after the password expires until the account is disabled	useradd -f 7 josec
-g	Specifies the primary group for the new user (either the group's name or its unique GID number can be used)	useradd -g ops josec
-G	Adds a list of additional groups of which the new user should be made a member (this information is stored in the /etc/group file, not in /etc/passwd)	useradd -G teamlead, party,emt josec
-m	Forces creation of the user's home directory, even if the default settings do not include creating a home directory	useradd -m josec
-M	Does not create a home directory, even if the default is set to include one	useradd -M josec
-n	Disables the User Private Group feature so that a group matching the new user name is not created	useradd -n josec
-s	Sets the user's login shell. The default shell in Linux is bash. The complete path to another shell program can be used with this option.	useradd -s /bin/zsh josec
-u	Sets a specific numeric value for the user ID of the new user (normally a UID is selected automatically—use this option if you need to force the use of a specific UID number)	useradd -u 509 josec

To display the default settings for the *useradd* command, use the *-D* option. Typical output of the *-D* option is shown here:

```
# useradd -D
GROUP=100
HOME=/home
INACTIVE=-1
EXPIRE=
SHELL=/bin/bash
SKEL=/etc/skel
```

The information returned by the *-D* option is described in the following list:

- *GROUP*: The group ID number for the group in which all new users are placed (as a primary group) if no other is indicated when the user is created

- *HOME*: The path in which home directories for new users are created

- *INACTIVE*: The number of days after a user's password expires that the account is disabled. Using a value of –1 (minus one) for this field disables this option (passwords do not expire).

- *EXPIRE*: The expiration date for a new user account

- *SHELL*: The path and program name for the default shell (command-line interpreter) to be used by each new user account

- *SKEL*: The path to the skeleton directory used to fill a new home directory with basic files (this directory is discussed later in this section)

You can change the defaults for *useradd* by editing the file /etc/default/useradd. You can also change them with the *useradd -D* option. For example, to change the default shell so that all new users use the C shell instead of the bash shell, use this command:

```
# useradd -D -s /bin/csh
```

Before anyone can log in using a newly created account, the account must be assigned a password. A password is not defined by *useradd* when a new user account is created unless you use the *-p* option. (But using the *-p* option is impractical in most cases because it requires that you enter the password in encrypted form—as it would appear in the /etc/shadow file.)

A system administrator might also choose to use the *passwd* command, which you learned about previously, to define or change a user's password. (This command has the same name as the /etc/passwd file.) When using this command as root, include the name of the user account whose password you want to define. For example, to change the password for account rsolomon, use this command (nothing appears on screen as you type in password entries):

```
# passwd rsolomon
```

If you are logged in as rsolomon, you can only change your own password, which you do by entering this command:

```
$ passwd
```

You can also lock a user's account using the *passwd* command to temporarily disable it. Use the *-l* (hyphen lowercase L) option:

```
# passwd -l thomas
```

To unlock an account that has been locked using the *-l* option, use the *-u* option:

```
# passwd -u thomas
```

Creating New Groups

Although modifying the /etc/group file in a text editor does not pose as great a danger as editing /etc/passwd, the preferred method for adding a new group is to use the **groupadd** command. This command is used much like the *useradd* command, but it supports fewer options.

 Graphical tools designed for creating users often allow you to create groups as well. These tools are useful if you prefer to work in a graphical environment. However, you should learn about the *groupadd* command as a backup and for troubleshooting.

To add a new group, include the group name as a parameter, as follows:

```
# groupadd managers
```

If you need to use a specific GID number for the new group, you can include it with the *-g* option. For example:

```
# groupadd -g 919 managers
```

11

Modifying User and Group Accounts at the Command Line

Shortly after setting up user and group accounts, you probably need to modify account information. To do this, use the *usermod* (for *user modify*) command or *groupmod* (for *group modify*) command. The **usermod** command uses the same options as the *useradd* command, but it operates on an existing user account. To use the *usermod* command to update a user's account information, type *usermod* followed by one of the *usermod* parameters and a value for that parameter. For example, suppose lizw gets married and wishes to have her full name changed from Liz Walters to Liz Osowski on her employment records and user account. Using the *-c* option, as with the *useradd* command to change the comment field of the user account, the command to update the lizw account to include the new name would be:

```
# usermod -c "Liz Osowski" lizw
```

You can change the user's login name from lizw to lizo with the *-l* option:

```
# usermod -l lizo -d /home/lizo lizw
```

Using the *-l* option alone leaves the home directory as it was before (/home/lizw). By using the *-d* option shown previously, the home directory path in /etc/passwd is updated as well (to /home/lizo). Note that the *usermod* command does not change the actual directory name. After using the *usermod -d* command, you must change the actual directory name as follows:

```
# mv /home/lizw /home/lizo
```

As another example, suppose you created an account for a new employee, using the default settings, and then discovered that the new employee (Steve Rubenstein) prefers to use a different login shell and needs to be part of several additional groups to accommodate his job responsibilities. The command to update his account might look like this:

```
# usermod -G taskforce,marketing -s /bin/tcsh srubenst
```

Much as you use *usermod* to modify users, you can use **groupmod** to modify groups. The difference is that groups do not have as many aspects that you can modify. The *groupmod* command supports two options: use the *-g* option with a group ID to change the GID of the named group; use the *-n* option with a new name to change the named group. For example, suppose you have an existing group named "managers" that contains 10 users as members. You want to change the name of the group to "teamlead" to match the users' job titles. You also want to change the GID from its current number to 600 in order to match the GID of a similar group on another Linux system. You can make both changes at the same time with this command:

```
# groupmod -g 600 -n teamlead managers
```

The 10 users would then be members of group teamlead, with a GID of 600. Any files that listed managers as their group, however, still have the previous GID. The GID assigned to files is not changed by the *groupmod* command. You use the *find* and *chmod* commands to make that change.

After making changes to groups, you can execute the **grpck** command to check the integrity of the /etc/group and /etc/gshadow files. This command tells you of any inconsistencies found, such as members listed in a group that are not actual user accounts, or misplaced commas or colons that can cause the group account to function incorrectly. This is especially useful when you are using group passwords to permit users to switch their current group so that they can access other files. (This is done by a user entering the **newgrp** or **sg** command, followed by a password, if one is assigned to the group using the **gpasswd** command.) The *grpck* command uses no parameters:

```
# grpck
```

Setting Password Options

A more complex utility is the **chage** command, which you can use to alter password aging information such as when a password expires or how many days before expiration a user is warned. You can use this utility in three ways. First, you can use the *-l* option to list the current settings. Any user can do this to see when his or her password expires:

```
$ chage -l nwells
```

When logged in as root, you can provide command-line options that specify each of the parameters you want to change for any account on the system. The supported options include the following:

- *-m days*: Specifies the minimum number of days a user must wait before his or her account password can be changed. If this is set to 0, the user can change the password anytime.

- *-M days*: Specifies the maximum number of days a user can wait before his or her password expires. You can use this option or the –E option. With this option, you specify a number of days, such as 30 or 60 days. When you use the –E option, you give a specific date for expiration.

- *-d lastday*: The last time the password was changed. You can specify this date to control the next time the user must change the password. For example, if you specify that the password was changed on a date that is 90 days ago, and you have set the –M option to a maximum days of 60, the user is prompted to change the password the next time he or she logs in. Use the format YYYY-MM-DD to specify this option.

- *-I days*: Specifies the number of days of inactivity after the password expires before the account is locked. Use this as a precaution to lock an inactive account so that someone cannot try to use the account to break into the system. If a user's password expires and does not ask you to make their account active again after a few days, let the system lock the account using this feature.

- *-E expiredate*: Specify the date on which the password expires using the format YYYY-MM-DD.

- *-W days*: Specify the number of days before the password expires that the system warns the user to change his or her password.

The third way you can use the *chage* command is in interactive mode. For this mode, you don't have to remember any of the options. Just provide the user account you want to review or modify. For example, while logged in as root, enter a command like this one:

```
# chage jthomas
```

The system displays each of the password expiration parameters in turn. For each, the current setting is shown in square brackets. You can press Enter to keep that setting, or enter a new setting. Figure 11-8 shows the *chage* command being used in this mode.

If you are working with an older Linux system that does not use the shadow password system by default, the encrypted passwords for all users are stored in /etc/passwd. You can use the **pwconv** utility to convert the older /etc/passwd password storage to /etc/shadow password storage. Conversely, if you need to convert an existing system that uses /etc/shadow (the default on most new Linux systems) to the older /etc/passwd system for compatibility with other systems, you can use the **pwunconv** utility. If you are using group passwords and need to convert between the older and newer systems, or vice versa, the respective utilities to perform those conversions are **grpconv** and **grpunconv**.

11

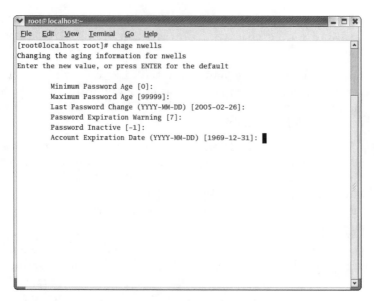

Figure 11-8 Using *chage* in interactive mode

After completing password editing tasks, you can check the validity of your password files (/etc/passwd and /etc/shadow) using the **pwck** command. This command informs you of formatting errors that make accounts unusable. All of these commands—*pwconv*, *pwunconv*, *grpconv*, *grpunconv*, and *pwck*—can be used without any command-line options.

Automating Home Directory Creation

You often want to include basic configuration files in the home directory of each new user that you create. This information might include:

- Company document templates and calendars
- Environment variable settings to access department printers and servers
- Terminal settings to make Linux work well with desktop PCs
- Commands (scripts) to automate basic tasks and set up the user's system each time the user logs in

Files contained in **/etc/skel** are automatically copied into each user's home directory at the time you create the account, whether you create it using a graphical utility such as system-config-users or with the *useradd* command. As system administrator, you should place files in /etc/skel when you first install Linux so that those files are automatically placed in each user's home directory that you create with *useradd*. Many of the files in /etc/skel are hidden configuration files. Use the *ls -la* command to list the contents of /etc/skel. Here is one version:

```
$ ls -la /etc/skel
total 28
drwxr-xr-x  3 root root   4096 Sep 18 17:11 .
drwxr-xr-x 58 root root   4096 Oct 17 08:07 ..
-rw-r—r—    1 root root     24 Apr 12 2002 .bash_logout
-rw-r—r—    1 root root    191 Apr 12 2002 .bash_profile
-rw-r—r—    1 root root    124 Apr 12 2002 .bashrc
-rw-r—r—    1 root root    118 Apr 15 2002 .gtkrc
drwxr-xr-x  3 root root   4096 Sep 18 17:08 .kde
```

The files shown here are used for graphical interfaces such as KDE and the bash default shell. If you want to have other files included in each user's home directory, simply copy those files to /etc/skel.

When you add files to /etc/skel, they are not added to the home directories of *existing* user accounts; they are only copied to the home directories of user accounts created *after* the new files are added. For existing accounts, you must use *cp* to copy additional files manually to each home directory.

Disabling User Accounts

You can temporarily or permanently disable a user account. You might need to do this because:

- An employee has left the organization (permanent deletion of the account).

- An employee is on vacation (temporary disabling as a security precaution).

- A guest user has not paid for the account or for computer time (temporary, perhaps permanent later).

- An employee is under disciplinary action and is not allowed to access company information (temporary, perhaps permanent later).

To temporarily disable a user's account, change the password with the *passwd* command so the user can no longer log in.

If you are concerned about having an active account with only a new password as security, you can use the command *passwd -l [username]* to lock the account. Then use *passwd -u [username]* to unlock the account so the user can log in again. Similarly, you can edit the /etc/shadow file in a text editor and place an asterisk before the encrypted password. (You must be logged in as root and override the read-only status of the file as you save your changes to the file.) This saves the password because you can simply remove the asterisk later to reenable the account. But while the asterisk is part of the password, Linux does not allow anyone to log in to the user account. The line in /etc/shadow before the edit might look like this:

```
nwells:$12$tJhxVO2kUgVU2/o0434jj0:10799:0:99999:7:-1:-1:134538468
```

11

And after the edit it looks like this:

```
nwells:*$12$tJhxVO2kUgVU2/o0434jj0:10799:0:99999:7:-1:-1:134538468
```

Another simple way to disable a user account is to place a # at the beginning of the line that defines that user account in /etc/passwd, making that line into a comment.

To delete a user account permanently, use the **userdel** command with the user account name. For example:

```
# userdel lizo
```

This command removes the user named lizo from /etc/passwd. The user can no longer log in because the user account no longer exists. But *userdel* does *not* remove the user's home directory or its contents. You will typically want to review and archive the home directory for a deleted user account. (If an employee is leaving the organization, friends or coworkers may be able to access part of the former employee's home directory because of common group membership, for example.)

A similar command to *userdel* is **groupdel**. Using this command is straightforward. For example, to delete a group called teamlead, use this command:

```
# groupdel teamlead
```

When you use this command, the group entry is deleted from the /etc/group file. You should be careful deleting groups. When you delete a group, any user account that has the deleted group's GID listed as its primary group in /etc/passwd will still have that number listed, even though it is now invalid (it refers to a nonexistent group). You should change those GID numbers in /etc/passwd using system-config-users, *vigp*, or another user management tool. In addition, any files that have the group's GID as owner will still have that GID, but it will be invalid. You should use the *chown* and *find* commands to locate any such files and change their group owner to a valid group.

In addition to the file permission issues that arise when you change the UID or a user or delete a user or group account, several more specialized file permission issues also relate to user and group accounts. These are discussed in the next section.

COMPLEX FILE PERMISSIONS

In Chapter 4 you learned about basic file permissions in Linux: the read, write, and execute permissions, which you can grant to the owner, group, or other system users for each file and directory. This is done using the *chmod* command or various graphical tools (such as the Properties window in the Nautilus file manager).

Several specialized file permissions are also supported in Linux. These are permissions that serve unusual functions and that you do not see very often. The standard file permissions can also have some unexpected uses. This section outlines some of the special uses and introduces you to the specialized file permissions, which are called Set User ID and Set Group ID.

Before learning about these permissions, you should also be familiar with a file permission called the sticky bit. The **sticky bit** was used on older UNIX systems to control how a program file would be treated with regard to swap space—that is, whether it was always kept in swap space to be quickly accessible to the kernel. The sticky bit is no longer used for program files—the Linux kernel ignores it. But the sticky bit does serve a special purpose for directories. When the sticky bit is set on a directory, files in that directory can only be renamed or unlinked by the user that owns them or by root. Without this permission set, any user who can write to the directory can also delete or rename files in that directory. The sticky bit is often used on directories where you want all users to be able to create files, such as /tmp. These features are discussed further in connection with group permissions on directories later in this section.

To set the sticky bit, you can use the *chmod* command with the letter *t* as the permission. A numeric method is also shown later in this section:

```
# chmod a+t /tmp
```

The **Set User ID** permission—often called **SUID** or the SUID bit—can be added to a file that has the execute permission set. When SUID is added, it causes the user who executes that file to take on the file permissions of the owner of the file.

For example, the file /bin/bash is the program that, when executed, gives a shell prompt. If a person is logged in as chris and then executes /bin/bash, that person has the permissions of user chris while working in bash. But if the file /bin/bash, which is owned by root, were to have the SUID permission set, then whenever chris (or any other user) executed /bin/bash, that user would have the permission of the file's owner (root in this case) while working with the program /bin/bash.

This feature is very useful for a few specialized programs. For example, the *chage* command that you just learned about must access the /etc/shadow file, which only root can read. Because any user is permitted to see when his or her password expires, the *chage* command must be able to "act as root" and read /etc/shadow when the command is executed by a regular (nonroot) user. You can see this by executing this command. The permissions for /bin/chage include the file permission *s* where the *x* would normally be.

```
$ ls -l /usr/bin/chage
```

Only about 10 commands on a typical Linux system have the SUID permission set. This permission is very dangerous if used on a program that you do not trust. For example, suppose a user on your system handed you a disk containing a utility program and asked you to install the program as root. He tells you the program requires SUID, like *chage*, in order to operate correctly. But the user could have modified the program so that it permitted *any* action using root permission, rather than just the functions you expected the utility to provide. In fact, SUID can be so dangerous that the Linux kernel ignores the SUID permission if it is used on a script file.

To set the SUID permission, use the *chmod* command to add the *s* permission to the user permissions:

```
# chmod u+s file
```

A file must have the execute permission set along with the SUID permission.

Permissions are not always what they seem at first. For example, suppose you have two files in a work directory. One is for your use only—no permissions are granted to group and other users. The second file is to be read by other users in a managers group that you have created, so it has group permission set to read. Because other managers sometimes create files in this working directory, the directory has the execute permission set for the group, allowing any member of the group to create files in the directory. The listing for the two files appears like this (using the *ls -l* command) (note the permissions on the left of the listing):

```
-rw-------    1 nwells    users    23411 Jun 22 21:40 private_report
-rw-r--r--    1 nwells    users    21390 Jun 22 21:40 public_report
```

The listing for the directory containing these two files appears like this (using the *ls -ld* command within the parent directory):

```
drwxrwx---    2 nwells    users     4096 Jun 22 21:40 reports
```

Now, suppose that another member of the managers group tries to read the private_report file:

```
$ less private_report
```

She can't do this because she does not have read permission. Only the owner of the file has read permission. Suppose she tries to copy a file over it using this command:

```
$ cp public_report private_report
```

Once again, the system reports that this is not allowed, this time because she does not have write permission to private_report, which is required to overwrite the file using copy. But suppose that she instead uses the *mv* command like this:

```
$ mv public_report private_report
```

This time, the system checks whether she has permission to create or rename files in this directory, which is controlled by the execute permission on the parent directory. In this case, the other manager is part of the group that is granted execute permission so that they can create new files in the directory. Because that permission also allows renaming files, the operation is permitted. She has not been able to read private_report, but she has erased it. You cannot set up a directory for all members of a group to create and share files without this consequence, but you need to understand that it exists.

The paragraphs that follow describe two other group-related techniques to help you manage file security.

CAUTION

Recall that the Set User ID bit (which appears as *s* in the Execute bit field for the owner of a file) causes the user who executes a program to assume the permissions of the owner of that file. This bit is often referred to as SUID. The SUID bit is necessary for some types of programs, such as the *su* utility. But it presents a real security hazard—if crackers are able to set other system files to have the Set User ID bit active, they may gain root access to the system simply by running a common system utility.

You can also add a **Set Group ID** permission to a file or directory—often called **SGID**. This causes the person who executes a program file to have the permissions of the file's group while executing the program. To set this permission, use an *s* with the group setting in *chmod*:

```
# chmod g+s file
```

The SUID and SGID permissions can also be set numerically. Recall that normal file permissions can be set using a 3-digit number, where each permission is assigned a value of 4, 2, or 1. The values for each set of permissions are added together to get the digit for the user, group, or other. To set SUID or SGID for a file or directory, you add a fourth digit. A 4 indicates SUID, a 2 indicates SGID, and a 1 indicates the sticky bit. So, for example, to set the file permissions on a program file to be read and execute for the user, with the SUID permission set, but nothing else, you use this command:

```
# chmod  4500 program_file
```

The same command without using numbers is:

```
# chmod u=rxs
```

These permissions are displayed by *ls -l* as follows:

```
-r-s------
```

If you see a file permission of *S* (uppercase S) in a listing using *ls -l*, this indicates that the SUID permission is set, but the execute permission is not set. SUID without execute permission is meaningless.

The SGID permission isn't of much use, and you'll rarely hear of SGID being used on a program file. But adding SGID to a directory serves a special purpose.

Consider first that when a user creates a new file, the group assigned to that file is normally the primary group for that user, as defined in /etc/passwd. For example, on Linux systems using the User Private Group system described previously, a new file lists the same name as both user and group, as shown in this example:

```
-rw-rw-r--    1 nwells   nwells    3971 Jun 22 21:44 test1
```

You can try this yourself by using the *touch* command to create an empty file and then using *ls -l* to see the ownership and permissions of the file. But when you set SGID on a directory, any file that is created within that directory is assigned to the group of the directory, rather than to the user that creates the file. This is a convenient method for creating a working

11

space for a collection of users who should be allowed to both create files and read each others' files, all without the system administrator intervening to permit access to each individual file.

To see how this works, suppose you had already created a group called managers with a number of users as members. Then you executed the following commands as root:

```
$ mkdir /workspace
$ chgrp managers /workspace
$ chmod g+rws /workspace
```

Now suppose that user thomas logs in. Within his home directory, he creates a test file and then views its permissions and ownership:

```
$ cd
$ touch test2
$ ls -l test2
-rw-rw-r--  1 thomas   thomas  3971 Jun 22 21:44 test2
```

Then thomas changes to the /workspace directory, creates a test file and views its permissions and ownership:

```
$ cd /workspace
$ touch test3
$ ls -l test3
-rw-rw-r--  1 thomas   managers 3971 Jun 22 21:44 test3
```

Because the file that thomas created—test3—is owned by the group managers, anyone else in the group can read and edit its contents. Files created by any member of group managers have the same characteristics.

A second technique allows you to deny access to members of a group. Remember that the "other" permissions on a file or directory still require that a user be logged in to Linux. So this technique allows you to say "the owner has a certain access level, and everyone else on the system has a certain access level, but the members of this group can't access the file or directory."

To set this up, you might use a series of commands like this, assuming you had created a group called no_finance that you didn't want to have access to a particular directory:

```
$ mkdir /finance_data
$ chmod 705 /finance_data
$ chgrp no_finance /finance_data
$ ls -l /finance_data
drwx---r-x 2 nwells no_finance 4096 Jun 22 21:40 finance_data
```

None of the members of the group no_finance can use the *cd* command to get into the /finance_data directory or list the files it contains. This is effective because Linux computes access rights first by checking whether the user requesting access is the owner and if the owner's rights permit the access requested. If the user is not the owner, Linux checks to see if the requesting user is a member of the group assigned to that file or directory. If so, the group permissions of the file or directory are used to assign access (or deny it in this case); the rights assigned to other users are never considered.

In the next section, you learn about several other commands for securely managing user access to Linux systems and for communicating with users who are logged in.

USER SECURITY ISSUES

File permissions are a critical part of user security. They control which files and directories a regular user can access, and determine what the users can do with those files and directories (execute them, create files in a directory, and so forth). This section describes some additional communications and user security mechanisms in Linux.

Communicating with Users

Two methods of communicating with users were popular before graphical desktops became the standard for Linux users. Knowing about these may still be useful to you on occasion.

On a system with many users, you often need to communicate with all the users on the system regarding planned system maintenance or some other aspect of how people are using the computer system. In Linux, each time a user logs in, the contents of the file **/etc/motd** are displayed just before the shell is started. This file, which is the "message of the day," is sometimes used for fun sayings or quotes, or (in a more serious environment), for news of upcoming maintenance, requirements about changing passwords or backing up files, or other system administrative functions that users need to be informed about. The /etc/motd file does not appear, however, unless the user opens a command line or logs in at a text-mode console.

A second method of communicating with users is the *wall* command (for write all). Use this command when you need to communicate an immediate message to all users who are logged in to the system. This command displays a broadcast message on the command line for all users who are working in text mode or have an open terminal window. Depending on the type of day you are having, you can use this for messages such as "Free bagels in the breakroom" or "Emergency system shutdown in 3 minutes—save your work!!" The format is simple. Here is an example of what you would enter as root:

```
# wall Meet in the conference room in 5 minutes for an
announcement from Evelyn
```

Using /etc/motd and the *wall* command are alternatives to using an e-mail addressed to each user. Each method has advantages and disadvantages.

In addition to communicating with users, you can learn about what users are doing with the *fuser* command. Recall that when you have file systems mounted, you cannot unmount a file system if any user is working in that file system. For example, if a user has a file from that file system open, or even has a directory in that file system as their current working directory,

11

you cannot unmount that file system. If you are trying to unmount a file system using the *umount* command, but the system informs you that the file system is in use, you can use the *fuser* command to learn which user is using the file system. Then you can ask that user to stop what they are doing or kill the process as root if it is an emergency.

 Be careful about killing a user's process when they have a file open, as this may cause the person to lose unsaved data!

The simplest way to use *fuser* is to list the file system that you want to learn about:

```
# fuser /home
```

The *fuser* command can also refer to a serial port or even a network connection:

```
# fuser /dev/ttyS1
# fuser telnet/tcp
```

The command to have *fuser* kill all processes (the *-k* option) using the named mounted file system (as specified by the *-m* option, which is /home in this example) is this:

```
# fuser -km /home
```

Granting Limited Root Access

Although you must guard the root account of a Linux system with great care, system administrators and even regular users may need to occasionally perform tasks that only root is allowed to handle. The **sudo** command lets you assign privileges to any user account so that that user can execute just the programs that the *sudo* configuration specifies. Examples of where this is useful include:

- The system administrator completing common system administration tasks without needing to su to root

- Users mounting and unmounting removable disks or CD-ROM discs on systems where they do not have root access

- Users being able to kill programs that have crashed or stopped responding

- Users who don't have root access but manage a particular service (such as printing or Samba) having access to the configuration tools for those programs

The *sudo* command uses the **/etc/sudoers** configuration file to determine which users can perform which tasks. Unfortunately, the syntax of this file can be very complex. If you don't follow the syntax correctly, *sudo* refuses to execute at all. (Conversely, you may edit the configuration file using correct syntax but without understanding exactly what actions the file permits, thus creating a security hole.) The man page for sudoers describes the syntax in exhaustive detail, but for those new to *sudo*, skip to the end of the man page and review the examples with explanations instead of wading through the syntax diagrams of all possible configurations. The basic format of a configuration line is:

```
user host = command_list
```

Part of the power (and possible confusion) of configuring *sudo* is that you can define aliases by which a single word represents any of the following:

- A collection of users who are granted permission
- A collection of hosts on which one or more users' permission is granted
- A collection of programs for which one or more users is granted permission
- A set of *sudo* options that are applied to any of the above collections.

To edit the /etc/sudoers file you *must* use the **visudo** program. This program prevents conflicts between multiple open files (assuming multiple users have root access to your system), and also checks the syntax of the /etc/sudoers configuration file upon exit. On Red Hat and Fedora Linux, you must include the path to this command to execute it:

```
# /usr/sbin/visudo
```

The default /etc/sudoers file includes sections in which various types of aliases can be listed, plus a couple of examples. Assume, for example, that you want all users to be able to mount and unmount the CD-ROM drive. The following line in /etc/sudoers permits that:

```
%users  ALL=/sbin/mount /cdrom,/sbin/umount /cdrom
```

The %users refers to a group on your system named "users"; you must create that group or make certain that all users are members of it for this configuration to work correctly. When used in /etc/sudoers, the ALL keyword always matches, so the host field in this example is not controlled. Finally, the two commands which users can execute are */sbin/mount /cdrom* and */sbin/umount /cdrom*. A user can execute the *mount* command like this:

```
$ sudo /sbin/mount /cdrom
```

After checking the /etc/sudoers file, the *sudo* command executes the command given as a parameter. For this to work properly, you must have an entry in /etc/fstab so that the /cdrom mount point is defined correctly. For example, /etc/fstab should define the CD-ROM as being mounted at /mnt/cdrom. Because *mount /mnt/cdrom* is not listed in sudoers, the user will be unable to mount the CD-ROM. This points out the need to carefully test *sudo* configurations, not just for syntax (*visudo* takes care of this), but for actual effect.

Part of the reason for complex *sudo* configuration options is that *sudo* can present security dangers if not properly configured. As with other parts of your system, a person should have exactly as much access as his or her job requires, and no more—everything is on a "need to know basis," as they say. The particular risk of *sudo* is that a clever or malicious user can try to use access to a single command to gain access to other commands. Suppose, for example, that you included this line in /etc/sudoers to permit a user to edit the printing configuration file:

```
jamesg    ALL=vi /etc/printcap
```

Once jamesg is in vi, editing this file with root permission, he simply enters :!bash and vi runs a bash command shell—with root permission. Many programs support shelling out in this way, or at least some limited capacity to execute other programs from within the original program. The *sudo* program cannot foresee or control all of this. The system administrator must hand out *sudo* power carefully.

Consider another example: Sarah helps the system administrator with a number of basic Web server administration tasks that require root access. The system administrator creates a subdirectory containing symbolic links to the commands that Sarah needs to use and makes the Web user www the owner of those programs (symbolic links, really). Using /etc/sudoers, the following line grants Sarah access to run any command in that directory on the local machine, all acting as user www:

```
sarah    myhost = (www) /usr/local/webcommands
```

A single configuration line can assign access to multiple commands, each while acting as a different user. By default, a user must enter a password to verify his or her identity before *sudo* executes the requested command. This can be overridden in /etc/sudoers for one or multiple specific commands. Dozens of other options let you control exactly what tasks a user can perform and how the user can perform them.

Using Pluggable Authentication Modules

The Linux password architecture that you have learned about (including the /etc/passwd and /etc/shadow files) provides security that is robust enough for many sites. However it is not robust enough for all sites, nor does it permit much of the flexibility in configuration that other operating systems have offered for a long time. In addition, adding Linux to a network of other systems (such as Windows NT/2000/Server 2003) can place a real burden on a system administrator, who must then keep two sets of configuration files updated with user information, rather than just one.

The **Pluggable Authentication Module (PAM)** architecture was developed by Sun Microsystems. It is now used on virtually every Linux system to provide improved user-level security, flexibility in managing user authentication, and smoother integration between Linux configuration data and user information stored on other systems. PAM is an architecture and set of libraries that let a programmer create a module to perform a specific security-related function, such as testing whether an updated password is too short or whether a user is permitted to log in at a certain time of day. System administrators can select, configure, and then use one or more modules to control the operation of any Linux program that is aware of PAM capabilities. Because PAM has been in widespread use for several years, many programs recognize PAM as a security mechanism.

You may have already seen PAM at work. If you are using a standard Red Hat Linux or Fedora installation, PAM is configured by default. As one example of its operation, you cannot enter a short word (for example, three characters) when you change your password unless you are root. Instead you see a message telling you that the password is "WAY too short!" and the password is not changed. This message comes from a PAM module that is configured by default in Red Hat Linux to stop users from entering insecure passwords.

To use PAM, you select which PAM modules you want to control the activity of a particular program. You list those modules in a configuration file for that program, with parameters to set how the module behaves. Some examples will help you see how this is done.

PAM is configured using either a single configuration file, /etc/pam.conf, or a series of configuration files in the directory /etc/pam.d. (The person compiling the software selects which configuration style is used.) Red Hat Linux and Fedora use the directory method because it makes it simple for a software package to add a file to your system in order to configure a newly added program. The /etc/pam.d directory contains a file with a name matching the program being configured. For example, the text file /etc/pam.d/login configures the login program. Each file contains a list of one or more modules that PAM uses when that program is run. The file named "other" is used if a program tries to use PAM but no specific configuration file is found in /etc/pam.d. The syntax of each line in a file within /etc/pam.d is shown here. Each element is described below.

```
module_type     control_flag     module_path     argumentscode
```

 Be careful working with PAM configuration files. If you were to delete the /etc/pam.d/login file, for example, you would be unable to log in to your system, even as root!

CAUTION

To discuss these elements, it is helpful to have a sample file to review. Below is the default /etc/pam.d/login file from Fedora. The lines are numbered for reference below; these numbers are not part of the actual file.

```
1 #%PAM-1.0
2 auth     required /lib/security/pam_securetty.so
3 auth     required /lib/security/pam_stack.so service=system-auth
4 auth     required /lib/security/pam_nologin.so
5 account  required /lib/security/pam_stack.so service=system-auth
6 password required /lib/security/pam_stack.so service=system-auth
7 session  required /lib/security/pam_selinux.so multiple
8 session  required /lib/security/pam_stack.so service=system-auth
9 session  optional /lib/security/pam_console.so
```

The first element on each line is the module_type, which defines when the module is used. Possible types include:

- *auth*: Authentication modules are used to identify a user, normally by prompting for a password.

- *account*: These modules manage the user's account once identity has been established by an auth module. These modules typically restrict access, for example, allowing access only during certain times of the day.

- *session*: These modules manage a user's current session, normally attending to tasks that must be completed before a user is allowed to work, such as creating log files or mounting a file system that the user needs.

- *password*: These modules are executed when a user needs to change a password (or other authentication tokens).

NOTE

Complete documentation on PAM and individual modules is located in /usr/ share/doc/pam-0.77 on Red Hat Linux and Fedora.

When a PAM-compatible program such as *login* or *passwd* is executed, it checks to see which applicable modules are configured for a given task. For example, when a user first logs in, *login* passes control to PAM, which must run all the modules listed as auth modules (lines 2, 3, and 4 in the above example file). When multiple modules are listed for a module type, modules are said to be stacked. Unless a control_flag dictates otherwise, PAM executes all of the modules in a stack in the order they are listed, and returns a result of Access Permitted or Access Denied based on the modules' results. The control_flag element determines how PAM processes stacked modules. The control_flag has two forms; the older and simpler syntax is still used in most configuration files. It supports four possible values:

- *required*: The module must succeed for the final result to be Access Permitted. Because later modules in the stack are also executed, the user cannot tell which module failed, but the final result is Access Denied if any required module fails.

- *requisite*: The module must succeed for the final result to be Access Permitted. If a requisite module fails, remaining modules in a stack are not executed; if a requisite module succeeds, remaining modules are also executed.

- *sufficient*: The final result can be Access Permitted even if this module fails, but if this module succeeds, that is sufficient for an Access Permitted result. If a sufficient module succeeds, no other modules are executed; if a previous required module in the stack did not fail, PAM returns immediately with a result of Access Permitted. If a sufficient module fails, later modules are executed without regard to the result of the sufficient module.

- *optional*: The result of an optional module does not affect the final result of a module stack. Optional modules are used to perform tasks such as logging that are not part of determining access but are helpful in system administration or meeting user needs.

As if this system were not sufficiently complicated, PAM also supports another syntax for the control_flag element. You can include one or more sets (separated by spaces) of instructions in the format *test=action*. The test is one of 30 codes, such as user_unknown or acct_expired. The action can be one of six codes such as ignore, done, or bad; or the action can be a number that indicates how many subsequent modules in the current stack should be skipped. Using this format for the control_flag lets you create a complex stack of PAM modules and control how they are executed based on the results of previous modules. Standard Linux systems don't implement this more complex system in their default configuration files, but you can read about it in the PAM documentation.

The last two elements in a PAM configuration file are the module_path and arguments. The module_path is the complete path and module name to be executed. The arguments are information that should be passed to that module as it is executed. Lines 2, 4, and 9 in the above sample file are examples of lines without any arguments. The other lines (besides 1, which is a comment line) have a single argument for the pam_stack module: *service=system-auth*.

The pam_stack module is a special module that acts like an "include" file. The service listed after a pam_stack module refers to another configuration file in /etc/pam.d. All of the modules listed in the named configuration file are executed at that point. For example, consider the lines above from the PAM login configuration file (again, line numbers are not part of the file):

11

```
2 auth       required    /lib/security/pam_securetty.so
3 auth       required    /lib/security/pam_stack.so service=system-auth
4 auth       required    /lib/security/pam_nologin.so
```

The file /etc/pam.d/system-auth contains these module configuration lines, which are generated automatically by the authconfig utility based on which security measures you select:

```
auth       required    /lib/security/$ISA/pam_env.so
auth       sufficient  /lib/security/$ISA/pam_unix.so likeauth nullok
auth       required    /lib/security/$ISA/pam_deny.so

account    sufficient  /lib/security/$ISA/pam_succeed_if.so uid < 100
account    required    /lib/security/$ISA/pam_unix.so

password   requisite   /lib/security/$ISA/pam_cracklib.so retry=3
password   sufficient  /lib/security/$ISA/pam_unix.so nullok use_authtok md5 shadow
password   required    /lib/security/$ISA/pam_deny.so

session    required    /lib/security/$ISA/pam_limits.so
session    required    /lib/security/$ISA/pam_unix.so
```

Given these two files, the *login* command would execute these modules—in this order—as part of the login process (the auth stack):

- pam_securetty.so   (from /etc/pam.d/login)

- pam_stack.so   (from /etc/pam.d/login—this module only starts the next three)

- pam_env.so   (from /etc/pam.d/system-auth)

- pam_unix.so   (from /etc/pam.d/system-auth)

- pam_deny.so   (from /etc/pam.d/system-auth)

- pam_nologin.so   (from /etc/pam.d/login)

The file /usr/share/doc/pam-0.77/html/pam-6.html in Red Hat Linux or Fedora contains reference information for each module, including examples and descriptions of all the supported arguments. These descriptions include information specific to any of the four module types for which the module is supported. For example, the pam_unix module can be used for auth, account, session, or passwd.

TIP Although you will want to review the PAM documentation to learn about the operation and options supported by each module, reviewing example configuration files and the most commonly used modules can help you understand how you can configure PAM to meet the needs of your own network. Keep in mind that PAM configurations can become quite complicated and that misconfigured systems may allow or prevent access in ways that you had not anticipated. As you learn about PAM, make changes to configuration files one at a time, testing the results after each change to see what happens.

Shown below is a sample PAM configuration file for the *halt* command: /etc/pam.d/halt. (Comment lines have been removed.) This command shuts down all Linux services so that you can safely turn your computer's power off.

TIP When you press Ctrl+Alt+Del to restart or shut down your Linux system, the *init* program executes a command to restart the system. Typically, the *shutdown* command is executed (you can see this in the /etc/inittab configuration file). You can also use the commands *halt* or *reboot* at the command line to either shut down or reboot your Linux system.

```
#%PAM-1.0
auth       sufficient    pam_rootok.so
auth       required      pam_console.so
#auth      required      pam_stack.so service=system-auth
account    required      pam_permit.so
```

The auth stack of PAM modules includes rootok and console. These modules operate as follows:

1. The rootok module checks whether the user who is executing the *halt* command is root (this is normally done by checking whether the user ID is 0). If it is, PAM sees that this condition is sufficient and immediately returns an Access Permitted result, so root can execute *halt*.

2. If the user is not root, the console module checks to see whether the user is working at the console (as opposed to logging in via a remote connection of some kind, such as over a network or modem). If the user is on the console, the user can execute *halt*. Otherwise, PAM denies access and the command does not execute.

Suppose that you let other users sit at the console of your Linux system but they could not log in as root. You don't want them to run the *halt* command. Because the default action of PAM is to deny access if no module specifically permits access, you can make this change so that only root can run *halt* by deleting or commenting out the second line in the above sample file. Then, if the rootok module fails (because the user is not root), the *halt* command cannot be run. No other checks will be performed.

Using Network Information Service

Network Information Service (NIS) is a program that lets a system administrator manage a single set of configuration files for multiple Linux (or UNIX) servers. For example, if you had 10 Linux servers, each of which provided file and print services for 25 users, you would normally have to manage the user accounts on each of those 10 servers independently. If any of the users needed to be granted access to one of the other nine servers, you would have to set up special access, including a user account on the additional server.

By using NIS, you can have a single file containing all 250 users (10 servers, 25 users on each). The file is located on one of the systems (the NIS server), and when a user logs in to any of the other nine servers, that server contacts the NIS server to see if the user has a valid user account.

The NIS service is sometimes called the yellow pages service, with the abbreviation *yp*. You see this in the /etc/rc.d/init.d directory, where you can see several programs for client and server programs supporting NIS. These include *ypserv*, *ypbind*, *yppasswdd*, and *ypxfrd*.

NIS is often provided in a more recent version called **NIS+** or NISplus. You can set up your system to use an NIS server by running the program *authconfig*. In this program, shown in Figure 11-9, you can enter the name of an NIS domain and server name. Setting up your own NIS server is beyond the scope of this book, though it can easily be done using Linux.

Figure 11-9   The *authconfig* program

One of the important files that is configured when you use NIS is the **/etc/nsswitch.conf** file. This file instructs various system programs in Linux where to look for the configuration information they need. For example, one line in the /etc/nsswitch.conf file looks like this:

```
passwd: files
```

This line instructs programs that need to read password information to refer to /etc/passwd on the local system. Other options that can be listed on the *passwd* line in /etc/nsswitch.conf include *yp* or *nis* for an NIS server, *nis+* or *nisplus* for an NIS+ server, *db* for database files, or *dns* for a DNS server. Not all of these are used for password information, but the /etc/nsswitch.conf file includes instructions for finding several types of information. For the present discussion, you should be aware that user account information can be located on an NIS server or other location besides /etc/passwd.

The configuration lines in /etc/nsswitch.conf often include multiple options. For example, the *passwd* line might look like this:

```
passwd: nis+, nis, files
```

This means that programs should try to find a user's password information by contacting an NIS+ system; if one cannot be found, try using an NIS system; if one cannot be found, check the local file /etc/passwd. In this way, you can centralize management of numerous user accounts while giving flexibility for special circumstances.

CHAPTER SUMMARY

❏ User accounts can be managed graphically using system-config-users, Webmin, YAST, or similar tools in various Linux distributions. User accounts can also be managed very effectively from the command line.

❏ When changing UIDs or GIDs, you must be careful not to leave files that have the old UID or GID assigned. When deleting user or group accounts, you must be careful not to reuse a user or group name inadvertently.

❏ The *useradd* command is used to create user accounts on the command line. It relies on default settings that you can view with the *-D* option. The *groupadd* command is used to create new groups.

❏ The *usermod* command is used to modify existing user accounts. The *groupmod* command is used to modify existing group accounts.

❏ Password expiration details can be configured using the *chage* command, or using most graphical user configuration tools.

❏ When new user accounts are created, the contents of the /etc/skel directory is copied into the new home directory of the user. The /etc/login.defs file also defines some default information for new user accounts.

❏ User accounts can be disabled using the *passwd* command or deleted using the *userdel* command. Some system administrators prefer to never delete a user account, but only disable them and remove the user's files.

❏ The SUID and SGID permissions cause a user to assume the permissions of the owner of an executable file when that program is executed. These special permissions are useful but can be very dangerous if used on untrusted program files.

❏ The sticky bit and several other special file permission arrangements permit a system administrator to carefully control how multiple users can work with files in shared directories.

❏ To set the sticky bit, SUID, or SGID, you can use *chmod* with either an additional digit (in the numeric mode) or an *s* or *t* (in letter mode).

❏ System administrators can communicate with users using *wall*, using the /etc/motd file, or via e-mail, selecting whichever method is most appropriate for the message to be delivered.

❏ The *sudo* program lets regular users perform tasks that require root privileges. The program is configured using the /etc/sudoers file, which you must edit using the *visudo* command.

❏ Each line in /etc/sudoers configures a user or group with permission to use certain commands on a certain computer system. Sample configurations make a basic setup easy to configure, but errors in *sudo* configuration can lead to serious security breaches.

❏ Pluggable Authentication Modules (PAMs) provide a flexible and powerful way for system administrators to configure exactly how user security is handled by relying on individual modules to perform different security tasks.

❏ Multiple systems can share user files such as /etc/passwd and /etc/shadow by using an NIS or NIS+ server. If such a server exists on the network, it can be used by configuring a system via the *authconfig* program.

COMMAND SUMMARY

Command	Description	Example
authconfig	Configure shadow passwords, NIS, and other authentication and security features in Red Hat Linux and Fedora in a text-mode menu-driven program.	authconfig
chage	View or change password aging information.	chage -l nwells
fuser	Display which users are using any file on a file system, other device, or network connection.	fuser /home
gpasswd	Assign or change the password for a group, permitting a person who knows that password to become a member of that group temporarily using the *newgrp* command.	gpasswd journalists
groupadd	Create a new group.	groupadd journalists
groupdel	Delete an existing group.	groupdel journalists
groupmod	Change the name or GID for an existing group.	groupmod -n press journalists
grpck	Check the integrity of the /etc/group and /etc/gshadow files.	grpck
grpconv	Convert an existing /etc/group file containing group passwords into the newer format (the default on most Linux systems) in which group password information is stored in /etc/gshadow.	grpconv
grpunconv	Convert existing /etc/group and /etc/gshadow password information into the older format in which group password information is stored solely in /etc/group.	grpunconv
newgrp	Change a user's primary group temporarily. May require entry of a group password if configured for the group to which the user wants to change.	newgrp journalists
pwck	Verify the integrity of the /etc/passwd and /etc/shadow files.	pwck

Command	Description	Example
pwconv	Convert an existing /etc/passwd file containing encrypted passwords into the newer format (the default on most Linux systems) in which all encrypted passwords are stored in /etc/shadow.	pwconv
pwunconv	Convert existing /etc/passwd and /etc/ shadow password information into the older format in which all encrypted passwords are stored in /etc/passwd.	pwunconv
sg	Change temporarily to a different group; same as *newgrp* command.	sg journalists
sudo	Permit access to a command normally reserved for root, based on configuration information in /etc/sudoers.	sudo mount /mnt/ cdrom
system-config-users	View and edit user account and group information with this graphical utility provided in Red Hat Linux and Fedora.	system-config-users
useradd	Create a new user account.	useradd cmoffett
userdel	Delete an existing user account.	userdel cmoffett
usermod	Modify the parts of an existing user account as stored in /etc/passwd.	usermod -c "Liz Osowski" lizw
visudo	Edit the /etc/sudoers file to configure the sudo command.	visudo
wall	Write all—send a broadcast message to all users who are logged in to the system.	wall Meet outside for lunch in 10 minutes

11

KEY TERMS

/etc/login.defs — File in which default information used to create new user accounts is stored.

/etc/motd — File in which a message of the day may be stored. Empty by default on most Linux systems, the contents of this file are displayed on a user's system when logging in to a text-based console or starting a shell in a terminal window.

/etc/nsswitch.conf — File that defines where to search for various system information such as password and networking configuration details. Supports directing programs to local files, NIS or NIS+ servers, or other centralized information repositories.

/etc/skel — A directory containing files that are copied to a new user's home directory at the time a new user account is created.

/etc/sudoers — Configuration file that determines what actions regular users are permitted to perform using the *sudo* command. Must be edited using the *visudo* command.

Network Information Service (NIS) — A network service that can provide (among other information) centralized user and password management across multiple Linux or UNIX systems.

NIS+ — A newer version of the Network Information Service. *See* NIS.

Pluggable Authentication Module (PAM) — A security system supported by Linux that permits each program needing security features to be configured independently using numerous modules, each of which provides a specific type of security check. Programs are configured using files located in /etc/pam.d.

Set Group ID (SGID) — A special-purpose file permission that causes the user executing a program to take the file permissions of the group assigned to the program file. Also used to permit special access rights to a directory.

Set User ID (SUID) — A special-purpose file permission that causes the user executing a program to take the file permissions of the owner of the program file.

sticky bit — A special purpose file permission, now ignored when used on files, that grants special access rights when used on a directory; only the owner of a file or root is permitted to rename or delete a file in a directory with this permission set.

REVIEW QUESTIONS

1. Name the command and corresponding file that control defaults used by the *useradd* command.

2. When you add a file to the /etc/skel directory, the file is added to the home directory of users:

   a. when you create new users after that time

   b. immediately

   c. when the next *usermod* command is executed

   d. based on the options set in the /etc/shadow file for each user

3. On which tab of the User Properties dialog box in system-config-users do you configure password aging information?

   a. User Data

   b. Account Info

   c. Password Info

   d. Groups

4. Why does the Groups tab of the User Properties dialog box in system-config-users include two lists of all groups on the system?

5. What is wrong with this command: *useradd -g sales -c "Ralph Barrow"*

   a. It doesn't include a user name.

   b. It uses an option that is invalid.

   c. It is not a valid command.

   d. It is missing a required option to create a new user account.

6. What is the command used to display the default settings that *useradd* relies on when creating a new user account?

7. Which option of the *usermod* command is used to define a list of multiple groups of which a user should be a member?

   a. -*g*

   b. -*c*

   c. -*M*

   d. -G

8. What is the purpose of the -*M* option of the *chage* command?

   a. It defines whether a home directory exists for the user or not.

   b. It sets the maximum number of days between times that a user must change his or her password.

   c. It defines the minimum number of days between times that a user must change his or her password.

   d. It causes the command to show the current status of a regular user's password (that is, when it needs to be changed).

9. What is wrong with this command: *moduser -c "Ralph W. Barrow" ralph*

   a. It doesn't include a valid user name.

   b. It uses an option that is invalid.

   c. It is not a valid command.

   d. It is missing a required option to modify a user account.

10. Describe a method of disabling a user account without using the *passwd* or *usermod* commands.

11. Which numeric mode includes the Set User ID permission?

    a. 4644

    b. 2755

    c. 2600

    d. 1666

12. Which numeric mode includes the Set Group ID permission?

    a. 4644

    b. 2755

    c. 5600

    d. 1666

11

13. Which characters are used in the output of the *ls -l* command to show the SUID and SGID permissions, respectively?

    a. s, t

    b. s, s

    c. t, s

    d. s, xg

14. You have just realized that the root file system is almost full and that you must immediately shut down the server to clean up some space before the kernel crashes. To let everyone know that they should immediately save their work and log off, you use:

    a. the *shutdown* command

    b. the /etc/motd file

    c. an e-mail message

    d. the *wall* command

15. Stacking PAM modules refers to:

    a. executing multiple modules of one module type in sequence

    b. the collection of modules of all types listed in a given PAM configuration file

    c. placing PAM data on a fixed memory location where other programs can access it

    d. a user determining the order in which PAM modules are executed to customize login security

16. What is the difference between a *required* and a *requisite* control_flag in a PAM configuration file?

17. When the SUID bit is set on a program file, Linux:

    a. makes the file completely unchangeable until root removes that bit

    b. allows only the program owner to execute that file

    c. executes the program with the file permissions of the program file's owner

    d. allows that program to be run using only root permission

18. The *auth* keyword in a PAM configuration file refers to:

    a. the module type indicating how the named module is being used

    b. the control_flag that defines module interaction with the calling program

    c. the parameters passed to the module

    d. whether users must be authorized in order for the PAM module to be executed

19. The actions of *sudo* are controlled by the file:

    a. /etc/sudo.conf

    b. /etc/visudo

    c. /etc/sudoers

    d. /etc/sudo/visudoers.conf

20. The *visudo* program:

    a. creates default configurations for *sudo* execution by regular users

    b. lets you safely edit the configuration file for *sudo*

    c. must be configured by each user who wants to have access to *sudo* functionality

    d. cannot be accessed without first setting up /etc/sudoers.conf

---

Hands-On Projects

HANDS-ON PROJECTS

Project 11-1

11

In this project, you practice managing user and group accounts. To complete this project you need an installed Linux system with root access. This procedure should work on any version of Linux, though the defaults assume you are working on Red Hat Linux or Fedora.

1. Log in to Linux, open a command-line window and use **su –** to change to root access.

2. Create a new group named "webmasters":

    `groupadd webmasters`

3. Display the group file and review the new group on the last line of the output:

    `cat /etc/group`

4. Review the default settings for *useradd*:

    `useradd -D`

    Notice the SHELL= setting refers to the bash shell.

5. Change the default shell to **tcsh** for all users created after this point:

    `useradd -D -s /bin/tcsh`

6. Review the contents of the /etc/skel directory:

    `ls /etc/skel`

    Why is nothing listed?

7. Review the contents of the /etc/skel directory again:

    `ls -a /etc/skel`

8. Examine the default .bash_profile script where you can place environment variables or aliases that were to be part of users' environments:

   `cat /etc/skel/.bash_profile`

9. Create a new user account with a primary group assignment, an expiration date, and a full name in the comment field:

   `useradd -g webmasters -e 12/31/07 -c "Haley Mendez" hmendez`

10. Display the user account file and review the new user account information in the last line of the output:

    `cat /etc/passwd`

11. Review the contents of the new user's home directory and compare it with what you viewed in /etc/skel:

    `ls -a /home/hmendez`

12. Set a password for the new user account:

    `passwd hmendez`

13. Enter a new password twice, as prompted.

14. Change to the new user account using the substitute user command:

    `su - hmendez`

    No password is required because you are logged in as root.

15. Display the aliases that are in effect for the new user:

    `alias`

16. Check which shell you are currently using:

    `echo $SHELL`

17. Return to the root account:

    `exit`

18. Change the shell used by the hmendez account with the following *usermod* command:

    `usermod -s /bin/bash hmendez`

19. Change the default shell used when creating new user accounts:

    `useradd -D -s /bin/bash`

20. Change to another virtual console by pressing **Ctrl+Alt+F2** if you are working in a graphical environment or **Alt+F2** if you are working in a text-mode console.

21. Log in using the new account you created and the password you assigned.

22. Change back to your previous virtual console by pressing **Alt+F7** for graphical mode or **Alt+F1** for the first text-mode console. Log out.

Project 11-2

In this project, you set password control information for a user account. To complete this project, you should have Red Hat Linux or Fedora installed with root access and at least one regular user account created. These steps should work on most Linux systems, though some systems may require different commands to configure user accounts and passwords than those shown in this project.

1. Log in using your regular user account to see that it functions correctly.

2. Use the **su** command to switch to root access.

3. Look at the entry for your regular user account in the /etc/shadow file. Notice what the first character of the encrypted password is (the first character after the first colon on that line).

4. Lock your regular user account.

    ```
    passwd -l user name
    ```

5. Log out of root access using the **exit** command and try to log in using your regular user account.

6. Use **su** to switch to root again and look at the first character in your encrypted password. The character you see there modifies the encryption and makes the password that you enter to log in invalid.

7. Unlock the account.

    ```
    passwd -u user name
    ```

8. Check the /etc/shadow file again to see that the extra character is gone. You can now log in using the original password.

9. If you are in a lab environment, try using the -d option to disable your regular account and then review /etc/shadow again.

    ```
    passwd -d user name
    ```

10. Set the minimum days that a password must remain before a user can change it to 100 (this is just an experiment; normally, you set the minimum at a day or two and the maximum at around 30 to 60).

    ```
    chage -m 100 user name
    ```

    Can you spot the field where this is stored in /etc/shadow on the line for your regular account?

11. Log out and log in again with your regular user account. Try to change your password using *passwd*.

12. Log out, then log in again as root if you wish and change the minimum days between password changes back to 0, which lets you change your password as often as you choose. Log out.

11

Project 11-3

In this project, you configure PAM settings for a system utility. To complete this project, you should have Red Hat Linux or Fedora installed with root access. Before completing this project, you should make a backup copy of the file that you will edit using this command: *cp /etc/pam.d/system-auth /etc/pam.d/system-auth-backup*. If you have trouble completing the project, you can restore the backup copy of the file.

1. Log in with root access using the su - command and open the file **/etc/pam.d/system-auth** in a text editor.

2. Locate the line on which the pam_cracklib module is referenced.

3. Change the *retry* parameter to **5** and add a *minlen* parameter with a value of **12**. The line should look like this:

   ```
   password requisite  /lib/security/$ISA/pam_cracklib.so retry=5 minlen=12
   ```

   (Note that the minimum length value gives "credit" when a password includes a variety of symbols, mixed case, and digits. So a well-formed password does not need to be 12 characters long.)

4. Among the lines in the file that begin with password (in the far left column), locate the line with the pam_unix module. Add the parameter **remember=15**. This causes the system to record the previous 15 passwords for each user so that they cannot be used again.

5. Log out and log in using your regular user account.

6. Try changing your password using various lengths and repeating previously used passwords to see how these settings affect what you can do. Log out.

Project 11-4

In this project, you continue working with PAM by altering the control_flag setting for a utility's PAM configuration. To complete this project, you should have Red Hat Linux or Fedora installed with root access and have just completed Project 11-3. The steps here assume you are working in a graphical interface. You should only complete this project if you are working in a lab where you are not concerned about the security of your system. Before completing this project, you should make a backup copy of each of the files that you will edit (see the example in the instructions for Project 11-3). If you have trouble completing the project, you can restore the backup copy of these files.

1. Log in as root using the **su -** command.

2. Edit the file /etc/pam.d/login. Change the control_flag on the pam_securetty line from *required* to **sufficient**.

3. Save the file.

4. Switch to a virtual console by pressing **Ctrl+Alt+F3**. On that virtual console, log in as root. What happened and why?

5. Switch back to the graphical interface by pressing **Alt+F7**. Edit the /etc/pam.d/ login file again and change *sufficient* back to **required**. Save the file.

6. Now open the /etc/pam.d/system-auth file in a text editor.

7. Just *above* the lines that begin with *password* insert this line, then save the file.

   ```
   password    optional  /lib/security/$ISA/pam_issue.so issue=/etc/printcap
   ```

   (You can refer to any brief text file that you choose instead of the /etc/printcap file; this file is used simply as an illustration.)

8. Switch to a virtual console by pressing **Ctrl+Alt+F3**. On that virtual console, log out (if you are still logged in) and log in again. Do you see any differences?

9. Switch back to the graphical interface by pressing **Alt+F7**. Edit the /etc/pam.d/ system-auth file again.

10. Just *below* the lines that begin with *auth* insert this line, then save the file.

    ```
    auth optional  /lib/security/$ISA/pam_issue.so issue=/etc/ printcap
    ```

11. Switch to a virtual console by pressing **Ctrl+Alt+F3**. On that virtual console, log out if you are still logged in.

12. Log in by entering your user name, but *enter the wrong password*.

    What do you see?

13. You are prompted again to log in. Use your correct user name and password. You can successfully log in. Now log out on the virtual console by entering the command **exit**.

14. Switch back to the graphical interface by pressing **Alt+F7**. Edit /etc/pam.d/system-auth and remove the extra lines you added to it. Save the changes and close the text editor. Why did the first extra line not have any effect? (See the documentation on the module for the answer.)

    Why was the optional control_flag appropriate here?

15. Log out.

11

CASE PROJECTS

Considering Security in User Management

1. One of the security systems that is growing in popularity—Kerberos—was not mentioned in relation to PAM modules. In fact, Linux PAM has very good support for Kerberos. Review the documentation on this feature, located in a separate directory on Red Hat Linux (/usr/share/doc/pam_krb5-2.0.10) plus the information listed under Kerberos at *http://www.us.kernel.org/pub/linux/libs/pam/modules.html*. Write a 1-page summary of how PAM implements Kerberos and what benefits or concerns this implementation raises for you.

2. Write a summary of policy statements regarding the use of *sudo* in a large company that relies on multiple system administrators for specific networking tasks such as print management, file server maintenance, and e-mail server maintenance. You may want to consult the *sudo* and *sudoers* man pages as well as example security policies that you locate on the Internet.

3. Describe how you would instruct and influence users in a corporate or academic department regarding the selection and protection of their passwords. Note that you are probably younger, less experienced professionally, and paid less than the people you are seeking to influence (and protect).

4. Review the contents of the /etc/login.defs file, noting which parts of the file you recognize and any that you might want to change as defaults when creating users on your system.

# CHAPTER 12

CONFIGURING NETWORKS

After reading this chapter and completing the exercises, you will be able to:

♦ Configure network interfaces using command-line and graphical utilities

♦ Set up a simple DHCP server

♦ Manage networked printing services

In the previous chapter you learned about creating and managing user accounts on your system. This involved basic operations such as creating new user and group accounts and making changes to those accounts. It also involved managing special file permissions that gave users additional access to files or directories for special purposes. The policies you learned about for managing users included security considerations such as granting root-level access, and using various systems to provide a network-wide database of user accounts for easier management.

In this chapter, you learn more about configuring network devices using both the underlying command-line utilities and the graphical utilities that make basic configuration tasks simpler. You also learn about setting up a DHCP server to provide IP address and related information to other computers on your network. Finally, you learn about setting up and managing complex printing services that include networked printers using both the traditional and more recent printing systems supported by Linux.

CONFIGURING LINUX NETWORKING

In Chapter 7, "Using Network Clients," you learned basic information about networking in order to use network client programs such as a Web browser or e-mail client. You also learned in Chapter 8, "Installing Linux," a little about the protocols and technologies used to network computers. In this section, you learn more about networking protocols and configuration.

Understanding Network Devices in Linux

As you know, devices in Linux are typically accessed via the /dev subdirectory of the file system, where hundreds of device names are listed. Not all devices named are actually present on your system; the name is there for convenience in case you install a corresponding device. You would expect that Linux networking devices would appear in the /dev directory and be configured similarly to other devices. However, Linux networking devices are not shown in the /dev directory, and in fact do not "exist" on the system until an appropriate device driver is installed in the Linux kernel.

Physical networking devices are easy to identify: routers, hubs, NICs, and so on. But it may help you to think of a networking device in Linux as a named channel over which network traffic can pass. Some Linux networking devices refer to physical Ethernet cards; others refer to logical networking channels, such as the loopback interface, which you saw in Chapter 7.

Because networking is handled in the Linux kernel, all device drivers for networking are actually kernel modules. **Kernel modules** are parts of the kernel that can be loaded or unloaded while Linux is running, but most system administrators configure their system so that the networking modules are loaded immediately at system startup. (Chapter 13, "System and Kernel Management," discusses kernel modules in depth.) When the appropriate kernel module is loaded, it locates a network device such as an Ethernet card and activates that card so the kernel can use it. The networking "device" is then available on the system. The first Ethernet card installed on a system is /dev/eth0.

Installing network devices is typically a nonevent: the system detects your networking card and configures the correct kernel module during installation. Chapter 13 describes how you can load and test kernel modules if you add networking hardware after installing Linux.

Every Ethernet card has a unique address assigned by the manufacturer, called its **Media Access Control (MAC) address**, or simply its hardware address. When one host on an Ethernet network wants to communicate with another host, it must obtain the MAC address of the destination Ethernet card. To obtain this MAC address, a host broadcasts a message to the entire network segment using the **Address Resolution Protocol (ARP)**. The message says, in effect, "I need the MAC address of the computer having the IP address aa.bb.cc.dd." All of the hosts on the network segment see the ARP request; the host that has the requested IP address responds with its MAC address directly to the computer that sent the ARP request (the source host). The source host then stores, or caches, that correspondence between MAC address and IP address so that it won't need to repeat the ARP request later on. With the correct MAC address available, the system can prepare packets and send them out on the network via the Ethernet card.

You can use the *arp* command to display the **ARP cache**, a mapping of IP addresses to hardware addresses. The *arp* command is used mainly for troubleshooting network connectivity. Most entries in the ARP cache are dynamic and are discarded if not referenced within two minutes.

Configuring Networking with Command-line Utilities

Most Linux distributions use a very similar set of commands and scripts to configure networking. In fact, the two core command line programs are the same on all versions of Linux: *ifconfig* and *route*. These commands are used by the script /etc/rc.d/init.d/network, which you learned about in Chapter 9, "Understanding System Initialization." Here you learn about how those underlying networking utilities operate.

You used **ifconfig** in Chapter 7 to review the existing network configuration. The same utility is used to set up that configuration in the Linux kernel. This command is used by the system startup scripts at boot time, though you can use it to manually reconfigure the network if needed. The parameters used by *ifconfig* include, at a minimum, a network interface (such as eth0), the IP address assigned to the interface, and the network mask. These three pieces of information allow packets to be sent. A **packet** is a unit of data that the network card transmits. Additional parameters that you can configure using *ifconfig* include the **broadcast address** (an address that will send a packet to all computers on the same part of the network), the **maximum transmission unit** or **MTU** (the maximum size of packet that the interface supports), and various special features such as point-to-point connections and IPv6 addressing (which are not discussed in this chapter).

When you are working at a command line in Linux, you can enter the *ifconfig* command with an interface name such as eth0 to see the status of that interface:

```
$ ifconfig eth0
```

```
eth0      Link encap:Ethernet  HWaddr 00:01:02:76:FC:69
          inet addr:192.168.100.3  Bcast:192.168.100.255  Mask:
          255.255.255.0
          inet6 addr: fe80::201:2ff:fe76:fc69/64 Scope:Link
          UP BROADCAST RUNNING MULTICAST  MTU:1500  Metric:1
          RX packets:0 errors:0 dropped:0 overruns:0 frame:0
          TX packets:16 errors:0 dropped:0 overruns:0 carrier:3
          collisions:0 txqueuelen:1000
          RX bytes:0 (0.0 b)  TX bytes:3012 (2.9 Kb)
          Interrupt:11 Base address:0x1080
```

By specifying an interface such as eth0 in the *ifconfig* command, you can start an interface ("bring it up") or stop it ("take it down"). To do this, you add *up* or *down* after the interface name. For example, to stop the Ethernet interface, enter this command:

```
# ifconfig eth0 down
```

To start it again, enter this command:

```
# ifconfig eth0 up
```

You shouldn't need to use this command directly (as explained in the next section). If you do, note that you still need to configure the route manually for the interface to work as expected with other computers on the network. The basic syntax of an *ifconfig* command looks like this:

```
ifconfig device ip_address netmask address broadcast address
```

A real example of configuring an Ethernet card at the command line might look like this:

```
# ifconfig eth0 192.168.100.1 netmask 255.255.255.0 broadcast
192.168.100.255
```

The second core networking command is ***route***, which lets you view or configure the routing table within the Linux kernel. The **routing table** tells the networking software where to send packets that aren't part of the local network. In fact, it even includes the local network, as you'll see.

As with *ifconfig*, the *route* command is executed by your Linux system at boot time when networking is initialized. You can always use it manually to view or change the configured routes. But you shouldn't plan on needing *ifconfig* and *route* regularly except to see a quick list of how the kernel is currently configured.

Using the *route* command with no parameters displays the kernel routing table. Sample output is shown here:

```
# route
Kernel IP routing table
Destination     Gateway          Genmask          Flags  Metric  Ref  Use  Iface
192.168.100.0   *                255.255.255.0    U      0       0    0    eth0
127.0.0.0       *                255.0.0.0        U      0       0    0    lo
default         192.168.100.5    0.0.0.0          UG     0       0    0    eth0
```

The next section walks you through each part of this output, which is labeled by the utility itself as the "Kernel IP routing table." The output for this host consists of three lines (after the column headings):

- A line defining where to send traffic for the 192.168.100.0 network (that's the network associated with the IP address of the eth0 device)

- A line defining where to send traffic for the 127.0.0.0 network (that's the localhost or loopback network address)

- A line defining where to send any packet with a destination address on a network other than the two just mentioned; those packets must go to the gateway, as this system doesn't know how to reach any other networks

Examining the columns in the output of the *route* command, you see:

- *Destination:* The network to which the routing table entry applies. If the destination address of an IP packet is part of the network listed on a line, then that entry is used to route the packet.

- *Gateway:* The computer that should receive a packet destined for the specified network. Because this output is from a host (not a machine acting as a dedicated router), the Gateway field contains either an asterisk (*) to indicate that the network is the one the host is a part of (no routing is needed) or the default gateway (send all nonlocal traffic to the named IP address).

- *Genmask:* Specifies the network mask used to identify the network ID portion of any IP address that is part of the destination network identified on that line

- *Flags:* Nine single-letter flags indicate information about this routing table entry. The U indicates that the route is up; the G indicates that the route refers to a gateway. Most of the other flags (all of which you can view in the *route* command's online man page by entering *man route*) are used for dedicated routers using dynamic routing protocols, as discussed later in this section, rather than single hosts, and refer to how the route was created or updated using routing daemons. (A **routing daemon**, as you'll learn later in this section, is a program that automatically generates routing table entries based on information received over the network via protocols dedicated to routing information.)

- *Metric:* The number of hops (how many routers) needed to reach the specified network (not used by the Linux kernel)

- *Ref:* How many references are made to this route (not used by the Linux kernel)

- *Use:* The number of times this route has been looked up by the routing software. This gives a rough measure of how much traffic is headed for the specified network.

- *Iface:* The network interface on which packets destined for the specified network should be sent.

As with *ifconfig*, you shouldn't plan on using *route* to set up your routing table initially; let the scripts described in the next section or the graphical tools do it for you. As you configure more complex networks, you will need to make changes to these default settings based on how your systems are arranged. A sample command to add a route might look like this:

```
# route add -net 192.168.100.0 netmask 255.255.255.0 dev eth0
```

This example adds a route to reach the network 192.168.100.0 by specifying the network mask for that network and the device to which packets should be sent in order to reach that network: eth0. Here's another example. This command adds a default gateway route, which indicates that traffic to any network for which a route has not been set up should be sent to the gateway system, which knows what to do with it.

```
# route add default gw 192.168.100.5
```

As you work with more complex networks than those described so far, you'll find it helpful to be familiar with the output and the options of the *route* command. At times you may need to modify or add routes to make your Linux system function as desired within a larger network that has multiple gateways or uses network prefixes that require manual configuration.

Recall that you normally use the *service* command to start or stop networking, and that this command relies on the script /etc/rc.d/init.d/network. This script, in turn, relies on information stored in the file /etc/sysconfig/network and the files located in the directories /etc/sysconfig/network-scripts and /etc/sysconfig/networking/devices. Within the latter directory, you see a file for each network device, such as ifcfg-eth0. The contents of the ifcfg-eth0 file might look like this:

```
# 3Com Corporation|3c905B 100BaseTX [Cyclone]
DEVICE=eth0
BOOTPROTO=none
BROADCAST=192.168.100.255
HWADDR=00:01:02:76:FA:79
IPADDR=192.168.100.25
NETMASK=255.255.255.0
NETWORK=192.168.100.0
ONBOOT=yes
TYPE=Ethernet
DHCP_HOSTNAME=inverness.xmission.com
USERCTL=no
PEERDNS=no
```

NOTE

If you are using DHCP to obtain IP address information, your ifcfg-eth0 file will look different from the one shown here.

The contents of all of these files are used by the /etc/rc.d/init.d/network script as it executes *ifconfig* and *route* commands. To change the IP address or other networking parameters for your computer, you can simply change the information in /etc/sysconfig/network-scripts/ ifcfg-eth0 and then execute this command:

```
# service network restart
```

CAUTION

You should not make haphazard changes in your networking. They might not only stop your system from working, but can interfere with other users' systems.

If you want to manage a single interface rather than all network interfaces that are configured on the system, you can use the *ifup* and *ifdown* scripts instead of the *service* command. These two scripts are located in the directory /etc/sysconfig/network-scripts. You can use these scripts to "bring up" or "take down" a specific network interface, without affecting other interfaces. Using one of these scripts is generally better than using the *ifconfig* command directly, because the scripts can carefully look at all the parameters and associated functionality needed to cleanly manage the interface. As an example, you can stop the Ethernet interface, eth0, using this command (assuming you are in the directory /etc/sysconfig/network-scripts):

```
# ./ifdown eth0
```

After making modifications to the Ethernet configuration, you can start the interface again using this command:

```
# ./ifup eth0
```

Normally, only the root account can use the network configuration commands and scripts. You can modify the USERCTL field in the device files, however, so that a regular user can start or stop a network interface using the *service*, *ifup*, or *ifdown* command. You can also configure this feature using the graphical utility described in the next section.

To see the flexibility and usefulness of this system and its many scripts and configuration files, consider how you would manually add a new interface. Suppose that you needed to assign a second IP address to your Ethernet card. This is called **IP aliasing**, when a single physical interface has more than one IP address assigned—a feature that is useful when hosting multiple Web sites on a single machine, for example. IP aliases are referred to by adding a number to the physical interface name. So, if the interface is eth0, the first additional IP address would refer to eth0:1, the second to eth0:2, and so on.

To create the IP alias you need, you simply create a new file in the /etc/sysconfig/network-scripts directory with the name ifcfg-eth0:1. The easiest way is to copy the existing file ifcfg-eth0. Then change the values of the DEVICE and IPADDR lines to refer to eth0:1 and the second IP address you wanted to assign to the Ethernet card. Then you restart networking to make the additional IP address automatically active. Every time you start up Linux, the additional IP address is started. To remove this IP alias, you just delete the additional file that you created and restart networking. You experiment with creating an IP alias in the Hands-On Projects at the end of the chapter.

Some systems have two or more physical network devices. For example, you might have two Ethernet cards, or an Ethernet card and a DSL Internet connection. By having two devices, you can connect to two networks at the same time. This illustrates the purpose of a gateway: packets arriving at the gateway computer via one of the network devices need to leave the computer via the other network device in order to reach their intended destination. To

12

permit this, you must enable IP forwarding. **IP forwarding** is a feature of the Linux kernel that allows packets to be passed between network interfaces. IP forwarding is required for any router. To enable IP forwarding, you use this command:

```
# echo 1 > /proc/sys/net/ipv4/ip_forward
```

Configuring Networking Using Graphical Tools

A good system administrator knows how things work "under the hood," rather than just relying on graphical tools. By knowing about the networking scripts and the *ifconfig* and *route* commands, you'll have a better grasp of how to diagnose any problems that arise on your network. Once you understand those things, however, there's no reason not to use the tools that make life easier. Every major version of Linux includes graphical utilities to help you set up and manage networking.

Red Hat Linux and Fedora include the system-config-network program. You can start this program from the command line or by choosing System Settings, then Network on the GNOME main menu. Figure 12-1 shows the Devices tab of this utility. As the text in the tab notes, multiple Linux networking devices can be associated with a single physical piece of hardware.

Figure 12-1 The Devices tab of system-config-network

This section discusses only the Hardware and Devices tabs. The Hosts and DNS tabs are discussed later in this chapter.

NOTE

On the Devices tab, you see a list of each Linux networking device name and the type of hardware driver associated with it. You can use the New button in the top section of the dialog box to configure many types of networking interfaces, though not nearly as many as Linux actually supports. Figure 12-2 shows the dialog box that walks you through creating a new device after you click New.

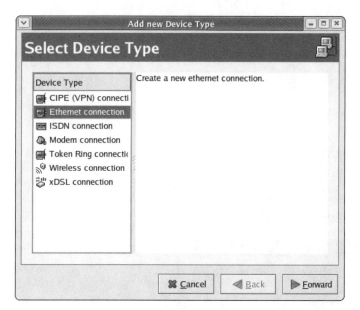

Figure 12-2 Beginning to create a new device in system-config-network

You can easily use this tool to set up IP aliasing, adding another IP address to a single Ethernet card. Just select Ethernet as the device type, then select the same Ethernet card in the second dialog box. When prompted to enter address information, enter the new (second) IP address. (See Figure 12-3.) The utility automatically assigns it an appropriate device name (such as eth0:1), which you see in the Devices tab when you complete the configuration.

If you select an existing device and click Edit, you can view and alter the configuration of that device. Figure 12-4 shows the dialog box that appears when you select an Ethernet device and click Edit. The General tab lets you decide whether to use DHCP to obtain an IP address or assign a static IP address. You can also define whether regular users can activate the networking device, whether the device should be started at boot time, and which parts of the configuration are provided by DHCP (DNS server, host name, or just an IP address).

12

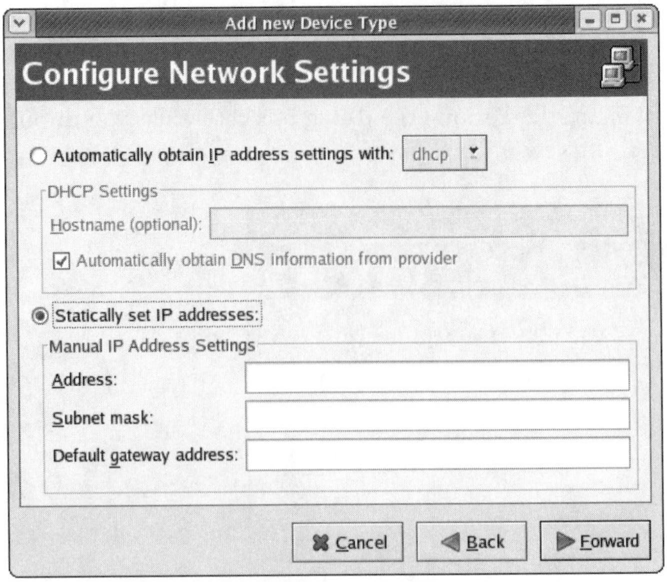

Figure 12-3 An IP alias's Ethernet device

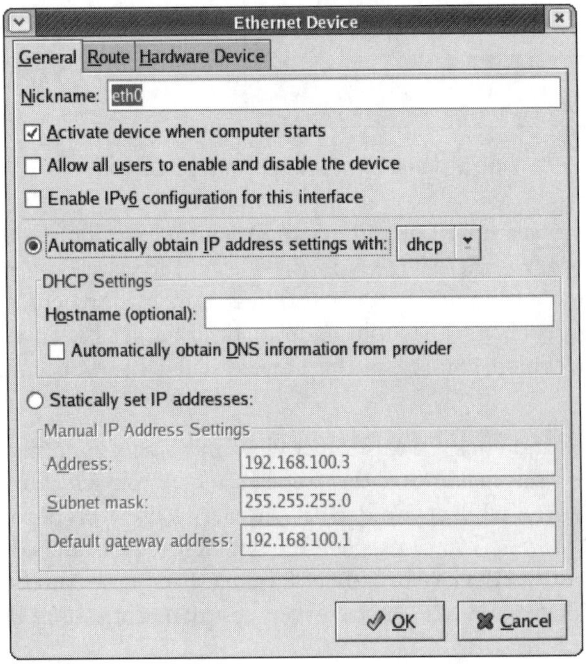

Figure 12-4 Editing an Ethernet device in system-config-network

On the Route tab, you can use the Add, Delete, and Edit buttons to manage entries in the kernel's routing table. In most cases, you can rely on the information configured by default in this tab. In the Hardware Device tab, you can view which physical device is associated with the logical device you are editing. Again, you are unlikely to need to change this information.

The Hardware tab in the Network Configuration window (see Figure 12-5) lists physical devices installed on your system. You can use the New button while viewing this tab to help you locate and configure the correct kernel module for any networking hardware you have added since you installed Linux.

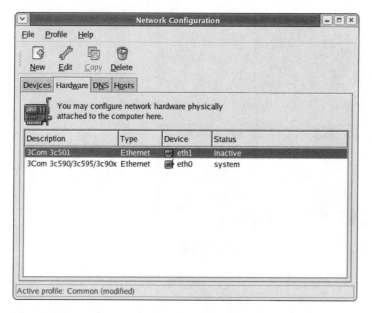

Figure 12-5 The Hardware tab in system-config-network

After you choose New in the Hardware tab, you select the type of networking hardware you are adding and click OK. A Network Adapters Configuration dialog box then appears. (See Figure 12-6.) In the Adapter field, you can select the type of hardware you are installing from a drop-down list of supported devices. If necessary, you can also enter other information in this dialog box. When you choose OK, the utility attempts to install the appropriate kernel module and activate the device. You see a message informing you if this was successful or failed because the device could not be located. In this case, you might need to provide additional information or select a different device and try the operation again.

You can select System Tools, then Network Device Control on the GNOME main menu to start a simpler utility that lets you activate or deactivate the networking devices that you saw on the Devices tab of system-config-network. Figure 12-7 shows this utility. Selecting the Configure button in this utility starts the system-config-network utility.

Figure 12-6 Configuring a new network adapter in system-config-network

Figure 12-7 The Network Device Control utility

Several other graphical tools are available to help you configure networking in different versions of Linux. For example, the **YAST2** utility is used in SUSE Linux; other versions use the **Webmin** tools (see *www.webmin.com*). The key point is that a graphical tool can help you configure networking, but you should still understand what's happening in the background and how to dig deeper into the system for when troubleshooting becomes necessary. Keep your eyes open for the tools that you prefer to use and that save time in the types of networking environments where you find yourself working.

Configuring the DNS Resolver

You learned previously that a domain name service is used to convert host and domain names such as *www.google.com* into IP addresses such as 128.54.12.4. This service is implemented by a server that supports the domain name service (DNS). A client can send a request to a DNS server saying, "I need to contact domain name X; what is the corresponding IP address?" The DNS server then responds (if it can) with the IP address. A client may also send an IP address to a DNS server and ask for the corresponding domain name. This is a feature called **reverse DNS** that helps prevent certain types of security breaches on the Internet. **Resolving** is the process of converting a domain name to an IP address, or vice versa.

The **resolver** is the client part of DNS: it makes requests to a DNS server so that other programs on your system can use the IP address of a given server to make a network connection. Networked programs such as a Web browser automatically use the resolver in Linux to resolve domain names into IP addresses.

If you included a DNS server address when installing Linux, the resolver should already be configured. If you are using DHCP, the address of the DNS server may also have been provided by the DHCP server that assigned your computer an IP address. You can test the resolver by pinging another system using a host name instead of an IP address. For example, enter *ping www.novell.com*.

The resolver is configured by a single file in Linux: **/etc/resolv.conf** (notice that "resolve" is missing an "e" in the file name). You configure the resolver by storing the IP address of one or more DNS servers in the resolv.conf file, preceded by the keyword *nameserver*. A keyword is simply a word to which the program reading the configuration file attaches a special meaning. You can use any DNS server on the Internet that allows you access, but the closer the server is to your local network segment, the faster the responses are to resolver requests. You can include up to three DNS servers in resolv.conf, each on a separate line. The resolver tries to reach each of the servers in the order you list them until a request succeeds.

You can also include other items in resolv.conf, such as the domain name of which your host is a part. This information guides the resolver in determining exactly what host name it should resolve. Because a DNS server often maintains information for a number of domains (including the domain name from which you are coming), including this information can make searches quicker. You can include multiple domain names to search using the search keyword. They must all be on a single line or only the last one is used. On most Linux systems you can list up to six domains to search. Here is an example resolv.conf file:

```
domain xmission.com
nameserver 198.60.22.2
nameserver 10.21.105.1
```

You can change the resolv.conf file in any text editor. This configuration file is checked before each query, so if you make a change in /etc/resolv.conf, you don't need to take any other action for the change to take effect.

12

You can review the man page for resolv.conf to learn about the *options* keyword, which you can include to control things such as the length of time that the resolver waits for a response from a name server and the number of retries it makes before giving up. Another keyword, *rotate*, causes the resolver to use each of the listed name servers in turn instead of always trying the first one listed. This spreads the load out among several name servers, which may be appropriate in some settings.

Linux includes a number of utilities for researching DNS problems. These include *dnsquery*, *nslookup*, *dig*, *whois*, and *host*. The most powerful of these, *dig*, is discussed in more detail in Chapter 15, "Advanced Topics and Troubleshooting," in connection with setting up a DNS server.

The hosts File

The DNS resolver is actually the more complicated way to convert an IP address to a domain name. The simpler method is to store the IP addresses and corresponding domain names in a text file on your host. The file where this information can be stored is called **/etc/hosts**. By default, it contains only the host name localhost and your own host's name (on some versions of Linux). All of the possible names that can be used to refer to the listed IP address are included on the same line, separated by spaces. A sample file might look like this:

```
127.0.0.1    sundance.xmission.com localhost
```

When you have a small network, you can create a hosts file that contains each host and the IP address of that host. By installing that file in the /etc directory of every host, you avoid the need for a DNS server. Each time the resolver needs to convert a domain name to an IP address, it can find the needed information on the local hard disk without relying on a network connection, which is much slower.

However, even if you have a small network and want to include the names and IP addresses of all local hosts in the /etc/hosts file, you may want to have nonlocal domain names resolved by a request to a DNS server. You can configure this in two ways. The older method is to set up the **/etc/host.conf** file to specify the order in which the resolver should consult resources to resolve the host name to an IP address. This file typically contains a single line:

```
order hosts,bind
```

This line tells the Linux resolver to check the /etc/hosts file first; if the domain name is not listed in /etc/hosts, the resolver uses the configuration in resolv.conf to query a DNS server. (DNS servers use the BIND protocol, hence the word "bind" in the host.conf file.) If you wanted to check the DNS server first, you switch the order of the words in /etc/host.conf. That would be unusual, however, except when testing your configuration.

More common than using /etc/host.conf in current Linux distributions is using the /etc/nsswitch.conf file, which you learned about in Chapter 11, "Managing Users." This file functions much like /etc/host.conf but is used by a number of different programs, not just the resolver. It tells the resolver where to look to resolve IP addresses and domain names. A sample line from /etc/nsswitch.conf to control the actions of the resolver might look like this:

```
hosts:      files nisplus dns
```

This line indicates that the resolver should first look in the /etc/hosts file, then try to use the NIS+ server, if available, and finally use the DNS server configured in /etc/resolv.conf.

Configuring the DNS Resolver Graphically

If you're trying to avoid using a text editor to configure Linux, you can use system-config-network to set up the resolver. Within this utility, choose the DNS tab, shown in Figure 12-8. On this tab, you can configure the host name for your system, which is not actually associated with the resolver (it is stored in /etc/sysconfig/networking). You can also enter the IP address for up to three DNS servers.

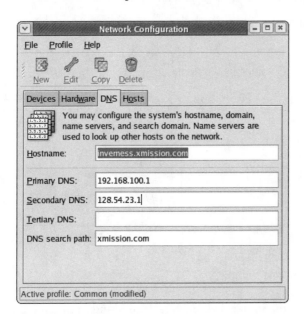

Figure 12-8   DNS tab of system-config-network

Dynamic Routing with Routing Protocols

The routing described previously is called **static routing**. The routing table in your Linux kernel is assembled by entries in your start-up scripts or by route commands that you enter to update or modify the routing table. This is straightforward and effective for a small, reliable network, but static routing is not the best choice for larger networks and unreliable connections. In most routing situations, dynamic routing is used. **Dynamic routing** is the process of using a specialized routing protocol to build and modify routing tables automatically through a network based on information shared by the routers, without constant human intervention.

To see the value of dynamic routing, consider the networking configuration shown in Figure 12-9. Host Abe wants to reach Host Bill. If static routing is used, Router 1 would have an entry showing that the Ethernet card connected directly to Router 2 was the correct way to reach Host Bill. However, if something breaks the network connection between Router 1 and Router 2—for example the phone connection is broken, or someone unplugs the wrong network cable in a server room—Host Abe is unable to reach Host Bill, even though Host Bill *could* be reached via Router 3 and Router 4. With static routing, Router 1 can't find this out; a system administrator would need to learn of the problem, determine an alternate route, and enter the information at a command line. Later, when the problem was fixed, the original route directly to Router 2 would need to be entered in Router 1's routing table in order to keep the network operating as efficiently as possible.

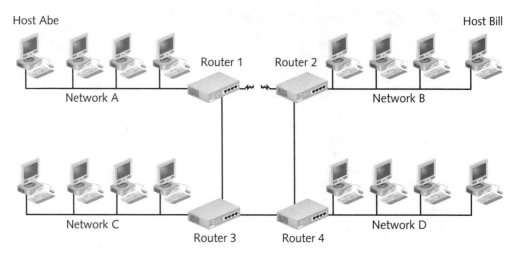

Figure 12-9   The need for dynamic routing

On the other hand, if all four of the routers in Figure 12-9 are using a routing protocol, they can exchange information often about the networks that they are capable of reaching. Before a minute had passed, Router 3 would have informed Router 1 that packets for Network B should be sent to it, passed on to Router 4, and then Router 2. Even on a large network, a well-configured routing protocol would have reestablished the connection between Host Abe and Host Bill via another route within a minute or two, without any administrator having to take action.

Many routing protocols are available, but only a few are widely used. Routing protocols are divided into two categories: interior and exterior. While the difference can seem vague at the outset, loosely stated, **interior routing protocols** are those designed for routing packets among networks under your control; they route packets based on mathematical models (though you won't need any math to implement them). **Exterior routing protocols** are designed for routing packets between networks controlled by different organizations; they route packets based on administration policies, often controlled by how much a particular organization's routing information is trusted.

All routing protocols are designed to exchange information among routers. They use broadcast messages or other techniques to inform other routers of the networks they know how to reach. For example, one router might send a message using a routing protocol that says, "I can reach network 198.60.12.0 in five hops." If another router sees that message and doesn't know how to reach the named network in four hops or less, it copies that information to its routing table. Then it can broadcast to other routers: "I can reach network 198.60.12.0 in six hops." (It adds one hop to reach the router from which it received the information.)

Routing Information Protocol (RIP)

Routing Information Protocol (RIP), an interior routing protocol, is the oldest routing protocol still in common use. Its usefulness is limited to smaller networks or routing that is not highly complex. RIP does not provide support for classless IP addresses except in RIP version 2, and it can only handle routing with up to 15 hops between source and destination.

NOTE A routing topic that is not discussed in detail in this book is IP address classes. Basically, blocks of IP addresses can be grouped in different ways to aid routing decisions; classes A, B, and C are commonly referred to. Other classes are also defined. Classless addresses provide more flexibility, but require more intelligence in the router (and more work from the system administrator).

RIP is implemented in Linux using the *routed* daemon, which is included with most Linux distributions, though it is typically not installed by default. The *routed* daemon is easy to configure and run, and it is the choice of most network administrators who maintain routers on Linux networks. It is not a strong solution, however, for larger networks because of the limitations of RIP.

Open Shortest Path First (OSPF) and gated

The **Open Shortest Path First (OSPF)** protocol is an interior routing protocol designed to work effectively even in very large networks. OSPF uses a technique called flooding. A router running OSPF periodically floods the network with everything it knows about its neighboring hosts. Other OSPF routers see information coming from other routers and use this data to intelligently construct a "chart" inside the router that defines the best way to reach the various networks. It's as if OSPF tries to let each router take the pulse of distant networks so that OSPF can determine which route to use for the most efficient connection from point A to point B.

Relatively few Linux network administrators need to use OSPF. The larger, often nation-wide networks for which OSPF was designed generally rely on dedicated router hardware such as that provided by Cisco Systems. Nevertheless, Linux does support OSPF using *gated*. This routing daemon is included in many Linux distributions, including Red Hat Linux and Fedora, but it is not installed by default.

gated is a powerful tool that supports multiple routing protocols and can combine routing information provided by those protocols to make the most intelligent routing decisions. The home page for the *gated* daemon is *www.gated.org*. The *gated* daemon supports RIP (including RIP version 2), OSPF, and an external routing protocol called **Border Gateway Protocol (BGP)**.

BGP is designed for routing between major national networks. Initial configuration of even BGP is not hard—that is, the configuration file is not long—but at this level, managing packet routing becomes very complex. In fact, some of the most highly specialized (and highly paid) Internet careers focus on the sometimes mundane task of keeping routers running efficiently.

CONFIGURING A DHCP SERVER

You have read many times that a DHCP server can automatically provide an IP address and other information to a computer. Although this book does not focus on Linux server capabilities, setting up a basic DHCP server is a simple and important task that you will often need to perform.

NOTE DHCP is backward compatible with the **BOOTP** protocol that has long been used by diskless workstations to obtain network configuration instructions. You can think of BOOTP and DHCP as being interchangeable terms, though they are really two separate protocols. Virtually all modern systems use DHCP.

The DHCP server is installed by default on many Linux systems. Configuring this server involves creating an **/etc/dhcpd.conf** file (the location can vary among Linux versions). This file instructs the DHCP server which IP address ranges are available for DHCP clients that request an address. It also may define addresses of DNS name servers, a broadcast address, a maximum time that a client can use the address, and many other options. Each time a client requests an IP address, the DHCP server is said to **lease** the address to the client for a specified time. After that time, the client must request a renewal of the lease, which may involve getting a different IP address. Once configured, however, the whole arrangement is transparent to the user on the client host. A sample dhcpd.conf file is shown here:

```
# Sample /etc/dhcpd.conf
default-lease-time 600;
max-lease-time 7200;
option subnet-mask 255.255.255.0;
option broadcast-address 192.168.1.255;
```

```
option routers 192.168.1.254;
option domain-name-servers 192.168.1.1, 192.168.1.2;
option domain-name "mydomain.org";

subnet 192.168.1.0 netmask 255.255.255.0 {
   range 192.168.1.10 192.168.1.100;
   range 192.168.1.150 192.168.1.200;
}
```

This file defines two ranges of addresses within the 192.168.1.0 network. Within these ranges, IP addresses are assigned randomly to any client that requests an address. You can tie a specific IP address to a specific host by using the MAC address of that host's Ethernet card. That portion of the configuration file would look like this:

```
host haagen {
   hardware ethernet 08:00:6b:3a:29:7f;
   fixed-address 192.168.1.5;
}
```

Many additional options are supported by dhcpd.conf. You can refer to the man page for a list of these. Once you have the DHCP server configured, you can start it using the standard script in /etc/rc.d/init.d or run this command:

```
# service dhcpd start
```

A DHCP client can run on any operating system. So long as it "speaks" DHCP, it can obtain an IP address from the Linux DHCP server. Windows DHCP clients, however, do not follow the DHCP standard, and require that you add a route on Linux so that they can use the Linux DHCP server (change the dev from eth0 to match your networking device as needed):

```
# route add -host 255.255.255.255 dev eth0
```

12

NETWORKED PRINTING SERVICES

In Chapter 3, "Using the Shell," you learned how to set up a local printer using a graphical utility, how to print files from the command line using the *lpr* command, and how to set up basic printing options using *lpoptions*. In this section, you learn more about printing functions in Linux, including the networking capabilities of Linux printing.

Using Traditional Linux Printing: LPRng

The traditional Linux printing system is based on the BSD version of UNIX and is called **LPRng**. (The name refers to the "next generation" of the LPR printing system, though LPRng is quite old at this point.) LPRng printing allows multiple users to print files at the same time to either local or networked printers.

Before a user can print files in Linux, the system administrator must define the printers that the system supports. The administrator creates one or more printer definitions that describe the type of printer and the features to be used when something is printed on it, such as the resolution or color settings and which users can print to it. These printer definitions are also called print queue definitions, and are often referred to simply as **print queues**. When you speak of printing a file, you normally say you're sending it to a certain *printer*, even though we really send it to a print queue: a set of attributes that is in turn associated with a physical printer.

The process of printing a file in the LPRng system includes the following steps:

1. An application submits a file to be printed, as directed by a user. The file submitted for printing is called a **print job**, and can include various options to describe how the printing should be accomplished, such as which printer to use and how many copies to print.

2. The print job is processed by a **print filter**. The print filter converts the information from a Linux application into formatting codes that produce the desired output on the printer. The printing system chooses which print filter to use based on the information configured for the printer that was specified when the print job was submitted.

3. After sending the print job through a print filter, the printing utility stores the print job in a **print spool directory**, which is a location in the file system set aside to hold files waiting to be printed. The default print spool directory for the LPRng system is /var/spool/lpd. Within this directory, subdirectories are created for each print queue. For example, if you had created a printer definition called hplj, print jobs submitted to that print queue would be stored in /var/spool/lpd/hplj.

4. The print server program, *lpd*, keeps track of all the print jobs in all the print queues on the system. When a printer is available (for example, it finishes what it was printing or is reactivated), *lpd* sends the next print job to the printer.

5. At any time after a print job is submitted, the user or system administrator can use various utilities to see what print jobs are waiting to be printed or are being printed, and modify the contents of print queues or the actions of the *lpd* print server.

The print spool directory, /var/spool/lpd, can consume a lot of disk space on a system where many users are printing. Users can submit files for printing much more quickly than printers can process them; be certain you have enough hard disk space to hold print jobs while they wait their turn to be printed.

The correlation between a print queue and a physical printer is not always one to one. That is, one print queue might be used to send print jobs to multiple printers. Conversely, several print queues might all specify the same physical printer.

To understand why LPRng printer definitions might not have a one-to-one correspondence to physical printers, consider two examples. In the first, imagine a large network where many users need to print files. By configuring a single print queue that sends print jobs to multiple printers, users can send files to a single location instead of trying to discover which printer isn't busy at the moment. The *lpd* print server sends print jobs from the single print queue to whichever printer is available. This arrangement is shown in Figure 12-10.

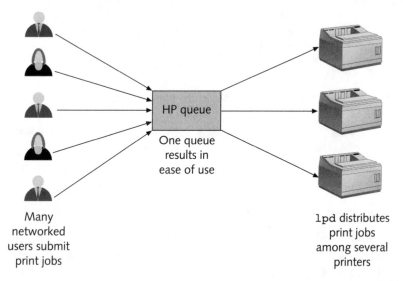

Many
networked
users submit
print jobs

HP queue

One queue
results in
ease of use

lpd distributes
print jobs
among several
printers

12

Figure 12-10   A single print queue can refer to multiple physical printers

The arrangement in Figure 12-10 can also be implemented using classes in the Common UNIX Printing System (CUPS), as described later in this chapter.

CAUTION

As a second example, suppose you have only a single printer. The system administrator on a small office network configures separate print queues for envelopes, color printing, legal-sized documents, and standard printing. Users on the network submit files to the print queues depending on the type of document being printed. The person maintaining the printer would activate the print queue for legal-sized documents (and disable all other print queues) only when legal-sized paper was inserted and ready to print. When envelopes were inserted in the single printer, the envelope queue could be activated, and so forth. This method requires that someone actively maintain the printer unless the printer holds multiple paper trays, and users must wait while each queue is processed in turn. But this may be much more convenient than trying to print an envelope while everyone else is printing out reports. Figure 12-11 shows this arrangement.

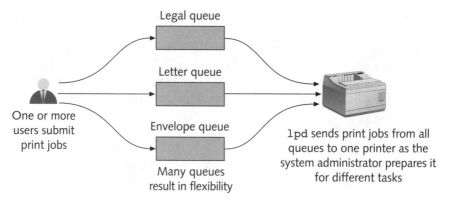

Legal queue

Letter queue

One or more
users submit
print jobs

Envelope queue

Many queues
result in flexibility

lpd sends print jobs from all
queues to one printer as the
system administrator prepares it
for different tasks

Figure 12-11   Many print queues can refer to a single physical printer

The arrangement in Figure 12-11 can also be implemented using multiple
instances of a single print queue in CUPS, as described later in this chapter.

NOTE

Understanding Print Filters and Drivers

To print different types of documents from Linux applications to a variety of printer devices,
Linux uses special programs called print filters, as described previously. A Linux print filter
is essentially the same as a printer driver in other operating systems: it converts documents
or images into a format that the printer can use.

Each printer uses a page description language to guide what it prints. A **page description
language** is a special set of codes that determine the graphics elements, text font, and
everything else about what appears on a printed page. The most widely used page
description languages are PostScript and Printer Control Language (PCL). If a printer uses
PostScript, for example, everything sent to that printer must be written in the PostScript
page description language.

The documents you create in text editors, word processors, spreadsheets, and other Linux
programs are not written in PostScript, PCL, or any other page description language. The
print filter converts each document that you want to print into instructions using the
appropriate page description language for the printer you want to use.

PostScript was developed by Adobe and is widely used in many types of printers. PCL,
developed by Hewlett-Packard, is supported by most Hewlett-Packard printers and by many
others as well. Many printers support multiple page description languages.

If you want to see what PostScript looks like, use the *cat* or *less* command to
view the file /usr/share/doc/HTML/en/kdvi/aboutkde.ps on Red Hat Linux or
Fedora. Use the command *locate .ps* to see what other PostScript files are on
your system.

TIP

Most Linux distributions use a "super print filter" or **magic filter** that can convert documents into formats for many different printers. This makes it convenient to support hundreds of printers on Linux, but it doesn't generally allow Linux to use the specialized features of each printer. For example, if you have used expensive laser printers on Microsoft Windows systems, you have seen graphical configuration utilities that let you access and configure dozens of features for your particular printer. Few manufacturers are yet providing such tools for Linux (one exception from Hewlett-Packard is mentioned in the next section), though the Linux printing architecture makes it easy to use such tools when they appear.

Red Hat Linux and Fedora are both good examples of how most Linux distributions handle print filters. When you configure a print queue (as described in the next section), the configuration utility lets you select a printer from a list of supported devices. The printer model that you select is stored in the printer configuration file and used to direct the print filter.

The main print filter in Red Hat Linux and Fedora is a script called /usr/share/printconf/util/mf_wrapper. You can view this script in any text editor, but don't alter it! This script starts the *magicfilter-t* program with a parameter describing the printer for which output should be generated. To see some of the details behind *magicfilter-t*, enter this command:

```
$ magicfilter-t --dump
```

The *magicfilter-t* program (sometimes just called the magic filter) accepts many different printing options and produces output for many different printers. You see the list of printers that the magic filter supports as you configure a printer in the next section. The magic filter uses several other programs such as *gs*, *enscript*, and *nenscript*, to convert documents for various formats.

NOTE

Another popular tool that manages filtering for multiple printer models is foomatic. You can learn more about this program at *www.linuxprinting.org*.

Besides not having access to all printer features, using multiple interpreted programs to convert each print job to the appropriate page description language is much slower than a single dedicated program. Later in this section you learn about **PostScript Printer Description (PPD)** files, which are a great improvement on the print filter system described here, but which LPRng does not use.

12

In fact, for many of the printers you are likely to use, the manufacturer has created a filter or driver designed to take advantage of the specific features of that printer. For example, dozens of Lexmark printers are fully supported by special Linux drivers available from *www.lexmark. com*. From the Lexmark Web site you can download both the drivers and a user guide more than 100 pages long for UNIX and Linux printing. Hewlett-Packard has created a separate Web site for Linux-related printing solutions. See *http://hpinkjet.sourceforge.net* and *www. linuxprinting.org*, where you can read about efforts to improve Linux printing. HP has even created a basic graphical interface that lets you select which available features you want to apply to the job you are submitting. It isn't integrated with graphical applications, but it's certainly a step in the right direction.

With all this progress by the major printer manufacturers, you still must rely on the printing architecture described in this chapter. For example, the impressive user guide from Lexmark still describes how to set up a printer and print files using the same command-line and graphical tools described in the following sections.

Besides Lexmark and HP, several other groups are working on high-quality Linux printer drivers that you can use in place of the all-purpose magic filter. IBM has created a multipurpose printer driver called Omni; the GIMP graphical program has a graphically oriented driver that supports many printers. Some manufacturers (for example, Canon) have done nothing with Linux, but others, such as Epson, are making a strong effort without providing official support for Linux-related software. Visit *www.epkowa.co.jp/english/index_ e.html* and click the Linux link for unofficial drivers supporting several high-end Epson color printers. Additional information on Epson printers, with several useful links for Linux printing, is available at the unofficial site *www.epsondevelopers.com*. Finally, try Xwtools, a set of utilities that permit high-quality color printing on Epson, Canon, and some HP inkjet printers. See *xwtools.automatix.de/*.

Configuring Local Printer Definitions

When you install most Linux systems, the printing system is configured and running. All you need to do is define one or more printers before you can print documents. On some Linux systems, you configure a printer as you install the operating system.

Each LPRng printer definition is created as a print queue entry in the /etc/printcap configuration file. The **/etc/printcap** (printer capture) file uses a complex format that can include dozens of options for each print queue. For this reason, you rarely configure the printcap file manually (in a text editor). Instead, you use one of the graphical tools described later in this chapter to set it up.

To use a local printer—one connected to the parallel or serial port of your computer—you must provide the appropriate Linux device name when you configure the printer. Parallel ports use the device name lp (lp stands for line printer) followed by a device number; serial ports use the name ttyS followed by a device number. For example, if your printer were attached to the first parallel port of the Linux computer, you refer to device /dev/lp0. If your printer were attached to the third serial port, you refer to /dev/ttyS2.

The format of a printcap entry consists of a print queue name, followed by a series of 2-character option codes that apply to that printer. Each option is separated from the next by two colons. In the example file that follows, one of the colons is at the end of each line, and the second is at the beginning of the next line. Multiple options could be listed on a single line, so that you see two colons together; you see here a standard formatting method for this file. Many options are followed by specific parameters. For example, the parameter lp=/dev/lp0 specifies that the physical printer is connected to the first parallel port. For readability, each option is typically placed on a separate line of the file, with a backslash after each option to indicate that the line break should be ignored when processing the file. A basic printcap entry taken from Red Hat Linux is shown here:

```
local:\
     :ml#0:\
     :mx#0:\
     :sd=/var/spool/lpd/local:\
     :af=/var/spool/lpd/local/local.acct:\
     :sh:\
     :lp=/dev/lp0:\
     :lpd_bounce=true:\
     :if=/usr/share/printconf/util/mf_wrapper:
```

You learned in Chapter 3 how to create a basic printcap entry using the *printconf-gui* command in Red Hat Linux and Fedora. Other Linux distributions provide different graphical tools, such as Webmin or YAST. None of these graphical tools lets you set up all the possible options, but they will usually get you started printing right away.

Printing Remotely Using LPRng

When you defined a printer in Chapter 3, you created a "local" printer—one attached to your computer. You can also define a **remote printer** so that the *lpd* print server daemon sends print jobs to another computer instead of to a printer connected to your computer.

To do this, you define a printer on your system that refers to the remote computer and a print queue on the remote system. The *lpd* daemon on your computer communicates with the *lpd* program on the remote computer, transferring the print job. This arrangement is shown in Figure 12-12.

Once a print job has been sent to a remote system using *lpd*, you have no direct control over it. If you want to see the status of the print job, you must have permission to log in to the remote printer and use the printer management tools on that system.

Within the /etc/printcap file, a simple remote printer definition looks like this:

```
lp:\
    :sd=/var/spool/lpd/lp:\
    :mx#0:\
    :sh:\
    :rm=brighton.xmission.com:\
    :rp=lexmark:
```

12

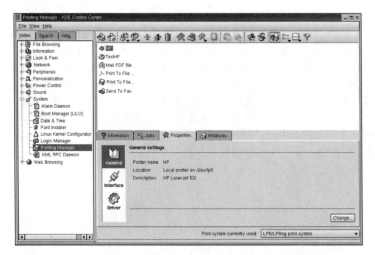

Figure 12-12   Printing to a remote printer using *lpd*

The key options to note here are *rm*, where the remote system is specified, and *rp*, where the remote print queue is specified.

Within the printconf-gui tool, you can select Networked UNIX (LPD) in the wizard where you define a printer. Then enter the remote system and queue name. See Figure 12-13.

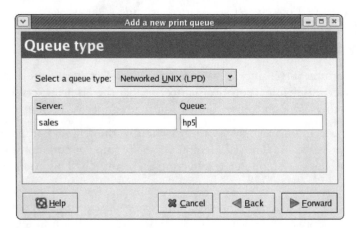

Figure 12-13   Configuring a remote printer in printconf-gui

The *lpd* daemon is configured by options in /etc/lpd.conf. Typically, *lpd* is not used in an environment where security is a big concern, because it is not considered highly secure. But you can set permissions for numerous *lpd* functions using /etc/lpd.perms. Both lpd.conf and lpd.perms have complete man pages describing *lpd* configuration options.

The *lpd* daemon is generally used only on Linux and UNIX systems, though it is available for other operating systems. Because of this limitation, you only use *lpd* when sharing a printer between two Linux or UNIX systems.

After you have defined a remote printer, you can print to the associated print queue just as you would a local printer. The *lpd* daemon takes care of submitting the print job to the remote computer.

Understanding the Common UNIX Printing System (CUPS)

The LPRng printing system and the *lpd* daemon have been used for many years. But they lack key features that system administrators like to have for a multiuser, network-capable printing system.

To understand what LPRng lacks, consider how some other operating systems manage printing. With Windows and NetWare systems, a user can "browse" the network to see what printers are available. Finding one that is appropriate, a user can send a print job directly to that printer, without first defining a local printer that refers to it. System administrators can use a single print management utility to see and control print jobs on multiple computers. And they can do this from anywhere on the network that has the appropriate utility installed, without needing additional user accounts on each system.

These are the capabilities that the **Common UNIX Printing System (CUPS)** provides to Linux and UNIX. CUPS is a fairly recent development. It provides a new architecture for Linux printing that lets users and system administrators browse the network to find and print to networked printers and other devices. It also lets system administrators manage printer definitions and print jobs across the network.

One of the less obvious problems with LPRng and other *lpd*-based printing systems has been that each UNIX vendor produced a slightly different version of the printing software. A system administrator who managed a network with several versions of UNIX and Linux systems faced numerous configuration obstacles to provide convenient printing services for users. Using CUPS overcomes this problem because the same architecture is available for all versions of UNIX and Linux.

CUPS is installed by default in Red Hat Linux and Fedora as a set of six software packages. The main print server daemon is *cupsd*, which is controlled by the cups script in /etc/rc.d/init.d. A number of configuration files are included in the /etc/cups subdirectory. You can use command-line utilities to interact with the CUPS server to submit print jobs or to manage the server. Many system administrators prefer to use the browser-based management interface described in this section.

12

You can learn more about CUPS at *www.cups.org*. CUPS implements a widely supported printing protocol called the Internet Printing Protocol (IPP), which you can learn about at *www.pwg.org/ipp*. An invaluable resource for information on all aspects of printing within Linux is *www.linuxprinting.org*, which has links to articles and other sites for CUPS, LPRng, numerous printer drivers and filters, and much more.

Configuring Printers within CUPS

The *cupsd* print server daemon operates much like a Web server. It uses the same HTTP protocol as Web servers and accepts requests and processes print jobs sent over the network. It also manages printers using a Web browser interface. This interface is configured by default in Red Hat Linux and Fedora. On other systems you might have to install the correct software packages and enable networking to use the CUPS features described here.

The CUPS architecture uses network port 631 to communicate between CUPS-enabled print servers. A **port** is like the address of an application on a networked computer. The *cupsd* daemon on one computer sends a message to the *cupsd* daemon on another computer by sending it to the predefined port address of 631, which you indicate by adding ":631" to the name of the CUPS server you want to contact.

You can start the CUPS user interface in Red Hat Linux or Fedora by starting a Web browser (for example, click on the "world" icon next to the main menu icon in GNOME to start Mozilla). Then enter this URL: *http://localhost:631/*. You see the main menu of the CUPS management utility, as shown in Figure 12-14.

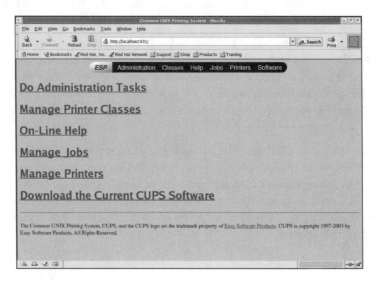

Figure 12-14 The main page of the CUPS browser-based interface

If you want to manage the printers or the print jobs on another system running CUPS anywhere on your network, you enter that system's name with the CUPS port, 631. For example, suppose you are working on host arizona and you want to manage CUPS on host colorado. You simply enter this URL in any browser: *http://colorado:631.*

 Before you can perform any management tasks, such as defining new printers, you should log in as root when prompted. This is true even when you are managing CUPS on your local system.

The *cupsd* program is configured in much the same way as the popular Apache Web server. The file /etc/cups/cupsd.conf contains directives that specify a setting for each active server option. Hundreds of comments in this file describe the current options, as well as options that are supported but not activated. For example, this file can configure CUPS to:

- Use a variety of authentication systems for determining which users can configure or manage printing.

- Use encryption techniques to protect your user and password information as you manage networked print servers.

- Manage how hosts can browse the network to see printers on each print server.

- Limit which hosts on the network can use certain printers.

To configure a new printer from the first page of the CUPS interface, choose the Manage Printers link or the Printers item on the bar across the top of the page. The page that appears shows any CUPS printers that you have already defined. These are taken from the /etc/printcap file, and CUPS generates a revised /etc/printcap file by default when you make changes using CUPS. (Printer information is also maintained in a separate file, /etc/cups/printers.conf.) To define a new printer (add a new printer definition, or print queue), click the Add Printer button. Enter the root user name and password when prompted. Then, on the pages that follow, enter printer information as you did for the printconf-gui and the KDE Control Center tools: you enter a name, a location, and a description; you select a device and a device URI for the printer; you select a make, model, and print filter. Once you have completed the definition, the printer you defined appears on the Printers page, as shown in Figure 12-15.

Behind the scenes in CUPS, many printers are configured using a PostScript Printer Description (PPD) file. Each PPD file describes the capabilities of a printer using a standardized language. By consulting the PPD file for a printer model, a graphical print configuration utility or a graphical application such as OpenOffice.org or GIMP can display all supported options for a specific printer. An appropriate graphical dialog box is built "on the fly" based on the information in the PPD file. By relying on PPD files, printer manufacturers can easily create a text-based configuration file that permits their printer to be graphically configured using standard utilities.

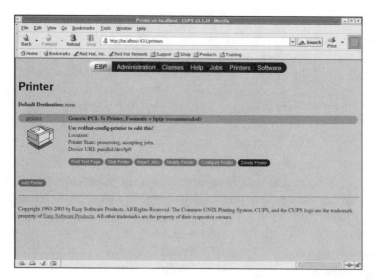

Figure 12-15　The Printers page in the CUPS browser-based interface

PPD files are sometimes available from printer manufacturers or from free software sites, in which case the PPD has been created by someone besides the printer manufacturer. Despite the name, PPD files are used for all types of printers, not just PostScript-capable printers.

In addition, some specialized programs can create a PPD file based on information taken from standard print filters. One example is the PPD-O-Matic program, which you can learn more about at *www.linuxprinting.org*.

As a system administrator, you should never need to explore the contents of a PPD file, though you may need to search for a PPD file to support a printer model that is not installed on your Linux system. You can also explore a PPD file to learn more about how they are constructed by viewing one of the files on your system. Red Hat Linux and Fedora each include over 1000 PPD files installed by default in /usr/share/cups/model. Most of the PPD files are located in subdirectories named for different manufacturers. You can view a sample file using this command:

```
$ zcat /usr/share/cups/model/laserjet.ppd.gz | less
```

Additional information about PPD files is available on the Linux Printing Web site at *www.linuxprinting.org/ppd-doc.html*.

NOTE

Setting up CUPS Classes

When many users share several printers, they may jockey for position, trying to get their print job completed quickly when another user is printing a very long document. Classes are a more elegant solution to this problem than the LPRng system shown in Figure 12-10. A

CUPS class is a group of printers to which a user can submit a print job. Whichever printer within the class is first available is used to print the job.

For example, suppose you manage the printing for a busy office that has three high-capacity laser printers that you have defined as lexmark1, lexmark2, and lexmark3. Without classes, users would try to guess which printer to send their print job to so it wouldn't have to wait for another long job to finish; polite users might send out a department-wide e-mail: "380 page job going to lexmark2." You decide to use CUPS and create a class called lexmarks that includes all three lexmark print queues. Now users send all print jobs to lexmarks. Each time any one of the three printers finishes a print job, CUPS sends the next print job to that printer. Users get the fastest possible service. In exchange, they have to check three different printers to see which one their print job came out on. (Printers within a class are typically located next to each other in an office.)

To create a class in CUPS, click the Classes button at the top of the CUPS page and then click the Add Class button on the Classes page. The page that appears lets you define a name, location, and description. You must include at least a name, such as "lexmarks." In a large department with many users or printers, it's also a good idea to enter a location and description, for example "Downstairs by Robin's Cube" and "Main dept. laser printers."

When you choose Continue, you see a listing of all printers defined within CUPS. You select all of the printers that should be included in the class you are defining. Then choose Continue. A confirmation page shows you that the class was successfully completed. If you return to the Classes page by clicking Classes at the top of the page, you see that your class is shown with most of the same options as a regular printer, except that the icon shows multiple printers, and many of the buttons differ. Figure 12-16 shows the Classes page.

12

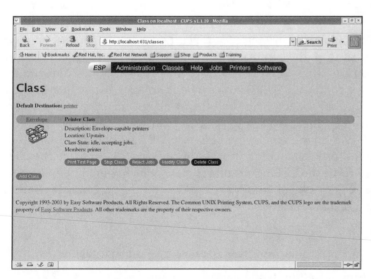

Figure 12-16   The Classes page within the CUPS configuration

Users can still send print jobs to an individual printer that is part of a class (such as lexmark2 in the previous example). But the class provides a more efficient method of distributing print jobs on a busy network with many users and more than one printer.

Managing Printing

You learned in Chapter 3 how to submit a print job from the command line. Printing from a graphical application is even easier: you typically select Print from the File menu and choose Print in the dialog box that appears.

Though submitting print jobs is easy, as a system administrator you are likely to spend a lot of time managing printing. Printers have many moving parts and are more subject to breakdowns than anything inside a computer. Printing also consumes resources such as paper and toner that must be replenished even when the system is working correctly. (Some companies have an employee designated to take care of these things who does not manage other aspects of printing.) For all of these reasons, many organizations establish a **printing policy**: a brief statement of rules describing how printing resources can be used and how printers should be managed.

Linux includes several utilities to help you manage printing resources. One of these is the *lpc* utility. This command-line utility lets you control LPRng or CUPS printing, specifying how print jobs are accepted and processed.

NOTE   Many Linux system administrators prefer to use one of the graphical utilities described later in this section instead of *lpc*.

Though it was not obvious in Chapter 3, Red Hat Linux and Fedora use an **alternatives printing system** that maps the command you enter to different programs based on which printing system you are using: LPRng or CUPS. You can view and configure this system using the *alternatives* command. The actual symbolic links are maintained in the directory /etc/alternatives. Both the *lpr* command and the *lpc* command are actually symbolic links. The *lpc* command, for example, is a link to /etc/alternatives/print-lpc, which in turn points to the appropriate control program for the LPR or CUPS printing system. In Fedora Core 2, the default control program referred to by this link is /usr/sbin/lpc.cups. The link is changed if you switch to the LPRng printing system, which would be unusual in Fedora because the newer CUPS system is the default. The control programs for both LPR and CUPS provide similar functionality, but act on different underlying systems..

Using *lpc* you can:

- Prevent new print jobs from being accepted by a print queue.
- Prevent print jobs from being sent to a printer.
- Cancel a print job that is currently being printed.

- See the status of any printer (such as whether it is enabled, whether the corresponding print queue contains any print jobs, or how much of the current document has been sent to the printer).

You must be logged in as the root user to use *lpc*. You can include an *lpc* command as a parameter on the command line. This command displays the status of the default printer:

```
# lpc status
```

You can also use *lpc* interactively to enter multiple commands. To begin using *lpc* in interactive mode, enter the utility name without any parameters:

```
# lpc
lpc>
```

Table 12-1 lists the commands that you can use at the *lpc* prompt or as parameters to the *lpc* command (if you prefer not to use the interactive mode for some tasks).

For each of the commands shown, *lpc* acts on the default printer (the first one listed in the printcap file) unless you specify a printer name. For example, if the first printer in printcap is hp, using this command brings down the hp printer:

```
# lpc down
```

If the printcap file contains a definition of another printer named stylus, you can use this command to bring down the stylus printer:

```
# lpc down stylus
```

Table 12-1   lpc Commands

Command	Description	Example (noninteractive mode)
help	Display a list of all *lpc* commands	lpc help
status	Display status of the lpd printer daemon and the print queue indicated (or the default if none is indicated)	lpc status
abort	Cancel the print job currently being printed (use the *start* command to restart printing)	lpc abort
stop	Stop sending print jobs to the printer after the current print job has finished printing	lpc stop
start	Start sending print jobs to the printer (used after *abort* or *stop*)	lpc start
disable	Prevent users from submitting new print jobs	lpc disable
enable	Allow users to submit new print jobs	lpc enable
down	Stop sending print jobs to the printer and prevent new print jobs from being submitted (equivalent to using *stop* and *disable*)	lpc down
up	Begin sending print jobs to the printer and allow new print jobs to be submitted (equivalent to using *start* and *enable*)	lpc up

12

Table 12-1   `lpc` Commands (continued)

Command	Description	Example (noninteractive mode)
exit or quit	Exit the *lpc* program	Used only in interactive mode
restart	Attempt to restart the lpd printer daemon (equivalent to using the command */etc/rc.d/ init.d/lpd restart*)	lpc restart
clean	Remove any temporary, data, or control files that could not be printed	lpc clean
topq	Move a print job to the top of the named print queue; this command requires a printer name (where the print job is placed) and the print job number (which you can obtain using the *lpq* command)	lpc topq hplj 16

When using any of the *lpc* commands (except *topq*), you can use *all* to refer to all printers. For example, to completely shut down printing, so that no print jobs can be submitted and all printing stops after the current print jobs are finished, use this command:

```
# lpc down all
```

NOTE
The *lpr* command you learned previously uses a *-P* parameter to define the printer name. For the *lpc* command you simply add the printer name as an additional parameter.

Figure 12-17 illustrates how some key *lpc* commands affect the printing process. The same terms you see in the figure are used in the *lpc* man page and in graphical print management tools.

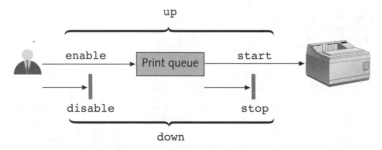

Figure 12-17   Using *lpc* to control the printing process

You can also use the *lpstat* command to see a quick summary of what each printer is doing.

Tracking Print Jobs

To view the print jobs in the default print queue, enter the command *lpq*. The **lpq** utility lists each of the print jobs in a print queue with the following information:

- Status of the print job, such as active (currently printing), ready, or error
- Owner (the user who submitted the print job)
- Class of the print job (its priority; normally A, unless the -C option is used with the *lpr* command)
- Job number assigned by the print server
- Size of the file in bytes (characters)
- Time that the print job was submitted

Any user can view the current print jobs using *lpq*. A sample *lpq* command is shown here:

```
$ lpq -P hplj
```

If you are working on a server where the print queue contains many documents, you may either want to use the -s option, to display a shorter format for each print job, or add a job ID to the *lpq* command. The job ID refers to the print job number assigned by the print server and displayed under the Job field in the sample *lpq* output above. To see a list of all print jobs submitted by user alexv, enter this command:

```
$ lpq alexv
```

If you have previously used *lpq* to identify the job number of a large print job, use that number to query the status of the job, as in this example:

```
$ lpq 572
```

You can delete print jobs from any print queue. If you are logged in as root, you can delete anyone's print jobs, or move a print job to another print queue or to the top of a print queue so that it is printed next. The **lprm** command deletes a print job from a queue. You need a job ID from *lpq* before you can use *lprm* to delete a specific print job. For example, if you decide after viewing the output of *lpq* that print job number 491 should be deleted before it is printed, use this command to remove it from the hplj print queue:

```
$ lprm -P hplj 491
```

You can remove all of a user's print jobs by referring to a user name. Each user can remove his or her own print jobs in this way; root can remove anyone's print jobs:

```
# lprm nwells
```

You can also remove all of the print jobs in a queue by using the - (hyphen) parameter:

```
# lprm -P hplj -
```

When you are using CUPS, the *cancel* command works just like the *lprm* command.

NOTE

Using Graphical Print Management Utilities

Instead of *lpc*, *lpq*, and *lprm*, you can choose System Tools, then Print Manager on the GNOME main menu. When the main window of the Print Manager appears, double-click the print queue that you want to manage. A dialog box listing all print jobs currently in that print queue appears. (See Figure 12-18.)

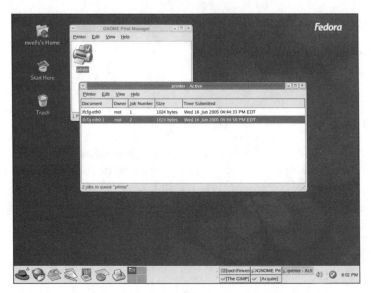

Figure 12-18 Managing print jobs in the GNOME Print Manager

Within that dialog box, you can review information about each print job and cancel any print job that is causing problems.

KDE also includes graphical utilities to manage printing. If KDE is installed, you can start the KDE Control Center (enter *kcontrol* at a command line), then open the Peripherals item on the left side of the Control Center, choose Printers, then choose the Jobs tab on the right side of the Control Center. (See Figure 12-19.) You can also use this section of the Control Center to configure print queues.

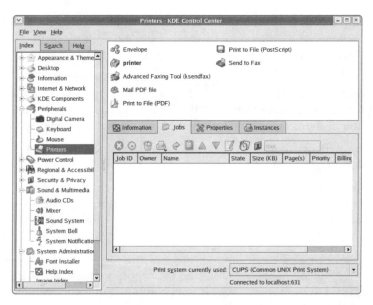

Figure 12-19   Managing print jobs in the KDE Control Center

When you are using CUPS for printing, you can manage print jobs in the same interface where you create and modify printer definitions. After starting a browser with the *localhost: 631* address, choose the Jobs link to view print jobs. You can use the options on that page to control each print job as needed.

The design of CUPS allows you to manage print jobs on any networked system where you have been granted permissions in the cups.conf configuration file. Compare this to *lpd*, for which you must have a shell account with root access to a system in order to manage print jobs, and then can probably only do so using command-line utilities.

CHAPTER SUMMARY

- Linux networking hardware differs from other devices—they are not available until an appropriate kernel module is installed in the kernel and configures the physical networking device.

- Each Ethernet card includes a unique MAC address. This address is used by the Address Resolution Protocol to permit a computer to locate other computers and routers on the same part of the network.

- The *ifconfig* command is used to configure a networking interface in the Linux kernel. Other scripts are also used to start or stop network devices when sufficient details are included in system configuration files. These scripts include *ifup*, *ifdown*, and the network script in /etc/rc.d/init.d.

❑ The *route* command modifies the internal routing table, which instructs the Linux kernel how to process packets that a computer receives that are not intended for that system. IP forwarding must be enabled for Linux to route packets between two network interfaces (and thus between two networks).

❑ Each Ethernet card can be assigned multiple IP addresses for purposes such as hosting multiple Web sites on one system. This is called IP aliasing and can be done manually using configuration files or graphically using system-config-network or other utilities.

❑ The system-config-network utility is one example of the graphical tools provided in each version of Linux to help you easily configure networking devices.

❑ The DNS resolver is configured using /etc/resolv.conf. Resolution of names is also controlled by /etc/host.conf and /etc/nsswitch, which determine where the resolver looks for name resolution, either the local /etc/hosts file, a configured DNS server, or other modes such as NIS+.

❑ The *route* command provides static routing. Routing protocols are also supported by Linux in order to provide dynamically changing routing information for large, complex networks. RIP, OSPF, and BGP and three examples of routing protocols. All are supported in Linux by the *routed* or *gated* daemons.

❑ Setting up a DHCP server on Linux requires configuring the /etc/dhcpd.conf file with IP addresses that can be assigned and a few other basic parameters. Having a Windows system use Linux as its DHCP server requires an additional *route* command to compensate for Windows' nonstandard DHCP.

❑ Linux printing relies on printer definitions, usually called print queues. Print jobs are submitted to these queues and are stored in directories until a print server sends the print job to a physical printer. In UNIX printing, multiple users can print to multiple printers either locally or across a network.

❑ Traditionally, UNIX used a printing system called LPRng and a print server daemon called *lpd*. This system uses commands such as *lpr*, *lpc*, *lprm*, and *lpq* to manage printing.

❑ A newer UNIX printing system called CUPS permits much easier network-wide management of both printers and print jobs without having separate user accounts on many systems. CUPS uses a Web browser interface to manage printing.

❑ Red Hat Linux and Fedora support both LPRng and CUPS printing using an alternatives printing system. Standard printing commands use symbolic links to refer to either LPRng or CUPS underlying commands based on the configuration tools used to set up printing.

❑ Printing in UNIX relies on print filters and printer description files to simplify the task of supporting thousands of diverse printer models. Manufacturers are just starting to provide strong support for Linux printing.

❑ Print jobs can be managed using the command line, with utilities such as *lpc*, *lpstat*, *lpq*, and *lprm*. Graphical utilities are also very useful. These include the GNOME Print Manager and the KDE Control Center.

COMMAND SUMMARY

Command	Description	Example
alternatives	Configure or view symbolic links to select among alternative printing or mail server systems	alternatives --config print
arp	Displays the internal cache of MAC-to-IP address mappings that was creating using the Address Resolution Protocol	arp
cancel	Removes (deletes) a pending print job from a print queue when using CUPS printing	cancel -P hplj 491
cupsd	Daemon that controls printing in the CUPS printing system; similar to the lpd daemon in LPRng printing	cupsd
gated	Gateway daemon used for complex routing; Supports the OSPF and BGP routing protocols (as well as the older RIP protocol)	gated
ifconfig	Displays currently configured network interfaces or configures new network interfaces	ifconfig
ifdown	Script used to stop a named network interface. Located in /etc/sysconfig/network-scripts	ifdown eth0
ifup	Script used to start a named network interface; Located in /etc/sysconfig/network-scripts	ifup eth0
lpc	Manages LPRng-based printing, showing status, permitting or stopping queue submission and physical printing, and performing other printing-related tasks; Table 12-1 shows *lpc* options	lpc status
lpq	Displays the print jobs in one or more print queues; the status of a single print job number, of all jobs submitted by a named user, or all print jobs in one or all print queues can be displayed	lpq -P hplj
lprm	Removes (deletes) a pending print job from a print queue; a single print job number, all jobs from a named user, or all print jobs in a named print queue can be deleted	lprm -P hplj 491
lpstat	Displays the current status of a print queue	lpstat

12

Command	Description	Example
route	Displays the kernel's routing table or modifies that table by adding or removing a network route	route add -net 192.168.100.0 netmask 255.255.255.0 dev eth0
routed	Daemon for basic network routing using the RIP protocol	routed

Key Terms

/etc/dhcpd.conf — Configuration file used to define the operation of the DHCP server daemon, dhcpd.

/etc/host.conf — Configuration file that specifies the order in which the resolver should consult resources to resolve the host name to an IP address. Not used in many Linux systems because /etc/nsswitch.conf is used instead.

/etc/hosts — Configuration file that stores IP addresses and corresponding domain names for hosts, usually those frequently accessed on a local network.

/etc/printcap — Configuration file that defines print queues, specifically used for the LPRng printing system.

/etc/resolv.conf — Configuration file that configures the Linux resolver by listing the computer's domain and the IP address of one or more DNS name servers.

Address Resolution Protocol (ARP) — A protocol that broadcasts a message to an entire network segment in order to obtain a host's MAC address, or, if the MAC address is known, to obtain a host's IP address.

alternatives printing system — A method used in Red Hat Linux and Fedora to permit both LPRng and CUPS printing systems to reside on the same Linux system using symbolic links for commonly used printing commands.

ARP cache — A list of IP address-to-hardware mappings maintained by the ARP protocol to assist in routing packets. Viewed using the *arp* command.

BOOTP — A protocol used by diskless computers to obtain configuration information. Rarely used now, but similar to DHCP, which is backwards compatible with BOOTP.

Border Gateway Protocol (BGP) — A widely used external routing protocol.

broadcast address — An IP address that a computer on a network can use to send a packet to all computers on that network.

Common UNIX Printing System (CUPS) — A printing system that permits browser-based configuration and print management. Intended to eventually replace the LPRng printing system.

dynamic routing — Collecting and updating routing table information automatically using a routing protocol such as RIP, OSPF, or BGP.

exterior routing protocols — Routing protocols designed for routing packets between networks controlled by different organizations; packets are routed based on administrative policies, often controlled by how much a particular organization's routing information is trusted.

interior routing protocols — Routing protocols designed for routing packets among networks controlled by a single organization; packets are routed based on mathematical models.

IP aliasing — A networking feature that allows a single physical interface to have more than one IP address assigned to it.

IP forwarding — A feature of Linux networking, required to act as a router, that instructs the Linux kernel to send network packets out on whichever network interface the routing tables dictate. Without IP forwarding, packets arriving on a given network interface can only be sent out on the same interface.

kernel modules — Small programs that are part of the Linux kernel but that can be added or removed independently of other parts of the kernel. Used for device drivers, network support, file system support, and other kernel features.

lease — The action a DHCP server takes in assigning an IP address to a client for a specific length of time.

LPRng — The traditional Linux printing system, based on the BSD version of UNIX.

magic filter — A program that can convert documents being printed into any of several formats for printing on a specific printer model.

maximum transmission unit (MTU) — The maximum size of a packet that a given network interface can transmit or receive.

Media Access Control (MAC) address — A unique hardware address assigned to each Ethernet card. Used in the process of routing packets. Obtained using the Address Resolution Protocol (ARP).

Open Shortest Path First (OSPF) — An interior routing protocol designed to work effectively even in very large networks.

packet — A set of data that is transmitted by the network, defined by the parameters of a particular protocol such as Ethernet or IP.

page description language — A special set of codes that determine the graphics elements, text font, and everything else about how information appears on a printed page. PostScript and PCL are examples of page description languages.

port — A networking parameter that permits one application to communicate with a specific application on a networked computer.

PostScript Printer Description (PPD) — A file containing a standardized printer description that can be used by several printing architectures on different operating systems. PPD files are used to describe many types of printers, not just PostScript printers.

print filter — A script that contains instructions for formatting documents using the page description language required by a specific printer. The print filter is used by the *lpr* program to prepare files to be sent to a physical printer.

print job — A file submitted for printing via the *lpr* command or a graphical dialog box.

print queue — A printer definition; also a subdirectory where files are stored to wait for a print server daemon (such as *lpd*) to retrieve them one by one and send them to the printer. Also called a print spool directory.

print spool directory — The directory where print jobs submitted to a print queue are stored until they are sent to a printer.

12

printing policy — A brief document that describes how printing resources can be used and how they should be managed within an organization.

remote printer — A printer attached to another computer on the network or to the network itself, rather than to the computer on which you are working.

resolver — The client portion of DNS, which makes requests to a DNS server so that other programs on a host can use the IP address of a named server to make a network connection.

resolving — The process of converting a domain name to an IP address, or vice versa.

reverse DNS — A method of using DNS in which a client sends an IP address to a DNS server and requests the corresponding domain name.

routing daemon — A program that automatically generates routing table entries based on information received over the network via protocols dedicated to transmitting routing information.

Routing Information Protocol (RIP) — An interior routing protocol; the oldest routing protocol still in common use.

routing table — A listing within a router containing the information needed to send packets to another network when they are not destined for the network in which they originated.

static routing — Assembling a routing table via entries in start-up scripts or by manually entered route commands.

Webmin — A browser-based configuration utility that can be installed on any version of Linux and is included by default with some versions.

YAST2 — A configuration utility provided in SUSE Linux.

REVIEW QUESTIONS

1. The purpose of a routing protocol is to:

    a. Route packets across multiple network segments.

    b. Facilitate the exchange of routing table entries among routers.

    c. Make static routing easier to configure on multiple hosts.

    d. Avoid the need to use DNS in larger networks.

2. Forwarding packets refers to:

    a. transferring them from the segment on which they originate to a different segment to which they are addressed

    b. storing packets in a router until they are requested by the destination host

    c. caching packet IDs using a routing protocol

    d. configuring an Ethernet card to handle multiple network data types on the same local network segment

3. Each Ethernet card has a number assigned to it by the manufacturer that is called the:

   a. NIC Header checksum

   b. Ethernet cyclic redundancy check

   c. Data Link protocol

   d. Media Access Control (MAC) address

4. Name services such as DNS are used to:

   a. Translate between human readable domain names and IP addresses.

   b. Translate headers between levels of the network architecture.

   c. Assign packet numbers to each network session initiated by an application.

   d. Locate services available on the Internet.

5. A default route is normally defined at the same time Linux networking is configured on any host. This allows Linux to:

   a. Accumulate routing table information passed on by a routing protocol such as RIP.

   b. Avoid duplicate packets being sent to the local segment and to the correct remote segment.

   c. Respond automatically to ISP requests for routing information.

   d. Send packets addressed to other segments to the "gateway" out of the local segment.

6. If an IP stack does not have the MAC address of the system it needs to communicate with, it must:

   a. Send the packet in question to the default router, which has the MAC address for the system.

   b. Consult the routing engine tables to obtain the correct IP address, which includes the MAC address as well.

   c. Use DNS to obtain the MAC address.

   d. Use ARP to obtain the MAC address directly, caching it for future communications with the same remote system.

7. Ports are used to:

   a. Attach security information to IP packets.

   b. Autoconfigure network protocol information.

   c. Identify a remote host by specific Ethernet hardware address.

   d. Provide an application-to-application path for network packets.

12

8. The Linux resolver:

   a. resolves a host or domain name to an IP address and vice versa

   b. resolves conflicts between multiple IP addresses on the same host

   c. resolves contention between multiple Ethernet cards in the same computer

   d. resolves authorization issues for X clients

9. Which is not a valid configuration file mentioned in this chapter?

   a. /etc/host.conf

   b. /etc/nsswitch

   c. /etc/resolve.conf

   d. /etc/hosts

10. The /etc/hosts file is checked before contacting a DNS server only if:

    a. The /etc/host.conf or /etc/nsswitch file says to use /etc/hosts first.

    b. A DNS server cannot be contacted.

    c. The search keyword in /etc/resolv.conf indicates a local domain name.

    d. A graphical tool was used to configure both /etc/resolv.conf and /etc/hosts.

11. Networking devices differ from other Linux devices in that:

    a. Networking devices use a different set of major and minor device numbers than devices that do not rely on kernel modules.

    b. Networking devices can transmit data much faster than other types of devices.

    c. Networking devices are not directly visible in the /dev subdirectory but are created on the fly when a networking device module is loaded into the kernel.

    d. Networking devices can only be accessed via shell scripts.

12. Which is not a valid *ifconfig* command?

    a. *ifconfig eth0 up*

    b. *ifconfig eth0 192.168.100.1 netmask 255.255.255.0 broadcast 255.255.255.0*

    c. *ifconfig*

    d. *ifconfig eth0 ifup*

13. Which information field is not part of the output of the *route* command?

    a. the gateway to reach the specified network

    b. the MAC address of the interface used to transfer packets to the specified network

    c. the interface through which the specified network can be reached

    d. the network address to which each routing table entry applies

14. Which statement is true about the following command:

    route add -net 192.168.20.0 netmask 255.255.255.0 gw 192.168.
    10.1 dev eth0.

    a. It is valid and defines the router that can reach network 192.168.20.0.

    b. It is valid and defines a default gateway for all traffic not destined for network 192.168.20.0.

    c. It is invalid because it does not specify the host IP address of the source of the packets to be routed.

    d. It is invalid in format because it lacks needed dashes before command-line options.

15. You would use the *arp* command to:

    a. Send a hardware address to a remote host per an ARP protocol request.

    b. Turn on and off ARP functionality for your network.

    c. Collect host name-to-IP address mappings for each of the hosts on your local network.

    d. View or modify the ARP cache containing hardware address to IP address mappings.

16. A correct device designation for an IP alias to the first Ethernet card is:

    a. eth00

    b. eth0:1

    c. Ethernet II

    d. eth1:0

17. IP forwarding is enabled by the following command:

    a. ifconfig eth0 ip_forward

    b. arp ip_forward

    c. route add default ip_forward -net 192.168.10.0 netmask 255.255.255.0

    d. echo 1 > /proc/sys/net/ipv4/ip_forward

18. Each time a user prints a file, a _____ is created.

    a. printer definition

    b. print queue

    c. print job

    d. printer instance

19. The two print server daemons described in this chapter are:

    a. lpd and cupsd

    b. printconf-gui and the KDE Control Center

    c. lpstat and lpc

    d. LPRng and CUPS

12

20. Printer definitions, or print queue definitions, are stored in which file?

    a. /var/spool/lpd/lp

    b. /var/adm/acct

    c. /etc/printcap

    d. /etc/lpd.conf

21. The graphical utility provided in Red Hat Linux and Fedora to configure a printer definition is:

    a. printconf-gui

    b. lpc

    c. cupsd

    d. lpoptions

22. Print filters are used to:

    a. Convert graphics formats before printing images.

    b. Prepare documents in a printer-specific format.

    c. Remove unprintable characters from documents.

    d. Compress print job files before transfer to a remote print server.

23. Multiple options in the printcap file are separated by:

    a. an equals sign

    b. two colons

    c. a carriage return/new line

    d. a tab

24. The CUPS printing architecture *does not* allow system administrators to:

    a. Use the same printing system on diverse UNIX and Linux systems.

    b. Check the status of print jobs on a remote server using a browser-based interface.

    c. Use multiple instances of a printer that include specific sets of printing options.

    d. Graphically configure features specific to one model of printer, such as duplex printing or dots-per-inch settings.

25. Explain the difference between the *lpc* commands *up*, *enable*, and *start*.

26. CUPS management is accomplished:

    a. by contacting a Web server-type server using port 631

    b. by using a browser to reach *linuxprinting.org*

    c. by using port 631 of printconf-gui or the KDE Control Center

    d. by using any standard Web server on a system with *cupsd* and the appropriate PPD files installed

27. The _____ utility displays the owner, size, and submission time for print jobs.

    a. *lpq*

    b. *lprm*

    c. *lpc*

    d. *lpd*

28. A CUPS class lets you:

    a. Aggregate print jobs for multiple printers using a single name for increased end-user convenience.

    b. Specify options that apply to a printer definition when you indicate the class name as the selected printer.

    c. Specify the features that a printer model supports, such as duplex printing, color printing options, scaling, or multiple paper trays.

    d. Control print jobs that were submitted to a remote printer.

29. Which *lpc* command stops the printing of the current print job?

    a. *lpc abort*

    b. *lpc cancel*

    c. *lpc stop*

    d. *lpc disable*

30. Describe how both LPRng and CUPS can be supported by the same commands such as *lpr* and *lpq*.

12

HANDS-ON PROJECTS

HANDS-ON PROJECTS

Project 12-1

In this project, you explore the Address Resolution Protocol (ARP). To complete this project, you should have a network connection configured with at least one other host on the network. An Internet connection is used for the last part of the project but is not strictly necessary.

1. Log in to Linux and open a command-line window. Change to root access using the **su –** command.

2. Enter the command **arp –a** to display the contents of the ARP cache on your Linux system. The result may be nothing—the cache is probably empty at this point if you have not done any networking in the last few minutes. Each entry is saved only for about two minutes.

3. If the ARP cache is not empty, note the contents carefully. See if you can identify a neighbor on the network (in your computer lab, for example) that is not listed in the output of the command. Obtain that neighbor's IP address.

4. Ping your neighbor using a command such as this (substitute the neighbor's IP address for 192.168.100.45):

   ```
   ping 192.168.100.45
   ```

5. Press **Ctrl+c** to exit the *ping* command. Run the *arp* command a second time:

   ```
   arp -a
   ```

   You should see your neighbor's system listed (as indicated by an IP address that you recognize).

6. Ping an Internet site such as 155.99.1.2 or 192.20.4.70. Press **Ctrl+c** to exit the *ping* command.

7. Run **arp –a** again. Why is no additional entry included for the new site that you pinged? Close all windows and log off.

HANDS-ON PROJECTS

Project 12-2

In this project, you create an IP alias by adding a second IP address to your Ethernet card. To complete this project, you must be connected to an Ethernet network using a static IP address (not DHCP) and have been assigned a second IP address for this project by your instructor or system administrator. You must be logged in as root to complete this project.

1. Log in to Linux and open a command-line window.

2. Enter **su –** to change to root access.

3. Enter **ifconfig** without any parameters to see that you have a correctly configured Ethernet (eth0) interface.

4. Change to the directory /etc/sysconfig/networking/devices using this command:

   ```
   cd /etc/sysconfig/network-scripts
   ```

5. Copy the configuration file for the eth0 interface as a basis for creating a new interface called eth0:1, which will be an IP alias to the same physical Ethernet card:

   ```
   cp ifcfg-eth0 ifcfg-eth0:1
   ```

6. Open the file ifcfg-eth0:0 in a text editor:

   ```
   vi ifcfg-eth0:1
   ```

7. Change the **DEVICE** parameter from eth0 to read **eth0:1**.

8. Change the **IPADDR** parameter to reflect the new IP address provided by your instructor. Remember, if you simply choose a random IP address, you may cause networking problems for others in your lab or on the Internet.

9. Save your changes to the ifcfg-eth0:1 file and exit the text editor.

10. Create a link from the new device definition you created in each of the networking configuration directories where the network management scripts expect to find them. Enter these two commands while still working in the /etc/sysconfig/network-scripts directory:

```
ln ifcfg-eth0:1 ../networking/device/
ln ifcfg-eth0:1 ../networking/profiles/default
```

11. Restart networking by entering **service network restart**.

12. Run the **ifconfig | less** command. Notice that you now have a new, third interface: eth0:1.

13. Ping the IP address of your eth0 interface. Ping the IP address of your eth0:1 interface. You could now use these independent interfaces to set up two separate Web sites or FTP servers on the same computer.

14. Delete the three files you created, confirming the deletion if prompted (these commands assume you are still working in the /etc/sysconfig/network-scripts directory):

```
rm ifcfg-eth0:1
rm ../networking/device/ifcfg-eth0:1
rm ../networking/profiles/default/ifcfg-eth0:1
```

15. Restart networking again: **service network restart**

16. Run the **ifconfig** command to verify that you once again have only two networking devices: lo and eth0. Close all windows and log off.

HANDS-ON PROJECTS

Project 12-3

In this project, you use the *ping* command to explore how the Linux resolver operates in conjunction with the configuration files you learned about in this chapter. To complete this project, you need Internet access and access to the root account on your Linux system. For each of the *ping* commands described in this project, you only need to let two or three response lines appear to verify that the command works, then press Ctrl+c to interrupt *ping* and continue with the next step.

1. Log in to Linux and open a command-line window.

2. Enter **su –** to change to root access.

3. Choose a site that allows you to ping it and execute the *ping* command to see that it is alive. We've used the University of Utah (one of the Internet's foundational members) as an example:

```
ping www.utah.edu
```

4. As the ping packets are returned, note how the domain name and a corresponding IP address for the site are shown on each line. Write down the IP address.

5. Press **Ctrl+c** to exit the *ping* command. Open the **/etc/hosts** file in a text editor and add a line like this one to the end of the file. Then save the file and close the text editor. (Use the domain name and IP address that you selected for Steps 3 and 4 if you prefer.)

   `155.99.1.2 www.utah.edu`

6. Ping the same site again. This time the IP address is taken from the /etc/hosts file instead of DNS. Do you know why?

   `ping www.utah.edu`

7. Press **Ctrl+c** to exit the *ping* command. Open **/etc/hosts** again and change the IP address that you entered in Step 5 so that it is incorrect. Save the file and close the text editor. For example, change the line to read like this:

   `155.99.255.255 www.utah.edu`

8. Ping the site a third time. This time is doesn't work; the /etc/hosts file is referenced instead of a DNS server, but the information in the /etc/hosts file is incorrect, so the server cannot be contacted.

9. Open **/etc/hosts** a final time and delete the line that you added. Save the file and close the text editor.

10. Ping the site a final time. Because a reference to the site is not included in /etc/hosts, the resolver must contact a DNS server to obtain an IP address, so ping works correctly again.

    `ping www.utah.edu`

11. Press **Ctrl+c** to exit the *ping* command. Close all windows and log off.

HANDS-ON PROJECTS

Project 12-4

In this project, you create a new print queue using a graphical utility and review how it affects the text configuration files. To complete this project, you need root access to a Red Hat Linux or Fedora system.

1. Log in to Linux and open a command-line window.

2. Enter **su –** to change to root access.

3. Start the **printconf-gui** program at the command line, or choose **System Settings**, then **Printing** on the GNOME main menu.

4. When the utility appears, note whether any local printers have been configured (perhaps from Chapter 3, if you have not reinstalled Linux since completing that chapter.) If a local printer is defined, delete it:

   a. Select the printer by clicking on it.

   b. Choose the **Delete** button.

   c. Choose **Quit** on the **Action** menu of the utility.

   d. Choose **Save** when prompted to save your changes.

   e. After the utility exits, restart it as you did in Step 3.

5. Click the **New** button to begin creating a new printer definition. The Add a new print queue window appears.

6. Click **Forward** to continue. The Queue name window appears.

7. Enter **lex** in the Name field, and enter **Project 12–4 test** in the Short description field.

8. Click **Forward** to continue. The Queue type window appears.

9. Make certain that **Locally-connected** is selected (it is the default) in the Select a queue type field.

10. Select a device from the list shown. You normally see /dev/lp0 and can choose this device. You could also click Custom Device and enter a specific device name, such as /dev/ttyS1 for the second serial port, but you will not be printing using this queue, so the device you select is not important.

11. Click **Forward** to continue. The Printer model window appears.

12. A drop-down list indicates Generic (click to select manufacturer). Click the arrow to the right of that label and select **Lexmark**.

13. The list of supported Lexmark printer models appears. Scroll down and then click on **5700**. Then click **Forward** to continue.

14. The window appears that is titled Finish, and create the new print queue. Click **Finish** to complete the printer definition.

15. A message box appears asking if you want to print a test page. Click **No**. The printer you defined is now listed in the main window of printconf-gui.

16. Click on **lex** in the main window of printconf-gui.

17. Click the **Edit** button to open the Edit a print queue dialog box.

18. Click the **Driver options** tab. After a moment, a list of options for this printer appears. These options are taken from the lex5700 Linux driver provided by Lexmark and included with Red Hat Linux and Fedora.

19. Set the Resolution to **1200x1200 dpi**.

20. Review the other tabs in the dialog box to learn what options are available.

21. Choose **OK** to close the Edit a print queue dialog box.

22. Choose **Quit** on the **Action** menu of printconf-gui.

23. When prompted, choose **Save** to save the changes you made. After a moment, the utility closes.

24. Open a command-line window if one is not already open.

12

25. View the /etc/printcap file:

    ```
    less /etc/printcap
    ```

    Can you see the lex print queue that you created? Note that this file includes a comment that refers you to the /etc/cups/printers.conf file, because CUPS is the newer, preferred printing system.

26. Press **q** to exit the *less* command. Review the contents of the other configuration file: **less /etc/cups/printers.conf**. Scroll to the bottom of that file and review the <DefaultPrinter lex> section.

27. Press **q** to exit the *less* command. Close all windows and log out.

Project 12-5

In this project, you create a remote print queue to access the print queue you created in Project 12-4. To complete this project you need a working Red Hat Linux or Fedora system with root access. In this project you should work as a team with another person working on a second computer. You should have completed Project 12-4 on one computer (referred to in this project as the server) and have another computer as well (referred to in this project as the client). Both systems must have networking correctly configured.

1. Log in to Linux on the server and open a command-line window.

2. Enter **su –** to change to root access.

3. On the server computer, display the host name of the computer:

    ```
    echo $HOSTNAME
    ```

    Note the output from this command.

4. Log in to the client computer, open a command-line window, and enter **su –** to change to root access.

5. On the client computer, enter **printconf-gui**.

6. Click **New** to begin defining a new print queue. The Add a new print queue window appears.

7. Click **Forward** to continue. The Queue name window appears.

8. Enter **remote-lex** in the Name field, and then enter **Project 12-5 test** in the Short description field.

9. Click **Forward** to continue. The Queue type window appears.

10. Select **Networked CUPS (IPP)** in the Select a queue type field.

11. In the Server field, enter the host name of the server computer that you determined in Step 3 of this project.

12. In the Path field, enter **/printers/lex**, to refer to the print queue that you defined on the server computer in Project 12-4.

13. Click **Forward** to continue. The Printer model window appears.

14. A drop-down list indicates Generic (click to select manufacturer). Click the arrow to the right of that label and select **Lexmark**.

15. The list of supported Lexmark printer models appears. Scroll down, click **5700**, then click **Forward** to continue.

16. The window appears that is titled Finish, and create the new print queue. Click **Finish** to complete the printer definition.

17. A message box appears asking if you want to print a test page. Click **No**. The remote-lex printer definition that you created is now listed in the main window of printconf-gui.

18. Choose **Quit** on the **Action** menu of printconf-gui.

19. When prompted, choose **Save** to save the changes you made. After a moment, the utility closes.

20. Still working on the client computer, print a file to the remote print queue that you just defined:

```
lpr -P remote-lex /etc/termcap
```

21. On the client computer, review the contents of your print queues using the command **lpc status**. Note in the output that the remote-lex print queue has no print jobs. Unless a networking problem occurred, the print job has already been sent to the server and is no longer associated with anything on the client system.

22. On the server computer, start the GNOME print manager by selecting **System Tools**, then **Print Manager** on the GNOME main menu.

23. When the utility opens, double-click on the **lex** printer icon. A separate dialog box appears that lists print jobs in that print queue. Note that the print job you submitted from the client is listed.

24. Click **Printer**, **Close** in the dialog box.

25. Click **Printer**, **Quit** to exit the GNOME Print Manager.

26. Still working on the server, review the contents of your print queues:

```
lpc status
```

Note that the lex print queue contains one print job.

27. Remove all print jobs on the server computer:

```
lprm -P lex
```

28. Close all windows on both client and server and log off.

12

CASE PROJECTS

Networking and Printing

You have been hired as a consultant by the law firm of Snow, Sleet, and Hale, based in Fairbanks, Alaska. The firm has been in business for many years, but is just now realizing the need to upgrade its information technology infrastructure. The firm consists of three offices, two in Fairbanks and one in Juneau. The Fairbanks headquarters is the largest, with 40 attorneys plus support staff of paralegals, secretaries, librarians, and others. They are divided into two practice groups, one for environmental work and another for energy work relating to oil, natural gas, hydrothermal, and hydroelectric. The work of the two groups doesn't intermingle much, though the attorneys from the two groups occasionally have a common client. All staff members share e-mail, of course, and occasionally need to access the same files. A second Fairbanks office is located about two miles away from headquarters. It consists of 10 lawyers who also do energy work, almost exclusively for a large company that occupies the same building. The Juneau office is relatively new and focuses on government-related work at the state capitol. It consists of seven lawyers and a few support staff. The firm is doing well, with very little employee turnover. Because of the static nature of the network information, you are considering taking some steps to reduce the burden on their system administrator.

1. Would you consider relying on an /etc/hosts file instead of a DNS server for the firm? For just one office? What are the costs and benefits of doing this?

2. Would you consider using DHCP instead of assigning IP addresses statically? Would you do this throughout the firm? If so, would you use a separate DHCP server in each office? What are the trade-offs you must consider in deciding this?

3. The law firm is preparing a court case involving a number of exhibits—presentations that they will make before a jury in court. They want these to look as good as possible. You want to make Linux look as good as possible. To help further both ends, use the Web resources described in the chapter text to locate the highest-end color printer that has good Linux support. What features make you select one model over another? What level of Linux support can you find for high-end color printers?

4. You select two very nice color printers and install them for the law firm. The management team is very happy with the results, but they call you a month later with a concern: they are spending a small fortune on supplies for the new printers. They have created a set of rules for employees that limits printing, but they want you to make the rules effective. Review the documentation for LPRng and for CUPS (check in /usr/share/doc/cups-1.1.20). Determine what methods are available to track printer usage in each system and write a one-page report on what kind of system and policy you think might be appropriate. Note any technical aspects that you feel should be highlighted to implement your plan. (*Hint*: This type of tracking is typically called print accounting, so you might search on that term in the documentation.)

13

SYSTEM AND KERNEL MANAGEMENT

After reading this chapter and completing the exercises, you will be able to:

♦ Establish a Linux backup strategy

♦ Configure and review system log files

♦ Understand the use of kernel modules and the features of a high-end kernel

♦ Upgrade and recompile the Linux kernel

In the previous chapter you learned about configuring network devices using both command-line utilities and graphical utilities that make basic configuration tasks simpler. You also learned about setting up a DHCP server to provide IP address and related information to other computers on your network. Finally, you learned about setting up and managing complex printing services that included networked printers using both the traditional and more recent printing systems supported by Linux.

In this chapter, you learn about establishing a Linux backup strategy to protect system data from unforeseen problems. You also learn how Linux system logs are configured and how to understand the information in those logs. The Linux kernel is the final topic of the chapter. You learn about using kernel modules to add features to a running kernel, and about viewing or modifying kernel information by using the /proc file system, either directly or using command-line utilities. You also learn about several methods you can use to modify your kernel, should this be necessary, by modifying source code and using configuration utilities before compiling the source code to create a new kernel.

Backing Up a Linux System

A **backup** is simply a copy of data on a computer system. Making a backup of critical data is a form of insurance. A system administrator takes on extra expense and effort to back up data with the understanding that systems sometimes fail; the small, regularly occurring cost of backups is better than the exorbitant, when-you-least-expect-it cost of a system failure that wipes out your data.

Designing a Backup Strategy

Backing up thousands of files owned by dozens or hundreds of users can be a complex process. A **backup plan** is a written document that outlines when, how, and perhaps even why various files are backed up, stored, and—when necessary—restored. As you might guess, implementing the backup plan normally falls to the system administrator.

NOTE   The information described in this section as part of a backup plan is often included in broader plans made by an organization, such as a security plan or a disaster plan. The name of the plan is much less important than having steps and rationale written down and then implemented.

Among other things, a backup plan normally specifies the type of backup media that the organization uses. **Backup media** is the item that holds backed-up data, such as a tape cartridge, writeable CD or DVD, or even a 3.5-inch disk. The backup plan also specifies how lost data can be restored. To **restore** data is to copy it from backup media (for example, a tape cartridge) back to the file system where that data is normally used, and from which it was lost.

Developing a backup strategy that works well for your organization is an ongoing process. As a system administrator, you can expect to work with many types of computer systems, a variety of applications and data storage needs, and computer users whose preferences and actions are rarely predictable. This section addresses some of the questions that you should consider when formulating a backup plan.

Consider some of these questions as you formulate a backup plan:

- *What files should be backed up?* Backing up everything on the system is an admirable goal, but time and cost restrictions might make it impractical. You should evaluate the various parts of your system to determine what data is easily restored from a vendor CD, such as the operating system or an application. If you are short on resources, these items can be re-created (and then reconfigured) from their original sources rather than from a backup that you create.

- *Who will back up files?* As mentioned previously, this task normally falls to the system administrator. You may decide, however, that users on a networked system should take on part of this responsibility themselves. For example, you could inform users that only data placed in a certain directory area will be backed up each night. Multiple system administrators can also share the responsibility for backups, either to reduce the work burden on one person or to make backups more accessible in case they are needed for restoring data.

- *Where are files located?* You probably know offhand where different types of data are located on your Linux system. A more thorough review lets you determine which specific directories on the system are being actively used, which contain data that is easily reconstructed, and which hold temporary files that don't warrant the effort of a regular backup. These are just three examples of the categories you might assign to parts of your system as you review the various file systems and devices that store data.

- *How should backups be performed?* The answer to this question might be determined by the equipment you purchase, as well as by how your organization operates its computer systems. Many system administrators must back up data during nonwork hours. This process can be automated in most cases using a *cron* job or other specialized utilities. You might also want certain events to trigger a regular backup, or a different type of backup than would normally occur. For example, you might want to back up the entire system before installing new hardware devices such as SCSI adapters.

- *Must you be able to restore data within a specific period of time?* When a problem occurs (and it will), several factors affect how rapidly you can restore lost data to the system. These factors include the size and location of the lost files and the media format on which the backup data was stored. Your backup plan should reflect the value of time within your organization. In some organizations, the ability to restore lost data immediately is essential. In others, speed is not as critical.

Ideally, your backup plan should prevent the headaches associated with having to locate files and figure out how to reconstruct damaged or lost data in the midst of a crisis. A well-designed backup plan makes it easy and convenient for you to regularly back up system data and restore files according to the needs of your organization. It also helps you justify to management the costs of the equipment and time needed to make your backup plan effective.

Determining the Value of Data

Many of the decisions you make as you create a backup strategy should be based on the value of the data you are backing up. The more expensive data is to create, acquire, or refine, the more you should spend to protect its integrity. Some data may be valuable only to one person in an organization, but if that person's time is required to re-create any data that is lost, the data still has value to the entire organization.

For example, a study of the value of data held by an organization might determine that a given set of files required 4000 hours of work by the employees of the firm to create. A different estimate might state that the data could be re-created given current experience and facts in about 2000 hours. If the average wage of the employees involved in the project is approximately $40 per hour, the data would have a value of $80,000. But the study doesn't end there.

NOTE   Cost-of-data calculations involving employee pay should include the benefits paid to the employee. When a company pays an employee a salary of $60,000 per year, the company also pays taxes, insurance, retirement benefits, and other costs that raise the total cost to the company for that employee by 35% to 100%—the $60,000 employee costs the company a total of $81,000 to $120,000. This is called the burdened cost of the employee.

The estimate of 2000 hours—about one workyear—is based on an experienced employee re-creating the data. If that well-trained employee spends time re-creating lost data, what current work will he or she not be able to do? This is called the opportunity cost. The employee might forgo a project worth many times $80,000 in order to re-create the lost data. Opportunity cost extends even further. How was the data that was lost going to be used? Was it part of a multimillion dollar advertising campaign? Or perhaps a financial merger? A great deal of money may be lost because the data is unavailable when needed. Even if $80,000 can be invested to re-create it, the moment of opportunity when the data was needed may be past.

CAUTION   This discussion doesn't address the anger or low morale of an employee who must re-create a project that was partially or completely finished. These factors can also affect the financial health of an organization and are worth considering as justification for spending money on a solid backup strategy.

Determining When to Back Up Data

Once you have created an initial backup or archive of important data, the question of how often to refresh the backup arises—that is, how often to back up the system again to account for changes in the data since you last backed it up. Having at least one backup of data is better than having none at all, but data changes frequently in most organizations. Regularly backing up the latest information stored on the system is a critical part of most system administrators' jobs.

The question of when to back up data is related to how valuable the data is to an organization. You can begin by asking, "How often does the data change?" and "Do changes to the data affect the value of the data?"

The answers to these questions vary according to which part of a Linux system you are evaluating. The operating system itself probably changes very little after the initial configuration. Applications installed on the system are also unlikely to change regularly. In contrast, user data, log files, and e-mail archives change daily and are normally the focus of frequent backups. This data constitutes the daily work of users within your organization. By maintaining regular backups, no one is ever likely to lose more than a few hours worth of work, even if the entire system crashes or a hard disk is destroyed.

Several backup strategies are commonly used. You can select a strategy based on how often data on your system changes and how valuable or critical each incremental piece of data is. The following discussion describes a widely used backup strategy for Linux.

A Linux Backup Strategy

Different backup strategies balance the desire for a complete backup of data at all times with the need for convenience in creating and maintaining backups. The method described here is a standard used for many Linux and UNIX systems. You can adjust the time frames according to how often the data on your system changes.

Using Backup Levels

This strategy relies on multiple backup levels. A **backup level** defines how much data is to be backed up in comparison to another backup level. A backup operation at a given backup level stores all of the data that has changed since the last backup of the previous level. For example, a backup at level one stores all files that have changed since the last level zero backup; a backup at level two stores all files that have changed since the last level one backup. A commonly used arrangement operates with three levels, as described here:

- Level zero is a full backup (also called an **epoch backup**). Everything on the system is backed up. A level zero backup might be performed on the first of every month.

- A level one backup might be done once per week. Every file that has been modified since the last level zero backup (on the first of the month) is included in the level one backup. Storing only files that have changed since a full backup is called a **differential backup**.

- A level two backup could then be done each day. Every file that has been modified since the first of the week (the last level one backup) is included in the level two backup. This is also considered a differential backup.

Figure 13-1 illustrates the three-level backup just described.

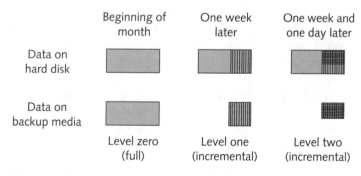

Figure 13-1   Backup levels

Another important backup term is **incremental backup**. The difference between a differential backup and an incremental backup can be confusing in this multilevel scheme. A differential backup stores all files that have been changed since the most recent full backup. An incremental backup only stores files that have been changed since the most recent incremental backup or differential backup. To restore a system using a differential backup, you only need the most recent full backup and the most recent differential backup, but to restore from incremental backups, you need a full backup plus all incremental backups, because each contains a different set of changes. As discussed in the next section, the three-level approach here uses two levels of differential backups, so you need the most recent backup from each level to completely restore a system.

The times associated with backup levels are arbitrary. A level zero backup is normally a full backup in which every file is backed up, but other levels can store data that has changed each month, week, day, or hour, as you choose. Each level always records all the changes since a backup of a previous level.

The advantage of using backup levels is that you can back up data frequently, so very little data is lost if a system fails, but you don't have to back up the entire system each time you do a backup.

Restoring a File from a Three-level Backup

Suppose you had backed up data using the system just described. A user comes to you and needs you to recover a file that was inadvertently deleted. The user can't recall when the file was last modified, but it was "recently." You can follow these steps to locate the file:

1. Check the most recent level two backup. If the file is there, it was changed in the last day. This backup probably doesn't include very many files compared to the size of the entire system, so it's easy to search for a file. If the file isn't there, then it wasn't modified in the last 24 hours, so proceed to Step 2.

2. Check the most recent level one backup. If the file is there, it was changed sometime after the first of the week, but not in the last 24 hours. This backup contains more files, so it takes a little longer to search. If the file is not found, proceed to Step 3.

3. Check the most recent level zero backup. The file will always be included on this backup because a full backup includes every file on the system. Searching through this backup may be time consuming because it is fairly large.

NOTE   Backup media such as tape drives and optical disks always have directories of their contents to help you locate files as rapidly as possible, but a tape cartridge must be rewound to the place where the file is stored. As a result, restoring a single file from a tape cartridge can be time consuming.

You might wonder why you shouldn't start searching for the file in the level zero backup, since it is certain to be part of that backup. You should always start with the most recent backup in order to find the most recent version of a file. If the file had been altered since the first of the month, the most recent copy of the file will not be on the level zero backup.

TIP

If a file was created and deleted on the same day, it wouldn't be part of any backup plan that backed up data each evening. If a user asks for help in this situation, you would need to rely on undelete utilities to find the deleted file on the hard disk. Examples of these utilities include e2undel, R-Linux (see *www. r-tt.com*), and *recover.*

Advantages to the three-level backup method include:

- Creating the level two daily backups requires little of the system administrator's time because few files are altered on any given day.

- No user ever loses more than a single day's work because the changes in the file system from each day are recorded in a level two backup.

- Files that rarely change are still backed up and available, but don't require daily maintenance by the system administrator.

Some backup utilities explicitly use the term "backup levels" to refer to how data is backed up and how backup media are tracked. The concept can be applied to any backup utility, however. For the system to work well, you need to keep careful records and label backup media clearly.

In the event that an entire system must be restored using a set of backup media that have been prepared using the three-level method, a system administrator would follow this procedure:

1. Restore everything from the most recent level zero backup.

2. Restore everything from the most recent level one backup.

3. Restore everything from the most recent level two backup.

Figure 13-2 illustrates how this procedure results in all of the latest information being included in the restored file system. (Compare the backup levels pictured in Figure 13-1 to the restore operation pictured in Figure 13-2.)

13

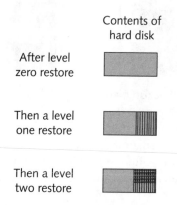

Figure 13-2   Restoring data from a three-level set of backup media

Managing and Storing Backup Media

As you create a backup plan that specifies backup levels and times appropriate to your organization's needs, you must determine how many backup media you will need (disks, tapes, cartridges) for each level. That is, a level zero full backup may require five tape cartridges, but a typical level two backup requires only a single cartridge (because relatively few files are modified each day). As an example, the three-level backup described previously might include the following:

- Three months of level zero backups; each month requires five tape cartridges, for a total of 15.

- Five weeks of level one backups (some months have five weeks); each month requires three tape cartridges, for a total of 15.

- Five to seven days of level two backups (some organizations run seven days per week); each requires one tape cartridge, for a total of five to seven.

You would therefore need a total of 35 tape cartridges for this plan for a standard workweek. Figure 13-3 illustrates this arrangement. The importance of carefully labeling each tape cartridge cannot be overstated. If you can't identify which backup media is the most recent of any given level, much of your backup effort will be useless when a serious problem arises.

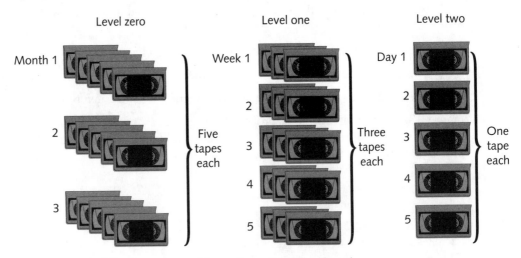

Figure 13-3 Multiple tapes used for a three-level backup plan

Most organizations would store one set of the monthly (level zero) backup media and perhaps the most recent weekly (level one) backup media off-site. The strategy for off-site storage depends on how critical data is and how often someone wants to take the responsibility of carrying the backup media to the chosen secure location (such as a bank vault).

CAUTION Most backup media are designed to be used repeatedly. For example, a rewriteable CD can be used about 1000 times, according to the manufacturer. But you should nevertheless plan on scheduled replacement of backup media to avoid problems with deteriorating, outdated products.

Using the plan just outlined, you can reuse the same set of level one weekly tape cartridges each month, starting with the oldest one. The same applies to the level two tape cartridges. For example, on any Wednesday afternoon, you should have five level two tape cartridges containing the following:

- Last Wednesday's backup, which you will overwrite this evening with new data
- Last Thursday's backup, which you will overwrite tomorrow evening with new data
- Last Friday's backup
- Monday's backup (from two days ago)
- Tuesday's backup (from last night)

In addition to being fairly easy to manage, this system provides data redundancy. If you have a problem and need to restore a file on this particular Wednesday, you first check the Tuesday backup that you made last night. If a problem occurs with that tape cartridge, you can also check Monday morning's level one backup, Monday evening's level two backup, or even last Friday's backup. A single user may lose more work if you cannot use the most recent backup, but the organization won't lose all its data, because many copies of the data exist on different media.

Backing Up the Root File System

The root file system requires special attention in your backup plan because it contains the tools that you normally use to restore damaged data, such as a deleted file or data from a corrupted hard disk partition. You should think about how to respond if the root file system is damaged, either by a hard disk failure or by corrupted configuration files that prevent you from booting the Linux operating system kernel.

As you prepare a backup plan, you'll want to consider the hardware and software that you'll use to implement that plan. The following section describes some key issues you face in making hardware and software choices.

Hardware and Software Issues

Once you have determined why, when, and how you want to back up your Linux system, you must determine the best tools to get the job done. Linux includes all the necessary software utilities for many backup tasks. You can also purchase commercial backup software. Both of these options are described later in this chapter.

The size of hard disks in standard PCs is growing very rapidly. A few years ago, a 500 MB hard disk was considered huge, but today hard disks with 80 to 250 GB are common and can be purchased for a few hundred dollars. Storage space is often measured according to its cost per megabyte or per gigabyte. For example, if an 80 GB hard disk costs $300, the cost per gigabyte is about $3.75 (about 0.375 cents per megabyte). Similarly, if a tape cartridge used to back up a system costs $90 and holds 200 GB, the cost per gigabyte is 45 cents.

You normally have multiple copies of the data on your system, backed up at different times. Backup media such as tape cartridges cost much less than a hard disk, but you use multiple tape cartridges (35 in the previous example) to back up the system. Optical media are also very popular and cost very little—under $5 for a blank DVD that can hold almost 5 GB of data—but they are inappropriate for backing up large systems because you would need to switch disks after every 5 GB.

Verification, Permissions, and Compression

Although problems are rare once you have a backup system up and running, you should verify your backups on a regular basis. Almost all backup utilities create log files that record their actions. This is especially important because they often run in the middle of the night. You should make a habit of checking the backup log each morning after a backup utility has run to see if any problems occurred during the night. You can then take immediate action to back up any files missing from the automated backup operation.

Verifying a backup is sometimes done as part of a backup utility, as described later in this chapter, but you can always perform your own verification using steps such as these:

1. Pick a backup tape or disk, either at random or according to a reasonable plan. For example, you might decide to test a randomly chosen level one backup tape once per week.

2. Check the file listing on the tape by querying for the contents of the backup media. (This is equivalent to using the *ls* command to see the contents of the backup media. With some media you can actually use the *ls* command; with others you need to use a backup utility.)

3. Restore a randomly selected file to the /tmp directory of your Linux system to be certain that the data in the file can be retrieved and reassembled without errors. If possible, do this step immediately after backing up data (on your regular schedule), and then compare the file you restored with the original file that you backed up to see that the size and contents match. (Use the *diff* command to compare the contents of two files.)

In addition to verifying the data, you should also know exactly what information is backed up. Does the backup include the contents of each file? What about the owner and file permissions associated with each file? Many times a system administrator encounters problems after restoring a large number of files because the owner and group assigned to the files and directories, or the file and directory permissions, are not stored as part of the backup. If this information is not backed up and then restored in a consistent way, access to all files may be denied to all users, or granted to all users. Either way, you would need to assign new file permissions to each file manually.

CAUTION A backup utility typically must run with root permission because only root can access all users' files on the system and the backup device itself. You must protect access to the backup utility and to the backed up data so that users who are not authorized to see data on the system also cannot access it as part of a backup operation or on backup media. Most system administrators keep all backup media in a locked cabinet or closet.

Backup utilities normally include options to maintain or ignore file ownership and permissions. Normally you want to maintain this information and check it carefully when you verify your backups by restoring selected files.

In most backup utilities, you can also choose whether to use a compression feature for your backed up data. Tape drives typically list a standard capacity and a compressed capacity; backup commands include options to compress data as it's being archived. Should you use these features? Probably, but you should also be aware of their limitations. By definition, when you compress data, you remove the redundancy from it. That is, compressed data can be re-created in its original form by restoring the redundant information using an established set of rules.

To understand compression better, consider this example. When you see the words "hllo my nm is Nchlas," you can probably understand their meaning even though part of the information is missing. The missing information is redundant—it's not needed for you to understand the sentence. You can also use standard rules (English grammar and spelling) to reconstruct the original sentence: "Hello my name is Nicholas."

The danger with using compression is that with all the redundancy removed from a set of information, all of the information and rules are needed in order to reconstruct the data. For example, if you don't speak English well, English words with missing letters are difficult to decipher. In the same way, if even a small part of some compressed data is lost, the original cannot be easily reconstructed. By leaving the redundancy in the data that you back up, you might make it easier to fix any problems that occur on backup media.

Most backup media formats are highly reliable, but when age, environmental factors such as heat and dust, and regular wear and tear are working against the data you have carefully saved, you should consider whether compression is always necessary.

Using Linux Backup Utilities

Many utilities are available to back up data from a Linux system in a secure and organized way. In Chapter 4, "Understanding Users and File Systems," you learned about the *tar* and *cpio* commands, both of which are widely used for simple backups. Two additional command-line utilities are ***dump*** and ***restore***, which you can use to back up and restore files, respectively. These commands are designed to work with the multilevel backup approach just described. They are powerful and flexible, and are easy to use within shell scripts (see Chapter 14, "Writing Shell Scripts"), but they are not as widely used as in years past because of the many quality graphical utilities that are so much easier to use. Still another command that is sometimes used for backup operations is **dd**. The *dd* command does a "data dump" between any two devices or files.

A number of the graphical utilities for backing up your system that are listed later in this section rely on *tar*, *cpio*, or *dump* and *restore* in the background. Popular commercial backup utilities include features such as tracking tapes for you, keeping online indexes of each backup that you have performed, and automating schedules for unattended backups (similar to the options provided by the *crontab* command).

It's common to use Linux backup utilities across a network—a single system equipped with a tape drive or other backup device is used to back up file systems located on machines all over the network. You can do this using many techniques, such as remotely mounting file systems using NFS or Samba software, or downloading files using Linux FTP server software. Most full-featured backup utilities create their own network connections between software components installed on the machine to be backed up and the machine where the tape drive is located. The documentation for specific utilities describes their networking capabilities; basic Linux utilities such as those described in the next section rely on services such as NFS to access networked data.

 NOTE   Networking topics such as NFS, Samba, FTP, and more are covered in *Guide to Linux Networking and Security* (Course Technology 2003, ISBN 0-619-00094-5).

The commands *tar*, *cpio*, *dump*, and *restore* can operate either with a tape drive or with backup devices that rely on a standard Linux file system or standard mounting operation, such as an Iomega Jaz drive or a writable DVD drive. When you are using tape drives that are not randomly accessible (as a CD is), you may want to use additional tools to manage tape indexes, tape rewinding and searching, and so forth. One graphical tool for managing data backup operations is **ark**, part of the KDE desktop.

The complexities of maintaining large numbers of backup media for large volumes of data led manufacturers long ago to create specialized software to help with the task. Fortunately, several of these tools have made their way to the Linux platform:

- BRU (Backup and Restore Utility) from Enhanced Software Technologies has been popular among Linux users for many years. It provides multiple levels of data verification, unattended operation with scheduled backups, and support for numerous types of backup devices. See *www.bru.com*.

- Arkeia is another popular Linux backup tool. Arkeia is an enterprise network backup solution that is designed to control backup of multiple remote systems from a single location, saving or restoring data from anywhere on the network. See *www.arkeia.com*. Figure 13-4 shows a sample Arkeia screen.

- Storix provides system backup and disaster recovery designed specifically for IBM AIX and Linux operating systems. You can learn more at *www.storix.com*.

Figure 13-4   The Arkeia commercial backup program

- HyperTape from BridgeHead Software provides automatic unattended backups to local or networked tape drives. See *www.BridgeHeadSoftware.com*.

- AMANDA is a freely available backup system that coordinates data backups from multiple servers on a network to a single master server. See *www.amanda.org*.

- Legato, a traditionally strong vendor in the UNIX market, now provides its high-end data management and backup/restore software on a variety of Linux platforms. See *www.legato.com*.

- Vendors of tape devices such as Hewlett-Packard, IBM, Quantum, and MTI increasingly include support options for Linux and even Linux software utilities.

Many other backup utilities are available—free and commercial, graphical and command-line.

Understanding Redundant Disk Systems and RAID

Two parts of the Linux kernel that are generally not implemented using kernel modules are RAID and logical volume management. Both of these disk management techniques are typically set up when you install Linux. This section and the next section introduce you to these high-end features of Linux.

One of the most vulnerable parts of a computer system is the hard disk. It contains many moving parts, and is often subjected to constant heavy use. If the data on your hard disks becomes unavailable because of a failure, the rest of the computer system is useless. For these reasons, much effort has gone into making hard disks redundant. Although specialized redundant hard disks have been available for mainframe computers for decades, most users now rely on groups of hard disks, known as **redundant arrays of inexpensive disks**, commonly called **RAID** subsystems or RAID arrays.

The idea behind RAID is simple: instead of trying to create a single hard disk that never fails (an expensive proposition) use a group, or array, of inexpensive hard disks. The assumption is that if one disk fails, the others can take over until the failed disk is replaced. RAID takes advantage of the statistical fact that multiple hard disks are unlikely to fail at the same time.

You can add RAID to your system using a separate hardware device, as described later, or by relying solely on features within the Linux kernel. It can contain as many disks as necessary to reach the storage capacity needed. A RAID system does not have a specific number of hard disks, a specific storage capacity, or even a specific platform. RAID systems are used by all operating systems. Instead, the different forms, or levels, of RAID are distinguished by the techniques used to store data, as explained in the following sections.

Within the Linux kernel, RAID capability is implemented as a device called /dev/md0 ("md" stands for meta-disk). /dev/md0 may be composed of several actual hard disk partitions. The Linux kernel processes requests to /dev/md0 so that they reach the correct physical hard disk partition.

Setting up RAID in Linux is not difficult. You can use the Disk Druid utility that you use during the installation of Red Hat Linux or Fedora (as described in Chapter 8, "Installing Linux").

Defining RAID Levels

RAID can be implemented in many forms, or levels. The levels differ in the amount of **fault tolerance** they provide (protection from unexpected failures), the speed of reading or writing data, and the cost of implementation. The next sections introduce the most popular RAID levels and define the terms and techniques associated with RAID.

TIP

Vendors differ in the features they associate with the different RAID levels. When reviewing RAID technologies or products, look for specific features rather than just a RAID level. When selecting hard disks to create your own software-RAID array, use hard disks of the same type, size, and manufacturer.

RAID-Linear lets you combine multiple physical devices into a single logical device. This allows one logical Linux file system to span multiple disk drives or partitions, which is useful when you want a file system to be larger than a single hard disk. For example, suppose you need a huge file system for the /home directory. By storing this file system on multiple disk drives, you avoid buying one very large (expensive) hard disk. Instead, you can purchase multiple disks of a more common size. But the /home directory can still be managed as a single file system because of RAID-Linear.

RAID-Linear is not truly a RAID level because it does not provide any redundancy or fault tolerance, nor does it improve system performance, as some RAID levels do. In fact,

RAID-Linear reduces fault tolerance: if any disk in a RAID-Linear array fails, the entire file system is unusable. RAID-Linear is illustrated in Figure 13-5.

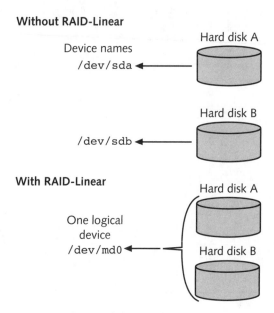

Figure 13-5 RAID-Linear

RAID-0 uses a data storage technique called **striping**, in which a single block of data is divided into pieces and stored on more than one hard disk. This allows faster access, because two disk drives work together to gather parts of any requested information at the same time. The performance gain is increased if each hard disk uses a separate hard disk controller (for example, using two SCSI cards); multiple hard disk controllers prevent a bottleneck in communicating from the hard disk to the CPU. However, if either hard disk fails in a RAID-0 setup, the entire file system is unusable. Hence, using RAID-0 without other measures described in this chapter reduces fault tolerance significantly. Figure 13-6 illustrates striping.

RAID-1 mirrors data across multiple hard disks. **Mirroring** refers to a system with two or more hard disks that contain identical information. Each time one hard disk is updated, the copy or copies (the mirrors) are also updated. If one hard disk fails, the mirrored hard disks continue to respond to data requests without interruption. **Duplexing** refers to mirrored hard disks that are on separate controller cards, which increases performance and reduces vulnerability to a hardware failure.

Mirrored and duplexed hard disks increase performance when reading from a hard disk because multiple hard disks respond to data requests at the same time. This technique also increases fault tolerance: if one hard disk fails, the duplicate disks continue to respond without interruption. But using mirroring or duplexing has two downsides. First, the time required to write files to a hard disk is increased because data must be written to each disk

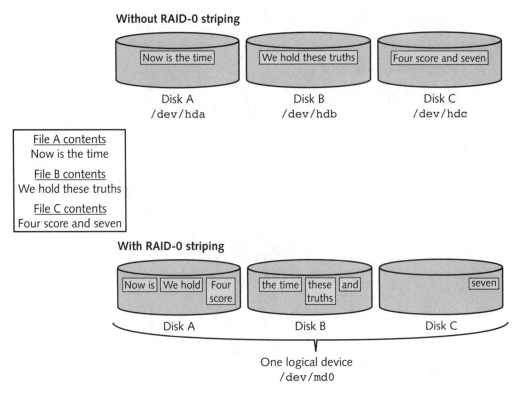

Figure 13-6   RAID-0 or data striping

instead of just one. Second, these techniques require extra hard disks that are used only for mirroring—they don't provide extra storage capacity. For example, if you want 120 GB of mirrored hard disk storage, you must pay for 240 GB of hard disk space. With the low price of hard disks today, this may be a very good investment, but it can be a limiting factor when planning a system with large amounts of storage (e.g., thousands of gigabytes of data). Figure 13-7 shows a mirrored hard disk system.

RAID-0 (striping) improves performance but makes a system more vulnerable to failure. **RAID-3** combines the performance advantages of striping data across multiple hard disks but provides additional protection against the failure of one of the hard disks by using parity. **Parity** is a technique that allows corrupted data to be reconstructed using an extra piece of information that is created as the data is stored. The parity information provides redundancy to the piece of data. In RAID-3, this extra information is stored in a **parity stripe**. If one of the hard disks fails, the system can use the parity information to reconstruct the data stored on that disk. Figure 13-8 illustrates a RAID-3 system.

RAID-3 provides good fault tolerance because of the parity stripe. If a hard disk fails, data is still usable; when the failed hard disk is replaced, the data is automatically rebuilt on the new hard disk. RAID-3 also improves performance on systems that perform many disk

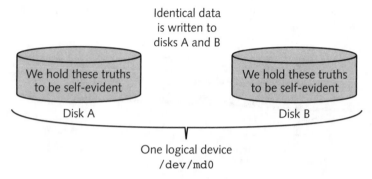

Identical data
is written to
disks A and B

We hold these truths
to be self-evident

Disk A

We hold these truths
to be self-evident

Disk B

One logical device
/dev/md0

Figure 13-7 RAID-1 with mirrored hard disks

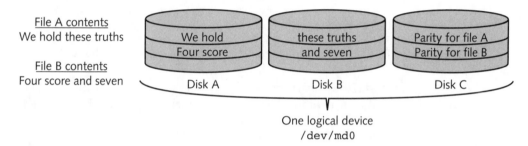

File A contents
We hold these truths

File B contents
Four score and seven

We hold
Four score

these truths
and seven

Parity for file A
Parity for file B

Disk A

Disk B

Disk C

One logical device
/dev/md0

Figure 13-8 RAID-3, striping with parity

reads. All the hard disks in a RAID-3 array can work in parallel to respond to multiple requests at the same time. Instead of waiting for a single disk, the chances are good that a hard disk that is not busy can immediately begin to service a read request. Also, unlike disk mirroring, with RAID-3 only one hard disk (the one containing the parity information) is unavailable for data storage. For example, to have 200 GB of usable storage space in a RAID-3 system, you need to purchase about 250 GB of hard disks. One disadvantage of RAID-3 is that the write performance suffers because parity information must be computed and several hard disks must store information for each write operation.

NOTE

Although RAID-2 and RAID-4 are listed in some definitions of RAID, they are not used in production systems and so are not presented here. These two RAID levels simply use different combinations of the techniques implemented by other RAID levels.

RAID-5 is similar to RAID-3 except that with RAID-5 both the parity information and the stored data are striped across multiple hard disks. This has the advantage of making read performance better, but it makes write performance even worse than RAID-3. As with RAID-3, if a hard disk fails, the parity information allows the information to be reconstructed once the disk is replaced. In the meantime, data remains available. Figure 13-9 illustrates how RAID-5 spreads information across multiple hard disks. Many vendors who sell RAID-5 hardware systems (see the next section) use built-in **write caching** to store new information in memory until it can be written to the multiple hard disks without degrading performance overall.

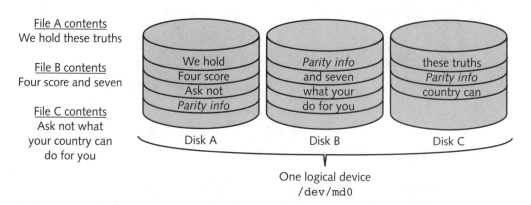

Figure 13-9   RAID-5, parity and striping over multiple disks

Table 13-1 compares the characteristics of the different RAID levels. By understanding these characteristics, a system administrator can select which system is the best choice for each file system.

Table 13-1   Comparing RAID Levels

Level	Fault tolerance	Speed: reading data	Speed: Writing data	Comments
RAID-L	Poor	Possible improvement over non-RAID	Good	Useful for managing multiple disk drives as one volume
RAID-0 (striping)	Poor	Good	Good	
RAID-1 (mirroring)	Good	Good	Fair	
RAID-3	Very good	Very good	Poor	Data striping with parity information
RAID-5	Very good	Very good	Poor	Similar to RAID-3 but stripes the parity information across all drives

Using Hardware-based RAID

A RAID system can be implemented as a separate device that connects to your Linux computer, such as an external printer or CD-ROM drive. This is called **hardware–based RAID** because the control and management of the disk array depends on a separate hardware system (called a **RAID subsystem**). Hardware-based RAID devices include

RAM, a CPU, and other components besides the array of hard disks; it is practically a separate computer with the sole purpose of providing data redundancy to your main system. The main advantage of using a hardware-based RAID system is that all of the special technology is contained in the RAID device. For example, a huge RAID subsystem connected to your Linux server by a SCSI controller appears to Linux as a single SCSI disk drive. No special utilities or management are needed on Linux.

Another advantage of hardware-based RAID systems is that they often allow **hot-swapping** disks, meaning that you can pull out and replace a failed hard disk without turning off the RAID subsystem. A system administrator normally keeps one or two spares on a shelf and swaps them with a failed hard disk when necessary. Hot-swapping is an expensive feature; it is also available as part of high-end Linux-based servers from companies such as Hewlett-Packard and IBM.

TIP

A hardware-based RAID system may include utilities that run on the host operating system and that are designed to manage or configure the RAID device. Check whether such utilities can be used on a Linux platform.

The main disadvantage of hardware-based RAID is its cost. Because the RAID system includes a CPU and other electronics to manage the hard disks, plus a separate case and software utilities, hardware-based RAID is much more expensive than simply using the RAID capabilities of the Linux kernel.

13

Understanding Logical Volume Management

Another important feature of Linux that has been added in recent years is the **Logical Volume Manager (LVM)**. Like RAID, the LVM is used to manage large hard disks. Also like RAID, you typically set up LVM during the installation of Linux, using the Disk Druid utility in Red Hat Linux or Fedora. LVM is designed to solve a simple problem: previously when you set up your system, you arranged disk partitions based on the amount of space you had. As the system grew, you needed to add more hard disk space, but doing so required you to back up a file system, install and configure new hard disks, then restore data onto the newly configured file systems.

Using a Logical Volume Manager avoids this problem. By separating the management of physical hard disks from the management of partitions, the LVM lets you add hard disks (and thus storage space) to a file system without doing the backup-reformat-restore procedure that can be so time consuming.

Figure 13-10 shows the basic concept of the LVM. You use the Disk Druid to set up "real" partitions on multiple hard disks. These are referred to as **physical volumes**. Multiple physical volumes are grouped together into a **logical volume group**. The logical volume group is then treated as you would normally treat a regular hard disk—you can partition it into separate file systems as needed for your data and operating system needs.

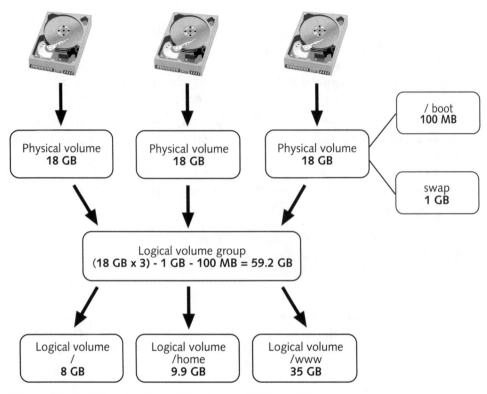

Figure 13-10   The structure of the Logical Volume Manager

The boot loader (LILO or GRUB) is not able to work directly with LVM or a logical volume group, so if you want to have your root file system be part of a LVM (which is not uncommon), you need to create a separate /boot partition containing the Linux kernel. This partition would not be part of the logical volume group managed by the LVM utilities.

Suppose you have three hard disks that you want to use for a Linux system that is acting as a Web server. You create /boot and swap partitions, but use the majority of space on all three disks for two partitions: / and /www. The operating system will be stored on /, and all the Web server data will be stored on /www.

After using the system for several months, you realize that you need to add much more storage space to your Web server. First, you must shut down your server and install a fourth hard disk. After you restart, you can use the LVM utilities that are included with Linux to add the fourth hard disk to the logical volume group. Then you can increase the size of the /www partition without reformatting it or losing any data. This is something that was not possible with older hard disk management utilities.

If you create a logical volume group in Disk Druid as you install Linux, you can use the collection of LVM utilities to manage logical volume groups and make changes such as those described in the previous example. The **lvm** program is the principal utility; enter the command *apropos* lvm to see a list of related utilities.

SYSTEM LOGS

On any ship, the captain keeps a log of information about each day, including where the ship has traveled, its cargo, and any noteworthy events. The log serves as a record not only for the captain and crew, but also for others who may need detailed information about the ship.

In much the same way, Linux keeps detailed records of events within the system. These records, known as **log files**, are created by many programs. As the system administrator, you can refer to the log files to determine the status of your system, watch for intruders, or look for data about a particular program or event. Table 13-2 lists some commonly logged events and the location of the corresponding log files. This section focuses on the main system log, which is typically located at /var/log/messages.

Table 13-2   Commonly Logged Events and Their Log Files

Event	Path and file name of the log
Main system messages	/var/log/messages
Web server transfers	/var/log/httpd/access_log
FTP server transfers	/var/log/xferlog
E-mail server information	/var/log/maillog
Automatic script executions	/var/log/cron

Many different programs write messages to /var/log/messages. A **message** is a description of what is happening within a program. The message may report information (someone has logged in), a warning (someone tried to log in unsuccessfully), or a serious error indicating that a program is about to crash. Several sample messages are shown later in this section. A number of daemons—such as the Web server, e-mail server, and login security programs—write to the file, as does the Linux kernel itself. The messages from the kernel tell you about low-level system activities such as when devices are first initialized and when daemons are started by the kernel.

The **messages file** uses a standard format. Each line of the file makes up an individual log message. Each message, in turn, contains the following information:

- The date and time when the event being logged occurred (often called the **timestamp**)
- The host name (or computer name) of the system on which the event occurred
- The name of the program generating the log message
- The message text itself, which may be more than one line long

13

A few sample lines from a messages log file are shown here. Notice that the host name for all these messages is brighton, the name of someone's computer. Also notice that several different programs have generated the log messages shown here, including the Linux kernel, the httpd daemon (the Web server), the sound system, and other programs.

```
Oct 26 06:42:29 brighton kernel:
 Installing knfsd (copyright (C) 1996 ok
Oct 26 06:42:29 brighton nfs: rpc.nfsd startup succeeded
Oct 26 06:42:29 brighton keytable: Loading keymap:
Oct 26 06:42:30 brighton keytable: Loading /usr/lib/kbd/keymaps/
i386/qwe
Oct 26 06:42:30 brighton keytable: Loading systemffont:
Oct 26 06:42:30 brighton rc: Starting keytable succeeded
Oct 26 06:42:30 brighton gpm: gpm startup succeeded
Oct 26 06:44:57 brighton rpc.statd[451]:
 gethostbyname error for brighto
Oct 26 06:45:01 brighton httpd: Cannot determine local host name.
Oct 26 06:45:01 brighton httpd:
 Use the ServerName directive to set it
Oct 26 06:45:01 brighton httpd: httpd startup failed
Oct 26 06:45:01 brighton sound: Starting sound configuration:
Oct 26 06:45:01 brighton sound: sound
Oct 26 06:45:01 brighton rc: Starting sound succeeded
Oct 26 06:45:02 brighton PAM_pwdb[582]:
 (su) session opened for user xfs
Oct 26 06:45:03 brighton PAM_pwdb[582]:
 (su) session closed for user xfs
Oct 26 06:45:03 brighton xfs: xfs startup succeeded
Oct 26 06:45:05 brighton rc: Starting local succeeded
Oct 26 06:45:08 brighton PAM_pwdb[629]: check pass; user unknown
Oct 26 06:45:09 brighton login[629]:
 FAILED LOGIN 1 FROM (null) FOR roopt, User not known to the
underlying authentication module
```

Right now you don't have to understand everything in the preceding log file lines. But you should become familiar with the format of a log line.

If you see a program in a log line that you don't recognize, you can use the *whatis* command to learn about it. This command looks at a database of program descriptions and prints a one-line description of the program you ask about. Sometimes the result is not too helpful, but it can give you a starting place and also refer you to a man page that may provide more information.

NOTE   The *whatis* command uses an internal database to find an answer to your query. That database should be prepared automatically, but if it is not available, you can create it by running the command *makewhatis*.

The syslogd and klogd Daemons

A programmer writing software for Linux can rely on the programming function named syslog to write a message to the /var/log/messages file or another configured location, as described shortly. All of the calls to the syslog function are managed by **syslogd**, the system logging daemon.

The *syslogd* daemon watches for messages submitted by programs; another daemon called **klogd** (kernel logging daemon) watches for messages submitted by the Linux kernel. The *klogd* daemon logs kernel messages to /var/log/messages (or another configured location). Both *klogd* and *syslogd* write messages to the same log file. Figure 13-11 shows how everything works together to record log messages.

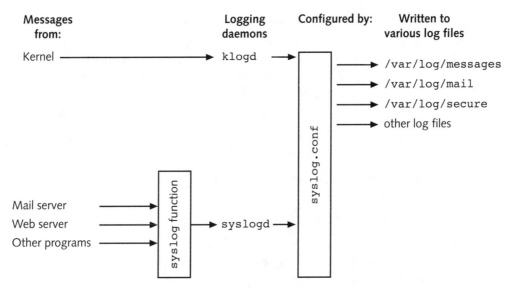

Figure 13-11   *syslogd* and *klogd* work together to process log messages

The *syslogd* and *klogd* daemons are started by the system initialization scripts in /etc/rc.d/init.d each time you start your Linux system. You should never need to start these programs manually.

Configuring the System Log

You can configure what information you want *syslogd* and *klogd* to store in the main system log (/var/log/messages by default) and what information you want stored in other files. Both *syslogd* and *klogd* rely on a single configuration file: /etc/**syslog.conf**. Figure 13-12 shows the format of each line in the syslog.conf file. The parts of the figure are described below it.

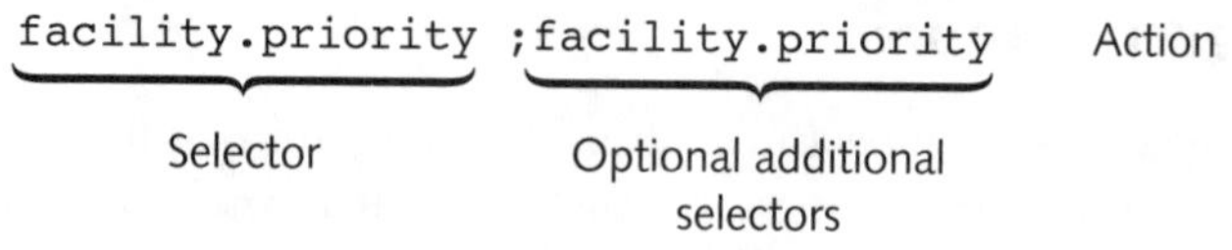

facility.priority ;facility.priority   Action

Selector   Optional additional
                       selectors

Figure 13-12 The format of each line in /etc/syslog.conf

NOTE

As with most configuration files, lines that begin with a hash mark (#) in /etc/syslog.conf are comments and are ignored by the logging daemons.

Each line in the syslog.conf file contains two parts:

- A **selector**, a set of code words that selects what events are being logged
- An **action**, a file name or user name that determines either the file in which the message describing an event is written or the users on whose screen the message appears (the action can also refer to a remote computer for networked logging, as described later in this section)

Each selector describing an event to be logged is composed of two parts:

- The **facility**, a code word that specifies which type of program is being selected (the category of program providing the log entry)
- The **priority**, a code word that specifies the type of messages being selected for logging

Consider this example log configuration line:

daemon.info   /var/log/messages

The left part of the line contains a selector: daemon.info. The facility of this selector is daemon. The priority is info. So, messages from any daemon program with a priority of info or higher are selected by these code words. On the right, the line contains an action: /var/log/messages. This action is a file name, which specifies that messages selected by the daemon.info selector are written to the file /var/log/messages.

The Facilities

When a Linux program wants to log a message, it issues a programming call to the syslog function. As part of that call, the program indicates its type, or category. For example, when the *login* program records a message about a user logging into the system, the *login* program specifies that the message is coming from an authentication (security-related) program. The *syslogd* daemon uses this category information to determine where to write the message, based on the syslog.conf configuration. The actual name of the program (*login*, in this example), rather than the category (authentication in this example), is written to the log file. Table 13-3 lists the different facilities, or types of programs, for which you can separately configure logging.

Table 13-3   Code Words Used to Specify Facilities in syslog.conf

Facility description	Facility name
Messages from user authentication utilities such as login	auth (formerly called security)
Special-purpose (private) user authentication messages	auth-priv
Messages from the cron program (used to control automated, scheduled tasks)	cron
Messages from all standard daemons or servers not otherwise listed by name here	daemon
Kernel messages (through klogd)	kern
Printer server messages	lpr
Mail server messages (from the Mail Transfer Agent)	mail
News server messages	news
Messages about the system logging process itself (such as starting the logging program)	syslog
Messages from programs started by end users	user
Messages from the uucp program (rarely used)	uucp
Eight special-purpose categories that a Linux vendor or programmer can define for specific needs not covered by the other categories	local0 through local7

NOTE

In many cases, multiple programs use the same facility. The daemon facility, in particular, is used by many programs.

13

The Priorities

All Linux programs generate different types of messages. Some messages are informational; they might describe how the program is using system resources, for example. Other messages indicate a potential problem. Still other messages indicate a serious or critical problem that will corrupt data or shut down the program. Each program can generate messages with different priorities, depending on the seriousness of the event. You can configure your system so messages of different priorities are logged in different ways.

Table 13-4 shows the different priorities available in syslog.conf, listed from lowest to highest priority.

Table 13-4   Message Priorities Used in syslog.conf

Priority description	Priority name
No priority	none
Debugging messages used by programmers or those testing how a program works	debug
Informational messages about what a program is doing	info

Table 13-4   Message Priorities Used in syslog.conf (continued)

Priority description	Priority name
Information about noteworthy events occurring as a program executes	notice
Warnings about potential problems with a program	warning (formerly called warn)
Notices about errors occurring within a program	err (formerly called error)
Critical error messages describing events that will likely cause a program to shut down	crit
Error messages that will cause a program to shut down and may also affect other programs	alert
Messages about events serious enough to potentially crash the system	emerg (formerly called panic)

As a software developer writes a program, he or she decides which events are associated with which priority levels. For example, the developer might design a program so that a certain event generates a message with the priority of warning. Another programmer might decide that the same event should generate a message with the priority of notice. Thus, the programs themselves determine to which facility they pertain and what priority individual events or messages should have. As a system administrator, you simply determine where messages are logged, based on their facility and priority.

The Actions

Once you set up a selector (consisting of a facility and a priority), you can assign an action to that selector. The action determines what *syslogd* and *klogd* do with the messages defined by the selector. Possible actions are listed here:

- Write the message to a regular file using the given file name. (This is by far the most commonly used action.)

- Write the message to the terminal indicated. This can be a standard virtual terminal name, from /dev/tty1 to /dev/tty6, or the console device, /dev/console.

- Write the message to the screen of any users who are logged in from a given list of users. For example, if the action is root,lsnow, the messages in the selector are written to the screen of users root and lsnow, if they are logged in. This ensures that root and perhaps other users are immediately informed when a serious error occurs that might cause a program to shut down.

- Write the message to the log file on a remote system. This is done using the symbol @ in the action. You could specify the action as @incline.xyz.com, for example, to send log messages for the given selector to the *syslogd* daemon running on the system named incline.xyz.com.

The option of writing messages to a remote system is useful in several circumstances:

- *To consolidate important messages*: Many systems in an organization can send log messages to a single system so they can be archived and studied as a group.

- *To safeguard information on a failed system*: When a system crashes because of a hardware failure, any system log files stored on the hard disk can be damaged, or at least rendered inaccessible until the system is restored. By storing log files on another system, you ensure that these messages can be reviewed even after the system that generated them fails.

- *To enhance security*: Storing log files remotely makes it more difficult for intruders to delete records of their activities that may be stored in system log files.

Configuration File Syntax

The following sample listing shows lines from a syslog.conf file. The comment lines (beginning with the # character) precede and explain the purpose of each configuration line.

```
# Log anything (except mail) of level info or higher.
# Don't log private authentication messages!
*.info;mail.none;authpriv.none              /var/log/messages
# The authpriv log file has restricted access.
authpriv.*                                  /var/log/secure
# Log all the mail messages in one place.
mail.*                                      /var/log/maillog
# Everybody gets emergency messages
*.emerg                                     *
# Save boot messages also to boot.log
local7.*                                    /var/log/boot.log
```

Some aspects of the configuration file syntax are not obvious even after reading about facilities and actions:

- An asterisk (*) used as the facility or the priority matches all facilities or all priorities, respectively. For example, the selector *.emerg selects all messages with the emerg priority from any facility.

- An asterisk (*) used as the action means that all users who are logged in can see matching messages on their screen (if they have a command line available to receive the message). The *.emerg selector in the sample lines above uses (*) as the action.

- The facility and the priority are separated by a period.

- Multiple selectors can be included on the same configuration line by separating them with a semicolon (;).

- Multiple facilities or priorities can be specified at the same time using a comma-separated list. For example, uucp,news.crit matches messages of priority crit originating from either the uucp or news facility.

- The keyword *none* as a priority excludes all messages from the named facility. For example, specifying *.info;mail.none matches messages of info priority or higher from any facility, but all messages from the mail facility are excluded.

- For any priority specified in a selector, all messages of that priority and all *higher* priorities (more serious problems) are included.

- The same messages can be logged to more than one place by including the same selector on multiple lines with different actions. For example, critical kernel messages might be displayed on the /dev/console device and also logged to a remote machine for later analysis using a configuration line such as this:

  ```
  *.crit      /dev/console,@logging_host
  ```

- Configuration lines in syslog.conf do not override previous configuration lines; each action configured by a line in syslog.conf adds to everything already configured.

In addition to these basic rules of syntax for syslog.conf, several special symbols are occasionally used to specify facilities or priorities with greater precision. The man page for syslog.conf has complete details on these rarely used features.

Table 13-5 describes the effect of several sample syslog.conf configuration lines.

Table 13-5   Sample syslog.conf Configuration Lines

Sample configuration line	Effect of the configuration line
#kern.* /dev/console	None; this line begins with a comment character
kern.* /dev/console	Log all kernel messages (of any priority) to the console (the computer screen)
*.info;mail.none;authpriv. none /var/log/messages	Log all messages from any facility with a priority of info or higher to the file /var/log/messages, but exclude all messages with a facility of mail or authpriv, no matter what priority
authpriv.* /var/log/secure	Log all messages from the authpriv facility to the file /var/log/secure
uucp,news.crit /var/log/ spooler	Write any messages of priority crit or higher for the facilities uucp or news to the file /var/log/spooler
*.emerg *	Display any messages with a priority of emerg on the screen of all users who are logged in
mail.* /var/log/maillog	Log all messages from the mail facility to the file /var/log/maillog
*.emerg @loghost	Send all messages of priority emerg (from all facilities) to the syslogd daemon running on the computer named loghost

After changing the syslog.conf configuration file, you must tell *syslogd* and *klogd* to reread the configuration file, so that your changes to the file are implemented on your system. You can do this using the *service* command (the syslog service restarts both logging daemons):

```
# service syslog restart
```

Another useful method to know about is sending a reconfigure signal to the logging daemons. Several Linux daemons store their process identifier (PID) in files for occasions when you need to send a signal to the process. The following command shows you the PID of *syslogd*:

```
# cat /var/run/syslogd.pid
```

The following command shows you the PID of *klogd*:

```
# cat /var/run/klogd.pid
```

Use the PID returned by these commands with *kill* to send a **SIGHUP** signal to each daemon. This signal tells the daemon to reread its configuration files. You can also use single backward quotation marks to execute the *cat* command and insert the resulting text as a parameter for the *kill* command. (Be sure to use single backward quotation marks rather than forward marks.) The following command causes *syslogd* to reread the syslog.conf configuration file:

```
# kill -HUP `cat /var/run/syslogd.pid`
```

Similarly, you can have *klogd* reread the configuration file using this command:

```
# kill -HUP `cat /var/run/klogd.pid`
```

Another acceptable method of sending the signal to the logging daemons is to use the *killall* command with the name of the daemon, as these two commands show:

```
# killall -HUP syslogd
# killall -HUP klogd
```

Using the logger Utility

The *logger* utility lets you send a message to the syslog function, just as programs do. You can use the *logger* utility from a command line or from a script (as described in Chapter 14, "Writing Shell Scripts"). You can use the *logger* command with just a message. For example, suppose you created a script to compress files automatically. The script can include a simple *logger* command like this:

```
$ logger Compression utility started
```

This logs the message using a default selector of user.notice. The message is logged wherever the syslog.conf file has configured messages matching that selector (normally in /var/log/messages). Because no additional information is specified, the user name of the user running the script is included in the log file as the program name providing the log message. The resulting log entry looks something like this (the timestamp, machine name, and user name would differ on your system):

```
Oct 26 11:42:25 brighton rajw: Compression utility started
```

You can also specify other selectors with the *logger* command. For example, to log a message to the mail facility with a priority of info and the name of the compression script as part of the log file, use this command:

```
$ logger -p mail.info -t compressor Mail folders compressed
```

This logs a message similar to the following:

```
Oct 26 11:46:13 brighton compressor: Mail folders compressed
```

Analyzing Log Files

Log files require attention because they contain a valuable record of what has occurred on your Linux system. You can use the information in the log files to check for various problems, watch for intruders, and compute statistics about your system. At the same time, log files can become very large, eventually filling up the hard disk on a busy system.

A system administrator should regularly check log files for indications of trouble. By reviewing log files and locating problems before they become critical, you can save a great deal of time and expense troubleshooting and recovering from security breaches and program failures. As you review log files regularly, you become accustomed to what is normal and what is unexpected. Table 13-6 lists some sample log file entries with possible interpretations. For the sake of brevity, only the program name and message text are shown in the table; the timestamp and computer host name have been removed from the log entries.

Table 13-6   Interpreting Sample Log File Entries

Sample log entry	System administrator considerations
`login: FAILED LOGIN 3 FROM(null) for nwells, Authentication failure`	Someone has tried to log in as user nwells and entered the wrong password three times in a row. If this happens repeatedly in a short period of time, someone may be trying to break in using that user account.
`login: ROOT LOGIN ON tty1`	Someone has logged in as root, but the timestamp (not shown here) indicates that the login occurred at 2 a.m. If no one is expected to be working at that time, an intruder may have access to the system.
`syslogd 1.3-3: restart`	The *syslogd* daemon was restarted. If you did not do this as system administrator, someone may have changed the logging configuration to try to circumvent a security check or cover a security break-in.
`kernel: eth0: NE2000 Compatible: port 0x300, irg 5, hw_addr 00:E0:98:05:77:B2`	The kernel successfully located the Ethernet card as the system booted. The parameters used to access the card are shown in the kernel log message.
`named[339]: Ready to answer queries`	The DNS server has successfully started and is able to respond to requests from clients to resolve domain names to IP addresses.

Table 13-6 Interpreting Sample Log File Entries (continued)

Sample log entry	System administrator considerations
`modprobe: can't locate module block-major-48`	The *modprobe* command (described in the next section of this chapter) was unable to initialize a device. Some device on the system may not be configured properly.
`kernel: cdrom: open failed`	A user has tried to mount or access the CD-ROM device and either used an incorrect *mount* command or has made some other mistake. The user might need instruction in using the CD-ROM device.
`--MARK--`	The *syslogd* program has inserted a marker to indicate that a fixed amount of time has passed (20 minutes by default). This helps you determine how many messages are written to the log file in each period, but not all systems use this feature. (Red Hat Linux and Fedora, for example, do not.)

You can use standard Linux tools such as *grep* to search for information in the log files. For example, to search for all lines in /var/log/messages that contain the program name login:, use this command:

```
# grep login: /var/log/messages
```

You can also use special log management utilities that watch your log files for conditions that you specify and notify you via e-mail about problems. One of the better log management tools is LogCheck, part of the Sentry Tools package, which you can download from *www.sourceforge.net*.

Rotating Log Files

Over time, log files become too large to leave on your system. Part of every system administrator's job is to rotate the log files regularly so they can be reviewed and then archived or discarded. The process of **rotating log files** can include:

- Erasing old log files to free up disk space for new log information
- Compressing log files and storing them on an archive medium as a long-term record of system activity
- Renaming and compressing the log files so they can be studied at some future time

A common log rotation system stores log files for a month, with a separate archive file for each week. Your particular circumstances must dictate whether you use a separate file for each day, each week, or each month, and how many of those files you maintain. Log files are normally moved to another directory and often to another file system (another hard disk or hard disk partition) to free up space on the root partition.

13

For example, suppose you want to maintain four weeks' worth of archived data for the /var/log/messages log. Each Monday morning you would rotate the log files using this process:

1. Rename all old log rotation files. For example, week4 is deleted, week3 is renamed to week4, week2 is renamed to week3, and week1 is renamed to week2.

2. Rename the /var/log/messages file to week1.

3. Create a new file named /var/log/messages using the *touch* command (initially the file is empty).

4. Send the *syslogd* and *klogd* programs a SIGHUP signal so they can begin to use the new /var/log/messages file. (This signal causes them to find the inode for the new /var/log/messages instead of continuing to write to the previously valid inode, which is now your renamed week1 file.)

You can create scripts to complete these tasks, but Red Hat Linux and Fedora provide a utility called **logrotate** that does all this (and more) for you. This utility is configured by default when you install Red Hat Linux or Fedora so that it runs weekly. If you view the contents of the /var/log directory, you see files ending in a number (such as messages.2). These are the weekly archives of the message log and other logs.

The configuration file /etc/logrotate.conf defines how log files are rotated. This utility manages many types of log files, not just the system log. Specific instructions are included in separate files in the /etc/logrotate.d directory. Review the man page for *logrotate* if you want to modify the default configuration for your system. Other Linux distributions may not include *logrotate*, but often include similar utilities or scripts.

EXPLORING KERNEL COMPONENTS

In this section you learn how Linux keeps track of the time. You also learn about the proc file system, which contains detailed information about the kernel. This section also discusses working with kernel modules and several high-end features of the Linux kernel. You may want to experiment with these if you work on large Linux servers or maintain data for large numbers of users.

Timekeeping in Linux

Each Intel-based computer contains an electronic clock with a small battery. This clock maintains the correct time, even when the computer is turned off. In the Linux community, this is called the **hardware clock**. Each time you turn on a Linux system, the kernel retrieves the time from the hardware clock and sets its own internal clock, called the **system clock**. This system clock is used for virtually all situations in which the time and date are needed. The system clock is maintained internally as a single number: the number of seconds since January 1, 1970. Fortunately, that number is converted to a more readable format by several utilities; you would only use the raw number stored in the system clock if you were working as a software developer.

You can see the current date and time, as recorded in the system clock, using the *date* command. You can see the current date and time, as recorded in the hardware clock, using the *hwclock* command. Neither command requires any parameters.

You can also use the *hwclock* command to change the time and date stored in the hardware clock. This has no effect on the system clock (the Linux kernel or any activities of the kernel or Linux programs) until the system is restarted. Unfortunately, if the system clock is inaccurate because the hardware clock was incorrectly set, it is dangerous to change the value of the system clock directly, though it can be done using the *date* command or other programming commands. Doing so is dangerous because so many parts of the Linux system rely on the system clock, and expect it to continue its forward progression.

Most system administrators working on a larger network with access to the Internet use a network time server. A **network time server** is a computer that maintains highly accurate time based on atomic clocks or radio clocks. Using the **Network Time Protocol (NTP)**, a Linux system can contact a network time server regularly and adjust the system clock (and, as needed, the hardware clock) without disturbing the operation of the kernel. By using NTP, many Linux systems located around the world can keep precisely the same time. This becomes important for coordinating various network events, time-stamping files and e-mails, and in other situations.

The NTP server is installed by default on Red Hat Linux and Fedora. To use it, you must add the name of a network time server to the **/etc/ntp.conf** file. You can read more about this protocol and how time servers are organized worldwide, plus find a time server near you, at *www.ntp.org*. After you have added the name of the network time server to your configuration file, you can start the NTP service using this command:

```
# service ntpd start
```

Kernel Management Using the /proc File System

As you work at your graphical desktop or command-line interface, the Linux kernel and many other programs are managing the system in the background. For example, while the kernel is managing memory and network traffic, one program might be sending files to a printer, and another logging many activities for later review.

In Chapter 6, "Managing Processes," you learned that you can view detailed information about any process running on a Linux system by looking in /proc and referring to the PID for a running program. The /proc file system provides much more information about what the kernel is doing. You can also set parameters within the kernel directly from the command line.

The /proc file system is similar to the /dev directory in that you use it to interact with system resources as if they were files. For example, you can read information within /proc or its subdirectories using a command such as *cat*. But the information you see from /proc is not stored on a hard disk. When you query a file name in /proc, the Linux kernel responds with live information about the status of a process, memory, or other resource. This information can change from moment to moment.

For example, you can query /proc to see the memory capacity of your system and how it is being used:

```
# cat /proc/meminfo
```

You can query /proc to learn about many parts of your system hardware. This information can be useful as you configure devices or software services. Table 13-7 lists the paths in your Linux directory structure where you can access various hardware information.

Table 13-7   Hardware Information Accessible through /proc

Hardware information	Path
Battery information for systems using advanced power management (APM) software	/proc/apm
CPU information	/proc/cpuinfo
Direct memory access (DMA) channels used by system devices	/proc/dma
Interrupts configured for system devices	/proc/interrupts
Ports (memory addresses) used to communicate with system devices	/proc/ioports
File systems currently available to the Linux kernel	/proc/mounts
Disk partitions known to the Linux kernel	/proc/partitions
Information on all PCI devices in your system, such as video cards and hard disk controllers	/proc/pci
Information on all SCSI devices in your system	/proc/scsi and its subdirectories
Swap device information	/proc/swaps

Many Linux system administration utilities use information from /proc. For example, utilities such as *free*, *ps*, and *vmstat*, described in Chapter 6, obtain information from /proc and present it in a format that is easier to read than the /proc files themselves.

You can also write information to some file names in /proc. For example, you can write a value to /proc/sys/fs/file-max to change the number of file handles that can be used at one time in Linux. (A **file handle** is an internal storage mechanism that allows a single file to be opened and used in Linux.) This command displays the number of file handles currently configured in the Linux kernel:

```
# cat /proc/sys/fs/file-max
19660
```

This command changes the number of file handles available in the Linux kernel to 48000:

```
# echo 48000 > /proc/sys/fs/file-max
```

The preferred method of viewing and updating many kernel parameters is to use the *sysctl* command. This command displays the value of a kernel parameter, or sets the parameter to a new value that you specify. Initial values of kernel parameters are set when the kernel is first compiled, but they can also be modified at startup by any values that are stored in the file /etc/sysctl.conf.

The *sysctl* command operates on values stored in /proc/sys. This directory contains numerous subdirectories. Some of these, such as /proc/sys/net/ipv4, contain dozens of kernel parameters that are very complex—you are unlikely to ever need to change most of these. A few parameters can be very helpful, however. For example, if you were operating a very large Web server, you might want to increase the maximum number of files that the kernel can have open at the same time by increasing the maximum number of file handles permitted, as shown by the previous parameter, /proc/sys/fs/file-max.

As another example, suppose that you have installed two Ethernet cards in your computer and want it to act as a router. To do this, you must enable IP forwarding, so that network packets can be transferred between the two Ethernet cards. You saw in Chapter 12, "Configuring Networks," how to do this using a *cat* command. The preferred method is to use the *sysctl* command. First, you might query the current status of the parameter. A period is used to separate levels of subdirectories when using *sysctl*. For example, to query a parameter stored in the net/ipv4 subdirectory under /proc/sys, you add net.ipv4. before the parameter name. The IP forward query would look like this:

```
# sysctl net.ipv4.ip_forward
```

If the value reported back to you is 0 then you know that IP forwarding is not enabled. You can enable it using this command:

```
# sysctl -w net.ipv4.ip_forward=1
```

If you want to have IP forwarding enabled each time your system is booted, you can add this line to the /etc/sysctl.conf file:

```
net.ipv4.ip_forward=1
```

Using Kernel Modules

One of the most useful features of Linux is its ability to add and remove parts of the kernel without restarting the computer. Linux **kernel modules** are files containing computer code that can be loaded into the kernel or removed from the kernel as needed. Many features of Linux can be created either as built-in parts of the kernel or as modules that can be inserted on the fly. Examples include:

- Support for a network adapter card
- Support for a SCSI hard disk controller card
- Networking features such as special firewall capability
- The ability to access other types of file systems
- Support for a sound card

13

Kernel modules can be automatically loaded based on the configuration you set up during the Linux installation. The ***lsmod*** command lists the modules that are installed in the Linux kernel. The names of most modules are not very helpful, but some are recognizable. For example, the *sound* module is used for sound card support, and the *scsi* module is part of the support for SCSI hard disk controllers (multiple modules are required for both sound and SCSI support). A standard Red Hat Linux or Fedora system includes about 30 kernel modules by default. When you see any module listed in the output of *lsmod*, you can use the ***modinfo*** command to learn a little more about that module. For example, use a command such as the following to see information about the ext3 module (you need to be logged in as root to use all of the module-related commands):

```
# modinfo ext3
```

Each kernel module is stored as a file on the hard disk. When the module is added to the kernel, it is copied from the hard disk to memory as part of the kernel.

Adding and Removing Modules

In most cases, the kernel modules needed to communicate with your computer hardware are loaded automatically. But as you explore more advanced Linux functions, you may need to add a module manually. You can do this using the ***modprobe*** command, which loads a module with any required supporting modules. For example, if you use the command *modprobe sb* to load the SoundBlaster module, other modules are automatically loaded as well so that the sound card functions correctly.

NOTE

The modprobe relies on a table of module dependencies that is created by the ***depmod*** command. This command is executed each time you start your system. In addition to modprobe, you can use the ***insmod*** command to insert (add) modules to the running Linux kernel. But the *insmod* command doesn't automatically load dependent modules, so you must know exactly what additional modules to load and the order in which to load them.

The ***rmmod*** command removes a module from the kernel. The module remains available on the hard disk so that you can load it again later.

Some modules require specific hardware information in order to function correctly. For example, when you add a module to support a network adapter card, you may need to include information about the card's IRQ (interrupt request line). **Module parameters** provide information needed by a module to locate system resources. When using the *insmod* or *modprobe* command, you add module parameters after the module name. For example, to support an NE2000 network adapter, you must load the *ne2* module. The following command includes the hardware's IRQ and I/O port address:

```
# modprobe ne2 irq=11 io_port=0x330
```

The 0x at the beginning of the last number in the preceding example indicates a hexadecimal value.

When you execute the *insmod* or *modprobe* command, the module attempts to communicate with any related system hardware as it is being loaded. If the module loads successfully, you see no feedback on the screen. If a problem occurs, you see a message stating that the module could not be loaded or could not be initialized. Such a message means that you selected the wrong module for your hardware or that the module parameters were incorrect or inadequate.

Locating Modules

When you see a module name (something like *sb* or *aic7xxx*), it's difficult to know which devices or kernel features that module supports. In addition, the parameters supported by each module are difficult to find. You can experiment with different modules until you finally locate the correct module for hardware that is not working correctly. But it is more efficient to contact the vendor of your Linux system or your hardware vendor and ask the technical support representative which module and parameters to use. (You still need to determine the values for the required parameters based on your computer's hardware configuration.)

13

The comments in the source code for each module contain detailed information about what devices and parameters that module supports. To explore the source code, install the kernel-source package, as described in the next section.

The module files are stored in /lib/modules/*version*/kernel, where *version* is the version number of the Linux kernel on the system (for example, /lib/modules/2.6.5-1.358/kernel). Within this directory are subdirectories for networking-related modules, device drivers, and other module types. For example, the subdirectory net/ipv4/netfilter contains 50 modules devoted to the firewall features of the Linux kernel. The subdirectory drivers/Bluetooth contains multiple modules to support Bluetooth wireless device communication.

When you enter an *insmod* or *modprobe* command, the command searches all the module subdirectories for the module name you have entered. The *-t* option of *modprobe* even lets you specify a subdirectory to which *modprobe* should refer, trying all modules in that subdirectory until one loads without an error.

In most situations, the kernel of Red Hat Linux or Fedora loads any necessary kernel modules without help from a system administrator. Although you should understand modules so you can set up complex devices manually, you rarely need to use the *modprobe* command.

Once you have figured out which kernel module you need and what parameters are appropriate for your hardware, you'll want that module to load each time you boot the system. Some versions of Linux automate that process for you. For example, Red Hat Linux and Fedora detect when a needed module is not loaded and load it for you. Other systems rely on a configuration file in /etc that lists the name of each module to be loaded at boot time. In either case, you need to specify any module parameters (such as IRQ number) that should be included when the module is loaded by the system.

In Red Hat Linux and Fedora, you must include an options line in /etc/modprobe.conf for each kernel module that requires kernel parameters when loaded. (The configuration file is /etc/conf.modules in some Linux distributions.) Two sample lines within /etc/modprobe.conf might look like this, depending on the networking hardware that you are using:

```
alias  eth0    3c59x
options 3c59x  irq=15 io=0x300
```

CONFIGURING AND UPGRADING KERNEL COMPONENTS

A standard Linux kernel such as the one installed as part of Red Hat Linux or Fedora provides many popular features and support for many types of hardware. Red Hat Software and other vendors configure the available features of the kernel to appeal to a broad collection of users. Many of these vendors also include multiple versions of the kernel and select which to install based on selections you make or the hardware detected during installation.

Occasionally, a new kernel is released by a Linux vendor such as Red Hat Software or SUSE to correct a security flaw that is discovered. Such flaws are typically part of a server program (like the DNS server), but when the kernel needs to be upgraded, a vendor can release a new rpm file that upgrades your system as needed. If you use the Red Hat Network service discussed in Chapter 10, "Managing Software Packages and File Systems," these updates can be downloaded for you automatically. Kernel updates are not automatically installed by default, however.

You can add features to the kernel by inserting kernel modules. But some kernel features are not available as modules; you can only use them if they are configured when the kernel is compiled from source code. It's unusual that you would need to recompile the Linux kernel. Some situations that might require it include:

- You want to activate a feature that the Linux kernel includes but that is not activated in the default kernel from your Linux vendor. For example, you might want to activate experimental networking features that cannot be added as modules.

- You want to disable an unneeded feature that is part of the default kernel. For example, knowing that you do not have any SCSI devices, you might decide to remove all support for SCSI devices in order to make your kernel smaller.

- You need to compile support for a hardware device into the kernel rather than loading it as a module.

- You want to use an updated version of the Linux kernel to add new features or fix a security problem that was discovered with your current version.

For any of these reasons, you can recompile the Linux kernel from source code, creating a new kernel. The file vmlinuz-2.6.5-1.358 contains the Linux kernel that is used when you start your system. It is usually located in the / directory or in the /boot directory.

When you create a new kernel from source code, that kernel is stored in a subdirectory of /usr/src/linux (based on the kernel version number you are working with). Creating a new kernel involves three steps:

1. Make certain the kernel source code and supporting packages are installed on your system.

2. Configure which features you want the new kernel to have.

3. Execute the commands to compile the source code with the features you selected.

Installing Kernel Source Code

Before recompiling the kernel, you must have several packages installed on your system, such as the source code itself, the compiler, and numerous supporting packages. In Red Hat Linux and Fedora, the source code is in a single (175 MB) rpm named kernel-source. You can use the *rpm* command with the *-q* option to see if this package is installed:

```
# rpm -q kernel-source
```

If this package is not installed, you can use the *rpm* command to install it, but you will probably see that other supporting packages are needed before you can install the kernel-source package. For this reason, the kernel source code was indicated in Chapter 8 as a category that was recommended for installation. If you need to install the kernel source code after installing Linux, use the *rpm* command to install whatever additional packages are needed, then install the kernel-source package.

TIP

You can always download raw source code (not in an rpm-format software package) from *www.linuxhq.com*.

Once the source code is installed, you can explore the source code files in the directory /usr/src/linux-2.6.5-1.358. When you recompile the source code to create a new kernel file, you are not changing the version of the kernel. You are only changing the features that are activated in the kernel. After you recompile the kernel, the timestamp on the kernel you create is different than the kernel that was installed by default on your system.

13

In addition to vendors providing new rpm files containing an updated Linux kernel, you might need to add a small piece of additional source code to the kernel. This is typically done as a patch. A **patch file** is a small file that contains new source code with instructions for where that source code should be inserted or replace existing source code. The *patch* command is used to insert and change lines based on the contents of the patch file. This operation is only rarely needed; the information provided when you download a patch file from your Linux vendor describes the exact steps and commands to use when upgrading your kernel source code with a patch.

Configuring Kernel Features

Once the source code has been installed and patched, if necessary, you can select which kernel options you want to include or activate for your system. The Linux kernel supports thousands of different options. The kernel source code package includes different utilities to help you configure which options you want to include in the kernel you are creating.

Three utilities are available. All of them create or edit the .config file in /usr/src/linux-2. 6.5-1.358. The data in this file is based on your selections in the configuration utilities, as well as information stored in the configs subdirectory (/usr/src/linux-2.6.5-1.358/configs). Each of the configuration files is used for a different type of system; the configuration utilities detect the type of CPU you have and use the appropriate configuration file. The three utilities are:

- *config*: A text-only question and answer session
- *menuconfig*: A text-mode menu-based program
- *xconfig*: A graphical program (renamed *qconf* in Red Hat and Fedora Linux)

You start each of these utilities using the *make* command. The **make** command is a programming utility that uses instructions in a configuration file (called Makefile) to execute a series of instructions. By using the name of a kernel configuration utility after make, you tell *make* which part of the Makefile to use for kernel configuration. You must be in the source code directory (/usr/src/linux-2.6.5-1.358) before using the *make* command. Then use any one of these three commands to run the configuration utility:

```
# make config
# make menuconfig
# make xconfig
```

After entering any of these commands, you see a number of strange lines of text scroll up your screen as the *make* command starts a compiler to prepare the configuration utility you have requested.

Figure 13-13 shows the text-mode questions presented by *make config*. This mode is useful for advanced users because you can use input redirection (the < operator) to feed configuration options to the configuration program. Most users, however, will not want to use this utility.

```
                          root@localhost:/usr/src/linux-2.6.5-1.358              [-][□][X]
 File   Edit   View   Terminal   Tabs   Help
* Power management options (ACPI, APM)

Power Management support (PM) [Y/n/?]
  Software Suspend (EXPERIMENTAL) (SOFTWARE_SUSPEND) [N/y/?]
  Suspend-to-Disk Support (PM_DISK) [N/y/?]
*
* ACPI (Advanced Configuration and Power Interface) Support

ACPI Support (ACPI) [Y/n/?]
  Sleep States (EXPERIMENTAL) (ACPI_SLEEP) [Y/n/?]
  AC Adapter (ACPI_AC) [M/n/y/?]
  Battery (ACPI_BATTERY) [M/n/y/?]
  Button (ACPI_BUTTON) [M/n/y/?]
  Fan (ACPI_FAN) [Y/n/m/?]
  Processor (ACPI_PROCESSOR) [Y/n/m/?]
    Thermal Zone (ACPI_THERMAL) [Y/n/m/?]
  ASUS/Medion Laptop Extras (ACPI_ASUS) [M/n/y/?]
  Toshiba Laptop Extras (ACPI_TOSHIBA) [M/n/y/?]
  Debug Statements (ACPI_DEBUG) [N/y/?]
  Power Management Timer Support (X86_PM_TIMER) [Y/n/?]
*
* APM (Advanced Power Management) BIOS Support

APM (Advanced Power Management) BIOS support (APM) [Y/n/m/?]
  Ignore USER SUSPEND (APM_IGNORE_USER_SUSPEND) [N/y/?]
  Enable PM at boot time (APM_DO_ENABLE) [N/y/?]
  Make CPU Idle calls when idle (APM_CPU_IDLE) [Y/n/?]
  Enable console blanking using APM (APM_DISPLAY_BLANK) [N/y/?]
  RTC stores time in GMT (APM_RTC_IS_GMT) [Y/n/?]
  Allow interrupts during APM BIOS calls (APM_ALLOW_INTS) [N/y/?]
  Use real mode APM BIOS call to power off (APM_REAL_MODE_POWER_OFF) [N/y/?]
*
* CPU Frequency scaling

CPU Frequency scaling (CPU_FREQ) [Y/n/?]
  /proc/cpufreq interface (deprecated) (CPU_FREQ_PROC_INTF) [N/m/y/?]
  Default CPUFreq governor
    1. performance (CPU_FREQ_DEFAULT_GOV_PERFORMANCE)
  > 2. userspace (CPU_FREQ_DEFAULT_GOV_USERSPACE)
  choice[1-2?]:
  'performance' governor (CPU_FREQ_GOV_PERFORMANCE) [Y/n/m/?]
  'powersave' governor (CPU_FREQ_GOV_POWERSAVE) [M/n/y/?]
  'userspace' governor for userspace frequency scaling (CPU_FREQ_GOV_USERSPACE) [Y/?] y
    /proc/sys/cpu/ interface (2.4. / OLD) (CPU_FREQ_24_API) [N/y/?] █
```

Figure 13-13   The *config* utility for setting kernel options

TIP   All three kernel configuration utilities provide access to exactly the same options; they simply give you a different interface to those options.

13

Figure 13-14 shows the text-mode menu–based configuration tool *menuconfig*. Use the arrow keys and other keys as directed in this interface to select kernel features that you want to activate. Over 1000 options are available in the 2.6 kernel. One advantage of this interface is that you can use it when you don't have the X Window System installed.

Figure 13-15 shows the graphical configuration tool *qconf*, which is launched using the *make xconfig* command shown previously. Both *menuconfig* and *qconf* include help buttons. The buttons next to each option provide a description of that option, with a recommendation for when you might use the option and when you should avoid it. The help text for all three utilities is identical.

Beyond its appearance, the *qconf* utility is a good choice for learning about kernel compilation because of how it displays options. Many kernel features can be either built-in (compiled into the kernel itself) or built as modules (which you can load into the kernel at any time). The advantage of modules is that you can have hundreds of features available and only use those you decide you need later on. The advantage of building in features is that you don't have to worry about managing modules to get a feature activated. Beyond that,

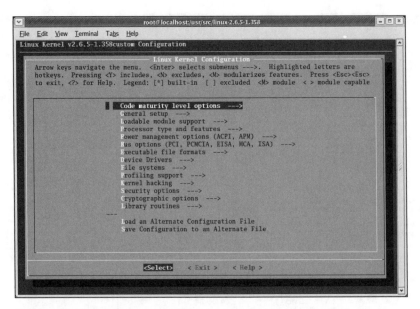

Figure 13-14 The *menuconfig* utility for setting kernel options

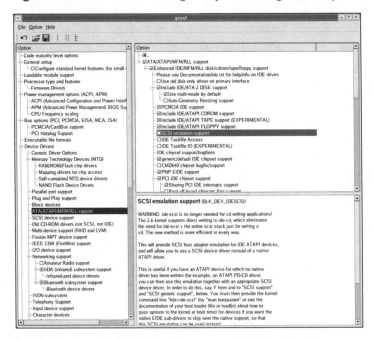

Figure 13-15 The *qconf* utility for setting kernel options

some features can only be built in. For example, the ext3 file system must be compiled into the kernel; it cannot be built in as a module. Such relationships between kernel components are probably easier to see in the *qconf* interface.

TIP Even if you do not need to recompile your kernel, exploring the kernel features and reading the help text in the *qconf* program is an excellent way to learn about Linux capabilities. Many help screens also include Web URLs to direct you to additional information on relevant topics.

When you exit *config*, *menuconfig*, or *qconf*, the utility saves any changes you have made to the configuration file. If you decide you want to revert back to the original configuration of your current kernel, enter this command from within /usr/src/linux-2.6.5–1.358:

```
# make mrproper
```

Compiling a New Kernel

After selecting a new kernel configuration, you are ready to compile the kernel source code into a new kernel file that you can use to start your system. To do this, you execute a series of make commands that prepare all the source code files and then compile them into a kernel image. You also compile and install new modules for the new kernel as a separate operation. Running all of these commands requires between 30 minutes and three hours, depending on the speed of your system. These commands are often placed on the same command line, separated by semicolons, so you can enter one command line and return to your computer after all the commands have completed. A typical command string is:

```
# make dep; make bzImage; make modules; make modules_install
```

You can also use *make bzdisk* in place of *make bzImage* to create a boot disk containing the new Linux kernel. This is a safe way to experiment with new kernels because your original kernel remains intact: you can try the new kernel by starting from a 3.5-inch disk, or eject the disk and return to your default kernel. The default configuration of the kernel is too large to fit on a floppy disk, however. You need to deactivate several features if you want to experiment with boot disks.

The *make bzImage* command creates a compressed kernel image called bzImage in the directory /usr/src/linux-2.6.5–1.358/arch/i386/boot. To use that kernel, you should make a backup copy of your current kernel in /boot, then copy the bzImage file to /boot. In Red Hat Linux or Fedora, the /boot/vmlinuz-2.6.5–1.358 file is a symbolic link to the actual kernel file (which includes lengthy version and release numbers). You can use the following commands to set up the new kernel:

```
# cd /boot
# cp /usr/src/linux-2.6.5-1.358/arch/i386/boot/bzImage ./vmlinuz-
new
# ln -s vmlinuz vmlinuz-new
```

If you are using the LILO boot manager, you must also run the *lilo* command to update the boot manager with information about the new kernel file. If you are using the default GRUB boot manager, this step is not needed. GRUB can locate the needed information based solely on the file name.

13

When you restart your system, the new vmlinuz file is used. After restarting, execute the *uname -v* command to see the timestamp of the kernel you are running.

NOTE   Recompiling the kernel can be much more complicated than what is outlined here. For further study, refer to the README file in /usr/src/linux-2.6.5-1.358, the help screens within the configuration utilities, and the copious documentation provided in /usr/src/linux-2.6.5-1.358/Documentation and on *www. linuxhq.com*.

CHAPTER SUMMARY

- ❏ A backup plan helps a system administrator create an orderly system for backing up Linux data on a regular basis and restoring lost data as needed.

- ❏ A backup plan must address questions such as who is responsible for maintaining backups, which parts of each Linux file system are backed up at what intervals, and how often backups are performed.

- ❏ The dollar value and time sensitivity of the data stored on your Linux systems determines how much expense you can justify in creating a backup plan. The value of data includes several factors beyond the money paid to an employee to create the data.

- ❏ A three-level backup method is commonly used. All data is backed up monthly (level zero), and changed files are backed up weekly (level one) and daily (level two). A multilevel backup system provides a reasonable trade-off between convenience and low cost on one side, and protecting data on the other.

- ❏ Backing up the root file system and preparing to restore critical applications are parts of a backup plan that may require special attention.

- ❏ Backups should be verified regularly to be certain that data is recoverable from the backup media.

- ❏ File permissions must be part of a valid backup in order to avoid problems when files are restored.

- ❏ Compression is commonly used when backing up data, but does increase vulnerability in case of corrupted data.

- ❏ The command-line utilities *tar, cpio, dump,* and *restore* are commonly used for simple backups.

- ❏ Many free and commercial utilities are available to help system administrators manage their backup strategy. Most of these are graphical applications and include facilities for networkwide backup, managing large sets of backup media, and verifying or restoring files from backup media.

- ❏ Log files record the activities of Linux programs. The main system log used by the kernel and many daemons is /var/log/messages.

❑ System and kernel messages are logged by the *syslogd* and *klogd* daemons using the configuration in /etc/syslog.conf.

❑ Each line in syslog.conf defines a set of messages and what action to take with those messages. Messages are defined using a selector, which is made up of a facility and a priority. The facility defines the type of program that generated the message; the priority defines the severity or type of message.

❑ Special characters in syslog.conf let you define multiple facilities or priorities, use multiple selectors, or implement other special features.

❑ The *logger* utility lets you send a message to the system logging daemon from any command line or script.

❑ Log files must be maintained by rotating them. This is typically done using the *logrotate* command. Analyzing log files can help a system administrator spot problems with security or performance.

❑ A system clock in the Linux kernel maintains a time and date for system events. This clock is initially set from the hardware clock, but can be more accurately maintained using a network time server that relies on the Network Time Protocol. The *date* and *hwclock* commands display the date and time from the system and hardware clocks, respectively.

❑ The /proc file system lets you view details about the kernel, running processes, and other system information. You can view process information using /proc or using a number of other utilities, such as *ps* and *top*.

❑ Kernel parameters in /proc/sys can be viewed and altered using the *sysctl* command. Parameter values stored in /etc/sysctl.conf are configured automatically at boot time.

❑ The Linux kernel supports loadable modules, which are managed using the *lsmod*, *insmod*, *rmmod*, and *modprobe* commands. Module parameters define information to help modules load and operate correctly.

❑ RAID systems let you improve speed, fault tolerance, or both, depending on the configuration you choose. Hardware-based RAID systems let you use RAID without configuring RAID as part of the Linux kernel, but they are expensive.

❑ RAID levels include features such as mirroring and duplexing to make data redundant, striping to make data access faster, and parity information to reconstruct data when one disk in the array fails.

❑ Using the Logical Volume Manager, you can combine multiple physical hard disks into a single logical volume group, which can then be split into partitions for separate file systems. These partitions can be expanded by adding physical storage to the system without destroying data on the existing file system.

❑ The Linux kernel is sometimes updated by Linux vendors via a new rpm file. You can also modify the kernel source code by adding a patch file or downloading new versions of the kernel source code.

13

❏ You can modify the configuration of the Linux kernel (without changing its source code) in order to activate or deactivate features, including making features built-in instead of loadable modules.

❏ The kernel source code is available as an rpm package or as raw source code from *www.linuxhq.com*. This site also has patches to let you upgrade to a newer version of the kernel, though that is rarely necessary.

❏ Three kernel configuration utilities are supported: *config*, *menuconfig*, and *xconfig* (*qconf*). Each uses the same help text and the same options, but each interface has its own advantages and disadvantages.

❏ Kernel configuration utilities are started using the *make* command, which is also used after configuration is completed to start the actual kernel compilation process. This process can take several hours on a slower machine.

❏ The new kernel is located in /usr/src/linux-2.6.5-1.358/arch/i386/boot. It must be copied to /boot to make it usable and may require that you update or modify your boot manager to use the new kernel. You can also create a boot floppy disk using *make bzdisk*, though the default kernel configuration cannot fit on a floppy.

COMMAND SUMMARY

Command	Description	Example
apropos	Displays any man pages with information on the specified term.	apropos lvm
ark	Graphical backup (archiving) utility; part of the KDE desktop.	ark
config	Option used to configure the Linux kernel using interactive command-line entries; must be used with the *make* command while in an appropriate Linux kernel source code directory (such as /usr/src/Linux-2.6.5-1.358).	make config
date	Displays the date and time stored by the system clock.	date
dd	Copies data from one device to another, without any processing by the command.	dd if=/mnt/cdrom/ images/bootdisk.img of=/dev/fd0
depmod	Creates a file listing dependencies between all kernel modules available on the system for use by the *modprobe* command. Normally executed only as part of system startup scripts.	/sbin/depmod –a
dump	Stores files for backup.	dump -0u -f /dev/ st0 /home
hwclock	Displays the date and time stored by the hardware clock, or updates those values.	hwclock

Command	Description	Example
insmod	Adds a kernel module to the running kernel. The *modprobe* command is normally used instead of this command because *modprobe* automatically adds modules that are prerequisite to the one requested.	insmod ne2000
klogd	A daemon used to log kernel messages according to the configuration given in the syslog.conf configuration file; started by scripts at start-up.	klogd
logger	A program that lets you send a message to the syslog function; messages are written to the log files according to the configuration in syslog.conf.	logger -p mail.info -t compressor Mail folders compressed
logrotate	A program that manages the rotation of multiple log files at regular intervals according to the logrotate.conf configuration file.	logrotate /etc/logrotate.conf
lsmod	Lists all modules currently installed in the Linux kernel.	lsmod
lvm	The Logical Volume Manager utility; only used when logical volume groups have been configured.	lvm
make	Performs actions defined in a Makefile, usually compiling a collection of source code into a finished binary program and preparing or installing that program.	make xconfig
makewhatis	Creates an internal database of man page information for use by the *whatis* command.	makewhatis
menuconfig	Option used to configure the Linux kernel using a text-based menu system; must be used with the *make* command while in an appropriate Linux kernel source code directory (such as /usr/src/Linux-2.6.5-1.358).	make menuconfig
modinfo	Displays information about a named kernel module.	modinfo ext3
modprobe	Adds a kernel module to the running kernel, including any prerequisite modules.	modprobe ne2000
patch	Updates source code files using a patch file that contains modifications to one or more source code files.	patch -p0 < *patch_ file*
restore	Restores files that have been archived using the *dump* command.	restore rf /dev/st0
rmmod	Removes a kernel module from the kernel.	rmmod ne2000
sysctl	Views or modifies a kernel parameter via the /proc file system.	sysctl -w net.ipv4.ip_ forward=1

13

Command	Description	Example
syslogd	Daemon that manages all of the calls to the syslog function, writing log messages according to the syslog.conf configuration; started by scripts at start-up.	syslogd
whatis	Displays a one-line description of any man page about the item queried.	whatis lvm
xconfig	Option used to configure the Linux kernel using a graphical utility (called *qconf* in Red Hat and Fedora); must be used with the *make* command while in an appropriate Linux kernel source code directory (such as /usr/src/Linux-2.6.5-1.358).	make xconfig

Key Terms

/etc/ntp.conf — Configuration file used by the Network Time Protocol (NTP) server.

action — A field in the syslog.conf configuration file that determines what to do with messages matching the selector on that line.

backup — A copy of data on a computer system.

backup level — A description of how much data is stored in a backup operation. A backup level is only relevant in comparison with another backup level. When performing a backup operation at a given level, all of the data that has changed since the last backup of the previous level is recorded.

backup media — A device on which data can be stored, such as a tape cartridge, writeable CD or DVD, or floppy disk.

backup plan — A written document that outlines when, how, and why various files and file systems are backed up, stored, and—when necessary—restored to prevent permanent data loss.

differential backup — A backup process that stores all files that have changed since a full backup was made.

duplexing — A redundancy technique in which hard disks are accessed via different hard disk controllers. Compare to "mirroring," a technique that provides identical information on two file systems but without redundant disk controllers.

epoch backup — A full backup, containing all the data on a system.

facility — A category assigned to a system message, identifying the type of program providing the message. Facilities are used in syslog.conf.

fault tolerance — The ability to respond gracefully when an unexpected hardware or software failure occurs, so as to prevent a complete shutdown of the system.

file handle — An internal storage mechanism that allows a single file to be opened and used in Linux.

hardware-based RAID — A RAID array that is contained in a separate hardware device (a RAID subsystem) and is controlled by a CPU and other components separate from the CPU of the Linux system.

hardware clock — The clock that is part of the hardware in every Intel-based PC. Used by the Linux kernel to initialize the system clock when the kernel is started.

hot-swapping — Removing and replacing a failed hard drive or other component without turning off the power to the device.

incremental backup — A backup process that stores all files that have changed since the last incremental or differential backup was made.

kernel modules — Files containing computer code that can be loaded into the kernel or removed from the kernel as needed.

log file — A file that contains detailed records of activity on a Linux system.

logical volume group — A collection of physical volumes (actual hard disk partitions) that are grouped together for use by the Logical Volume Manager utilities to provide a level of abstraction for ease in adding space to file systems later on.

Logical Volume Manager (LVM) — A feature of Red Hat Linux and Fedora that provides a collection of utilities to permit multiple physical storage devices to be managed as single storage volumes, dividing them into file systems as needed and adding space to those file systems without the need to reformat hard disks.

message — A description of what is happening within a program.

messages file — The main system log file in Linux, usually stored in the directory /var/log.

mirroring — A redundancy technique in which the contents of two file systems contain identical information. Mirroring improves data access speed and provides fault tolerance in the event that one of the file systems fails.

module parameters — Information needed by a module to locate system resources. The parameters are added after the module name when using the *insmod* or *modprobe* command.

Network Time Protocol (NTP) — A protocol used to coordinate highly accurate timekeeping between servers on a network or the Internet.

network time server — A computer that maintains accurate time by relying on a radio clock, atomic clock, or similar device, and that can provide accurate time to other networked servers using the Network Time Protocol (NTP).

parity — A redundancy technique that allows corrupted data to be reconstructed using an extra piece of information (the parity information) that is created as the data is stored.

parity stripe — Parity information stored as part of a RAID-3 or RAID-5 system.

patch file — A text file containing updates to one or more source code files, with instructions for how those source code files should be updated. The *patch* command is used to apply a patch file to existing source code files.

physical volumes — The underlying physical partitions used by the Logical Volume Manager. Multiple physical volumes together are a logical volume group, which is divided into standard partitions data storage.

priority — A label indicating the severity of a message submitted for logging. Priorities are used in syslog.conf.

RAID (redundant arrays of inexpensive disks) — A storage technique using multiple inexpensive hard disks arranged in a predefined pattern (an array) to improve performance, increase fault tolerance, or both.

13

RAID-0 — A RAID level that uses striping to improve disk performance without adding any fault tolerance.

RAID-1 — A RAID level that uses disk mirroring to significantly improve fault tolerance. Disk read performance is also improved, but disk write performance suffers.

RAID-3 — A RAID level that uses striping with parity information to improve performance and increase fault tolerance.

RAID-5 — A RAID level in which striping with parity is spread across all disks in the RAID array (compared to RAID-3, in which the parity information is stored on a single hard disk).

RAID-Linear — A storage technique in which multiple physical devices are combined into a single logical device.

RAID subsystem — A hardware-controlled RAID device containing a CPU and other components to control the array of hard disks.

redundant arrays of inexpensive disks — *See* RAID.

restore — To copy data from a backup location (for example, a tape cartridge) onto the file system where that data is normally used, and from which it was unintentionally lost.

rotating log files — The process of moving existing log files to another file name and location for archiving or review.

selector — A field in the syslog.conf file that determines what events are being logged. A selector is composed of a facility and a priority.

SIGHUP — A signal sent to a logging daemon to instruct the daemon to reread its configuration files and the log file to which it writes. Sometimes called HUP.

striping — A data storage technique in which parts of a file are written to more than one disk in order to improve performance. *See* RAID-3 and RAID-5.

syslog.conf — The configuration file used to control how and where messages are logged by *syslogd* and *klogd*.

system clock — An internal clock maintained by the Linux kernel whenever the system is turned on. Initialized based on the hardware clock. Maintained accurately on large networks by relying on a network time server using the Network Time Protocol (NTP).

timestamp — The date and time when an event being logged occurred.

write caching — A feature of some storage systems in which information that is to be written to a file system (particularly a RAID file system) is stored in memory temporarily in order to improve the overall read/write performance of the file system.

Review Questions

1. A backup plan does *not* normally include the following:

    a. a list of tape drive prices

    b. times when backups are performed

    c. the location of critical files on the system

    d. a recommended time to replace old tape cartridges with new ones

2. Explain how the speed with which files need to be restored affects a backup plan.

3. Why might you back up operating system files as well as user data files?

4. Name two parts of a Linux system that are likely to change daily.

5. Explain why a level one backup is called a differential backup.

6. Using backup levels has the advantage of:

   a. reducing the time required to back up the entire file system

   b. making it easier to recover a file that has not been changed in several weeks

   c. allowing a system administrator to spend less time with backups but keep data backed up very frequently

   d. causing all system backups to be available via a single file index

7. Using a standard three-level backup plan with the time intervals described in the chapter text, a user would expect never to lose more than _____ worth of work.

   a. a week's

   b. a day's

   c. an hour's

   d. 20 MB

8. Explain why a system administrator must use backup media from three backups in order to completely restore a system that used three backup levels.

9. As a rule, tape cartridges can hold much more than optical media. True or False?

10. The burdened cost of an employee includes:

    a. the costs an employee must pay for benefits such as health insurance

    b. the costs an employer must pay that are not part of the employee's salary

    c. the value of data that an employee created for an organization but that is lost because of unverified backups

    d. two to three times the employee's salary

11. Explain how redundancy relates to compressed data and why that is relevant to data backup operations.

12. The _____ utility is a commercial backup utility.

    a. BRU

    b. kdat

    c. Arkeia

    d. mke2fs

13. Describe the special considerations that must be taken to restore the root file system of Linux after a hardware failure.

14. In the long term, backup media are likely to cost more than the backup device used to access them. True or False?

15. Log files are generally *not* used for which of the following tasks?

    a. watching for security problems

    b. calculating system usage statistics

    c. calculating memory usage for applications

    d. determining the cause of system failures

16. Given the log entry,

    ```
    Oct 26 06:45:01 brighton httpd:
    Cannot determine local host name
    ```

    the word httpd refers to which of the following?

    a. the system name on which the event being logged occurred

    b. the program that generated the event being logged

    c. the daemon handling the logging of the event

    d. the configuration file used to control logging of this event

17. Explain the differences between the *syslogd* and the *klogd* logging daemons.

18. The *syslogd* and *klogd* logging daemons depend upon which configuration file?

    a. logrotate.conf

    b. syslog.conf

    c. They are internally configured and use no configuration file.

    d. the syslog function called by individual applications

19. A configuration pair consisting of a facility and a priority is called:

    a. an action

    b. the timestamp

    c. a selector

    d. a SIGHUP signal

20. If *.info appears in the log configuration file, the following will be logged:

    a. messages from all facilities with a priority of info or higher

    b. messages without a facility assigned with a priority of info

    c. messages with a facility of info and any priority

    d. messages from the info command that are posted on the screens of all users who are logged into the system

21. Which of the following is not a valid facility name?

    a. auth

    b. httpd

    c. user

    d. mail

22. This configuration line

    `*.emerg   @brighton`

    causes which of the following to occur?

    a. All messages with a facility of emerg are logged to a file matching the system name (the host name).

    b. All messages with a priority of emerg or lower are logged to the file configured as an alias to brighton.

    c. All messages with a priority of emerg are sent to the machine named brighton for logging.

    d. All messages of any priority but emerg are displayed on the screen of user brighton, if that user is logged in.

23. This configuration line

    `*.info:mail,news.none:authpriv.none   -/var/log/messages`

    is invalid because:

    a. A colon cannot be used to separate multiple selectors.

    b. Each selector can only include one facility.

    c. The *none* keyword cannot be used as a priority.

    d. The hyphen can only be used in the action field when associated with a set of user names.

24. Describe why the system logging daemons must be reinitialized using a HUP signal in order to access new configuration files.

25. The *logger* utility does which of the following?

    a. sends messages to the syslog function for logging according to the syslog.conf file

    b. writes messages to /var/log/messages

    c. rotates log files according to a predetermined configuration

    d. restarts the logging daemons with a SIGHUP signal

26. Which of the following is a valid reason to rotate your log files?

    a. Leaving them open for long periods can cause file corruption.

    b. The files become too large to store permanently on the root partition.

    c. System administrators cannot study live log files.

    d. Security-minded individuals feel rotated log files are safer.

13

27. If you saw the message

    ```
    login:
    FAILED LOGIN 3 FROM (null) for rajw, Authentication failure
    ```

    you might reasonably assume any of the following *except*:

    a. Someone is trying to break into your system using the rajw account.

    b. User rajw has forgotten his password.

    c. The login program has become corrupted.

    d. A user on your system is trying to break into the files owned by rajw.

28. The module files loaded by the *modprobe* command are located in a subdirectory of:

    a. /etc/modules

    b. /lib/modules

    c. /usr/lib/modules

    d. /boot/modules

29. Name four commands used to work with kernel modules.

30. Redundant arrays of inexpensive disks (RAID) are used to provide:

    a. lower-cost systems than single disks

    b. redundant superblock information

    c. improved reliability

    d. high-efficiency multi-processing

31. Striping refers to which of the following?

    a. spreading a single file across multiple hard disks

    b. duplicating file information on multiple hard disks

    c. adding error-correcting codes to a file

    d. duplicating inode data

32. Define the advantages and disadvantages of using hot-swapped disk drives.

33. Which RAID level provides redundancy and fault tolerance at the *highest cost*?

    a. RAID-0

    b. RAID-1

    c. RAID-3

    d. RAID-5

34. When using the Logical Volume Manager, a collection of physical volumes that can be split into logical partitions for individual file systems is called a:

    a. logical volume group

    b. physical volume

    c. mirrored partition

    d. partition module

35. Which of the following statements is correct?

    a. The graphical utility for configuring the kernel provides access to additional configuration options compared to the other two utilities.

    b. The command-line utility for configuring the kernel provides access to additional configuration options compared to the other two utilities.

    c. The three available configuration utilities for the kernel differ only in their interface to select kernel options.

    d. When configuring kernel options, you must determine which configuration utility has been preinstalled on the system by your Linux vendor because attempting to configure the kernel with a nonsupported utility can damage the kernel configuration and can, in extreme cases, require reinstalling the operating system.

HANDS-ON PROJECTS

HANDS-ON PROJECTS

Project 13-1

In this project, you experiment with the KDE graphical archive utility Ark. To complete this activity you must have a working Linux system with KDE and GNOME installed. The recommended installation in Chapter 8, "Installing Linux," includes both GNOME and KDE, and includes the Ark utility. The steps taken to add files to the archive assume you are running Red Hat Linux or Fedora and using the GNOME desktop, but any standard version of KDE includes the Ark program.

13

1. Log in to Linux and open a command-line window.

2. Open a Nautilus window by selecting Browse Filesystem on the GNOME main menu.

3. In the Location field of the window, enter this directory name:

    /usr/share/doc/pam-0.77/txts

4. Start the KDE archiving utility called Ark by entering **ark &** at a command line. Wait for the Ark window to open.

5. In the Nautilus window, click and drag to select a number of the text files in the directory you specified in Step 3.

6. Click on one of the selected items in the txts window and drag your mouse to the blank area in the middle of the Ark window, then release your mouse button.

7. You are asked whether you want to create a new archive file using these files. Click **Yes**.

8. A file-browsing window appears allowing you to select the directory in which you want your new archive file created and to enter a name for that archive file. Your home directory is shown by default, which is fine for this project. In the Location field of the Create New Archive – Ark window, enter **testark.tgz**. Then click **Save**.

   The files you dragged and dropped are listed in the Ark main window. The title bar also changes to show the name of the archive you created, testark.tgz.

9. In the Ark window, open the **Action** menu and click **Add Folder**.

10. Use the directory browser in that window (or enter in the text field below the directory browser) to select the directory **/usr/share/dict**, then click **OK**. All the files from that directory are added to the testark.tgz file and are also listed on the screen.

11. Right-click any file name in the Ark main window. What options are available for any file in the archive?

12. Choose **File**, then **Quit** from the menu of Ark. If prompted to select Save, Discard, or Cancel, click **Save**.

13. Delete the archive file you created by entering this command at the command line:

    ```
    rm ~/testark.tgz
    ```

14. Confirm the deletion if prompted, then close the command-line window and log out.

HANDS-ON PROJECTS

Project 13-2

In this project, you watch the system log file as new messages are written to it by the *syslogd* daemon. To complete this project you need a Linux system with a graphical interface and root access.

1. Log in to Linux and open two command-line windows.

2. In each of the command-line windows, use **su –** to change to root access.

3. In one command-line window, enter this command to display the last 15 lines of the system log file, updating the display every few seconds

   ```
   tail -f /var/log/messages
   ```

4. In the second command-line window, enter this command to restart the *syslogd* daemon:

   ```
   killall -HUP syslogd
   ```

   Notice that a message is added to the first window stating that the *syslogd* program was restarted.

5. In the second window, enter **killall –HUP cron** to restart the scheduling daemons. Were any messages added?

6. Try to find other actions that write information to the system log shown in the first window. For example, try opening a Web browser, restarting other system services (using the *service* command), changing a user's password, or switching to a virtual console and logging in. Why do you think some actions write to the log file and others do not?

7. Press **Ctrl+c** to exit the *tail* command in the first command-line window. Close all open windows and log out.

Project 13-3

In this project, you use the *logger* command to send a message to /var/log/messages. To complete this project you need a Linux system with a graphical interface and root access.

1. Log in to Linux and start the graphical environment.

2. Open two command-line windows. In both windows, use the **su –** command to change to root access.

3. In one of the windows, enter this command to display the last 15 lines of the system log file, updating the display every few seconds:

```
tail -f /var/log/messages
```

4. In the second window, enter this command:

```
logger -p user.info -t TESTING This is a logging test.
```

5. Notice the message that is added to the /var/log/messages file shown in the first window.

6. Using the facility and priority names you have learned, try sending one or two other messages using the *logger* program. In particular, try sending a message with the priority emerg. For example, you might use this command:

```
logger -p user.emerg -t TESTING Emergency message test.
```

What do you notice about how this command is treated compared to the other *logger* commands you entered? Can you explain why, based on the information in the syslog.conf file?

7. Press **Ctrl+c** to exit the *tail* command in the first command-line window. Close all open windows and log out.

Project 13-4

In this project, you practice selecting kernel configuration options using the graphical configuration tool. To complete this project you need a Linux system with the kernel-source rpm and supporting packages installed. (If you selected all the recommended packages in Chapter 8, you have all needed packages.) You also need root access. If you want to complete the final steps of compiling a new kernel image, you may need up to an hour or more while the kernel is compiled (though you do not need to be sitting at the computer during this time).

 NOTE   The configuration you see as you work in the configuration utility does not necessarily match the kernel you are currently running. Your installation program may select from among various kernels based on your installation selections and your hardware, but the kernel-source package has a set of default options that you see when you start configuring the kernel.

1. Log in to Linux and start the graphical environment.

2. Open a command-line window and use **su –** to change to root access.

3. Change to the kernel source code directory:

   cd /usr/src/linux-2.6.5-1.358

4. Start the graphical kernel configuration utility:

   make xconfig

   You see many lines of text scroll by as the utility is prepared and launched. After a moment, the utility should appear. (This may take as much as 3-4 minutes on an older system.)

5. On the main window of the utility that appears, which is labeled qconf, locate the **Processor type and features** item within the Option panel on the left side of the qconf window. This item is the fourth top-level item in the list. Click that item.

6. In the right side of the qconf window, a list of options appears for Processor type and features. Locate the section labeled **Processor family** and review the processors for which the kernel can be optimized. Select the processor in your computer if you know it. If you do not, leave this field unchanged. (When you click on any item, a brief help screen related to that item appears in the bottom right of the window.)

7. Look again at the list on the left side of the qconf window. Locate the **File systems** item and click on it.

8. On the right side of the qconf window, make certain that Quota support is selected (the check box next to that item should have a check in it).

9. With the File systems item still selected in the left side of the window, locate the item on the right side labeled Reiserfs support. If you see a dot instead of a check mark in the box next to this option, this indicates that support for the Reiserfs file system will be created as a loadable kernel module rather than in the kernel itself. Suppose you wanted to have your root file system based on Reiserfs instead of ext3. Click the check box next to this option to change the dot to a check box.

10. Information about any mounted Reiserfs file systems are not included in the /proc file system by default. Make certain the check box next to the line Stats in /proc/fs/reiserfs is also checked.

11. Looking again on the left side of the qconf window, click on **Network File Systems** below the File Systems item.

12. With Network File Systems selected, look at the right side of the window and locate SMB file system support (to mount Windows shares, etc.). Click the checkbox next to that item so that it contains a check.

13. On the left side, below the Network File Systems item, click **Native Language Support**.

14. On the right side of the window, scroll down the list to see what character sets the Linux kernel supports. By default, most are created as kernel modules. Select one of them near the top of the list that includes the label "Codepage" with a number. Write down the code page number of that item.

15. On the left side of the window, click **Cryptographic options**, near the bottom of the list.

16. None of the cryptographic options are compiled into the kernel by default, but the kernel can support many different methods of encrypting network traffic. Review the options listed.

17. Choose File, then Quit on the menu of the qconf window.

18. When prompted, click **Save Changes** to create a new configuration file based on the selections you have made.

19. The kernel configuration you created is stored in the file .config in the /usr/src/linux-2.6.5-1.358 directory. Open that file in a text editor with this command:

```
vi .config
```

20. Search for the text CONFIG_NLS_CODEPAGE to find the list of native language support options. In vi, type / then type the search text and press **Enter**. When you find that part of the file, locate the line matching the code page that you selected in Step 16.

21. Explore the .config file as you wish, then exit the text editor.

22. If you have sufficient time and your instructor's permission, compile a new kernel based on your configuration by entering this command while in the /usr/src/linux-2.6.5-1.358 directory:

```
make dep; make bzImage; make modules
```

You see hundreds of lines scroll by as the kernel is compiled. Remember that the new kernel file is being created, but that this does not affect the kernel that you are running (including the next time you restart). The finished kernel is stored as a file called bzImage in the directory /usr/src/linux-2.6.5-1.358/arch/i386/boot.

13

CASE PROJECTS

Backups and Complex File Systems

Choose one of the case projects that you have worked on for a previous chapter. Use your work on that project as the basis for your decisions in Questions 1 and 2.

1. Based on the needs of the project you selected, what basic backup strategy will you use? Specifically, how often will you run a complete backup? How often will you perform a differential (level 2) backup? Will you back up applications and operating system configurations regularly or focus on user data? Provide business justifications for each of your responses.

2. Determine the amount of data that you must back up, making reasonable assumptions about the size of hard disks you have used for the project you selected. Go online to a site such as *www.cdw.com* and review the available tape devices. Based on your answers to the previous question and the business environment of your client, what tape device will you select? What will the total cost be for the device and a full set of media to implement your backup plan? Prepare a backup program budget for the next 12 months with brief but specific justifications based on protecting your client's data.

3. If you are comfortable installing Linux, had little difficulty with Linux recognizing your hardware, and have a few hours to experiment, do the following. Reinstall Linux, but instead of creating basic swap and root partitions, divide your hard disk into multiple logical partitions using the Disk Druid utility. Define either a RAID device or an LVM setup. Finish installing Linux and explore the characteristics of your file systems, including using the available RAID or LVM utilities, and standard utilities such as *df*, *mount*, and *tune2fs*.

# CHAPTER 14

WRITING SHELL SCRIPTS

> **After reading this chapter and completing the exercises, you will be able to:**
>
> ♦ Understand how shell scripts operate
>
> ♦ Collect user input and write to the screen from within a script
>
> ♦ Control command execution using tests and loops
>
> ♦ Debug shell scripts
>
> ♦ Understand other types of programming available on Linux

In the previous chapter you learned about establishing a Linux backup strategy to protect system data from unforeseen problems. You also learned how Linux system logs are configured and about the information contained in those logs. You also learned about using kernel modules to add features to a running kernel and about viewing or modifying kernel information via the /proc file system, either directly or using command-line utilities. Finally, you learned about several methods of changing your kernel by modifying source code or using configuration utilities to activate different kernel features before compiling the source code to create a new kernel.

In this chapter, you learn how to create shell scripts in any text editor. These scripts can contain any command that you can execute at the command line, as well as many special commands that are usually only found within scripts. You learn about managing input and output in a script, and about controlling which parts of a script are executed based on tests and various looping structures. You also learn about debugging shell scripts to find problems with your syntax or logic. Finally, you learn a little more about other methods of programming on Linux and some of the developer tools that support those methods.

SCRIPTING BASICS

As a Linux system administrator, you often enter a series of commands in a shell to accomplish an administrative task. In many cases, the commands you enter are identical—or nearly so—to commands you have recently entered. You can automate the process of entering frequently used commands by creating a shell script. A **shell script** is an executable file containing lines of text as you would enter them at a command line, including special commands to control the order in which lines in the file are executed. To execute the commands in a shell script, you simply execute the shell script as you would any other program.

Shell scripts are used on every Linux system. You have already learned about many shell scripts:

- The system initialization scripts in the /etc/rc.d subdirectory (such as rc and rc.local)

- The scripts in /etc/rc.d/init.d that start system services (such as networking or system logging daemons)

- The /etc/profile and /etc/bashrc scripts that Linux executes each time you log in

- The scripts that the X Window System uses to start initial graphical programs (for example, /etc/X11/xinit/xinitrc and /etc/X11/xdm/Xsession)

All of the functionality in these scripts could be implemented using standard Linux programs, as described in the next section, rather than using shell scripts. But shell scripts have two advantages for you as a system administrator. First, they let you study what is happening on the Linux system because you can view the contents of the scripts that control various system events. Second, you can change the way anything on the system occurs simply by altering the relevant shell script.

Interpreting and Compiling Programs

Before you can create shell scripts, you need to be familiar with some basic programming concepts. There are two basic types of computer programs: interpreted programs and compiled programs. Both are written using a computer language. A **computer language**, or **programming language**, is a set of words and syntax rules that can be arranged in predefined ways to cause a computer to perform tasks defined by the person using the language. The words used in a computer language are often called **keywords**, because they have special meanings when used within a computer program. For example, later you will learn the keyword *for*, which defines certain actions when used in a shell script.

A software developer or programmer writes a computer program using a computer language, storing the keywords and related programming in a file. This file is called the program's **source code**. The keywords that make up the computer language are human readable, though you must be familiar with the computer language to understand what the program does. The computer cannot act directly on the keywords of the computer language. The keywords must first be converted to numeric code that the computer's CPU can process. The collection of numeric codes is called the **binary file**, or **executable file**. To use a program, the user runs the appropriate executable file.

The process of converting computer language keywords into computer-readable numeric codes can occur in two ways:

- When the computer language is a compiled language, the source code is converted to a binary file immediately after the programmer writes the source code. The binary file is given to people who want to use the program. (Linux and related programs are unusual in that the source code is also available, but few people need to access it.) A **compiled language** is one for which the source code is converted to a binary file before the program is run by users. A **compiler** is a special program that converts the source code of a compiled language into a binary file.

- When the computer language is an **interpreted language**, the source code is converted into numeric codes at the instant a user runs the program. This conversion takes place each time the user runs the program. The source code is given to people who want to use the program. The user running the program must have an **interpreter** to convert the source code of an interpreted language into numeric codes.

NOTE Because conversion to numeric codes in an interpreted language takes place during program execution, interpreted languages are slower than compiled languages.

A shell script is an **interpreted program**, that is, a program written in an interpreted language. The commands that you learn in this chapter are part of the interpreted language for the bash shell. The shell is the interpreter that acts on the keywords that you include in shell scripts. All of these keywords can also be used at the shell prompt. Thus, a script is a text file that can be interpreted or executed by another program. You read in Chapter 5, "Understanding Text Processing," about the *awk* and *sed* interpreters; others are mentioned at the end of this chapter.

Understanding Programming Concepts

Writing a shell script, though not overly difficult, is really computer programming. In order to write effective shell scripts, knowledge of a few programming concepts is helpful.

A computer program is executed one command at a time. Execution normally proceeds from the first line of the program to the last. Each command within the program is also called a **statement**. A statement is often a single keyword, but a statement can also be a group of keywords and other elements that the computer language syntax requires or allows to be used together. One such keyword, described later in this chapter, is *if*. You can never use the *if* keyword without also using two other keywords: *then* and *fi*.

You can define a list of statements that are executed once, many times, or not at all depending on what happens at some other point in the program. When you group several statements together and use a keyword to control how they are executed, the group of statements is often called a block, or a **statement block**. Statement blocks often contain many statements. They can even contain other statement blocks. This is called **nesting**, when one statement block contains another statement block.

Components of a Shell Script

You can create a shell script in any text editor, including vi, Emacs, or a graphical editor within KDE or GNOME. Any text file that adheres to three basic rules is considered a shell script:

- The first line of the text file must indicate the name of the shell (or other program) that should be used to interpret the script.

- The text file must have the execute file permission set for the user, group, or other category (whichever you want to be able to run the script).

- The text file must contain valid commands that the interpreter can recognize.

TIP

A shell script is sometimes called a shell program. The process of writing a shell script is also called shell programming, because you must adhere to a shell's programming syntax.

When you execute a shell script, you are running a program. The program just happens to be contained in a human-readable text file rather than a binary file. But to the shell, running a shell script and running a program such as a Web browser both require a similar process. In order for the shell to identify a text file as an executable script, the execute file permission must be set. Both of the following example commands allow anyone to execute the script stock_quote (remember, you must be the file's owner or root to change file permissions):

```
$ chmod ugo+x stock_quote
```

or

```
$ chmod 755 stock_quote
```

After using either of these *chmod* commands, the file permissions for the file look like this, indicating to the shell that the file can be executed as a program:

```
-rwxr-xr-x
```

One difference between running a shell script and running a program like a Web browser is that the shell must start another program to interpret the shell script. This is why the first line of the shell script must contain the name of the interpreter that executes the script.

When you execute a shell script by entering the script name at a shell prompt, the shell examines the first line of the file and starts the interpreter named there, with the file you indicated as a parameter. If you are running the bash shell and start a shell script that requires bash, the shell starts a second copy of bash to execute the shell script.

The format of the first line of a shell script consists of a hash mark (#), followed by an exclamation point, followed by the complete path to the interpreter. For example, the first line of a script written for the bash shell looks like this (the path shown is the standard on most Linux systems):

```
#!/bin/bash
```

Conversely, the first line of a shell script written to be executed by the TC shell looks like this:

```
#!/bin/tcsh
```

CAUTION

If you don't include the name of the interpreter on the first line of a script, your default shell tries to execute the script itself. This can generate unexpected results if you created the script to run under a different shell or programming language.

Many of the script examples in this chapter use the *echo* command. The *echo* command prints the text that you enter after the *echo* command to the STDOUT channel—to the screen unless output has been redirected. For example, to print the message "Hello world" to the screen, you use the command *echo Hello world*. If the text after the *echo* command includes special characters, such as a single parenthesis or an asterisk, you should enclose the text in quotation marks so the shell does not try to give the character a special meaning. Suppose you created a file named testscript containing the following lines (you can do this in any text editor):

```
#!/bin/bash
echo This is a sample shell script.
```

TIP

It doesn't matter what file name you use for your shell scripts. You can use any file name and any file extension, so long as you adhere to the three rules listed previously.

To test a new script, enter the name of the file as a command at a Linux command line. Use a period and a forward slash (./) before the file name to tell the shell that the file is located in the current directory rather than in a directory that is part of the PATH environment variable. For example:

```
$ ./testscript
```

After you enter *./testscript* at the command line, the following steps occur:

1. The shell you are working in looks at the first line of the testscript file and sees #!/bin/bash.

14

2. The shell you are working in starts a new bash shell with the file name testscript as a parameter. In effect, the shell executes this command for you:

```
bash ./testscript
```

3. The new copy of bash loads the testscript file and executes each of the lines in the file as if they had been entered at a shell prompt, printing output from commands on the screen.

4. When the new copy of bash reaches the end of the testscript file, it exits, returning control of the screen to the shell from which the shell script was originally started.

When any program exits, it returns a numeric code to the program that started it. This code is called the **exit code** or exit status. You can reference this code at the command line or in a script using the variable $?. If the program completed its task without any problems, the exit code is typically zero. A nonzero exit code usually indicates some type of problem or error. For example, suppose you are working at the command line and successfully create a new directory called data_dir using the command *mkdir data_dir*. The exit code would be zero, though you don't see that code anywhere. If you then execute the same command again, *mkdir data_dir*, that command returns a nonzero exit code—an error occurred because the directory you tried to create already existed. Again, you do not see the exit code, but it is passed to the shell.

Exit codes are important when creating shell scripts because they let you check the status of commands executed within your script. You can determine whether a command was completed correctly or generated an error, and you can choose which actions to take in your script based on the result. A script also returns an exit code. This code is either the exit code of the last command executed within the script, or else the code indicated by the exit keyword. For example, if you determine within your script that a certain command has failed, you can use this as the last command in your script:

```
exit 1
```

The program that started your script (which may be another script) can examine the exit code and determine what to do next.

The sections that follow describe how to create shell scripts based on bash shell programming syntax. As you recall from Chapter 3, "Using the Shell," other shells use different programming syntax rules. bash shell programming is more common than other types of shell programming on Linux systems, but note that the shell you are working in and the shell used to execute a script can be different.

Suppose, for example, that you prefer to work in the TC shell because of its interactive shell features, but you want to execute a shell script written for bash. This is fine, so long as the first line of the script contains #!/bin/bash and bash is installed on your system. As in Step 2 above, the TC shell would start a copy of the bash shell in order to execute the shell script. When the shell script finished, the bash shell would exit, and you would again be working in the TC shell.

INPUT AND OUTPUT

Some Linux commands are used mostly within shell scripts rather than directly at the command line. This section describes some of these commands and explains how you can use them within simple shell scripts. For example, consider the following sample shell script contained in a file named clean:

```
#!/bin/bash
#
# Author:        dave lambert, dave@xyz.org
# Date:          12 October 2005
# Description:   Collect info on core dump files
# and create file with directory sizes
#
find /home -name core -exec rm {} \;
du /home >/tmp/home_sizes
```

The purpose of the second line of this script is to locate and remove all files named core within all users' home directories. In the third line, the *du* command creates a summary of the size of every subdirectory under /home, storing that information in a file named home_sizes. This script is not long, but the commands are lengthy. By storing these lines in a script, you can execute both complex commands by entering one simple script name, for example:

```
./clean
```

14

TIP

The files named core that the preceding script finds are produced when a Linux program ends unexpectedly. These are called **core dump** files, and they can be quite large (over 1 MB). They contain many types of system information as it existed at the moment a program exited unexpectedly or with an error. By reviewing a core dump file, a software developer can determine why a program ended and fix the program. The core dump files are not needed unless someone is troubleshooting a recurring problem; so deleting any core files on the system saves disk space.

The clean script above doesn't produce any output on the screen. All of the commands in the script work directly with files. Other scripts write information to the screen or require input from the keyboard to process the statements in the script. The following script, called filesize, uses the *read* command. The **read** command causes the shell to pause for a user to enter information at the keyboard. The information entered is assigned to a variable provided with the *read* command. The variable, a named location in memory that holds a value, can then be referenced later to retrieve its value.

```
#!/bin/bash
#
# Author:        dave lambert, dave@xyz.org
# Date:          12 October 2005
```

```
# Description:  Read filename with READ;
# process file size information with wc
#
echo Enter a filename to process:
read THEFILE
echo The number of lines in $THEFILE is:
wc -l $THEFILE
echo The number of words in $THEFILE is:
wc -w $THEFILE
echo End of processing for $THEFILE
```

You have learned previously about environment variables. You can create your own variables to store values within a script. You can define a variable by simply assigning a value to a name that you choose. For example, including this line in a script defines a new variable named MYFILE and assigns it a value of index.html:

```
MYFILE="index.html"
```

The previous script used a variable with the *read* command. This command causes a script to pause for keyboard input. The text that a user enters at the keyboard is assigned as the value of the variable given in the *read* command. Once a value is assigned to a variable using either of these methods (a direct assignment or using a *read* command), the script can refer to the variable in other commands. In the example script just referred to, the script references the variable THEFILE as it executes the *wc* command. Just as with environment variables, when you use a $ symbol at the beginning of a variable name, the shell retrieves the value of that variable.

If the above script were stored in a file called filesize, any user with execute permission to the file could start the script using this command:

```
./filesize
```

The output from the filesize script is shown here. The script pauses after displaying the first line of this output so that the user can enter a file name. The file name shown (report.txt) is entered by the user running the script.

```
Enter a filename to process:
report.txt
The number of lines in report.txt is:
    453 report.txt
The number of words in report.txt is:
    3215 report.txt
End of processing for report.txt
```

Although the *read* command is useful for collecting input from a user, you should make sure your scripts test the validity of values entered by the user. For example, if the user running the filesize script entered a file name that did not exist on the system, the other commands in the script (the *wc* commands in this example) would generate error messages. Later in this chapter, you will learn how to create scripts that can test values entered by the user.

Because scripts use standard Linux commands that write information to the screen, they can also use the Linux redirection operators to change the flow of information to and from commands. As you learned in Chapter 3, you can use redirection operators to change how the standard input and standard output for any command are treated. For example, suppose you start the filesize script using this command:

```
./filesize > /tmp/output
```

Because of the > redirection operator, all of the data that is normally written to the screen is instead written to the file /tmp/output. When you view the contents of the /tmp/output file, you see exactly what you would have seen onscreen if you ran the filesize command without a redirection operator.

You can use any of the Linux redirection operators (<, >, >>, <<, or |) in conjunction with shell scripts. By using these operators, you can treat a shell script as you would treat any regular Linux command, using pipes to connect scripts with other commands, storing script output to files, and so forth. You will see other examples of using redirection operators later in this chapter.

Using Variables in Scripts

The filesize sample script in the previous section uses a variable to store information entered by a user. A variable used in a shell script in this way is sometimes called a **shell variable**, though shell variables and environment variables are essentially the same thing. Shell variables are usually defined by a person writing a shell script; environment variables are predefined by scripts that came with the operating system or by programs running on Linux. When you define a variable within a shell script, you should **initialize** the variable by assigning it a value such as zero or "" (an empty string).

As you write shell scripts, you are likely to refer to many variables. For example, a command in your shell script may need to copy a file into the home directory of the user running the shell script. To do this, you can refer to the HOME environment variable. The following sample command copies the file report.txt to a user's home directory:

```
cp /tmp/report.txt $HOME
```

Instead of the HOME environment variable, you can use the following command in the script, but this type of command only works if user rajw is running the script.

```
cp /tmp/report.txt /home/rajw/
```

By using the HOME environment variable, you ensure that the script works for any user who starts the script. As a system administrator, you should use techniques such as this to create shell scripts that are as flexible as possible. This allows the scripts to be used safely by different system administrators and users. Not all users can execute every script, however. Some scripts access parts of the system that only the root user can access. If another user runs such a script, an error occurs; even if the user has execute permission on the script file itself, he or she may not have permission to access the files that the script tries to access.

Shell scripts often use special variables called positional variables. Rather than taking on a value assigned to it within the script, a **positional variable** (or **positional parameter**) takes a value based on the information that the user includes on the command line. If the filesize script shown earlier incorporated a positional variable, the user could enter the file name at the command line with the command to execute the script. For example, the user would enter the following command to process the file report.txt:

```
./filesize report.txt
```

Within a script, you indicate positional variables using a dollar sign and a number. The notation $0 indicates the first item on the command line (the script name: ./filesize in the example above). A $1 indicates the second item on the command line (report.txt in the example above). A $2 indicates the third item on the command line, and so forth. To incorporate a file name entered at the command line as data within a script, you could rewrite the filesize script as shown here. As you compare this script with the previous version, notice that the *read* command is not used. Instead, the user executing the script must provide a file name on the command line. The shell assigns the file name on the command line to the variable $1 as it starts the script. The $1 positional variable is used in place of the THEFILE variable throughout the script.

```
#!/bin/bash
#
# Author:       dave lambert, dave@xyz.org
# Date:         12 October 2005
# Description:  Read filename from command line;
# process file size information with wc
#
echo The number of lines in $1 is:
wc -l $1
echo The number of words in $1 is:
wc -w $1
echo End of processing for $1
```

TIP

A script that uses positional parameters to read data supplied on the command line makes it easier for a system administrator to execute your script, but checking for information on the command line and prompting the user if it isn't supplied makes a script easier to use.

When working with positional variables, it's helpful to know how many items the user running the script has included on the command line. For example, you may want to have your script verify that the correct number of items is included on the command line before having the script proceed. Each time you execute a script, the shell defines a special variable called $# that contains the number of items on the command line used to execute the script. Later you will learn how to test the value of $# to determine how many items a user provided on the command line when the script was started. The following version of filesize reports the value of $# but does not alter its action based on that value:

```
#!/bin/bash
# Author:        dave lambert, dave@xyz.org
# Date:          12 October 2005
# Description:   Read multiple filenames from command line;
# process each with wc
#
echo The script you are running is $0
echo The number of filenames you provided is $#
echo The number of lines in file $1 is:
wc -l $1
echo The number of lines in file $2 is:
wc -l $2
echo The number of lines in file $3 is:
wc -l $3
echo The number of lines in file $4 is:
wc -l $4
```

Suppose you ran the script above with this command:

```
./filesize data1 data2 data3 data4
```

The shell assigns the name of the script—the first item on the command line—to the positional variable $0. The shell also assigns the file names included on the command line to the positional variables $1, $2, $3, and $4, respectively. Finally, the shell assigns the value of 4 to the $# variable (which you see on the third line of the script) because the command line used to execute this script contains four items besides the name of the script.

The output of the script would look like this (depending on the size of the data files):

```
The script you are running is filesize
The number of filenames you provided is 4
The number of lines in file data1 is:
123
The number of lines in file data2 is:
11241
The number of lines in file data3 is:
2321
The number of lines in file data4 is:
3159
```

Positional variables are a useful way to provide information to the commands in a script. But the previous example expected precisely four file names. You can make a more flexible script by testing the value of a variable and taking action based on the results of the test.

14

CONDITIONAL AND LOOPING STRUCTURES

The real power of a computer program lies in its ability to decide which parts of the program to execute based on factors that the program itself examines. For example, if you make a shell script that retrieves a stock price from the Web, you could cause the script to execute one set of statements if the stock price is over a certain value, and another set of statements if the price is below that value. This is done with a selection statement. A **selection statement** lets a computer programmer determine which parts of a program will execute according to values that are determined as the program is executed. Using a selection statement means that all lines in a shell script are not necessarily executed when the script is run—the results of the tests in the selection statements determine which steps are executed. Figure 14-1 illustrates a selection based on the results of a test.

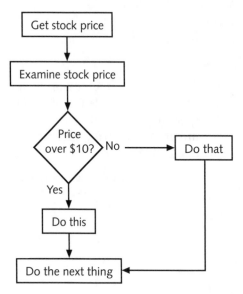

Figure 14-1   A selection statement chooses among alternative options

Most shell scripts include selection statements. They can be very complex, with many options, or very simple, with only a single test such as "if this number is 4, do this; otherwise, don't." The tests performed in shell scripts (and in any computer programming language) only have two possible outcomes (values): true or false. You must design your script to respond to these two possible values. Tests used in a shell script usually check the status of a file or the value of an environment variable. They are not designed for mathematical computations, though you can perform math functions using Linux commands within the script.

The **test** command creates a type of selection statement that lets you determine if a condition is true or false. For example, you can test:

- Whether a file name entered by a user or included on the command line actually exists
- Whether two numeric values are identical
- Whether a file is empty
- Whether the number of parameters on the command line is correct, so the script can function as intended

Using if Statements

A test statement uses a rule to examine a file or variable, returning a result of true or false. The script chooses which commands to execute according to the test result. The **if** command introduces a test in a shell script. An *if* command must be followed by a **then** command, which lists the commands to be executed if the test succeeds (returns a value of true). The **fi** command marks the end of the *if* statement. When the *if* test succeeds (returns true), all the commands between *then* and *fi* are executed. When the test fails (returns false), none of those commands are executed. The *test* command evaluates parameters you provide and returns either true (a value of 1) or false (a value of 0). The results of the *test* command are evaluated by the *if* command. An example of an *if* command used with a *test* command is shown here (the parameters after *test* are described shortly):

```
if test $1 -eq report
```

Instead of the *test* keyword, you often use square brackets around the parameters of the test, followed by a semicolon, like this:

```
if [ $1 -eq report ];
```

Figure 14-2 shows conceptually how an *if-then* statement is organized.

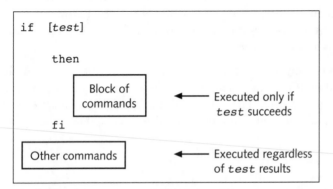

Figure 14-2 Structure of an *if-then* statement

Each test includes either one or two items being tested and a test operator that defines what aspect of the item you want to test. Table 14–1 lists the test operators available in bash.

Table 14-1 File-testing Operators in the bash Shell

Test operator	Description
-d	Test whether the item is a directory name
-e	Test whether the file name exists
-f	Test whether the file exists and is a regular file
-h or -L	Test whether the file exists and is a symbolic link
-r	Test whether the file exists and is readable
-w	Test whether the file exists and is writable
-x	Test whether the file exists and is executable
-lt	Test whether the numeric variable on the left (of the operator) is less than the numeric variable or value on the right
-gt	Test whether the numeric variable on the left (of the operator) is greater than the numeric variable or value on the right
-le	Test whether the numeric variable on the left (of the operator) is less than or equal to the numeric variable or value on the right
-ge	Test whether the numeric variable on the left (of the operator) is greater than or equal to the numeric variable or value on the right
-eq	Test whether the numeric variable on the left (of the operator) is equal to the numeric variable or value on the right
-ne	Return a value of true if the numeric variable on the left (of the operator) is not equal to the numeric variable or value on the right

An **if-then-else statement** is another kind of selection statement. It specifies that if a test returns a value of true, then one set of commands should be executed; if a test returns a value of false, then another set of commands should be executed.

The *else* command extends the capability of an *if-then* statement by adding a block of commands that are *only* executed if a test returns a value of false (that is, if the test fails). You can use an *else* command only as part of an *if-then* statement. The structure of an *if-then-else* statement is shown in Figure 14–3. Notice especially that the *else* block of commands is skipped if the test returns a value of true.

The following sample statement shows how *if-then-else* is used. As with a simpler *if-then* statement, the *fi* keyword ends the entire statement. The commands between *then* and *else* are executed only if the test succeeds. The commands between *else* and *fi* are executed only if the test fails. Commands after *fi* (none are shown here) are executed regardless of the results of the test.

```
if [ -f /etc/samba/smb.conf ];
    then
            echo The Samba server appears to be configured.
    else
            echo The Samba server cannot be started.
    fi
```

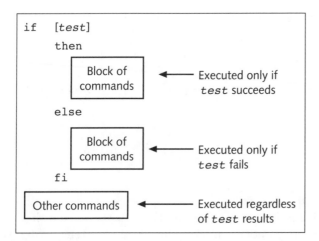

if   [*test*]
    then

    Block of
    commands   ◄——— Executed only if
                          test succeeds

    else

    Block of
    commands   ◄——— Executed only if
                          test fails
    fi

    Other commands   ◄——— Executed regardless
                                of *test* results

Figure 14-3   The structure of an *if-then-else* statement

TIP

The indentation of lines using tabs and spaces is a convention designed to make the script easier for a person to read. Tabs and spaces included in a program are called **white space**. White space between commands or lines has no effect on a shell script's operation.

The **exit** command stops the execution of a script immediately and returns the exit code that is provided with the *exit* command. You should generally avoid using *exit* within a loop. Good programming style demands that you finish each loop and conditional statement that you begin, using appropriate tests to exit them (and the entire script) as needed without "skipping" from the middle of a loop or *if-then-else* statement. But *exit* is sometimes used as a crutch to exit when a difficult situation develops.

TIP

A **comment** is a line within a script that is not processed by the shell, but is only included to help someone reading the file understand the purpose of the script or how it functions. To include a comment, begin a line with a hash mark, #. (The first line of a script that begins with #! is a special case and is not a comment.)

The following script includes a test using the *-ne* (not equal) operator within an *if-then* statement to determine whether the $# variable has a value of 2 or not. This script includes several comment lines. You should include numerous comments to help other system administrators understand the scripts you write (and to remind yourself how and why you created a script when you review it months later).

```
#!/bin/bash
#
# Author:      dave lambert, dave@xyz.org
# Date:        12 October 2005
# Description: Add a user for database access
```

14

```
# Requires a user name and database table name on the
# command line
#
if [ $# -ne 2 ];
then
      echo You must provide a user name and a database table name.
      exit
fi
# Begin processing:
# Store command line parameters in shell variables
DB_USER=$1
DB_TABLE=$2
```

If you review the scripts in /etc/rc.d/init.d, you see complex test expressions using multiple environment variables. Studying these scripts is a good way to learn about shell scripting, though you may not immediately understand everything you see. Refer to the bash man page to learn about more advanced types of tests available for shell scripts.

Although each test can only return either a true or false, you often need to determine the value of a variable or file name that may have any one of several values. You could use multiple *if-then-else* statements to check for different values, as shown here. When you are using an *if-then-else* statement and the first command in the else block is another *if-then-else* statement, you can use the **elif** keyword instead of *else*, as shown here :

```
if [ $# = 4 ] ; then
echo "Ready to process four files."
elif [ $# = 3 ] ; then
echo "Ready to process three files."
elif [ $# = 2 ] ; then
echo "Ready to process two files ."
elif [ $# = 1 ] ; then
echo "Ready to process one file."
else
echo "No filenames to process."
fi
```

The *case* statement is a more elegant way to do this. The **case** statement lets you specify a number of possible values for a variable, with a statement block to be executed for each matching value. Of all the statement blocks in a *case* statement, only one is executed. The previous code can be rewritten using a *case* statement like this:

```
case $# in
4)
echo "Ready to process four files." ;;
3)
echo "Ready to process three files." ;;
2)
echo "Ready to process two files." ;;
1)
echo "Ready to process one file." ;;
```

```
*)
echo "Invalid number of filenames provided." ;;
esac
```

In the above example, the statement block following the *) case is executed if the $# variable does not match any of the previous cases (4, 3, 2, or 1). A double semicolon indicates the end of the statement block for each case. The **esac** keyword ("case" spelled backward) is used to indicate the end of the *case* statement. After one of the statement blocks in the *case* statement is executed (such as *echo "Ready to process four files."*), the next statement executed is the line after the *esac* keyword.

TIP

The scripts in /etc/rc.d/init.d are a good place to see examples of *case* statements.

Adding Loops to a Script

A selection statement is used to determine whether part of a computer program should be executed. A **loop statement** is used to determine whether part of a computer program should be executed more than once. A loop statement has several parts:

- A counting variable, which is assigned a different value each time the loop is repeated; the counting variable is often called the **index** of the loop, because it tracks how many times the loop has executed a list of statements

- A list of values that should be assigned to the counting variable

- A list of statements to be executed each time through the loop

A loop statement causes a block of commands to be repeated a certain number of times or until a condition is met. You can define several types of loops in bash shell scripts.

The *for* command creates a **for loop**, which repeats a statement block once for each item in a list. You can include a list of items when you write the script, or you can design the loop so that the list items are provided on the command line when the script is executed. The syntax of the *for* command is shown here. The keywords *for*, *in*, *do*, and *done* are all part of a *for* loop:

```
for <counting variable> in <list of items>
do
      <statement block>
done
```

The *<statement block>* is executed once for each item in *<list of items>*. Each time through the loop is called an **iteration**. The *<counting variable>* is assigned the value of the next item in the *<list of items>* each time the *<statement block>* is executed—each iteration. The *do* and *done* commands are keywords used to begin and end a statement block within a *for* loop (and in other places, as you'll see).

14

The *<list of items>* can be, among other things, any of the following (an example of the first line of a *for* loop is shown for each):

- Numbers: for COUNT in 1 2 3 4 5 6 7

- Words: for NAME in george ali maria rupert kim

- A regular expression used to match file names: for db_filename in *html

- The special variable $@, described below: for db_filename in $@

When you use a regular expression (such as *c) as the *<list of items>* in a *for* loop, the shell replaces the regular expression with all matching file names. Using the example of *html, the shell substitutes all the file names in the current directory that end with the letters "html." This substitution occurs before the shell executes the *for* loop.

A special variable used in *for* loops is **$@**. This variable contains all the parameters that were included on the command line when the script was executed. If you include a regular expression on the command line, such as *txt or *html, the shell finds all matching file names and includes them as part of $@ when the script is executed. By using $@ as the *<list of items>* in a *for* loop, you automatically include all items from the command line.

The following example script shows a *for* loop that compresses each file name given on the command line:

```
#!/bin/bash
# Author:       dave lambert, dave@xyz.org
# Date:         12 October 2005
# Description:  Compress each filename given on the command line
#
for counter in $@
do
    gzip $counter
done
```

Suppose the above script was stored in a file called squash and you started the script using the following command line:

```
./squash phoebe.tif charon.tif europa.tif
```

The *for* loop would execute the commands between *do* and *done* (the *gzip* command in this example) three times, once for each file name on the command line. The counting variable *counter* takes the value of each of the three file names in turn during the three iterations through the statement block enclosed by *do* and *done*.

A second type of loop uses a test such as an *if-then* statement. As long as the test returns a value of true, the statement block within the loop is executed again and again. As soon as the test returns a value of false, the loop exits. You use the **while** command to create such a loop. The syntax of a *while* loop is shown here. The three keywords *while*, *do*, and *done* must be used together:

```
while <test>
do
      <statement block>
done
```

A *while* loop uses the same tests as an *if-then* statement. Consider, for example, the following *while* loop:

```
DB_FILE=""
while [ ! -f $DB_FILE ];
do
      echo Please enter the database file to archive:
      read DB_FILE
done
```

First, the DB_FILE variable is initialized as an empty string. This prevents the *while* loop from behaving unexpectedly the first time the variable is tested. The loop then begins by testing whether the file name defined by DB_FILE exists. This test uses the *-f* operator to test whether a file exists, and a ! character to reverse the result of the test. You could read this test as "While not DB_FILE exists," or "As long as the file name stored in DB_FILE doesn't exist." While this condition is met, the statement block between *do* and *done* is executed, requesting a file name from the user.

The reason to use this loop is to make sure the user enters a valid file name before the script continues and tries to use that file. The loop will repeat the statement block indefinitely until the user enters a valid file name.

> You normally can exit any shell script by pressing Ctrl+c.
> **TIP**

When you create a loop using *for* or *while*, you sometimes want to exit from the loop in the middle of the statement block rather than at its end. Other times, you might want to return to the top of the loop (do the next iteration of the loop or run the *while* test again), without executing the rest of the statements in the statement block. The **break** and **continue** commands let you do this.

For example, suppose you want to process a number of file names that are provided on the command line. You need to test whether each file name is valid before you begin processing it. If the name is valid, you want to process that file, otherwise, you want to skip to the next file name. The *continue* command shown here causes the script to perform the next iteration of the *for* loop if a file name is not valid.

```
for NEXTFILE in $@
do
if [ ! -f '$NEXTFILE' ] ; then
echo "$NEXTFILE cannot be found!"
continue
```

```
fi
# Everything looks OK for the current file name.
# Begin processing it
done
```

TIP

The scripts in this section are examples of nested control structures, such as a *for* loop that contains an *if-then* statement, or a *while* loop that contains a *case* statement.

In a similar way, you can use the *break* command to exit from the loop completely. The example here uses a *while* loop with no test at all. This creates an infinite loop—the nonexistent test never fails, so the loop continues until the user presses Ctrl+c or the *break* command is executed. Notice that in the script fragment that follows, the user does not need to press Ctrl+c to exit from the script. The script never exits based on testing a value in the *while* statement, but it does exit if a user enters q or Q because of the *break* command in the *case* statement.

```
while  :
do
echo "Enter a file to see how many lines it contains (q to quit):"
read NEXTFILE
case $NEXTFILE in
[qQ])  break ;;
*) wc -l $NEXTFILE ;;
esac
done
```

Using Functions in a Script

If you write many shell scripts (and as a system administrator, that is likely the case), you will find that you need to perform the same tasks repeatedly. By creating a **function**, you can create a small shell script, give it a name, and then refer to that script from other locations. Suppose, for example, that you often write scripts that manipulate a set of database files. In each of these scripts, you want to set certain variables that you use to refer to the database files. You can create a function that sets those variables, and then include that function in each of your scripts. The function might look like this:

```
init_db_files() {
DB_FILE="/data/newport/users.db"
ADMIN="nwells"
SQL_MODE="standard"
}
```

To define a function, you choose any name, as with a variable, but you follow the name with () (open and close parentheses) to indicate a function. All the statements enclosed in the braces { } are considered part of the function. If you had included the above function at the beginning of a script, you could refer to it by name later in the script. At that point, all the commands that make up the function are executed. There are several advantages to using a function:

- You can copy the function from one script to another and know exactly what it will do, and that it has been written correctly (it doesn't have any bugs) because you've used it previously.

- You can call the same function multiple times in a single script, so you don't have to rewrite and retest the same commands again and again.

- You can separate the actions of your script into groups and make the script more readable, as the next example shows.

Using the previous function as an example, the first part of a script might look like this:

```
#!/bin/bash
# Author:       dave lambert, dave@xyz.org
# Date:         12 October 2005
# Description:  Database analysis, main script
#
init_db_files() {
DB_FILE="/data/newport/users.db
ADMIN="nwells"
SQL_MODE="standard"
}
#  Main part of script
#  First, initialize the database variables
init_db_files
# Now, let's begin reading data from the database file and
# making calculations
```

SHELL SCRIPT DEBUGGING

As you use the example scripts in this chapter, it is fairly easy to locate any problems that occur—the scripts are short and the design is simple. As you create or examine much longer scripts, you will find that it becomes more difficult to quickly see syntax errors or logic problems. A **syntax error** is an error in how a statement is entered—the shell cannot understand what you mean because you have misspelled a keyword, left off a semicolon, or done something similar. A **logic error** refers to what the commands are trying to accomplish. For example, your script has a command to delete a temporary file that is referred to by a variable name, but you never set the value of the variable, so the delete command can't function correctly.

To find and fix both types of errors, you can use the debugging features of the shell. Recall that when you enter a script name, another copy of the shell is started and that copy runs the shell. You can also start another copy of the shell yourself, including a debugging option and providing the name of the script you want to debug. For example, suppose you have created a long script called startnet. You can start that script using this command:

```
$ bash ./startnet
```

Before executing any large script you have written, you should check that the script does not contain syntax errors. These errors are easy for the shell itself to identify. By checking for syntax errors, you can fix them before the script is executed. To do this, use the *-n* option when you start the script:

```
$ bash -n ./startnet
```

When you use the *-n* debugging option, the shell looks at each line of the script and prints a message when it finds any syntax errors, but it does not actually execute any commands in the script. If the script contains no syntax errors, there is no output from the above command.

You can also use the *-v* option to have the script display each line of the script as it reads it. This can be helpful with the *-n* option to see how the shell is progressing during the syntax check:

```
$ bash -nv ./startnet
```

Using Shell Tracing

More in-depth debugging help is provided by the shell tracing feature. A **shell trace** displays on the screen each line of the script as it is executed. This differs from the *-v* option, which displays each line as it appears in the script file. Recall that the shell must perform numerous substitutions based on regular expressions, variable values, and so on as a command is executed. The shell trace displays each command with the data that is actually used or operated upon.

Shell tracing is activated with the *-x* option. For example, suppose a line in your startnet script looks like this:

```
for loopvar in $@
```

You need to debug the script, so you start it with the *-x* option and the file names that you want the script to process:

```
bash -x./startnet *conf
```

The *-x* option causes the shell to print each line as it will be executed. So when the shell reaches the *for* statement, it displays the line as it has expanded it, containing all the matching names from the $@ variable. If your working directory contains four files matching the pattern *conf, then the shell prints something like this:

```
for loopvar in eth0.conf lo.conf eth1.conf ppp.conf
```

A shell trace lets you see if the script is really using the values you expect, and if it is executing commands in the order that you expect.

Debugging within a Script

Although it can be very useful to start a script with the -*x* option, a large script generates a great deal of output that can make it hard to locate errors. For this reason, it is often more helpful to turn on debugging within a script just at the point where the script appears to be working incorrectly. You can do this using the **set** command with the -*x* option. For example, if your script includes a *for* loop that does not function as expected, you can enclose that loop within two *set* commands, enabling and then disabling the shell trace debugging function. By doing this, debugging information is only displayed for the loop causing the problem, making it easier to spot the problem:

```
set -x
for loopvar in $@
do
# process each file name that was provided on the command line
done
set +x
```

Software developers or system administrators who write many scripts often create debugging functions that they can call from different points in their scripts. Their scripts, or sometimes the debugging functions themselves, may rely on environment variables. For example, a developer might write a large script that includes several debugging features. But none of the debugging features are active by default. But when any user sets an environment variable called DEBUGME (a random variable name selected by the developer) to the value of true before executing the script, the script changes behavior, providing debugging information automatically. Resetting the DEBUGME environment variable to false causes the script to act normally, displaying no debugging information.

You can experiment with different arrangements using the *set -x* command and various functions within your own scripts to see what arrangement is most helpful to you. Examining scripts written by experienced administrators and developers (including those you find on a standard Linux system) is a great way to see how different tasks have already been accomplished.

14

OTHER PROGRAMMING METHODS

You have learned the basics of creating shell scripts, but many other types of scripts and compiled languages are used in Linux. The statements in a shell script must follow specific syntax rules for tests, loops, and so forth. Other types of scripts are written using different computer languages and interpreted by different interpreters (rather than the bash shell). The specific syntax rules a script must follow depend on the interpreter that will execute the script.

Other Scripting Languages

Different scripting languages are used for different purposes. As you learn more about the types of scripts available, you can decide which type is best suited for a given programming task.

Table 14-2 lists some of the popular scripting languages used in Linux. An interpreter for each of these languages is included in most Linux distributions. Many books are available to teach you how to write programs using these scripting languages.

Table 14-2   Popular Scripting Languages

Language	Comments
Awk	Used for system administration work, often processing text files in conjunction with the *sed* program (see Chapter 5). The most widely used version of the *awk* interpreter used on Linux is the *gawk* program from the GNU project. Enter *man awk* to learn more.
Perl	Used extensively to process data on Web servers. Very popular and well-known. See *www.perl.org*.
PHP	A very popular scripting language used for managing dynamic content on a Web site. See *www.php.org*.
Python	A more recently developed language, popular for creating graphical programs. Used by Red Hat Software to create many system administration utilities in Red Hat Linux and Fedora. See *www.python.org*.
Tcl/Tk	A popular language for creating graphical applications. See *www.scriptics.com*.

By convention, scripts often use standardized file extensions to help users identify them. For example, perl scripts often end in .pl, Python scripts in .py, and Tcl/Tk scripts in .tcl. These file extensions are for convenience, however, and don't affect the interpreters' ability to run the script. The next two sections describe some of these scripting languages in more detail.

Perl Scripts

The **perl** programming language was developed by Larry Wall, a famous free software developer. perl is especially well suited to processing text strings and was very popular for years as a tool for managing data submitted by Web page forms. When you submitted information through a Web page, a perl script on the Web server examined your input and returned a new Web page based on it. Although many Web servers now use PHP or specialized Web programs such as ColdFusion, perl remains a reliable workhorse in this area.

TIP

The first line of a perl script typically includes the following line, though the exact location of the perl interpreter varies on some Linux distributions:
#!/usr/bin/perl

perl scripts and scripts written in other languages interact with Web servers using a communication standard called the **Common Gateway Interface**, or **CGI**. CGI uses the standard input and standard output channels to permit communications between two programs. These steps outline how a perl script and a Web server interact using CGI:

1. A user running a Web browser enters data in a form, such as the user's name and e-mail address.

2. The browser sends the user's data to a Web server running on Linux.

3. The Web server starts a perl script designed to process the data from the form.

4. The perl script retrieves the form data submitted by the browser and acts on it (perhaps adding it to a file or sending an e-mail to the user).

5. The perl script creates a customized response for the user based on the data that the user entered and writes that response text to standard output.

6. The Web server collects all the output of the perl script and sends it back to the browser as a document.

The interaction between the perl script and the Web server in Steps 5 and 6 unfolds according to the standards of CGI. By using CGI standards, the Web server can rely on standard communication channels as a gateway between two programs. Other methods of processing Web server data can provide higher performance because they do not require running a separate perl interpreter. But CGI allows a Linux Web server to communicate with any other Linux program.

Scripts for Graphical Programs

Scripting languages such as Tcl/Tk and Python let you create graphical programs that include dialog boxes and menus. Creating graphical programs in a scripting language is easier than using a compiled language such as C or C++, but interpreted graphical programs execute much more slowly.

Tcl/Tk is a scripting language developed by John Ousterhout. The name Tcl/Tk stands for *tool command language/toolkit*. The word *toolkit* refers to the graphical toolkit, a set of programming functions that you can use within Tcl/Tk scripts to create graphical interfaces. (Tcl/Tk is often referred to as "tickle-tee-kay.")

Scripts written in Tcl/Tk are executed by an interpreter called *wish*. The first line of a Tcl/Tk script includes a line resembling this (depending on how your Linux distribution is configured):

```
#!/usr/bin/wish
```

The **Python** scripting language uses the same Tk graphical programming toolkit as Tcl. Python is an object-oriented language, meaning that parts of a Python program can be reused in another program with minimal effort. Python was developed by Guido van Rossum. You can use either Tcl/Tk or Python to create powerful and complex graphical program scripts. Figure 14-4 shows an example of a graphical program written in Python.

14

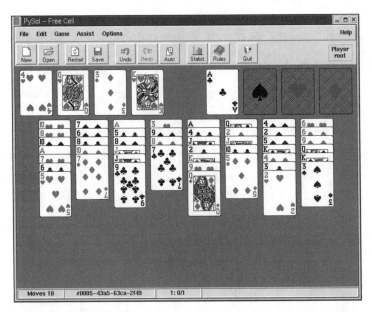

Figure 14-4 A program written using the Python scripting language

Compiled Languages

Scripting languages are useful for many tasks, but the Linux kernel and the utilities that you use regularly in Linux are written using compiled languages. The most widely used compiled languages for Linux are C and C++, though Linux supports dozens of other languages. Some that you may have heard of that Linux supports are:

- Pascal
- Java
- FORTRAN
- Smalltalk
- Lisp
- Objective C

A collection of basic programming tools is included with every Linux distribution. These tools enable any user to modify and rebuild software from the source code that is included with Linux programs. The tools include the following:

- *gcc* — A C language compiler
- *g++* — A C++ language compiler
- *gdb* — A debugging tool for C and C++ programs

- *gnumake* — The *make* program (which you learned about briefly in Chapter 13, "System and Kernel Management")

- *configure* — A programming tool that creates a configuration file for the *make* utility based on system parameters and user information

- bash and other shells

- vi, Emacs, and other editors

- Various other programming and analysis utilities

Writing a simple computer program is not hard once you know something about the syntax of the programming language you are using and you become familiar with the tools used to create the compiled program. For example, the following lines, placed in a text file (call it hello.c) are the source code for a complete C language program:

```
#include <stdio.h>

int main()
{
printf("Hello world\n");
exit(0);
}
```

If you create the above as a text file, then execute the following commands, you will have compiled the source code into a binary program, made that program executable, and executed it. (This program relies on a set of library functions that are referenced with the term stdio.h in the source code above.)

```
$ gcc -o hello hello.c
$ chmod a+x hello
$ ./hello
```

From here, however, things can quickly become much more complicated. Even simple programs can run into thousands of lines of source code. Careful debugging is required to complete such a program. They generally rely on dozens or hundreds of functions that are found in **libraries** with which you must become familiar to use those functions correctly. Graphical programs and programs that interact with the network or the Linux kernel have special requirements that you must learn. And yet, creating such programs can be very rewarding. When working with open source software, in particular, you have the advantage of being able to review existing programs to see how something was accomplished, then copying part of that program and modifying it for your own needs.

Several very powerful tools are available to help you create large, complex software projects. These tools are sometimes called **Integrated Development Environments (IDEs)** because they integrate in a single (usually graphical) interface, a text editor, access to a compiler with tracking of the compiler's output, a debugger, commonly needed documentation, and other functions. Several free and commercial IDEs are available for Linux. One that is included with the KDE desktop (and that is installed on your Linux system if you have installed Red Hat Linux or Fedora using the recommendations in Chapter 8, "Installing

Linux"), is called KDevelop. This tool is shown in Figure 14-5; you can start it by selecting Programming, then KDevelop on the GNOME main menu.

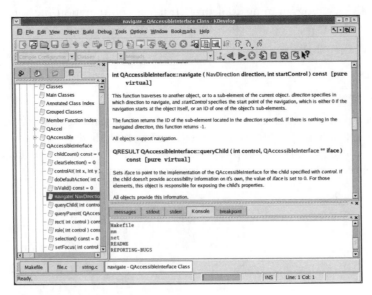

Figure 14-5   The KDevelop programming IDE

Another type of programming tool is called a **Rapid Application Development (RAD)** tool. RAD packages try to simplify the development of complex software projects by providing prewritten modules, by helping you track multiple parts of a project and reusing parts of the software you have written, and by using many other advanced techniques. One powerful example of a RAD package for Linux is OmniStudio, currently marketed by Raining Data Corporation (see *www.rainingdata.com*).

You can learn about programming for Linux using C, C++, or other interpreted or compiled languages by reviewing the documentation that comes with your Linux distribution. But a beginning guide to computer programming or classroom training usually provides a much better learning experience. Red Hat Software offers 5-day programming courses for beginning Linux software developers, or for more advanced developers to learn about converting applications from other systems to Linux, programming for devices, programming for the Linux kernel, and other related topics. Information about these courses is available at *www.redhat.com/training*.

Many independent training companies also offer programming courses for working professionals. At least a basic understanding of computer programming in Linux with commonly used languages is an important skill for system administrators who hope to advance in their careers.

CHAPTER SUMMARY

- Shell scripts let you execute a complex set of commands by entering a single script name. Scripts can include control statements and tests to determine which commands in the script file are executed. Every Linux system includes dozens of examples of shell scripts.

- Each script uses keywords from a programming language. An interpreter converts the source code of the script to an executable format as you run it. Compilers perform a similar conversion before a program is executed. The bash shell interpreter is often used for shell scripts.

- Each script file must start with a line identifying the interpreter to use for that script; it must have the execute permission set; and it must use only correctly formed statements for the interpreter you are using.

- Environment and positional variables are often referenced in scripts. You can also create shell variables to hold information the script needs to process.

- When a program closes unexpectedly, the operating system creates a record of the state of the system at the time the program ended and stores this information in a file named core. These core dump files can be used by developers to diagnose what caused the program to end.

- Well-written scripts include many comments to help developers understand how a script was designed and what each part of it does.

- The *read* command waits for users to enter information at the keyboard and assigns that information to a variable.

- The *if-then-else* statement tests a condition and executes statements if the condition is present.

- The *case* statement is a cleaner way to provide multiple tests of a variable, with a statement block to be executed for each matching value.

- Loops using *for* and *while* repeatedly execute a statement block based on either a fixed number of iterations or a condition being tested.

- The normal flow of a loop statement can be altered using a *break* statement (to exit the loop immediately) or a *continue* statement (to begin the next iteration of the loop immediately).

- Functions let a programmer create a set of commands to complete a chosen task, assign those commands a name, and then complete the task by referring to the name at a later time in the script or program. Complex scripts make extensive use of functions.

- Shell scripts can be debugged using shell options to check syntax, or to print out each line of the script, either as it is read from the script file or as it is executed by the shell (after all substitutions have been made by the shell). The latter method is called shell tracing.

14

❑ Many scripting languages are used on Linux systems, including perl, PHP, Python, and Tcl/Tk. Some are appropriate for use with Web servers via CGI; some are appropriate for creating graphical programs.

❑ Linux includes support for many computer languages. The C and C++ languages are the most widely used. Each relies on a compiler to convert source code to an executable file. IDEs and RAD programs are commonly used to ease the complexity of developing large programs.

❑ A knowledge of programming languages and tools is very useful for advanced system administrators.

COMMAND SUMMARY

Command	Description	Example
break	Used within a *for* or *while* loop to exit from the loop immediately	[qQ]) break ;;
case	Introduces a test that is compared against a set of values, each followed by a statement block to be executed if the value matches the variable being tested	case $# in
configure	Creates a configuration file for the *make* command based on various parameters	configure
continue	Used within a *for* or *while* loop to immediately begin with the next iteration of the loop (return to the top of the loop)	continue
do	Used with the *done* command to enclose a statement block as part of a *for* loop or a *while* loop	do
done	Used with the *do* command to enclose a statement block as part of a *for* loop or a *while* loop	done
elif	Introduces an *if-then-else* statement that is the first statement in the *else* block of another *if-then-else* statement. Used in place of *else if*	elif [$# = 3] ; then
else	Extends the capability of an *if-then* statement by adding a statement block that is only executed if the test after *if* returns a value of false (that is, if the test fails)	else
esac	Ends a *case* statement block	esac
exit	Stops the execution of a script immediately; can optionally include an exit code	exit 1
fi	Marks the end of an *if-then* or *if-then-else* statement block	fi
for	Repeats a statement block one time for each item in a list	for NEXTFILE in $@
if	Introduces a test within a shell script. An *if* command is always followed by a *then* command.	if [! -f '$NEXT-FILE'] ;
in	Used as part of a *for* loop, before the list of items to be used as variable values for each iteration of the loop	for NEXTFILE in $@

Command	Description	Example
perl	Starts the perl language interpreter	perl ./myscript.pl
read	Pauses for a user to input data at the keyboard and assigns that input to a variable	read FILENAME
set	Views or sets environment variables or shell options	set -x
test	Evaluates the arguments provided after the command name and returns either true (a value of 1) or false (a value of 0)	if test $1 -eq report
then	Begins a statement block of commands to be executed if the test introduced by an *if* command succeeds (returns a value of true)	then
while	Creates a loop based on a test. The loop executes a statement block as long as the test returns true.	while [! –f $DB_FILE];
wish	Starts the Tcl/Tk language interpreter	wish ./myscript.tcl

KEY TERMS

$@ — A special shell variable that includes all of the parameters on the command line.

binary file — *See* executable file.

comment — A line in a script or source code that is not processed by the interpreter or compiler, but is only included to help someone reading the file understand the purpose or operation of the script or source code. Comments in shell scripts and many other languages are created by beginning a line with the # character.

Common Gateway Interface (CGI) — A method of communication between two programs using the standard input and standard output channels.

compiled language — A computer language for which the source code is converted to a binary file before the program is executed.

compiler — A program that converts the source code of a compiled language into a binary file.

computer language — A set of words and syntax rules that can be arranged in predefined ways to cause a computer to perform tasks defined by the person using the language.

core dump — A diagnostic file (named core) that is created by the operating system when a program ends unexpectedly (crashes).

executable file — A file containing numeric codes that a computer can execute. Created from a source code file by a compiler, the executable file is the program that a user can run.

exit code — A numeric code provided by a program or shell script to indicate success or failure of the expected operation.

for loop — A list of commands that is repeatedly executed according to the parameters provided with the *for* command.

function — A collection of commands that have been given a name and can be executed at a later time by referring to that name.

14

if–then–else statement — A set of commands used to determine whether other commands in a script are executed. An *if-then-else* statement is one kind of selection statement.

index — A counting variable used within a loop statement. The index acts as a marker to count how many times the loop has executed a list of commands.

initialize — To set a variable to a predefined value such as zero or "" (an empty string) so a script can use the variable without uncertainty about its initial value.

Integrated Development Environment (IDE) — A program (usually graphical) that provides a convenient working environment for programmers by integrating many of the tools that a programmer uses regularly, such as a text editor, compiler, debugger, and documentation.

interpreted language — A language for which the source code of a program is converted to numeric codes at the time a user runs the program. This conversion takes place each time the user runs the program.

interpreted program — A computer program that is converted from human-readable form to a format that can be used by a computer (numeric codes) at the moment you execute the program.

interpreter — A program that converts the source code written in an interpreted language into numeric codes that a computer can execute.

iteration — An occurrence of an event or process that can or must be done many times.

keyword — A word used in a computer language to define a specific task or meaning.

libraries — Files containing programming functions that can be used by any program; prebuilt programming functionality.

logic error — A programming error caused by the design of the program or script as a whole and the arrangement of commands. Compare to a syntax error, which is caused by malformed commands.

loop statement — A statement used to determine whether part of a computer program should be executed more than once.

nesting — A programming method in which one selection or loop statement contains another selection or loop statement.

Perl — A popular programming language developed by Larry Wall.

positional variable — A variable used within a shell script that contains data included on the command line when the script is started. Also called a **positional parameter**.

programming language — *See* computer language.

Python — A scripting language developed by Guido van Rossum. Often used for creating graphical programs.

Rapid Application Development (RAD) — A software program that simplifies the development of complex software projects by providing prewritten modules, by helping track multiple parts of a project, permitting reuse of parts of the software, and by using many other advanced techniques.

selection statement — A statement that lets a computer programmer determine which parts of a program are executed according to values that are calculated by testing as the program is executed. The *if-then* statement is an example of a selection statement used in shell scripts.

shell script — An executable file containing lines of text as you would enter them at a command line, with special commands to control the order in which lines in the file are executed.

shell trace — A method of debugging a shell script that displays each command on screen as the shell executes it.

shell variable — A variable used within a shell script to store information for use by the script.

source code — The file that a programmer writes using the keywords and syntax rules of a computer language.

statement — A command within a computer program. A statement is often a single keyword, but the term may also refer to a group of keywords that the computer language syntax requires or allows to be used together.

statement block — A list of commands (or statements) that are controlled by a selection or loop statement.

syntax error — An error in a script or source code file caused by misuse of the structure, keywords, or punctuation required by the computer language being used. A syntax error can be found before executing the program.

Tcl/Tk — A scripting language developed by John Ousterhout; often used to create graphical programs.

white space — Tabs or spaces included in a program or script file that make the script easier for a person to read but have no effect on how the interpreter or compiler works with the file.

14

REVIEW QUESTIONS

1. Name four shell scripts that are included on a standard Linux system, and describe the use of each one.

2. The first line of a standard shell script must contain:

   a. a comment defining the user name of the person creating the script

   b. a valid command as you would enter it from a command line

   c. the path and file name of the shell used to execute the script

   d. a time specification for when the script will be executed

3. In order to be executed by any user (including root), a shell script must have the _____ file permission set.

   a. execute

   b. write

   c. other

   d. owner

4. Which of these statements contains a standard positional variable?

   a. *gzip $file*

   b. *gzip $1*

   c. *gzip /tmp/listing 2>&1*

   d. *gzip HOME*

5. Which two commands involve a test value of true or false?

   a. *if* and *while*

   b. *while* and *for*

   c. *for* and *do*

   d. *exit* and *break*

6. The *test* command is equivalent to using square brackets around a test expression, but the *test* command is less frequently used. True or False?

7. Briefly explain why comments are an important part of any shell script.

8. Describe the difference in control methods between a *for* loop and a *while* loop.

9. A loop beginning with the command *for i in 2 4 6 8* will be executed how many times?

   a. eight

   b. four

   c. the preset value of i

   d. It cannot be determined without knowing what files are in the current working directory.

10. Name three nonshell scripting languages. Include a statement on the use, characteristics, or author of each one.

11. CGI is popular for which of the following purposes?

    a. creating Web servers

    b. interfacing between scripts and Web servers

    c. automating system administration work

    d. creating graphical programs

12. Which of the following list contains only interpreted languages?

    a. perl, C++, Tcl/Tk, C, Java

    b. perl, bash, Tcl/Tk, Python

    c. C++, FORTRAN, C, Java

    d. perl, bash, Objective C

13. Explain why a compiled program is typically much faster than an interpreted program.

14. If an *if-then* statement block includes another *if-then* statement block, and that block in turn includes a simple *while* loop, all of these statements taken together are a good example of:

    a. recursion

    b. RAD

    c. iterations

    d. nesting

15. Which of the following is not a valid first line for a script file?

    a. #!/bin/bash

    b. #!/bin/tcsh

    c. !#/bin/perl

    d. #!/bin/wish

16. If the *exit* command is not used in a bash shell script, then the exit code provided by the script to the program that started the script is:

    a. the exit code of the last command executed as part of the script

    b. 0

    c. undefined

    d. dependent on the value of the *set* command when the script was started

17. A file named _____ is created by the operating system when a program crashes; this file is called a _____ .

    a. core; debugging output

    b. set; shell trace

    c. break; statement block

    d. core; core dump

18. Using a *case* statement is a good alternative to which of the following?

    a. multiple *if-then* statements

    b. a *for* loop

    c. a *while* loop

    d. using *break* and *continue* repeatedly

14

19. Which statement is correct about a *for* loop?

    a. The list of items can be numeric or text, but cannot include regular expressions or variables of any kind.

    b. The value of the counting variable remains unchanged during each iteration of the loop, but can be referenced within the statement block enclosed by *do* and *done*.

    c. The counting variable takes on a new value from the list of items in the *for* command during each iteration of the loop.

    d. The statement block must include a list of items to define the number of iterations for the loop.

20. What syntax error exists in the following *case* statement?

```
case $NEXTFILE in
   [qQ]) break ;
   *) wc -l $NEXTFILE ;
esac
```

    a. The ending keyword is incorrect.

    b. The semicolon at the end of each case is incorrect.

    c. The variable referred to after the *case* keyword should not have a $.

    d. The *) case is invalid because it is a regular expression where a fixed value must be provided.

21. Which of the following is a valid first line defining a shell script function called init_db_files?

    a. init_db_files() {

    b. init_db_files {

    c. $init_db_files {

    d. init_db_files=(

22. To start a bash shell script called network with shell tracing active, which of the following commands do you use?

    a. *bash -x ./network*

    b. *bash -n ./network*

    c. *bash -nv ./network*

    d. *bash set x ./network*

23. The standard C language compiler included with Linux is called:

    a. make

    b. g++

    c. gcc

    d. wish

24. Looking at the following line from a bash shell script, what does the ! symbol indicate?

```
if [ ! -f '$NEXTFILE' ] ; then
```

a. The test indicated by the brackets should be performed twice.

b. The value of the test being done should be reversed (negated).

c. The test being done should only be performed if the variable contains a valid file name (based on the *-f* operator).

d. a syntax error

25. The following line is an example of what?

```
DB_FILE=""
```

a. variable initialization

b. a function definition

c. a counting variable

d. a selection statement

HANDS-ON PROJECTS

HANDS-ON PROJECTS

Project 14-1

14

In this project, you review scripts that are part of your default Linux installation. You must have an installed Linux system to complete this project. The steps here refer specifically to scripts found on a Red Hat Linux or Fedora system, though similar scripts are part of virtually every popular Linux distribution.

1. Log in to Linux using your regular user account.

2. If you are working in a graphical desktop, open a command-line window.

3. Change directories using this command:

   cd /etc/rc.d/init.d

4. List the files that are in this directory: **ls**. All of them are shell scripts.

5. You don't have permission to change these scripts while logged in as a regular user, but you can still view them. Open the functions script in a text editor:

   vi functions

6. Search for the daemon function. In vi, press **/** then enter **daemon**. How can you tell that this is a function?

7. Review the commands in this function, especially the lengthy case statement and the tests used in the *if-then* statements that follow it.

8. Exit your text editor.

9. Open the anacron script, which is used to start the cron daemon, in your text editor:

   vi anacron

10. Search in this file for the word **daemon**, if necessary. Notice that the daemon function is called from within another function called start. Notice also that where the daemon function is called, it has several parameters after it. These are used as positional parameters within the daemon function you reviewed previously.

11. Because the daemon function is called from within the start function, search for the word **start** to see where that function is called. Notice that the start function is called in several places, including when a user starts this daemon and when a user restarts this daemon (in the case statement, you see cases of start and restart that both include calls to the start function).

12. Exit the text editor.

13. Open the network script in your text editor:

    vi network

14. Scroll down in the network script using the down arrow or Page Down keys. If you are working in a standard graphical desktop, comments should appear in blue text. (Keywords, variables, and other text appear in separate colors as well.) How helpful are the comments to you? Would you like to see more comments? If so, remember this when you write your own scripts.

15. Exit the text editor after you finish exploring the network script. Close the command-line window and log off.

HANDS-ON
PROJECTS

Project 14-2

In this project, you create a simple shell script, then execute that script at the command line. To complete this activity you should have Linux installed.

1. Log in to Linux using your regular user name and password.

2. If you are using a graphical environment, open a command-line window.

3. Make certain you are in your home directory, then start vi (or another text editor) using the name of the script you will be creating:

   cd; vi fileinfo

4. If you are using vi, press **i** to change to insert mode.

5. Enter the following lines in vi:

```
#!/bin/bash
if [ $# -lt 1 ] then
        echo You must include a filename on the command line.
        exit
fi
```

```
echo Beginning to process files.
for i in $@
do
        echo Number of lines in $i
        wc -l $i
        echo Number of words in $i
        wc -w $i
done
```

6. Press **Esc** to return to command mode.

7. Type **:wq** and press **Enter** to exit vi and save the file. If you are using a different text editor, such as gedit, save the file you entered as fileinfo and close the text editor.

8. Change the file permissions on fileinfo to include the execute permission:

chmod 755 fileinfo

9. Check the syntax of the file by executing it with the –n option:

bash -n ./fileinfo

10. The program stops when it finds a syntax error. It can be difficult to determine what is wrong from the output of the shell. Try using the verbose option as well to see the lines of the script as the syntax is checked:

bash -nv ./fileinfo

This time you see the lines from your script. It's still not easy, but because the shell appears to think *fi* is unexpected, you might guess that the *if* statement didn't end properly, so the shell doesn't think it should see *fi* yet. (Experience helps you recognize where to look for syntax errors.)

11. Start your text editor and add a semicolon after the closing bracket in the *if* statement, so the line looks like this:

if [$# -lt 1]; then

12. Save the file and exit your text editor.

13. Run the syntax checking again:

bash -n ./fileinfo

If you see no output, you know that the syntax of each command in your program is correct.

14. Enter **./fileinfo** to execute the command without any parameters. What happens? What result is returned by the test in the second line of the script? What other methods could you use to test for the presence of a command-line parameter? What would happen if you removed the *if-then* test but didn't include any file names on the command line?

15. Enter **./fileinfo /etc/syslog.conf** to execute the command with a parameter. What happens? How many times was the *for* loop executed?

16. Execute the command with the parameter shown here:

    ```
    ./fileinfo /etc/m*conf
    ```

    What happens? How could you alter the script to test the validity of each file name that was provided on the command line before using the *wc* command? (*Hint*: Use the *-r* file test from Table 14-1.)

17. Pipe the results of a longer set of output through *less* to see if the script is using STDOUT:

    ```
    ./fileinfo /etc/[ms]*conf | less
    ```

18. Exit the command-line window and log out. (Don't delete the script file, because you will use it in the next project.)

**HANDS-ON
PROJECTS**

Project 14-3

In this project, you continue to work with the fileinfo script you created in Project 14-2, experimenting with the debugging features and modifying the script. To complete this activity you should have Linux installed.

1. Log in to Linux using your regular user account and open a command-line window.

2. Run your script with these parameters:

   ```
   ./fileinfo /etc/[ms]*conf
   ```

3. Now run the script again, but using the shell tracing option:

   ```
   bash -x ./fileinfo /etc/[ms]*conf
   ```

   You see that lines beginning with a + symbol are the shell trace, showing a line of your script exactly as the shell is executing it (with a file name, for example, instead of a regular expression or variable name). After each line beginning with +, you see the output of that command, if the command generated any screen output.

4. Because the output from Step 3 was too long to display on one screen, you cannot review all of it. Try redirecting the output of the script to a file (use the up arrow to display the command you just entered, then add to it, rather than retyping the entire command):

   ```
   bash -x ./fileinfo /etc/[ms]*conf > scriptsave
   ```

   You see only the lines that start with +. These are written to the STDERR channel rather than STDOUT, so the scriptsave file contains what the script would have written to the screen, but the shell trace still appears on screen. This can be very helpful because you see exactly what lines the shell is executing.

5. Assuming this is still too much information, suppose that you realized that a problem was occurring in your script when it tried to process files starting with "w", but not with other letters. You decide to modify your script so you can find this pesky bug. Open the fileinfo script in a text editor:

   ```
   vi fileinfo
   ```

6. In the *for* loop, right after the *do* line, before the first *echo* command, insert the following lines to turn on shell tracing only for file names starting with w:

```
case $i in
   w*)   set -x ;;
   *)    set +x ;;
esac
```

7. Save your file and exit the text editor.

8. Test the syntax of your script. You should see no output:

bash -n ./fileinfo

9. Now you can run the script without using the *-x* option on the command line, because you are setting the shell trace feature inside the script. Try this command:

./fileinfo /etc/[msw]*conf > scriptsave

You see no shell tracing output, though you thought you had set up the script to turn it on for file names starting with w.

10. After some head scratching, you realize that the file names you are using all start with /etc/—the script doesn't know that you mean the file name without any path before it. You could add commands to strip that information off, but you choose to take an easier approach for now. First, change to the /etc directory, so you can refer to the configuration files without including /etc/ in front of the file names:

cd /etc

11. Now execute the script in your home directory:

~/fileinfo [msw]*conf > ~/scriptsave

You see on the screen shell tracing output only for file names that begin with "w". The rest of the script output is stored in your home directory in the scriptsave file.

12. Exit the command-line window and log off.

14

CASE PROJECTS

Writing Shell Scripts

The Starwood movie studio has asked for your help. The computer graphics specialists creating their next feature film want to automate some of their CPU-intensive graphics commands so they can schedule them to run during lunch or after hours. You teach the staff how to submit a *cron* job to accomplish this, but after a few days, it becomes obvious that your training session was not sufficient:

1. Write a shell script that asks a user to input a single-line command that they want to have executed once each week. Ask the user to input the day of the week on which they want the command to be executed. Submit their command as a correctly formatted *cron* job. (You may need to review the last part of Chapter 6, "Managing Processes," to refresh your memory on how to use *cron* and *crontab*.)

2. As part of a larger project for several clients, you need to help the Starwood system administrator prepare for possible system failures. Write a script that queries relevant system information from the /proc file system, the *uname* command, the output of *dmesg*, and possibly other sources on the system. The script should collect this information in variables, format it, then store it in a text file. (System administrators will run this script, then give you the file it creates so you can develop disaster plans for each site.)

3. The director of Starwood has asked that you prepare a special game as a skill-building device for the studio's employees. The game displays a series of random numbers or letters on the screen for a brief time, then clears the screen and asks the user to enter what they saw. The game develops short-term memory and visual acuity. Skilled "players" can view a 12-digit number for one second and reenter it accurately. Create a script to implement this game using the RANDOM variable (see the bash man page), the *sleep* command to pause for a length of time, and the *clear* command to clear the screen after pausing. Format the random string for easy reading, read in the user's response and compare it with the string displayed, then report how the user did. After creating a basic version, you might expand your script to permit the user to define the length of the string (perhaps starting at three digits and growing if the user scores well); to include scoring information displayed on the screen and saved to a file for comparison with later progress; to keep track of which types of strings the user does best on; or to select whether to include only digits or both digits and letters, among other features. If you decide the game is useful, you can add features over time to play it over the network with other users and to make it graphical. These last two features can be added by creating the script using Python, Tcl/Tk, or other languages.

ADVANCED TOPICS AND TROUBLESHOOTING

After reading this chapter and completing the exercises, you will be able to:

♦ Understand X Window System scripts and remote access

♦ Implement basic system security

♦ Use simple features of common network services

♦ Troubleshoot common hardware and software problems

In the previous chapter you learned how to create shell scripts in a text editor. These scripts were used to automate commands that you might otherwise execute at the command line, and they also included special commands that are usually only found within scripts. You learned about managing input and output in a script, and about controlling which parts of a script are executed based on tests and various looping structures. You also learned about debugging shell scripts to find problems with your syntax or logic. Finally, you learned a little about other methods of programming on Linux and some of the developer tools that support those methods.

In this final chapter, you learn about several advanced topics and about some basic troubleshooting techniques and tools in Linux. First, you learn more about the X Window System, including the scripts it uses when started, and, more importantly, how to provide remote graphical access using X. You also learn about basic system security and the types of security problems and tools that a Linux administrator typically uses. A large section on network services introduces the most widely used Linux network services, such as Web servers, DNS servers, and e-mail servers. You will learn enough about these services to get them running in a lab environment and perform basic configuration steps. Finally, you will learn some troubleshooting and rescue tips.

X WINDOW SYSTEM ADVANCED CONFIGURATION

Improvements in both installation programs and in the XFree86 X server over the last few years mean that challenges configuring your graphical system are rare. Your video card is either supported or it isn't. If it is, your installation program configures it and places you in a graphical desktop; if it is not, nothing you can do will permit X to run, short of buying a new video card. Previous versions of Linux included special configuration utilities for setting up X. These included Xconfigurator (in Red Hat Linux), xf86config, XF86Setup, SaX (in SUSE Linux), lizardx (in Caldera OpenLinux), and others. You will rarely find any of these utilities installed on a newer Linux system because they are no longer needed.

In this section, you learn more about what is happening behind the scenes in the X Window System, including how to adjust your video configuration and how the separate start-up files for the X Window System operate.

Configuring X

When you installed Linux, the XFree86 X server was installed on your hard disk. In addition, you have many supporting XFree86 packages, such as a window manager and a desktop interface.

NOTE On any Linux system, you can choose not to run X to save system resources (both memory and CPU processing time). To do this, make sure you are working in run level 3, as described in Chapter 9, "Understanding System Initialization."

The X software is normally located in the directory /usr/X11R6. This directory is sometimes called the X-root directory. The file name X11R6 refers to X version 11, release 6. The configuration file for the XFree86 server is located either in the /etc/X11 directory, or in the /usr/X11R6/lib/X11 directory. (Red Hat Linux and Fedora use the former location.) The configuration file is called xorg.conf. In years past, you would have to understand and edit this file by hand when you had trouble with your video configuration. This is almost never necessary now, but you can review the configuration file to learn how X operates.

TIP If you experiment with different video configuration settings and end up with a blank or garbled screen, try pressing the key combination Ctrl+Alt+Backspace to exit X and return to character mode.

If you have purchased a commercial X server, that program uses a different configuration file with a different format. For example, the Accelerated-X server from Xi Graphics uses the configuration file /etc/Xaccel.ini. Commercial X servers include graphical configuration tools similar to what you saw when you installed Linux. When working with a commercial X server, you should review the documentation accompanying the product to learn how to use the product's configuration utility to prepare a configuration file.

Newer Linux systems often do include utilities to adjust your video display, even though the initial configuration is handled by the installation program. The **xvidtune** program is part of the X Window System. It lets you adjust the finer details of your display, but can damage your monitor if used carelessly (a warning message tells you this when you start the program). Figure 15-1 shows the main window of the *xvidtune* program.

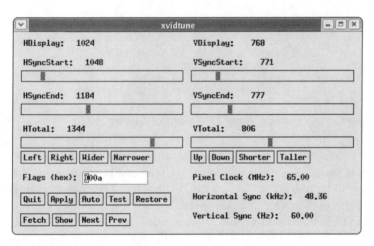

Figure 15-1 The *xvidtune* graphical adjustment utility

Even when your video display looks good (so *xvidtune* is not needed), you might want to change your screen resolution to suit your preferences. For example, if the installation program set up the screen with a resolution of 800x600, you might prefer to use 1024x768. If you have installed KDE, you can change the resolution setting in the KDE Control Center. Under the Peripherals category on the left side of the Control Center, choose the Display item, then make sure the Size & Orientation tab is selected. Figure 15-2 shows this window. On most systems, you are only able to change the size, rather than the orientation. Further, KDE might not let you change to a resolution as high as you might like. It limits itself to protect your monitor from damage, because in former times, a poorly configured X Window System could damage a monitor.

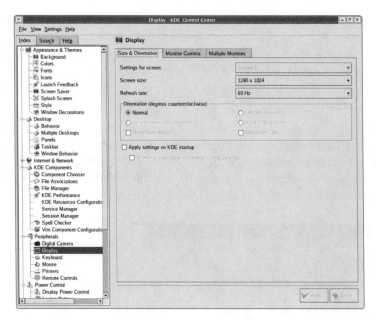

Figure 15-2   Setting display options in the KDE Control Center

When using Red Hat Linux or Fedora, you can also configure your screen using the *system-config-display* program, shown in Figure 15-3. In this program, you can configure the screen resolution and number of colors on the Settings tab. The choices available depend on your video card and the amount of video memory you have. On the Hardware tab, you see the video card and monitor listed as they are currently configured. If you need to (which would be rare), you can click Configure to choose a different video card or monitor from the list of supported hardware.

Using X Window System Start-up Scripts

If you configured X while installing Linux and used the default settings for a graphical login prompt, the X Window System starts automatically every time you log in at the graphical prompt. (This is because you are working in run level 5 by default, as configured in the /etc/inittab file.)

If you are not using a graphical login prompt, the standard method of starting X is to log in to Linux on a character-mode console and then execute the *startx* command. This command automatically executes a number of other commands that start the X server and run the programs that make up the graphical environment.

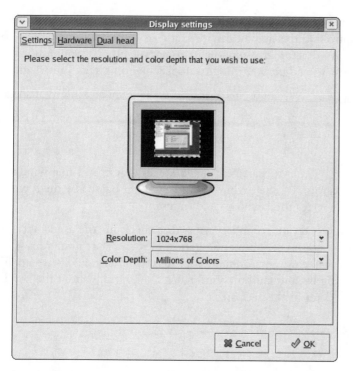

Figure 15-3   Setting display options using *system-config-display*

The *startx* program is actually a script located in /usr/X11R6/bin. This script starts another program called ***xinit***, which looks for several scripts in various locations in the Linux directory structure, including ~/.xinitrc, ~/.Xclients, /etc/X11/xinit/xinitrc, and /etc/X11/xinit/Xclients. A system administrator can place scripts in a user's home directory (~/.xinitrc and ~/.Xclients) to define a unique graphical configuration for that user. All of the scripts listed here specify which programs should start along with X. For the most part, these programs are X clients. (Remember, an X client is an application that runs in X.)

Each X client is started as a background application. A **background application** is an application that does not prevent the program that started it (the *xinit* program in this case) from going on to other tasks (starting other X clients). In this case, the *xinit* scripts can start an X client and then go on to start another (and another, and another, and so on) without waiting for the first one to finish execution. The X clients that *xinit* starts from the initialization scripts include the window manager, and desktop applications such as a file manager and a toolbar that includes the main menu for the desktop.

The window manager is the last X client that the *xinit* program starts. The window manager is responsible for controlling the graphical screen, and its features are used by all of the X applications that are started before the window manager; the other X applications wait until the window manager is started before trying to display any on screen information.

A very simple script that *xinit* could use to start one X client and a window manager might look like this:

```
xterm &
fvwm
```

If this script were used by *xinit* to start X, a single xterm (command-line window) would appear on a blank background. (The background would be provided by the fvwm window manager, which also manages the keyboard and mouse.)

In practice, Linux vendors create complex scripts that check for the availability of default window managers, look at a variety of configuration files, and start numerous X clients to provide a convenient working environment for users. The standard start-up process is outlined in the following list and illustrated in Figure 15-4. Details about the last few items in the list are provided later in this section.

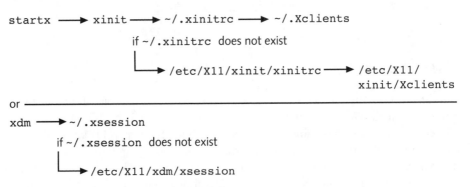

Figure 15-4 The start-up scripts used by the X Window System

1. The user logs in at a graphical login prompt or executes the *startx* command.

2. The *startx* command or the graphical login prompt (the display manager, described in the next section) initiates the *xinit* command.

3. The *xinit* command starts the X server program.

4. The *xinit* command attempts to start a script called .xinitrc located in the user's home directory.

5. If the file is found, the commands in .xinitrc are executed by *xinit*. This script normally executes commands in other scripts, particularly the .Xclients script, which can also be located in each user's home directory, if the system administrator implements a different graphical configuration for each user.

6. If the .xinitrc file is not found in the user's home directory, the *xinit* program looks for the file /etc/X11/xinit/xinitrc. (Notice that this file name does not begin with a period as do those in a user's home directory.)

7. If the /etc/X11/xinit/xinitrc file mentioned in Step 6 is found, the commands in it are executed by *xinit*. The /etc/X11/xinit/xinitrc script normally executes commands in other scripts, particularly the /etc/X11/xinit/Xclients script. (Again, the file name has no initial period.) These two scripts (located in /etc/X11/xinit) are systemwide graphical configuration scripts that are used for any user who does not have files in his or her home directory as described in Steps 4 and 5.

The scripts xinitrc, .xinitrc, Xclients, and .Xclients often include calls to execute other scripts, such as Xclients_default. The names and arrangement of these additional scripts vary by Linux distribution, but you can learn more about them by reviewing the contents of the xinitrc or .xinitrc file. All of the standard scripts (such as xinitrc), and the additional scripts that may be used by a particular Linux distribution, are shell scripts.

Notice in the previous steps that you can use a separate configuration file in each user's home directory so each user can use a different graphical configuration. One user might choose to use fvwm as a window manager; another user might select GNOME or KDE as a graphical environment.

Adjusting the Display of Graphical Applications

You can use several utilities that come with the X Window System to adjust how applications are displayed and how X behaves in different situations.

Each graphical application uses a number of separate screen elements, such as scroll bars, text fonts, mouse pointers, and title bars for windows or dialog boxes. Each of these elements is called an **X resource**. This is a term used by programmers, but you should be familiar with it because as a system administrator you can configure the appearance of the X resources used in each application.

A collection of default X resource settings applies to all X applications. These default settings govern how windows in the application are displayed, which colors and fonts are used, and which features of the application are active when the application starts. You can also set up additional X resource settings that apply only when a specific user runs a specific application. These resource settings are compiled into a **resource database** file. Collectively, the information in this file defines how an X resource should appear onscreen.

The main resource database file is called app–defaults. It is located at /usr/X11R6/lib/X11. In addition to this set of resource information, each user's home directory can contain additional settings that override the default appearance of specific applications. A file named .Xresources or .Xdefaults contains this information. For example, the following sample lines in an .Xresources file define how an *xterm* window appears and what features it includes.

These same features can be set or changed once the *xterm* program is running, but when a user creates an X resource database, the application is started with the user's preferences already active.

```
XTerm*cursorColor: gold
XTerm*multiScroll: on
XTerm*jumpScroll: on
XTerm*reverseWrap: on
XTerm*curses: on
XTerm*Font: 6x10
XTerm*scrollBar: on
XTerm*scrollbar*thickness: 5
XTerm*multiClickTime: 500
XTerm*charClass: 33:48,37:48,45-47:48,64:48  XTerm*cutNewline:
 off
XTerm*cutToBeginningOfLine: off
XTerm*titeInhibit: on
XTerm*ttyModes: intr ^c erase ^? kill ^u XLoad*Background: gold
```

X resource database files are activated within one of the startup scripts such as .xinitrc or .Xclients by using the command xrdb. The **xrdb** command loads an initial X database resource file or adds resource configuration details from files such as .Xresources. An *xrdb* command such as the one shown here is part of the X startup scripts described previously:

```
xrdb -load $HOME/.Xresources
```

When there are additional resource settings to be loaded, the *-merge* option is used instead of the *-load* option. You rarely need to set up the *xrdb* command, because it is part of the default configuration when you install X. But you may want to add information to an .Xresources file to configure the appearance of an application. The online manual page for a graphical application tells you about options you can configure via X resources.

NOTE   Linux desktop environments (such as KDE and GNOME) include an X resource database that is designed to give a standard look and feel to all programs that you run. Instead of using an .Xresources file to configure the appearance and options of the desktop, these environments use their own configuration tools, typically on a Preferences menu or in a Control Center window, as discussed in Chapter 2, "Exploring the Desktop."

You can use the **xfontsel** command to see the fonts supported by the X Window System. Fonts are processed for use in each application by a font server (called xfs) that receives requests for font information from applications. Within the *xfontsel* program, click on each category below the two buttons shown to select from a drop-down list of available items. Within modern desktop interfaces such as KDE and GNOME, the *xfontsel* program is not used because they rely on separate Preferences windows in which you select the font for display of graphical applications.

Although the configuration file and scripts described thus far control many aspects of X, you can use the *xset* command to adjust the behavior of X to suit your preferences. Execute *xset* at any command line to see a list of the options that you can use with this command to control X. They include:

- Turn keyclick on or off.
- Set the keyclick volume.
- Choose keyboard autorepeat settings.
- Activate EnergyStar features of compliant monitors.
- Set mouse acceleration levels.
- Set font locations and other font settings.
- Alter properties of the X screen blanker (this is separate from the screen saver that is part of GNOME or KDE).

For example, suppose you notice that the screen of your system goes completely blank after a few minutes without using the system. To turn off this feature, execute this command:

```
$ xset s noblank
```

To see the current settings for all the features that *xset* controls, use this command:

```
$  xset q
```

Using a Graphical Login Screen

If your installation program successfully configures the video card, most Linux distributions start the system in run level 5 rather than run level 3. After Linux starts and initializes, it switches immediately to graphics mode and displays a graphical login screen. Once the user name and password have been entered, a standard graphical system such as GNOME or KDE is opened.

TIP

To change the run level used by default as the Linux system starts, set the value in the initdefault line of the /etc/inittab file.

The graphical login screen is provided by the X display manager. This program is called **xdm**; versions specific to KDE and GNOME are called **kdm** and **gdm**, respectively. Each operates in much the same way. xdm is started by the *init* program as Linux boots. Any time a user exits the graphical desktop, xdm is restarted automatically to provide a graphical login screen. Thus the user never encounters a character-mode screen—a fact that can make new users much more comfortable with Linux. The xdm program is installed as part of the X Window System.

15

When a user logs in using an xdm graphical login screen, xdm selects which programs to start based on the session chosen by the user. A **session** defines a set of graphical programs to run when a user logs in.

A configuration file called Xsession specifies which programs are started by a particular session name. When xdm starts X (after a user logs in), it executes the file/etc/X11/xdm/ Xsession to determine which X clients to run. The Xsession file contains a set of instructions that match the names of sessions defined for xdm. For example, if the user selects the failsafe session, the Xsession script only starts an *xterm* program; if the user selects a KDE session, Xsession starts all of the standard KDE components. A per-user configuration file named .xsession (all lowercase, beginning with a period) can be placed in a user's home directory to control which sessions that user has available. The available session types are normally common to all users, however, so using an .xsession file in a home directory is unusual.

You can configure the features of xdm in various text files in the /etc/X11/xdm subdirectory. Most users rely on either kdm or gdm, both of which you can configure using graphical tools in KDE and GNOME. In KDE or GNOME, choose System Settings, then Login Screen to set up the login screen. (On versions of Linux besides Red Hat and Fedora, the location of the configuration utility on the KDE menus may vary.) Figure 15-5 shows a sample configuration screen from the Login Screen configuration window.

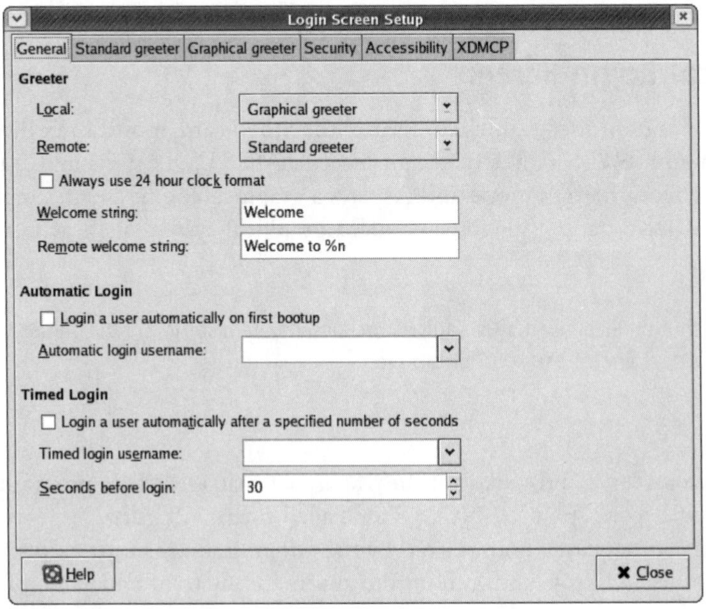

Figure 15-5   The GNOME Login Screen configuration window

Displaying X Clients Remotely

The X Window System actually uses its own protocol (the X protocol) to communicate between the X server and each X client. This protocol can be used over network connections. That is, you can use an X server to display the window for an X client running on any computer on a network. For example, suppose you have StarOffice (the X client) installed on one computer (call it computer A). Many different users on other computers (B, C, and D in the example) can log in to computer A over the network and start a copy of StarOffice. All of the copies of StarOffice are actually running on computer A, but the X server program on computers B, C, and D, where all of the users are physically located, displays the X client application on those computers as shown in Figure 15-6. The X server on computers B, C, and D receives requests from the X client (StarOffice) on computer A to display windows and collect keyboard and mouse input.

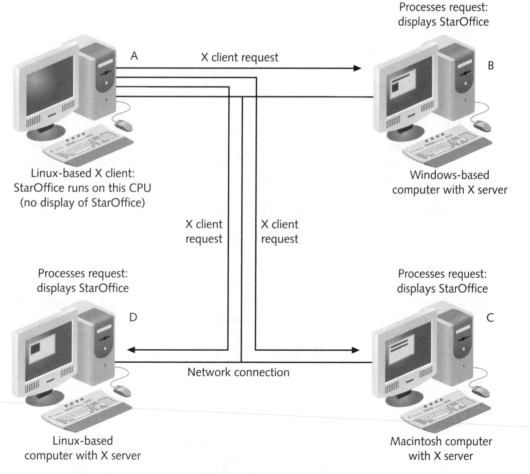

Figure 15-6 Remotely displaying an X client

Any type of computer can run the X server that displays windows and collects input for an X client. For example, by installing an X server on a Microsoft Windows computer, you can open an application on a Linux computer and use that application while sitting at the Windows computer. Two examples of commercial X servers for Windows are X-Win32 (*www.starnet.com*) and Exceed (*www.hummingbird.com.*—Use the search feature of this Web site to locate Exceed, which is an older product and not easy to locate.).

Each time you start a graphical application, the application decides which X server to use—that is, it decides where to display its windows and collect keyboard and mouse input. By default, it uses the X server on the same computer where the X client is executed. But you can specify a different X server in two ways:

- Set the DISPLAY environment variable to the name of the computer whose X server you want the X client to use. The format of the computer name includes a special code that all Linux systems use to determine X server behavior: :0.0. For example, the commands to set this variable to display graphical applications on host nevada are:

  ```
  DISPLAY=nevada:0.0
  export DISPLAY
  ```

- Add the *display* option to the command you are executing. For example, the following command starts the GIMP application and displays it on host oregon:

```
gimp display oregon:0.0
```

Each user on a system has a different set of environment variables, so all users can log in and have the programs they run displayed on different remote hosts. The *display* option overrides the DISPLAY environment variable.

Configuring Remote Display Security

Before an X client can display its windows on a remote host, the X server on the remote host must be configured to allow other computers to display programs there. You can do this in two ways: one easy and insecure, the other more work but more secure. The easy method is to execute the **xhost** command on the remote host. This command specifies the name of a remote computer that is permitted to use the local X server. Any user on the remote computer can then display an application on the computer where *xhost* was executed. For example, if this command is executed on host idaho, any user on host oregon can start an application and display it on idaho:

```
# xhost +oregon
```

Some users even use this highly insecure command to permit *anyone* to use their X server:

```
# xhost +
```

A more secure system uses the **xauth** command. With this system you can restrict access to those users on a remote system who have a specific token (a long number) in order to use the X server. This token is commonly called a **cookie**. The cookie used by the *xauth* command is also called an **MIT Magic Cookie**.

In work environments, the *xauth* program should be used in connection with SSH, so that security information is not transmitted over the network without being encrypted.

When using the *xauth* system, programs follow this process:

1. Suppose you start a program on host oregon that is to be displayed by the X server on host nevada. The program you execute on oregon examines the **.Xauthority** file in your home directory on oregon to see whether a token is given for the remote host nevada.

2. Assuming that a token is available (you must put it there yourself, as you will shortly see), the token is sent to nevada over the network as oregon tries to initiate a connection to use the X server on nevada.

3. The X server on nevada looks in *its* .Xauthority file for a token that corresponds to host oregon. If it finds one, it allows the connection to proceed. If not, the connection is refused and the program on oregon does not run (because it has been instructed to use nevada for its display and nevada won't allow that).

The .Xauthority files mentioned in this process are stored in a user's home directory. So each user must have the necessary tokens to use another user's X server. Of course, the most common situation is that you have accounts on two systems and you copy the token between your home directories so that you can run and display programs on any of the systems to which you have access. In any case, *xauth* is designed to be a user-to-user security system, rather than a host-to-host security system.

You can see the .Xauthority file in your home directory using the *ls -a* command (it's a hidden file). To view or alter the file's contents, you use the *xauth* program, which you can start from any command line. When you start *xauth*, you see a prompt where you can enter commands interactively to manage your tokens.

A few helpful commands are *help* to show all the *xauth* commands, *list* to list all the tokens currently stored, and *add* to place a token into the authority file for use by a remote host. For example, if the *add* command shown here is executed on oregon, it permits oregon to use the X server on nevada (the information in the command was first obtained from nevada):

```
add nevada:0  MIT-MAGIC-COOKIE1 6da29c0a7399aa179c90cba39426dd5f
```

The .Xauthority file should always include a token for the host where you are working. A new token is generated each time you log in to X. If your file doesn't include a token for your local host, use the *generate* command within *xauth* to create one. Here, you see *xauth* started, followed by the *list* command to show all the known tokens on host nevada:

```
[thomasj@nevada thomasj]# xauth
Using authority file /home/thomasj/.Xauthority
xauth> list
```

15

```
nevada/unix:0  MIT-MAGIC-COOKIE-1 da29c0a7399aa179c90cba39426dd5f
nevada:0  MIT-MAGIC-COOKIE-1 6da29c0a7399aa179c90cba39426dd5f
xauth>
```

If you have a file such as this one and you want host oregon to be able to use nevada as an X server (that is, to display programs on it), you must get the information from this file into your .Xauthority file on oregon. Once you have done this, oregon will have a valid token to send to nevada so that nevada will allow oregon to connect for remote program display.

NOTE You can transfer an *xauth* cookie between systems in several ways. Typically, you use a networking program such as *telnet*, *rlogin*, or *ssh* to connect to a remote computer over the network, then copy and paste the information between two windows.

Don't be surprised if remote display of graphical applications doesn't work correctly on your first attempt. The many components of X can make it difficult to configure. If you are having problems, be certain that your DISPLAY variable is correctly set. Check with your system administrator to see if X was started with the *-nolisten tcp* argument, which stops it from listening for remote connections. Make certain that the host name you have specified is reachable on the network (try *ping*, for example). Check again that the tokens in the two .Xauthority files match and that a problem such as an expired token is not interfering with your efforts. Finally, review the man pages (for X, *xauth*, and so on.) and HOWTO documents related to X to see what else might be preventing your setup from functioning as expected.

Remote Graphical Login

A special type of remote display occurs when you want a person to be able to log in to your Linux system and use a graphical environment as if they were sitting at the Linux system. This is commonly done when people working in a company run graphical applications on a large central server but work at independent graphical workstations. When the workstation is turned on (this can also apply to a Microsoft Windows System running an X Server such as Exceed, mentioned previously), the workstation uses the xdm control protocol (**XDMCP**) to communicate with the Linux server. The Linux server provides a graphical login screen at which the remote user can log in. After logging in, the entire graphical environment (such as GNOME) is provided to the remote user.

Using XDMCP requires some configuration of the remote user's software, configuration on the Linux server to run XDMCP, and appropriate security mechanisms, as discussed in the previous section. In the Login Screen configuration window of GNOME, you can see on the Security and XDMCP tabs, shown in Figures 15-7 and 15-8, some of the options that are supported when using this advanced feature of the X Window System.

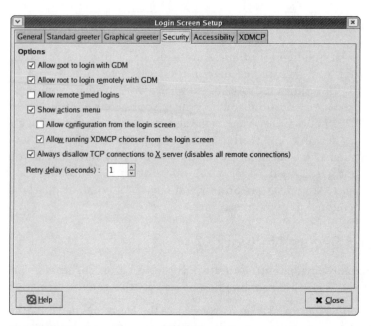

Figure 15-7   The Security tab of the GNOME Login Screen configuration dialog box

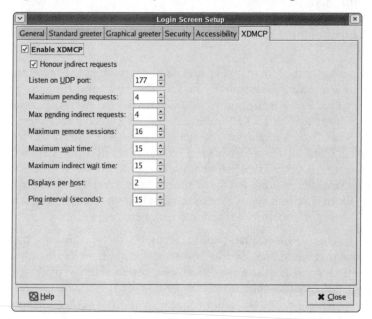

15

Figure 15-8   The XDMCP tab of the GNOME Login Screen configuration dialog box

SECURITY ISSUES

You have learned about hundreds of utilities, protocols, and administration tasks, of which the topic of security is only one, placed here in the last chapter of this book. Yet as you become familiar with the utilities and tasks of your daily work, security concerns will loom much larger. In fact, the more advanced you become in your system administration skills, the more you will be placed in positions where your biggest concern is maintaining the security of your organization's networks and the information they contain. With that introduction, this section only scratches the surface of computer security by introducing you to some general guidelines and terms used. Much more information is available in Course Technology's *Guide to Linux Networking and Security* and *Guide to Firewalls and Network Security*, and similar books dedicated to computer security.

The Structure of a Secure Network

Security can be roughly divided into four areas. By focusing on challenges in all of these areas, you are more likely to eliminate breaches of security that can threaten your network.

- *Physical security*: Can an attacker gain access to the hardware used for your network? This is most often taken care of by locking the servers in a closet. Only system administrators have access, because a person who can get to the servers can restart them with a floppy disk to change the operating system options, remove a hard disk to extract data from it at another location, or simply turn off the server to disrupt people's work.

- *User security*: Each user has an account with a password. Maintaining strong passwords and teaching users not to disclose them ensures that only the person authorized to use a user name and password actually can. Attackers sometimes use **social engineering**—clever lies or persuasive skills—to convince users to divulge their passwords. For example, an attacker can pose as a system administrator or security officer and ask for a password to "test" a user's account. User security also involves setting resource limits on what users can do on the system, such as how much disk space they can use and what times of the day they can log in. Although networks (fourth in this list) are a more broadly known security concern, employees cause most of the security breaches in an organization.

- *File security*: This involves maintaining accurate file permissions on files and directories so that when user security is working properly, users are only allowed to access information for which they have permission. File security also involves tracking the status of files so that if a change is made to a file that could indicate a security problem, the system administrator will notice that change and can investigate. A popular tool for catching unauthorized changes to files is called Tripwire (see *www.tripwire.com*).

■ *Network security*: Networking makes computer systems much more useful, but also much more vulnerable to attack, because people far away can attempt to breach your security. Network security involves many issues and can take place at many levels. In the next section of this chapter you will read about several ways of improving network security in Linux, including NetFilter packet filtering, TCP Wrappers, and application-specific access controls. Network security can also be as simple as using the **/etc/nologin** file, which blocks anyone from logging in remotely, or editing the **/etc/securetty** file, which defines from where root can log in.

Types of Security Attacks

Security attacks come in many forms. Because many of the security subjects related to user and file security have been addressed in previous chapters, much of the rest of this section is devoted to exploring network security in more depth. Categories of security attacks include the following:

■ **Password cracking** is a technique in which an attacker obtains a user's password, either by using a program that examines millions of passwords until the correct one is found, or by guessing based on personal knowledge about the user (don't ever use your pet's name as a password). With a valid password in hand, an attacker can log in to your system (usually remotely) without any signs of suspicious activity.

■ **Trojan horse** attacks occur when you run a program that you obtained from an untrustworthy source or that was installed on your machine by an attacker without your knowledge. The program appears to function normally but actually performs hidden tasks that render your system insecure and allow the cracker to gain access. E-mail viruses are a common way for Trojan horse programs to enter a computer system, though these viruses themselves are rarely a problem for Linux servers because of the way that Linux multitasking operates. More common on Linux servers are Trojan horses that run with root access, appearing to be valid system utilities or kernel modules.

TIP
If you are not familiar with the term "Trojan horse," it refers to the time around 1200 BC when the Greeks laying siege to Troy built a large wooden horse. They hid their best soldiers inside it and presented the horse as a gift to the Trojans. The Trojans pulled the horse into their fort and were subsequently defeated as a result of this trick. The story is recounted in Homer's *The Iliad* and is the basis of the saying "Beware Greeks bearing gifts," or as it has been said in this context, "Beware of geeks bearing gifts."

■ **Buffer overflow attacks** rely on a weakness in the design of a program. These weaknesses are usually very difficult to find because they are based on complex logic within a large program (such as a DNS server). However, once discovered by a skilled attacker, the buffer overflow is generally not hard to exploit as a security hole, and the attacker may inform others of the problem. An attacker must find a specific sequence of steps, or specific input to give to a network program, so that the program becomes confused and tries to use computer memory inappropriately: The buffer, or memory space, reserved for a part of the program overflows. The result can be corruption of system data, a crashed server, or even direct root access, any of which may be the goal of the attacker.

- **Denial-of-service (DoS)** attacks try to overwhelm a server so that valid users cannot access it. This is often done by attacking numerous insecure systems and using all of them at the same time to send requests to a server. This is called a **distributed DoS (DDoS)** attack. Services such as DNS and the Web are among those vulnerable to this type of attack. Because a server is designed to accept any incoming connection, this type of attack can be very hard to anticipate and prevent, though features in modern routers and in newer protocols make prevention easier.

- **Port scanning** is a technique used by both attackers and system administrators checking the security of their network. Networked applications in Linux typically (but not always) communicate with other systems by using ports. A **port** is a number, like an address, associated with an application running on a computer. Many port numbers are predefined for standard services; others are used on as-needed basis. A port-scanning program sends packets to a server to gain information about the server based on its response. Port scanning normally involves sending packets to many ports or sending malformed packets to gain knowledge that the host is not intentionally sharing.

CAUTION

If you are a network administrator with responsibility for the security of a particular network, feel free to use port scanning and packet-sniffing tools to learn about your network's weaknesses and improve your security. For any other networks, ask before you act or you risk causing yourself and the other network administrator many problems.

- **Packet sniffing** (also called **network traffic analysis**) is another technique used by both attackers and skilled network administrators studying the network. Sniffing lets you see the headers and data contained within every packet on a network, not just those that are addressed to your own host.

Security Tools

The most widely used port-scanning utility is *nmap*, the network mapper. *nmap* is a powerful command-line utility that can use a variety of different scanning methods. *nmap* is installed by default on Red Hat Linux and Fedora.

The home page for the *nmap* utility is *www.insecure.org/nmap*, where you can also find a number of very interesting security-related articles. One of the most valuable is the list of 75 most used security utilities, from a survey of hundreds of network administrators. You can find this list at *www.insecure.org/tools.html*. A simple example of using *nmap* to scan a host is shown here:

```
# nmap -sS www.myplace.net
```

Although *nmap* is not difficult to use, the **nmapfe** utility provides a nice graphical interface that is useful both when you are learning to use the utility and when you expect to collect a lot of data that is more easily viewed in a graphical environment. Figure 15-9 shows this utility, which is part of the Nmap Front End package, located on Fedora CD 3 (this package is not installed by default).

Figure 15-9   The *nmapfe* port-scanning utility

The IPTraf program is a popular tool for viewing network activity on a LAN. It doesn't display the data within packets, but instead displays individual network connections, with protocol and other data listed for each one. It also displays statistics by protocol, by interface, by host name, or IP address. You can set up filters to track only certain protocols, certain host names, or certain IP addresses. The home page of IPTraf is *http://cebu.mozcom.com/riker/iptraf/*, but it is included on CD 3 of Fedora (it is not installed by default). Start it with the command *iptraf*. Figure 15-10 shows a configuration menu within IPTraf.

The **tcpdump** command-line utility provides functionality similar to the IPTraf program, but it also includes more detailed information about packets on your network. This utility is installed by default on Red Hat Linux and Fedora using the categories recommended in Chapter 8, "Installing Linux." Using *tcpdump*, you can examine the headers for each packet and save that information to a file for later analysis. You can also save the data within packets to a file, having *tcpdump* act as a network sniffer.

Figure 15-10   The IPTraf network traffic analysis program

One of the best packet-sniffing tools is **Ethereal**, a graphical network traffic analysis tool. Though it's not installed by default on Red Hat Linux or Fedora, you can add it to your system by installing the following two packages from Fedora CD 3: ethereal and ethereal-gnome.

The first of these packages includes documentation; the second includes the actual Ethereal program and setup instructions for the GNOME graphical desktop. If you're running other versions of Linux, packaged binaries are also likely to be available for your system. Visit the Ethereal home page at *www.ethereal.com* or your favorite Linux download site (such as *rpmfind.net* or *freshmeat.net*). To start the program, execute the ***ethereal*** command from any graphical command-line window. Figure 15-11 shows the Ethereal window.

The Ethereal packages also include a text-mode version called ***tethereal***.

TIP

A special type of security software is called an **intrusion detection system (IDS)**. An IDS watches the network for activity that may indicate that an attacker is looking for a way to enter your server. For example, when a person uses the *nmap* program to perform a port scan of your server, an intrusion detection program sees that certain network activity is coming from a port scanner, which indicates the presence of an attacker.

A freely available IDS is the **Linux Intrusion Detection System (LIDS)**. LIDS is a challenge to use, but provides a level of protection that's hard to match with most other tools. LIDS adds a module to the Linux kernel that blocks access to resources for all users—including root—except as configured by LIDS. You can download LIDS from *www.lids.org*. Specific features of LIDS include:

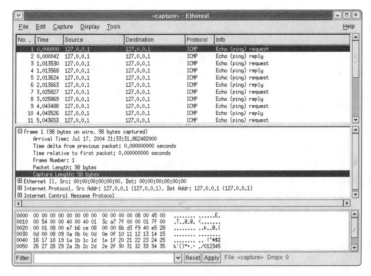

Figure 15-11   The Ethereal network traffic analysis program

- Port scanner detection within the kernel

- Ability to hide files completely or make them read-only, even to root

- Ability to hide processes completely or block which other processes can send signals to them (effectively blocking the use of the *kill* command to stop or restart an application)

- **Access Control Lists (ACLs)** (data structures that define who can access individual directories and programs)

- Time-based restrictions stating a task can only be performed or a file accessed during specific times during the day (this is similar to features offered by such services as Pluggable Authentication Modules, but LIDS performs this directly in the Linux kernel)

After you have started using security tools, you can test the security of your servers by performing a **security audit**, a review or test of how secure your system really is and what needs to be done to improve its security. Such an audit can take many forms. For example, if you work in an organization that has a well-defined security policy, one type of security audit would consist of a careful review of that policy to see where the systems, system administrators, management team, or end-users fall short in implementing that policy. Software can also be used to perform an automated attack on your servers using known weaknesses and typical attacker techniques.

The **Security Administrator's Integrated Network Tool (SAINT)** is a utility that uses a Web browser interface to manage an "attack" on your network and report to you the vulnerabilities it finds. It is similar to using a port scanner to locate potentially open network

15

ports; SAINT uses different methods and looks for different vulnerabilities than the *nmap* tool. To learn about SAINT, visit the home page at *www.saintcorporation.com*.

Viruses and Worms

Viruses and worms are security threats designed to replicate themselves once they have been installed on your system. A virus usually tries to replicate as part of another program (for example, as an e-mail attachment), while a worm attempts to infiltrate other systems on its own. Linux is rarely the subject of virus attacks, because programs running on Linux have access to system resources based solely on the user permissions of the person running the program. Unless a program is running as root and is not security oriented (a rare situation in Linux), a virus can't do much damage. In addition, because Linux lacks support for common viral "carriers" such as Microsoft Word and Excel, few viruses can run on Linux, and those that can have a hard time affecting other programs (unless you run everything as root, which should always be avoided).

Worms pose a greater threat than viruses because they are independent programs, not files attached to other programs or macros. A worm is like an automated attacker: if you protect your system against attackers by regularly updating network services, as discussed in Chapter 10, "Managing Software Packages and File Systems," the worm will have trouble finding a hole on your system.

Security Organizations

To help you learn more about computer security, several organizations are available as clearinghouses of security-related information, training centers, and professional consultants. The **CERT Coordination Center (CERT/CC)** is a U.S. federal government-funded software engineering institute operated by Carnegie-Mellon University. It was formerly called the Computer Emergency Response Team and focused on handling computer security incidents; most security experts likely still think of it in those terms. The CERT/CC Web site, *www.cert.org,* maintains lists of security vulnerabilities, alerts, incident reports, and similar information.

The **System Administration, Networking, and Security (SANS) Institute** (or simply SANS) is a prestigious and well-regarded education and research organization. Its members include most of the leading computer security experts in the country. To take advantage of SANS information, start by visiting the Web site at *www.sans.org*. You can subscribe to mailing lists of security alerts for various platforms. You can also review information about the SANS Storm Center at *www.incidents.org*. This is a statistical summary of what attacks are taking place at more than 3000 firewalls in over 60 countries around the world. By analyzing these attacks, SANS security experts are able to provide guidance to other network administrators before new attacks become widespread.

SANS also coordinates with the FBI to provide a Top 20 list of the most widely used strategies for attacking computer systems. You can review this list to make certain that your systems are protected against known security threats.

The information on the SANS Web site is continually updated and includes a number of Linux-specific security resources. Beyond this, SANS maintains a highly regarded hands-on certification program for security professionals: the **Global Information Assurance Certification (GIAC)** program. Related to this effort, SANS focuses a great deal of energy on providing technical conferences in cities around the world. These are amazing conferences, where top security experts teach hands-on courses to network administrators who face security threats each day.

Other useful Web sites that contain computer security information include *www.securityfocus.com* and *www.securitymanagement.com*.

Using Network Services

In several previous chapters you have learned about many aspects of networking. In this section, you are introduced to a number of different network services that typically run on Linux. Most of these are installed by default and are controlled using a script in the /etc/rc.d/init.d directory, or using the *service* command (as discussed in Chapter 9). Although the level of detail provided in this section for each of these services is minimal, it should be enough to acquaint you with the service, start it up, and explore how it operates using the commands and documentation referenced. After reading this section, you should expect to both experiment and study before you feel ready to implement these services on a production server—each of these topics deserves a book of its own.

Using NetFilter for Firewalls

A **firewall** is a hardware device or software program that prevents unintended network access. A **packet filter** is a firewall that performs this function by examining the information stored in each packet and deciding how to process that packet based on rules established as part of the firewall. The Linux kernel includes the ability to filter network packets. The packet-filtering feature in older Linux kernels was called **IP chains**, and you can still see information about this feature in various kinds of Linux documentation.

The latest Linux kernels use a feature called **NetFilter**, which includes an enhancement of the IP chains system called **IP tables**. Both IP chains and IP tables let you define a list of rules (a chain or a table, respectively). Each network packet is compared against the rules that you define as the kernel decides what to do with it: discard it, forward it to another system, change information within the packet and pass it on, and so on. Although the NetFilter system is harder to configure than some commercial firewall products, it provides a very powerful firewall. Once you are familiar with configuring NetFilter, you can use a separate Linux system as a firewall and save thousands of dollars compared to buying a special-purpose hardware firewall.

Packets are processed by the kernel in different stages of their journey between computers. During each stage, the kernel processes the rules defined for that stage. The principal stages of packet processing are listed here. A set of rules can be assigned to each of them, and you can create additional named tables for special purposes that contain separate lists of rules:

- Input: Packets coming from outside the system on which the rule is executed

- Forward: Packets coming from outside the system on which the rule is executed and that need to be routed to another computer

- Output: Packets coming from within the system on which the rule is executed and that are destined for other systems

The basic operation of an IP table is shown in Figure 15-12. Each rule in the table specifies one or more parameters. If a packet matches those parameters, the packet is handled as the rule directs. If the packet doesn't match the parameters in the rule, the next rule is tried. If none of the rules match, a default policy defines what happens to the packet.

You create and manage rules in a table using the *iptables* command. The rules can be simple or complex. A simple rule might indicate that the default policy for the input table is DROP, meaning that if an incoming packet does not match one of the rules in the table, it should be rejected with no response sent back to the sender. This rule is shown here:

```
# iptables -P INPUT DROP
```

Rules in a table can take any of the following basic actions for a packet: ACCEPT, DROP, QUEUE, and RETURN. DROP means that the packet is completely ignored. QUEUE and RETURN take different actions depending on the default policy associated with the table containing the rule. Much more complex actions can be associated with special types of tables that permit NetFilter to perform complex routing tasks. Here is one basic example of a rule, defined by an *iptables* command:

```
iptables -A INPUT -p udp -s 0/0 --sport 67:68 -d 0/0 --dport 67:
68 -i eth0 -j  ACCEPT
```

The command above adds a rule to the input table that says to accept a packet coming from any source IP address and destined for any IP address if it is using the UDP protocol, arrives on the eth0 network interface, and uses either port 67 or 68 for both the source and destination addresses.

You can list the rules in all tables with the -*L* option (the -*n* option tells the command to go on if IP addresses can't be resolved through DNS):

```
# iptables -n -L
```

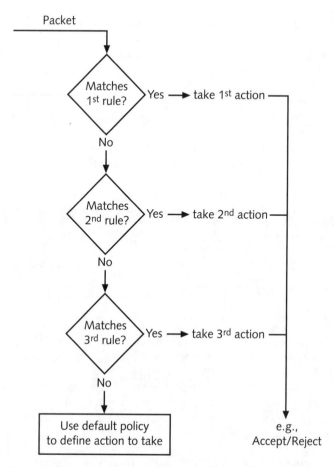

Packet

Matches
1st rule?
Yes ⟶ take 1st action

No

Matches
2nd rule?
Yes ⟶ take 2nd action

No

Matches
3rd rule?
Yes ⟶ take 3rd action

No

| Use default policy to define action to take |

e.g.,
Accept/Reject

15

Figure 15-12 Basic operation of rules stored in IP tables

Rules are executed in the order that you place them in the chain. For example, suppose you have the following two rules. The first accepts packets from a single network; the second denies packets for all networks.

```
# iptables -A INPUT -s 192.168.10.0/0 -j ACCEPT
# iptables -A INPUT -j DROP
```

As with certain other configuration files that you have seen, the order of the rules is important. If you reversed the above two rules, packets coming from the 192.168.10.0 network would be denied before they could be permitted access by the more specific rule.

In general, firewall rules should go from more specific at first to more general at the end, with "catchall" rules at the very end so that nothing gets through unexpectedly.

The NetFilter rules configured on your system are activated by the *iptables* service when the system is started, before networking is activated. The file /etc/sysconfig/iptables contains the rules configured on your system. During installation of Red Hat Linux or Fedora, you answer a question about the level of firewall protection that you want to implement. The level that you select—low, medium, or high—determines what *iptables* commands are executed each time you start your Linux system. Those commands normally form only the beginning of your firewall; a server connecting an organization to the Internet might use hundreds of *iptables* commands to set up its network access.

Table 15-1 lists the most commonly used options for the *iptables* command. All of the options are case sensitive. With the information in this table you should be able to review *iptables* commands that you find in your default installation and practice new configurations on your network. Refer to the *iptables* man page for a more complete listing.

Table 15-1   Commonly Used Options for the *iptables* Command

Option	Description
-A *table*	Append a rule to the end of the named table
-D *table index*	Delete rule number index from the named table
-F *table*	Flush (delete) all rules from the named table, or from all tables if no table is named
-L *table*	List all the rules from all tables, or from the named table if given
-P *table policy*	Set the default policy of the named table to the named policy
-s *address port*	Define a source IP address against which to compare a packet; you can include a port number after the address to indicate which TCP or UDP port should match the rule
-d *address port*	Define a destination IP address against which to compare a packet; a port number can be included as with the *-s* option
-i *interface*	Specify the network interface (such as eth0) that a packet must use to match the rule
-p *protocol*	Indicate the protocol field of the IP address that will match the rule; the protocol can be TCP, UDP, or ICMP (The protocol specification is not case sensitive)
-j *target*	Define an action for packets matching the packet specifications (such as the *-p* and *-s* options)

Network Address Translation

The IP tables feature provides special routing functionality called **network address translation (NAT)**. This is a routing technique that alters the addresses or other information in a packet. One popular type of NAT is **IP masquerading**, a type of network address translation in which packets from many computers on a LAN are altered to appear as if they came from a single computer. This technique is very useful for organizational or home networks that connect to the Internet, as shown in Figure 15-13.

Using IP masquerading, a single IP address can permit an entire LAN to connect to the Internet or to larger organizational networks. DSL and cable routers often use this technique to permit multiple computers to access the Internet. IP masquerading acts almost like a

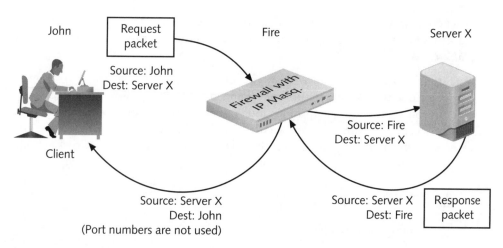

Figure 15-13 IP masquerading

firewall because a remote computer cannot connect to a client within a masqueraded LAN. If you configure the router carefully, IP masquerading effectively hides your entire network.

Setting up IP masquerading requires a rule that says in effect, "Any network traffic coming from this network should be masqueraded." Suppose you have a LAN (using device eth0) with the network address 192.168.100.0 that you connect to the Internet through a cable modem. Using the following command on the server would cause all network traffic from the internal network to be masqueraded; all clients on the LAN would then be able to access the Internet (though the ISP would see all traffic as coming from the gateway system). The nat table (per the –t option) refers to the network address translation table; the –A POSTROUTING option appends this rule to the list of rules used after other routing decisions have been made.

```
# iptables -t nat -A POSTROUTING -o eth0 -j MASQUERADE
```

Graphical Firewall Configuration Utilities

Although the syntax of the *iptables* command is straightforward once you are accustomed to it, a graphical utility can still be very helpful in setting up a Linux firewall.

You need to understand how IP tables and the networking protocols operate before a graphical utility will be of much help in configuring a secure firewall.

Red Hat Linux and Fedora, like many other Linux distributions, include basic firewall configuration tools to help new users give their systems some level of protection. When you install Red Hat Linux or Fedora, you answer basic questions about your network security. These questions are posed using the *system-config-securitylevel* program, which you can execute at any time from the command line. (A text-mode program to perform the same task is **system-config-securitylevel-tui**; you can also start this program using its old name, **lokkit**.)

Figure 15-14 shows a screen from the graphical *system-config-securitylevel* program. This program doesn't ask you about "rules," but instead sets up reasonable rules based on how secure you want your system to be and any specific protocols that you want to leave more open. (Remember that "more secure" means "harder to use" if you are in a trusted environment such as a testing lab, where you want to run many network services without reconfiguring the firewall for each one.)

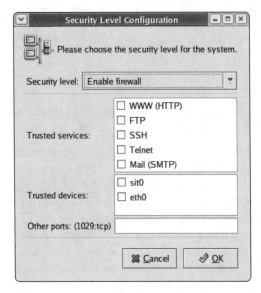

Figure 15-14   The *system-config-securitylevel* program

Because this program only sets a generalized "security level," a system administrator is well advised to download (or purchase, as warranted) a more complete graphical solution if the *iptables* command alone seems inefficient. Several examples are listed here:

- The GNOME program Firestarter includes a firewall creation wizard to help you set up a basic firewall. Then you can modify the basic *iptables* rules as needed within the graphical interface. You can also watch real-time monitors to see when a packet matches a specific rule. You can find this program through the download link on *firestarter.sourceforge.net*.

- Mason is a firewall tool that uses a different approach appropriate for less experienced Linux administrators. Instead of defining rules at the outset, you start Mason, then start all the other services that you want to support on your server. Mason prepares a list of rules that intelligently allows only those services and blocks all others. For more information, visit *http://mason.stearns.org*.

- KMyFirewall is a KDE-based program that lets you set up a "personal firewall" or protect a larger network using IP tables. It includes a setup wizard for less experienced users, plus a more advanced interface to help you create complex rules. You can save a copy of your firewall rules to a separate file and then use that file to easily configure other firewalls running KMyFirewall when the same rules should be applied. For information, visit *http://kmyfirewall.sourceforge.net*.

- One of the most full-featured firewall configuration utilities for Linux is GuardDog. GuardDog can use either a graphical interface or its own command-line utility. For details, see *www.simonzone.com/software/guarddog/*.

Setting up a DNS Name Server

In Chapter 12, "Configuring Networks," you learned how to configure the DNS resolver using configuration files such as /etc/resolv.conf, /etc/hosts, /etc/host.conf, and /etc/nsswitch.conf. In this section you learn how to create a DNS server on Linux on which other systems can rely to resolve host names and IP addresses.

You can think of the information in DNS as an Internet-wide inverted hierarchical tree, as Figure 15-15 illustrates. The very top of the tree is called root and is represented by a period: "." The root is typically only mentioned in regard to the **root name servers**—DNS servers that the organizations that run the Internet have designated as a starting point for DNS queries. More commonly, you see the last part of domain names referred to as top-level domains such as .org, .com, .edu, and .net, along with many others.

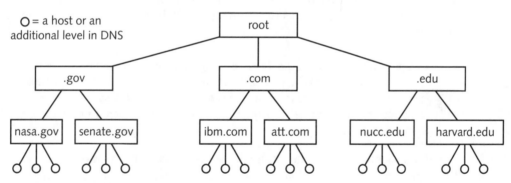

Figure 15-15   The structure of DNS

To resolve a host name or IP address, a client asks a DNS server for the needed information (for example, "What is the IP address of www.google.com?"). The DNS server can either find another DNS server that has that information already stored (cached), or it can locate the server where the managers of google.com officially defined what the IP address is for their server. Finding the official google.com DNS server takes longer, but the google.com address is cached in many DNS servers, so doing that is rarely needed.

15

If you operate your own domain, you can set up a DNS server that provides information on your domain to others on your network or the Internet. This would be the **master DNS server** or **primary DNS server** for your domain. Often your ISP provides this service for you if you register a domain name with them. You or your ISP would also have a backup copy of your DNS information on a **slave DNS server** or **secondary DNS server**.

Even if you don't have your own domain name to maintain, you can speed things up for users on your network by setting up a DNS server that simply caches information that it collects from other DNS servers. When DNS query results are stored on a machine within your network, the average time required for each DNS query can drop significantly.

Creating a Basic Name Server

The program that implements a DNS server is called *named*, the name daemon. This program is found in the BIND package on most Linux systems, including Red Hat Linux and Fedora. BIND (Berkeley Internet Name Domains) is the name of a collection of programs that implement the DNS protocol. If you selected the name server component when installing Red Hat Linux or Fedora, you also have the *system-config-bind* program, a graphical configuration utility.

A **caching name server** is one that doesn't have any preconfigured information on domains (except local host, as described below). That is, it is not a master or slave server for any domain. Instead, it simply queries other DNS servers and caches the results. By running a caching DNS server on your network, you ensure that all queries are cached close to your users. If you normally connect through a slow network connection, this can dramatically reduce the traffic over the connection compared with having all name servers on the remote side of the connection.

TIP One program that can act *only* as a caching name server (it can't be a master or slave server) is *dnscache*, part of the djbdns package. You can find this package at *http://cr.yp.to*. Because *dnscache* is much smaller and faster than *named*, networks that don't need to respond to outside DNS queries might choose *dnscache* instead of *named*.

The *named* daemon is controlled using the *service* command. The most recent version of the BIND programs (including *named*) is 9. But many servers still run the older version 4. You can recognize version 4 because BIND version 4 uses the /etc/named.boot configuration file. BIND version 8 or 9 uses the /etc/named.conf configuration file. If you find a server running BIND 4, try to upgrade it to BIND 9 to prevent security breaches.

The /etc/named.conf file determines how the *named* daemon operates, such as defining which domains it acts as a master DNS server for and which clients are allowed to query the DNS server for information. When a DNS server maintains information for at least part of a domain, that part is called a **zone**. Besides the /etc/named.conf file, a *named* daemon that is acting as a master or slave server must have **zone information files** configured that define host names and corresponding IP addresses. This permits the DNS server to respond when queries arrive. Each line in a zone information file is called a **resource record** and defines something about a host on a network that the DNS server knows about. For example, a resource record might define the IP address of a host name, or the e-mail server to use for mail being sent to a given host name, or an alternate name (like an alias) by which a host can be known.

A good way to experiment with a DNS server is to install the caching name server package on Fedora CD 3. This package contains only configuration files. It sets up your system as a caching name server so that clients can query your computer for DNS information. After installing this package, other computers on your network can configure your IP address in their /etc/resolv.conf files. You can review the zone information files stored in /var/named to see examples of resource records. (For example, see the named.ca and localhost.zone files.) Because these records have very precise formatting requirements, it is helpful to use the *system-config-bind* utility to configure a DNS server. This lessens the risk of small typographic errors causing problems.

After installing the caching-name server package, if you start the *redhat-config-bind* program, you see an indication that basic information is stored for localhost. See Figure 15-16, in which a configuration dialog box for the localhost domain has been opened.

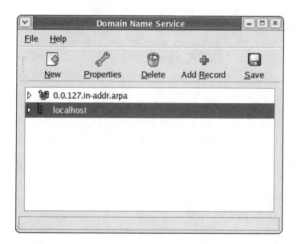

Figure 15-16   The *system-config-bind* program

The **rndc** utility is part of the bind package and is used to control the *named* daemon from a command line. *rndc* can operate over a network connection, but is used only locally by default. You use the *rndc* command to reload configuration files, write out a status file, or perform other related tasks. The command you are most likely to use is this one, to reload the /etc/named.conf configuration file and all zone information files:

```
# rndc reload
```

Using Other Command-line Utilities

Once you have a DNS server up and running, you normally want to test it to see that it responds as expected to queries. You can use the *dig* utility to query any DNS server (including one running on the same machine) to gather data from its zone information files.

TIP

A program called **nslookup** is similar to the *dig* command, but *dig* is generally preferred.

A simple *dig* query looks like this:

```
$ dig www.npr.org
```

A more complex query looks like this:

```
$ dig @ns.xmission.com www.xmission.com any
```

This query goes directly to the DNS server *ns.xmission.com*, rather than the DNS server configured in /etc/resolv.conf, and looks for information about *www.xmission.com*. It returns all types of resource records for that address.

A related utility is **whois**. This utility tells you information about the people or organization that registered a domain name. Project 15-3 explores how to use this utility.

File Sharing with NFS

The **Network File System (NFS)** lets you work with hard disks located all over the local network (or even a remote network) as if they were part of the local directory structure. So, for example, when you execute a command such as *ls /data/aircraft*, you might actually be viewing the contents of the /parts/data/reports/aircraft directory on a host located in the next room or the next county.

As you learned in Chapter 10, "Managing Software Packages and File Systems," the *mount* command can be used to access a file system located on an NFS server using a command such as this one, which makes the contents of a file system located on the server appear as directory /data/aircraft on Linux:

```
# mount -t nfs parts:/parts/data/reports/aircraft  /data/aircraft
```

In this section you learn how to set up Linux as an NFS server so that other computers (clients) can remotely access file systems on your Linux server.

One popular use of NFS is to install Linux on numerous systems over a network connection. This is easier and faster than hovering over each workstation and swapping CD-ROMs. If an NFS server has been set up with the Linux operating system files available for remote access (as described later in this section), you can install Linux via NFS by starting the installation program, selecting the NFS installation method, then entering the appropriate NFS server name and file system path to reach the Linux installation files.

The NFS protocol is implemented by several daemons, each handling a different set of tasks. These daemons are not started up by default in Linux. You should start them yourself and set them to start automatically only after you have configured the NFS system as described in this section. The *rpc.mountd* daemon lets clients establish new connections to mount a file system on your server using NFS. Once mounted, the *nfsd* daemon handles file transfers based on the settings that the *rpc.mountd* daemon has validated. Some systems (including Red Hat Linux) add one or two peripheral programs to these two programs to help manage NFS-mounted file systems. The first is *rpc.rquotad*, which permits tracking user disk space quotas for remotely mounted file systems, just as you can on local Linux file systems. The second is *rpc.statd*, which helps manage NFS-mounted file systems when the remote NFS server crashes (or otherwise breaks its connection) and then comes up again.

All of these programs are normally started by a script in the /etc/rc.d/init.d directory. In some versions of Linux, they are listed individually by name; in others they are grouped for management by a few scripts. For example, in Red Hat Linux and Fedora, you can use this command to start the three standard daemons *rpc.mountd*, *nfsd*, and *rpc.rquotad*. (You start the *rpc.statd* daemon using the *nfslock* service in the same directory.)

```
# service nfs start
```

Exporting File Systems Using NFS

To make parts of your file system accessible over the network to other systems, you must have the NFS daemons running (as described previously), and you must allow the NFS traffic to pass between the two hosts (without a firewall blocking it). Beyond these requirements, you must set up the **/etc/exports** file to define which of your local directories you want to be accessible to remote users (that is, which directories are exported) and how each can be used.

Once you have /etc/exports carefully set up, run the **exportfs** command to activate the contents of /etc/exports, then start the NFS daemons using the scripts in /etc/rc.d/init.d.

The syntax of a line within /etc/exports is shown here. You can include multiple hostname(option) settings for the same directory, separating each by a space.

```
/directory-path hostname(option,option,...)
```

The host name can be defined in several ways. You can use a complete host name to define a specific host; you can use a domain name to define all hosts within a domain; or you can use an IP address, either for a single host or for a network or part of a network. The *exports* man page lists all of the possible permutations.

An /etc/exports file can be as simple as this:

```
/projects
```

This /etc/exports file allows anyone who can reach your host via NFS to mount the /projects directory, as no host name or access options are specified. Well, that's almost true. When you use an NFS client to access a remote file system, the NFS server must decide what user to treat you as, because you never "log in" or provide a password when you use the NFS client (as you saw in Chapter 10's discussion of the *mount* command). The default action is that the *mount* command sends your user ID and group ID on the client, then the NFS server uses the same user ID and group ID on the server system. Your file permissions match those of the corresponding user and group. This is designed for a situation where a single user has accounts on multiple systems, with the same user ID and group ID on each one. (This is a lot like the *rlogin*, *rsh*, and *rcp* commands you learned about in Chapter 7, "Using Network Clients.")

This arrangement is not always easy to achieve, nor is it always appropriate. For this reason, you normally include options in /etc/exports to **map** incoming client user and group IDs to user and group IDs on the NFS server.

NFS uses a security concept called **squashing** to prevent a user from gaining access to a user account on the NFS server simply because the user has the same ID on the NFS client. The most important use of this is squashing the root account: you shouldn't have root access on the NFS server just because you have root access on an NFS client! Squashing of the root account is done automatically unless you use the no_root_squash option. One method of squashing incoming client user IDs is to define an anonymous user account and tell NFS to map all incoming users to that account. Thus, all NFS clients have access only to areas that you have specifically granted to this "anonymous" user. Reviewing a few examples should make the uses of this system apparent:

```
/                 scout(rw,no_root_squash)
```

This line shows a very trusted host, scout, for which squashing is not used (remember, root_squash is the default action). The root user can thus have root access to the / directory on the NFS server. This type of entry would be used for a trusted network in which a single system administrator wanted to have complete access to multiple hosts' file systems via NFS.

The next example assumes that everyone on the myplace.net domain has a user account with a matching user ID on the NFS server. They all are permitted to access the /projects directory, reading and writing according to the file permissions within /projects on the NFS server.

```
/projects         *.myplace.net(rw)
```

Accessing Remote NFS File Systems

When you need to access a remote NFS file system, as shown previously, you can either include all needed options on the command line, or create an entry for the NFS server in the /etc/fstab file. About 20 special options are available when you mount a file system on an NFS server. Some of the most useful are listed here:

- *rsize=8192,wsize=8192*—Used together, these options alter the default buffer size for NFS transfers. Using these options avoids the speed problems sometimes associated with NFS on Linux.

- *ro* and *rw*—You can mount a file system as read-only (*ro*) or read-write (*rw*).

- *hard* or *soft*—You can **hard mount** an NFS file system, which means your programs wait—without limit—for the NFS server to respond. If the remote server goes down and then comes up again a while later, your program continues without a hitch. Alternatively, you can **soft mount** an NFS file system, which means that NFS waits for a while and then gives up. The documentation recommends not using the *soft* option unless the NFS server you are working with is quite unreliable.

- *noauto*—This option causes the NFS file system not to be mounted automatically at system start-up.

This example line from /etc/fstab shows how NFS options appear in that file:

```
rome:/home/public   /mnt/rome
nfs    rsize=8192,wsize=8192,rw,noauto 0 0
```

Setting up a Samba Server

The **Samba** suite is a collection of programs that implement file and print sharing using the SMB and CIFS protocols, which are the standards used by Microsoft Windows operating systems. Samba includes two server daemons: **nmbd**, which implements the NetBIOS name service, and **smbd**, which handles file and print services. Both of these daemons must be running. On Red Hat Linux and Fedora, you can manage these daemons together as the smb service; on some Linux distributions, the service is called Samba. After you have set up the configuration file and created appropriate user accounts as outlined in this section, you can start the Samba service on Red Hat Linux or Fedora using this command:

```
# service smb start
```

Once you have configured Samba, you can use the *chkconfig* command to make it start automatically whenever you start Linux.

Samba configuration files are typically stored in /etc/samba, though the location may vary in different Linux distributions. The main configuration file is smb.conf. A sample or default smb.conf file is provided. It contains many comments, but not enough to understand all the

15

configuration options. Still, you should review that file and add your own settings before running a Samba server. A very basic smb.conf file is shown here:

```
[global]
workgroup = MYPLACE
netbios name = sundance
server string = Samba on Linux posing as Windows 2000
hosts allow = 192.168.100.
printcap name = /etc/printcap
load printers = yes
printing = lprng
log file = /var/log/samba.log
max log size = 0
security = user
encrypt passwords = yes
smb passwd file = /etc/samba/smbpasswd
socket options = TCP_NODELAY SO_RCVBUF=8192 SO_SNDBUF=8192
dns proxy = no

[homes]
comment = User home directories
browseable = no
writable = yes

[printers]
comment = Linux printers
path = /var/spool/samba
browseable = no
guest ok = no
printable = yes
```

The smb.conf file is divided into sections. The [global] section defines the overall operation of the server. Other sections define how the server handles shared resources: either the printers or specific file system **shares** (directories that you want to share). The [homes] and [printers] sections are standard names that refer to the home directories of each user who logs in and the Linux printers, respectively. You can create other sections to define other shares.

Creating Samba Users

Although the sample configuration file settings above are sufficient to start a basic Samba server, the recommended user-based security model requires that each user must log in with a valid user name and password before using a share on the Samba server. It's common to allow everyone with a Linux user account to also log in via Samba. Several utilities included with the Samba suite make this easy to implement. Assuming that you have created all your Linux user accounts, the following command creates a Samba password file for all your Linux users:

```
# cat /etc/passwd | mksmbpasswd.sh > /etc/samba/smbpasswd
```

No passwords are transferred in this process; you must enter a password for each user (twice) using the *smbpasswd* command. For example, this command lets you set the Samba password for user nwells in the smbpasswd file:

```
# smbpasswd nwells
```

User nwells can then use the password entered to access a share on the Samba server from a Windows system. (The Samba server simply appears as part of the Windows network—it can take some time after activating the Samba server before the Windows systems displays it.)

If you add Linux users to your system after setting up Samba, you can add them to your smbpasswd file using the ***smbpasswd*** command with the *-a* option. This command has no effect on the Linux users on your system. For example, you could add a new Samba user and define a password for that user (when prompted) using this command:

```
# smbpasswd -a abutler
```

A more comprehensive user management utility for Samba is the ***pdbedit*** utility. To add a Samba user with this utility, you can use this format:

```
# pdbedit  -a -u abutler
```

Using SWAT to Configure SMB

The example smb.conf configuration file described previously contains only a fraction of the hundreds of options supported by Samba. Exploring them all can be a challenge, especially if you are new to Windows networking. A graphical tool that can help you both configure Samba and learn about its options is **SWAT**, a browser-based graphical interface that sets up the smb.conf file, restarts the Samba servers, and provides some status information on how the server is being utilized.

SWAT runs as a network service managed by the superserver, which is discussed at the end of this section. After enabling SWAT in your superserver configuration (either in /etc/ inetd.conf or /etc/xinetd.d/swat), you can use your browser from any system to reach SWAT and manage your Samba server. However, SWAT transfers are not encrypted, so unless you are using SWAT to manage Samba on the same machine, you risk exposing your root password to someone snooping around on your network. (You can configure *ssh* to protect you from this danger and permit safe remote management.)

To access SWAT once you have the network capabilities configured, start your Web browser and enter the URL *http://localhost:901/* (assuming you are configuring SWAT on your own machine.) You are prompted for a user name and password. You must enter the user name root and the root password for your host.

Creating a Proxy Server with Squid

A **proxy server** is similar in function to the network address translation and IP masquerading features discussed previously in this section. A proxy lets one server make a request for another server. This is typically done either to improve the efficiency or the security of the network as a whole. As two examples, a proxy server that requests Web pages for hundreds of clients in a large company can cache many of the pages that it retrieves so that they are returned more quickly if another client requests the same page (such as *www.cnn.com*). A proxy that retrieves Web pages can also be configured to block client access to any Web server (such as *www.espn.com*).

The Apache Web server discussed in the next section can act as a proxy Web server, retrieving Web pages for clients. But the most widely used Linux proxy server is **Squid**. This proxy server is installed on Fedora if you selected the recommended software categories in Chapter 8. It is managed using the *service* command as the Squid service, but it requires significant configuration before use. Typically, you first configure Squid and then you configure each client on your network to use a proxy server, referring to the server name where Squid was installed and the port number that you had configured it to use.

An alternative to this standard configuration is to use the transparent proxy feature of IP tables. **Transparent proxy** lets you redirect a network packet based on the port to which the packet is addressed. This lets you leave all client Web browsers unchanged, but effectively "catch" their Web requests as they pass through the server on the way to the Internet, redirecting them to the Squid proxy server for processing. This extra step is transparent to the client.

To configure Squid, you edit the file /etc/squid/squid.conf (on Red Hat Linux and Fedora systems). This file initially contains over 3200 lines of comments; none of the roughly 190 configuration options is active by default. The Squid Web site at *www.squid-cache.org*, contains a lot of useful reference information, including quick-start and comprehensive configuration guides. To use Squid in standard Web proxy mode (for which you must configure client Web browsers with the appropriate server name and port number), you can search for and configure (or uncomment) the following four options in the squid.conf file:

- Define a directory where Web pages will be stored. You must create the directory and should specify the maximum size to which the cache can grow (100 MB is the default). A sample line for a 500 MB cache is: `cache_dir ufs /squid-cache 500`

- Define the port that Squid will use. This is the port that clients should be configured to use for proxy access. A sample line is: `http_port 3128`

- Define who can use your Squid server. By default, localhost can access Squid. You can use this line for testing to let all other computers on your local network use Squid: `http_access allow all`

- Define the user and group that Squid operates as, if Squid is started by root (which is typical). A Squid user and a Squid group are created by default in Red Hat Linux and Fedora. You should create these accounts if they do not exist on your system, then use these configuration lines:
  `cache_effective_user squid`

  `cache_effective_group squid`

Creating a Linux Web Server with Apache

The most widely used Web server in the world is **Apache**. Apache is included with Red Hat Linux and is installed as part of Fedora if you selected the software categories listed in Table 8-4. Some of the features of Apache that make it popular include:

- A regular development cycle that keeps up with Web technology and provides a very reliable product

- Virtual hosting, which allows a single Web server to provide documents for multiple Web sites (multiple domain names)

- A modular design that lets Web administrators add and remove functionality to meet their site's needs

- Many security options and performance tuning settings

- A broad support base, despite being free software (for example, see *www.apacheweek.com*)

The Apache server runs as a daemon named *httpd*. Although you can control it using the *service* utility, the preferred method is to use the **apachectl** program. For example, after you have configured Apache as described in this section, you can check that the syntax of your configuration file is valid by entering this command:

```
# apachectl -t
```

Start the server using this command:

```
# apachectl -k start
```

15

Apache configuration files are stored in /etc/httpd/conf. The main configuration file, /etc/httpd/conf/httpd.conf, contains hundreds of configuration options, along with comments describing most of them. Each configuration option in this file is called a directive. Whenever you change the configuration file, you should restart Apache using this command:

```
# apachectl -k restart
```

Because the configuration file contains examples of all the directive types you are likely ever to need for Apache, exploring that file and reading the comments it contains can give you a solid understanding of what Apache is capable of and how to take advantage of those capabilities. The online documentation provided at *www.apache.org* is also worth researching when you have questions about specific directives that you are considering using. But more immediately, you can start your Web browser, choose Open File on the File menu, and browse to the directory /var/www/manual/. Within that directory, the files ending with the .en file extension are English language documentation files that you can view directly in your browser.

The DocumentRoot directive in httpd.conf defines where the server looks for documents that are returned to clients. If a client requests a document from the root of the server (without giving a path name in the URL), that document actually comes from the directory specified by the DocumentRoot. The documents that the server sends to clients are stored in /var/www/html by default on Red Hat Linux and Fedora; other Linux systems may store them in /home/http or /usr/httpd. If you configure **virtual hosting** on your Web server, you can define multiple DocumentRoot directives, each of which will appear as a separate Web server on the network, though they are being processed by the same copy of Apache, and data is being retrieved from the same hard disk (or wherever you specify).

To experiment with the server, you can change the DocumentRoot directive from its default (on Red Hat Linux and Fedora) of /var/www/html to be /var/www/manual. Restart Apache, then start your Web browser and enter the URL *http://localhost/*. The Apache manual is delivered to your browser by the Apache server running on the same computer, even though the files you view are stored locally.

The directives in the first part of httpd.conf affect the global operation of Apache. Directives in the latter part of httpd.conf control features that are specific to one directory of the document collection, or to one virtual host. Many of the directives are fine with their default values, but if you are concerned about the security of your Web server, or are trying to create a Web server to receive a large number of client requests, then you should learn more about the directives and make adjustments based on the requirements of your server.

CAUTION

Do not casually start a Web server and make it available on the Internet unless the computer contains no private data. Apache is not configured initially to be highly secure, and setting up adequate security features is a complex process.

Many features of Apache are implemented as loadable modules; you define what your copy of Apache can do by which modules you select for inclusion. Each module is controlled by various directives that you include in the httpd.conf configuration file. Much like the Linux kernel, **Apache modules** can be included when you compile Apache from source code or can be loaded on the fly as shared objects. This is equivalent to using *modprobe* to load a kernel module, but you must list the modules for Apache in the httpd.conf file and include the module itself in a subdirectory. You can learn more about all available Apache modules by visiting *modules.apache.org*.

Much of the httpd.conf file is organized into containers. A **container** is a special type of directive that activates other directives only if a condition is met or only within a particular context. One container example that appears several times in httpd.conf is the <directory> container. Each directory container starts with a <directory> line and ends with a </directory> line, similar to some HTML tags. The container defines how Apache handles requests for files within the named directory. Security features or access restrictions are often configured within containers. The standard <directory> container for the default document root of Apache is shown here:

```
<Directory "/var/www/html">
      Options Indexes FollowSymLinks
         AllowOverride None
         Order allow,deny
```

```
        Allow from all
</Directory>
```

The Options line defines what types of files can be accessed in this directory.

- Indexes means that a Web page listing the contents of the directory is generated by Apache if no index.html file is available. (The DirectoryIndex directive defines the default file name index.html, which you can add to or change.)

- FollowSymLinks lets Apache follow a symbolic link in this directory to a file in another directory.

- "Includes" allow Apache to process special statements within the text of files in this directory. These are called **server-side includes** (or **server-parsed documents**) and allow Apache to alter documents dynamically (as they are requested). This feature can add significantly to the load of a Web server. (It also presents security issues, as do many of the features listed here. See Chapter 12 for more information.)

- ExecCGI allows Apache to run a script in this directory and return the output of the script to the requesting browser.

- You could also use the None or All keywords after Options to use all the above (for very open access) or none of the above (for very restrictive access).

The AllowOverride line defines which parts of the directory access information defined in this container can be changed if a configuration file called .htaccess (by default—you can change this) is present in the named directory. Using .htaccess lets you allow multiple users to control their own subdirectories on a Web site, but AllowOverride lets you also limit their freedom to choose settings that might endanger the rest of the site. AllowOverride can use any of these keywords:

- *FileInfo*: Defines how different data types are handled

- *Options*: As described for the Options directive above

- *AuthConfig*: Controls the authentication options by which a user must provide a user name and password before accessing a file

- *Limit*: A separate container that can be included within a <directory> container to limit access to a file or to a set of host names or IP addresses

- *None* or *All*: Provides a blanket answer, giving .htaccess no ability to change the configuration or letting it set everything differently

The Order, Allow, and Deny directives (Deny is not shown above) define which hosts can access files in this directory. Order defines which is processed first—Allow directives or Deny directives. This is similar to what you have learned about the /etc/hosts.allow and /etc/hosts.deny files. For example, the following lines permit access only by hosts on the 192.168.0.0 network:

```
Order deny,allow
 Allow from 192.168.
 Deny from all
```

The following lines allow access to everyone except clients from the trouble.net domain:

```
Order allow,deny
 Allow from all
 Deny from trouble.net
```

Think carefully about what you want to achieve when you set up your access statements. Besides httpd.conf, the only access control mechanism for your Web server will be any firewalls that block packets at the network level.

In httpd.conf you see several other examples of <directory> containers, <limit> containers, and other containers to help you understand how these are used. The information in a <directory> container applies to all subdirectories of the named directory unless another <directory> container defines different settings for the subdirectory.

The version of Apache included with Red Hat Linux and Fedora includes dozens of directives for **Secure Socket Layer (SSL)** operation, though these are not activated by default. SSL allows a Web server to communicate securely with a browser for e-commerce or similar applications. For more information on the SSL features of Apache, visit *www. apache.org*.

Configuring a Basic E-mail Server

E-mail is one of the most important services provided by Internet servers. To provide e-mail service, a **Mail Transfer Agent (MTA)** moves mail between e-mail servers; the MTA is commonly referred to as the e-mail server program. A **Mail Delivery Agent (MDA)** examines messages and delivers them to a user's mailbox file (such as /var/spool/mail/ nwells). A **Mail User Agent (MUA)** such as Netscape, Evolution, Kmail, elm, or pine lets a user view the messages stored in the mailbox and create new messages that are handed to the MTA for delivery to the recipient.

E-mail servers rely on DNS servers to determine which MTA should receive e-mail for a given recipient. Once the correct e-mail server is located, your e-mail server can initiate a connection using the SMTP protocol and begin sending all messages to the destination e-mail addresses that are handled by that e-mail server.

 The SMTP protocol has been extended since its original introduction, so you may see occasional references to the Extended Simple Mail Transport Protocol, ESMTP. Most administrators just refer to SMTP.

NOTE

A number of e-mail servers are available for Linux. The most popular are **sendmail** (the most widely known e-mail server in the world (see *www.sendmail.com* or *www.sendmail.org*); Qmail, popular because of its enhanced security compared to sendmail; Postfix; and Smail, a smaller e-mail server based on sendmail.

The sendmail program is installed on Red Hat Linux and Fedora as a single rpm package called sendmail. You should also install the sendmail-cf and sendmail-doc packages from

Fedora CD 3. These are not installed automatically, but contain needed configuration files and documentation for the program.

Sendmail is managed using a standard script in /etc/rc.d/init.d. You can use the *start*, *stop*, *restart*, and *status* commands to control the daemon. The start-up parameters of sendmail are controlled by information stored in the /etc/sysconfig/sendmail file. For example, the parameter QUEUE=1h tells sendmail to attempt to send out stored messages each hour.

Starting sendmail takes a few moments. If the start-up script hesitates rather than starting up sendmail, check that your host name is correctly defined in your /etc/hosts file. By default, sendmail uses this to determine the host on which it is operating, information that it must have.

The operation of sendmail is configured using the file /etc/sendmail.cf. You should review this file briefly in a text editor, being careful not to change its contents. The sendmail.cf file is widely considered to be the single most difficult Linux configuration file to master. You can study the comments in this file and the documentation for sendmail to learn how the file is organized and operates; some administration tasks may require you to edit this file directly. The file README.cf acts as an online manual for the sendmail.cf file. It contains over 3000 lines of text. In Red Hat Linux or Fedora, this file is located at /usr/share/doc/sendmail after you have installed the sendmail-doc package.

Most e-mail administrators prefer to rely on the *m4* program to configure sendmail. The **m4** program uses a text file containing configuration parameters and generates a complete sendmail.cf file based on those parameters. The *m4* parameters are stored in sendmail.mc. To create a new sendmail.cf file, you edit the sendmail.mc file and then execute this command:

```
# m4 /etc/mail/sendmail.mc > /etc/sendmail.cf
```

15

The default configuration provided with Red Hat Linux and Fedora provides a workable sendmail environment, but you must make a few changes to use it as an Internet e-mail server.

TIP

Setting up a sendmail configuration file is difficult, but managing any e-mail server is an ongoing challenge because of such issues as trying to get e-mail from various operating systems to interoperate, dealing with spam, and numerous potential security threats.

You can review the README file to learn about key options in the sendmail.mc file. After making a backup copy of sendmail.mc, you can experiment by making changes to that file and creating a new sendmail.cf file using the *m4* command.

Using Forwarding and Aliases

Several techniques are available in sendmail to route mail among different e-mail accounts without sending a message to a different e-mail server. One of the more popular is the /etc/aliases file. An **e-mail alias** is another name that can deliver e-mail messages to a user. (Don't confuse this with a shell alias that replaces text you type with different text.) The aliases file contains a list of alternate names or e-mail addresses to which e-mail messages might be addressed. Each e-mail alias in this file is followed by text that defines what sendmail should do with a message so addressed. For example, suppose that your e-mail address is *kcarver@myplace.net*. Because different companies use specific formats for e-mail addresses, you would also like to receive e-mail using the following e-mail addresses: *kim.carver@myplace.net*, *kim_carver@myplace.net*, and *kimc@myplace.net*. Using e-mail aliases lets you do this if you include the following lines in /etc/aliases:

```
kim.carver: kcarver
kim_carver: kcarver
kimc: kcarver
```

Aliases are also commonly used for assigning topical e-mail to a specific individual. For example, you can define a webmaster alias that sends e-mail to the accounts of Kim Carver and Thomas Jennings, who work at a company that helps manage your Web server:

```
webmaster: kcarver, tjennings@webstuff.com
```

Each time you make a change in /etc/aliases, you must run the ***newaliases*** command to create a database of aliases that sendmail can use. This is done automatically each time sendmail is started, but you can rebuild the database with newaliases at any time without restarting sendmail.

Individual users can't alter the /etc/aliases file, but they can create a .forward file in their home directories. If sendmail finds a **.forward** file in a user's home directory, e-mail for that user is processed according to the text in .forward instead of simply being sent to the user's standard inbox in /var/spool/mail. Common uses of .forward include forwarding e-mail to another system when you prefer to receive your e-mail at another host (this method requires you to have a user account on the e-mail server) and piping your messages through a mail filter to remove spam or sort messages. For example, if you were on assignment with a subsidiary company for a month, you could include the following line in your .forward file:

```
kcarver@myplace_germany.net
```

All e-mail that would have been delivered to your mailbox is instead forwarded to the e-mail address given.

Watching sendmail Work

The sendmail daemon creates copious logs of what it does. Each message received and each message sent out are logged along with daemon-specific messages about the server configuration, starting and stopping, and so on. These messages are written to the standard system logger, *syslogd*, based on the configuration in /etc/syslog.conf. The default setting in Red Hat Linux and Fedora is to store messages from any mail server in /var/log/maillog.

In addition to learning about sendmail activity by reviewing the log files, you can use several other programs that will keep you informed about the state of your e-mail server, such as:

- ***hoststat***: Displays the status of hosts that have recently sent e-mail to your sendmail daemon. By default, information for a host is maintained for 30 minutes.

- ***mailq***: Displays a list of messages waiting to be sent out. Messages wait in the queue while you are not connected to the Internet, while sendmail waits for a domain name to be resolved, or a message has not been accepted by a remote mail server (by default, sendmail will try again later).

- ***mailstats***: Displays a summary of the amount of e-mail traffic that sendmail has handled. Fields in the output of *mailstats* include messages received, bytes received, messages sent, bytes sent, messages rejected, and messages discarded.

Using Superservers for Network Services

On a Linux system providing many network services, it can be wasteful to have 30 or more different services running at the same time. Many services are only needed occasionally. Yet you still want client requests for each service to be handled without you intervening to start the needed service. The solution is the **superserver** (also called a **metaserver**), which listens on multiple network ports and starts the appropriate service when a client connection arrives for that port. The most widely used superserver program is called *inetd*, for Internet daemon. Another superserver that is gaining in popularity is *xinetd*, for extended Internet daemon. *xinetd* is used by default on Red Hat Linux and Fedora.

NOTE   Some network services do not rely on the superserver mechanism; they are designed to run in **standalone mode**, without being started by *inetd* or *xinetd* as new client requests arrive.

Examples of network services that often rely on a superserver are FTP, Telnet, SSH, and standard e-mail servers. The mapping of services to default port numbers is done via the **/etc/services** file.

Many different programs refer to /etc/services to determine which port to use for a particular network service. The superserver daemons use the port numbers in /etc/services to determine which ports to watch for client connections. When a client tries to connect to a given port number, the superserver starts the appropriate network service to handle the client's request. After that request has been handled, the network service exits, so its resources are freed for other programs. The only program that has to be running all the time is the superserver itself.

Both *inetd* and *xinetd* are configured using text files within /etc. The configuration files indicates to which ports the superserver should listen and which program the superserver should start if a client request arrives on one of those ports. *xinetd* has a more complex configuration model and better security, though *inetd* is perfectly adequate when used in conjunction with certain security measures you'll learn about in the next section.

Using xinetd

The *xinetd* program is a revised version of *inetd* that focuses on creating a more secure environment, and happens to be more sound in its configuration architecture as well. *xinetd* as shipped with Red Hat Linux and Fedora (which do not include *inetd*) includes a configuration file /etc/xinetd.conf that refers to the contents of the /etc/xinetd.d directory. Within that directory, each service is configured by a separate file. A sample file, /etc/xinetd. d/wu-ftpd, is shown here:

```
# default: on
# description: The wu-ftpd FTP server serves FTP connections.
 It uses \
#normal, unencrypted usernames and passwords for authentication.
service ftp
{
socket_type= stream
wait= no
user= root
server= /usr/sbin/in.ftpd
server_args= -l -a
log_on_success+= DURATION USERID
log_on_failure+= USERID
nice= 10
disable= yes
}
```

The format of each file in /etc/xinetd.d names a service, as in the *service* line above. Brackets then enclose options that apply to that service. Some of these options match those described in the next section for the inetd.conf file, such as *socket_type*, *user*, and *server*. Several other options extend the functionality of *xinetd* beyond what the older *inetd* program offers. For example, various logging options are provided to determine what information *xinetd* writes to the system log when a connection is attempted, and several security options are available to control access to services. For example, the parameters *only_from, no_access, access_time*, and *deny_time* determine which hosts can access a service and when they can access it.

The extensive man page for xinetd.conf describes its available options. One particular option to note is the *disable* option. Several services in Red Hat Linux are fully configured but are disabled, so no connections are accepted. You can enable them by changing the line in the appropriate configuration file to *disable=no*. By default, the configuration files located in /etc/xinetd.d/ in Red Hat Linux include the line *disable=yes* so that the service is not active (available to clients) until you manually alter this default setting.

You should also restart *xinetd* after making any changes to its configuration files:

```
# service xinetd restart
```

Using inetd

The *inetd* program is configured using /etc/inetd.conf. A few sample lines from this file are shown here:

```
ftp      stream  tcp     nowait  root    /usr/sbin/tcpd in.ftpd -l -a
telnet   stream  tcp     nowait  root    /usr/sbin/tcpd in.telnetd
```

```
pop3     stream   tcp      nowait   root     /usr/sbin/tcpd ipop3d
imap     stream   tcp      nowait   root     /usr/sbin/tcpd imapd
telnet   stream   tcp      nowait   root     /usr/sbin/tcpd in.telnetd
```

You only need to notice two of the fields on these lines from inetd.conf, the first and the last. The first field, on the far left, is the service name. This name must correspond to a service name in /etc/services. The service name tells *inetd* which port to listen to. The far-right item on each line defines the server program that *inetd* starts when a client request arrives on the corresponding port.

TCP Wrappers

If you look back at the sample lines from inetd.conf, you will notice that the last part of each line, right before the name of the server to be started, contains the text "/usr/sbin/tcpd." This is a security mechanism. For nearly every service managed by *inetd*, the program that *inetd* actually starts is *tcpd*. **tcpd** is a security program known as **TCP Wrappers** that examines the incoming network connection and compares it to a configuration file to determine whether the connection is allowed. If so, the "real" program is started (such as *in.ftpd* or *in.telnetd*). If access is not allowed, the packet requesting a connection is simply dropped.

TCP Wrappers—*tcpd*—is an application-level access control program. It is not a firewall in the traditional sense, because it operates only for a specific application. In theory, TCP Wrappers is not as secure as a firewall because the packet in question is already being examined by the software running on your system. That said, TCP Wrappers provides a good way to add security to a system that is already protected with a firewall. You should use both whenever you have any concerns about who accesses your Linux system.

TCP Wrappers is configured by two files: **/etc/hosts.allow** and **/etc/hosts.deny**. The interaction of these two files in controlling access to network services is shown in Figure 15-17. Getting started with these files is easy, but be aware that you should test the configuration carefully before relying on it. This flexibility in configuration means that you may not be configuring exactly what you *think* you are configuring! The format is simple. You list a service, followed by the host name or IP address that should be allowed or denied access to that service. A few keywords are supported as well, such as ALL and EXCEPT. For example, suppose the hosts.deny file contains this line:

```
in.telnetd ALL
```

And the hosts.allow file contains this line:

```
in.telnetd 192.168.
```

This indicates that only users whose IP addresses begin with 192.168 are allowed access to the Telnet server. Similarly, suppose the hosts.allow file contains this line:

```
in.telnetd *.myplace.net EXCEPT ns.myplace.net
```

This indicates that users from the myplace.net domain name, except the name server (ns.myplace.net), are allowed to use Telnet. Of course, these examples only touch upon the

15

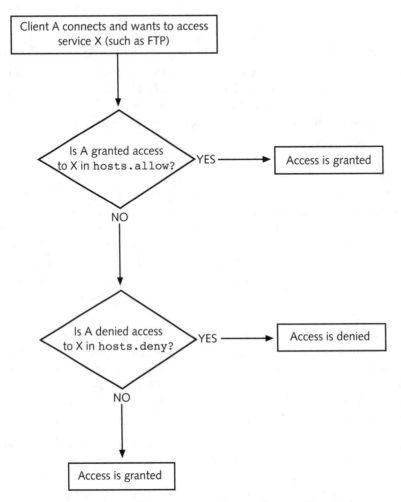

Figure 15-17   Controlling access via hosts.allow and hosts.deny

complexity of the assignments you can create. The ALL and EXCEPT keywords (plus several others) can be used in the service name field as well to protect a number of fields at the same time. For example, the hosts.deny file can contain this line to block access to all services for all users:

ALL ALL

Whenever you make a change in the inetd.conf file, you must restart the *inetd* program using a system script with a command like this:

/etc/rc.d/init.d/inetd restart

Note that the default action of *tcpd* is to allow access. The hosts.allow file is checked first, and if an entry matching a pending connection request is found, the connection is accepted. If no entry is found, hosts.deny is checked. If an entry is found there, the connection is denied;

otherwise, it is accepted. The safest configuration you can make for TCP Wrappers is therefore to block all services to all users, then in hosts.allow you specifically allow any service to which you want users to have access, with corresponding IP addresses, hosts, or even an ALL designation. To learn about these options, carefully review the hosts_access man page.

TIP

Besides the *man* command, you can view both info and man pages using the ***pinfo*** command, which presents info or man pages in a color-coded format with hypertext links to other referenced documents. The program looks first for an info page, then for a man page for the utility you name on the command line. Other similar programs that provide a more attractive interface for viewing info or man pages include ***xman***, ***xinfo***, and ***tkman***. Of these, only *pinfo* is included by default on Red Hat Linux and Fedora.

TROUBLESHOOTING AND RECOVERY

Your success at troubleshooting problems in Linux is largely dependent on how well you understand the services and protocols involved in a problem, and how comfortable you are with the utilities described in this book (and others that you will learn about on your own). Still, having an appropriate methodology can make it much easier to locate and fix problems. Again, the success of any methodology depends in part on how well you understand system services and the utilities and configuration files that control them. Otherwise, you will not be able to answer the questions posed in any reasonable troubleshooting method.

A basic methodology for troubleshooting in Linux might present the following questions:

- Is this problem being caused by hardware failure, hardware configuration, software internal errors, software configuration, or user error?

- What system or service is causing this problem?

- Can I eliminate other possible causes to limit the scope of the problem?

Starting with the least complex element, or lowest-common-denominator that might cause the problem, check the status of that item so you can eliminate it as a reason for the trouble. Then move to the next most complex item.

Walking through an example or two can illustrate this process. Suppose that when you turn on your Linux server, it doesn't appear to boot. You might go through the following series of inquiries to locate the trouble:

1. Did the system boot yesterday? It did, so you know the operating system has been correctly installed. If not, maybe an operating system has never been installed (or installed correctly) on this system.

15

2. Is the power cord attached to the system? Yes, you can hear a fan blowing when you turn it on. Other parts of the system could still have failed, so if nothing else is found as the cause, you would want to examine hardware components, such as the hard disk.

3. Is the power cord attached to the monitor? Yes, you see a light on the bottom of the monitor. Otherwise, the system may have started up normally, you just cannot see any evidence of that on screen.

4. Has the system been moved lately? No. Otherwise, a loose expansion card in the system could cause it to fail on startup.

5. Is the hard disk being accessed to find the boot manager for Linux? It appears not, because there is no on screen display of the boot manager.

6. Is a different device being used to boot the system instead of the hard disk? Yes, a floppy disk was inadvertently left in the disk drive, so the system is trying to boot from that disk. When you remove that disk and reboot, the system starts normally.

An experienced system administrator considers all of these questions without really thinking about them. Only less common problems, or problems involving systems you are unfamiliar with, require a more formal process of eliminating possible causes of a problem.

Consider another example: You are trying to use your Web browser, but cannot connect to your home page, *www.yahoo.com*. You might think of questions such as these:

1. Is the network cable correctly attached to my system?

2. Is the DNS server I use unavailable, so that my browser cannot resolve *www. yahoo.com* into an IP address?

3. Is my connection to the Internet unavailable?

4. Is my connection to this site being blocked by software on my local network?

5. Is my local network using a proxy or other service that I need to configure on my system before I can access the Internet?

6. Is the Yahoo! server down?

You can investigate all of these questions according to how likely each is, and how much effort it takes to check each one. As you gain experience, you will learn about the order to ask questions for different situations. For example, you may recall that you can test whether your DNS server is the problem by trying to establish a network connection using an IP address rather than a domain name (using either your Web browser or the *ping* command). Or, someone at your organization may have made changes in the network (such as adding a proxy server) of which you are unaware.

Troubleshooting is most difficult when you ignore possible causes because they seem unlikely to you. For example, you may know that your own network cable is not unplugged, but when a user calls you to ask for help with a networking problem, you would probably check the network cable before trying more complex solutions. Because Linux is so widely used, you can often find the solution to a problem, once you have narrowed down its cause, by searching online. You can search specific sites, such as the documentation on Red Hat Software's Web site (*www.redhat.com/docs/*), or the Linux Documentation project site (*www. tldp.org*). You will often find a solution by typing in key words on the Google search engine, at *www.google.com*.

Troubleshooting Linux Installation

Linux installation *can* be trouble free, completed in about 15 minutes plus the time it takes to copy files from the CD-ROM to your hard disk. But that doesn't always happen. The following sections provide ideas on solving some common problems you might encounter during a difficult Linux installation.

The Installation Program Doesn't Boot

If the Linux installation program does not start, the following are likely causes:

- The boot disk was created incorrectly. Try using a new disk and recreating the boot disk using the *rawwritewin* or *dd* programs. The *dd* program is more likely to cause trouble if you are unfamiliar with Linux utilities.

- The BIOS is configured to start the operating system from the hard disk without first checking the floppy disk or CD-ROM (whichever you are trying to use). This is a handy security feature that some systems implement by default; it also saves time because most people boot their systems from a hard disk. Edit the BIOS settings as needed.

- If the installation program starts but then appears to crash, the installation program may not be able to detect your video card. Try starting the installation by entering the word "text" at the first screen of text.

After Linux Is Installed, the System Doesn't Boot

Once you install Linux, the system sometimes does not boot into the newly installed Linux system. Here are some likely causes:

- You may have installed the boot manager on the active partition (as selected by default), but another boot manager installed in the MBR causes control to pass to another partition (not the active partition). Use the boot disk you created at the end of the installation to boot into your new Linux system—the boot disk "knows" which partition on your system contains Linux. You can also reinstall Linux, placing the Linux boot manager on the MBR.

15

- The system may have trouble identifying hardware on your system that was not detected during the installation process. In this case it may help to specify information about the hardware via a boot parameter. The boot manager starts the Linux kernel with this parameter attached. These parameters are used both to affect how Linux recognizes hardware devices, and to alter the enabled features of the operating system.

The Graphical Interface Doesn't Work

Sometimes the graphical interface doesn't work even though the installation program appears to detect your video hardware without a complaint. In this case, you probably selected a color depth or resolution that is not supported by the Linux driver. This can be true even if higher resolutions are supported on Windows—the Linux driver may still be in development or the developers lack critical technical information to make the video card perform to its capabilities.

Some video cards that are not supported by XFree86 are supported by commercial X Window System products that you can purchase and add to your Linux system after installing Linux. One such server is available from Xi Graphics (see *www.xig.com*). In the rare case that your card is not supported by any of these products, you can only use Linux in text mode. This is typical for many server installations, but if you want to use a graphical desktop, you need to invest in a different video card.

A Device or Part of Memory Isn't Available

Sometimes hardware that is included on the list of supported hardware on the Linux vendor's Web site is nevertheless not available after starting Linux. This is often because the hardware is not correctly configured. As with a system that won't boot, the configuration can sometimes be corrected by adding a boot parameter when starting Linux. For example, some computers running Linux cannot access the CD-ROM drive correctly unless the device name is added as a boot parameter, like this:

```
linux cdrom=/dev/hdc
```

Or, Linux may not access all of the available system RAM because of limitations in the computer's BIOS. (The *free* command displays the amount of memory available to Linux.) You can tell Linux the amount of RAM on the system using this format:

```
linux mem=<<amount of memory>>M
```

So to indicate 512 MB of RAM, you use the following command:

```
linux mem=512M
```

Be sure to use the correct value for the amount of RAM on your computer, or Linux crashes as it tries to work with nonexistent memory.

You can combine multiple boot parameters on a single line separated by spaces. For example:

```
linux cdrom=/dev/hdc mem=512M
```

Diagnosing Device Status

Linux includes a number of utilities to help you learn about devices attached to your system and configure those devices for use in Linux. Some of these require a fairly detailed knowledge of the hardware in question.

The directories of the /proc file system can provide information about many devices. For example, looking in the /proc/interrupts, /proc/ioports, /proc/pci, or /proc/dma displays helpful device information. Linux also includes specific utilities to display this and other device information in a useful format. These utilities include *lspci*, *setserial*, and *usbmodules*.

Similar information is available graphically using the Hardware Browser in Red Hat Linux and Fedora (choose System Tools, then Hardware Browser on the GNOME main menu).

Troubleshooting Network Connections

Networking can become very complex; the larger the network and the more diverse the technologies it uses, the more difficult troubleshooting becomes. Table 15-2 lists some common networking problems that you can diagnose and troubleshoot with the tools you have learned about.

15

Table 15-2   Basic Networking Troubleshooting Review

Trouble	Things to check
Networking doesn't appear to function at all	Use the *ifconfig* command to see whether networking is up and running; if not, try the network script in /etc/rc.d/init.d. (Remember to check things that seem too obvious: Is the cable plugged into the Ethernet card? Is an Ethernet card installed? Is the cable plugged into the wall or a hub?)
The network script doesn't appear to work	Use the *lsmod* command to see whether any network modules are installed in the kernel; if not, use *modprobe -t* or a graphical utility to install the right kernel module for your networking card
Can't *ping* any other systems on the local network segment	Check the cables; check with *ifconfig* to see whether a valid IP address has been assigned; check the routing tables to see that a route is listed for the local network
Can't *ping* any system on another segment within the organization	Check the cables at the hub or server room; check with *ifconfig* to see if a valid IP address is assigned and how that address compares or conflicts with those on the other network segment; does the routing table include a route for the other network that refers to an intermediate router, if necessary?

Table 15-2 Basic Networking Troubleshooting Review (continued)

Trouble	Things to check
Traffic to another segment seems very slow	Check the routing table to see whether the most direct route is defined, and check whether another system has the same IP address assigned. Review the output of the *ifconfig* command to see whether a large number of collisions are occurring—if so the network may be overloaded. Check *ifconfig* output to see whether a large number of errors are occurring—if so the NIC may be defective. Review whether fragmentation problems between the two segments could be slowing down traffic; use *traceroute* to see at what point along the way the transmission slows down significantly.

Creating Rescue Disks

A fairly common system failure is a hard disk problem or other trouble with booting the system. Sometimes this takes the form of a complete crash, in which case you may have to restore all of the data to a new hard disk from a backup archive. In other cases, part of the disk is corrupted so that the system cannot boot. Sometimes a hard disk problem can even be caused by something that the system administrator has done to the system. In the case of many hard drive failures, you cannot boot the Linux system normally from the hard disk; you must boot from a removable disk or bootable CD-ROM before you can access the hard disk and solve the problem.

A **rescue disk** is a 3.5-inch disk that you can use to boot a Linux-based computer. It may have only a boot manager and enough information to locate the Linux partition on your hard disk. Often, it includes a minimal version of Linux and enough system utilities to diagnose and repair problems in hard disk files. After booting the system from a rescue disk, you can mount the hard disks where Linux is installed to correct problems. One popular preconfigured rescue disk is Tom's Boot disk, which you can download from *www.toms.net/rb*.

Some system administrators always boot their servers from a 3.5-inch disk. This takes more time than booting from a hard drive, but because a server is rarely rebooted, speed of booting is not really a concern. By doing this, the system administrator can control how the system boots and easily maintain a backup of the removable disk in case of problems. A separate rescue disk is used when the boot disk or hard disk fails.

Ideally, you create a boot disk for your system when installing Linux, as described in Chapter 8. This guarantees that the boot disk and the boot manager information on the computer's hard disk are compatible. You can also use the **mkbootdisk** command to create a boot disk after your system is running.

When you are working with Red Hat Linux or Fedora and have problems booting the system, or have a hard disk crash or other serious hard disk problem, you can start the system in **rescue mode** using Fedora CD 1. After booting from that CD, enter *linux rescue* at the first prompt. The system boots from the CD and then asks you to select a language, keyboard, and whether to start networking devices (which you may want to access as needed to repair the system). After this, the system informs you that it will search for Fedora installations. You can either select Continue to mount the installation under /mnt/sysimage, Read-Only to make that file system read-only, or Skip to not mount any file systems. In any case, you then see a text-mode shell prompt. At this shell prompt, you can use whatever utilities are appropriate to diagnose and repair problems. If you selected Skip at the last prompt while entering rescue mode, you need to manually mount the correct disk partition before you can access any data on your Fedora installation. Entering exit in the rescue shell causes the system to reboot.

CHAPTER SUMMARY

- ❑ X Window System configuration is handled by the Linux installation program, but can be adjusted using several graphical tools such as *xvidtune* and *system-config-display*.

- ❑ Many scripts are used by the X Window System to determine exactly what programs to start as the graphical environment is started. These scripts are less relevant when using a desktop such as GNOME or KDE.

- ❑ Features of X such as resources, fonts, and interaction with the mouse can all be configured using simple command-line utilities. Some features overlap those controlled by desktop interfaces such as GNOME, which are also configurable using graphical preferences tools in those desktops.

- ❑ The graphical login screen is handled by a program called *xdm*, or *gdm* and *kdm* in GNOME and KDE. This screen can be accessed remotely using the XDMCP protocol.

- ❑ Graphical programs in Linux can be displayed remotely to any system that has an X server installed. Security for this feature is provided by either *xhost* or *xauth* security, the second being harder to configure but much more secure. Remote applications are often run over an SSH connection to prevent security breaches.

- ❑ Computer security is often divided into categories that include physical, user, file, and network security.

- ❑ Examples of security attacks include password cracking, Trojan horses, buffer overflow attacks, DoS and DDoS attacks, viruses, and worms.

- ❑ Both attackers and system administrators use a variety of security software tools. These include tools for port scanning (such as *nmap*), for packet sniffing (such as *tcpdump* and Ethereal), IDS programs, and security auditing tools such as SAINT.

- ❑ Several organizations support computing professionals as they try to maintain secure systems. Two of the most important are CERT/CC and SANS.

15

❏ Linux uses a firewalling and packet-filtering system called NetFilter, which uses IP tables to define rules used to process network packets. This feature of Linux supports IP masquerading, transparent proxying, and other advanced routing and packet control features.

❏ A DNS server on Linux is implemented using the *named* daemon, with zone information files stored on a master or slave DNS server providing data in response to client requests. A caching name server does not act as a master or slave for any domain, but only stores information for quicker local access.

❏ NFS permits remote users to mount a file system on an NFS server as a part of their directory structure. The directories that are available are defined on the server in the /etc/exports file.

❏ The Samba suite provides Microsoft Windows-compatible file and print services using the SMB and CIFS protocols. The Samba server can be configured manually by editing the smb.conf file or using the SWAT browser-based configuration tool.

❏ Squid is a proxy server that provides caching and many other features to clients on a local network.

❏ Apache is a Web server that is included with most Linux distributions. It is configured using the httpd.conf file, and controlled using the *apachectl* program. It supports such advanced features as virtual hosting and a modular architecture.

❏ The most popular MTA (e-mail server) is sendmail. It is challenging to configure, but provides many useful features such as forwarding and aliases. The *m4* program is usually used to simplify configuration of sendmail.

❏ Superservers such as *inetd* and *xinetd* are often used to manage multiple network services. These programs start the needed network service only when a client request for that service arrives. These programs use built-in security to control who can access each network service, or else they rely on the TCP Wrappers program, which in turn uses the hosts.allow and hosts.deny files to determine which connections should be permitted for a specific network service.

❏ Systematically eliminating possible problems is a sound methodology for troubleshooting. The more you understand about the underlying technology and helpful utilities, the easier it is to locate and fix problems.

❏ Linux includes numerous utilities to help you learn about and configure hardware. Networking problems can be very challenging, but basic programs such as *ping* and *traceroute* can help isolate problems.

❏ A boot disk or rescue disk is a huge time saver when a system goes down. When these are not available, using a Red Hat Linux or Fedora CD to enter rescue mode is also useful. In this mode, you can mount hard disk partitions and use a variety of system utilities to track down and fix problems.

COMMAND SUMMARY

Command	Description	Example
apachectl	Control program used to manage the Apache Web server	apachectl -k start
dig	A utility used to query specific DNS servers for specific resource records	dig @ns.xmission.com www. xmission.com any
dnscache	A minimalist DNS caching server	dnscache
ethereal	Graphical program that displays the contents of and statistical information about network packets; a packet sniffer	ethereal
exportfs	Causes the NFS daemon to use an updated (recently edited) version of the /etc/exports file	exportfs
hoststat	Displays the status of hosts that have recently sent e-mail to your sendmail daemon	hoststat
inetd	A widely used superserver program	inetd
iptables	Configures rules within the IP tables (packet filtering/firewall) part of the Linux kernel; common options are listed in Table 15-1	`iptables -A INPUT -p udp -s 0/0 --sport 67:68 -d 0/0 --dport 67:68 -i eth0 -j ACCEPT`
iptraf	A popular "packet sniffer" program for viewing network activity on a LAN	IPTraf
lokkit	A text-mode program that sets up basic firewall rules according to the level of security protection desired	lokkit
lspci	Lists information about PCI devices on the system	lspci
m4	A program that converts a text file containing configuration parameters into a complete sendmail.cf file	m4 /etc/mail/sendmail.mc > /etc/sendmail.cf
mailq	Displays a list of messages waiting to be sent out	mailq
mailstats	Displays a summary of the amount of e-mail traffic that sendmail has handled	mailstats
mkbootdisk	Creates a boot disk	mkbootdisk --device /dev/fd0 2.4.22
named	The Linux program that implements the DNS protocol to create a DNS server; part of the BIND collection of programs	named

15

Command	Description	Example
newaliases	Reconfigures the aliases (alternate names) stored in /etc/aliases after changes have been made to that file; used in connection with the sendmail e-mail server	newaliases
nfsd	The main daemon used by NFS to provide access to local file systems by remote clients	nfsd
nmap	The most widely used port-scanning utility	nmap -sS www.myplace.net
nmapfe	A utility that acts as a graphical front end to the nmap command; requires the GNOME desktop	nmapfe
nmbd	The Windows name-server component of the Samba suite of programs	nmbd
nslookup	A utility used to query DNS servers for resource records	nslookup www.xmission.com
pdbedit	Edit the Samba user account database	pdbedit -a -u abutler
pinfo	Provides color-coded display of info and man pages	pinfo bash
rndc	A control program used to manage the named daemon	rndc reload
rpc.mountd	Daemon used by NFS to permit mounting of local file systems by remote clients	rpc.mountd
rpc.rquotad	Daemon that tracks user disk space quotas for remotely mounted file systems	rpc.rquotad
rpc.statd	Daemon that manages NFS-mounted file systems when the remote NFS server to which a mount point refers has crashed	rpc.statd
setserial	Used to display and configure serial port settings	setserial /dev/ttyS0
smbd	The file and print sharing daemon for the Samba suite of programs	smbd
startx	Starts the X Window System from a text mode prompt	startx
system-config-bind	Graphical utility for configuring the named DNS server	system-config-bind
system-config-display	Graphical program used to change screen resolution or color depth	system-config-display
system-config-securitylevel	Graphical utility for configuring an overall security level in Red Hat Linux and Fedora	system-config-securitylevel

Command	Description	Example
system-config-securitylevel-tui	Text and menu-based utility for configuring an overall security level in Red Hat Linux and Fedora	system-config-securitylevel-tui
tcpd	The daemon that implements TCP Wrappers	tcpd in.ftpd
tcpdump	Command-line network traffic analysis utility	tcpdump
tethereal	Text-based program similar to Ethereal, used to display and analyze the contents of network packets; a packet sniffer	tethereal
tkman	Graphical display tool for man pages (not included in Red Hat Linux and Fedora)	tkman bash
usbmodules	Information and configuration tool for USB devices	usbmodules
whois	A utility that queries an Internet database to learn about the person who manages a specific domain	whois www.law.gw.edu
xauth	A security system for managing display of graphical programs on remote computers by sharing a numeric token called a cookie; also the program used in Linux to manage this security system and the numeric cookies associated with it	xauth
xfontsel	Graphical program that displays available fonts in the X Window System and lets you select the default font to use for title bars, menus, etc.	xfontsel
xhost	A program that can control access by X clients to an X server for display of graphical programs; xhost is not a secure system	xhost +
xinetd	A superserver with extended configuration options; standard on Red Hat Linux instead of the more usual *inetd* program	xinetd
xinfo	Graphical display tool for info pages (not included in Red Hat Linux and Fedora)	xinfo ls
xinit	Program that starts the X server; called by the *startx* script	xinit

15

Command	Description	Example
xman	Graphical display tool for man pages (not included in Red Hat Linux and Fedora)	xman nmap
xrdb	Manages X resource database information for graphical programs	xrdb -load $HOME/.Xresources
xset	Sets options within the X Window System	xset s noblank
xvidtune	Graphical utility that adjusts display characteristics of the X Window System	xvidtune

KEY TERMS

.forward — Configuration file placed in a user's home directory to define where e-mail messages should be forwarded by sendmail.

.Xauthority — Configuration file containing tokens (cookies) used by the *xauth* program to enable remote display of graphical programs.

/etc/exports — File containing a description of local file systems and directories to be made available using NFS.

/etc/hosts.allow — Configuration file that defines services and hosts that should be permitted access by TCP Wrappers.

/etc/hosts.deny — Configuration file that defines services and hosts that should be denied access by TCP Wrappers.

/etc/nologin — A file whose existence prevents all users except root from logging in to the system. Regular users attempting to log in see the contents of the file /etc/nologin.

/etc/securetty — Configuration file that lists locations from which root is permitted to log in. Used to prevent root from logging in via a remote connection, such as a modem.

/etc/services — Configuration file that maps service names to port numbers. Used by many programs, including the superservers *inetd* and *xinetd*.

Access Control Lists (ACLs) — Data structures that define who can access individual directories and programs.

Apache — A popular Web server program.

Apache modules — Program code that can be loaded independently into the Apache Web server.

background application — An application that does not prevent the program that started it from immediately interacting further with the user.

buffer overflow attack — A technique for gaining access to a computer system by exploiting a weakness in the design of a computer program. When a cracker follows a specific sequence of steps or provides specific input to a program, the program becomes confused and tries to use computer memory inappropriately; consequently, the buffer, or memory space, reserved for a part of the program overflows. The result can be either corruption of system data, a crashed server, or even direct root access.

caching name server — A DNS server that contains no preconfigured information on domains (except localhost), but simply queries other DNS servers and caches the results.

CERT Coordination Center (CERT/CC) — A federally funded software-engineering institute that focuses much attention on computer security issues and provides information to security and system administration professionals around the world; operated by Carnegie-Mellon University.

container — A special type of Apache configuration directive that activates other directives only if a condition is met or only within a particular context.

cookie — A numeric token used by a program to identify information about a host or user.

denial of service (DoS) — A cracker activity that ties up the attacked server or a particular program with so much bogus network traffic that it cannot respond to valid requests.

distributed DoS (DDoS) — A special type of denial-of-service attack in which a cracker infiltrates many systems and installs a program that executes a DoS attack on an assigned target at the cracker's command.

e-mail alias — An alternative name that can be used to e-mail messages to a user account.

Ethereal — A powerful graphical network traffic analysis tool.

firewall — A program that filters (blocks) IP packets based on their characteristics and according to a set of rules.

gdm — The display manager included with GNOME; used to provide a graphical login prompt.

Global Information Assurance Certification (GIAC) — A hands-on security certification program run by the SANS Institute.

hard mount — A method of mounting an NFS file system in which programs will wait—without limit—for the NFS server to respond.

intrusion detection system (IDS) — A type of software that aids network intrusion detection.

IP chains — An older packet-filtering (firewalling) technique used in the Linux kernel.

IP masquerading — A type of network address translation in which packets from many computers on a LAN are altered to appear as if they came from a single computer.

IP tables — The lists of rules associated with one of the programming hooks provided in the networking stacks by the NetFilter architecture.

kdm — The display manager included with KDE; used to provide a graphical login prompt.

Linux Intrusion Detection System (LIDS) — A complex intrusion detection system that alters the Linux kernel to remove root's comprehensive access to a Linux system.

Mail Delivery Agent (MDA) — A program that places e-mail in a user's mailbox so that it can be read. This function is often subsumed by an MTA.

Mail Transfer Agent (MTA) — A program that moves e-mail messages from one server on the Internet to another. Also called an e-mail server.

Mail User Agent (MUA) — A program that displays and manages e-mail messages for a user.

map — A technique in which user account information for an incoming client request is assigned to a user account on the server that processes that request.

15

master DNS server — The authoritative name server for a zone, typically containing database files that provide IP addresses for hosts within that zone.

metaserver — *See* superserver.

MIT Magic Cookie — The name given to a cookie used by the *xauth* program for X display authentication.

NetFilter — The packet-filtering and advanced routing architecture in Linux 2.4 and 2.6 kernels.

network address translation (NAT) — A routing technique in which the addresses or other header information in a packet is altered during routing.

Network File System (NFS) — A network service that permits remote users to mount and work with a file system as part of their directory structure.

network traffic analysis — *See* packet sniffing.

packet filter — A technique in which network packets are processed according to their contents, usually based on a series of rules that compose a firewall. Handled in the Linux kernel using rules defined by the *iptables* command.

packet sniffing — A network activity in which the headers and payload of all packets on the network are captured and examined (also called network traffic analysis).

password cracking — A cracker activity by which the cracker obtains the password for a valid user account, either by using a program that examines millions of passwords until the correct one is found, or by guessing based on personal knowledge about the user.

port — A number that is associated with a network-capable application.

port scanning — A network activity in which packets sent to a host are analyzed to learn about that host.

primary DNS server — *See* master DNS server.

proxy server — A server that receives a client request that is intended for a different server. The proxy server then makes the request as if the proxy server itself were the client; when the intended server responds, the proxy server sends the response to the client.

rescue disk — A disk created specifically to boot a Linux system in the event of a system failure. Contains the software tools most likely to be of help in diagnosing and repairing problems with the failed system.

rescue mode — A mode of operation in Red Hat Linux. Used to repair a system failure that blocks normal booting and operation.

resource database — A file that defines how an X resource should appear on screen.

resource record — A line within a DNS zone information file, defining how the DNS server should resolve a given host or IP address, or provide related information.

root name servers — DNS servers designated as a starting point for DNS queries.

Samba — A collection of programs that emulates Microsoft networking functionality—both client and server—on Linux and various other operating systems.

secondary DNS server — *See also* slave DNS server.

Secure Socket Layer (SSL) — A protocol that allows a Web server to communicate securely with a browser for e-commerce or similar applications.

Security Administrator's Integrated Network Tool (SAINT) — A popular security-auditing program.

security audit — A review or test of how secure a system really is and what needs to be done to improve its security.

sendmail — The most widely used Linux e-mail server.

server-parsed documents — *See* server-side includes.

server-side includes — Statements within a text file that are processed on the fly by a Web server when that document is requested.

session — A configuration that defines a set of graphical programs to run when a user logs in.

slave DNS server — A backup to a master DNS server, containing the same database files as the master DNS server.

share — A Microsoft Windows term referring to a resource intended to be shared over a network.

social engineering — A method used by attackers to violate user security measures, typically by using clever lies or persuasion to convince a user to divulge a password or other crucial system information. The attacker typically poses as a system administrator or similar person.

soft mount — A method of mounting an NFS file system in which NFS will wait for a while if a data request is made and the NFS server does not respond, then the client will give up.

squashing — A method of preserving user security in NFS by preventing a user with root access on one system from automatically acquiring root access on an NFS server by virtue of mounting an exported NFS directory.

Squid — The most widely used Linux proxy server.

standalone mode — Using a network program without support from a superserver such as *xinetd* or *inetd*.

superserver — A program that listens on multiple network ports and starts appropriate network service daemons when a client connection arrives for that port. Also called a metaserver. Examples include *inetd* and *xinetd*.

SWAT — A browser-based graphical configuration interface for setting up and managing the Samba SMB server.

System Administration, Networking, and Security (SANS) Institute — A prestigious and well-regarded education and research organization whose members include most of the leading computer security experts in the country. Also called simply SANS.

TCP Wrappers — An application-level access control (security) program that examines incoming network connections when requested by a superserver, then compares the connection details to a configuration file to determine whether the connection is allowed.

transparent proxy — A networking technique in which a packet is redirected to a different port on the same computer.

Trojan horse — A technique for gaining access to a computer system by having a system administrator execute a program that appears normal but which actually creates a security hole for a cracker or destroys data on the host when it is run.

virtual hosting — A feature of the Apache Web server that lets a single copy of Apache serve documents for several Web sites (several domains).

15

X resource — The separate screen elements of a graphical application, such as scroll bars, text fonts, and titles bars.

xdm — The program that provides a graphical login screen in Linux. Replaced by the very similar program gdm in GNOME, or kdm in KDE.

XDMCP — A protocol that allows remote hosts to use X running on a Linux system to provide a graphical login display.

zone — A part of the DNS domain tree for which a particular DNS server has authority to provide information.

zone information files — The files referred to in named.conf that contain detailed information about specific zones: the information that a DNS query seeks.

REVIEW QUESTIONS

1. Describe at least one advantage and one disadvantage of using *xauth* instead of *xhost*.

2. The DISPLAY environment variable:
   a. is used only by *xhost*, not by *xauth*
   b. must be used in conjunction with the *--display* command-line option
   c. is only used when connecting via Telnet or SSH
   d. often includes a 0.0 specification

3. The *inetd* superserver typically starts:
   a. TCP Wrappers
   b. an Internet service daemon such as in.ftpd
   c. *xinetd*
   d. standalone services such as a Web server

4. TCP Wrappers is configured using:
   a. /etc/hosts
   b. /etc/inetd.conf
   c. /etc/hosts.allow and /etc/hosts.deny
   d. /etc/services

5. Select the meaning of the *in.telnetd 192.168.0* line within /etc/hosts.allow:
   a. Deny access to the Telnet service for all hosts on any network ID starting with 192.168.0.
   b. Permit access to the Telnet service for all hosts on any network ID starting with 192.168.0.

    c. Deny access to the Telnet service for any host except those on any network ID starting with 192.168.0.

    d. Permit access to the Telnet service for all hosts except those on any network ID starting with 192.168.0.

6. Using a server in standalone mode refers to:

    a. relying on information in /etc/services so that *inetd* can initiate it correctly

    b. not using a superserver to control the server

    c. resting the server by connecting only to localhost

    d. relying on TCP Wrappers for security rather than built-in security functions

7. To what does the term "metaserver" refer?

8. Describe the difference between a DoS attack and a DDoS attack.

9. Linux firewalls consist of _____ organized into_____ or _____ .

    a. commands, packets, datagrams

    b. utilities, secure, insecure

    c. chains, protocols, filters

    d. rules, chains, tables

10. The three default rule sets used by IP tables are:

    a. INPUT, FORWARDING, OUTPUT

    b. INPUT, FORWARD, OUPUT

    c. DENY, REJECT, ACCEPT

    d. NETFILTER, IPTABLES, SSH

11. IP tables rules can specify the following actions:

    a. ACCEPT, REJECT, OUTPUT, RETURN

    b. ACCEPT, DENY, QUEUE, RETURN

    c. ACCEPT, REJECT, DENY, RETURN

    d. ACCEPT, DROP, QUEUE, RETURN

12. IP masquerading is a popular example of:

    a. network address translation

    b. transparent proxy

    c. combining TCP/IP with other protocols

    d. a new feature that NetFilter introduced to Linux

13. IP masquerading is configured using which option within an *iptables* command?

    a. *-j MASQUERADE*

    b. *-j DROP*

15

    c. *-i MASQUERADE*

    d. *-A FORWARD*

14. By using a transparent proxy configuration, a system administrator can:

    a. securely transmit packets over the Internet using a variety of ciphers

    b. hide logging and other security features from users sending packets through a LAN

    c. redirect packets destined for a given port on a remote system to a different port on the router

    d. cache packets in the router to provide higher performance for all users on the LAN

15. The _____ utility is the preferred tool for querying name servers for administrative or troubleshooting purposes.

    a. *nslookup*

    b. *named*

    c. *dig*

    d. host.conf

16. Modules allow the Apache Web server to:

    a. Interact cleanly with the Linux kernel.

    b. Load and unload functionality by recompiling Apache.

    c. Make new functionality part of Apache as it is running.

    d. Use LoadModule to specify programs that are loaded when a user requests a certain Web document.

17. Server-parsed documents are:

    a. documents stored on the Web server that Apache examines or processes at the moment they are requested by a client

    b. module information files that Apache examines or processes when the server starts up

    c. document files that Apache can preload into memory to speed responses to browser queries

    d. another name for virtual-hosted documents

18. Computer security for a host is often divided into four areas of concern:

    a. physical, user, file, and network

    b. network, firewall, VPN, and tunneling

    c. physical, user, firewalls, intrusion detection

    d. Trojan horse, buffer overflow, password cracking, worms and viruses

19. What is the purpose of /etc/nologin?

20. The X Window System files are normally located in which subdirectory in Linux?

    a. /etc/X

    b. /usr/share

    c. /opt/kde

    d. /usr/X11R6

21. Choosing not to run X:

    a. is pointless because it runs in the background anyway

    b. can cause configuration problems on server-based systems

    c. saves the system resources that the X server would have consumed

    d. would be unreasonable on a Linux system used as an Internet server

22. The _____ program provides an insecure but easy-to-use method of permitting other computers to use your X server.

    a. *xhost*

    b. *xauth*

    c. *Xsession*

    d. *xinit*

23. Graphical programs use the X server that is:

    a. defined by the --*display* option of the command, unless a DISPLAY variable defines a different X server

    b. always on the same system as the program that is running

    c. defined by the DISPLAY environment variable, or the --*display* option if it is included with the command

    d. listed in the *xinitrc* script file

24. The command normally used to start the X Window System from a text-mode prompt in run level 3 is:

    a. *xinit*

    b. *startx*

    c. *xdm*

    d. *xinitrc*

25. The xdm, gdm, or kdm display manager is initially started by the _____ program (or script).

    a. *init*

    b. *startx*

    c. *xinit*

    d. *xrdb*

15

Hands-On Projects

Project 15-1

In this project, you experiment with the *xauth* program to remotely display a graphical application. To complete this project, you need a working Linux system with a graphical (X) display, and a friend in your classroom or lab with a similar system. You will work as a team on this project.

1. Log in to Linux. Instead of using the *xauth* command interactively as the chapter text described, use command-line options as shown here. Start with the list option (no dashes) to dump to the screen the cookies stored in your .Xauthority file:

```
xauth list
```

2. Now use the *nextract* option to create output in the cookielist file that can be merged into another .Xauthority file. You must include the display for which cookies are being extracted, which would be :0 on most systems. The DISPLAY environment variable is a consistent way to refer to the current display in the command:

```
xauth nextract cookielist $DISPLAY
```

3. Give this file to your trusted friend (e-mail it, use FTP, copy it to a disk, or whatever means you prefer).

4. Move to your friend's computer and copy the file containing the cookie from your system into your friend's home directory. (The easiest way to transfer the file if you don't have all your networking services already set up is to use the *mcopy* command to transfer the file to a removable disk and then from the disk onto the other host.)

5. On your friend's computer, execute this command, inserting the file name containing the cookie from your system. This command merges the *xauth* cookies from the named file into the .Xauthority file on your friend's system:

```
xauth merge cookielist
```

6. On your friend's system, execute this command to start a graphical program. You can use any graphical program that is installed, but be certain to substitute your own host name where the command says *hostname*:

```
gedit -display hostname:0.0
```

7. You and your friend should see the program appear on your system.

8. Move back to your system and execute this command, substituting the program name if you used a different program in Step 6:

```
ps aux|grep gedit
```

9. You see that the program that appears on your system's screen is not running on your system; it is running on your friend's system.

10. Close the program by pressing **Ctrl+c** on your friend's system or choosing **Quit** from the **File** menu on your screen (within *gedit*).

11. Though you trust your friend, the next time you log out of X and log in again, a new *xauth* cookie is generated automatically, so your friend is not able to use your system as an X server unless you hand over your cookie again. Log off.

Project 15-2

**HANDS-ON
PROJECTS**

In this project, you experiment with the *nmap* port-scanning utility. You should work in a lab for this project. In the steps, the host name *target.edu* has been used; replace this with the IP address or host name of any single system in your computer lab. To complete this project you should have Linux installed and have root access. The second part of the project requires the Nmap Front End package, which can only be used on Red Hat Linux or Fedora (or other systems using the GNOME desktop).

> *Do not complete this project on a production network; work only in an isolated lab environment.*
>
> **CAUTION**

1. Log in to Linux, open a command-line window, and change to root access. Use this scan to determine which hosts are "listening" on your local network:

    ```
    nmap -sP target.edu/24
    ```

    This scan may take several minutes to complete, depending on the size of your LAN. You see a report listing each system that appears to be running on the network. This gives you the information you need to start reviewing the services offered by each host.

2. Use the following command to determine the OS used by one of the hosts in your network and see a list of ports discovered to be open using a basic port scan. This scan takes a couple of minutes to complete:

    ```
    nmap -O target.edu
    ```

3. You would want to try a stealthier scan if you were concerned that the default scan might alert the server to your actions and block your subsequent access. In that case you might try a scan such as this one. The resulting list should look the same: you see which ports appear to be open, so that you could attack them based on the service they are providing to the network:

    ```
    nmap -sN target.edu
    ```

4. Suppose you knew of a vulnerability in DNS, but didn't know which hosts on the network were running a name server. You can use the following command to scan the DNS port (53) on all systems in your LAN to identify which ones are running a DNS server:

    ```
    nmap -sS -p 53 target.edu/24
    ```

15

5. You decide to scan the hosts in the LAN in random order, so you use this command instead:

```
nmap -randomize_hosts -sS -p 53 target.edu/24
```

6. Because you are concerned that someone running a tool to watch for port scanning might block your scans, you decide to slow your scans down in hopes that no one will detect them. Try this command:

```
nmap -randomize_hosts -T 0 -sS -p 53 target.edu/24
```

7. When you tire of waiting, press **Ctrl+c** and read the man page for *nmap* to discover how long *nmap* waits between each packet sent when the –T 0 timing option is used.

8. Load the Nmap Front End package from Fedora CD 3 if you have not previously installed it (it is not installed as part of the recommended packages in Chapter 8).

9. Start the graphical utility:

```
nmapfe
```

10. Use *nmapfe* to complete any three of the six scans given in the preceding steps. You can check your use of the utility by seeing whether the command-line output for *nmap* shown just below the output window (the field labeled Command) matches the command you are trying to duplicate from one of the steps above. (The order of parameters is not critical and may vary.) Log off.

HANDS-ON PROJECTS

Project 15-3

In this project, you use *whois* to look for information about a domain name. To complete this project you need a working Linux system and an Internet connection.

For this project, you are helping a friend set up the new computer lab at Alexandria High School in Northern Virginia. Because this will be a small lab, you want to have a couple of backup DNS servers that you can include in your configurations in case you need to stop your local DNS server for maintenance. You decide that Northern Virginia Community College (NVCC) probably wouldn't mind if you pointed to their site for your secondary and tertiary DNS servers.

1. Log in to Linux and open a command-line window. Suppose you've seen two different URLs for the NVCC site. Try the first one, *nvcc.vccs.edu*, in a *whois* query. What result do you see?

```
whois   nvcc.vccs.edu
```

2. If this didn't work, maybe you need to reference the whois server that is specific to the .EDU domain. Use *whois.educause.net* and query again for *nvcc.vccs.edu*.

```
whois   -h whois.educause.net nvcc.vccs.edu
```

3. If this still didn't work, consider the address itself. It apparently refers to NVCC within some larger unit, vccs—probably the Virginia Community College System, or something like that. With this theory in mind, try a query to the Educause whois server using just *vccs.edu*. What results do you see?

```
whois    -h whois.educause.net  vccs.edu
```

4. You are concerned that the VCCS people may not have direct authority over the NVCC servers, so you decide to try the other NVCC address to see if you can locate someone at that school. Run a *whois* query for *nv.cc.va.us*. (You might want to view both *www.nv.cc.va.us* and *www.nvcc.vccs.edu* in your Web browser first to check that they are valid domains.) Where did you query for *nv.cc.va.us*? What result did you see, and why did you get that result?

```
whois    -h whois.educause.net  nv.cc.va.us
```

5. Concerned that you haven't been able to find the contact person yet at NVCC, you decide to try the University of Virginia site, *uva.edu*. Make this *whois* query. Sometimes a query directly to *whois.internic.net* can connect directly to another whois server such as *educause.net*. Other times you may need to specify Educause.net as your whois server.

```
whois    -h whois.educause.net  uva.edu
```

6. From the information listed, obtain the IP addresses of the DNS servers and the name, phone, and e-mail address of the contact person. You should check with the contact person as a courtesy before referencing their DNS servers. Log off.

HANDS-ON
PROJECTS

Project 15-4

In this project, you experiment with the NFS protocol. The steps describe the procedure on Red Hat Linux and Fedora, but they should be substantially equivalent for any Linux distribution. To complete this project, you should have the NFS daemons installed. Be aware that if you used a High Security setting when you installed Linux, or otherwise set up firewalling, the procedure may not work. If you are in a safe lab environment, you can delete all firewall rules on the system and set all default firewall policies to ACCEPT by issuing the following commands while logged in as root:

```
iptables -F
iptables -P INPUT ACCEPT
iptables -P FORWARD ACCEPT
iptables -P OUTPUT ACCEPT
```

For this project you should work in teams; one Linux system should be designated as the NFS server and the other as the NFS client. You should have root access to both systems.

1. Log in to the server, open a command-line window and change to root access. Then edit the /etc/exports file and add the following line, substituting the host name of your client system where indicated:

```
/usr/share/doc    client_host(all_squash,rw)
```

2. Also on the server, edit the /etc/hosts.deny file by adding this line:

```
portmap            client_host
```

3. What steps need to be taken to activate these two changes?

4. On the client, log in as root and create a mount point directory for the NFS server. Here is an example:

```
mkdir /mnt/server_hostname
```

5. Edit the /etc/fstab file on the client by adding this line:

```
server_hostname:/usr/share/doc /mnt/server_hostname nfs
o=ro,rsize=8192,wsize=8192 0 0
```

6. Use the *mount* command on the client to mount the NFS file system you exported:

```
mount /mnt/server_hostname
```

Why did it not work?

7. On the server, edit /etc/hosts.deny, removing your addition.

8. On the client, try the *mount* command again.

9. Change to the mount point directory that you created.

10. Noting that the directory is exported as rw on the server, create a new directory in that directory:

```
mkdir mydocs
```

11. Give three reasons why this didn't work. Log off.

Project 15-5

In this project, you set up and test a caching name server using the standard packages provided with Red Hat Linux and Fedora. To complete this project, you should have Fedora installed, with networking established, root access to the system, and an Internet connection.

1. Log in to Linux, open a command-line window, and change to root access.

2. Check that the necessary packages are installed using the following commands:

```
rpm -q bind
rpm -q bind-utils
rpm -q caching-nameserver
```

You will probably need to install the last package from Fedora CD 3 using this command (after mounting the CD and changing to the appropriate directory):

```
rpm -Uvh caching-nameserver*
```

3. Start the name server:

```
service named start
```

4. Use this command to query for a domain name. You have not changed your /etc/ resolv.conf file, so your previously configured DNS server can still be used.

   dig www.sony.com

5. Notice the Query time and SERVER lines in the last part of the output of *dig*.

6. Now, try out your caching name server with this command:

   dig @localhost www.sony.com

7. Notice the same two lines at the end of the output. How do they differ?

   Why was the time not faster when the response was already cached at your preconfig- ured name server?

8. Open the /etc/named.conf file in a text editor.

9. Within the options section near the top of the file, right after the line directory "/var/named", insert the following lines. Substitute the IP address of your primary DNS name server at your ISP for the IP address shown here:

   ```
   forward first;
   forwarders {
           198.60.22.2;
   };
   ```

10. Save the file and exit the editor.

11. Run the **named-checkconf** command to see whether any syntax errors were introduced as you edited the configuration file. If so, correct them.

12. Reload the configuration using this command (you may see a warning message about the name key, which you can safely ignore for this project):

    rndc reload

13. Select another domain name for testing. You should select one that others in your class have not selected and that you would not expect to have been visited often; a somewhat obscure domain name is better for this test. Use *dig* with your localhost to query for the domain you selected:

    dig @localhost www.cern.org

14. Notice how long the query time is, given near the end of *dig*'s response.

15. Perform the same query again. How does the query time differ? From where is the information being taken? What advantage does forwarding have over simply using a caching name server?

16. If you wish, you can have your system always use the local DNS server (the daemon running on the same computer) for name resolution. To do this, edit your /etc/ resolv.conf file to contain only this line (plus any comment lines you choose to include):

    nameserver 127.0.0.1

15

If you choose to do this, use the following command to make *named* start each time your system is started:

```
chkconfig --level 35 named on
```

17. Log off.

Project 15-6

In this project, you check the contents of remote name servers using the *dig* command. To complete this project, you should have Linux installed (any version that includes the *dig* utility), with networking established, and an Internet connection.

Sometimes the results you receive from a name resolution are unexpected. This can be caused by several problems, such as a poorly configured DNS server, a DNS server without a slave that temporarily goes down, or slow propagation of a change in a DNS file. In this project, you query step by step through several name servers to get a complete name resolution. This project uses the sample domain name *ftp.hq.nasa.gov*, but feel free to experiment on any domain name you choose once you understand the process being illustrated.

1. Log in to Linux, open a command-line window, and change to root access.

2. Query your ISP's name server for the address you want to find. Instruct the DNS server not to search "down the tree," but to give you only the first piece of information that it has, using the "norecurse" option (to stop recursion) to arrive at the requested domain:

```
dig ftp.hq.nasa.gov NS +norecurse
```

3. The result is a list of the addresses of authoritative DNS servers for the .gov domain, unless the server you queried happens to have cached the authoritative servers for nasa.gov as well. In that case, you might choose to use this command to get the .gov NS records specifically:

```
dig gov NS +norecurse
```

4. The *dig* command shows a list of name servers that manage the .gov top-level domain. From that list of servers, choose any three and write them down.

5. To each of those three name servers, make the following query to check the next part of the domain:

```
dig @gov-ns-server nasa.gov NS +norecurse
```

6. For each of the three *dig* queries you make in Step 5, write down the server that is listed as handling the nasa.gov domain (it has "NS" next to the server name, to indicate a name server). Does the ANSWER section of the *dig* output show the same server in all three *dig* queries of Step 5?

7. If so, continue as follows. Execute the command below. Where you see *nasa-ns-server* below, insert one of the server names that you wrote down in Step 6 from the output of the three commands you executed in Step 5. (Many domains do not have three name servers, but NASA has a huge network, and so includes numerous name servers.)

```
dig @nasa-ns-server hq.nasa.gov NS +norecurse
```

8. The output of the *dig* command you executed in Step 7 shows you a list of name servers that have information about *hq.nasa.gov* servers. Each of the name servers is listed with an "NS" after it. One of the name servers listed is probably *mx.nsi.nasa.gov* (though these name servers can change over time within an organization). Query that name server, or one of the others listed with "NS" in the output of Step 7 using this *dig* command (substitute a different name server for *mx.msi.nasa.gov* if you choose to try a different name server):

```
dig @mx.nsi.nasa.gov ftp.hq.nasa.gov
```

Below is the output from the above command. The exact output that you see may differ.

```
; <<>> DiG 9.1.3 <<>> @mx.nsi.nasa.gov ftp.hq.nasa.gov
;; global options: printcmd
;; Got answer:
;; ->>HEADER<<- opcode: QUERY, status: NOERROR, id: 49505
;; flags: qr aa rd ra; QUERY: 1, ANSWER: 1,
;; AUTHORITY: 4, ADDITIONAL: 4

;; QUESTION SECTION:
;ftp.hq.nasa.gov. IN A

;; ANSWER SECTION:
ftp.hq.nasa.gov. 86400 IN A 198.116.65.46

;; AUTHORITY SECTION:
hq.nasa.gov. 86400 IN NS ns3.hq.nasa.gov.
hq.nasa.gov. 86400 IN NS mx.nsi.nasa.gov.
hq.nasa.gov. 86400 IN NS ns1.hq.nasa.gov.
hq.nasa.gov. 86400 IN NS ns2.hq.nasa.gov.

;; ADDITIONAL SECTION:
ns3.hq.nasa.gov. 86400 IN A 198.116.65.241
mx.nsi.nasa.gov. 3600 IN A 128.102.18.31
ns1.hq.nasa.gov. 86400 IN A 131.182.230.28
ns2.hq.nasa.gov. 86400 IN A 131.182.1.28

;; Query time: 290 msec
;; SERVER: 128.102.18.31#53(mx.nsi.nasa.gov)
;; WHEN: Tue Apr 23 22:09:43 2002
;; MSG SIZE rcvd: 188
```

15

9. Look at the SERVER line, third from the bottom. This identifies which name server responded to the query. See if you can locate this address in the ADDITIONAL section.

   What is the host name of the responding name server?

10. Look in the AUTHORITY section. Is the responding name server listed as being authoritative for the hq.nasa.gov domain?

   What does this process tell you about the quality of the information you just obtained? How could you use this process if you were seeing unexpected results from standard DNS operations?

11. Log off.

HANDS-ON PROJECTS

Project 15-7

In this project, you experiment with e-mail aliases and sendmail. To complete this project, you should have Linux installed, with root access to the system. For simplicity's sake, the directory names referred to are specific to Red Hat Linux and Fedora, but most distributions should use the same location for the files named.

1. Log in to Linux, open a command-line window, and change to root access.

2. View the mail log using this command (this will occupy this text window for the duration of this project):

```
tail -f /var/log/maillog
```

3. Use a text editor to add the following lines to the end of the /etc/aliases file:

```
supervisor:root
spam:/tmp/spamcan
```

4. Save the file, then execute the following command:

```
newaliases
```

5. Use a mail program to send a message to the address "supervisor". The following command is one way to do this, sending the contents of a text file as the body of the message:

```
mail -s "testing aliases" supervisor < /etc/syslog.conf
```

6. Watch the window where the maillog is displayed. When you see a line indicating that your message has been delivered, open an e-mail reading program to see that the message addressed to supervisor was delivered to root.

7. Send another e-mail message to spam. An example command to do this is shown here:

```
mail -s "still testing aliases" spam </etc/syslog.conf
```

8. Watch the window where the maillog is displayed to see when the message has been delivered by sendmail.

9. Look in the /tmp directory to see whether the spamcan file was created.

10. Enter the command **mailstats** to see a summary of activity for your sendmail server. Have any messages been discarded (see the msgsdis column)? If not, what happened to the message addressed to spam? Log off.

Project 15-8

In this project, you create a boot disk and start your computer using it. To complete this project you must have a working Linux system with root access, a blank 3.5-inch disk, and Internet access.

1. Log in to Linux.

2. Start your Web browser using an icon on the panel or a menu item.

3. Enter **www.toms.net/rb** in the Address bar of the browser and then press **Enter**. The tomsrtbt Web page appears.

4. Click the link to download **tomsrtbt**.

5. Click on one of the mirror sites. After a moment, you see a list of files.

6. Click on the file **tomsrtbt-2.0.103.tar.gz** or whatever the latest version of the file is named. When prompted, save the file on your hard disk and note the location where you saved it. (Using /tmp is a good choice.)

7. Uncompress the file you just downloaded. Read the tomsrtbt.FAQ file and note the installation instructions.

```
tar xvzf /tmp/tomsrtbt-2.0.103.tar.gz
```

8. Following the instructions in the tomsrtbt.FAQ file, change to the appropriate directory by entering **cd /tomsrtbt**, then type **./install.s** at the command prompt and follow the onscreen directions to install the program.

9. Shut down your Linux system.

10. With the floppy disk inserted, restart your system. The boot disk should load the operating system and eventually display a login prompt.

11. Log in as root. The onscreen instructions will tell you that a password is needed and what the password is.

12. You are now logged in to a real Linux operating system. Feel free to explore the file system and utilities included with this single-disk version of Linux.

13. When you have finished experimenting, remove the 3.5-inch disk and restart the system. Your regular Linux system returns.

15

CASE PROJECTS

**CASE
PROJECTS**

The Future of Network Security

1. One of the biggest legal clients of Snow, Sleet & Hale is an energy company that runs an oil pipeline across the Alaskan wilderness. Recently, a group of antiglobalization protesters traveled cross-country to a remote part of the pipeline and sabotaged it, then made the resulting oil spill public. Snow, Sleet & Hale are handling the lawsuit against the protest group for property damage and cleanup costs. At the same time, they are trying to press criminal charges and handle the public relations disaster while the energy company cleans up the oil spill.

   Because of the law firm's involvement and public exposure in this case, protesters from various antiglobalization groups around the world have started attacking the law firm's servers. You have just noticed this activity.

   What do you think the protesters' goals are in attacking the systems? Is it too late to use a security-auditing tool? What possible attacks or vulnerabilities are you most concerned about? Which concern you the least? What actions might you take with your network configurations, services, or daily practices to help you weather this attack? How long would you remain in "siege mode"? What are the main costs and disadvantages of operating in constant expectation of a serious attack? (Consider the benefits and disadvantages to you as system administrator as well as monetary costs to the firm and to end-users on the firm's networks.)

2. As it turns out, one of the legal secretaries working in the Fairbanks office is a secret supporter of the largest antiglobalization protest group. Though he doesn't participate in the demonstrations for fear of losing his job, he appears to feel he can contribute to the cause by making your networks more vulnerable to the cyberattacks.

   What parts of your well-designed security policy protect your networks from this employee? If he attempts to attack the network from inside the firm, can your safeguards detect his actions and protect against them? How can you protect the networks against internal attackers without excessively reducing ease of use for everyone and without creating a working environment so overburdened with paranoia that no one wants to work at your firm?

3. The dust settles, the protesters depart, the lawsuits begin (they won't be over for many years), and your success in dealing with this difficult situation comes to the attention of a number of people through stories in computer trade magazines. As a result, you are asked to join a Presidential Commission run in cooperation with the National Infrastructure Protection Center (see *www.nipc.gov*) and The SANS Institute. The commission will study the current landscape of network security and future trends affecting corporate and governmental risks created by the increased use of networks around the world.

As an industry luminary, your first task is to prepare brief remarks for a hearing before the Senate Select Committee on Intelligence (see *www.intelligence.senate.gov*).

The special committee would like to hear: (a) what you feel should be the greatest network security concerns of corporations and government organizations based on current technologies; (b) what new security-related technologies are in the wings and their possible effects on corporate and government security efforts; (c) how international efforts to standardize security protocols and strengthen encryption technologies may affect the work of the U.S. intelligence community (e.g., the C.I.A.); (d) what government action, if any, you would recommend to make computer networks more secure in the future. (You may want to review the list of statements made to Congress by the NIPC. See *www.nipc.gov/pressroom/pressroom2.htm*.)

15

RED HAT CERTIFIED TECHNICIAN OBJECTIVES

This appendix contains objectives for the Red Hat Certified Technician (RHCT) program. The objectives listed here are based on outlines of the two courses that Red Hat Software recommends you take to prepare yourself to pass the RHCT exam. The exam is administered only by Red Hat Software and its affiliated testing centers. Visit *www.redhat.com/training* to locate a testing center and sign up to take the RHCT exam.

More advanced certifications are also offered by Red Hat Software, including the Red Hat Certified Engineer program (RHCE) and the Red Hat Certified Architect program (RHCA). The two courses referred to in this Appendix, 033 and 133, are also part of the curriculum for these more advanced certifications.

OBJECTIVES BASED ON COURSE RH 033—RED HAT LINUX ESSENTIALS

Unit 1: Overview

Description of Objectives	Location in This Book (Chapter, Heading)
UNIX History and Principles	Chapter 1, "A Brief History"
GNU Project, FSF, and the GPL	Chapter 1, "A Brief History"
Linux Origins and Benefits	Chapter 1, "A Brief History"
Red Hat Offerings	Chapter 1, "Linux in the Market"
Recommended Hardware Requirements	Chapter 8, "Reviewing Your Computer's Hardware"
Logging in	Chapter 1, "Starting to Use Linux"
Running Commands	Chapter 1, "Starting to Use Linux" and "Exploring the File System"
Red Hat Graphical Environments	Chapter 2, "Linux Graphical Desktops"

Unit 2: Command-line File System Browsing

Description of Objectives	Location in This Book (Chapter, Heading)
Linux File Hierarchy Concepts	Chapter 1, "Exploring the File System" Chapter 4, "Introducing the File System"
Current Working Directory	Chapter 1, "Exploring the File System"
Changing Directories	Chapter 1, "Exploring the File System"
Listing Directory Contents	Chapter 1, "Exploring the File System"
The Home Directory	Chapter 1, "Exploring the File System"
Absolute Pathnames	Chapter 1, "Exploring the File System"
Relative Pathnames	Chapter 1, "Exploring the File System"
File Names	Chapter 1, "Exploring the File System"
Copying Files and Directories	Chapter 1, "Exploring the File System"
Copying Files and Directories: The Destination	Chapter 1, "Exploring the File System"
Moving and Renaming Files and Directories	Chapter 1, "Exploring the File System"
Moving and Renaming Files and Directories: The Destination	Chapter 1, "Exploring the File System"
Removing and Creating Files	Chapter 1, "Exploring the File System"
Creating and Removing Directories	Chapter 1, "Exploring the File System"
Viewing an Entire Text File	Chapter 1, "Exploring the File System"
Viewing Files One Screenful at a Time	Chapter 1, "Exploring the File System"
slocate	Chapter 1, "Exploring the File System"
Getting Help: man pages	Chapter 1, "Finding Command Help"
Other Help Utilities	Chapter 1, "Finding Command Help"

Unit 3: GNOME and KDE Desktops

Description of Objectives	Location in This Book (Chapter, Heading)
The X Window System	Chapter 2, "Linux Graphical Desktops" Chapter 15, "X Window System Advanced Configuration"
GNOME and KDE	Chapter 2, "Configuring GNOME and KDE"
Starting XFree86	Chapter 2, "Linux Graphical Desktops" Chapter 15, "X Window System Advanced Configuration"
Switching Between GNOME and KDE	Chapter 2, "Configuring GNOME and KDE"
The nautilus File Manager	Chapter 2, "Core Graphical Utilities"
Graphical Terminals, Editors, and Browsers	Chapter 2, "Core Graphical Utilities"
OpenOffice.org Office Suite	Chapter 2, "Popular Graphical Programs"
Useful Keystrokes in X	Chapter 2, "Linux Graphical Desktops" Chapter 15, "X Window System Advanced Configuration"

Unit 4: The Bash Shell

Description of Objectives	Location in This Book (Chapter, Heading)
Shell History	Chapter 3, "Exploring the Bash Shell"
Command Line Shortcuts	Chapter 3, "Exploring the Bash Shell"
Command Line Expansion and Protecting from Expansion	Chapter 3, "Exploring the Bash Shell"
Command Line History and Editing Tricks	Chapter 3, "Exploring the Bash Shell"

Unit 5: Users, Groups, and Permissions

Description of Objectives	Location in This Book (Chapter, Heading)
Users, Groups, and the root User	Chapter 4, "Linux Users and Groups"
The Linux Security Model: File and Process Security	Chapter 4, "File Permissions" Chapter 15, "Security Issues"
Examining Permissions	Chapter 4, "File Permissions"
File Permission Types	Chapter 4, "File Permissions"
Changing Permissions: Symbolic and Numeric Methods	Chapter 4, "File Permissions"

Unit 6: vi and vim Editor Basics and Printing

Description of Objectives	Location in This Book (Chapter, Heading)
Starting vi and vim	Chapter 3, "Editing Text with vi" Chapter 5, "More Advanced Text Editing"
Three Modes of vi and vim	Chapter 3, "Editing Text with vi"

Description of Objectives	Location in This Book (Chapter, Heading)
Cursor Movement	Chapter 3, "Editing Text with vi"
Entering and Leaving Insert Mode	Chapter 3, "Editing Text with vi"
Changing, Deleting, Yanking, and Putting Text	Chapter 3, "Editing Text with vi"
Undoing Changes	Chapter 3, "Editing Text with vi" Chapter 5, "More Advanced Text Editing"
Searching for Text	Chapter 5, "More Advanced Text Editing"
Saving and Exiting	Chapter 3, "Editing Text with vi" Chapter 5, "More Advanced Text Editing"
Printing in Linux	Chapter 3, "Printing from the Command Line" Chapter 12, "Networked Printing Services"

Unit 7: The Linux File System

Description of Objectives	Location in This Book (Chapter, Heading)
Partitions and Filesystems	Chapter 4, "Introducing the File System" Chapter 8, "Reviewing Your Computer's Hardware" Chapter 10, "Understanding the File System"
Inodes, Directories, and the cp, mv, and rm Commands	Chapter 4, "Introducing the File System"
Symbolic Links and Hard Links	Chapter 4, "Introducing the File System"
The Seven Fundamental Filetypes	Chapter 4, "Introducing the File System"
Checking Free Space	Chapter 4, "Introducing the File System"
Finding and Processing Files	Chapter 4, "Introducing the File System"
Mounting Removable Media	Chapter 4, "Introducing the File System"
Formatting a Floppy	Chapter 4, "Introducing the File System"
Archiving Files	Chapter 4, "Managing File Archives"
Compressing Files	Chapter 4, "Managing File Archives"
Compressing Archives	Chapter 4, "Managing File Archives"
tar to Unformatted Floppies	Chapter 4, "Managing File Archives" Chapter 13, "Backing up a Linux System"

Unit 8: Configuring GNOME, KDE, and X-based Tools

Description of Objectives	Location in This Book (Chapter, Heading)
A Layered Vision of the X Window System	Chapter 2, "Linux Graphical Desktops" Chapter 15, "X Window System Advanced Configuration"
Window Managers	Chapter 2, "Linux Graphical Desktops" Chapter 15, "X Window System Advanced Configuration"

A

Description of Objectives	Location in This Book (Chapter, Heading)
The GNOME and KDE Control Centers	Chapter 2, "Configuring GNOME and KDE"
The panel Application	Chapter 2, "Configuring GNOME and KDE"
Configuring nautilus and gnome-terminal	Chapter 2, "Core Graphical Utilities"
Saving Desktop Configuration Across Logins	Chapter 2, "Configuring GNOME and KDE"
X-based E-mail Clients and Configuring evolution	Chapter 2, "Popular Graphical Programs"

Unit 9: The Bash Shell and Configuration

Description of Objectives	Location in This Book (Chapter, Heading)
The bash Shell and Configuration	Chapter 3, "Exploring the Bash Shell"
Variables	Chapter 3, "Shell Variables"
Configuring the Shell: Local Variables	Chapter 3, "Shell Variables"
Common Local Variables	Chapter 3, "Shell Variables"
Aliases	Chapter 3, "Exploring the Bash Shell"
Other Shell Configuration Methods	Chapter 3, "Exploring the Bash Shell"
Configuring Commands: Environment Variables	Chapter 3, "Shell Variables"
Common Environment Variables	Chapter 3, "Shell Variables"
The TERM and PATH Environment Variable	Chapter 3, "Shell Variables"
How the Shell Expands the Command Line	Chapter 3, "Exploring the Bash Shell"
Shell Startup Scripts	Chapter 3, "Exploring the Bash Shell-"Chapter 14, "Scripting Basics"
Login Shells	Chapter 4, "Linux Users and Groups" Chapter 11, "Creating and Managing User Accounts"

Unit 10: Advanced Topics in Users, Groups, and Permissions

Description of Objectives	Location in This Book (Chapter, Heading)
User and Group ID Numbers	Chapter 4, "Linux Users and Groups" Chapter 11, "Creating and Managing User Accounts"
/etc/passwd, /etc/shadow, and /etc/group Files	Chapter 4, "Linux Users and Groups" Chapter 11, "Creating and Managing User Accounts"
System Users and Groups	Chapter 4, "Linux Users and Groups"
Changing Your Identity	Chapter 4, "Linux Users and Groups"
User Information Commands	Chapter 4, "Linux Users and Groups"
Default File Permissions	Chapter 4, "File Permissions"
Special Permissions	Chapter 11, "Complex File Permissions"

Unit 11: Advanced Uses of the vi and vim Editors

Description of Objectives	Location in This Book (Chapter, Heading)
File and Screen Repositioning	Chapter 5, "More Advanced Text Editing"
Filtering	Chapter 5, "More Advanced Text Editing"
Search and Replace	Chapter 5, "More Advanced Text Editing"
Advanced Reading and Saving	Chapter 5, "More Advanced Text Editing"
Configuring vi and vim	Chapter 5, "More Advanced Text Editing"
Expanding Your Vocabulary	Chapter 5, "More Advanced Text Editing"

Unit 12: Standard I/O and Pipes

Description of Objectives	Location in This Book (Chapter, Heading)
Redirecting Input, Output, and Error	Chapter 3, "Data Redirection"
Overwriting or Appending	Chapter 3, "Data Redirection"
Using Pipes to Connect Processes	Chapter 3, "Data Redirection"
The tee Command	Chapter 3, "Data Redirection"
Piping into the mail Command	Chapter 3, "Data Redirection"

Unit 13: Introduction to String Processing

Description of Objectives	Location in This Book (Chapter, Heading)
Showing the Beginning and End of Files	Chapter 5, "Manipulating Files"
Counting Words, Lines, and Characters	Chapter 5, "Manipulating Files"
Sorting Data	Chapter 5, "Manipulating Files"
Printing Unique Lines of Files	Chapter 5, "Manipulating Files"
Rearranging Columns and Fields	Chapter 5, "Manipulating Files"
Version Comparison	Chapter 5, "Manipulating Files"
Spell Checking	Chapter 5, "Manipulating Files"
Formatting Tools	Chapter 5, "Manipulating Files"

Unit 14: String Processing with Regular Expressions

Description of Objectives	Location in This Book (Chapter, Heading)
Pattern Matching with Regular Expressions	Chapter 5, "Regular Expressions"
Wildcards, Modifiers, and Anchors	Chapter 5, "Regular Expressions"
Regular Expressions in Combinations	Chapter 5, "Regular Expressions"
Searching for Patterns in Files	Chapter 5, "Manipulating Files"
Modifying Streams of Data	Chapter 5, "Manipulating Files"
Regular Expressions in Pagers and Editors	Chapter 5, "Manipulating Files"
Extended Regular Expressions	Chapter 5, "Regular Expressions"
Using awk	Chapter 5, "Using sed and awk"

Unit 15: Introduction to Processes

A

Description of Objectives	Location in This Book (Chapter, Heading)
What is a Process?	Chapter 6, "Defining Processes"
How Processes Are Created: Process Ancestry	Chapter 6, "Defining Processes"
Process States	Chapter 6, "Defining Processes"
Viewing Processes	Chapter 6, "Managing Linux Processes"
Sending Signals to Processes	Chapter 6, "Managing Linux Processes"
Terminating Processes	Chapter 6, "Managing Linux Processes"
Altering Process Scheduling Priority	Chapter 6, "Managing Linux Processes"
Running a Process in the Foreground and Background	Chapter 6, "Managing Linux Processes"
Suspending a Process	Chapter 6, "Managing Linux Processes"
Listing and Resuming Background and Suspended Jobs	Chapter 6, "Managing Linux Processes"
Compound Commands	Chapter 6, "Managing Linux Processes"
Scheduling a Process to Execute Later	Chapter 6, "Scheduling Processes"
Scheduling Periodic Processes	Chapter 6, "Scheduling Processes"

Unit 16: Bash Shell Scripting

Description of Objectives	Location in This Book (Chapter, Heading)
Scripting Basics	Chapter 14, "Scripting Basics"
Creating Shell Scripts	Chapter 14, "Scripting Basics"
Making Scripts Executable	Chapter 14, "Scripting Basics"
Generating Output	Chapter 14, "Input and Output"
Handling Input	Chapter 14, "Input and Output"
Using Positional Parameters	Chapter 14, "Input and Output"
Using Functions in Shell Scripts	Chapter 14, "Conditional and Looping Structures"
Exit Status	Chapter 14, "Scripting Basics"
File and String Tests	Chapter 14, "Conditional and Looping Structures"
Control Structures and Conditional Execution	Chapter 14, "Conditional and Looping Structures"
Selection Structures: if and case Statements	Chapter 14, "Conditional and Looping Structures"
Repetition Structures: for and while Loops	Chapter 14, "Conditional and Looping Structures"
Breaking Out of Loops	Chapter 14, "Conditional and Looping Structures"
Shell Script Debugging	Chapter 14, "Shell Script Debugging"

Unit 17: Basic Networking Clients

Description of Objectives	Location in This Book (Chapter, Heading)
Logging into Remote Computers Securely	Chapter 7, "Remote Login"
Secure Network Copying	Chapter 7, "Remote Login"

Description of Objectives	Location in This Book (Chapter, Heading)
Insecure Protocols: telnet and the "r" Service	Chapter 7, "Remote Login"
FTP, Web, and Email Clients	Chapter 7, "Data Services" Chapter 15, "Using Network Services"
Keeping Files Synchronized Across the Network	Chapter 7, "Data Services"
Mirroring Web Sites	Chapter 7, "Data Services"
Network Diagnostic Tools	Chapter 7, "Networking and Network Diagnostic Tools" Chapter 15, "Using Network Services"

Unit 18: Programming and Administration

Description of Objectives	Location in This Book (Chapter, Heading)
Programming Tools	Chapter 14, "Other Programming Methods"
Programming Languages	Chapter 14, "Other Programming Methods"
Integrated Development Environment (IDE)	Chapter 14, "Other Programming Methods"
Red Hat Programming Classes	Chapter 14, "Other Programming Methods"
System Administrator Duties	Chapter 1, "The Work of a System Administrator"
Red Hat Administration Classes	Chapter 1, "Linux in the Market"

OBJECTIVES BASED ON COURSE RH 133—RED HAT LINUX SYSTEM ADMINISTRATION

Unit 1: Hardware, Device Configuration, and Installation

Description of Objectives	Location in This Book (Chapter, Heading)
Hardware Compatibility and Resources	Chapter 8, "Reviewing Your Computer's Hardware"
CPU and Memory	Chapter 8, "Reviewing Your Computer's Hardware"
Filesystem Device Nodes and Device Node Table	Chapter 8, "Reviewing Your Computer's Hardware"
Block Device Support	Chapter 8, "Reviewing Your Computer's Hardware"
System and Hot-swappable Bus Support	Chapter 8, "Reviewing Your Computer's Hardware"
Peripheral Device Ports	Chapter 8, "Reviewing Your Computer's Hardware"
Laptops	Chapter 8, "Reviewing Your Computer's Hardware"

A

Description of Objectives	Location in This Book (Chapter, Heading)
Console and Graphics	Chapter 8, "Reviewing Your Computer's Hardware"
Disk Partitioning	Chapter 8, "Reviewing Your Computer's Hardware"
Block Devices and Filesystem Schemes	Chapter 8, "Reviewing Your Computer's Hardware" Chapter 10, "Understanding the File System"
Red Hat Installer Features	Chapter 8, "Installing Linux"
Red Hat Linux Installation	Chapter 8, "Installing Linux"
Partitioning Hard Drives	Chapter 8, "Installing Linux"
Configuring Software RAID at Installation	Chapter 13, "Backing up a Linux System"
Configuring Flexible Filesystems with LVM	Chapter 13, "Backing up a Linux System"
Network Configuration and Firewall Setup	Chapter 8, "Installing Linux" Chapter 15, "Using Network Services"
Package Selection	Chapter 8, "Installing Linux" Chapter 10, "Managing Packages"
Validating the Installation	Chapter 8, "Installing Linux"
Serial Console Installation	Chapter 15, "Troubleshooting and Recovery"
Noprobe Mode	Chapter 15, "Troubleshooting and Recovery"
Driver Disks	Chapter 8, "Configuring Disk Space" (these disks are not used in Fedora)
Post-Install Configuration	Chapter 8, "Installing Linux"

Unit 2: Linux File System Management

Description of Objectives	Location in This Book (Chapter, Heading)
System Initialization: Device Recognition	Chapter 9, "Hardware Initialization"
Managing Partitions	Chapter 10, "Understanding the File System"
Filesystem Basics and Attributes	Chapter 10, "Understanding the File System"
Filesystem Creation	Chapter 10, "Understanding the File System"
Ext3: Journaling for Ext2 Filesystems	Chapter 10, "Understanding the File System"
ReiserFS and JFS	Chapter 10, "Understanding the File System"
The Filesystem Hierarchy	Chapter 1, "Exploring the File System"
Mount options and configuration	Chapter 10, "Understanding the File System"
Connecting Network Resources	Chapter 10, "Understanding the File System" Chapter 15, "Using Network Services"
Unmounting Filesystems	Chapter 4, "Introducing the File System" Chapter 10, "Understanding the File System"
The Auto-Mounter	Chapter 10, "Understanding the File System"
Virtual Memory Files	Chapter 10, "Understanding the File System"
Filesystem Maintenance	Chapter 10, "Understanding the File System"

Description of Objectives	Location in This Book (Chapter, Heading)
Determining Filesystem Usage	Chapter 4, "Introducing the File System" Chapter 10, "Understanding the File System"
Adding a Drive	Chapter 10, "Understanding the File System"

Unit 3: System Initialization and Services

Description of Objectives	Location in This Book (Chapter, Heading)
BIOS Initialization	Chapter 9, "Hardware Initialization"
The Boot Sequence	Chapter 9, "Hardware Initialization"
The Boot Loader	Chapter 9, "Hardware Initialization"
Kernel Initialization	Chapter 9, "Hardware Initialization" Chapter 13, "Exploring Kernel Components"
init Initialization	Chapter 9, "init and its Scripts"
Run Levels	Chapter 9, "init and its Scripts"
Daemon Processes	Chapter 9, "init and its Scripts"
The rc.sysinit Script	Chapter 9, "init and its Scripts"
System V Run Levels	Chapter 9, "init and its Scripts"
The rc.local Script	Chapter 9, "init and its Scripts"
Virtual Consoles	Chapter 9, "init and its Scripts"
System Shutdown and Reboot	Chapter 9, "Controlling Services"
Controlling Services	Chapter 9, "Controlling Services"

Unit 4: User Administration

Description of Objectives	Location in This Book (Chapter, Heading)
User Policy Considerations	Chapter 4, "Linux Users and Groups" Chapter 15, "Security Issues"
The User Account Database	Chapter 4, "Linux Users and Groups" Chapter 11, "Creating and Managing User Accounts"
Adding a New User Account	Chapter 11, "Creating and Managing User Accounts"
Modifying/Deleting Accounts	Chapter 11, "Creating and Managing User Accounts"
Password Aging Policies	Chapter 4, "Linux Users and Groups" Chapter 11, "Creating and Managing User Accounts"
Authentication Configuration	Chapter 4, "Linux Users and Groups" Chapter 11, "User Security Issues" Chapter 15, "Security Issues"
NIS Configuration	Chapter 8, "Installing Linux" Chapter 11, "User Security Issues"
Group Administration	Chapter 4, "Linux Users and Groups" Chapter 11, "Creating and Managing User Accounts"
Switching Accounts	Chapter 4, "Linux Users and Groups"
File Ownership	Chapter 4, "Linux Users and Groups"
Linux File Permission	Chapter 4, "File Permissions"
SUID / SGID Executables	Chapter 11, "Complex File Permissions"

A

Description of Objectives	Location in This Book (Chapter, Heading)
The Sticky Bit and Setgid Access Mode	Chapter 11, "Complex File Permissions"
Default File Permissions	Chapter 4, "File Permissions"
User Private Groups	Chapter 4, "Linux Users and Groups"

Unit 5: Network Configuration

Description of Objectives	Location in This Book (Chapter, Heading)
Network Device Recognition	Chapter 7, "Network and Network Diagnostic Tools"
Network Interfaces	Chapter 7, "Network and Network Diagnostic Tools" Chapter 8, "Installing Linux" Chapter 15, "Using Network Services"
Address Resolution Protocol	Chapter 15, "Using Network Services"
Bringing Network Interfaces Up and Down	Chapter 15, "Using Network Services"
Interface Configuration Files	Chapter 7, "Network and Network Diagnostic Tools" Chapter 15, "Using Network Services"
Configuration Utilities	Chapter 7, "Network and Network Diagnostic Tools" Chapter 15, "Using Network Services"
Multiple NICs	Chapter 15, "Using Network Services"
Binding Multiple IP Addresses	Chapter 15, "Using Network Services"
DHCP/BOOTP	Chapter 15, "Using Network Services"
Allowing User Control of Network Interfaces	Chapter 11, "User Security Issues"
Basic IP Routes	Chapter 15, "Using Network Services"
System Default Route	Chapter 15, "Using Network Services"
IP Forwarding	Chapter 15, "Using Network Services"
Global Network Parameters	Chapter 8, "Installing Linux"
Name Resolution	Chapter 7, "Network and Network Diagnostic Tools" Chapter 8, "Installing Linux" Chapter 15, "Using Network Services"
DNS Client Configuration	Chapter 7, "Network and Network Diagnostic Tools" Chapter 15, "Using Network Services"
DNS and Network Diagnostics and Troubleshooting	Chapter 15, "Using Network Services"

Unit 6: System Administration Tools

Description of Objectives	Location in This Book (Chapter, Heading)
Using the Alternatives System	Chapter 12, "Networked Printing Services"
The Print System User Interface	Chapter 12, "Networked Printing Services"
LPRng/CUPS Configuration	Chapter 12, "Networked Printing Services"
LPRng/CUPS Queue Management	Chapter 12, "Networked Printing Services"
Task Automation With at and cron	Chapter 6, "Scheduling Processes"
Controlling Access to Task Automation	Chapter 6, "Scheduling Processes"

Description of Objectives	Location in This Book (Chapter, Heading)
crontab format	Chapter 6, "Scheduling Processes"
System crontab Files	Chapter 6, "Scheduling Processes"
Using anacron	Chapter 6, "Scheduling Processes"
Using tmpwatch	Chapter 6, "Scheduling Processes"
Configuring, Maintaining, and Montoring System Logs	Chapter 13, "System Logs"
Managing the whatis Database	Chapter 1, "Finding Command Help"
System Monitoring and Process Control	Chapter 6, "Scheduling Processes"
Tape Backups	Chapter 13, "Backing up a Linux System"
Archiving with tar, dump/restore, and cpio	Chapter 4, "Managing File Archives" Chapter 13, "Backing up a Linux System"
Remote Backups	Chapter 13, "Backing up a Linux System"

Unit 7: RPM, Boot Loaders, and Kickstart

Description of Objectives	Location in This Book (Chapter, Heading)
Installing and Removing Software with RPM	Chapter 10, "Managing Packages"
RPM Queries and Verification	Chapter 10, "Managing Packages"
RPM Utilities and Features	Chapter 10, "Managing Packages"
Red Hat Network in the Enterprise	Chapter 10, "Updating the System Automatically"
Red Hat Network Registration	Chapter 10, "Updating the System Automatically"
The up2date utility	Chapter 10, "Updating the System Automatically"
Remote Administration	Chapter 10, "Updating the System Automatically"
Boot Loader Components	Chapter 9, "Configuring Boot Loaders"
LILO and lilo.conf	Chapter 9, "Configuring Boot Loaders"
GRUB and grub.conf	Chapter 9, "Configuring Boot Loaders"
Starting the Boot Process	Chapter 9, "Configuring Boot Loaders"
Multiboot Systems	Chapter 8, "Configuring Disk Space" Chapter 9, "Configuring Boot Loaders"
Configuring a Red Hat Linux Network Installation Server	Chapter 8, "Installing Linux" Chapter 15, "Using Network Services"
Using Kickstart to Automate Installation	Chapter 8, "Kickstart Installations"
The Kickstart Configuration File	Chapter 8, "Kickstart Installations"

A

Unit 8: Kernel Services and Configuration

Description of Objectives	Location in This Book (Chapter, Heading)
Kernel Modules and Their Configuration	Chapter 13, "Exploring Kernel Components"
Updating a Kernel RPM	Chapter 10, "Managing Packages" Chapter 13, "Configuring and Upgrading Kernel Components"
The /proc Filesystem	Chapter 13, "Exploring Kernel Components"
/proc/sys Configuration with sysctl	Chapter 13, "Exploring Kernel Components"
The Linux Quota System	Chapter 10, "Understanding the File System"
Software RAID Configuration and Recovery	Chapter 13, "Backing up a Linux System"
Flexible Filesystems with LVM	Chapter 13, "Backing up a Linux System"

Unit 9: The X Window System

Description of Objectives	Location in This Book (Chapter, Heading)
The X Protocol	Chapter 15, "X Window System Advanced Configuration"
X Security	Chapter 15, "X Window System Advanced Configuration"
xauth with ssh	Chapter 15, "X Window System Advanced Configuration"
X Modularity	Chapter 2, "Linux Graphical Desktops" Chapter 15, "X Window System Advanced Configuration"
X Extensibility	Chapter 15, "X Window System Advanced Configuration"
Window Managers	Chapter 2, "Linux Graphical Desktops" Chapter 15, "X Window System Advanced Configuration"
Display Managers	Chapter 2, "Linux Graphical Desktops" Chapter 15, "X Window System Advanced Configuration"
XFree86 Startup	Chapter 15, "X Window System Advanced Configuration"
X Server Configuration	Chapter 15, "X Window System Advanced Configuration"
The X Font Server	Chapter 15, "X Window System Advanced Configuration"

Unit 10: Troubleshooting

Description of Objectives	Location in This Book (Chapter, Heading)
Troubleshooting X	Chapter 15, "Troubleshooting and Recovery"
Troubleshooting Services	Chapter 15, "Troubleshooting and Recovery"
Troubleshooting Networking	Chapter 15, "Troubleshooting and Recovery"
Troubleshooting Boot Problems	Chapter 15, "Troubleshooting and Recovery"
Filesystem Corruption and Recovery	Chapter 10, "Understanding the File System" Chapter 15, "Troubleshooting and Recovery"
Recovery Run Levels	Chapter 9, "init and its Scripts"
Boot Floppies	Chapter 15, "Troubleshooting and Recovery"
Rescue Environment Utilities	Chapter 15, "Troubleshooting and Recovery"
Rescue Environment Details	Chapter 15, "Troubleshooting and Recovery"

B

LINUX PROFESSIONAL INSTITUTE LPI CERTIFICATION—LEVEL 1 OBJECTIVES

This appendix contains the official testing objectives for the Linux Professional Institute (LPI) Certification, Level 1—LPIC 1, Junior Level Administrator (see *www.lpi.org*). This certification requires that you pass two exams (numbered 101 and 102). More advanced LPI certifications—LPIC 2 and LPIC 3—are also available or planned.

Many (though not all) of the objectives covered in the LPIC 2 and LPIC 3 advanced certifications are discussed in this book. Only objectives for LPIC 1 are included in this appendix. Additional information on advanced topics is available in a companion book, *Guide to Linux Networking and Security* (ISBN 0-619-00094-5).

In the charts that follow, a weight is assigned to each objective. The weights range from 1 to 10; a higher weight indicates that the topic will be covered by more exam questions. The numbering of the objectives is not consecutive (for example, the first two objectives are 1.101.1 and 1.101.3). This is because of changes in the objectives from their original release. The information here reflects the latest available version at the time of this writing.

OBJECTIVES FOR EXAM 101

Topic 101 Hardware and Architecture

1.101.1 Configure Fundamental BIOS Settings

Weight	Description of Objective	Location in This Book (Chapter, Heading)
1	Candidates should be able to configure fundamental system hardware by making the correct settings in the system BIOS. This objective includes a proper understanding of BIOS configuration issues such as the use of LBA on IDE hard disks larger than 1024 cylinders, enabling or disabling integrated peripherals, as well as configuring systems with (or without) external peripherals such as keyboards. It also includes the correct setting for IRQ, DMA, and I/O addresses for all BIOS administrated ports and settings for error handling. Key files, terms, and utilities include: /proc/ioports, /proc/interrupts, /proc/dma, /proc/pci	Chapter 8, "Reviewing Your Computer's Hardware" and "Installing Linux"
		Chapter 15, "Troubleshooting and Recovery"

1.101.3 Configure Modem and Sound Cards

Weight	Description of Objective	Location in This Book (Chapter, Heading)
1	Candidates should ensure devices meet compatibility requirements (particularly that the modem is NOT a win modem), verify that both the modem and sound card are using unique and correct IRQs, I/O, and DMA addresses; if the sound card is PnP install and run sndconfig and isapnp, configure modem for outbound dial-up, configure modem for outbound PPP	SLIP	CSLIP connection, set serial port for 115.2 Kbps.	Chapter 8, "Reviewing Your Computer's Hardware"
		Chapter 15, "Troubleshooting and Recovery"

B

1.101.4 Set up SCSI Devices

Weight	Description of Objective	Location in This Book (Chapter, Heading)
1	Candidates should be able to configure SCSI devices using the SCSI BIOS as well as the necessary Linux tools. They also should be able to differentiate between the various types of SCSI. This objective includes manipulating the SCSI BIOS to detect used and available SCSI IDs and setting the correct ID number for different devices, especially the boot device. It also includes managing the settings in the computer's BIOS to determine the desired boot sequence if both SCSI and IDE drives are used. Key files, terms, and utilities include: SCSI ID, /proc/scsi/, scsi_info.	Chapter 8, "Reviewing Your Computer's Hardware" Chapter 13, "Exploring Kernel Components" Chapter 15, "Troubleshooting and Recovery"

1.101.5 Set up Different PC Expansion Cards

Weight	Description of Objective	Location in This Book (Chapter, Heading)
3	Candidates should be able to configure various cards for the various expansion slots. They should know the differences between ISA and PCI cards with respect to configuration issues. This objective includes the correct settings of IRQs, DMAs, and I/O ports of the cards, especially to avoid conflicts between devices. It also includes using isapnp if the card is an ISA PnP device. Key files, terms, and utilities include: /proc/dma, /proc/interrupts, /proc/ioports, /proc/pci, pnpdump(8), isapnp(8), lspci(8).	Chapter 8, "Reviewing Your Computer's Hardware" Chapter 13, "Exploring Kernel Components" Chapter 15, "Troubleshooting and Recovery"

1.101.6 Configure Communication Devices

Weight	Description of Objective	Location in This Book (Chapter, Heading)
1	Candidates should be able to install and configure different internal and external communication devices like modems, ISDN adapters, and DSL switches. This objective includes verification of compatibility requirements (especially important if the modem is a winmodem), necessary hardware settings for internal devices (IRQs, DMAs, I/O ports), and loading and configuring suitable device drivers. It also includes communication device and interface configuration requirements, such as the right serial port for 115.2 Kbps, and the correct modem settings for outbound PPP connection(s). Key files, terms, and utilities include: /proc/dma, /proc/interrupts, /proc/ioports, setserial(8).	Chapter 8, "Reviewing Your Computer's Hardware" Chapter 13, "Exploring Kernel Components" Chapter 15, "Troubleshooting and Recovery"

1.101.7 Configure USB Devices

Weight	Description of Objective	Location in This Book (Chapter, Heading)
1	Candidates should be able to activate USB support, and use and configure different USB devices. This objective includes the correct selection of the USB chipset and the corresponding module. It also includes the knowledge of the basic architecture of the layer model of USB as well as the different modules used in the different layers. Key files, terms, and utilities include: lspci(8), usb-uhci.o, usb-ohci.o, /etc/usbmgr/, usbmodules, /etc/hotplug.	Chapter 8, "Reviewing Your Computer's Hardware"
		Chapter 13, "Exploring Kernel Components"
		Chapter 15, "Troubleshooting and Recovery"

Topic 102 Linux Installation and Package Management

1.102.1 Design Hard Disk Layout

Weight	Description of Objective	Location in This Book (Chapter, Heading)
5	Candidates should be able to design a disk partitioning scheme for a Linux system. This objective includes allocating filesystems or swap space to separate partitions or disks, and tailoring the design to the intended use of the system. It also includes placing /boot on a partition that conforms with the BIOS' requirements for booting. Key files, terms, and utilities include: / (root) filesystem, /var file system, /home filesystem, swap space, mount points, partitions, cylinder 1024.	Chapter 8, "Configuring Disk Space"
		Chapter 10, "Understanding the File System"

1.102.2 Install a Boot Manager

Weight	Description of Objective	Location in This Book (Chapter, Heading)
1	Candidates should be able to select, install, and configure a boot manager. This objective includes providing alternative boot locations and backup boot options (for example, using a boot floppy). Key files, terms, and utilities include: /etc/lilo.conf, /boot/grub/grub.conf, lilo, grub-install, MBR, superblock, first stage boot loader.	Chapter 8, "Installing Linux"
		Chapter 9, "Configuring Boot Loaders"

1.102.3 Make and Install Programs from Source

Weight	Description of Objective	Location in This Book (Chapter, Heading)
5	Candidates should be able to build and install an executable program from source. This objective includes being able to unpack a file of sources. Candidates should be able to make simple customizations to the Makefile, for example changing paths or adding extra include directories. Key files, terms, and utilities include: gunzip, gzip, bzip2, tar, configure, make.	Chapter 14, "Other Programming Methods"

1.102.4 Manage Shared Libraries

Weight	Description of Objective	Location in This Book (Chapter, Heading)
3	Candidates should be able to determine the shared libraries that executable programs depend on and install them when necessary. Candidates should be able to state where system libraries are kept. Key files, terms, and utilities include: ldd, ldconfig, /etc/ld.so.conf, LD_LIBRARY_PATH.	Chapter 6, "Managing Memory"

1.102.5 Use Debian Package Management

Weight	Description of Objective	Location in This Book (Chapter, Heading)
8	Candidates should be able to perform Debian package management. This objective includes being able to use command-line and interactive tools to install, upgrade, or uninstall packages, as well as find packages containing specific files or software (such packages might or might not be installed). This objective also includes being able to obtain package information like version, content, dependencies, package integrity and installation status (whether or not the package is installed). Key files, terms, and utilities include: unpack, configure, /etc/dpkg/dpkg.cfg, /var/lib/dpkg/*, /etc/apt/apt.conf, /etc/apt/sources.list, dpkg, dselect, dpkg-reconfigure, apt-get, alien.	Chapter 10, "Managing Packages"

B

1.102.6 Use Red Hat Package Manager (RPM)

Weight	Description of Objective	Location in This Book (Chapter, Heading)
8	Candidates should be able to perform package management under Linux distributions that use RPMs for package distribution. This objective includes being able to install, reinstall, upgrade, and remove packages, as well as obtain status and version information on packages. This objective also includes obtaining package information such as version, status, dependencies, integrity, and signatures. Candidates should be able to determine what files a package provides, as well as find which package a specific file comes from. Key files, terms, and utilities include: /etc/rpmrc, /usr/lib/rpm/*, rpm, grep.	Chapter 10, "Managing Packages"

Topic 103 GNU and UNIX Commands

1.103.1 Work on the Command Line

Weight	Description of Objective	Location in This Book (Chapter, Heading)
5	Candidates should be able to interact with shells and commands using the command line. This includes typing valid commands and command sequences; defining, referencing, and exporting environment variables; using command history and editing facilities; invoking commands in the path and outside the path; using command substitution; applying commands recursively through a directory tree; and using man to find out about commands. Key files, terms, and utilities include: bash, echo, env, exec, export, man, pwd, set, unset, ~/.bash_history, ~/.profile.	Chapter 1, "Starting to Use Linux" and "Exploring the File System"
		Chapter 3, throughout

1.103.2 Process Text Streams Using Filters

Weight	Description of Objective	Location in This Book (Chapter, Heading)
6	Candidates should be able to apply filters to text streams. Tasks include sending text files and output streams through text utility filters to modify the output, and using standard UNIX commands found in the GNU textutils package. Key files, terms, and utilities include: cat, cut, expand, fmt, head, join, nl, od, paste, pr, sed, sort, split, tac, tail, tr, unexpand, uniq, wc.	Chapter 5, "Manipulating Files"

B

1.103.3 Perform Basic File Management

Weight	Description of Objective	Location in This Book (Chapter, Heading)
3	Candidates should be able to use the basic UNIX commands to copy, move, and remove files and directories. Tasks include advanced file management operations such as copying multiple files recursively, removing directories recursively, and moving files that meet a wildcard pattern. This includes using simple and advanced wildcard specifications to refer to files, as well as using find to locate and act on files based on type, size, or time. Key files, terms, and utilities include: cp, find, mkdir, mv, ls, rm, rmdir, touch, file globbing.	Chapter 1, "Exploring the File System"
		Chapter 4, "Introducing the File System"
		Chapter 5, "Regular Expressions"

1.103.4 Use Streams, Pipes, and Redirects

Weight	Description of Objective	Location in This Book (Chapter, Heading)
5	Candidates should be able to redirect streams and connect them in order to process textual data efficiently. Tasks include redirecting standard input, standard output, and standard error, piping the output of one command to the input of another command, using the output of one command as arguments to another command, and sending output to both stdout and a file. Key files, terms, and utilities include: tee, xargs, <, <<, >, >>, |, ' '.	Chapter 3, "Data Redirection"

1.103.5 Create, Monitor, and Kill Processes

Weight	Description of Objective	Location in This Book (Chapter, Heading)
5	Candidates should be able to manage processes. This includes knowing how to run jobs in the foreground and background, bringing a job from the background to the foreground and vice versa, starting a process that will run without being connected to a terminal, and signaling a program to continue running after logout. Tasks also include monitoring active processes, selecting and sorting processes for display, sending signals to processes, killing processes, and identifying and killing X applications that did not terminate after the X session closed. Key files, terms, and utilities include: &, bg, fg, jobs, kill, nohup, ps, top.	Chapter 6, "Defining Processes" and "Managing Linux Processes"

1.103.6 Modify Process Execution Priorities

Weight	Description of Objective	Location in This Book (Chapter, Heading)
3	Candidates should be able to manage process execution priorities. Tasks include running a program with higher or lower priority, determining the priority of a process, and changing the priority of a running process. Key files, terms, and utilities include: nice, ps, renice, top.	Chapter 6, "Managing Linux Processes"

1.103.7 Search Text Files Using Regular Expressions

Weight	Description of Objective	Location in This Book (Chapter, Heading)
3	Candidates should be able to manipulate files and text data using regular expressions. This objective includes creating simple regular expressions containing several notational elements. It also includes using regular expression tools to perform searches through a file system or file content. Key files, terms, and utilities include: grep, regexp, sed.	Chapter 5, "Manipulating Files"

1.103.8 Perform Basic File-editing Operations Using vi

Weight	Description of Objective	Location in This Book (Chapter, Heading)
1	Candidates must be able to edit text files using vi. This objective includes vi navigation, basic vi nodes, inserting, editing,	Chapter 3, "Editing Text with vi"
	deleting, copying, and finding text. Key files, terms, and utilities include: vi, /, ?, h, j, k, l, G, H, L, i, c, d, dd, p, o, a, ZZ, :w!, :q!, :e!, :!.	Chapter 5, "More Advanced Text Editing"

Topic 104 Devices, Linux File Systems, and File System Hierarchy Standard

B

1.104.1 Create Partitions and File Systems

Weight	Description of Objective	Location in This Book (Chapter, Heading)
3	Candidates should be able to configure disk partitions and then create file systems on media such as hard disks. This objective includes using various mkfs commands to set up partitions to various file systems, including ext2,ext3, reiserfs, vfat, and xfs. Key files, terms, and utilities include: fdisk, mkfs.	Chapter 4, "Introducing the File System"
		Chapter 8, "Configuring Disk Space"
		Chapter 10, "Understanding the File System"

1.104.2 Maintain the Integrity of File Systems

Weight	Description of Objective	Location in This Book (Chapter, Heading)
3	Candidates should be able to verify the integrity of file systems, monitor free space and inodes, and repair simple file system problems. This objective includes the commands required to maintain a standard file system, as well as the extra data associated with a journaling file system. Key files, terms, and utilities include: du, df, fsck, e2fsck, mke2fs, debugfs, dumpe2fs, tune2fs.	Chapter 10, "Understanding the File System"

1.104.3 Control Mounting and Unmounting File Systems

Weight	Description of Objective	Location in This Book (Chapter, Heading)
3	Candidates should be able to configure the mounting of a file system. This objective includes the ability to manually mount and unmount file systems, configure file system mounting on bootup, and configure user-mountable removable file systems such as tape drives, floppies, and CDs. Key files, terms, and utilities include: /etc/fstab, mount, umount.	Chapter 4, "Introducing the File System"
		Chapter 10, "Understanding the File System"

1.104.4 Managing Disk Quotas

Weight	Description of Objective	Location in This Book (Chapter, Heading)
3	Candidates should be able to manage disk quotas for users. This objective includes setting up a disk quota for a file system, editing, checking, and generating user quota reports. Key files, terms, and utilities include: quota, edquota, repquota, quotaon.	Chapter 10, "Understanding the File System"

1.104.5 Use File Permissions to Control Access to Files

Weight	Description of Objective	Location in This Book (Chapter, Heading)
5	Candidates should be able to control file access through permissions. This objective includes access permissions on regular and special files as well as directories. Also included are access modes such as suid, sgid, and the sticky bit, the use of the group field to grant file access to workgroups, the immutable flag, and the default file creation mode. Key files, terms, and utilities include: chmod, umask, chattr.	Chapter 4, "File Permissions"
		Chapter 11, "Complex File Permissions"

1.104.6 Manage File Ownership

Weight	Description of Objective	Location in This Book (Chapter, Heading)
1	Candidates should be able to control user and group ownership of files. This objective includes the ability to change the user and group owner of a file as well as the default group owner for new files. Key files, terms, and utilities include: chmod, chown, chgrp.	Chapter 4, "File Permissions"

1.104.7 Create and Change Hard and Symbolic Links

Weight	Description of Objective	Location in This Book (Chapter, Heading)
1	Candidates should be able to create and manage hard and symbolic links to a file. This objective includes the ability to create and identify links, copy files through links, and use linked files to support system administration tasks. Key files, terms, and utilities include: ln.	Chapter 4, "Introducing the File System"

B

1.104.8 Find System Files and Place Files in the Correct Location

Weight	Description of Objective	Location in This Book (Chapter, Heading)
5	Candidates should be thoroughly familiar with the File System Hierarchy Standard, including typical file locations and directory classifications. This objective includes the ability to find files and commands on a Linux system. Key files, terms, and utilities include: find, locate, slocate, updatedb, whereis, which, /etc/updatedb.conf.	Chapter 1, "Exploring the File System" and "Finding Command Help"

Topic 110 The X Window System

1.110.1 Install and Configure XFree86

Weight	Description of Objective	Location in This Book (Chapter, Heading)
5	Candidates should be able to configure and install X and an X font server. This objective includes verifying that the video card and monitor are supported by an X server, as well as customizing and tuning X for the video card and monitor. It also includes installing an X font server, installing fonts, and configuring X to use the font server (may require a manual edit of /etc/X11/XF86Config in the "Files" section). Key files, terms, and utilities include:XF86Setup, xf86config, xvidtune, /etc/X11/XF86Config, .Xresources.	Chapter 2, "Linux Graphical Desktops"
		Chapter 15, "X Window System Advanced Configuration"

1.110.2 Set up a Display Manager

Weight	Description of Objective	Location in This Book (Chapter, Heading)
3	Candidates should be able set up and customize a display manager. This objective includes turning the display manager on or off and changing the display manager greeting. This objective includes changing default bitplanes for the display manager. It also includes configuring display managers for use by X stations. This objective covers the display managers XDM (X Display Manager), GDM (Gnome Display Manager), and KDM (KDE Display Manager). Key files, terms, and utilities include: /etc/inittab, /etc/X11/xdm/*, /etc/X11/kdm/*, /etc/X11/gdm/*.	Chapter 2, "Linux Graphical Desktops"
		Chapter 15, "X Window System Advanced Configuration"

1.110.4 Install and Customize a Window Manager Environment

Weight	Description of Objective	Location in This Book (Chapter, Heading)
5	Candidates should be able to customize a system-wide desktop environment and/or window manager, to demonstrate an understanding of customization procedures for window manager menus and/or desktop panel menus. This objective includes selecting and configuring the desired X terminal (xterm, rxvt, aterm etc.), verifying and resolving library dependency issues for X applications, and exporting X display to a client workstation. Key files, terms, and utilities include: .xinitrc, .Xdefaults, xhost, DISPLAY environment variable.	Chapter 2, "Linux Graphical Desktops"
		and "Configuring GNOME and KDE"
		Chapter 15, "X Window System Advanced Configuration"

OBJECTIVES FOR EXAM 102

Topic 105 Kernel

1.105.1 Manage/Query Kernel and Kernel Modules at Runtime

Weight	Description of Objective	Location in This Book (Chapter, Heading)
4	Candidates should be able to manage and/or query a kernel and kernel-loadable modules. This objective includes using command-line utilities to get information about the currently running kernel and kernel modules. It also includes manually loading and unloading modules as appropriate. It also includes being able to determine when modules can be unloaded and what parameters a module accepts. Candidates should be able to configure the system to load modules by names other than their file name. Key files, terms, and utilities include: /lib/modules/kernel-version/modules.dep, /etc/modules.conf & /etc/conf.modules, depmod, insmod, lsmod, rmmod, modinfo, modprobe, uname.	Chapter 13, "Exploring Kernel Components"

B

1.105.2 Reconfigure, Build, and Install a Custom Kernel and Kernel Modules

Weight	Description of Objective	Location in This Book (Chapter, Heading)
3	Candidates should be able to customize, build, and install a kernel and kernel-loadable modules from source. This objective includes customizing the current kernel configuration, building a new kernel, and building kernel modules as appropriate. It also includes installing the new kernel as well as any modules, and ensuring that the boot manager can locate the new kernel and associated files (generally located under /boot, see objective 1.102.2 for more details about boot manager configuration). Key files, terms, and utilities include: /usr/src/linux/*, /usr/src/linux/.config, /lib/modules/kernel-version/*, /boot/*; make, make targets, config, menuconfig, xconfig, oldconfig, modules, install, modules_install, depmod.	Chapter 13, "Configuring and Upgrading Kernel Components"

Topic 106 Boot, Initialization, Shutdown, and Run Levels

1.106.1 Boot the System

Weight	Description of Objective	Location in This Book (Chapter, Heading)
3	Candidates should be able to guide the system through the booting process. This includes giving commands to the boot loader and giving options to the kernel at boot time, and checking the events in the log files. Key files, terms, and utilities include: dmesg, /var/log/messages, /etc/conf.modules or /etc/modules.conf, LILO, GRUB.	Chapter 9, "Hardware Initialization" and "Configuring Boot Loaders"
		Chapter 13, "Exploring Kernel Components"

1.106.2 Change Run Levels and Shut Down or Reboot System

Weight	Description of Objective	Location in This Book (Chapter, Heading)
3	Candidates should be able to manage the run level of the system. This objective includes changing to single-user mode, shutdown, or rebooting the system. Candidates should be able to alert users before switching run level, and properly terminate processes. This objective also includes setting the default run level. Key files, terms, and utilities include: shutdown, init, /etc/inittab.	Chapter 9, "init and its Scripts"

Topic 107 Printing

1.107.2 Manage Printers and Print Queues

Weight	Description of Objective	Location in This Book (Chapter, Heading)
1	The candidates should be able to manage print queues and user print jobs. This objective includes monitoring print server and user print queues and troubleshooting general printing problems. Key files, terms, and utilities include: lpc, lpq, lprm, lpr, /etc/printcap	Chapter 3, "Printing from the Command Line"
		Chapter 12, "Networked Printing Services"

1.107.3 Print Files

Weight	Description of Objective	Location in This Book (Chapter, Heading)
1	Candidates should be able to manage print queues and manipulate print jobs. This objective includes adding and removing jobs from configured printer queues and converting text files to PostScript for printing. Key files, terms, and utilities include: lpr, lpq, mpage.	Chapter 3, "Printing from the Command Line"
		Chapter 12, "Networked Printing Services"

1.107.4 Install and Configure Local and Remote Printers

Weight	Description of Objective	Location in This Book (Chapter, Heading)
1	Candidates should be able to install a printer daemon, and install and configure a print filter (e.g., apsfilter, magicfilter). This objective includes making local and remote printers accessible for a Linux system, including PostScript, non-PostScript, and Samba printers. Key files, terms, and utilities include: lpd, /etc/printcap, /etc/apsfilter/*, /var/lib/apsfilter/*/, /etc/magicfilter/*/, /var/spool/lpd/*/.	Chapter 3, "Printing from the Command Line"
		Chapter 12, "Networked Printing Services"

Topic 108 Documentation

1.108.1 Use and Manage Local System Documentation

B

Weight	Description of Objective	Location in This Book (Chapter, Heading)
4	Candidates should be able to use and administer the man facility and the material in /usr/share/doc/. This objective includes finding relevant man pages, searching man page sections, finding commands and man pages related to them, and configuring access to man sources and the man system. It also includes using system documentation stored in /usr/share/doc/ and determining what documentation to keep in /usr/share/doc/. Key commands and terms: man, apropos, whatis, MANPATH.	Chapter 1, "Finding Command Help"

1.108.2 Find Linux Documentation on the Internet

Weight	Description of Objective	Location in This Book (Chapter, Heading)
3	Candidates should be able to find and use Linux documentation. This objective includes using Linux documentation at sources such as the Linux Documentation Project (LDP), vendor and third-party Web sites, newsgroups, newsgroup archives, and mailing lists.	Chapter 1, "Finding Command Help"

1.108.5 Notify Users on System-related Issues

Weight	Description of Objective	Location in This Book (Chapter, Heading)
1	Candidates should be able to notify users about current issues related to the system. This objective includes automating the communication process, e.g., through login messages. Key files, terms, and utilities include: /etc/issue, /etc/issue.net, /etc/motd.	Chapter 11, "User Security Issues"

Topic 109 Shells, Scripting, Programming, and Compiling

1.109.1 Customize and Use the Shell Environment

Weight	Description of Objective	Location in This Book (Chapter, Heading)
5	Candidates should be able to customize shell environments to meet users' needs. This objective includes setting environment variables (e.g., PATH) at login or when spawning a new shell. It also includes writing bash functions for frequently used sequences of commands. Key files, terms, and utilities include: ~/.bash_profile, ~/.bash_login, ~/.profile, ~/.bashrc, ~/.bash_logout, ~/.inputrc, function (Bash built-in command), export, env, set (Bash built-in command), unset (Bash built-in command).	Chapter 3, "Exploring the Bash Shell" and "Shell Variables"

1.109.2 Customize or Write Simple Scripts

Weight	Description of Objective	Location in This Book (Chapter, Heading)
3	Candidates should be able to customize existing scripts, or write simple new (ba)sh scripts. This objective includes using standard sh syntax (loops, tests), using command substitution, testing command return values, testing of file status, and conditional mailing to the superuser. This objective also includes making sure the correct interpreter is called on the first (#!) line of scripts. This objective also includes managing location, ownership, execution, and suid-rights of scripts. Key files, terms, and utilities include: while, for, test, chmod.	Chapter 14, "Scripting Basics," "Input and Output," "Conditional and Looping Structures," and "Shell Script Debugging"

Topic 111 Administrative Tasks

1.111.1 Manage Users and Group Accounts and Related System Files

Weight	Description of Objective	Location in This Book (Chapter, Heading)
4	Candidates should be able to add, remove, suspend, and change user accounts. Tasks include to add and remove groups, and to change user/group info in passwd/group databases. This objective also includes creating special purpose and limited accounts. Key files, terms, and utilities include: chage, gpasswd, groupadd, groupdel, groupmod, grpconv, grpunconv, passwd, pwconv, pwunconv, useradd, userdel, usermod, /etc/passwd, /etc/shadow, /etc/group, /etc/gshadow.	Chapter 11, "Creating and Managing User Accounts"

1.111.2 Tune the User Environment and System Environment Variables

Weight	Description of Objective	Location in This Book (Chapter, Heading)
3	Candidates should be able to modify global and user profiles. This includes setting environment variables, maintaining skel directories for new user accounts, and setting the command search path with the proper directory. Key files, terms, and utilities include: env, export, set, unset, /etc/profile, /etc/skel.	Chapter 3, "Shell Variables"
		Chapter 11, "Creating and Managing User Accounts"

1.111.3 Configure and Use System Log Files to Meet Administrative and Security Needs

Weight	Description of Objective	Location in This Book (Chapter, Heading)
3	Candidates should be able to configure system logs. This objective includes managing the type and level of information logged, manually scanning log files for notable activity, monitoring log files, arranging for automatic rotation and archiving of logs, and tracking down problems noted in logs. Key files, terms, and utilities include: logrotate, tail -f, /etc/syslog.conf, /var/log/*.	Chapter 13, "System Logs"

1.111.4 Automate System Administration Tasks by Scheduling Jobs to Run in the Future

Weight	Description of Objective	Location in This Book (Chapter, Heading)
4	Candidates should be able to use cron or anacron to run jobs at regular intervals and to use at to run jobs at a specific time. Tasks include managing cron and at jobs and configuring user access to cron and at services. Key files, terms, and utilities include: at, atq, atrm, crontab, /etc/anacrontab, /etc/at.deny, /etc/at.allow, /etc/crontab, /etc/cron.allow, /etc/cron.deny, /var/spool/cron/*.	Chapter 6, "Scheduling Processes"

1.111.5 Maintain an Effective Data Backup Strategy

Weight	Description of Objective	Location in This Book (Chapter, Heading)
3	Candidates should be able to plan a backup strategy and backup file systems automatically to various media. Tasks include dumping a raw device to a file or vice versa, performing partial and manual backups, verifying the integrity of backup files and partially or fully restoring backups. Key files, terms, and utilities include: cpio, dd, dump, restore, tar.	Chapter 13, "Backing Up a Linux System"

1.111.6 Maintain System Time

Weight	Description of Objective	Location in This Book (Chapter, Heading)
4	Candidates should be able to properly maintain the system time and synchronize the clock over NTP. Tasks include setting the system date and time, setting the BIOS clock to the correct time in UTC, configuring the correct time zone for the system and configuring the system to correct clock drift to match NTP clock. Key files, terms, and utilities include: date, hwclock, ntpd, ntpdate, /usr/share/zoneinfo, /etc/timezone, /etc/localtime, /etc/ntp.conf, /etc/ntp.drift.	Chapter 13, "Exploring Kernel Components"

Topic 112 Networking Fundamentals

1.112.1 Fundamentals of TCP/IP

Weight	Description of Objective	Location in This Book (Chapter, Heading)
4	Candidates should demonstrate a proper understanding of network fundamentals. This objective includes the understanding of IP addresses, network masks, and what they mean (i.e., determine a network and broadcast address for a host based on its subnet mask in "dotted quad" or abbreviated notation, or determine the network address, broadcast address, and netmask when given an IP address and number of bits). It also	Chapter 7, "Networking and Network Diagnostic Tools"
	covers the understanding of the network classes and classless subnets (CIDR) and the reserved addresses for private network use. It includes the understanding of the function and application of a default route. It also includes the understanding of	Chapter 8, "Installing Linux"
	basic Internet protocols (IP, ICMP, TCP, UDP) and the more common TCP and UDP ports (20, 21, 23, 25, 53, 80, 110, 119, 139, 143, 161). Key files, terms, and utilities include: /etc/services, ftp, telnet, host, ping, dig, traceroute, whois.	Chapter 12, "Configuring Linux Networking"

1.112.3 TCP/IP Configuration and Troubleshooting

Weight	Description of Objective	Location in This Book (Chapter, Heading)
7	Candidates should be able to view, change, and verify configuration settings and operational status for various network interfaces. This objective includes manual and automatic configuration of interfaces and routing tables. This especially means to add, start, stop, restart, delete, or reconfigure network interfaces. It also means to change, view, or configure the routing table and to correct an improperly set default route manually. Candidates should be able to configure Linux as a DHCP client and a TCP/IP host and to debug problems associated with the network configuration. Key files, terms, and utilities include: /etc/HOSTNAME or /etc/hostname, /etc/hosts, /etc/networks, /etc/host.conf, /etc/resolv.conf, /etc/nsswitch. conf, ifconfig, route, dhcpcd, dhcpclient, pump, host, hostname (domainname, dnsdomainname), netstat, ping, traceroute, tcpdump, the network scripts run during system initialization.	Chapter 7, "Networking and Network Diagnostic Tools" Chapter 8, "Installing Linux" Chapter 12, "Configuring Linux Networking" Chapter 15, "Troubleshooting and Recovery"

1.112.4 Configure Linux as a PPP Client

Weight	Description of Objective	Location in This Book (Chapter, Heading)
3	Candidates should understand the basics of the PPP protocol and be able to configure and use PPP for outbound connections. This objective includes the definition of the chat sequence to connect (given a login example) and the setup commands to be run automatically when a PPP connection is made. It also includes initialization and termination of a PPP connection, with a modem, ISDN, or ADSL, and setting PPP to reconnect automatically if disconnected. Key files, terms, and utilities include: /etc/ppp/options.*, /etc/ppp/peers/*, /etc/wvdial.conf, /etc/ppp/ip-up, /etc/ppp/ip-down, wvdial, pppd.	Chapter 12, "Configuring Linux Networking" Chapter 15, "Using Network Services"

B

Topic 113 Networking Services

1.113.1 Configure and Manage inetd, xinetd, and Related Services

Weight	Description of Objective	Location in This Book (Chapter, Heading)
4	Candidates should be able to configure which services are available through inetd, use tcpwrappers to allow or deny services on a host-by-host basis, manually start, stop, and restart Internet services, and configure basic network services including Telnet and FTP. Set a service to run as another user instead of the default in inetd.conf. Key files, terms, and utilities include: /etc/inetd.conf, /etc/hosts.allow, /etc/hosts.deny, /etc/services, /etc/xinetd.conf, /etc/xinetd.log.	Chapter 15, "Using Network Services"

1.113.2 Operate and Perform Basic Configuration of sendmail

Weight	Description of Objective	Location in This Book (Chapter, Heading)
4	Candidates should be able to modify simple parameters in sendmail configuration files (including the "Smart Host" parameter, if necessary), create mail aliases, manage the mail queue, start and stop sendmail, configure mail forwarding, and perform basic troubleshooting of sendmail. This objective includes checking for and closing open relays on the mail server. It does not include advanced custom configuration of sendmail. Key files, terms, and utilities include: /etc/sendmail.cf, /etc/aliases or /etc/mail/aliases, /etc/mail/*, ~/.forward, mailq, sendmail, newaliases.	Chapter 15, "Using Network Services"

1.113.3 Operate and Perform Basic Configuration of Apache

Weight	Description of Objective	Location in This Book (Chapter, Heading)
4	Candidates should be able to modify simple parameters in Apache configuration files, start, stop, and restart httpd, and arrange for automatic restarting of httpd upon boot. Does not include advanced custom configuration of Apache. Key files, terms, and utilities include: apachectl, httpd, httpd.conf.	Chapter 15, "Using Network Services"

B

1.113.4 Properly Manage the NFS, smb, and nmb Daemons

Weight	Description of Objective	Location in This Book (Chapter, Heading)
4	Candidates should know how to mount remote file systems using NFS, configure NFS for exporting local file systems, start, stop, and restart the NFS server. Install and configure Samba using the included GUI tools or direct edit of the /etc/smb.conf file (Note: this deliberately excludes advanced NT domain issues but includes simple sharing of home directories and printers, as well as correctly setting the nmbd as a WINS client). Key files, terms, and utilities include: /etc/exports, /etc/fstab, /etc/smb.conf, mount, umount.	Chapter 15, "Using Network Services"

1.113.5 Set up and Configure Basic DNS Services

Weight	Description of Objective	Location in This Book (Chapter, Heading)
4	Candidates should be able to configure hostname lookups and troubleshoot problems with local caching-only name server. Requires an understanding of the domain registration and DNS translation process. Requires understanding key differences in configuration files for bind 4 and bind 8. Key files, terms, and utilities include: /etc/hosts, /etc/resolv.conf, /etc/nsswitch.conf, /etc/named.boot (v.4) or /etc/named.conf (v.8), named.	Chapter 12, "Configuring Linux Networking"
		Chapter 15, "Using Network Services"

1.113.7 Set up Secure Shell (OpenSSH)

Weight	Description of Objective	Location in This Book (Chapter, Heading)
4	Candidates should be able to obtain and configure OpenSSH. This objective includes basic OpenSSH installation and troubleshooting, as well as configuring sshd to start at system boot. Key files, terms, and utilities include: /etc/hosts.allow, /etc/hosts.deny, /etc/nologin, /etc/ssh/sshd_config, /etc/ssh_known_hosts, /etc/sshrc, sshd, ssh-keygen.	Chapter 7, "Remote Login"
		Chapter 15, "Using Network Services"

Topic 114 Security

1.114.1 Perform Security Administration Tasks

Weight	Description of Objective	Location in This Book (Chapter, Heading)
4	Candidates should know how to review system configuration to ensure host security in accordance with local security policies. This objective includes how to configure TCPwrappers, find files with SUID/SGID bit set, verify packages, set or change user passwords and password aging information, and update binaries as recommended by CERT, BUGTRAQ, and/or distribution's security alerts. Includes basic knowledge of ipchains and iptables. Key files, terms, and utilities include: /proc/net/ip_fwchains, /proc/net/ip_fwnames, /proc/net/ip_masquerade, find, ipchains, passwd socket, iptables.	Chapter 15, "Security Issues" and "Using Network Services"

1.114.2 Set up Host Security

Weight	Description of Objective	Location in This Book (Chapter, Heading)
3	Candidates should know how to set up a basic level of host security. Tasks include syslog configuration, shadowed passwords, setup of a mail alias for root's mail, and turning off all network services not in use. Key files, terms, and utilities include: /etc/inetd.conf or /etc/inet.d/*, /etc/nologin, /etc/passwd, /etc/shadow, /ets/syslog.conf.	Chapter 11, "Creating and Managing User Accounts" and "User Security Issues"
		Chapter 13, "System Logs"
		Chapter 15, "Security Issues"

1.114.3 Set up User-level Security

Weight	Description of Objective	Location in This Book (Chapter, Heading)
1	Candidates should be able to configure user-level security. Tasks include limits on user logins, processes, and memory usage. Key files, terms, and utilities include: quota, usermod.	Chapter 10, "Understanding the File System"
		Chapter 11, "Creating and Managing User Accounts"and "User Security Issues"

SAIR/GNU CERTIFIED LINUX ADMINISTRATOR (LCA) LEVEL 1 OBJECTIVES

This appendix contains the official testing objectives for the SAIR/GNU Linux Certified Administrator (LCA), Level 1. These objectives are called competencies, and are available online, with additional information about the SAIR/GNU LCA certification program, at *www.linuxcertification.org*. This certification requires you to pass four exams: Installation, Administration, Networking, and Security. Not all of the requirements for the Networking and Security examinations are covered in this book, but most are covered at least sufficiently to familiarize you with the concepts you need to know. Additional detail on these advanced topics can be found in a companion Course Technology book, *Guide to Linux Networking and Security* (ISBN 0-619-00094-5).

In the tables that follow, a chapter and heading reference is normally provided only for each third-level heading (for example, 1.1.10). The reader should assume that headings at a more granular level (for example, 1.1.50.1.d) are included in the most recently provided reference at the third-level heading.

NOTE

Although every effort has been made to provide timely and relevant information in this book to ensure that the reader will be prepared to pass all applicable certification exams, please note that the competencies provided here, though taken directly from the SAIR/GNU Web site, refer in many cases to older technologies that are no longer available on the market. Familiarity with similar current technology should enable the test taker to easily pass each exam.

NOTE

The numbering in the competencies listed here is not consecutive in all cases. No competencies are missing—the numbering appearing on the SAIR/GNU site is also not consecutive.

Course 3X0-101—Linux Installation and Configuration

1.1 Theory of Operation

Competency	Location in This Book (Chapter, Heading)
1.1.10 History of Open Source and Free Software	**Chapter 1, "A Brief History" and "Linux in the Market"**
1.1.10.1 Describe the historical trends in free software	
1.1.10.2 Define the cost of free software	
1.1.10.3 Describe the advantages and disadvantages of free software	
1.1.20 The GNU General Public License (GPL)	**Chapter 1, "A Brief History" and "Linux in the Market"**
1.1.20.1 Briefly explain the history of the GNU GPL	
1.1.20.2 Define the use of copyright to enforce copyleft	
1.1.30 Third-party Analysis of open source software	
1.1.30.1 Describe the Microsoft Halloween memos and conclusions	
1.1.40 Living with Free Software	**Chapter 1, "Linux in the Market" and "The Work of a System Administrator"**
1.1.40.1 Describe the nature of free software development	
1.1.40.2 Explain the business of selling free software	
1.1.40.3 Compare and contrast free software warranty issues with those of proprietary software	
1.1.50 Linux System Concepts	*See below*
1.1.50.1 Explain the modular structure of Linux	Chapter 1, "A Brief History"
1.1.50.1.a Describe the modular concepts of the Linux kernel	Chapter 13, "Exploring Kernel Components"
1.1.50.1.b Explain the modular nature of the Linux networking subsystem	Chapter 12, "Configuring Linux Networking"
1.1.50.1.c Describe the role of the init process in Linux	Chapter 9, "init and its Scripts"

Competency	Location in This Book (Chapter, Heading)
1.1.50.1.d Describe the role of daemons in the Linux operating system	Chapter 9, "init and its Scripts"
1.1.50.1.e Explain how user-level processes are different from kernel-level processes	Chapter 6, "Defining Processes"
1.1.50.1.f Describe the modular components of the X Windows System and how they relate to Linux as a whole	Chapter 15, "X Window System Advanced Configuration"
1.1.60 Mainboard Configuration Issues	**Chapter 8, "Reviewing Your Computer's Hardware" and "Installing Linux" Chapter 13, "Exploring Kernel Components"**
1.1.60.1 Describe the IBM-PC Bus System Architecture	
1.1.60.1.a Identify and describe the various system busses	
1.1.60.1.b Explain the procedure for configuring a peripheral's I/O addresses	
1.1.60.1.c Explain the procedure for configuring a peripheral's IRQs	
1.1.60.1.d Describe DMA or Shared memory	
1.1.60.2 Identify RAM requirements and configuration issues given specific system usage scenarios	
1.1.60.3 Given the appropriate criteria, determine settings for the PCBIOS, the kernel, and peripheral devices	
1.1.60.5 Peripheral Configuration Issues	
1.1.60.5.1 Identify the need for primary or extended partitions and configure them appropriately	
1.1.60.5.2 Identify the need for multi-boot systems and configure them appropriately	
1.1.60.5.3 Describe issues that may affect installation with legacy CD-ROM controllers	
1.1.60.5.4 Describe the process for locating a supported graphics adapter and configuring it appropriately	
1.1.60.5.5 Define resolution and its relationship with video memory	
1.1.60.5.6 Describe refresh rates and the trade-offs with resolutions	
1.1.60.5.7 Identify the characteristics of the monitor and configure the graphics adapter appropriately	
1.1.60.5.8 Identify the need for vendor maintenance floppies and use them to properly configure adapter cards	
1.1.70 Network Configuration	**Chapter 8, "Reviewing Your Computer's Hardware" and "Installing Linux" Chapter 12, "Configuring Linux Networking"**
1.1.70.1 Identify and configure the correct IP address	
1.1.70.2 Identify and configure the correct Network Mask	
1.1.70.3 Identify and configure the correct Gateway	
1.1.70.4 Identify and configure the correct Domain Name Service (DNS) addresses	

C

1.2 Base System

Competency	Location in This Book (Chapter, Heading)
1.2.10 Installation Media	**Chapter 8, "Installing Linux" Chapter 15, "Using Network Services"**
1.2.10.1 Describe installation procedures using CD-ROM media	
1.2.10.2 Describe installation procedures using sources mounted on an MS-DOS partition	
1.2.10.3 Describe installation procedures using floppy disks	
1.2.10.4 Describe installation procedures using sources remotely mounted through FTP	
1.2.10.5 Describe installation procedures using sources remotely mounted through NFS	
1.2.10.6 Describe installation procedures using sources remotely accessible with Samba	
1.2.20 Component Compatibility and Configuration Responsibilities	**Chapter 8, "Understanding Your Computer's Hardware"**
1.2.20.1 Identify components that are supported by default configurations of Linux	
1.2.30 Describe Six Linux Distributions and Their Tradeoffs	**Chapter 1, "Linux in the Market"**
1.2.40 Installation of Linux	**Chapter 8, throughout**
1.2.40.1 Describe proper hard disk allocation strategies	
1.2.40.2 Describe the steps common to all Linux installations	
1.2.40.3 Use fdisk or a similar utility to create partitions	
1.2.40.4 Configure boot loaders, such as LILO	
1.2.40.5 Configure network parameters during the installation process	
1.2.40.6 Configure the X Windows System during the installation process	
1.2.50 Compare and Contrast Six Different Distributions of Linux	**Chapter 1, "Linux in the Market"**
1.2.60 Start Up and Shut Down Sequences	**Chapter 9, "Hardware Initialization" and "Controlling Services"**
1.2.60.1 Describe and configure the Linux Loader (LILO)	
1.2.60.2 Describe bootup kernel initialization and the init process	
1.2.60.3 Identify the different run levels and describe the differences between them	
1.2.60.4 Describe the process of logging in and logging out	
1.2.60.5 Describe the process that should be used to shut down a Linux system	
1.2.70 File System Hierarchy	**Chapter 1, "Exploring the File System" Chapter 4, "Introducing the File System"**
1.2.70.1 Describe the traditional UNIX file system layout	
1.2.70.2 Describe the procedure for mounting and un-mounting file systems	
1.2.70.3 List the considerations when mounting removable media	
1.2.70.4 Explain the advantages of the MTOOLS suite for quick access to floppy drives	
1.2.70.5 Describe and give usage examples of file system abstractions (/dev, /proc)	
1.2.80 Basic System Navigation	**Chapter 1, "Starting to Use Linux" and "Exploring the File System" Chapter 2, "Linux Graphical Desktops"**
1.2.80.1 Describe case sensitivity	

C

Competency	Location in This Book (Chapter, Heading)
1.2.80.2 Describe the use of the cd and ls commands	
1.2.80.2.a Describe file permissions	
1.2.80.3 Determine which programs are running (ps command)	
1.2.80.4 Demonstrate process management (kill, nice, etc.)	
1.2.80.5 Determine who is using the system (w and who commands)	
1.2.80.6 Describe proper use of the superuser account	
1.2.80.7 Start an X11 display or window manager (e.g., kdm & KDE)	
1.2.80.8 Describe the X Window System initialization files	
1.2.80.9 Describe the X Window System Graphical User Interface	
1.2.80.9.a The virtual display	
1.2.80.9.b X Window scrollbars	
1.2.80.9.c X Window resize	
1.2.80.9.d X Windows copy and paste	
1.2.80.9.e X Windows Fonts	
1.2.80.10 Identify the GUI Administration Utilities	
1.2.90 Manage User Accounts	**Chapter 11, "Creating and Managing User Accounts"**
1.2.90.1 Create a user account	
1.2.90.2 Use the adduser	
1.2.90.3 Use the following user management utilities: Useradd, userdel, and newusers	
1.2.90.4 Add accounts with Linuxconf, YaST, and Lisa/COAS	

1.3 Shells and Commands

Competency	Location in This Book (Chapter, Heading)
1.3.10 The Shell	**Chapter 3, "Exploring the Bash Shell," "Shell Variables," and "Data Redirection"** **Chapter 6, "Managing Linux Processes"**
1.3.10.1 Describe shell initialization files	
1.3.10.1.a System-wide initialization files	
1.3.10.1.b Individual user initialization files	
1.3.10.2 Environment and shell variables	
1.3.10.3 The path variable	
1.3.10.4 Passing special characters to the shell	
1.3.10.5 Command history and tab completion	
1.3.10.6 Command aliases	
1.3.10.7 I/O redirection	
1.3.10.8 Program-to-program I/O channels (pipes)	
1.3.10.9 Background program creation	
1.3.20 Single-character commands with stty (interrupt, erase, etc.)	**Chapter 1, "Exploring the File System"**

Competency	Location in This Book (Chapter, Heading)
1.3.30 The ls command - directory listing	Chapter 1, "Exploring the File System"
1.3.30.1 File system security (permissions)	
1.3.40 The cd command - change directory	Chapter 1, "Exploring the File System"
1.3.50 The more and less commands - pager utilities	Chapter 1, "Exploring the File System"
1.3.60 The cp command - copy a file	Chapter 1, "Exploring the File System"
1.3.70 The ln command - duplicate a directory or filename	Chapter 4, "Introducing the File System"
1.3.80 The mv command - move or rename a file	Chapter 1, "Exploring the File System"
1.3.90 The mkdir command - make a directory	Chapter 1, "Exploring the File System"
1.3.100 The rm command - remove a file	Chapter 1, "Exploring the File System"
1.3.110 The rmdir command - remove a directory	Chapter 1, "Exploring the File System"
1.3.120 The head and tail commands - peek at beginning or end of a file	Chapter 5, "Manipulating Files"
1.3.130 The file command - view the file type	Chapter 4, "Introducing the File System"
1.3.140 The grep command - search files for a target string	Chapter 5, "Manipulating Files"
1.3.150 The du and df commands - show disk usage and free space	Chapter 4, "Introducing the File System"
1.3.160 The tar command - places multiple files into one archive	Chapter 4, "Managing File Archives"
1.3.170 The gzip, gunzip, and zcat - un/compression utilities	Chapter 4, "Managing File Archives"
1.3.180 The mtools - read and write MS-DOS files quickly	Chapter 4, "Introducing the File System"
1.3.190 The find and locate - search for names in the file system	Chapter 1, "Exploring the File System"
1.3.200 The Vi editor	Chapter 4, "Editing Text with vi"

1.4 System Services

Competency	Location in This Book (Chapter, Heading)
1.4.10 Device Driver Utilities	Chapter 8, "Installing Linux" Chapter 13, "Exploring Kernel Components"
1.4.20 Printer Configuration	Chapter 12, "Networked Printing Services"
1.4.20.1 Linux printer drivers	
1.4.20.2 The lpd server and the lpr client	

Competency	Location in This Book (Chapter, Heading)
1.4.20.3 Configuring printers with GUI utilities (YaST, Printtool, etc.)	
1.4.20.4 The /etc/printcap file	
1.4.20.5 Printer filters	
1.4.20.6 Printer request (lpr)	
1.4.20.7 Printer control (lpq, lprm, lpc)	
1.4.30 The X Window System Architecture	**Chapter 2, "Linux Graphical Desktops" Chapter 15, "X Window System Advanced Configuration"**
1.4.30.1 Conceptual overview of system architecture	
1.4.30.2 Components of the X Window Systems	
1.4.30.3 X32 for MS-Windows	
1.4.30.4 Xhosts and the DISPLAY shell variable	
1.4.30.5 Location of X11 configuration files	
1.4.30.6 Format of the XF86Config file	
1.4.30.7 X11 Configuration utilities	
1.4.30.7.a SuperProbe - Determine the graphics chip set	
1.4.30.7.b xf86config, XF86Setup, Xconfigurator, SaX	
1.4.40 Window Managers	**Chapter 2, "Linux Graphical Desktops" Chapter 15, "X Window System Advanced Configuration"**
1.4.40.1 AfterStep	
1.4.40.2 KDE	
1.4.40.3 Window Maker	
1.4.40.4 FVWM and FVWM95	
1.4.40.5 Enlightenment	
1.4.40.6 Blackbox	

1.5 Applications

Competency	Location in This Book (Chapter, Heading)
1.5.10 Gathering Information	**Chapter 1, "Finding Command Help"**
1.5.10.1 Help switches (--help, -h, etc.)	
1.5.10.2 Man pages	
1.5.10.3 The locate command	
1.5.10.4 The find command	
1.5.10.5 Info command	
1.5.10.6 Xman, xinfo, tkman	
1.5.10.7 Gathering information from online sources	
1.5.10.7.a Linux Documentation Project	
1.5.10.7.b Deja News	
1.5.10.7.c Search engines	
1.5.10.7.d Linux breaking news (slashdot.org, linuxhq.com, freshmeat.org)	

C

Competency	Location in This Book (Chapter, Heading)
1.5.20 Network Applications	**Chapter 2, "Popular Graphical Programs"** **Chapter 7, "Data Services"**
1.5.20.1. WWW browser software	
1.5.20.2 FTP clients	
1.5.20.3 Telnet clients	
1.5.20.4 Mail clients	
1.5.30 Text Processing Programs	**Chapter 2, "Popular Graphical Programs"** **Chapter 5, "Manipulating Files"**
1.5.30.1 WordPerfect	
1.5.30.2 StarOffice Suite	
1.5.30.3 Applix Ware Suite	
1.5.30.4 WYSIWYG vs. mark-up word processing	
1.5.30.5 Ispell - Spell Checker	
1.5.40 Graphics Applications	**Chapter 2, "Popular Graphical Programs"**
1.5.40.1 GNU image manipulation program (GIMP)	
1.5.40.2 X-Fig - Interactive vector-based drawing tool	
1.5.40.3 ImageMagick	

1.6 Troubleshooting

Competency	Location in This Book (Chapter, Heading)
1.6.10 Installation Troubleshooting	**Chapter 15, "Troubleshooting and Recovery"**
1.6.10.1 Read Error or File Not Found error	Chapter 15, "Troubleshooting and Recovery"

COURSE 3X0-102: LINUX SYSTEM ADMINISTRATION

2.1 Theory of Operation

Competency	Location in This Book (Chapter, Heading)
2.1.10 File System Structure	**Chapter 4, "Introducing the File System"**
2.1.10.1 Describe Inodes	
2.1.10.2 Describe the concept of mounting volumes	
2.1.20 Explain the Detailed File System Hierarchy Standard (FHS)	**Chapter 1, "Exploring the File System"**

Competency	Location in This Book (Chapter, Heading)
2.1.30 Give the design tradeoff of backup	Chapter 13, "Backing Up a Linux System"
2.1.40 Explain the scheduling batch (cron) jobs	Chapter 6, "Scheduling Processes"
2.1.50 Explain the Client/Server printing design tradeoffs	Chapter 12, "Networked Printing Services"
2.1.60 Describe the basics of system tuning	Chapter 13, "Configuring and Upgrading Kernel Components"
2.1.70 Describe standard emergency procedures	Chapter 15, "Troubleshooting and Recovery"
2.1.70.1 Detail the process of creating a rescue floppy	
2.1.70.2 Describe how to single-user boot with root read/write access to the disk	
2.1.70.3 Describe the process of patching a file system	
2.1.70.4 Explain how to restore from back-up	
2.1.80 Give the tradeoffs of compressing and archiving	Chapter 4, "Managing File Archives"
2.1.90 Explain monitoring system resources	Chapter 6, "Defining Processes" and "Managing Memory"
2.1.90.1 Describe CPU, memory, I/O, network	

2.2 Base System

Competency	Location in This Book (Chapter, Heading)
2.2.10 Describe the process of adding and removing users	Chapter 11, "Creating and Managing User Accounts"
2.2.10.1 Explain default account configurations	
2.2.10.2 Explain shadow passwords	
2.2.20 Describe group management	Chapter 11, "Creating and Managing User Accounts"
2.2.10.1 Describe group creation	
2.2.10.2 Explain group switching	
2.2.10.3 Explain how to create access control lists	
2.2.30 Explain how to change ownership of files	Chapter 4, "File Permissions"
2.2.40 Describe adding email accounts	Chapter 2, "Popular Graphical Programs"
2.2.50 Explain creating mail aliases	Chapter 15, "Using Network Services"
2.2.60 Explain Run levels (/etc/inittab)	Chapter 9, "init and its Scripts"
2.2.70 Explain fstab and volume mounting	Chapter 10, "Understanding the File System"
2.2.80 Describe how to recompile the kernel	Chapter 13, "Configuring and Upgrading Kernel Components"

C

Competency	Location in This Book (Chapter, Heading)
2.2.90 Describe system shutdown techniques	Chapter 9, "Controlling Services"
2.2.100 Describe the various file permissions	Chapter 4, "File Permissions"
2.2.110 Explain the boot process	Chapter 9, "Hardware Initialization"
2.2.120 Describe the system startup files	Chapter 9, "init and its Scripts"
2.2.130 Explain good housekeeping	Chapter 15, "Security Issues"
2.2.140 Describe effective hard disk management	Chapter 10, "Understanding the File System"

2.3 Shells and Commands

Competency	Location in This Book (Chapter, Heading)
2.3.10 Describe when to use the superuser account	Chapter 1, "Exploring the File System"
2.3.10.1 Describe how to act as another user "su – *account*"	
2.3.10.2 Describe how to change users passwords	
2.3.20 Describe various methods of communicating with users	Chapter 10, "User Security Issues"
2.3.30 Describe different tools used to move from DOS/WIN to Linux	Chapter 8, "Configuring Disk Space"
2.3.40 Describe the configure and make commands	Chapter 14, "Other Programming Methods"
2.3.50 Explain the purpose of various shell scripts	Chapter 9, "init and its Scripts"; 14, *throughout*
2.3.50.1 Write a script using simple commands	
2.3.50.2 Describe the shell variables	
2.3.50.3 Explain the usage of the for loop	
2.3.50.4 Explain the usage of the while loop	
2.3.50.5 Explain the usage of command line arguments	
2.3.50.6 Explain the usage of the if statement	
2.3.50.7 Explain the usage of the case statement	
2.3.60 Describe system message logging /var/log files	Chapter 13, "System Logs"
2.3.70 Describe the usage of file system specific commands	Chapter 10, "Understanding the File System"
2.3.80 Explain the use of various commands for System Administrators	Chapter 1, "Exploring the File System"

2.4 System Services

Competency	Location in This Book (Chapter, Heading)
2.4.10 Archive Utilities	**Chapter 4, "Managing File Archives"**
2.4.10.1 Describe Gzip, tar, and libraries	
2.4.20 Backup Techniques	**Chapter 13, "Backing up a Linux System"**
2.4.20.1 Describe the Epoch backup techniques	
2.4.20.2. Describe incremental backups	
2.4.20.3 Describe differential backups	
2.4.20.4 Describe file ghost backups	
2.4.30 Volume Integrity	**Chapter 10, "Understanding the File System"**
2.4.30.1 Explain the removable media integrity problem	
2.4.30.2. Describe the function of fsck	
2.4.40 Process management	**Chapter 6, "Managing Linux Processes"**
2.4.40.1 Describe the ps, top, kill, nice, and nohup commands	
2.4.50 Describe file system accounting	**Chapter 10, "Understanding the File System"**
2.4.60 Describe printer configuration and restarting	**Chapter 12, "Networked Printing Services"**
2.4.60.1 Describe the background line printer daemon (lpd) server	
2.4.60.2 Describe the foreground line printer requester (lpr) client	
2.4.60.3 Describe detailed control with /etc/printcap	
2.4.60.4 Describe Queue management	
2.4.70 Describe software package management	**Chapter 10, "Managing Packages"**
2.4.70.1 Describe Red Hat RPMS	
2.4.70.2 Describe Debian dselect	
2.4.70.3 Describe examples of software package installation	

2.5 Applications

Competency	Location in This Book (Chapter, Heading)
2.5.10 AMANDA	**Chapter 13, "Backing up a Linux System"**
2.5.20 ORL's VNC	**Chapter 13, "Backing up a Linux System"**
2.5.30 Mail Exchange and Virtual Email	**Chapter 15, "Using Network Services"**
2.5.30.1 System mail aliases	
2.5.30.2 User mail aliases	
2.5.40 News	**Chapter 2, "Popular Graphical Programs"**
2.5.50 Apache Web Server	**Chapter 15, "Using Network Services"**

C

Competency	Location in This Book (Chapter, Heading)
2.5.50.1 Configuration files	
2.5.50.2 Modules	
2.5.50.3 Virtual hosts	
2.5.50.4 Virtual e-mail	
2.5.60 Configuration of X Window Desktops	**Chapter 15, "X Window System Advanced Configuration"**
2.5.60.1 fvwm95	
2.5.60.2 AfterStep	
2.5.60.3 Window maker	
2.5.60.4 KDE	
2.5.60.5 Gnome	
2.5.70 Benchmarks	**Chapter 15, "Security Issues"**

2.6 Troubleshooting

Competency	Location in This Book (Chapter, Heading)
2.6.10 Daemons	**Chapter 15, "Troubleshooting and Recovery"**
2.6.20 File system	**Chapter 15, "Troubleshooting and Recovery"**
2.6.30 Hardware	**Chapter 15, "Troubleshooting and Recovery"**
2.6.40 Log files	**Chapter 15, "Troubleshooting and Recovery"**
2.6.50 Core dump control	**Chapter 15, "Troubleshooting and Recovery"**
2.6.60 Ulimit in bash	**Chapter 15, "Troubleshooting and Recovery"**
2.6.70 Limit in tcsh or rlimit ksh	**Chapter 15, "Troubleshooting and Recovery"**

COURSE 3X0-103 LINUX NETWORKING

NOTE

As noted at the beginning of this appendix, this book doesn't cover these objectives. They are provided for information only. Additional detail on these advanced topics can be found in Course Technology's *Guide to Linux Networking and Security*.

3.1 Theory of Operation

3.1.10 LAN/WAN and the Internet

3.1.10.1 Contrast LAN with point-to-point transmission

3.1.10.2 Describe the speed/distance tradeoff for copper versus fiber-optic cables

3.1.10.3 Describe the LAN/WAN boundary and Internet subnet characteristics

3.1.20 Communication Technology

3.1.20.1 Define the IPv4; address format

3.1.20.2 Describe IPv4 address classes and design tradeoff

3.1.20.3 Describe IPv4 classless address conservation

3.1.20.4 Contrast IPv4 and IPv6 design tradeoffs

3.1.30 Network Physical versus Logical Topology

3.1.30.1 Define Ethernet singlecast, multicast, and broadcast routing

3.1.30.2 Describe store and forward point-to-point networking with explicit routing

3.1.30.3 Describe point-to-point emulation of broadcast and its tradeoff

3.1.30.4 Define subnet addressing and logical versus physical broadcasting

3.1.30.5 Contrast multicast protocol and network topology

3.1.40 Internet Architecture Networking Protocols

3.1.40.1 Describe IP host-to-host addressing

3.1.40.1 Describe host-relative ports or program-to-program addressing

3.1.40.2 Contrast the functions of TCP with UDP

3.1.40.3 Describe the role of the boundary zone and contrast network IP, ICMP, and ARP

3.1.50 Network adapter and software relationships

3.1.50.1 Contrast physical and logical addresses

3.1.50.2 Describe the Address Resolution Protocol (ARP)

3.1.50.2.a Describe the role of the address resolution cache

3.1.50.2.b Describe ARP routing and precedence over IP routing

3.1.50.3 Describe device driver and adapter connectivity

3.1.50.4 Describe network interface name and device drive connectivity

3.1.50.5 Describe network interface and logical address connectivity

3.1.50.6 Describe logical address and network interface routing

3.1.60 Domain Name Service (DNS)

3.1.60.1 Describe the role and general structure of the boot.named configuration file

3.1.60.2 Describe the record look up mechanism and explain the role of the dot (.) operator

3.1.60.3 Contrast A, CNAME, PTR, and NS resource records

3.1.60.4 Contrast authoritative resource records, non-authoritative resource records, and name updates

3.1.70 Manual address assignment

3.1.70.1 Describe the reverse name lookup and route table configuration problem

3.1.70.2 Contrast adding hosts, subnets, and gateways

3.1.70.3 Describe default route creation when routing multiple subnets

3.1.80 UUCP subsystem

3.1.80.1 Describe the overall design and tradeoff of using UUCP

3.1.80.2 Contrast uucico and uucp

3.1.90 Short Message Block (SMB)

3.1.90.1 Describe the overall design of SMB

3.1.90.2 Contrast smbd and nmbd servers

3.1.90.3 Describe the general structure of the smb.conf file

3.1.100 Describe the overall design of IPX and Novell compatibility

3.1.100.1 Describe general IPX interface configuration and detection issues

3.1.100.2 Describe general IPX router specification with RIP & SAP protocols

3.1.110 Describe the overall design of the Network File System (NFS)

3.1.110.1 Contrast the role of the /etc/fstab versus exports configuration files

3.1.110.2 Display and interpret NFS statistics

3.1.110.3 Show the mount information for an NFS server

3.2 Base System

3.2.10 Network device configuration

3.2.10.1 Describe BIOS device enabling

3.2.10.2 Describe how to confirm kernel recognition of network devices

3.2.10.3 Describe run-time network device driver installation

3.2.10.4 Describe the relationship between logical device names and network drivers

3.3 Shells and Commands

3.3.30 Explain the problem with DNS and network troubleshooting

3.3.40 Interpret netstat's output to describe the state of network connections

3.3.50 Describe how to construct network connections

3.3.60 Explain how to view and manipulate routes

3.3.70 Explain how to view and manipulate logical to physical address translations

3.3.80 Explain how to attach network addresses to a device driver

3.3.90 Explain how to load a NIC device driver

3.3.100 Describe the use of /etc/resolv.conf for DNS

3.3.110 Describe the use /etc/hosts for shorthand names

3.3.120 Explain how to configure firewalls and private networks

3.3.130 Explain Point-to-Point Protocol (PPP) configuration

3.4 System Services

3.4.10 Describe the domain name service (DNS) and give its tradeoff

3.4.10.1 Top-level domain names and root servers

3.4.10.2 SOA and forward versus reverse names

3.4.10.3 Multiple domains (zones) and transfers

3.4.10.4 Primary, secondary, and tertiary servers

3.4.20 FTP

3.4.20.1 Anonymous

3.4.20.2 Incoming

3.4.20.3 /etc/ftpaccess

3.4.30 NFS

3.4.30.1 /etc/exports

3.4.40 Internet super server

3.4.40.1 daemon (inetd)

3.4.40.2 /etc/inetd.conf

3.4.40.3 /etc/services

3.4.40.4 TCP/UDP wrappers

3.4.50 Samba

C

3.6.40 Nslookup

3.6.50 Local service

3.6.60 Internet weather

COURSE 3X0-104 LINUX SECURITY, ETHICS, AND PRIVACY

4.1 Theory of Operation

4.1.10 Why Security?

4.1.10.1 A few definitions of security

4.1.10.2 A few conclusions from CERT/CC statistics

4.1.10.3 Points of concern

4.1.20 Ethics

4.1.30 Privacy

4.1.40 Policies and Guidelines

4.1.50 Security -- Definitions and Types

4.1.60 Physical Security

4.1.60.1 Clear your screen, lock your system, and put a note on your computer if necessary

4.1.70 Trust Me

4.1.80 Passwords -- the number ONE weakness

4.1.90 Daemons as superusers and the buffer overflow problem

4.1.100 Common Forms of attacks (An Overview)

4.1.110 CERT/CC

4.1.120 U.S. Law

4.1.130 General Recommendations

4.1.130.1 Tradeoffs between security, morale, and getting the job done

4.1.130.2 General steps to defend system and basic precautions

4.1.140 New protection scheme for net class

4.1.150 Daily system check

4.2 Base System

4.3 Shells and Commands

4.3.50 Trojan horse and shell scripts

4.3.50.1 su command -- use full path

4.3.60 Baseline and monitoring -- daily system checks

4.3.70 CGI applications

4.4 System Services

4.4.10 Firewalls

4.4.20 TCP Wrappers

4.4.30 IPCHAINS/IPFWADM/IP Filters

4.4.50 UUCP

4.4.60 TCP/IP

4.4.70 WWW

4.4.80 PPP

4.4.90 Telnet

4.4.100 FTP

4.4.110 SMTP

4.4.120 Mail

4.4.130 NIS, RPC, NIS+, and Kerberos

4.4.140 Daemons

4.4.140.1 Disable all unnecessary daemons running on the system

4.5 Applications

4.5.10 Trojan horses

4.5.20 Worms

4.5.30 Viruses

4.5.40 Encryption

4.5.40.1 MD5 checksums

4.5.50 Samba

4.5.60 Apache

4.5.70 Hidden logfile backup

4.5.80 Security tools

4.5.80.1 cops, crack, Tripwire, Tiger, Gabriel, TCP/Wrappers, Satan, Kerberos

C

4.6 Troubleshooting

4.6.10 Do not Panic

4.6.20 Know Thy Enemy

4.6.20.1 Daily cron checks

4.6.20.2 Look at the taxonomy

4.6.30 Denial of Service (DoS) Attacks

4.6.40 Intruder detection

4.6.40.1 Hidden logfile backup

4.6.40.2 Find –cnewer suspect-file

4.6.40.3 Find –mtime –x break-in time

4.6.40.4 Find –perms 4000

4.6.50 Intruder removal

4.6.60 Greater detail on the steps to clean a system

4.6.70 How to contact CERN

D

LINUX+ CERTIFICATION OBJECTIVES

This appendix lists objectives for the CompTIA (Computing Technology Industry Association) Linux+ certification. The objectives listed here were considered "beta" at the time of writing, but are expected to become the official Linux+ objectives. To review these objectives and any possible updates, as well as to learn about taking the Linux+ certification exam, visit *www.comptia.com*.

The objectives for Linux+ are divided into six knowledge domains. CompTIA suggests that each of the domains consume the following percentages of the Linux+ exam:

Domain	Percentage of Examination
1.0 Installation	19%
2.0 Management	26%
3.0 Configuration	20%
4.0 Security	21%
5.0 Documentation	6%
6.0 Hardware	8%
TOTAL	100%

For each domain, the tables that follow indicate the chapter and section heading within the chapter where information on that topic is found in this book. For more in-depth coverage of networking services and security topics than is provided in this book, consult Course Technology's *Guide to Linux Networking and Security* (ISBN 0-619-00094-5) or *Guide to Firewalls and Network Security: Intrusion Detection and VPNs* (ISBN 0-619-13039-3).

Domain 1.0 Installation

Objective Description	Location in This Book (Chapter, Heading)
1.1 Identify all system hardware required (e.g., CPU, memory, drive space, scalability) and check compatibility with Linux distribution	Chapter 8, "Installing Linux"
1.2 Determine appropriate method of installation based on environment (e.g., boot disk, CD-ROM, network (HTTP, FTP, NFS, SMB))	Chapter 8, "Installing Linux"
1.3 Install multimedia options (e.g., video, sound, codecs)	Chapter 8, "Installing Linux"
1.4 Identify purpose of Linux machine based on predetermined customer requirements (e.g., appliance, desktop system, database, mail server, Web server, etc.)	Chapter 8, "Installing Linux"
1.5 Determine what software and services should be installed (e.g., client applications for workstation, server services for desired task)	Chapter 8, "Installing Linux" Chapter 15 "Using Network Services"
1.6 Partition according to preinstallation plan using fdisk (e.g., /boot, /usr, /var, /home, Swap, RAID/volume, hotfix)	Chapter 8, "Configuring Disk Space" Chapter 10, "Understanding the File System" Chapter 13, "Backing up a Linux System"
1.7 Configure file systems (e.g., (ext2) or (ext3) or REISER)	Chapter 10, "Understanding the File System"
1.8 Configure a boot manager (e.g., LILO, ELILO, GRUB, multiple boot options)	Chapter 8, "Configuring Disk Space" and "Installing Linux" Chapter 9, "Configuring Boot Loaders"
1.9 Manage packages after installing the operating systems (e.g., install, uninstall, update using RPM, tar, gzip)	Chapter 4, "Managing File Archives" Chapter 10, "Managing Packages"
1.10 Select appropriate networking configuration and protocols (e.g., inetd, xinetd, modems, Ethernet)	Chapter 7, "Networking and Network Diagnostic Tools" Chapter 8, "Installing Linux" Chapter 12, "Configuring Linux Networking"
1.11 Select appropriate parameters for Linux installation (e.g., language, time zones, keyboard, mouse)	Chapter 8, "Installing Linux"
1.12 Configure peripherals as necessary (e.g., printer, scanner, modem)	Chapter 8, "Installing Linux" Chapter 12, "Networked Printing Services" Chapter 15, "Troubleshooting and Recovery"

Domain 2.0 Management

Objective Description	Location in This Book (Chapter, Heading)
2.1 Manage local storage devices and file systems (e.g., fsck, fdisk, mkfs) using CLI commands	Chapter 10, "Understanding the File System"

D

Objective Description	Location in This Book (Chapter, Heading)
2.2 Mount and unmount varied file systems (e.g., Samba, NFS) using CLI commands	Chapter 4, "Introducing the File System" Chapter 10, "Understanding the File System" Chapter 15, "Using Network Services"
2.3 Create files and directories and modify files using CLI commands	Chapter 1, "Exploring the File System" Chapter 5, "Manipulating Files"
2.4 Execute content and directory searches using find and grep	Chapter 4, "Introducing the File System" Chapter 5, "Manipulating Files"
2.5 Create linked files using CLI commands	Chapter 4, "Introducing the File System"
2.6 Modify file and directory permissions and ownership (e.g., chmod, chown, sticky bit, octal permissions, chgrp) using CLI commands	Chapter 4, "File Permissions" Chapter 11, "User Security Issues"
2.7 Identify and modify default permissions for files and directories (e.g., umask) using CLI commands	Chapter 4, "File Permissions"
2.8 Perform and verify backups and restores (tar, cpio)	Chapter 4, "Managing File Archives" Chapter 13, "Backing up a Linux System"
2.9 Access and write data to recordable media (e.g. CDRW, hard drive, NVRAM)	Chapter 10, "Understanding the File System"
2.10 Manage run levels and system initialization from the CLI and configuration files (e.g., /etc/inittab and init command, /etc/rc.d, rc.local)	Chapter 9, "init and its Scripts"
2.11 Identify, execute, manage, and kill processes (e.g., ps, kill, killall, bg, fg, jobs, nice, renice, rc)	Chapter 6, "Managing Linux Processes"
2.12 Differentiate core processes from noncritical services (e.g., PID, PPID, init, timer)	Chapter 6, "Defining Processes"
2.13 Repair packages and scripts (e.g., resolving dependencies, file repair)	Chapter 10, "Managing Packages"
2.14 Monitor and troubleshoot network activity (e.g., ping, netstat, traceroute)	Chapter 7, "Networking and Network Diagnostic Tools" Chapter 15, "Using Network Services"
2.15 Perform text manipulation (e.g., sed, awk, vi)	Chapter 3, "Editing Text with vi" Chapter 5, throughout
2.16 Manage print jobs and print queues (e.g., lpd, lprm, lpq)	Chapter 3, "Printing from the Command Line" Chapter 12, "Networked Printing Services"
2.17 Perform remote management (e.g., rmon, ssh)	Chapter 7, "Remote Login"
2.18 Perform NIS-related domain management (yppasswd, ypinit, etc.)	Chapter 11, "User Security Issues"
2.19 Create, modify, and use basic shell scripts	Chapter 14, throughout
2.20 Create, modify, and delete user and group accounts (e.g., useradd, groupadd, /etc/passwd, chgrp, quota, chown, chmod, grpmod) using CLI utilities	Chapter 11, "Creating and Managing User Accounts"

Objective Description	Location in This Book (Chapter, Heading)
2.21 Manage mail queues (e.g., sendmail, postfix, mail, mutt) using CLI utilities	Chapter 7, "Data Services" Chapter 15, "Using Network Services"
2.22 Schedule jobs to execute in the future using at and cron daemons	Chapter 6, "Scheduling Processes"
2.23 Redirect output (e.g., piping, redirection)	Chapter 3, "Data Redirection"

DOMAIN 3.0 CONFIGURATION

Objective Description	Location in This Book (Chapter, Heading)
3.1 Configure client network services and settings (e.g., settings for TCP/IP)	Chapter 7, "Networking and Network Diagnostic Tools" Chapter 8, "Installing Linux" Chapter 15, "Using Network Services"
3.2 Configure basic server network services (e.g., DNS, DHCP, SAMBA, Apache)	Chapter 15, "Using Network Services"
3.3 Implement basic routing and subnetting (e.g., /sbin/route, ip forward statement)	Chapter 15, "Using Network Services"
3.4 Configure the system and perform basic makefile changes to support compiling applications and drivers	Chapter 13, "Configuring and Upgrading Kernel Components" Chapter 14, "Other Programming Methods"
3.5 Configure files that are used to mount drives or partitions (e.g., fstab, mtab, SAMBA, nfs, syntax)	Chapter 10, "Understanding the File System" Chapter 15, "Using Network Services"
3.6 Implement DNS and describe how it works (e.g., edit /etc/hosts, edit /etc/host.conf, edit /etc/resolv.conf, nslookup, dig, host, named)	Chapter 15, "Using Network Services"
3.7 Configure a Network Interface Card (NIC) from a command line	Chapter 7, "Networking and Network Diagnostic Tools" Chapter 15, "Using Network Services"
3.8 Configure Linux printing (e.g., cups, BSD LPD, SAMBA)	Chapter 12, "Networked Printing Services"
3.9 Apply basic printer permissions	Chapter 12, "Networked Printing Services"
3.10 Configure log files (e.g., syslog, remote log file storage)	Chapter 13, "System Logs"
3.11 Configure the X Window system	Chapter 2, "Linux Graphical Desktops" Chapter 15, "X Window System Advanced Configuration"
3.12 Set up environment variables (e.g., $PATH, $DISPLAY, $TERM, $PROMPT, $PS1)	Chapter 3, "Shell Variables"

DOMAIN 4.0 SECURITY

Objective Description	Location in This Book (Chapter, Heading)
4.1 Configure security environment files (e.g., hosts.allow, sudoers, ftpusers, sshd_config)	Chapter 7, "Remote Login" Chapter 11, "User Security Issues" 15, "Using Network Services"
4.2 Delete accounts while maintaining data stored in that user's home directory	Chapter 11, "Creating and Managing User Accounts"
4.3 Given security requirements, implement appropriate encryption configuration (e.g., blowfish 3DES, MD5)	Chapter 15, "Security Issues"
4.4 Detect symptoms that indicate a machine's security has been compromised (e.g., review log files for irregularities or intrusion attempts)	Chapter 15, "Security Issues," "Using Network Services," and "Troubleshooting and Recovery"
4.5 Use appropriate access level for login (e.g., root level vs. user-level activities, su, sudo)	Chapter 11, "User Security Issues"
4.6 Set process and special permissions (e.g., SUID, GUID)	Chapter 11, "Complex File Permissions"
4.7 Identify different Linux Intrusion Detection Systems (IDS) (e.g., Snort, PortSentry)	Chapter 15, "Security Issues" and "Using Network Services"
4.8 Given security requirements, implement basic IP tables/chains (note: requires knowledge of common ports)	Chapter 15, "Using Network Services"
4.9 Implement security auditing for files and authentication	Chapter 15, "Security Issues" and "Using Network Services"
4.10 Identify whether a package or file has been corrupted / altered (e.g., checksum, Tripwire)	Chapter 10, "Managing Packages" Chapter 15, "Security Issues" and "Using Network Services"
4.11 Given a set of security requirements, set password policies to match (complexity / aging / shadowed passwords) (e.g., convert to and from shadow passwords)	Chapter 11, "Creating and Managing User Accounts" and "User Security Issues"
4.12 Identify security vulnerabilities within Linux services	Chapter 15, "Security Issues" and "Using Network Services"
4.13 Set up user-level security (i.e., limits on logins, memory usage, and processes)	Chapter 11, "User Security Issues" Chapter 15, "Security Issues"

D

DOMAIN 5.0 DOCUMENTATION

Objective Description	Location in This Book (Chapter, Heading)
5.1 Establish system performance baseline	Chapter 1, "Finding Command Help"
5.2 Create written procedures for installation, configuration, security, and management	Chapter 1, "Finding Command Help" Chapter 8, "Installing Linux" Chapter 15, "Security Issues"

Objective Description	Location in This Book (Chapter, Heading)
5.3 Document installed configuration (e.g., installed packages, package options, TCP/IP assignment list, changes, configuration and maintenance)	Chapter 1, "Finding Command Help" Chapter 10, "Managing Packages"
5.4 Troubleshoot errors using systems logs (e.g., tail, head, grep)	Chapter 5, "Manipulating Files" Chapter 15, "Troubleshooting and Recovery"
5.5 Troubleshoot application errors using application logs (e.g., tail, head, grep)	Chapter 5, "Manipulating Files" Chapter 15, "Troubleshooting and Recovery"
5.6 Access system documentation and help files (e.g., man, info, readme, Web)	Chapter 1, "Finding Command Help"

DOMAIN 6.0 HARDWARE

Objective Description	Location in This Book (Chapter, Heading)
6.1 Describe common hardware components and resources (e.g., connectors, IRQs, DMA, SCSI, memory addresses)	Chapter 8, "Reviewing Your Computer's Hardware"
6.2 Diagnose hardware issues using Linux tools (e.g., /proc, disk utilities, ifconfig, /dev, knoppix, BBC, dmesg)	Chapter 8, "Reviewing Your Computer's Hardware" Chapter 15, "Troubleshooting and Recovery"
6.3 Identify and configure removable system hardware (e.g., PCMCIA, USB, IEEE1394)	Chapter 8, "Reviewing Your Computer's Hardware" Chapter 15, "Troubleshooting and Recovery"
6.4 Configure advanced power management and Advanced Configuration and Power Interface (ACPI)	Chapter 8, "Reviewing Your Computer's Hardware" Chapter 15, "Troubleshooting and Recovery"
6.5 Identify and configure mass storage devices and RAID (e.g., SCSI, ATAPI, tape, optical recordable)	Chapter 8, "Reviewing Your Computer's Hardware" Chapter 13, "Backing up a Linux System"

Glossary

/etc/dhcpd.conf — Configuration file used to define the operation of the DHCP server daemon, dhcpd.

/etc/exports — File containing a description of local file systems and directories to be made available using NFS.

/etc/fstab — A configuration file that contains a file system table with devices, mount points, file system types, and options. Used by the *mount* command.

/etc/group — A configuration file in which group information (group names and membership lists) is stored.

/etc/hosts — Configuration file that stores IP addresses and corresponding domain names for hosts, usually those frequently accessed on a local network.

/etc/hosts.allow — Configuration file that defines services and hosts that should be permitted access by TCP Wrappers.

/etc/host.conf — Configuration file that specifies the order in which the resolver should consult resources to resolve the host name to an IP address. Not used in many Linux systems because /etc/nsswitch.conf is used instead.

/etc/hosts.deny — Configuration file that defines services and hosts that should be denied access by TCP Wrappers.

/etc/hosts.equiv — A systemwide database of remote hosts and user names that are permitted to access the host using r-utilities. *See also* .rhosts.

/etc/login.defs — File in which default information used to create new user accounts is stored.

/etc/motd — File in which a message of the day may be stored. Empty by default on most Linux systems, the contents of this file are displayed on a user's system when logging in to a text-based console or starting a shell in a terminal window.

/etc/nologin — A file whose existence prevents all users except root from logging in to the system. Regular users attempting to log in see the contents of the file /etc/nologin.

/etc/nsswitch.conf — File that defines where to search for various system information such as password and networking configuration details. Supports directing programs to local files, NIS or NIS+ servers, or other centralized information repositories.

/etc/ntp.conf — Configuration file used by the Network Time Protocol (NTP) server.

/etc/passwd — A configuration file in which user account information is stored.

/etc/printcap — Configuration file that defines print queues, specifically used for the LPRng printing system.

/etc/profile — A script containing configuration information that applies to every user on the Linux system.

/etc/resolv.conf — Configuration file that configures the Linux resolver by listing the computer's domain and the IP address of one or more DNS name servers.

/etc/securetty — Configuration file that lists locations from which root is permitted to log in. Used to prevent root from logging in via a remote connection, such as a modem.

/etc/services — Configuration file that maps service names to port numbers. Used by many programs, including the superservers *inetd* and *xinetd*.

/etc/shadow — A configuration file in which encrypted user passwords and password configuration data are stored.

/etc/skel — A directory containing files that are copied to a new user's home directory at the time a new user account is created.

/etc/sudoers — Configuration file that determines what actions regular users are permitted to perform using the *sudo* command. Must be edited using the *visudo* command.

/proc file system — A collection of information about the Linux kernel and other system resources that you access as a file system.

$@ — A special shell variable that includes all of the parameters on the command line.

.bashrc — A configuration script that is executed each time the user starts a bash shell.

.exrc — A configuration file for vi, which can be stored in any directory. Any vi settings stored in this file are applied when vi is used to edit any text file in the same directory.

.forward — Configuration file placed in a user's home directory to define where e-mail messages should be forwarded by sendmail.

.profile — A configuration script that can be located in each user's home directory. A script that is executed each time any user on the system starts a bash shell. This script is not included by default on all Linux distributions, but can be created if needed.

.rhosts — A file stored within a user's home directory to determine who is allowed to access that user's account via r-utilities commands such as *rsh* and *rcp*. *See also* /etc/ hosts.equiv.

.Xauthority — Configuration file containing tokens (cookies) used by the *xauth* program to enable remote display of graphical programs.

absolute path — A complete description of how to access a desired subdirectory or file, specified from the root of the file system to the subdirectory or file. It must begin with a forward slash. *See also* relative path.

Access Control Lists (ACLs) — Data structures that define who can access individual directories and programs.

access mode — The file permissions assigned to a file or directory; the access permitted to that object.

action — A field in the syslog.conf configuration file that determines what to do with messages matching the selector on that line.

active partition — The bootable partition; the partition that the MBR passes control to if the MBR does not itself contain a boot manager.

Address Resolution Protocol (ARP) — A protocol that broadcasts a message to an entire network segment in order to obtain a host's MAC address, or, if the MAC address is known, to obtain a host's IP address.

alias — A string of characters that the shell substitutes for another string of characters when a command is entered. Created in the shell using the *alias* command.

alternatives printing system — A method used in Red Hat Linux and Fedora to permit both LPRng and CUPS printing systems to reside on the same Linux system using symbolic links for commonly used printing commands.

Apache — A popular Web server program.

Apache modules — Program code that can be loaded independently into the Apache Web server.

application — A program (such as a word processor or spreadsheet) that provides a service to a person using the computer, rather than simply managing the computer's resources.

ARP cache — A list of IP address-to-hardware mappings maintained by the ARP protocol to assist in routing packets. Viewed using the *arp* command.

at job — A command or script that you have scheduled to be executed at a specific time in the future using the *at* command.

authenticate — To prove to a computer that a person or program is in fact who it claims to be.

autofs — A system service that watches for users to enter configured mount points and then automatically mounts the corresponding file system. Managed via the autofs script in /etc/rc.d/init.d. Configured using the /etc/auto.master file.

background application — An application that does not prevent the program that started it from immediately interacting further with the user.

backup — A copy of data on a computer system.

backup level — A description of how much data is stored in a backup operation. A backup level is only relevant in comparison with another backup level. When performing a backup operation at a given level, all of the data that has changed since the last backup of the previous level is recorded.

backup media — A device on which data can be stored, such as a tape cartridge, writeable CD or DVD, or floppy disk.

backup plan — A written document that outlines when, how, and why various files and file systems are backed up, stored, and—when necessary— restored to prevent permanent data loss.

bang — In Linux jargon, an exclamation point character.

bash — Short for Bourne Again shell, an enhanced and extended version of the Bourne shell created by the GNU project for use on many UNIX-like operating systems. bash is the default Linux shell.

binary file — *See* executable file.

binary code — Machine-readable instructions used to execute a program.

BIOS (Basic Input/Output System) — Information stored in ROM that provides instructions to the operating system for using the devices on a computer.

bit — A binary digit; a bit can hold a value of either one or zero.

block — A unit of hard disk space; typically one that contains 1024 bytes, or two sectors.

bootable CD-ROM drive — A CD-ROM drive that can start an operating system (or other program) directly from a CD without accessing the hard disk. (This feature of the CD-ROM drive must be enabled by the BIOS.)

boot disk — A removable disk that can start an operating system, especially one that starts a Linux installation program.

boot image — A Linux kernel that can be started by a boot loader.

boot manager — A program that lets you start one or more operating systems each time you start a computer. (Examples include GRUB and LILO.)

boot parameter — A parameter provided to a boot loader, which is in turn passed to the Linux kernel at boot time in order to control how the kernel operates or to assist the kernel in working with hardware components.

BOOTP — A protocol used by diskless computers to obtain configuration information. Rarely used now, but similar to DHCP, which is backward compatible with BOOTP.

boot record — A small area on each partition that contains a program to start the operating system on that partition.

Border Gateway Protocol (BGP) — A widely used external routing protocol.

Bourne shell — The original shell for UNIX, written by Stephen Bourne.

broadcast address — An IP address that a computer on a network can use to send a packet to all computers on that network.

buffer — Memory used by an application for data storage.

buffer overflow attack — A technique for gaining access to a computer system by exploiting a weakness in the design of a computer program. When a cracker follows a specific sequence of steps or provides specific input to a program, the program becomes confused and tries to use computer memory inappropriately; consequently, the buffer, or memory space, reserved for a part of the program overflows. The result can be either corruption of system data, a crashed server, or even direct root access.

byte — Storage space sufficient to store one character; eight bits.

C shell — A shell developed by Bill Joy in the 1970s. He focused on adding easy-to-use features for interactive work at the shell prompt. (Most of these features were later added to the bash shell as well.) The C shell is not popular for shell programming because its syntax is more complex than that of the Bourne, bash, and Korn shells.

caching name server — A DNS server that contains no preconfigured information on domains (except localhost), but simply queries other DNS servers and caches the results.

CERT Coordination Center (CERT/CC) — A federally funded software-engineering institute that focuses much attention on computer security issues and provides information to security and system administration professionals around the world; operated by Carnegie-Mellon University.

chained boot loaders — Multiple boot loaders that refer to each other, located at different positions on one or more hard disks in a single computer, such as on the MBR, and on one or more boot records of distinct partitions.

chief information officer (CIO) — The executive in an organization who determines how information systems are used within the organization to further its goals or mission effectively.

child directory — A subdirectory of a parent directory.

child process — A process that was started by another process. All processes are child processes of the init process, some further removed than others.

client — A program or computer that is requesting information or service from another program or computer. *See also* server.

CMOS RAM — A special memory chip in which computer configuration details are stored. The data is maintained by a tiny battery and is modified as needed using a BIOS utility.

command history — A feature of the shell that records in a list (the history list) each of the commands that you enter at the shell prompt.

command interpreter — A program that accepts input from the keyboard and uses that input to start commands or otherwise control the computer system.

command-line interface (CLI) — A method of communicating with the operating system by entering textual commands at a prompt.

comment — A line in a script or source code that is not processed by the interpreter or compiler, but is only included to help someone reading the file understand the purpose or operation of the script or source code. Comments in shell scripts and many other languages are created by beginning a line with the # character.

Common Gateway Interface (CGI) — A method of communication between two programs using the standard input and standard output channels.

Common UNIX Printing System (CUPS) — A printing system that permits browser-based configuration and print management. Intended to eventually replace the LPRng printing system.

compiled language — A computer language for which the source code is converted to a binary file before the program is executed.

compiler — A program that converts the source code of a compiled language into a binary file.

computer language — A set of words and syntax rules that can be arranged in predefined ways to cause a computer to perform tasks defined by the person using the language.

console — A text-only interface to the operating system, providing a command-line interface. Not part of a GUI.

container — A special type of Apache configuration directive that activates other directives only if a condition is met or only within a particular context.

cookie — A numeric token used by a program to identify information about a host or user.

copyleft — An ironic term that refers to the GNU General Public License (the GPL), signifying a radical departure from standard copyright.

core dump — A diagnostic file (named core) that is created by the operating system when a program ends unexpectedly (crashes).

cron **job** — A command or script that you have scheduled to be executed repeatedly at specific times in the future.

current working directory — The directory in which you are working. Displayed using the *pwd* command.

cylinder — A set of tracks at the same location on all the platters of a hard disk.

daemon — A background process that typically doesn't have any screen output but waits for certain system activity and then acts on it.

defragment — A procedure that arranges each file so that the parts of the file are next to each other on the hard disk; places all sectors composing a file into contiguous disk locations.

denial of service (DoS) — A cracker activity that ties up the attacked server or a particular program with so much bogus network traffic that it cannot respond to valid requests.

desktop interface — *See* graphical user interface (GUI).

device driver — Software used to communicate with or control a hardware component.

DHCP server — A computer that responds to requests from hosts on a network, providing them with an IP address and other network configuration information.

differential backup — A backup process that stores all files that have changed since a full backup was made.

direct memory access (DMA) channel — A communication method within a computer that allows a device to read and write directly to the computer's RAM, without going through the microprocessor first.

directory record — A special type of file that contains the names and inode numbers of other files.

disk image — A single file that contains an exact copy of a floppy disk.

disk quotas — Limits assigned to each user or group that restrict the total amount of space that the user or group can consume on a file system.

distributed DoS (DDoS) — A special type of denial-of-service attack in which a cracker infiltrates many systems and installs a program that executes a DoS attack on an assigned target at the cracker's command.

DNS server — A server that responds to requests from clients needing a domain name converted to (resolved to) an IP address.

Domain Name System (DNS) — The protocol used to convert domain names such as *www.course.com* into IP addresses such as 198.60.22.5.

domain name — A name assigned to a collection of computers on a network.

dual-boot system — A computer that allows a user to choose which operating system to start each time the computer is started.

duplexing — A redundancy technique in which hard disks are accessed via different hard disk controllers. Compare to "mirroring," a technique that provides identical information on two file systems but without redundant disk controllers.

Dynamic Host Configuration Protocol (DHCP) — The protocol used by clients and DHCP servers to provide an IP address and other network configuration data to computers on a network. *See also* DHCP server.

dynamically linked applications — Linux programs that do not include within themselves the library functions that they require to operate. The libraries must be installed (as shared libraries) on the Linux system on which the applications are executed.

dynamic routing — Collecting and updating routing table information automatically using a routing protocol such as RIP, OSPF, or BGP.

effective UID — The user ID that is used to determine what access to the file system a user is permitted. The *su* command changes the effective UID.

emacs — A powerful editor that provides macros, programming tools, customization, and hundreds of keyboard shortcuts.

e-mail alias — An alternative name that can be used to e-mail messages to a user account.

end user — An individual who uses the computer systems in an organization to accomplish assigned tasks, but who often relies on a system administrator to keep those systems running smoothly.

environment variable — Variable defined by the Linux shell so that all programs can access its value.

epoch backup — A full backup, containing all the data on a system.

Ethereal — A powerful graphical network traffic analysis tool.

Ethernet — The most widely used type of networking hardware.

executable file — A file containing numeric codes that a computer can execute. Created from a source code file by a compiler, the executable file is the program that a user can run.

execute permission (x) — A file permission that allows a user to start a file as a program or see a file within a directory. Represented by the letter "x".

exit code — A numeric code provided by a program or shell script to indicate success or failure of the expected operation.

exterior routing protocols — Routing protocols designed for routing packets between networks controlled by different organizations; packets are routed based on administrative policies, often controlled by how much a particular organization's routing information is trusted.

face browser — A feature of the graphical login screen that causes it to display a small graphic image for each user.

facility — A category assigned to a system message, identifying the type of program providing the message. Facilities are used in syslog.conf.

FAT (File Allocation Table) — The file system type used by DOS and older versions of Windows.

FAT32 — (32-bit FAT) The file system type used by some versions of Windows (such as Windows 98).

fault tolerance — The ability to respond gracefully when an unexpected hardware or software failure occurs, so as to prevent a complete shutdown of the system.

File Transfer Protocol (FTP) — Protocol designed for transferring files between a server and one or more client computers.

file extension — The last part of a file name, traditionally the last three letters, separated from the rest of the file name by a period. Used in some cases to indicate the type of information the file contains, such as a document or graphic image of a particular format.

file handle — An internal storage mechanism that allows a single file to be opened and used in Linux.

file manager — A graphical utility used to manage files and subdirectories. Nautilus in the GNOME desktop is one example. Konqueror is the default file manager in the KDE desktop.

file permissions — Access rights that define the type of access a user has to a file or directory on the Linux system. Also called the access mode of a file or directory.

file record — A record within a Linux file system that contains a file name and an inode number or else, if a symbolic link, a file name and another file name to which the link refers.

file system — An organized collection of information on a storage device, typically a hard disk.

filtering — The process of adding, removing, or altering data in the text file based on complex rules or patterns.

FIPS — A program that creates two separate partitions from an existing Windows partition. Used to create an empty partition that can be deleted and the resulting free space used for installing Linux. Can not be used with the NTFS file system (Windows NT, 2000, XP, or Server 2003).

firewall — A program that filters (blocks) IP packets based on their characteristics and according to a set of rules.

for loop — A list of commands that is repeatedly executed according to the parameters provided with the *for* command.

fork — Method used to create a new process in Linux by starting it from within an existing process.

forking — Starting a new free software project based on an existing project.

Free Software Foundation (FSF) — An organization founded by Richard Stallman to promote his ideals of freely available software and to create and distribute that software.

function — A collection of commands that have been given a name and can be executed at a later time by referring to that name.

gateway — A computer attached to two or more networks such that computers on one network can reach other networks by sending data packets to the gateway computer.

gcc — A C language compiler. Probably the best-known product of the GNU Project.

gdm — The display manager included with GNOME; used to provide a graphical login prompt.

gigabyte (GB) — A measure of space on computers equal to 1024 megabytes, or roughly enough space to store 1 billion characters.

Global Information Assurance Certification (GIAC) — A hands-on security certification program run by the SANS Institute.

GNOME desktop (guh-NOME) — A graphical interface used by many Linux distributions, including Red Hat Linux.

GNOME System Monitor — A graphical utility for the GNOME desktop that is used to monitor and control processes running on Linux.

GNU General Public License (GPL) — The free software license that Richard Stallman of the Free Software Foundation developed for the programs created by the GNU Project.

GNU Project — An effort by the Free Software Foundation to create a free UNIX-like operating system. Many of the programs in every Linux distribution come from the GNU Project.

graceful shutdown — The technique used to stop all Linux services and shut down all file access in an orderly way before turning off or restarting the computer.

graphical libraries — Collections of programming functions that an X client can use to create and manage the elements of a graphical environment more efficiently.

graphical user interface (GUI) — Software that provides mouse-driven applications with menu bars, buttons, and so forth.

group — A named account that consists of a collection of users. Each member of a group has access to files owned by that group.

group permissions — A set of three file permissions (r, w, and x) that may be granted to members of the group assigned to a file or directory.

grpquota — Option that can be used within the /etc/fstab file that causes a file system to track disk space quotas for each group. Used in conjunction with the *quotaon* and *edquota* commands.

GRUB — A Linux boot manager; used by default on Red Hat Linux and Fedora distributions.

hard link — A file record that points to an inode that is already pointed to by at least one other file record.

hard mount — A method of mounting an NFS file system in which programs will wait—without limit—for the NFS server to respond.

hard wired — Computer functionality that is arranged in the wires and other components that make up a computer. Hard-wired functionality cannot be easily altered.

hardware-based RAID — A RAID array that is contained in a separate hardware device (a RAID subsystem) and is controlled by a CPU and other components separate from the CPU of the Linux system.

hardware clock — The clock that is part of the hardware in every Intel-based PC. Used by the Linux kernel to initialize the system clock when the kernel is started.

help desk — A service in many organizations that assists end users in solving problems related to information technology.

hexadecimal (hex) — A numbering system using base 16. Hex uses 0 to 9, plus the letters A through F (usually capitalized) to count the numbers 10 through 15.

history list — A list that contains the most recently executed commands. (Normally at least 100 commands are included in the history list.)

home directory — An area of the file system in which a particular user is permitted to store data. Each regular user account has an associated home directory, named after the user account login name. These are typically subdirectories of the /home directory in Linux.

hot-swapping — Removing and replacing a failed hard drive or other component without turning off the power to the device.

HOWTOs — Documents within the Linux Documentation Project that cover specific topics.

IDE — A low-cost, easy-to-manage interface used by most computers to connect hard disks and CD-ROM drives to the CPU.

IDE controller — A hardware component used to communicate between an IDE-compatible hard disk or other IDE device and the microprocessor.

if-then-else statement — A set of commands used to determine whether other commands in a script are executed. An *if-then-else* statement is one kind of selection statement.

incremental backup — A backup process that stores all files that have changed since the last incremental or differential backup was made.

index — A counting variable used within a loop statement. The index acts as a marker to count how many times the loop has executed a list of commands.

info page — A source of information for many Linux commands. Accessed using the *info* command. *See also* man page.

Information Systems (IS) department — A department within many organizations. IS staff are responsible for maintaining computer and information systems for other employees. (IS is called IT in some organizations.)

Information Technology (IT) department — *See* Information Systems (IS) department.

init **program** — A master control program that starts many other processes on the system, such as those providing a login prompt. The first process started after the Linux kernel is loaded and initialized.

initialize — To set a variable to a predefined value such as zero or " " (an empty string) so a script can use the variable without uncertainty about its initial value.

inode — A data record, identified by a unique number within a file system, which contains detailed information about a set of data blocks commonly called a "file."

installation source — The set of files from which Linux is installed. These files are normally stored on a Linux CD-ROM.

installation type — A specification indicating which Linux software to install; the appropriate installation type depends on how the Linux system will be used.

install disk — A disk used to start the Linux installation program on some distributions of Linux. *See* boot disk.

instance — A version of a printer definition that has particular options set.

Integrated Development Environment (IDE) — A program (usually graphical) that provides a convenient working environment for programmers by integrating many of the tools that a programmer uses regularly, such as a text editor, compiler, debugger, and documentation.

interior routing protocols — Routing protocols designed for routing packets among networks controlled by a single organization; packets are routed based on mathematical models.

Internet Protocol (IP) — Protocol used for all network communication in Linux. Used in conjunction with other protocols such as TCP.

interpreted language — A language for which the source code of a program is converted to numeric codes at the time a user runs the program. This conversion takes place each time the user runs the program.

interpreted program — A computer program that is converted from human-readable form to a format that can be used by a computer (numeric codes) at the moment you execute the program.

interpreter — A program that converts the source code written in an interpreted language into numeric codes that a computer can execute.

interrupt request (IRQ) — A numbered signal that a device sends to the operating system to request service.

intrusion detection system (IDS) — A type of software that aids network intrusion detection.

I/O ports — Special addresses (resembling memory addresses) used by a device for port-mapped I/O.

IP address — A numeric address such as 198.60.45.5 that is uniquely associated with one computer on the network.

IP aliasing — A networking feature that allows a single physical interface to have more than one IP address assigned to it.

IP chains — An older packet-filtering (firewalling) technique used in the Linux kernel.

IP forwarding — A feature of Linux networking, required to act as a router, that instructs the Linux kernel to send network packets out on whichever network interface the routing tables dictate. Without IP forwarding, packets arriving on a given network interface can only be sent out on the same interface.

IP masquerading — A type of network address translation in which packets from many computers on a LAN are altered to appear as if they came from a single computer.

IP tables — The lists of rules associated with one of the programming hooks provided in the networking stacks by the NetFilter architecture.

iteration — An occurrence of an event or process that can or must be done many times.

jobs — Within a shell, processes that have been started as child processes of that shell.

journaling file system — A file system that tracks each disk operation to be certain that it is either completed or not done at all. A journal is kept that permits the operating system to "back out" of a disk operation if it is not completed successfully. Linux supports several journaling file systems, including the ext3 file system, which is used by default.

Journaling File System (JFS) — A high-performance journaling file system developed by IBM and available on most Linux systems.

KDE desktop — A graphical interface used by many Linux distributions.

KDE System Guard — A graphical utility that displays a process list and lets you interact with that list to rearrange or kill processes.

kdm — The display manager included with KDE; used to provide a graphical login prompt.

kernel — The core of the operating system. The kernel interacts directly with the computer hardware and manages computer memory, the time allocated to each program running on a system, and other system resources.

kernel modules — Small programs that are part of the Linux kernel but that can be added or removed independently of other parts of the kernel. Used for device drivers, network support, file system support, and other kernel features.

kernel ring buffer — A memory area within the Linux kernel where some kernel messages are stored. When the buffer is full, the oldest message in the buffer is discarded as new messages are written. The contents of the buffer can be viewed using the *dmesg* command.

keyword — A word used in a computer language to define a specific task or meaning.

KGet — Graphical utility used to manage downloads of Web pages.

kickstart configuration file — The text file used to control a Kickstart installation, named ks.cfg.

Kickstart — A method of controlling the installation of Red Hat Linux or Fedora using a prebuilt configuration file instead of responding to questions at the keyboard during the installation.

Korn shell — A revision of the Bourne shell that includes the interactive features of the C shell but that maintains the Bourne shell programming style. The Korn shell was written by David Korn.

lease — The action a DHCP server takes in assigning an IP address to a client for a specific length of time.

LGPL (Library GPL) — A special version of the GNU General Public License intended to govern both free and commercial software use of software libraries.

library — A file containing prewritten programming functionality that any program can use.

LILO (Linux Loader) — A Linux boot manager.

link — A file record that refers to the same physical file data as another file record. *See* symbolic link and hard link.

Linux distribution — A Linux operating system product that includes the Linux kernel plus many software components, installation tools, documentation, and so forth.

Linux Documentation Project (LDP) — One of the first efforts to document how Linux is used. Started by Matt Welsh.

Linux Intrusion Detection System (LIDS) — A complex intrusion detection system that alters the Linux kernel to remove root's comprehensive access to a Linux system.

live CD — A CD-ROM containing a Linux distribution that can be run in computer memory and using the data on the CD-ROM, without ever performing a traditional Linux installation. No information is ever written to the hard disk.

log file — A file that contains detailed records of activity on a Linux system.

log in — To identify yourself to the operating system so that it knows that you are authorized to use the system, and which parts of the system to permit you to access.

logic error — A programming error caused by the design of the program or script as a whole and the arrangement of commands. Compare to a syntax error, which is caused by malformed commands.

Logical Volume Manager (LVM) — A feature of Red Hat Linux and Fedora that provides a collection of utilities to permit multiple physical storage devices to be managed as single storage volumes, dividing them into file systems as needed and adding space to those file systems without the need to reformat hard disks.

logical partition — A hard disk partition that exists within one of the four partitions that a hard disk can traditionally manage. Logical partitions are numbered beginning with 5. *See also* primary partition.

logical volume group — A collection of physical volumes (actual hard disk partitions) that are grouped together for use by the Logical Volume Manager utilities to provide a level of abstraction for ease in adding space to file systems later on.

loop statement — A statement used to determine whether part of a computer program should be executed more than once.

LPRng — The traditional Linux printing system, based on the BSD version of UNIX.

Lynx — A text-mode Web browser.

macro — A set of commands that can be executed at one time by referring to the name of the macro.

magic filter — A program that can convert documents being printed into any of several formats for printing on a specific printer model.

Mail Delivery Agent (MDA) — A program that places e-mail in a user's mailbox so that it can be read. This function is often subsumed by an MTA.

Mail Transfer Agent (MTA) — A program that moves e-mail messages from one server on the Internet to another. Also called an e-mail server.

Mail User Agent (MUA) — A program that displays and manages e-mail messages for a user.

Management — A middle level of Red Hat Network functionality (available for a fee). Permits additional upgrade services, such as comparing two systems to see if they have the same packages installed.

man page — An online manual page for a Linux command. The man pages are accessed using the *man* command.

map — A technique in which user account information for an incoming client request is assigned to a user account on the server that processes that request.

mark — A place holder within a text file being edited in vi. Similar to a bookmark on the Web. Setting a mark lets you immediately return to that spot in the file.

Master Boot Record (MBR) — A small area on the first hard disk that contains a program to decide how to start an operating system. Control passes from the BIOS to the program in the MBR when a computer is first booted.

master DNS server — The authoritative name server for a zone, typically containing database files that provide IP addresses for hosts within that zone.

maximum transmission unit (MTU) — The maximum size of a packet that a given network interface can transmit or receive.

Media Access Control (MAC) address — A unique hardware address assigned to each Ethernet card. Used in the process of routing packets. Obtained using the Address Resolution Protocol (ARP).

megabyte (MB) — A measure of space on computers equal to 1,048,576 bytes, or enough space to store roughly 1 million characters.

message — A description of what is happening within a program.

messages file — The main system log file in Linux, usually stored in the directory /var/log.

metaserver — *See* superserver.

mirroring — (1) A redundancy technique in which the contents of two file systems contain identical information. Mirroring improves data access speed and provides fault tolerance in the event that one of the file systems fails. (2) Making a copy of a Web site, FTP site, or other collection of files, typically across a network connection.

MIS (management of information systems or **manager of information systems)** — Another term for the IS or IT department or the staff who work in or manage that department.

MIT Magic Cookie — The name given to a cookie used by the *xauth* program for X display authentication.

modal editor — A text editor that uses multiple modes for editing text and entering commands to apply to that text.

module parameters — Information needed by a module to locate system resources. The parameters are added after the module name when using the *insmod* or *modprobe* command.

mount point — The path in the Linux directory structure where a file system is accessed.

multiprocessing — Operating with more than one CPU in a single computer (for example, a dual-Pentium system).

Nautilus — The graphical file manager provided with the GNOME desktop.

nesting — A programming method in which one selection or loop statement contains another selection or loop statement.

NetFilter — The packet-filtering and advanced routing architecture in Linux 2.4 and 2.6 kernels.

Network File System (NFS) — A network service that permits remote users to mount and work with a file system as part of their directory structure.

Network Information Service (NIS) — A network service that can provide (among other information) centralized user and password management across multiple Linux or UNIX systems.

Network Time Protocol (NTP) — A protocol used to coordinate highly accurate timekeeping between servers on a network or the Internet.

network address — An address that identifies the local network of which a computer is a part. This address is used to determine how data is routed to its intended destination.

network address translation (NAT) — A routing technique in which the addresses or other header information in a packet is altered during routing.

network mask — A numeric code that resembles an IP address. Used to correctly route data packets between different networks.

network time server — A computer that maintains accurate time by relying on a radio clock, atomic clock, or similar device, and that can provide accurate time to other networked servers using the Network Time Protocol (NTP).

network traffic analysis — *See* packet sniffing.

nice level — The priority level assigned to a Linux process, which determines how much CPU time the process is allocated compared to other processes.

NTFS (NT File System) — File system used by recent versions of the Windows operating system such as Windows NT, 2000, 2003, and XP. Linux supports read access to this file system.

Open Shortest Path First (OSPF) — An interior routing protocol designed to work effectively even in very large networks.

OpenSource — A trademarked name often used to refer to software licensed under the GPL.

OpenSSH — The free version of SSH utilities included in most Linux distributions.

operating system — Software that provides a set of core functionality for other programs to use in working with the computer hardware and interfacing with the user.

option — Information added to a command that determines how the command operates.

other permissions — A set of three file permissions (r, w, and x) that can be granted for all users on the Linux system who are not the owner of the file or directory in question and are not members of the group assigned to the file or directory.

owner — The user assigned to a file or directory, typically the user that created the object.

packet — A set of data that is transmitted by the network, defined by the parameters of a particular protocol such as Ethernet or IP.

packet filter — A technique in which network packets are processed according to their contents, usually based on a series of rules that compose a firewall. Handled in the Linux kernel using rules defined by the *iptables* command.

packet sniffing — A network activity in which the headers and payload of all packets on the network are captured and examined (also called network traffic analysis).

page — A block of 4 KB of memory. A page is the unit of memory in which the Linux kernel moves data to and from swap space.

page description language — A special set of codes that determine the graphics elements, text font, and everything else about how information appears on a printed page. PostScript and PCL are examples of page description languages.

Panel — A bar displayed across the bottom of the GNOME or KDE desktop interface that includes icons for commonly used applications, a button to access the main menu, and other informational or management features.

parameter — Information added to a command that defines what the command operates on, such as a file name or directory name.

parent directory — A directory that is above another directory, closer to the root of the file system.

parity — A redundancy technique that allows corrupted data to be reconstructed using an extra piece of information (the parity information) that is created as the data is stored.

parity stripe — Parity information stored as part of a RAID-3 or RAID-5 system.

parted — A free partition-editing tool that can be used to change partition sizes, including changing the size of an older Windows partition to make room for Linux. Comparable to the FIPS utility, but more powerful and more recently updated.

partition — A distinct area of a hard disk that has been prepared to store a particular type of data.

partition table — Information on a hard disk that defines the size and file system type of each partition on that hard disk.

password cracking — A cracker activity by which the cracker obtains the password for a valid user account, either by using a program that examines millions of passwords until the correct one is found, or by guessing based on personal knowledge about the user.

patch file — A text file containing updates to one or more source code files, with instructions for how those source code files should be updated. The *patch* command is used to apply a patch file to existing source code files.

path — A description of all the subdirectories in the file system hierarchy by which a particular subdirectory or file is accessed. Each part of the path—each subdirectory—is separated from others with a forward slash. *See also* relative path, absolute path.

PATH — An environment variable containing a list of directories on the Linux system that the shell searches each time a command is executed.

Perl — A popular programming language developed by Larry Wall that developers use to create scripts for working on text files and completing other complex tasks.

physical volumes — The underlying physical partitions used by the Logical Volume Manager. Multiple physical volumes together are a logical volume group, which is divided into standard partitions for data storage.

pico — A simple text editor that includes onscreen information about the Control key sequences used to perform editing functions.

pipe — A connection between two commands (indicated by the (|) character) that causes the output of one command to be used as the input of a second command.

Pluggable Authentication Modules (PAM) — A security system supported by Linux that permits each program needing security features to be configured independently using numerous modules, each of which provides a specific type of security check. Programs are configured using files located in /etc/pam.d.

port — A number that is associated with a network-capable application.

port scanning — A network activity in which packets sent to a host are analyzed to learn about that host.

port-mapped input/output (port-mapped I/O) — A device communication technique that uses a separate range of memory addresses called I/O ports as a place for a device to send and receive data. Essentially, each device-specific port address works like a post office box.

positional variable — A variable used within a shell script that contains data included on the command line when the script is started. Also called a positional parameter.

PostScript Printer Description (PPD) — A file containing a standardized printer description that can be used by several printing architectures on different operating systems. PPD files are used to describe many types of printers, not just PostScript printers.

primary DNS server — *See* master DNS server.

primary partition — One of the four partitions that traditional hard disk electronics can effectively manage. *See also* logical partition.

print filter — A script that contains instructions for formatting documents using the page description language required by a specific printer. The print filter is used by the *lpr* program to prepare files to be sent to a physical printer.

print job — A file submitted for printing via the *lpr* command or a graphical dialog box.

print queue — A printer definition associated with a physical printer; also a subdirectory where files are stored to wait for a print server daemon (such as *lpd*) to retrieve them one by one and send them to the printer. Also called a print spool directory.

print spool directory — The directory where print jobs submitted to a print queue are stored until they are sent to a printer.

printing policy — A brief document that describes how printing resources can be used and how they should be managed within an organization.

priority — (1) A label indicating the severity of a message submitted for logging. Priorities are used in syslog.conf. (2) In the context of process management, a value assigned to a process running on Linux that determines how much CPU time is granted to the process. Also called the nice level.

process — A program that has been started via the Linux kernel and about which data is maintained by the kernel for purposes of controlling that program and allocated system resources (especially CPU time and system memory).

process ID (PID) — A number from 1 to about 65,000, assigned to each process by the Linux kernel when that process is first started. The PID is used in many utilities to define which process can be affected by the utility.

programming language — *See* computer language.

Project Athena — The project sponsored by DEC and MIT to create a graphical environment or windowing system for UNIX.

protocol — An organized pattern of signals or words used to communicate efficiently.

Provisioning — The highest level of Red Hat Network functionality (available for a fee). Permits additional upgrade services, such as upgrading applications as well as operating system files, and upgrading multiple systems simultaneously from "bare metal."

proxy server — A server that receives a client request that is intended for a different server. The proxy server then makes the request as if the proxy server itself were the client; when the intended server responds, the proxy server sends the response to the client.

public key encryption — A method of encrypting information using a public and private key, such that the private key is never sent over the network.

public domain — Creative work (such as a software program) to which no one has a copyright ownership interest.

Python — A scripting language developed by Guido van Rossum. Often used for creating graphical programs.

RAID (redundant arrays of inexpensive disks) — A storage technique using multiple inexpensive hard disks arranged in a predefined pattern (an array) to improve performance, increase fault tolerance, or both.

RAID subsystem — A hardware-controlled RAID device containing a CPU and other components to control the array of hard disks.

RAID-0 — A RAID level that uses striping to improve disk performance without adding any fault tolerance.

RAID-1 — A RAID level that uses disk mirroring to significantly improve fault tolerance. Disk read performance is also improved, but disk write performance suffers.

RAID-3 — A RAID level that uses striping with parity information to improve performance and increase fault tolerance.

RAID-5 — A RAID level in which striping with parity is spread across all disks in the RAID array (compared to RAID-3, in which the parity information is stored on a single hard disk).

RAID-Linear — A storage technique in which multiple physical devices are combined into a single logical device.

random access memory (RAM) — Volatile electronic storage within a computer.

Rapid Application Development (RAD) — A software program that simplifies the development of complex software projects by providing prewritten modules, helping track multiple parts of a project, permitting reuse of parts of the software, and using many other advanced techniques.

read-only memory (ROM) — Nonvolatile electronic storage within a computer. Used to store information about how the computer starts and how the devices in the computer are configured.

read permission (r) — A file permission that allows a user to read the contents of a file or browse the files in a directory. Represented by a letter "r".

recursive — To repeat a procedure on successive sets of data or levels.

Red Hat Network (RHN) — A service provided via subscription by Red Hat Software using the Internet. This service automatically provides any security fixes, package upgrades, or other information needed to keep a Red Hat Linux system running smoothly and securely.

Red Hat Package Manager (rpm) — A software package format developed by Red Hat Software and used by numerous Linux distributions.

redirection — The act of changing either from where a Linux program receives its input or to where it sends its output.

redundant arrays of inexpensive disks — See RAID.

regular expression — A format that uses characters with special meanings (such as * or ^) to define patterns of characters or digits within Linux programs.

ReiserFS — A file system type that provides high performance and journaling. Used by default on several Linux systems, including SUSE and Gentoo.

relative path — A description of how to access a desired subdirectory or file, specified relative to another location in the file system (typically the current working directory) rather than from the root of the file system (for which an absolute path is used). A relative path does not begin with a forward slash. See also absolute path.

remote printer — A printer attached to another computer on the network or to the network itself, rather than to the computer on which you are working.

rescue disk — A disk created specifically to boot a Linux system in the event of a system failure. Contains the software tools most likely to be of help in diagnosing and repairing problems with the failed system.

rescue mode — A mode of operation in Red Hat Linux. Used to repair a system failure that blocks normal booting and operation.

resolve — To convert a domain name into an IP address using the DNS protocol.

resolver — The client portion of DNS, which makes requests to a DNS server so that other programs on a host can use the IP address of a named server to make a network connection.

resolving — The process of converting a domain name to an IP address, or vice versa.

resource database — A file that defines how an X resource should appear onscreen.

resource record — A line within a DNS zone information file, defining how the DNS server should resolve a given host or IP address, or provide related information.

restore — To copy data from a backup location (for example, a tape cartridge) onto the file system where that data is normally used, and from which it was unintentionally lost.

reverse DNS — A method of using DNS in which a client sends an IP address to a DNS server and requests the corresponding domain name.

root — The superuser, or administrative user account, on each Linux system.

root name servers — DNS servers designated as a starting point for DNS queries.

rotating log files — The process of moving existing log files to another file name and location for archiving or review.

router — A computer connected to two or more networks that transfers data packets between those networks to reach their correct destination. Also called a gateway.

routing — The process of determining where to send data packets on a network based on factors such as the sender's IP address and network mask.

routing daemon — A program that automatically generates routing table entries based on information received over the network via protocols dedicated to transmitting routing information.

Routing Information Protocol (RIP) — An interior routing protocol; the oldest routing protocol still in common use.

routing table — A listing within a router containing the information needed to send packets to another network when they are not destined for the network in which they originated.

run level — A mode of operation that defines which Linux system services are activated.

r-utilities (for "remote utilities") — Programs that allow a user to access remote hosts to run programs, transfer files, or perform other functions within a trusted network.

SAGE (System Administrators Guild) — A professional organization for system administrators.

Samba — A collection of programs that emulates Microsoft networking functionality—both client and server—on Linux and various other operating systems.

script — A list of commands stored in a text file. Instead of entering each command one by one at the command line, a script automates the execution of a series of commands.

SCSI — A high-performance interface used by many types of devices to connect to a computer.

secondary DNS server — *See* slave DNS server.

sector — A unit of data storage on a hard disk. Normally a sector contains 512 bytes.

Secure Shell (SSH) — A protocol that provides network connectivity equivalent to an encrypted version of Telnet, plus additional support to allow encryption of other protocols.

Secure Socket Layer (SSL) — A protocol that allows a Web server to communicate securely with a browser for e-commerce or similar applications.

Security Administrator's Integrated Network Tool (SAINT) — A popular security-auditing program.

security audit — A review or test of how secure a system really is and what needs to be done to improve its security.

selection statement — A statement that lets a computer programmer determine which parts of a program are executed according to values that are calculated by testing as the program is executed. The *if-then* statement is an example of a selection statement used in shell scripts.

selector — A field in the syslog.conf file that determines what events are being logged. A selector is composed of a facility and a priority.

sendmail — The most widely used Linux e-mail server.

server — A computer or program that provides data or a service to another program or computer. *See also* client.

server-parsed documents — *See* server-side includes.

server-side includes — Statements within a text file that are processed on the fly by a Web server when that document is requested.

session — A configuration that defines a set of graphical programs to run when a user logs in.

Set Group ID (SGID) — A special-purpose file permission that causes the user executing a program to take the file permissions of the group assigned to the program file. Also used to permit special access rights to a directory.

Set User ID (SUID) — A special-purpose file permission that causes the user executing a program to take the file permissions of the owner of the program file.

Shadow Password Suite — A set of password-related utilities that implement a security system used to restrict access to encrypted password text in /etc/shadow.

share — A Microsoft Windows term referring to a resource intended to be shared over a network.

shared library — A single copy of a function library that has been loaded into memory for use by multiple dynamically linked applications.

shell — A command interpreter that provides a command-line interface in a terminal window.

shell out — To start a program as if working at the Linux command line (the shell) from within another program (such as the vi editor).

shell prompt — A set of words or characters indicating that the shell is ready to accept commands at the keyboard.

shell script — An executable file containing lines of text as you would enter them at a command line, with special commands to control the order in which lines in the file are executed.

shell trace — A method of debugging a shell script that displays each command on screen as the shell executes it.

shell variable — A variable used within a shell script to store information for use by the script.

SIGHUP — A signal sent to a logging daemon to instruct the daemon to reread its configuration files and the log file to which it writes. Sometimes called HUP.

signal — A message (one of a fixed set defined by the Linux kernel) that can be sent to any process and responded to according to how that program is written.

slave DNS server — A backup to a master DNS server, containing the same database files as the master DNS server.

social engineering — A method used by attackers to violate user security measures, typically by using clever lies or persuasion to convince a user to divulge a password or other crucial system information. The attacker typically poses as a system administrator or similar person.

soft mount — A method of mounting an NFS file system in which NFS will wait for a while if a data request is made, and if the NFS server does not respond, then the client will give up.

software — Instructions that control the physical computer components, but can be changed because they reside on a changeable media such as a hard disk.

software license — A legal definition of who can use a piece of software and how it can be used.

software package — A collection of multiple files, along with descriptive information, security data, and installation instructions. Permits a user to install or upgrade an application or set of utilities with a single command. The Red Hat Package Manager (rpm) format and the Debian format are the two widely used software package formats on Linux.

source code — The file that a programmer writes using the keywords and syntax rules of a computer language to create a piece of software.

squashing — A method of preserving user security in NFS by preventing a user with root access on one system from automatically acquiring root access on an NFS server by virtue of mounting an exported NFS directory.

Squid — The most widely used Linux proxy server.

ssh-agent — A part of the SSH suite that helps manage key pairs and authentication among multiple SSH-capable systems.

Stallman, Richard — Founder of the Free Software Foundation and the GNU Project.

standalone mode — Using a network program without support from a superserver such as *xinetd* or *inetd*.

standard error (STDERR) — The communication channel used by most Linux programs to send information about errors in program execution.

standard input (STDIN) — The communication channel used by most Linux programs to collect input (normally from the keyboard).

standard output (STDOUT) — The communication channel used by most Linux programs to write output (normally to the screen).

statement — A command within a computer program. A statement is often a single keyword, but the term may also refer to a group of keywords that the computer language syntax requires or allows to be used together.

statement block — A list of commands (or statements) that are controlled by a selection or loop statement.

statically linked applications — Linux programs that include library functions in the program itself so that they are not dependent on the libraries loaded on the Linux system.

static routing — Assembling a routing table via entries in start-up scripts or by manually entered route commands.

sticky bit — A special-purpose file permission, now ignored when used on files, that grants special access rights when used on a directory; only the owner of a file or root is permitted to rename or delete a file in a directory with this permission set.

striping — A data storage technique in which parts of a file are written to more than one disk in order to improve performance. *See* RAID-3 and RAID-5.

subdirectory — A directory that is contained within another directory, and thus further from the root of the file system.

superblock — A record containing detailed status information about an ext2 or ext3 file system. Stored at multiple locations on each ext2 or ext3 file system. Viewed or altered with *tune2fs*.

superserver — A program that listens on multiple network ports and starts appropriate network service daemons when a client connection arrives for that port. Also called a metaserver. Examples include *inetd* and *xinetd*.

superuser — The system administrative account; the root account.

swap out — The act by the Linux kernel of copying data occupying a portion of RAM to the swap space so that the RAM can be used by another application for a time.

swap space — Storage space—typically on a hard disk—that the Linux kernel uses as extra memory when RAM is insufficient or a process is inactive. Also called virtual memory.

SWAT — A browser-based graphical configuration interface for setting up and managing the Samba SMB server.

symbolic link — A file that refers to another file name rather than directly to data in a file (via its inode). Also called a soft link.

syntax error — An error in a script or source code file caused by misuse of the structure, keywords, or punctuation required by the computer language being used. A syntax error can be found before executing the program.

syslog.conf — The configuration file used to control how and where messages are logged by *syslogd* and *klogd*.

System Administration, Networking, and Security (SANS) Institute — A prestigious and well-regarded education and research organization whose members include most of the leading computer security experts in the country. Also simply called SANS.

system clock — An internal clock maintained by the Linux kernel whenever the system is turned on. Initialized based on the hardware clock. Maintained accurately on large networks by relying on a network time server using the Network Time Protocol (NTP).

system utilities — Programs that are used to manage a Linux system. *See also* utility programs.

tab completion — A feature of the shell that lets you enter part of a file or directory name and have the shell fill in the remainder of the name.

tar archive — A file created by the *tar* command.

target hard disk partition — The location on the system's hard disk where Linux is installed. Also known as target partition.

Tcl/Tk — A scripting language developed by John Ousterhout; often used to create graphical programs.

TCP Wrappers — An application-level access control (security) program that examines incoming network connections when requested by a super-server, then compares the connection details to a configuration file to determine whether the connection is allowed.

Telnet — A terminal emulation program that allows a user to log in to a remote computer as if sitting at that computer's keyboard.

TENEX/TOPS C shell (TC shell) — An enhancement of the C shell. This is the version of the C shell that is commonly used on Linux systems.

terminal window — A command-line interface within a graphical desktop.

theme — A collection of colors, fonts, and images that give a display a certain look and feel.

thrashing — Excessive movement of processes between RAM and swap space, resulting in reduced system performance and excessive wear on the hard disk.

time slice — An allocation of CPU time assigned to a process by the Linux kernel. Used to implement multitasking.

timestamp — A record of the date and time when an event being logged occurred.

Torvalds, Linus — Originator of the Linux kernel; formerly a student in Helsinki, Finland.

total cost of ownership (TCO) — The sum of all costs involved in providing a technology solution, including components such as the initial cost of purchasing software and required hardware; support contracts; training for administrators, programmers, and end users; upgrade charges; and recovery costs if the technology fails unexpectedly.

track — One of many concentric circles of data storage area on each platter of a hard disk.

Transmission Control Protocol (TCP) — A protocol that works with the Internet Protocol (IP) to provide stable connections for data transfer services such as the Web or FTP.

transparent proxy — A networking technique in which a packet is redirected to a different port on the same computer.

Trojan horse — A technique for gaining access to a computer system by having a system administrator execute a program that appears normal but which actually creates a security hole for a cracker or destroys data on the host when it is run.

UNIX — An operating system created at AT&T Bell Labs (now part of Lucent Technologies) about 30 years ago by Ken Thompson and Dennis Ritchie. UNIX is still widely used, and it provided the technical basis for Linux.

USB (Universal Serial Bus) — A method of connecting peripherals, including storage drives, to a computer. USB devices are typically attached via an external cable.

user account — A set of permissions to use the system, with an associated user name and password.

user permissions — A set of three file permissions (r, w, and x) that can be granted to the owner of a file or directory.

User Private Group — A security model that creates a new group containing one user when that user is first created.

usrquota — Option that can be used within the /etc/fstab file that causes a file system to track disk space quotas for each user. Used in conjunction with the *quotaon* and *edquota* commands.

utility programs — Software that provides assistance in managing the hardware and operating system features (as opposed to doing other types of work such as word processing). *See also* system utilities.

vi — (stands for "visual editor") The most widely used text editor on UNIX and Linux systems. Different versions of vi, such as vim and elvis, are usually launched with the command *vi*.

virtual hosting — A feature of the Apache Web server that lets a single copy of Apache serve documents for several Web sites (several domains).

virtual console — A separate login screen that you access by pressing a combination of keys on your keyboard. It allows you to start multiple text-based login sessions on the same computer.

virtual file system — A method used by the Linux kernel to generalize access by programs to file data so that the kernel can support multiple, modularized file system types.

virtual memory — *See* swap space.

VT100 — The most widely supported dumb terminal standard.

Webmin — A browser-based configuration utility that can be installed on any version of Linux and is included by default with some versions.

wheel — A special system administrative group, not used officially in Linux.

white space — Tabs or spaces included in a program or script file that make the script easier for a person to read but have no effect on how the interpreter or compiler works with the file.

window manager — A special-purpose graphical application (X client) that controls the position and manipulation of the windows within a graphical user interface.

workspace — An empty background on a desktop interface, where you can open application windows.

write caching — A feature of some storage systems in which information that is to be written to a file system (particularly a RAID file system) is stored in memory temporarily in order to improve the overall read/write performance of the file system.

write permission (w) — A file permission that allows a user to add or change information in a file or create files within a directory. Represented by a letter "w".

X client — A graphical application.

X resource — The separate screen elements of a graphical application, such as scroll bars, text fonts, and titles bars.

X server — The program that communicates with the video card to create images on the screen.

X Window System — A graphical software environment used by almost all UNIX and Linux operating systems.

xdm — The program that provides a graphical login screen in Linux. Replaced by the very similar program gdm in GNOME, or kdm in KDE.

XDMCP — A protocol that allows remote hosts to use X running on a Linux system to provide a graphical login display.

xterm window — A type of terminal window. Used generically to refer to a command-line window within a graphical desktop interface.

YAST2 — A configuration utility provided in SUSE Linux.

zone — A part of the DNS domain tree for which a particular DNS server has authority to provide information.

zone information files — The files referred to in named.conf that contain detailed information about specific zones: the information that a DNS query seeks.

Index